An Annotated Bibliography
of the Pike, *Esox lucius*
(Osteichthyes: Salmoniformes)

E. J. Crossman is Curator in the Department of Ichthyology and Herpetology, Royal Ontario Museum, and Professor in the Department of Zoology, University of Toronto.

J. M. Casselman is Research Scientist in the Research Section, Fisheries Branch, Ontario Ministry of Natural Resources, and Research Associate in the Department of Ichthyology and Herpetology, Royal Ontario Museum.

Richard C. Hoffmann is Associate Professor History and Social Science in the Faculty of Arts, York University, Toronto.

An Annotated Bibliography of the Pike, *Esox lucius* (Osteichthyes: Salmoniformes)

E. J. Crossman and J. M. Casselman

With a foreword by Richard C. Hoffmann

RŎM

A Life Sciences Miscellaneous Publication
of the Royal Ontario Museum, Toronto

Canadian Cataloguing in Publication Data

Crossman, E. J., 1929–

An annotated bibliography of the pike, Esox lucius (Osteichthyes: Salmoniformes)

(Life sciences miscellaneous publications, ISSN 0082–5093)
Includes index.
ISBN 0–88854–331–X

1. Pike – Bibliography. 2. Pike fishing – Bibliography. I. Casselman, J. M. (John Malcolm), 1940–   . II. Royal Ontario Museum. III. Title. IV. Series.

Z7996.F5C77   1987   016.597'53   C87–093734–0

Cover art: Peter Buerschaper

Publication date: 30 June 1987
ISBN 0–88854–331–X
ISSN 0082–5093

© Royal Ontario Museum, 1987
100 Queen's Park, Toronto, Canada, M5S 2C6

Printed and bound in Canada at the University of Toronto Press

Contents

The Protohistory of Pike in Western Culture

Richard C. Hoffmann

Why in a bibliography of a fish is this foreword an essay about people? Because human minds and behaviour are at least as responsible for this book and all it contains as is *Esox lucius*. Bibliographers compile lists of special human cultural products, written and printed texts. The texts are intentional records of ways that people have perceived and understood something they had identified in the natural world around them. The conscious identification ("This thing is a pike and not something else") the mode of perception ("Examining the gonads of this pike tells me something about this kind of organism" or "If I catch this pike, I have food") and the purposeful keeping of a record ("Spawning Behaviour of *E. lucius* in a Mesotropic Estuarian System" or "Fly North for Lunker Northerns") are all human activities which tell as much about the cultural assumptions of the actors as they tell about pike. So, too, does the idea of compiling and publishing an organized list of such published information. As a natural organism the pike may be thought to have no "history" in the normal sense of the term, but the encounters of humans with that organism are, at least potentially, part of human history. How have people thought about the pike they encountered?

Most items in this bibliography approach the creature we now call *Esox lucius* in the distinctively modern cultural contexts of fishing arts or ichthyological science. The highly self-conscious activity we now know as science emerged slowly from older European cultural patterns. So, too, did today's understanding of fishing. People in earlier Western cultures took cognizance of fish, and specifically of pike, but their consciousnesses did not produce records easily assimilated to scientific or bibliographic modes of presentation. Their cultural mentality and its surviving products were prescientific and, in comparison with the subsequent written record of *E. lucius*, any treatment thereof must be protohistorical, a piecing together of unintentional fragments of a record.

This introductory essay thus explores what traces now remain of early Western encounters with *E. lucius* and ascertains what these sources can and cannot tell us of that fish's place in European minds up to the 16th and 17th centuries. It aims to recapture what those people thought of pike, less for the sake of checking whether their "facts" are now acceptable than for that of reconstructing the contexts and mental frameworks which gave meaning to their "facts". The concern is with *how* Europeans apprehended this fish before they established the systematic cultural tradition of writing about ichthyology, pisciculture, and fishing, which made intellectually conceivable a bibliography like this one.

The entry of pike into European consciousnesses

The first and most humans who confronted *E. lucius* left no, or merely indirect, traces in the surviving record. In prehistoric and undocumented pasts Europeans treated pike as a food object. Pike remains from human occupation sites affirm this for all periods since the early Neolithic, but the material evidence of bones and scales can carry only limited information. Early Europeans evidently brought pike to campsites, huts, halls, and castles generally across the native range of the species. At sites where careful modern archaeologists have recovered many fish remains, those of pike are often well represented. We may infer that in the minds of the people who once lived there the creature we call pike was "food," perhaps even "preferred food," but all else can be but speculation. Did they distinguish by name this fish from others? Did they intentionally seek this fish rather than just accept the luck of the net, trap, hook, or spear? Did they have and use knowledge of its haunts and habits? Analogy with other hunting and gathering cultures suggests affirmative answers, but to confirm them requires products of human minds more conscious than a garbage heap where a few vertebrae landed after a meal. Perhaps because the native European range of *E. lucius* only slightly overlaps that of early literate civilizations in the Mediterranean basin, consciously produced evidence to give a sense of what at least some person or people *thought* about pike comes late.

When the fish identifiably enters the extant verbal record, it bears a less than flattering reputation. A late Roman poet and teacher of rhetoric, Decimus Magnus Ausonius (310–393), travelled from Bordeaux northeast to Trier to tutor the future emperor Gratian. The trip inspired Ausonius to write the *Mosella*, a Latin poem on the Rhine tributary of the same name. When he there catalogued the fishes of the river, he introduced to the world of letters what he called *lucius*.[1] This first known written reference to pike deserves quotation in the original:

> Hic etiam latio risus praenomine cultor
> stagnorum, querulis vis infestissima ranis,
> lucius, obscuras ulva caenoque lacunas
> obsidet. Hic nullos mensarum lectus ad usus
> feruet fumosis olido nidore popinis.
>
> [*Mosella*, lines 120–124]

The precise sense and connotation of such typically stylized late classical Latin poetry is hard to put into English. Something like this comes close:

> A dweller in backwaters does enjoy a proper Latin name.
> Lucius besieges the complaining frogs
> in obscure holes among sedges and mud.
> His meat is not for the dining table
> but sold at cheap shops smoky with its reeking stink.

At the very end of ancient civilization, then, Ausonius first articulated a perception of pike as fish and as resource. This creature lives in a swampy habitat and preys, from concealment, on other animals. Enmity between pike and frogs will be a regular theme of later literature. For late Roman consumers, however, Ausonius thought the pike poor fare (a status which some later writers will dispute).

Along the wake of the "water wolf"

The two elements in Ausonius's introduction—object of nature and usefulness for humans—provide a frame for considering much of the subsequent record medieval Europeans left of the pike. Scattered references and allusions rank *lucius* with trout and carp among the freshwater fishes best known to humans, but this familiarity and knowledge long remained unsystematized.

Pike and other natural objects or phenomena belonged to what medieval Europeans long understood as a material veil which separated them from an ultimately spiritual reality. Some of them conceived the world of nature as actively hostile to humankind and to the divine plan for human salvation; for these any concern for the material was but foolish sin. Others conceded a godly origin to this imperfect creation but thought it worth attention only in so far as it might thus dimly reflect the divine plan for ultimate perfection. In the latter context things of nature either served the mundane (and hence uninteresting) needs of life in this transient world or signified with their characteristics analogous powers and truths of the supernatural.

People who saw signs in nature focused on the fearsomeness and the predatory habits of pike. One early text asserts that the great Theodoric, king of the Ostrogoths, died in terror in 526 after seeing in the face of a pike brought to his dining table the visage of his recently executed enemy Symmachus. When Ruodlieb, hero of an 11th-century Bavarian fairy tale, caught by quasi-magical means a whole list of fishes, pike were among the few given more than just a name: "Lucius...are the wolves among fishes, for they devour fish whenever they can catch them."[2]

Folk tales and popular practices that perhaps originated in assimilation of Christian notions by early medieval Europeans treated in mythic ways the pike and its attributes. In a widespread story the markings on the pike's head were seen as displaying the implements of Christ's passion: cross, ladder, hammer, nails, thorns, whip, and sponge. The tale explained that as Christ carried his cross through a brook where the pike lived, the fish looked out and was forever marked by what it saw. One variant of Scandinavian provenance listed the pike among the harmful things created by the devil to vex God. When angels captured these creatures and brought them before God, he saw on the pike's head a cross. So he blessed the fish and made it good and useful to humankind. A Latvian legend told how the pike grew very large and, forgetting in its pride God's command to eat only fish, caught and ate a fisherman. As a reminder, lest the pike again so err, the tale continued, God ordered the pike to carry in its head all the tools of the fisherman: the set net as jaws, the spear as teeth, the hooks as gills. What enters the set net is trapped; what the spear grasps is held firm; what reaches the hooks sticks tight. Of freshwater species only the pike appears as a protagonist in any of the family of stories about a competition (which collapsed in disorder) to be king among the fishes. Perhaps the idea of the pike as a fish of superior standing explains why in 1177 nobles in charge of a great knightly tournament held in Champagne offered a trophy pike to the champion.

Men of formal learning, who until the 12th century came almost exclusively from a monastic environment, used natural history more formally to explicate moral or doctrinal points. A late exponent of this approach, the English canon and teacher Alexander Neckam, assembled in his *De naturis rerum* of the 1180s many such allegorical interpretations. For Alexander, *lucius* was the "aquatic wolf" and "tyrant of the waters" that fish could no more escape than humans could old age. When this greedy eater swallows fish too big for its stomach, it digests them by halves. In another passage Neckam tells how, when the perch sees the pike, it raises its prickly fins in defence while the bream flees into the mud; so thwarted, the pike attacks other fishes. As wolfish as the pike, the writer continues, are the human despoilers of churches, but their subjects, being neither perch nor bream, must suffer their evil deeds. When shaped by a doctrine of signs, observations of nature gave understanding in ways alien to modern sensibilities.

Into (and, in some instances, beyond) the 12th century, then, those literate Europeans who thought to write about the pike did so with emphasis on the predatory "water wolf." At the same time and for much longer, however, other Europeans, mostly illiterates, were perceiving in wild pike populations objects of use and value.

Human exploitation of pike drew in the middle ages only occasional literate attention, though the record grows from the 12th century onwards. A 10th-century Anglo-Saxon schoolmaster, Aelfric of Eynsham, taught his pupils Latin with made-up stories, including one about a fisherman who earned his living taking pike and other species with hooks and nets. Just about the same time Aelfric was composing his schoolbook, real fishermen in and around the estuary of the Odra (Oder) River on the south coast of the Baltic were angling for pike with iron and bronze spoons. (The shape of those lures found by archaeologists is familiar to any modern pike fisher.) Then, too, the Count of Anjou reserved the pike for his own use when he donated a fishery to the abbey of Marmoutier. Comparable passing references or incidental local evidence of pike fishing continue thereafter. The species was important in the yield of fisheries for which in the late 14th century the church of Troyes in Champagne kept income accounts. By that time pike were mentioned in contracts made between land owners and commercial fishermen near Arles and in records of disputes among the same kinds of people in Prussia. The earliest medieval sport fisher we can so far document, a late 12th-century canon of Châlons-sur-Marne called Gui of Bazoches, listed pike among the fishes he enjoyed catching on a holiday at his uncle's country estate. Still, for long thereafter the techniques of fish capture remained unworthy of coherent and intentional written consideration by contemporaries.

The fishing, growth of human populations, clearance of land for farming, and development of the European economy during the 10th through 13th centuries brought wild pike populations under noticeable pressure. Expanding state authorities and literate administrations took measures to conserve valued fishery resources. In 1289 King Philip IV of France issued for all public waters a fisheries ordinance that established general gear restrictions and closed seasons and specified size limits for various fishes. No pike so small as to be worth 2 denier or less on the market could be legally taken. Comparable royal decrees went out regularly thereafter, though little is known of their enforcement or effect. In areas with less precocious central governments than had France, local and regional authorities took the lead. In the 15th century communities along the upper Rhine closed fishing for small pike from early spring until dates in late July or August to give the fish a chance to grow. In 1506 the Emperor Maximilian I, himself an enthusiastic and self-advertised devotee of field sports, decreed in his hereditary capacity as duke of Lower Austria minimum size and season regulations for numerous species in that territory. To invalidate the excuse of misidentification, the copy of the decree used by the city government in Vienna included coloured illustrations of each fish. The pike is unmistakable.

Maximilian and other authorities wanted to protect fish populations, including those of pike, because these were perceived as important sources of food. Medieval Europeans evidently thought pike far better meat than had Ausonius. In excavations of 10th- through 14th-century levels at Novgorod, remains of *E. lucius* ranked second in number only to those of zander (*Stizostedion lucioperca*). Popes at Avignon had purchasing agents obtain pike on buying trips to Burgundy. Inventories and account books kept by officials of Teutonic Order houses in late 14th-century Bohemia list pantry supplies of pike, both preserved (salted, pickled, dried) and fresh. Contemporaries in France paid 60 sous for a pike when a carp went for 15. At Eger in western Bohemia the municipal price-fixing ordinance of 1465 set fresh pike at 36 heller per pound, below only salmon; salt pike at 30 heller per pound were the most expensive preserved fish. These price relationships probably explain why, when all prices in Europe rose during the 16th century, pike slowly gave way to carp in the extant menus of hospitals, convents, and orphanages, though they continued to grace the tables of the elite.

By then pike had also appeared in a developing but poorly studied genre of writing that offered readers a mix of medical, dietary, and culinary advice. Hildegard of Bingen was a mystic and abbess from the middle Rhine who in the 1150s carefully investigated the foods available for her nuns. She noted that what she called the *hecht* preferred pure water and ate fish rather than mud or weeds and she concluded that it had good healthful flesh. She thus recommended pike meat for both the sick and the well, and to promote good digestion, the eating of pike livers. The housekeeping manual compiled in the 1390s by an elderly Parisian for his young wife advised male in preference to female pike except if she wished to make *rissoles* from the eggs. He offered particular recipes suited to pike in their ascending order of size: "lanterel, brochet, quarrel, lux et luceau."[3] In what is now recognized as the earliest known printed book on fishing, a manual done in Heidelberg in 1493 and many times reprinted in German, Flemish, and French (sometimes called *Dit Boecxken* after the Flemish title), the anonymous author also favoured the milter (male) over the roe (female), but emphasized that any large pike was good eating all year round except when it was spawning. This advice on size and seasons— along with the traditional notion that pike was "like a wolf"—Gregor Mangolt of Zürich copied into his early 16th-century handbook on the purchase and preparation of fish from the Bodensee (Lake Constance). The pirated edition of 1557 highly recommends a specimen taken in October and cooked whole either in its own juices, in a broth of sweet wine and salt, or "blue [*sic*]" in vinegar. If we better understood the history of such medieval cookbooks and medico-dietary thinking, we might detect therein early systematic knowledge about one aspect of the pike.

The pike enters scholarship

The institutional and intellectual setting of the 12th century, which yielded some of Hildegard's knowledge and in which Alexander Neckam worked, laid the foundations for modern scholarly and scientific traditions. New intellectual movements then justified the study of man and of nature without necessary reference to the supernatural, so that secular learning, though still subordinated to theology, could claim autonomous legitimacy. Scholastics at Paris and elsewhere recovered Aristotle's writings, including those on natural history, and compiled and updated what they learned from them. The great 13th-century natural philosophers like Thomas of Cantimpré, Vincent of Beauvais, and Albertus Magnus devoted to fish whole sections of their encyclopaedias.[4] Perhaps more significantly, they organized their learning to distinguish between the general and the particular and to indicate the sources of their data. High medieval scholasticism thus took the necessary first step from mere incidental comment to the accumulation of knowledge that is one characteristic of scientific scholarship.

The authors of surviving 13th-century encyclopaedias copied extensively from one another and from an earlier generation of writers (whose works they so effectively superseded as to cause their disappearance). As a result, much the same things were repeated in most scholastic discussions of pike. They point out that *lucius* is known as the "aquatic wolf" from its predatory habits. They describe it as a fish of fresh waters, with a wide mouth and many sharp teeth, that eats frogs and smaller fishes, preferably those without sharp spines and scales, but not sparing even its own kind or fish almost its own size. The prey is taken in head first, for otherwise the scales and fins would prevent the pike from swallowing it. Albertus, who grew up in the vicinity of the Rhine, adds at this point in his treatment that he had seen that the pike first catches its prey crosswise to the body and, after carrying it a while and puncturing it with its teeth, releases it to turn it about and swallow it whole head first. There is discussion of the shape of the pike's stomach and of a crystalline stone to be found in its head. Vincent alleges Aristotle (who had not in fact written about *E. lucius*) as his source for the claim that female pike are made gravid by the south wind and ascend rivers to spawn where they do not live, so that their children will not be a burden to them. Other authorities, Vincent continues, see in the spawning movement a search for purer water. He and his colleagues did not know that, a half century before, Hildegard of Bingen had recorded direct observations of spawning behaviour.

What the high medieval schoolmen had to say about pike must be understood in terms of their principal intellectual concern: to assemble statements from authoritative earlier writers into a coherent body of learning, which could then be examined through the tools of logic. The method had originated in the disciplines of law and metaphysics and subsequently spread into theology, history, and natural history. Because they achieved that purpose, the scholastic encylopaedists dominated learned European understandings of nature, of fish, and of pike into the 16th century.

Towards conscious manipulation and systematic knowledge
Late 12th- and 13th-century schoolmen were, therefore, the first Europeans to write extensively and with broad intellectual purpose about *lucius*. Rarely, however, did medieval intellectuals connect their work directly with observed natural phenomena or see it as affecting what people actually did in the world of nature. But during the later Middle Ages and the 16th century some Europeans who encountered pike did come to link observation, thought, writing, and action in three separate areas: pisciculture, fishing, and an emerging science of ichthyology. Though these activities, or at least the literatures of them, display occasional interconnections, they mainly evolved and can be examined independently.

Artificial fish culture in medieval Europe differed from the Roman emphasis on warm brackish-water coastal store ponds serving the private needs of luxurious epicures. By processes not yet well investigated, medieval Europeans established and spread a pisciculture using regulated complexes of artificial freshwater ponds to segregate by yearclasses large numbers of cyprinids (mainly carp) for reproduction, growth, fattening, and subsequent market sale. Incidental references in documents transferring land or reporting court proceedings suggest that the technical features of this system were available in northern and central France around 1200. The evidence thereafter becomes voluminous, first in western, then in east- central, Europe.

Intentional use of pike as a biological control agent in and byproduct of carp culture by the 13th century in at least some regions of Europe is revealed in incidental and administrative records, but, like fish culture in general, is not then the object of comprehensive, integrated, or synthetic discussion. A brief passage on fishponds in the late 13th-century Anglo-French manual of property management called *Fleta* recommended against admission of "aquatic wolves" that would eat other fish. However, 13th- through 15th-century texts from regions as far apart as England, central France, and Bohemia do show pond owners purposely exploiting the pike's piscivorous habits by placing a few in their finishing ponds to keep down the numbers of small carp and thus encourage growth of the large. In 1258 Count Thibaut V of Champagne stocked 6 large pike along with 3520 carp and 10000 bream and roach. Ponds belonging to the Duke of Burgundy a century later yielded at harvest numbers like 4638 carp, 650 bream, and 533 pike from Sarée or 5740 carp and 268 pike from l'Eperviére. In late 14th-century England, where the exotic carp was still very rare or absent and the elaborated multi-pond technology likely not common, Chaucer described the well-to-do franklin of the

Canterbury Tales as having ''many a breme and luce'' in his pond.

Conscious use of knowledge about the predatory pike and its effect on populations of other species as a tool for managing domesticated fish production thus long antedated codification of this knowledge into intentionally composed manuals of fish culture. A specialized technical literature on the operation of artificial fishponds developed only with the late 15th- and early 16th-century proliferation of carp culture in east-central Europe, notably Bohemia, Moravia, Silesia, and parts of southern Poland and Germany. Handbooks like *De piscinis* (''On fishponds'') by the Moravian prelate Jan Skaly z Dubravka (Dubravius), composed privately for the rich merchant Anton Fugger in 1525 and printed in Wrocław in 1547, or *O sprawie, sypaniu, wymierzeniu, i rybnieniu stawów* (''On the operation, excavation, surveying, and stocking of ponds'') by the veteran Polish pond master Olbrycht Strumieński printed in Kraków in 1573, or others known only in manuscript or done somewhat later make explicit little about pike which cannot now be inferred as earlier known to late medieval operators of piscicultural enterprises. These manuals advise keeping the predator out of the spawning ponds but stocking it in the third pond to eat the superfluous offspring of precocious three-year-old carp, which would otherwise inhibit the growth of the market-destined parents. They point out as well that pike from these well-managed and clean waters will be delicious for the pond owner's dining or remunerative for sale. The 16th-century writers on artificial fish culture also affirmed more clearly than may be shown before that pike spawn in weeds and shallows like the other fishes of their ponds and earlier in the season than carp.

In the present context, however, the intellectual role of the writers on fish culture has greater importance than the particular data they offered. Their observational knowledge of pike was integrated and systematized in ways hitherto unknown. The whole empirical technology of rearing fish, which had developed outside the ambit of literate social groups, these authors brought into that cultural setting, organized for communication through the written word, and disseminated by its new means of handling information, the printed book. Their works were translated and adapted into other languages and used in the writings of other commentators. A cumulative literate body of applied knowledge had been established.

European thought about catching pike and other fishes emerged, like that on fish rearing, from scattered unintentional traces of illiterate and disorganized empirical practice to coherent consideration in written and then printed treatises. Before the 14th-century no known text purports to describe or instruct in the arts and crafts of fishing; as mentioned above, our knowledge of medieval capture techniques comes from passing and often obscure references in writings done for other ends, chiefly literary or regulatory. Thereafter, however, works now extant make more visible for angling than for pisciculture the cultural process whereby a ''literature'' evolved from lists of prescriptions and short tracts to extended, comprehensive, and self-conscious didactic treatments.

The few brief early discussions of fish-capture techniques now known to have been written in 14th-century Italy, Germany, and England do not specify target species for the attractants, piscicides, baits, and gear they prescribe, but comparable or larger notes from the 15th century do. The pike, notably piscivorous among the easily seen European fishes of fresh waters, thus required treatment different from that for fishes susceptible to bread pastes, maggots, or live or simulated insects. A 15th-century German translator of the section on fishing from the 14th-century agricultural manual by the Bolognese Pietro de Crescenzi interpolated in a passage on angling the comment that a single hook baited with a small fish was good for ''all predators like pike.''[5] The interpolator adds that strong hooks and a line covered with wire are needed because of the pike's teeth.

Several of the more numerous English manuscript tracts offer similar advice. One in a 15th-century paper manuscript (Harley 2389) at the British Library goes into more detail, prescribing "to catch a pyke at all tymes" a double hook mounted two fathoms below a large cork and baited with a small roach, gudgeon, or bleak that has been rubbed with camphor and oil to make it shine and with asafoetida to attract by odour. Especially in May, September, and October a frog is the preferred bait and from January through March the pike will bite at a worm, but the small fish properly anointed is otherwise the best. A monk at the Bavarian abbey of Tegernsee, who about 1500 wrote down the methods of the professional fishers employed there, described techniques like the English ones, but also mentioned the use of a hook wrapped with purple silk and a special mix of feathers.

   The long Tegernsee manuscript still only listed baits, but by its time a genuine angling literature, which offered to a reading public organized treatment of the subject, was already appearing. The pamphlet printed in Heidelberg in 1493 (see above) combined advice on baits, a fisherman's calendar, and a curious satirical comparison of fish to human society ("The pike is a robber"). Its printer, Jacob Köbel, expressed surprised delight at finding a written discourse on the useful and pleasant activity of fishing. Earlier still, the anonymous English *Treatyse of Fysshynge wyth an Angle* (at times ignorantly ascribed to a mythical "Dame Juliana Berners" or "Barnes"), probably composed about 1420 and surviving in its initial form only as a fragmentary mid-century manuscript, had articulated the sporting quality of angling, described the necessary tackle, and detailed its use in general and for particular fishes. The extant portion, however, gives for pike only the recommendation to dye a chalk line brown and protect it with a wire. When the complete *Treatyse* appeared in print in the second *Boke of St. Albans* in 1496, some revision had occured and larger coverage was given to pike fishing. This begins with moral opprobrium for the pike's predatory behaviour, though these habits then explain the recommended baits and tactics: thread a roach or herring on a hook and float it in likely pike habitat; hook a frog through the skin of the neck and cast it into those places; soak a small fish in asafoetida before using it as bait; "and yf ye lyst to haue a good sporte, thenne tye the corde [with baited hook] to a gose fote [goose's foot] and ye shall se god halynge [a good tug-of- war] whether the gose or the pyke shall haue the better."[6]

   With the German tract of 1493, republished dozens of times in the next century and incorporated into other continental works, and the printing of the English *Treatyse*, fishing as the practical application of observed data from nature entered the world of public literary culture. On the European continent a tradition of angling literature subsequently faltered, but in England it grew and with it a cumulative angling perspective on the pike. At least some fishers read and some writers fished. In *The Arte of Angling* published anonymously in 1577 William Samuel, a Huntingdonshire clergyman, labelled the pike (here "pickerel") the "freshwater wolf" for the first time in English and noted its difference from other fishes in lacking a fear of man. Samuel advised familiar capture techniques suited to the pike's size and predatory nature: the wire-protected and heavy line; the roach, dace, frog, or large worm as bait, a drifting or still presentation. A new suggestion he offered was to hook a dead bait through the nose and move it actively in the water, and then, when the pike took, to wait until it carried, released, retook, and swallowed the bait before setting the hook. The conceptions of pike and pike fishing given in both the *Treatyse* and the *Arte* became commonplaces in English angling books done about 1600 and later in *The Compleat Angler* of Izaak Walton. This was in part because these authors lifted whole passages from the earlier works. In angling, then, a second systematic literate tradition about pike had emerged from the changing European consciousness.

For knowledge of pike, William Samuel drew in 1577 on more than angling experience and the written precedent of the *Treatyse*. His fictive expert, Piscator, tells his neophyte companion about a reputed 267-year-old pike captured in Germany which, says he, "Gesnerus doth make report of...."[7] He refers to the Swiss physician and naturalist Konrad von Gesner (1516–1565), a cofounder of modern ichthyological and of modern bibliographical science. Gesner and his fellow 16th-century students of fishes established the third context in which European perceptions of *lucius* departed from the protohistorical and the pre-systematic.

This foreword can provide no history of 16th-century ichthyology, just a sketch of how *lucius* was handled in that cultural setting. Gesner's principal work on fishes, the third volume of his *Historia animalium*, "which is on the nature of fishes and aquatic animals," was published at Zürich in 1558. Its author exploited scholarship by French, Italian, and German writers, as well as his own extensive network of correspondents. Gesner's treatment of *lucius* conformed to what had already become a standard mode of topical organization. His text begins with the nomenclature of Latin and the European vernaculars, for scientific inquiry requires consensus on the object of discussion. Thus he cited Ausonius but rejected as synonyms for *lucius* Pliny's *esox*, Strabo's *oxyrynchus*, and Aristotle's *lupus*. In his examination of recorded distribution Gesner noted the absence of pike from Spain. Physical descriptions, external and internal, follow. Gesner referred to writings of his contemporary Pierre Belon, and of his medieval predecessor Thomas of Cantimpré. After giving the latter's report on a crystal stone in the brain of pike, Gesner specified that he could not confirm this from his own observations. He then mentioned that some people saw in the head markings the instruments of the Passion.

Further sections in Gesner's discussion treat similarily the habitat, habits, capture, and dietary value of *lucius*. This dweller in quiet fresh waters "besieges, as Ausonius says" its prey, fishes and frogs, from cover. Feeding habits are described with reference to Thomas of Cantimpré and Albertus Magnus and then amplified with contemporary reports of the pike's voracity: one from the Rhone is said to have seized the lip of a mule brought to water; a man from Kraków told of pike eating small dogs and biting the feet of servant girls who swam in a fishpond. "Ein Hecht ist ein Rauber" ("A pike is a robber") is acknowledged as coming from the German "Iocularia piscium," the satirical comparison printed in 1493. Do pike reproduce by spontaneous generation? Gesner summarized earlier arguments and then pointed out that spawning pike and pike fry had been seen in the Elbe and in Switzerland. He listed techniques for catching pike and reported on size, season, and gear restrictions in force in various south German jurisdictions. He contrasted Ausonius's disdain for its food value with the favour of contemporary practice and writers. Gesner offered as well exemplary recipes, culinary and medicinal, including some taken from his compatriot Gregor Mangolt. In this concluding section he reported both that some people eat raw pike skin as a prophylactic against fever and that pike ashes relieve pains in "shameful places," though noting that the latter claim is "uncertain."

To develop knowledge about pike, Konrad von Gesner and his contemporaries read, observed, and catalogued.[8] They gathered data from all available sources, linked that data to the organism to which it referred, and began to sort out that data. The pike had become an object of inquiry or, if you will, of science. But 16th-century science was still closely connected to humanistic scholarship, for its practitioners had first to find and summarize the information in earlier writings done for whatever purpose. Hence

Gesner's place as a father of bibliography (his *Biblioteca universalis* of 1545 listed some ten thousand Latin, Greek, and Hebrew works) cannot be separated from his approach to ichthyology. The flood of information released by the printing press allowed, even demanded, that knowledge become an ordered but open-ended accumulation of data for collaborative consideration and incremental change.

Sixteenth-century shifts in the form, content, and context of scientific thinking about *E. lucius* thus replicated those then occurring in writings on the culture and capture of this fish. Information once confined to the unsystematic empiricism of illiterate practitioners or to an intellectual elite of professional scholars now became accessible to a wider array of people through publication in many identical copies. Writers of treatises and manuals sorted this data, organized it, and made it potentially subject to the tests of observation and subsequent revision. William Samuel's use of Gesner's writings and Gesner's of the 1493 tract even suggest new possibilities of cross-fertilization among hitherto separate groups interested in the pike. The "aquatic wolf" remained in the 16th century a creature of awe and mystery for Europeans, witness the tales of its age and ferocity Gesner thought proper to relate. Europeans now possessed about the pike, however, a corpus of shared and intentionally shaped information available to those interested in it for whatever reason—human food, sport, management, or scientific curiosity. What here follows in the bibliographic listing of writings on *E. lucius* is the latest descendant of that cultural creation.

Notes

[1] The only recorded Latin name for pike is *lucius* which, as Ausonius says, was also a common Roman personal name. No useful explanation for the homonymy has ever been suggested. The Latin root *luc-* is subsequently attached to this fish in all Romance languages, in Gaelic, and, into the 17th century, in English (as *luce*). French gradually abandoned the Latinate form for another of possible Gallic origin, *brochet* (literally "poker," "spear," and hence in an English under French influence, "pike"). German *Hecht* (< *hachit*, compare Old English *haecit*) carries the same connotation. *Esox* is a Latin word derived from the Celtic term for salmon and was until the time of Linnaeus used not for pike but for various salmonids.

Editorial policy for Life Science Publications of the Royal Ontario Museum discourages the use of footnotes. This foreword provides fewer exact citations than is normal in historical scholarship. These notes therefore give detailed references only for extended direct primary quotations and for those few modern studies which have most importantly influenced the interpretations here offered. The author welcomes inquiries about the source of any evidence here inadequately described.

[2] *The Ruodlieb. Linguistic Introduction, Latin Text, and Glossary*, ed. Gordon B. Ford, Jr (Leiden, 1966), fragment X, lines 39–40: "Lucius et rufus, qui sunt in piscibus hirpus, Pisces namque vorant, illos ubi prendere possunt." Translation from Gordon B. Ford, Jr, tr., *The Ruodlieb. The First Medieval Epic of Chivalry from Eleventh-Century Germany* (Leiden, 1965), p. 74.

[3] *Le Menagier de Paris*, ed. G. E. Brereton and J. M. Ferrier (Oxford, 1981), pp. 173, 181–183, and 231–232. Late medieval French texts do not always agree on the size sequence of names given to *lucius*.

[4] Christian Hünemörder, "Die Geschichte der Fischbücher von Aristoteles bis zum Ende des 17 Jahrhunderts," *Deutsches Schiffahrtsarchiv*, 1 (1975), 188–198 surveys formal scholarship in medieval and early modern times.

[5] "alle rawbfisch als hechte....," Kurt Lindner, ed., *Das Jagdbuch des Petrus de Crescentiis in deutschen Übersetzungen des 14. und 15. Jahrhunderts* (Berlin, 1957), p. 159. This passage in Book 10, chapter 38 of the 15th-century translation is absent from the same section of both a 14th-

century German version and de Crescenzi's original (there 10:39), which make no reference to particular fish species.

[6]John McDonald, *The Origins of Angling* (New York, 1963), p. 220, is a facsimile of the printed text; the manuscript passage occurs on p. 154.

[7]*The Arte of Angling 1577*, ed. Gerald E. Bentley (Princeton, 1958), facsimile fols. D.iii. verso - D.iiii. recto, and modernized text pp. 46–47. Identification of the reference to Gesner was made by D. E. Rhodes, "A new line for the angler, 1577," *The Library*, 5th series 10 (1955), 123–124, who traced the passage to Gesner's *Nomenclator aquatilium animantium* (Zürich, 1560), p. 316. Gesner had earlier published the tale, however, in the dedication to his *Historia animalium*, III. *De piscium & aquatilium animantium naturae* (Zürich, 1558), fols a3 recto - a6 verso, where he attributed it to his own teacher, the German humanist Conrad Celtis.

[8]These final paragraphs are influenced by Elizabeth L. Eisenstein, *The Printing Press as an Agent of Change* (Cambridge, 1979), abridged as *The Printing Revolution in Early Modern Europe* (Cambridge, 1983).

Acknowledgements

As a result of the magnitude of this project, work on it has spread over many years. More intensive activity, starting in 1980, occurred sporadically as individuals or small amounts of funding were available to commit to the project. During that time incidental funds were derived solely from the ROM and Fisheries Branch, Ontario Ministry of Natural Resources. We extend our thanks for that continuing encouragement. The real opportunity to complete the bibliography resulted from a contract from the Department of Supply and Services (DSS). Funds were made available from the Unsolicited Proposals Programme (UPP), in cooperation with the Freshwater Institute, Department of Fisheries and Oceans. That contract provided funds for salary for someone to complete the preparation of the computer version and partial support for publication. Computer support was also provided at that time by D. E. McAllister, National Museum of Natural Sciences, Ottawa. The DSS contract made it possible, finally, to commit a single person over a significant period of time to the tasks of drawing together the past efforts of others and completing the file. We thank Lois Casselman for all the work she did seeing the bibliography through to completion and for assistance with the bibliography over the years. She not only worked with care, enthusiasm, and commitment, but contributed ideas on how the bibliography should be done.

In addition there is a large group of people who assisted in a variety of ways, from searching references, typing cards and input sheets, preparing annotations, providing reprints or lists of references, to assisting with the many complexities of generating the computer and printed versions of this bibliography. That assistance is gratefully acknowledged. We list the names here alphabetically without references to the extent of each person's contribution and we offer our sincere thanks to all involved: R. Berka, V. Brull, M. Burridge-Smith, C. W. Casselman, B. Chong, J.-P. Cochain, M. Cook, J. F. Craig, M. Dornfeld, B. Flerov, L. Fuiman, N. Giles, D. Green, P. Grouette, L. Hawrysh, L. Hess, S. Hick, R. C. Hoffmann, C. Horkey, L. Johnson, S. Kirkpatrick, K. Korpacz, H. Lehtonen, A. London, R. Lutticken, W. C. Mackay, M. W. Malley, M. Meili, J. C. Pena, M. Pike, A. J. P. Raat, K. Reid, R. Riehl, C. Rutland, W. Takaki, G. Wilburn, and R. A. Wright.

Introduction

The pike, *Esox lucius* Linnaeus 1758, or northern pike as it is called in North America, is the second largest species in the family Esocidae but has the broadest geographical distribution. It extends in fresh waters, in a circumpolar band in the northern hemisphere, approximately from 35° to 75° north latitude, in North America, the United Kingdom, Europe, and Asia. The pike occurs over the major portion of all of those continental masses, except in narrow arctic or subarctic fringes, arctic islands, some coastal areas, and certain interior drainages (e.g., the Kawartha Lakes of Ontario and the Amur River of Asia). In these interior drainages the pike appears to be replaced by the closely related muskellunge, *Esox masquinongy*, or Amur pike, *E. reicherti*. The range of the pike has been extended south of its native limits in the United States and Europe, and north in the United Kingdom. Introductions have been attempted even in places such as the the Atlas Mountains of Morocco (Anonymous 1965a). It is considered a primary freshwater species but does occur in waters of low salinity in parts of the Baltic Sea.

In most countries this species has both a commercial and a recreational value. In certain European locations it is intensively managed for food in a virtual pond culture situation. The total commercial harvest in the Old World in 1984 was listed as 19966 tonnes, whereas in North America the figure was 3200 tonnes. In Europe the pike enjoys the same popularity as a sportfish that in America is reserved for the larger, closely related muskellunge.

It is obvious that man has been interested in this species for a variety of reasons over a considerable period of time (see Foreword by Richard C. Hoffmann). As a result of that and of the pike's broad distribution, the species became entrenched in a number of cultures, and in their folklore and language. One consequence is that there is an extensive list of names for this fish, most of which are given here in alphabetical order of language.

Croatian - štuka	Norwegian - gjedde
Czech - stika obecná	Polish - szczupak
Danish - gedde	Portuguese - lúcio
Dutch - snoek	Rumanian - stiuca
Finnish - hauki	Russian - shchuká
French - brochet	Slovakian - štuka
Gaelic - liús	Spanish - lucio
German - Hecht	Swedish - gädda
Greek - toúrna	Turkish - turna baliği
Hungarian - csuka	Yugoslavian - ščuka
Italian - luccio	

The English language name in the old world is pike, by which the species has been known for many hundreds of years. The origin of the name pike is debated—Norse and Saxon are cited as sources. All arguments utilize some relationship to "pointed" (snout or body). Several other English names still current are said to have been used at one time in England to describe the animal at various growth stages, from smaller to larger—jack, pickerel, pike, and luce. The populations in North America were long suspected to be sufficiently distinct from those in Europe to deserve a separate name. As a result, the names northern pike and great northern pike came into use. In the mid-1800s the pike in North America was often referred to by the name pickerel, or northern pickerel. The name pickerel, now properly restricted to the three smaller members of the pike family (chain, redfin, and grass pickerel), can cause confusion when using the older literature. This confusion is increased by the lingering practice in Ontario, Canada, of referring to the walleye, *Stizostedion vitreum*, by the name pickerel.

It is unfortunate that the pike is still referred to in English by two "official" common names. The name northern pike is presently the standard in North America, even though the distinction of North American populations is no longer given credence. For convenience and brevity we will use, in general discussion, the older name—pike—since the bibliography is not limited to North American references.

The scientific name *Esox lucius* is said to have been formed by the combination of two ancient common names, "esox" and "luce" or "lucius", long in use in Europe. Even Pliny employed the name "esox" (see Foreword), but he appears to have done so in reference to what would seem to be a much larger fish (the size of a tuna). Readers must also be cautious regarding the scientific name of the pike. Literature prior to 1900 will include references to this species in the genus *Lucius*. In addition, from approximately 1840 to 1900, the distinction between the pike and the muskellunge was poorly understood and some scientific names were used interchangeably. Since descriptions at that time were brief and fragmentary, it is often difficult, or even impossible, to determine which species was intended. This was particularly true for the names *E. estor*, *E. nobilior*, *E. nobilis*, and *E. lucioides*, or any of these trivials used with the genus *Lucius*.

The large size of the pike has always been a major part of its interest to humans. Its size is also prominent in the folklore. There are oft-quoted stories of pike in Europe that had been released after being fitted with a gold ring or collar, which were recaptured as many as 162 and 267 years later. The older of those fish was purported to have been 5.2 m long, though the displayed skeleton of another monster was found to have been made up of bones of several individuals. Pike do grow to an impressive size, and to a venerable age, for freshwater fishes. Individuals of 25 kg are regularly reported from Europe and claims go as high as 34 kg in the USSR. The present angler record in North America is held by a pike that weighed 20.9 kg. We are beginning to have a better understanding of the true age of pike since the establishment of the cleithral bone, rather than scales, as the indicator structure (Casselman 1979). It is quite probable that some large pike seen in Europe are between 20 and 30 years of age. A valuable source of information on large pike are the publications of Buller (1971, 1979, 1981).

This bibliography was prepared in order to make available the references accumulated as a result of our activities starting in 1957. As was true for the two previous esocid bibliographies (Crossman and Lewis 1973, *Esox niger*, Royal Ontario Museum Miscellaneous Publications; and Crossman and Goodchild 1978, *Esox masquinongy*, Royal Ontario Museum Miscellaneous Publications), other workers showed interest in access to these literature files, and it seemed appropriate to make them available in print. Since the preparation of the muskellunge bibliography there have been considerable advancements in the opportunity to mount bibliographies of this sort on microcomputers. This pike bibliography is so mounted. The computer version was used to generate the printed version and will be kept up-to-date. We request that all readers using the bibliography contribute to its updating by sending us corrections, reprints, or lists of new or missing titles. With assistance in maintaining the file, we should be able to provide people interested in the pike a computer print-out, for a particular subject category, of references received or discovered after the production of the printed version.

We wish to remind users of this bibliography that it is intended only as an indication of the source of the original articles. The annotations are meant simply to assist the reader in determining whether or not he or she should attempt to locate the original.

Annotations are not meant as a substitute for referring to the original. In addition, this list cannot be guaranteed to be without error. The presence here of an annotation could be construed as indicating that the entry was prepared from a copy of the paper. This is true for most entries, but not for all. An annotation was provided only if the publication cited was seen by us, or if an abstract was available in a bibliographic aid. Annotations were also derived from author abstracts when these were available.

Wherever possible, references were checked for accuracy. We felt, however, that we would serve the user better by listing unverified citations in the form available to us rather than by omitting them because they had not been verified. Many references were copied from the literature cited sections of various publications, at times perpetuating errors created by others. Any obvious errors were corrected, but the user of this bibliography is encouraged to locate the original. An n.d. (or n.d.a., n.d.b., etc.) notation implies that a copy of the article was seen, but that it carried no date of writing or publication. For entries that have no date and no n.d. notation, the indication is that although the original may have carried a date, we were unable to discover it.

Normally references in ROM publications are verified by ROM librarians prior to publication. The magnitude of the ''reference list'' in this publication made that impossible, and we accept responsibility for problems that will arise as a result. We apologize in advance to librarians everywhere who may be requested to locate a reference cited in the bibliography only to find that the listing is incomplete or in error.

The references come from a variety of sources: copies of publications, and references, gathered by each author; the list of references in papers cited in the bibliography; references and abstracts in printed bibliographic aids (e.g., ASFA1); lists of references made available by key-word searches of on-line bibliographic files (e.g., Fish and Wildlife Reference Service, Rockville, Maryland), lists of titles sent us by biologists, authors, bibliographers, anglers, etc., in North America and Europe. The references are not limited to professional publications. They also include popular titles we were able to acquire over the many years during which the bibliography was being accumulated. The bibliography is far from complete, and is more complete for North American than for Eurasian literature. An extensive campaign of written requests and notices at European meetings was mounted to attempt to attract submission of references to studies published in countries over the whole geographic distribution of the species. Response to these requests was very helpful but went only a short way towards accessing the voluminous Eurasian literature. We realize that the appearance of this bibliography will elicit a flood of notices advising us of references that were not included.

June 1986 was set as the termination date for adding new entries to the bibliography. A few that appeared after that date were added, including the new and very useful FAO synopsis of biological data on this species (Raat 1987).

In spite of the bibliography's shortcomings, we hope that its appearance, in conjunction with the appearance of the FAO synopsis, will make results of past work on the species much more available to teachers, researchers, resource managers, anglers, and interested naturalists. Other publications that summarized available information on the pike are Clark (1958), Buss (1961a), Toner, E. D. (1966), Carlander (1969), Toner and Lawler (1969), and Inskip (1982b).

The ROM format for publishing literature citations calls for spelling out the name of the source document. This we have done, except for abbreviations in a few references in languages other than English. Rather than risk creating errors by attempting to complete those abbreviations, we left them as found. Editors often require that authors spell out their given names, but authors citing other authors sometimes reduce given names to initials, or two initials to one. The result is that in this bibliography there are series of author citations that differ only in having sometimes one initial, sometimes two, and sometimes three, though one might assume that it is the same author in all instances. In addition, the names of authors in the USSR and Scandinavia are often transliterated in reference lists in English to avoid use of the Cyrillic alphabet and accents. This can result in the surname of an author appearing with two or three different spellings. In this bibliography we have retained the citations as found. Some deviations from ROM format (e.g., punctuation, square brackets) result from the need to list references not seen by us in the form in which they were found in other publications.

We apologize for the absence of accents and diacritical marks on words in languages in which they occur. The program used to prepare the computer-based version did not include them, and it was intended from the outset that this publication would be generated directly from the computer diskettes. We felt that the absence of the marks would not prevent any reader from being able to locate the original and decided to proceed without them in the printed version.

The bibliography consists of three sections: 1) the historical foreword by Richard C. Hoffmann, 2) the bibliography comprising citations and annotations in normal alphabetical and chronological order, and 3) the subject index. In the bibliography, the anonymous entries are in alphabetical position, rather than at the beginning as they are in many lists and in the earlier esocid bibliographies. Unlike the arrangement in the previous bibliographies, Mac and Mc entries are separated and in alphabetical position. Annotations are of two general types—descriptive and informative. The type chosen for each article depended on the subject, the length of the article, and the amount of data provided. We are not bothered by the fact that many annotations do not convey actual results, since we hope, as stated above, that the annotations will be used only in a decision regarding searching for the original.

The subject index consists of 37 categories chosen by us on the basis of the best organization of the subject matter contained in the references, and a decision on how readers would be most likely to categorize the information for which they were searching. The categories reflect subjects we have learned people are most interested in and most likely to search for.

For those articles not seen in the original, or in a bibliographic listing that included an abstract, it was often impossible to assign the paper to a subject category. As a result, there are references that cannot be located by using the subject index. They can, however, be located in the text if the name(s) of the author(s) is known. For that reason we felt it better to include them than to omit them. Many articles provide information on several subject categories and are indexed accordingly.

Because of the magnitude of even the subject index, an attempt was made to provide the reader with further assistance in selecting the papers to be located in the bibliography. Whenever the information was available, entries in the subject index include an indication of the geographic location of the study.

Subject Categories

Accounts by Geographical and Political Areas. Includes mainly publications entitled "The Fishes of" a particular political area. Such accounts generally involve at least brief comments for the species on several subjects. References in this category are not cross-indexed unless the account contains a significant contribution to one or more of the other subject categories. It is in papers or books indexed here that the reader will find at

4

least basic information on the pike specific to his or her country, region, province, or state.

Age and Growth Determination. Includes papers on the methodology of determining age and estimating growth. Deals specifically with the techniques and procedures.

Age and Growth Studies. Includes age and growth data, comprising age and size distribution, size at age, and growth rate. Papers that deal with the relationship of length and weight without associating them with age are indexed under *Length-Weight Relationships.* See also *Population Dynamics.*

Anatomy, Morphology, and Histology. Includes references on external anatomy, internal anatomy, osteology, and studies of structures that might otherwise be listed under embryology and cytology. It does not include systematics nor references that list external anatomical features as part of a simple description of the animal; those appear under *Taxonomy, Nomenclature, and Systematics.*

Angling and Record Catches. Includes stories and reminiscences about angling and notices of record catches. Most often these are articles in popular books, outdoor magazines, and periodicals.

Behaviour. Includes only those references dealing with ethology; concepts of behaviour that could be considered simply as habits are included under *Life History and Habits.*

Commercial Fishing. Includes articles dealing with the capture of pike for sale. Government publications listing commercial fisheries catches were not included in the bibliography. Anyone interested in this type of information should check government reports, such as Reports of the Commissioner of Fisheries, Annual Reports, and Overseers' Reports. Since government departments are frequently reorganized these reports can be found under various department names throughout the years.

Creel Census and Angling Statistics. Includes articles which present information usually allied to studies on age and growth, or population dynamics. However, publications describing methods or results of creel census do not always indicate the intended application, so they are indexed separately.

Culture and Artificial Propagation. Includes references dealing with artificial spawning, hatching, and rearing. Natural spawning was included here only if the study was carried out as an adjunct to fish culture. References to natural spawning appear under *Spawning.*

Distribution and Range. Includes references that vary from obvious ones dealing with the total range of this species to those that include the species in a checklist of a specific watershed or region, to those that list the species as present at a single location.

Early Development. Includes papers on early growth, development, and associated conditions for various young life stages such as eggs, yolk sac fry, larvae, and fingerlings.

Food and Feeding Habits. Includes all discussions of food items or feeding activity except those that allude to cannibalism or predator-prey relationships, which are listed

5

under *Predator-Prey Relationships*.

Fossils and Archaeology. Includes records of fossilized remains identified as this species, and "near fossils" from archaeological digs.

General Accounts. Includes a miscellany of articles much like that in *Accounts by Geographical and Political Areas*, giving brief comments on several aspects of this fish, but lacking any geographic orientation in the general discussion.

Genetics. Includes papers on electrophoresis, proteins, and enzymes and references to these other than in their physiological role. Depending on the application of the results, some of these apply to *Taxonomy, Nomenclature, and Systematics*.

Habitat and Environmental Factors. Includes not only general descriptions of the habitat, but also of specific environmental requirements, as well as lethal or sublethal environmental conditions, and contents of chemicals and other foreign materials dangerous to the fish or its captor.

Historical Accounts. Includes early historical information, as well as myths and legends.

Hybrids. Includes references that deal with hybrids in nature or cultured in the hatchery or laboratory. All references to *Esox lucius* X *E. masquinongy* are included here. In the subject categories in the index, any entry with the designation "H" after the geographic notation is a reference to a hybrid.

Identification. Includes descriptions of methods and characteristics used for identifying pike and distinguishing it from other fish, especially other esocids.

Introductions and Stocking. Includes references on release into areas beyond the natural range (introductions), and the re-establishment or support of populations within the natural range by fish culture practices (stocking).

Length-Weight Relationships. Includes all compendia of length or weight and comparisons of length and weight, and condition factor, except when any of these refer strictly to individual fish taken by anglers. Comparisons of length and weight are often associated with studies of age and growth, but there were so many references to works specifically giving length and weight data that they were indexed separately.

Life History and Habits. Includes those general discussions of aspects of the biology of the animal in nature that cannot be separately categorized. The category does not include papers on habitat, which are indexed separately. It includes discussions of activities usually referred to in general as habits but not described in ethological terms; the latter are indexed in *Behaviour*.

Management. Includes papers that deal with broad, general subjects allied to the management of pike populations for man's benefit, encompassing papers dealing with production, yield, and catch per unit of effort. There may be some crossover between this category and *Population Dynamics*. Most of the Dingell-Johnson Reports indexed under *Project Reports* probably could be equally well classified here.

6

Marking and Tagging. Includes studies that make extensive use of marks by mutilation, application, or implantation, whether numbered or electronic, regardless of the reason for the mark.

Movement and Activity. Includes references to migration, telemetry, movement patterns, and activity involving seasonal and diel cycles.

Nutrition. Includes studies on energy requirements, usually associated with artificial rearing and culture.

Parasites, Pathology, and Diseases. Includes references to the effect on the fish and its biology of these problems and their effect on the well-being of pike and pike populations.

Physiology and Biochemistry. Includes papers on the internal functions of the body, and response to stress and other environmental factors when results are expressed in terms of physiological processes. Includes chemical analysis of the parts of the animal in regard to percentage of constituents.

Popular Accounts. Includes descriptions of the animal in general terms—much like *General Accounts*—but usually those found in outdoor magazines, such as sporting periodicals, or interpretative publications such as conservation publications of state and provincial agencies. Popular articles that deal solely with stories of angling are indexed under *Angling and Record Catches.*

Population Dynamics. Includes references to abundance, density, mortality, natality, recruitment, and age-class structure; articles on assessment of population size and factors affecting population size, such as survival and natural and fishing mortalities. See also *Management, Creel Census and Angling Statistics,* and *Age and Growth Studies.*

Predator-Prey Relationships. Includes references to works with the word "predation" in the title, or texts in which predation of, or by, pike is implicit. References are set aside in this discrete category as a result of the interest in esocids as predatory control of the numbers of other fishes. Otherwise references on fishes eaten appear in *Food and Feeding Habits.*

Project Reports. Includes Dingell-Johnson Reports that describe projects supported under United States federal aid to fisheries. These are not in general circulation, and were largely derived from computer listings provided by Fish and Wildlife Reference Service, P.O. Box 6044, Rockville, Maryland 20850. Only some are annotated and for that reason they were difficult to categorize. We felt that readers might find it valuable to have all Dingell-Johnson Reports indexed as such. Any that could readily be categorized will appear in the appropriate part of the index. Almost all of these reports could have been indexed under *Management.*

Reproduction. Includes information associated with reproduction not directly related to spawning and includes physiological and biochemical information associated with reproduction.

Sampling Techniques. Includes studies examining specific methods for collecting, vulnerability, selectivity, availability, variability; the gear is usually being examined.

Spawning. Includes papers that describe natural spawning, habitat requirements for spawning, and production of young from natural spawning as opposed to fish culture.

Taxonomy, Nomenclature, and Systematics. Includes references to adequate taxonomic descriptions of the animal and various means of distinguishing it from other fishes.

Toxicology and Contaminants. Includes studies of anything that causes toxicity and is toxic to the normal biology of the species; anything that is considered to be present at levels that are not normal; the effects of toxic substances on survival.

Bibliography

ABASHIDZE, V. S.
　1969　Contribution to the innervation of the fish digestive tube. *In* Dzhavakhishvili, N. A., et al., eds., Transactions of the 7th All-Union Conference of Anatomists, Histologists, and Embryologists. Tibilsi, Publishing House, pp. 579–580.

ABBASOV, G. S.
　1980　The ichthyofauna of the main freshwater bodies of Azerbaidzhan. Journal of Ichthyology 20(4):140–143.
　　　　Based on a summary of data collected over 20 years (1958–1978). Mentions pike in list of species present.

ABROSIMOVA, A. M.
　1975　Study of fish orientation in homing. Vestnik Zoologii 1975(4):3–8.

ABROSIMOVA, A. M., S. G. VASINA and S. B. GUMENYUK
　1971　Effect of some sense organs on fish distance orientation. Vestnik Zoologii 5(2):79–80.

ACKERMAN, B.
　1955　Handbook of fishes of the Atlantic seaboard. Washington, American Printing. 144 pp.

ACOLAT, L.
　1955　Recherches relatives a la reaction du coeur isole du brochet (*Esox lucius* L.) au passage du courant galvanique. Annales Scientifiques de l'Universite de Besancon Zoologie et Physiologie 4:9–16.

ADAMS, C. C. and T. L. HANKINSON
　1928　The ecology and economics of Oneida Lake fish. Roosevelt Wildlife Annals 1(3 and 4):241–358.
　　　　Shows stomach contents of eight specimens and summary of others' findings.

ADELMAN, I.
　1969　Survival and growth of northern pike in relation to water quality. Ph.D. thesis, University of Minnesota. 195 pp.

ADELMAN, I. R. and L. L. SMITH, Jr.
　1970a　Effect of oxygen on growth and food conversion efficiency of pike. Progressive Fish-Culturist 32:93–96.
　　　　Growth and food consumption rates of juveniles decreased gradually, over 42 and 48 days, with reduction in oxygen concentrations from 7.20 to 3 ppm, and decreased more rapidly at lower levels. Food conversion efficiency was constant from 7.20 to 2.91 ppm, but decreased abruptly below 2.91 ppm.
　1970b　Effect of hydrogen sulfide on northern pike eggs and sac fry. Transactions of the American Fisheries Society 99:501–509.
　　　　Bioassays were conducted on eggs and sac fry to test the effects of hydrogen sulfide at two oxygen concentrations, 2 ppm and 6 ppm. Mean median tolerance limits are provided. Eggs subjected to hydrogen sulfide produced yolk sac fry with increased anatomical malformations and fry that were smaller than the controls. The maximum possible safe level of hydrogen sulfide for eggs was between 0.014 and 0.018 ppm and for sac fry between 0.004 and 0.006 ppm for 96 hours of exposure.

ADOLFSON, I.
   1949   Hur en sjosakning inverkar pa goddans fort plantnings formaga. Svensk Fisk-
           eritidskrift 58:7–8.
AGAPOV, J. D. and V. N. ABROSOV
   1967   On the selectivity in the feeding of fish and the fish cultural role of pike.
           Voprosy Ikhtiologii 7:123–128. [in Russian]
AGASSIZ, J. L. R.
   1854   Notice of collection of fishes from the southern bend of Tennessee River.
           American Journal of Science Ser.17, 2:297–308.
           Indicates mid-1800's confusion in names and distinction of forms of *Esox* in
           North America. Wrongly uses pike for muskellunge in Tennessee River and
           fails to recognize pike of Europe occurs in North America.
AGASSIZ, L.
   1842   Notice sur les poissons fossiles et l'osteologie du genre brochet (*Esox*). Neu-
           chatel:57–84.
   1850   Lake Superior: its physical character, vegetation, and animals, compared
           with those of other and similar regions. Boston, Gould, Kendall, Lincoln.
           428 pp.
   1857   Remarks on young bony pikes. Annals and Magazine of Natural History
           Ser.2, 19:190–191.
AHNE, W.
   1978   Isolation and characterization of infectious pancreatic necrosis virus from
           pike *Esox lucius* L. Archives of Virology 58:65–70.
           A nonenveloped icosahedral virus measuring 60 (.5) nm in diameter was iso-
           lated from pike fry. The isolate was stable to heat, lipid solvent, and acid.
           Serologically, the virus was related to the major European strains of infec-
           tious pancreatic necrosis virus Sp and Ab. The isolate was neutralized by
           normal trout serum and was not pathogenic for young pike. A line of CHSE-
           214 cells persistently infected with the isolate was established and was passed
           30 times.
   1980   Experimentelle Egtvedvirusinfektion beim Hecht (*Esox lucius* L.). [Experi-
           mental infection of pike (*Esox lucius*) with Egtvedvirus]. Tieraerztliche
           Umschau 35:225–229.
           Pike are susceptible to an infection with Egtvedvirus via water, food, and by
           infection of virus. Infected fish showed extensive haemorrhages in skin and
           muscle 3–4 days after infection. Mortality rate was 100%, and the virus
           could be re-isolated from a variety of organs.
AHO, I.
   1967   Besked om kvicksilvret: Alandska gaddan riskfri. Fiskarbladet 22, 14, 1 & 4
AHOKAS, J. T., N. T. KARKI, A. OIKARI and A. SOIVIC
   1976   Mixed function mono oxygenase of fish as an indicator of pollution of aquatic
           environment by industrial effluent. Bulletin of Environmental Contamination
           and Toxicology 16:270–274.
AISA, A.
   1976   Cisti da larve plerocercoidi di *Triaenophorus lucii* (Muller, 1776) nelle ovaie
           di *Tinca tinca* e di *Esox lucius*. Atti della Societa Italiana delle Scienze
           Veterinarie 29:613–620.

AISA, A. and P. GATTAPONI

1974   *Triaenophorus lucii* in Lake Trasimeno. Parassitologia 16:96–97.

AKHERMOV, A. K. and E. A. BOGDANOVA

1961   Data on the parasitofauna of fish in the region of the future Stalingrad water basin (in the region of the flood-land lakes and Eruslan River). *In* Petrushevskii, G. K., ed., Parasites and diseases of fish. Jerusalem, Israel Program for Scientific Translations, pp. 141–154.

AKOS, H.

1981   The growth of the pike *Esox lucius* in the section of the Tisza River near Tiszafured, Hungary. Allattani Kozlemenyek 68(1–4):67–76.

ALDINGER, H.

1965   Der Hecht. Hamburg. 178 pp.

ALEEV, Y. G.

1969   Function and gross morphology in fish. Jerusalem, Israel Program for Scientific Translations. 268 pp.

ALESSIO, G.

1975a   Ricerche sulla biologia del luccio *Esox lucius* L. (Osteichthyes, Esocidae) in Lomellina occidentale ed in una 'valle' veneta. [Investigations on the biology of the pike in the western Lomellina and a Venetian 'valley']. Bollettino di Pesca Piscicoltura e Idrobiologia 30:235–256.

1975b   Accrecimento lineare e ponderate del luccio, *Esox lucius* L. (Osteichthyes, Esocidae), in Lomellina occidentale ed una 'valle' veneta. [Growth in length and weight of the pike *Esox lucius* L. (Osteichthyes, Esocidae) of the western Lomellina and a Venetian 'valley']. Bollettino di Pesca Piscicoltura e Idrobiologia 30:257–275.

1976   Indagini preliminari sul luccio in Lomellina. Pavia Caccia Pesca e Sport 4(4):17–24.

1983   Quelques aspects de la biologie et de l'elevage du brochet (*Esox lucius* L.) en Italie. *In* Billard, R., ed., Le brochet gestion dans le milieu naturel et elevage. Paris, Institute National de la Recherche Agronomique. 371 pp.
    Summarizes several aspects of pike biology in natural waters and hatcheries in Italy, with special emphasis on growth, population structure, food, parasites, number of eggs for each spawning time.

1984   Le black-bass, *Micropterus salmoides* (Lacep.), dans les eaux italiennes. Un antagoniste du brochet? Bulletin Francais de Pisciculture 292:1–17.
    Discusses interspecific competition between largemouth bass and pike.

ALLAN, J. W.

1957   Tagging pike in Inner Long Point Bay. Ontario Department of Lands and Forests, unpublished internal report.

ALLDRIDGE, N. A. and A. M. WHITE

1980   Spawning site preferences for northern pike (*Esox lucius*) in a New York marsh with widely fluctuating water levels. Ohio Journal of Science 80:13.
    Pike spawned in open water over any available vegetation at depths of 6 to 24 inches. Spawning occurred at temperatures above 5.5 C; on days when the area was iced, spawning was delayed until late afternoon.

ALLEN, A. A.

1913   The red-winged blackbird. A study in the ecology of a cat-tail marsh. Proceedings of the Linnaean Society of New York 24–25:43–128.
    Noted pike running at Ithaca with the disappearance of the ice, and while the

inlet of Cayuga Lake was still full of floating ice pike were along the shore trying to enter the marshes, and here they spawned in large numbers during March and April.

ALLEN, J. L., C. W. LUHNING and P. D. HARMAN

1972   Residues of MS-222 in northern pike, muskellunge, and walleye. U.S. Fish and Wildlife Service, Investigations in Fish Control 45:3–8.

Residues of MS-222 in muscle tissue were measured by a modified Bratton-Marshall colorimetric method and confirmed by thin-layer chromatography. The residues dissipate rapidly when the fish are withdrawn from the anesthetic and are under the background readings of the controls within 24 hours.

ALLEN, K. R.

1939   A note on the food of pike (*Esox lucius*) in Windermere. Journal of Animal Ecology 8:72–75.

Stomach contents of 103 pike were examined. They fed almost entirely on fishes, mostly perch. The only invertebrate food was nymphs of *Ephemera danica*. Small pike ate smaller fish than did large pike. A high percentage of pike had empty stomachs, especially in winter.

ALLIS, E. P., JR.

1905   The laterosensory canals and related bones in fishes. Monatsschrift fuer Anatomie und Physiologie 21:401–502.

A short but detailed description and four schematic figures to illustrate the bone structure and the canal system in pike.

ALLISON, D. and H. HOTHEM

1975   An evaluation of the status of the fisheries and the status of other selected wild animals in the Maumee River Basin, Ohio. Ohio Department of Natural Resources, Division of Wildlife. 16 pp.

Lists 108 species of fish with comments on distribution, relative abundance, and the probable future of each species. Pike were common and found in Maumee, Tiffin, and St. Joseph rivers and Swan Creek. Spawning occurs in many small tributaries.

ALLISON, L. N.

1953   Advancements in prevention and treatment of parasitic diseases. Transactions of the American Fisheries Society 83:221–228.

Describes the pond-treatment method of control of fish disease caused by external organisms. Gives methods of treating external and internal parasites, as well as fungus, in both fish and eggs.

ALM, G.

1940   Gott resultat av gaddodling. Svensk Fiskeri Tidskrift 49:184.

1957   Avkastningen av Gadd—och Abborfisket vid Sveriges Ostersjokust Aren 1914–1955. [The yield of the pike and perch fisheries along the Baltic coasts of Sweden during the years 1914–1955]. Institute of Freshwater Research Drottningholm, Report 38:5–69.

1959   Connection between maturity, size, and age in fishes. Institute of Freshwater Research Drottningholm, Report 40:5–145.

A summary of age, growth, and maturity of pike from various countries.

ALT, K.

1977   The northern pike in Alaska. Alaska Department of Fish and Game, Wildlife Notebook Series. 2 pp.

A brief description, life history, and some sport fishing information on pike.

ALT, K. T.
1965   Food habits of inconnu in Alaska. Transactions of the American Fisheries Society 94:272–274.

1968   Sport fish investigations of Alaska: sheefish and pike investigations of the upper Yukon and Kuskokwim drainages with emphasis on Minto Flats drainages, 1967–1968. Alaska Department of Fish and Game, Dingell-Johnson Project F-S-R-9/17-B/:1–16.

1969   Sport fish investigations of Alaska: sheefish and pike investigations of the upper Yukon and Kuskokwin drainages with emphasis on Minto Flats drainages. Alaska Department of Fish and Game, Dingell-Johnson Project F-9-1, Report 17-B: 1–16.

1973   A life history study of sheefish and whitefish in Alaska. Alaska Department of Fish and Game 14:1–31.

1977   Inventory and cataloging western Alaska waters. Alaska Department of Fish and Game.

1980   Inventory and cataloging western Alaska waters. Alaska Department of Fish and Game.

ALTMAN, P. L. and D. S. DITTMER, eds.
1972   Biology data book. 2nd ed. Bethesda, Federation of American Societies for Experimental Biology, vol. 1. 606 pp.

AMBROSINUS, B.
1642   Paralipomena accuratissima historiae omnium animalium, quae in voluminibus Aldrovandi desiderantur. Bononiae.
        Description of the swim bladder of pike.

AMIN, O. M.
1979   Lymphocystis disease in Wisconsin fishes. Journal of Fish Diseases 2:207–218.

1981   *Fessisentis tichiganensis* new species Acanthocephala Fessisentidae from Wisconsin fishes with a key to species. Journal of Parasitology 66:1039–1045.

ANANICHEV, A. V.
1961   Comparative biochemical data for some freshwater invertebrates and fish. Biochemistry 26:16–26.

1963   Amino acid content of proteins of some freshwater invertebrates and fish. Data on biology and hydrology of the Volga region reservoirs. USSR Academy of Scientific Biology, Institute of Internal Waters, pp. 38–41

ANDERSON, A. W. and C. E. PETERSON
        Fisheries statistics of United States, U.S. Fish and Wildlife Service. U.S. Fish and Wildlife Service, Statistical Digest 27:1–492.

ANDERSON, R. G., G. LEIDAHL and C. K. BRASHIER
1971   Some algae isolated from fresh water fish. Journal of Phycology 7 (Suppl.):10.

ANDERSON, R. M.
1913   My life with the Eskimo. *In* Stefansson, V. New York, Macmillan, pp. 450–455.
        Notes on distribution and use by natives.

ANDERSON, R. O.

1973   Application of theory and research to management of warmwater fish popula-
        tions. Transactions of the American Fisheries Society 102:164–171.
        Pike were stocked in 12 reservoirs. Introduction and maintenance of large
        piscivorous species may add valuable sport fishing opportunities and enhance
        the yield of other sport fishes. The pike-muskellunge hybrid may have poten-
        tial south of the normal range of the parent species.

ANDERSON, R. O. and S. J. GUTREUTER

1981   Evolution and evaluation of structural indices of fish populations and com-
        munities. 43rd Midwest Fish and Wildlife Conference.

ANDERSON, R. O. and A. S. WEITHMAN

1978   The concept of balance for coolwater fish populations. American Fisheries
        Society Special Publication 11:371–381.
        State of balance of coolwater fish populations and communities is examined.
        Minimum stock and quality sizes are defined for several species, including
        pike (35 and 53 cm respectively). Balanced fish communities are defined.

ANDERSSON, G., H. BERGGSEN, G. CRONBERG and C. GELIN

1978   Effects of planktivorous and benthivorous fish on organisms and water chem-
        istry in eutrophic lakes. Hydrobiology 59:9.
        Enclosures were used to study the impact of fish on eutrophication in lakes
        that contained pike.

ANDERSSON, O. and G. BLOMKVIST

1981   Polybrominated aromatic pollutants found in fish in Sweden. Chemosphere
        10:1051–1060.
        The maximum level of polybrominated biphenyl ethers detected in muscle
        was 0.15 mg/kg (27 mg/kg fat) in a pike caught in the southwest part of
        Sweden. The liver contained 22 mg PBBEs/kg (110 mg PBBEs/kg fat).

ANDORFER, B.

1980   The school behaviour of *Leucaspius delineatus* (Heckel) in relation to
        ambient space and the presence of a pike (*Esox lucius*). Oecologia
        47:137–140.
        At a water depth of 60 cm (without pike) school concentration was very much
        lower than at 20 cm, both at 980 lux and at 0.02 lux. At 0.02 lux in the
        absence of the predator, the shapes of the water space cannot be ascertained
        to have an influence. At 980 lux (with and without pike) shape had an intense
        effect on school concentration. In the dark (0.02 lux) the effect of a pike in
        intensifying school formation was smaller, the larger the quantity of water.

ANDREASSEN, J. and H. MADSEN

1970   On *Diphyllobothrium latum* in Denmark. Nytt Magasin for Zoologi 18:99.

ANDREEV, V. L.

1968   A simple model of open controlled system of predator prey. Vch. Zap. Dal-
        nevastochnogo Univ. 15(2):145–153.

ANDREW, W.

1959   Textbook of comparative histology. New York, Oxford University Press.

ANDRIASHEV, A. P.

1937   K poznaniyu ikhtiofauny Berigova i Chukotskogo morey. Explor. Mers.
        URSS 25:292–355. [English summary]

ANDRIC-ESPERANTO, M. J.

1985 *Bothriocephalus echeilognathis* Yamaguti 1934 (*Bothriocephalus gowkongensis* Yeh 1935) in some regions in Yugoslovia. *In* E. Tumboy et al., eds. The Fourth European Multi-Colloquium of Parasitology, Izmer, Turkey. Izmer, Bilgehan Publishing, pp. 201–202.

Pike was one of the species that was discovered as a new host.

ANDRZEJCZYK, T.

1972 Wadkarstwo jeziorow. [Lake angling.] Warsaw, PWRiL. 284 pp.

ANISHCHENKO, V.

1965 Bliznetsovyi tral s elektropodboroi dlya lova karasa i shchuki. [Pair trawl with electric mainline for fishing crucian carp and pike]. Rybnoe Khozyaistvo 7.

ANNETT, C. S. and F. M. D'ITRI

1978 Mercury in fish and sediments in two eutrophic Michigan lakes with respect to time and urbanization. *In* Adriano, D. C., and I. L. Brisbin, Jr., eds., Environmental chemistry and cycling processes, U.S. Department of Energy Symposium Series, 1976. Springfield, U.S. Department of Commerce, pp. 866–878.

ANON, W. T.

1884 Fishing the Ottawa River. [In 3 parts]. The American Field 22(14–16):313–367.

Historical records of distribution, size, and angling success in the Ottawa and Grand rivers, Ontario, in 1876.

ANONYMOUS

1550 The art of angling. English manuscript annotated "from an old vellum ms. written probably about 1550 in my (Thomas Gosden?) possession."

1877 Pike, pickerel and maskalonge. Forest and Stream 8(20):320.

Distinguishing features and description.

1888 Big pike. The American Angler, p. 221.

Records of pike caught in England and Ireland obtained from a column contributed by "Vanderdecken, a well-known English angling writer".

1892 Sztuczne zapladnianie ikry szczpuaka. [Artificial fertilization of pike eggs.] Okolnik 8:45–46.

Practical suggestions on artificial fertilization of pike eggs.

1902a Pike, pickerel, mascalonge. Forest and Stream 59(3):50–51.

1902b Pike, pickerel and mascalonge. Forest and Stream 59(4):71.

1903 Kilka slow w obronie szczupaka. [Some comments in favour of pike.] Okolnik Rybacki 65:195–197.

Characteristic details concerning life and behaviour of this "shark" of fresh waters.

1906 Spory szczupak. [What a pike.] Okolnik Rybacki 83:142.

Information on a pike weighing 32 pounds, of body length 115 cm.

1908 Szczupak. [The pike.] Okolnik Rybacki 101:231–234.

Value of pike as a sport fish. Methods of artificial fertilization of pike eggs.

1928 Choroba szczupakow w Prusach Wschodnich. [Pike disease in eastern Prussia.] Przeglad Rybacki 1:322.

A note about the appearance of "pike disease" in inland waters of Eastern Prussia. The disease was of an epizootic character with slight symptoms.

1933   Tempo wzrostu szczupaka i jego zdolnosc wykorzystywania pokarmu. [Rate of growth of pike and its ability to utilize food.] Przeglad Rybacki 6:164–166.
        Studies on the rate of growth in particular stages of the life of pike.

1934   Ciekawostki o szczupaku. [Comments on pike.] Przeglad Rybacki 7:304–307.
        Studies on the utilization of food by pike. Description of interesting cases of finding live fish in pike stomachs after their consumption.

1937   Szczupak. [The pike.] Wiadomosci Wedkarskie 2(9):69.
        Method of catching pike with a rod.

1938   Jeszcze jeden sposob lowienia szczupakow. [One more method to catch pike.] Wiadomosci Wedkarskie 3(8):92–93.
        A method of catching pike using the so-called "szanca".

1946   Pike, pickerel and maskinonge. Royal Ontario Museum of Zoology, Circular 1, 3 pp.
        Discussion of the use of the names pike, pickerel, and maskinonge and of the species to which each refers.

1952   Monkeying with nature. Northern Sportsman 7(4):14–15, 27.

1957   Poradnik rybaka jeziorowego. [Manual of lake fisherman.] Warsaw, A. Rudnickiego, PWRiL. 483 pp.

1958   Wobronie szczupaka. [In favour of pike.] Wiadomosci Wedkorskie 3:1.
        Protective measures and a program of activities undertaken to protect pike against poaching and excessive angling.

1960a   Big fish of 1959 listed. North Dakota Outdoors, Feb. 1960, p. 13.

1960b   Fishing guide—1960. North Dakota Outdoors, May 1960, pp. 11–14.

1961a   List of species known to occur in la Verendrye Parc. Journal de bord, de l'office de biologie Ministere des pecheries et de la chasse 4:76.

1961b   Bekampfung der Fleckenseuche bei Hechten durch Antibiotika. Der Fischwirt 11.

1964   Wszystko o szczupaku. [All about pike.] Wiadomosci Wedkorskie 3:11.
        Basic knowledge on pike biology.

1965a   Pike in Morocco. Fishing Club du Moyen-Atlas, July 1965, pp. 22–23.
        Introduced pike have produced a successful sport fishery in temperate, interior waters. Their rate of growth is very satisfactory, often higher than in Europe.

1965b   Hodowla ryb w stawach. [Fish culture in ponds.] Warsaw, A. Rudnickiego, PWRiL. 635 pp.

1966   Northern pike stocking in Murphy Flowage. Wisconsin Conservation Department, Dingell-Johnson Project F-83-R-2, Job III-A: 1–20.
        Anglers' catch in 1966 was similar to that in 1965 but only 38–47% of the yearly catch for the 10-yr period 1955–1964. Survival of stocked pike over one year was 19% and only 6.5% of pike stocked in December 1963 had been caught by anglers.

1969   Ryby Hodowlane. Material zarybieniowy szczupaka. [Cultured fish. Stocking material of pike.] Wydawnictwa Normalizacyjne, Warsaw. 8 pp.
        Standards for fertilized eggs, eyed eggs, larvae, summer and autumn fry of pike. The standards define origin, health conditions, size of fry, external features and conditions of pike fry transport and storage.

1970   Joint meeting—Freshwater Biological Association, Windermere, 23 and 24 September 1969. Proceedings of the Challenger Society 4:67–76.

1973a   All-time Saskatchewan fishing derby records. Outdoor Saskatchewan 21(3):1–12.
         Provides angler's name, weight, and location of capture for the 605 largest pike ever entered in the Saskatchewan derby. The largest, caught in 1954, was 42 lb. 12 oz.

1973b   Maly slownik zoologiczny. Ryby. [Compact zoological glossary. Fishes.] Warsaw, Wiedza Powszechna. 310 pp.

1975a   Great northern pike introductions. Oklahoma Department of Wildlife Conservation, Dingell-Johnson Project F-22-R, Job 4: 1–18.

1975b   Northern pike after the turnover. In'Fisherman, Segment 1, Study Report 3, pp. 18–21.
         Provides information to the angler on feeding habits, habitat, condition, and movement of pike during autumn.

1976a   Al Lindner's pike challenge. In'Fisherman, Segment 1, Study Report 4, Unit 1, pp. 1–3.

1976b   Lunker pike lakes. In'Fisherman, Segment 1, Study Report 4, Unit 2, pp. 4–8.
         An angler's discussion of lake types according to limnology and forage (especially various members of the whitefish family) and the size of pike that each of these types produces.

1976c   Pike activity in cold water. In'Fisherman, Segment 1, Study Report 4, Unit 3, pp. 9–13.
         Advice to anglers on strategy. Included are prey search activity, metabolism, digestion, food preference, and how each varies with size of pike and season.

1976d   Predators relating to prey. In'Fisherman, Segment 1, Study Report 4, Unit 4, p. 14.

1976e   Cold water delivery systems. In'Fisherman, Segment 1, Study Report 4, Unit 5, pp. 21–29.
         Discussion of an angler's experiences with lures, baits, and techniques for catching pike.

1977   Early season northern pike techniques; hammerhandles or lunkers. Fins & Feathers, June 1977, pp. 12–16, 53–56.
         Describes techniques for angling large pike early in the season.

1983   Netherlands fish farming. In Brown, E. E., ed., World fish farming: cultivation and Economics. Westport, Connecticut, Avi. pp. 113–114.
         Five species of fish, including pike, are cultured in Holland. Pond culture, raceways, controlled conditions in glass houses, and cage culture in warmwater effluents are the four systems used.

1985   Fria gaddvatten. Fiske Journalen 7–8 (July-August):40–43.

n.d.a   Effects of temperature on physiology of northern pike. Dingell-Johnson Report F-57-R-3, Job 5h:1–23.
         A fish biomass model was re-arranged to work for young-of-the-year esocids. Standard metabolic rates, food consumption rates, and an activity factor were used in two equations to estimate oxygen and food consumption at any temperature.

n.d.b   12. Experimental northern pike and muskie propagation. Job XII-A. Stock ponds with northern pike fry and adult carp (amended to stock ponds with muskie fingerlings and adult carp). Annual Report Delafield Studies, pp. 18–19.

Two attempts to use *Cyprinus carpio* as forage for fingerling pike in small rearing ponds "left much to be desired". In contrast, carp as pike forage in Rush Lake was believed to result in excellent production and growth.

n.d.c   Fish and wildlife: major issues and problems. pp. 6s-7s.

A summary of factors limiting pike production, and objectives for increasing the populations to meet angler demands.

n.d.d   Fishin'formation. Northern pike. Folder published by Saskatchewan Government, Extension Services.

Information on pike given under the following headings: characteristics, distribution, reproduction, growth, habitat requirements, feeding habits, commercial importance, gamefish qualities, and management.

n.d.e   Harvest of northern pike. Ohio Department of Natural Resources, Dingell-Johnson Report F-57-R-3, Job 5-f.

n.d.f   Master Angler update, northern pike division. In-Fisherman, pp. 95–97.

Brief accounts of successful angling for pike.

ANTHONY, D. D. and C. R. JORGENSEN

1977   Factors in the declining contributions of walleye (*Stizostedion vitreum vitreum*) to the fishery of Lake Nipissing, Ontario, 1960–76. Journal of the Fisheries Research Board of Canada 34:1703–1709.

Suggests that walleye population was probably affected by interaction with pike.

ANTONESCU, C. S.

1933   Recherches sur les conditions d'existence et de nutrition des poissons dans les lacs eutropes profunds. Annales Scientifiques de l'Universite de Jassy 17:337–392.

ANTOSIAK, B.

1958   Regulacja liczebnosci drapieznikow jako jeden z elementow prawidlowej gospodarki jeziorowej. [Regulation of the abundance of predatory fishes as an element of proper lake management.] Gospodarka Rybna 10(6):7–12.

Food composition of pike. Elements of dependence between predatory fishes and their prey.

1961   Wzrost szczupaka (*Esox lucius* L.) w jeziorach okolic Wegorzewa. [The rate of growth of pike in Wegorzewa District lakes]. Roczniki Nauk Rolniczych 77:581–602.

Analysis of the rate of body length and weight growth in pike. The analysis is connected with studies on pike food, and an attempt is made to estimate the role of this species in regulating abundance of other fish species in lakes.

1963   Pokarm szczupaka (*Esox lucius* L.) niektorych jezior okolic Wegorzewa. [Pike food in some lakes of Wegorzewa District] Polish Agr. Ann., Ser.B, 82:295–317. [in Polish, English summary]

The effect of pike predation on the abundance of other fishes, based on the analysis of food tract content of 952 pike originating from 20 lakes.

ANWAND, K.

1963   Die Wirkung von Hypophysen und Gonabioninjektionen auf Hechtmilchner. [The effect of hypophysis and gonabion (chorionic gonadotrophin) injections on male pike.] Deutsche Fischerei Zeitung 10(7):202–207.

Injections achieved artificial ripening of spawning products that had been lost

18

through prolonged holding at near-ripeness, and increased strippable amounts in specimens that were flowing slightly.

1965a   Hinweise zur erfolgreicheren Hechterbrutung. [Suggestions for more successful pike feeding.] Deutsche Fischerei Zeitung 12(2):33–39.

Experiments to improve fertilization and incubation considered the following: use of mouth pipette, urea solution, suitable water quality, "resting" of eggs (temporary dry state), and effect of transport of eggs by water current.

1965b   Uber den Zeitpunkt des Assetzens von Hechtbrut. [The time for stocking pike fry.] Deutsche Fischerei Zeitung 12(2):40–44.

1966a   Die Ernahrung der Hechtbrut wahrend der Vorstreckperiode in Teichen. Deutsche Fischerei Zeitung 13(4):99–106.

1966b   Die Anreicherung von ^{45}Ca und ^{91}Y in Brut von *Esox lucius* L. und *Anguilla anguilla* (L.). International Association of Theoretical and Applied Limnology Proceedings 16:1124–1129.

1967a   Transport von Hechtbrut und vorgestreckten Hechten in Plastikbeuteln. Deutsche Fischerei Zeitung 14:323–328.

1967b   Moderne Verfahren zur Erzeugung von vorgestreckten Hechten. Deutsche Fischerei Zeitung 14(1):7–10.

1968   Ergebnisse der Besatzversuche mit signierter Hechtbrut. Deutsche Fischerei Zeitung 15(8):195–198.

1969   Zur Methode der Alterbestimmung des Hechtes an Schuppen. Zeitschrift fuer Fischerei und deren Hilfswissenschaften 17(1–4):165–176.

1971   Zusammensetzung der Fange von *Esox lucius* L. aus fischereilich genutzten Seen der DDR nach Lange und Alter. [Composition according to length and age of captured material of *Esox lucius* L. from lakes in East Germany used as fisheries.] International Association of Theoretical and Applied Limnology Proceedings 18(Part 2):1171–1181.

1972   Dynamik der Bestande des Hechtes (*Esox lucius*) in Produktionsgewassern. Zeitschrift fuer Binnenfischerei der DDR 19(2):44–48.

ANWAND, K. and G. GROHMANN
1967   Besatzversuche mit Hechtbrut in Karpfenteichen. Zeitschrift fuer Fischerei und deren Hilfswissenschaften 14(5/6):383–391.

ARAI, H. P. and S.-M. CHIEN
1973   A note on some Monogenea (Trematoda) from Albertan fishes. Canadian Journal of Zoology 51:1318.

Gills from 7 of 21 specimens of pike were infected with *Tetraonchus monenteron*, ranging in intensity from 1 to 9 with a mean of 3.4.

ARENDT, E.
1822   De capitis ossei *Esocis lucii* structura regularis. n.p.

ARGILLANDER, A.
1753   Ron om Gjadd-leken. Svensk. Vetensk. Acad. Handl. 15:74–77.

ARKHIPTSEVA, N. T.
1974   The growth and feeding of the predatory fishes of Lake Vuoksa. Hydrobiological Journal 10(2):66–69.

ARMBRUSTER, D.
1966   Hybridization of the chain pickerel and northern pike. Progressive Fish-Culturist 28:76–78.

The study suggests that the heterotic effect often associated with growth of hybrids did not appear in this pike-chain pickerel hybrid. The hybrids grew at a rate intermediate between the rates of the parent species. The colour pattern of the hybrids more nearly paralleled that of pike, as no tendency towards a chain-like effect was noted.

ARMSTRONG, F. A. J. and D. P. SCOTT

1979   Decrease in mercury content of fishes in Ball Lake, Ontario, since imposition of controls on mercury discharges. Journal of the Fisheries Research Board of Canada 36:670–672.

Ball Lake received mercury from 1962–1970, but controls since have been increasingly rigorous. In 1971, 1972, and 1976 adjusted mean white muscle mercury concentrations for pike 594 mm were 5.05, 5.72, and 1.80 mg/kg. Mercury in suspension may be a controlling factor.

ARRIGNON, J.

1966   Action d'une population de brochets (*Esox lucius* L.) sur le cheptel trutticole Leberge par les eaux de premiere categorie. Bulletin de l'Ecole Nationale Superieure Agronomique de Nancy 8:39–47.

Describes several river habitats and man-made alterations in relation to distribution of pike predation, especially on trout.

1972   Station experimentale d'elevage du brochet du Vivier du Gres (Oise). Bulletin Francais de Pisciculture 246:33–44.

ARSENAULT, M.

1982   *Eusthenopteron foordi*, a predator on *Homalacanthus concinnus* from the Escuminac formation, Miguasha, Quebec. Canadian Journal of Earth Science 19:2214–2217.

ARTAMOSHIN, A. S.

1978   Distribution of plerocercoids of the broad tapeworm in fish tissues. Meditsinskaya Parazitologiya i Parazitarnye Bolezni 47(5):15–18.

ARTAMOSHIN, A. S. and V. I. KHODAKOVA

1976   The effect of waste water on the infestation of underyearlings in the Kama Reservoir by broad tapeworm plerocercoids. Hydrobiological Journal 12(6):79–81

ARTAMOSHIN, A. S. and L. I. PROKOPENKO

1980   Rol'shchuk virashchivaemykh v ribovodnykh prudakh v podderzhanii ochaga difildobotrioza. [On the possible role of pike grown in fish-breeding ponds in the maintenance of diphyllobothriasis focus]. Meditsinskaya Parazitologiya i Parazitarnye Bolezni 49(3):51–53.

Considers the participation of pike bred in fishpond farms in the turnover of diphyllobothrial invasion caused by *Diphyllobothrium latum*.

ARTHUR, J. R., L. MARGOLIS and H. P. ARAI

1976   Parasites of fishes of Aishihik and Stevens lakes, Yukon Territory, and potential consequences of their interlake transfer through a proposed water diversion for hydroelectrical purposes. Journal of the Fisheries Research Board of Canada 33:2489–2499.

A list of parasites found in eight species, including pike, from both lakes.

ASH, G. R., N. R. CHYMKO and D. N. GALLUP

1974   Fish kill due to "cold shock" in Lake Wabamun, Alberta. Journal of the Fisheries Research Board of Canada 31:1822–1824.

Pike died from "cold shock" caused by mechanical failure in the steam electric generating unit when the temperature dropped from 21.8 to 4.9 C.

20

ASTANIN, L. P.

1947   On the determination of the ages of fishes. Zoological Journal 26:287–288.
Seasonal changes in NADPH production via the pentose shunt were examined in pike. No kinetic differences in glucose-6-phosphate dehydrogenase were observed in summer vs winter caught fish.

ASTER, P. L.

1975   Seasonal changes in glucose 6 phosphate dehydrogenase activity in two species of freshwater fish. American Zoologist 15:809. [Abstract]

1976   The influence of temperature and seasonal acclimatization on glucose-6-phosphate dehydrogenase and 6-phosphogluconate dehydrogenase from three teleost species. M.S. thesis, University of Alberta. 124 pp.

ATTON, F. M., R. P. JOHNSON and N. W. SMITH

1974   Bibliography of limnology and aquatic fauna and flora of Saskatchewan. Saskatchewan Department of Tourism and Renewable Resources, Report 10. References dealing with the limnobiology of lakes and streams from 1836 to 1972; includes indices and key words.

ATWATER, W. O.

1892   The chemical composition and nutritive values of food fishes and aquatic invertebrates. Report of the U.S. Commissioner of Fisheries for 1888:679–869.

AUGORAYA

1973   Fishing significance of pike in Kremenchug Reservoir. Rybnoe Khozaistvo.

AUSTIN, P.

1954a   Growth rate of pike. Part 1. The Fishing Gazette, April 17.

1954b   Growth rate of pike. Part 2. The Fishing Gazette 136(4020):445–446.

1958   Growth rates of trout and pike. The Fishing Gazette, June 28.

AUTKO, B. F.

1960   An evaluation of the state of pike stocks in Kuybyshev Reservoir, based on data from 1958 and 1959. Izvestiya Gosudarstvennogo Nauchno-Issledovatel'skogo Instituta Ozernogo i Rechnogo Rybnogo Khozvaistva 9:316–331.

1964   Commercial and biological characterization of pike in the Kuibyskev Reservoir on the basis of 1960–63 data. Izvestiya Gosudarstvennogo Nauchno-Issledovatel'skogo Instituta Ozernogo i Rechnogo Rybnogo Khozvaistva 10:249–259.
Change in water level during reproduction and reduced spawning area resulted in a decrease in the pike stock. The effect of the fishery was considered to be less important. Age distribution, year class strength, and growth are presented. Size at age decreased from 1959 to 1963.

AVDOS'EV, V. S., I. R. DEMCHENKO, I. M. KARPENKO and O. P. KULAKOVSKAYA

1962   The treatment and prophylaxis of pike infested by leeches. Veterinariya 7:60.

AYRES, W. O.

1849   Some remarks on a species of pike (*Esox lucius*). Proceedings of the American Association for the Advancement of Science 2:173.

BABALUK, J. A., B. M. BELCHER and J. S. CAMPBELL

   1984   An investigation of the sport fishery on Dauphin Lake, Manitoba, 1982.
           Canadian Manuscript Report Fisheries and Aquatic Sciences 1777:1–27.
           Results of a creel census, cottage residents' angling survey, and biological
           investigation between May 15 and Sept. 17, 1982. The catch was mainly pike
           (78.1%).

BACHOP, W. E.

   1958   Studies on the developmental anatomy of *Esox masquinongy ohioensis* Kirt-
           land. M.S. thesis, Ohio State University. 160 pp.

BACKIEL, T.

   1968   Ageing of coarse fish. European Inland Fisheries Advisory Committee, Food
           and Agriculture Organization of the United Nations, FI/EIFAC 68/SC I-
           6:1–30.

   1971   Production and food consumption of predatory fish in the Vistula River.
           Journal of Fish Biology 3:369–405.
           Samples of pike collected at 11 sites were used to assess food consumption,
           content (weight) of food in alimentary canals, growth in weight, natural and
           fishing mortality. Records of commercial catches were also used.

BACKUS, R. H.

   1957   The fishes of Labrador. Bulletin of the American Museum of Natural History
           113:277–377.

BADSHA, K. S. and C. R. GOLDSPINK

   1982   Preliminary observations on the heavy metal content of four species of fresh-
           water fish in northwest England. Journal of Fish Biology 21:251–267.
           Data on concentrations of zinc, lead, and cadmium in whole body samples
           and in tissues of brain, muscle, liver, kidney, heart, gonad, bone, and gills.

BAERENDS, G. P.

   1957   The ethological analysis of fish behavior. *In* Brown, M. E., ed., The physiol-
           ogy of fishes, vol. 2. New York, Academic Press, pp. 229–269.

BAGDZJUS, B. K.

   1959   Materialy po promyslovo-biologiceskoj charakteristike scuki (*Esox lucius* L.)
           zaliva Kursju-Marjos. Trudy Akademii Nauk Litovskoi Ser.B, 1(17).

BAGENAL, T. B.

   1967a   A short review of fish fecundity. *In* Gerking, S. D., ed., The biological basis
           of freshwater fish production. IBP Symposium, Reading, England, 1966, pp.
           89–111.

   1967b   A method of marking fish eggs and larvae. Nature 214(5083):113.

   1970a   An historical review of the fish and fisheries investigations of the Freshwater
           Biological Association, mainly at the Windermere Laboratory. Journal of
           Fish Biology 2:83–101.
           Studies on pike carried out by the Association at Windermere include general
           natural history, population studies, egg and young stages, and production stu-
           dies.

   1970b   Fish eggs and the next generation. Journal of Fish Biology 2(4):383.
           [Abstract].
           Considers variations in egg numbers and size. Discusses effects of these vari-
           ations on the next generation (i.e., annual variations in number, related to fish
           of same length). Shows relationship between egg number and population
           density.

1971   The interrelation of the size of fish eggs, the date of spawning and the production cycle. Journal of Fish Biology 3:207–219.
    Range of egg volumes is provided for pike. *Bosmina* is reported as an important food item of young pike. The feeding chronology of young pike is reviewed. It is reported that the spawning season of pike in Windermere is as closely associated with the hatching of perch *Perca fluviatilis* as with the production cycle of entomostraca, which is the first food.

1972   The variability of the catch from gill nets set for pike *Esox lucius* L. Freshwater Biology 2:77–82.
    The variability of the catch of pike from gill nets in Windermere over the period 1961–71 was analysed. A representative value of the residual between catch variance was used to estimate the reliability of the means of catches based on different numbers of net settings. It was shown that many settings of gill nets are required to get a reliable mean catch.

1977   Effects of fisheries on Eurasian perch *Perca fluviatilis* in Windermere. Journal of the Fisheries Research Board of Canada 34:1764–1768.
    Experimental gill net fishery (1944–1975) on pike reduced their average size and increased growth rate. Thus, predation on younger perch increased.

1979   EIFAC fishing gear intercalibration experiments. European Inland Fisheries Advisory Committee, Food and Agriculture Organization of the United Nations, Technical Paper 34:1–87.

1982   Experimental manipulations of the fish populations in Windermere. Hydrobiologia 86(1–2):201–206.

BAILEY, J. and M. PAGE
1985   Pike. The predator becomes the prey. Ramsbury, England, Crowood Press.
    Advice on how to angle for pike.

BAILEY, R. M., J. E. FITCH, E. S. HERALD, E. A. LACHNER, C. C. LINDSEY, C. R. ROBINS and W. B. SCOTT
1970   A list of common and scientific names of fishes from the United States and Canada. 3rd ed. American Fisheries Society Special Publication 6: 1–150.

BAJKOV, A.
1927   Reports of the Jasper Park lakes investigations, 1925–26. I. The fishes. Contributions to Canadian Biology and Fisheries 3(16):379–404.
    Gives world range generally, Jasper Park range specifically.

1930   Fishing industry and fisheries investigations in the Prairie Provinces. Transactions of the American Fisheries Society 60:215–237.
    A brief account of annual production, growth rate, food, spawning.

1932   Native game fish in Manitoba. Transactions of the American Fisheries Society 62:377–379.
    Discusses the variety and abundance of game fish in Manitoba, including pike.

BAJKOV, A. D. and A. H. SHORTT
1939   Northern pike (jackfish) as predator on waterfowl and muskrats. Published by Ducks Unlimited, Winnipeg.

BAKHTIN, Y. K.
1976   Morphology of the olfactory organ of some fish species and a possible functional interpretation. Journal of Ichthyology 16:786–804.
    The study of the olfactory organ of different fish species by optical and electron microscope has established that several types of cells, displaying

23

numerous ultrastructural differences, comprise this organ. An attempt is
made to describe the function of each type of cell.

BAKSHTANSKII, E. L. and V. D. NESTEROV

1976   The hunting activity of pike and its possible effect on the diurnal pattern of
downstream migration of young Atlantic salmon. *In* Biological basis and
ways of increasing the efficiency of valuable commercial fish culture, pp.
39–42.

BAKSHTANSKII, E. L., V. D. NESTEROV and M. N. NEKLYUDOV

1980   Behaviour of young Atlantic salmon *Salmo salar* in the period of downstream
migration. Voprosy Ikhtiologii 20:694–701.

BALAGUROVA, M. V.

1967   Materials on the nutrition of the pike. Izvestiya Gosudarstvennogo
Nauchno-Issledovatel'skogo Instituta Ozernogo i Rechnogo Rybnogo Khozvaistva 62:195–205.

BALAYEV, L. A.

1981   The behaviour of ecologically different fish in electric fields. II. Threshold of
anode reaction and tetanus. Journal of Ichthyology 21:134–143.

BALDWIN, N. S.

1946   A note on the removal of northern pike (*Esox lucius*) from Lake Marie
Louise, Sibley Park. Unpublished manuscript, Ontario Department of Lands
and Forests. 14 pp.
As many pike as possible were removed from the lake prior to the introduction of smallmouth bass. Recommended continued removal of pike during
1947, commencing approximately May 1, when pike begin to move into shallow water.

BALDWIN, N. S., R. W. SAALFELD, M. A. ROSS and H. J. BUETTNER

1979   Commercial fish production in the Great Lakes 1867–1977. Great Lakes
Fishery Commission Technical Report 3:1–187.
Canadian and United States data for each lake are presented in tables.

BALDWIN, R. E., D. H. STRONG and J. H. TORRIE

1961   Flavour and aroma of fish taken from four fresh-water sources. Transactions
of the American Fisheries Society 90:175–180.
Taste-panel studies were conducted on fish taken from four fresh-water
sources which included a cold deep lake, a shallow mixed water lake, and
flowages above and below the entry of effluent from industrial plants. Pike
were least affected.

BALFOUR-BROWNE, F.

1906   On the early stages in the life histories of certain fresh-water fishes. Transactions of the Norfolk-Norwich Naturalists' Society 8:478–488.
Found that in Sutton Broad the first food of young pike fry was Entomostraca,
including fairly large daphnids.

BALK, L., J. W. DEPIERRE, A. SUNDVALL and U. RANNUG

1982   Formation of mutagenic metabolites from benzo-alpha-pyrene and 2-
aminoanthracene by the S-9 fraction from the liver of the northern pike *Esox
lucius*; inducibility with 3-methylcholanthrene and correlation with benzo-
alpha-pyrene mono-oxygenase activity. Chemical-Biological Interaction
41:1–14.

BALK, L., A. KNALL and J. W. DEPIERRE

1982   Separation of the different classes of conjugated formed by metabolism of benzo-alpha-pyrene in the northern pike *Esox lucius*. Acta Chemica Scandinavica, Series B, Organic Chemistry and Biochemistry, 36:403–405.

BALK, L., S. MAANER, A. BERGSTRAND and J. W. DEPIERRE

1985   Preparation and characterization of sub-cellular fractions from the intestinal mucosa of the northern pike (*Esox lucius*) with special emphasis on enzymes involved in xenobiotic metabolism. Biochimica et Biophysica Acta 838:277–289.

The purity of different microzonal fractions obtained by differential centrifugation, as well as the recovery of different organelles, was determined by using both enzyme markers and morphological examination by electron microscopy. The subcellular distributions of several enzymes involved in drug metabolism were also examined. Within the limitations discussed, the subfractions prepared here are suitable for further characterization of drug-metabolizing systems in the intestinal mucosa.

BALK, L., S. MAANER, J. W. DEPIERRE and A. BERGESTRAND

1984   Subfractionation of the head and trunk kidneys of the northern pike (*Esox lucius*). *In* Stegeman, J. J., ed., Responses of marine organisms to pollutants. pp. 444–445.

A study of the metabolism of xenobiotics in pike, initiated because of the high tumor frequency in the species, its stationary habitat, and the fact that it is a top predator.

BALK, L., J. MEIJER, A. ASTROM, R. MORGENSTERN, J. SEIDEGAARD and J. W. DEPIERRE

1980   Subcellular fractionation of the liver from northern pike *Esox lucius*. Acta Chemica Scandinavica, Series B, Organic Chemistry and Biochemistry 34:224–226.

BALK, L., J. MEIJER, A. BERGSTRAND, A. AASTROEM, J. SEIDEGAARD and J. W. DEPIERRE

1982   Preparation and characterization of subcellular fractions from the liver of the northern pike, *Esox lucius*. Biochemical Pharmacology 31:1491–1500.

Microzonal fractions were prepared suitable for the study of xenobiotic metabolism. The purity of the different fractions obtained by differential centrifugation, as well as the recovery of different organelles, was determined using both enzyme markers and morphological examination with the electron microscope. Attempts were also made to increase the recovery of fragments of the endoplasmic reticulum in the microsomal fraction. The subcellular distribution of several drug-metabolizing enzymes was determined.

BALK, L., J. MEIJER, J. W. DEPIERRE and L.-E. APPELGREN

1984   The uptake and distribution of (^{3}H)benzo(a) pyrene in the northern pike (*Esox lucius*). Examination by whole-body autoradiography and scintillation counting. Toxicology and Applied Pharmacology 74:430–449.

BALL, R. C.

1950   Fertilization of natural lakes in Michigan. Transactions of the American Fisheries Society 78:145–155.

Merely mentions that pike were present in one lake and that fishing was fair.

BALON, E. K.

1964   On relative indexes for comparison of the growth of fishes. Acta Societatis Zoologica Bohemoslovakia 28:369–379.

1965   Wachstum des Hechtes (*Esox lucius* L.) in Orava-Stausee. Zeitschrift fuer Fischerei und deren Hilfswissenschaften 23:113–158.

1968a   Urgeschichte det donauichthyofauna (vor dem einfluss seitens des menschen). Archiv fuer Hydrobiologie 3:204–227.
        Pike were present in the pre-Danube of the Miocene and were considered to be among the first fishes inhabiting the Danube.

1968b   Die Anwendung der Pisciziden fur die Bestimmung von Fischabundation und Ichthyomasse in den Inundationsgewassern der Donau. Zeitschrift fuer Fischerei und deren Hilfswissenschaften 16(3/4):169–195. [English summary]

1974   The theory of saltation and its application in the ontogeny of fishes: steps and thresholds. Environmental Biology of Fishes 4:97–101.

1975a   Reproductive guilds of fishes: a proposal and definition. Journal of the Fisheries Research Board of Canada 32:821–864.

1975b   Terminology of intervals in fish development. Journal of the Fisheries Research Board of Canada 32:1663–1670.

1984   Reflections on some decisive events in the early life of fishes. Transactions of the American Fisheries Society 113:178–185.

BALVAY, G.

1983   L'alimentation naturelle des alevins de brochet (*Esox lucius* L.) durant leur premier mois de vie. *In* Billard, R., ed., Le brochet gestion dans le milieu naturel et elevage. Paris, Institute National de la Recherche Agronomique, pp. 179–198.
        Active feeding of pike starts between filling of the gas bladder and complete resorption of the yolk sac. The food selected follows a sequence of entomostraca, insects, and vertebrates. In extensive rearing, pond management must stimulate the production of natural food adapted to fry needs to reduce cannibalism.

BANENENE, Y. K.

1978   Biology of the pike in waters of the Lithuanian-SSR. Part 2. Sexual maturation and fertility of the Lake Dusya pike. Lietuvos TSR Mokslu Akademijos Darbai, Serija C, Biologijos Mokslai 2:95–100.

BANFIELD, W. G., C. J. DAWE, C. E. LEE and R. SONSTEGARD

1976   Cylindroid lamella-particle complexes in lymphoma cells of northern pike *Esox lucius*. Journal of the National Cancer Institute 57:415–420.
        Description of cylindroid structure and of cross and longitudinal sections of the lamellae.

BANGHAM, R.

1946   Parasites of northern Wisconsin fish. Transactions of the Wisconsin Academy of Science, Arts, and Letters 36:291–325.

BANGHAM, R. V. and J. R. ADAMS

1954   A survey of the parasites of freshwater fishes from the mainland of British Columbia. Journal of the Fisheries Research Board of Canada 11:673–708.
        Two small specimens of pike yielded only the cestode *Proteocephalus pinguis*.

BANGHAM, R. V. and G. HUNTER

1939   Studies on the fish parasites of Lake Erie. Distribution studies. Zoologica 24:385–448.

Of eight specimens of pike examined, six from the eastern end of Lake Erie and one from the western end were infected with *Proteocephalus pinguis* and two from the eastern end carried *Neoechinorhynchus tenellus*.

BANINA, N. N.

1969   Changeability of ciliates of the genus *Apiosoma*. Folia Parasitiologica 16:289–295.

BANIONIENE, J.

1979   Biology of pike of the reservoirs of the Lithuanian SSR. 3. Pike fecundity in Lake Galstas. Trudy Akademii Nauk Litovskoi SSR Ser.C, 4(88):71–78.

BANKS, J.

1965   The biology of pike from three lowland waters. Proceedings of the 2nd British Coarse Fish Conference, University of Liverpool, pp. 29–39.

BANKS, J. W.

1970   Observations on the fish population of Rostherne Mere, Cheshire. Field Studies 3:357–379.

Gives curves of length for age and regressions of weight on length for pike. Growth of pike is rather slow. Pike fed predominantly on perch. Although large pike took many fry, the bulk of their food was a small number of large prey.

BARAUSKAS, R.

1978   Effect of single electrical stimuli on the activity of neurons in the medulla oblongata of the pike *Esox lucius*. Journal of Evolutionary Biochemistry and Physiology 14:505–507.

A study of neuron responses to stimulating impulses applied to immobilized pike. To verify that behavioural reactions were due to action on peripheral formations of nervous system, experiments were performed on specimens in which body surfaces were anesthetized.

BARTA, A.

1877   Przyczynek do ryboznawstwa krajowego i gospodarstwa rybnego. Zapiski o rybach z Dniestru, polawianych we wsi Pobereze, kolo Jezupola. [Selected elements of local fisheries and fishery management. Notes on fishes from the Dniestr River, and fish catches in Pobrzeze, near Jezupol.] Kosmos 2(8, 9, 10):448–451.

Description of fishes and their catches based on practical knowledge of fishermen.

BARTEHLMES, D. and H. WALDOW

1978   Long term biological changes in the Grosse Mueggelsee (Berlin), some characteristics of its present status and previous fishing effects. 5. A summary of the fishing value of the biological changes observed in Grosse Mueggelsee. Zeitschrift fuer Binnenfischerei DDR 25(7):209–214.

Disappearance of weed reduced the yield of pike.

BARTHOLOMEW, M. A., J. DIVALL and J. E. MORROW

1962   Silver pike, an atypical *Esox lucius*, in Alaska, a first record. Copeia 1962:449–450.

The first record of this mutant from west of the Rocky Mountains.

BARTLES, B.

1973   Coarse fishing. London, A. & C. Black.

BARTMANN, W.

1973   Eine Prelzsymbiose Zwischen Stichling (*Gasterosteus aculeatus* L.) und Hecht (*Esox lucius* L.) im Aquarium. [A cleaning symbiosis between threespine stickleback on pike in the aquarium]. Zeitschrift fuer Tierpsychologie 33(2):153–162.

BARYSHEVA, A. F. and O. N. BAUER

1961   Fish parasites of Lake Ladoga. *In* Petrushevskii, G. K., ed., Parasites and diseases of fish. Jerusalem, Israel Program for Scientific Translations, pp. 171–224.

BASHMAKOVA, A. Y.

1930   Material on the age and growth rate of the pike (*Esox lucius* L.) of Lake Chany. Trudy Sibirskogo Otdela Gosudarstvennogo Nauchno-Issledovatel'skogo Instituta Ozernogo i Rechnogo Rybnogo Khozyaistva 5:187–205. [in Russian]

BASTL, I., J. HOLCIK and A. KIRKA

1975   Ichthyological investigation of the protected habitat of the Danubian salmon *Hucho hucho* on the River Turiec and suggestions for its management. Zbornik Slovenskeho Narodneho Muzea Prirodne Vedy 21:191–224.

BAUDO, R., G. GALANTI, B. LOCHT, H. MUNTAU and P. G. VARINI

1981   Heavy metal concentrations of pike (*Esox lucius*) and four other fish species from the Pallanca Basin. Memorie dell'Istituto Italiano di Idrobiologie Dott Marco de Marchi 38:409–414.

BAUER, P.

1971   Too easy to catch. National Wildlife June-July, 1971.
        Briefly describes some medieval pike legends, feeding habits, and two theories on how the pike's distribution became circumpolar.

BAUMANN, P. C., J. F. KITCHELL, J. J. MAGNUSON and T. B. KAYES

1974   Lake Wingra, 1837–1973. A case history of human impact. Transactions of the Wisconsin Academy of Science, Arts, and Letters 62:57–94.

BAUMGARTEN, H. G., B. FALCK and H. WARTENBERG

1970   Adrenergic neurons in the spinal cord of the pike *Esox lucius* and their relation to the caudal neuro secretory system. Zeitschrift fuer Zellforschung und Mikroskopie Anatomie 107:479–498.

BAUMGARTEN, H. G. and H. WARTENBERG

1970   Adrenergic neurons in the lower spinal cord of the pike *Esox lucius* and their relation to the neuro secretory system of the neurophysis spinalis caudalis. Aspects of Neuroendocrinology, 5th International Symposium on Neurosecretion. Berlin, West Germany, pp. 104–111.

BAXTER, G. T. and J. R. SIMON

1970   Wyoming fishes. Wyoming Game and Fish Department, Bulletin 4:1–168.
        A single specimen was caught from a sand pit near Torrington in 1966. The species is considered to be introduced since it certainly either moved into the state from populations introduced into Nebraska or was introduced into Wyoming illegally.

BAYLIS, H. A.

1928   Records of some parasitic worms from British vertebrates. Annals and Magazine of Natural History 10th S 1:329–343.

1939   Further records of parasitic worms from British vertebrates. Annals and Magazine of Natural History 11th S 4:473–498.

BEAMISH, R. J.
1973   Design of a trapnet with interchangeable parts for the capture of large and small fishes from varying depths. Journal of the Fisheries Research Board of Canada 30:587–590.
        Pike is listed as one of the species caught in these nets.

BEAMISH, R. J., M. J. MERRILEES and E. J. CROSSMAN
1971   Karyotypes and DNA values for members of the suborder Esocoidei (Osteichthyes: Salmoniformes). Chromosoma 34:436–447.
        Diploid chromosome number is 50 and total DNA 30–39% of human, as in all species of *Esox*. Values for other members of the suborder (except *Umbra krameri*) are given also.

BEAN, T. H.
1891a   The pike family—I. Forest and Stream 34(11):210.
1891b   The pike family—II. Forest and Stream 34(12):233.
1892   The fishes of Pennsylvania. Report of the State Commissioner of Fisheries 1889, 1890, 1891, pp. 89–94.
1897   Notes upon New York fishes received at the New York Aquarium, 1895 to 1897. New York Commissioners of Fisheries, Game, and Forests, 2nd annual report, 1896, pp. 229–232.
1902   The food and game fishes of New York. New York State Forest, Fish, and Game commission, 7th annual report, 1901, pp. 251–460.
1903a   The food and game fishes of New York: notes on their common names, distribution, habits and mode of capture. New York State Forest, Fish, and Game Commission. 427 pp.
1903b   Catalogue of the fishes of New York. New York University Bulletin 278, New York State Museum Bulletin 60, Zoology 9. 784 pp.
1911   The pike family. Transactions of the American Fisheries Society 1910:210, 233, 333.

BEARD, T. D.
1971   Statewide fishery research. Impact of an overwinter drawdown on feeding activities of northern pike. Wisconsin Department of Natural Resources Project F-83-R-7/Job 1:1–6.
        During overwinter drawdowns in 1967, 1968, and 1969 feeding of pike in Murphy Flowage, Wisconsin, increased. Due to the predator-prey ratio, this increase was unlikely to have a noticeable impact on the panfish populations.

BEARD, T. D. and H. E. SNOW
1970   Statewide fishery research. Impact of winter drawdown on slow-growing panfish population and associated species. Wisconsin Department of Natural Resources Project F-83-R-5/Job 5:1–18.
        Information on feeding activity of pike.

BEAULIEU, G.
1961   Fecondite de quelques especes de poisson de la province de Quebec. Actualities Marines 5(2):22–27.

BECKMAN, L. G. and J. H. ELROD
1971   Apparent abundance and distribution of young-of-year fishes in Lake Oahe 1965–1969. American Fisheries Society Special Publication 8:333–347.

BECKMAN, W. C.
 1948   The length-weight relationship, factors for conversions between standard and
        total lengths, and coefficients of condition for seven Michigan fishes. Tran-
        sactions of the American Fisheries Society 75:237–256.
        The ratio of standard to total length increases as length increases. The
        coefficients of condition and the n values in the length-weight equation W =
        cLn are listed.

BEKESI, L., G. MAJOROS and E. SZABO
 1984   Mass appearance of a rhabdovirus in pike fry (*Esox lucius* L.) in Hungary.
        Magyar Allatorvosok Lapja 39:231–234. [in Hungarian, English summary]

BELINA, T.
 1956   Obserwacje dotyczace produkcji narybku karpia i palczakow szczupaka.
        [Observation on the production of carp fry and pike fingerlings.] Gospodarka
        Rybna 8(9):12–13.
        Possibilities of maximal utilization of properly kept nursery ponds for the
        breeding of pike fingerlings and carp *Cyprinus carpio* fry during the same
        year.

BENECKE, B.
 1880   Systematische Uebersicht der Fische von Ost- und Westpreussen. *In* Fische,
        Fischerei und Fischzucht in Ost- und Westpreussen. Konigsberg, pp.
        165–167.
 1885   Utilizing water by fish culture. 7. The raising of fish of prey spawning in
        summer. Report of the U.S. Fish Commission, 1883, p. 1129. [Translated
        from German by Herman Jacobson].

BENNETT, G. W.
 1962a Management of artificial lakes and ponds. New York, Reinhold. 283 pp.
 1962b Management of small artificial lakes. A summary of fisheries investigation.
        Bulletin of the Illinois Natural History Survey 22:357–376.

BENNETT, L. H.
 1947   Separation of northern pike eggs. Progressive Fish-Culturist 9:169–171.
        Yellow clay was used successfully as a separating agent, and the per cent
        hatch was high.
 1948   Pike culture at the New London, Minnesota, station. Progressive Fish Cultu-
        rist 10:95–98.
        Describes experiences in collecting and hatching pike eggs and raising the
        fry.

BENOIT, D. S. R. and J. G. HALE
 1969   Automatic live brine shrimp feeder. Transactions of the American Fisheries
        Society 98:532–533.
        The automatic feeder has been successful for culturing pike. It requires less
        time than hand feeding and ensures an adequate supply of live food
        throughout the day.

BENSLEY, B. A.
 1915   The fishes of Georgian Bay. *In* Contributions to Canadian biology being stu-
        died from the biological stations of Canada, 1911–1914. Fasciculus II—
        Freshwater fish and lake biology. Canada Department of Marine Fisheries,
        Supplement to the 47th Annual Report, Sessional Paper 39b: 1–52.

BENSON, N. G.
  1968   Review of fishery studies on Missouri River main stem reservoirs. Bureau of Sport Fisheries, Wildlife Research Report 71:1–61.
  1976   Water management and fish production in Missouri River main stem reservoirs. *In* Osborn, J. F., and Alman, C. H., eds., Instream flow needs. American Fisheries Society, vol. 2, pp. 141–147.
          Modification of water levels and peaking schedules has been shown to benefit pike.
  1980   Effects of post-impoundment shore modifications on fish populations in Missouri River reservoirs. U.S. Fish and Wildlife Service Research Report 80:1–32.
          Pike was one of the species that appeared to be adversely affected by shore changes resulting in a loss of flooded vegetation for spawning.
BENSON, N. G., J. R. GREELEY, M. I. HUISH and J. H. KUEHN
  1961   Status of management of natural lakes. Transactions of the American Fisheries Society 90:218–224.
          Size limits are useful for pike, which are long-lived and particularly vulnerable to capture.
BERG, L. S.
  1899   On division and formation of the parablast in the pike (*Esox lucius*). Journal of the Zoological Society, Zoological Museum, Imperial Moscow University 2(9/10):29–52.
  1932   Les poissons des eaux douces de l'U.R.S.S. et des pays limitrophes. 3rd ed. Leningrad, L'Institut Peches Pisciculture, vol. 1, 543 pp.
  1933   Les poissons des eaux douces de l'U.R.S.S. et des pays limitrophes. 3rd ed. Leningrad, L'Institut Peches Pisciculture, vol. 2, pp. 544–899.
  1936   On the suborder Esocoidei. Institut Recherches Biologie de Perm., Bulletin 10:389–391. [in Russian, English summary].
          Brief notes on anatomy.
  1947   Classification of fishes, recent and fossil. Ann Arbor, Edwards. 517 pp.
  1948   Freshwater fishes of the U.S.S.R. and adjacent countries, 4th ed. Academy of Science, USSR, 1(27):1–504. (Translated from Russian by Israel Program for Scientific Translations, 1962)
  1962   Freshwater fishes of the U.S.S.R. and adjacent countries. Vol. 1. Jerusalem, Program for Scientific Translations. 504 pp.
  1965   Freshwater fishes of the USSR, and adjacent countries. Jerusalem, Israel Program for Scientific Translations, vol. 3.
BERG, R. J. and J. J. MAGNUSON
  1970   Variability of winterkill survival in fishes. Technical Report OWRR A-024-Wis., 40 pp.
BERGER, B. L., R. E. LENNON and J. W. HOGAN,
  1969   Laboratory studies on antimycin A as a fish toxicant. U.S. Bureau of Sport Fisheries and Wildlife Investigations in Fish Control 25:1–12.
BERGH, K.
  1977   Northern pike fishing. Minneapolis, Dillion.
BERKA, R.
  1980   Produkee stiky a candata v Europe a v CSSR. [Production of pike and pike-perch in Europe and Czechoslovakia]. Buletin Vyzkumy Ustav Rybarsky a Hydrobiologicky Vodnany 16(2):40–46.

Production data analysis of market-size and young pike with chronological statistical data given for German Democratic Republic, Yugoslavia, Netherlands, Finland, Poland, Switzerland, Turkey, USSR, and Czechoslovakia. Except for Finland and Switzerland, pike production trend was decreasing. Advanced intensive production methods for natural waters and/or cultural operations were expected to improve the situation.

BERKES, F. and M. MACKENZIE
1978   Cree fish names from eastern James Bay, Quebec, Canada. Arctic 31:489–495.

BERNARD, H.
1934   Would a muskrat attack a pike? Canadian Field-Naturalist 48(3):53.
        Describes seeing a large muskrat appear to chase a 12-inch pike.

BERNATOWICZ, S.
1938   Szczupak w wodach otwartych. [Pike in surface waters.] Przeglad Rybacki 11:153–156.
        A description of pike stockings in Polish conditions in view of German literature on the subject.

1948   Budowa przewodow pokarmowych u ryb. [Anatomy of the feeding tract of fishes.] Wiadomosci Wedkarskie 5(5):7–9.
        Morphology and functioning of food tracts of various freshwater fishes viewed on the example of pike food tracts.

1955   Stadia rozwojowe niektorych roslin naczyniowych jako wskaznik czasu tarla ryb. [Development stages of certain vascular plants as an indication of the spawning time of fish.] Roczniki Nauk Rolniczyck, Ser.B, 69:547–557. [in Polish].
        Relation between spawning time and development stages of vascular plants, presented in tables.

1962   Obserwacje nad fenologia rozrodu ryb. [Observations of the phenology of fish spawning.] Roczniki Nauk Rolniczyck, Ser.B, 81:307–333. [in Polish, English summary].

BERZINS, B.
1962   Populationstyper hos gadda (*Esox lucius* L.) i sydsvenska smasjoar. Skrifter Sodra Sveriges Fiskeriforening Lund 1961–1962:82–86.

BESRUKOW, E. A.
1928   Die Entwicklung des Chondrocraniums bei *Esox lucius*. Revue de Zoologie Russe 8:89–111.

BEUKEMA, J. J.
1970   Acquired hook-avoidance in the pike *Esox lucius* L. fished with artificial and natural baits. Journal of Fish Biology 2:155–160.
        Catch of tagged pike in a drainable pond by spinner fishing decreased to a very low level after about half the population had been caught this way. Catch by live bait fishing remained unaffected by both spinner and live bait fishing. It was difficult to capture pike more than once by spinning. In live bait fishing the number of recaptures closely matched the number expected if catchability remains unaffected by earlier capture.

BEVELHIMER, M. S.
1983   Assessing significance of physiological differences among three esocids with a bioenergetics model. M.S. Thesis, Ohio State University. 49 pp.
        Differences in metabolism, food consumption, conversion efficiency, and

growth among pike, muskellunge, and pike-muskellunge hybrid were determined in the laboratory over a range of 5–30 C. Growth modelling enabled
comparison of success of each esocid in different environments.

BEVELHIMER, M. S., R. A. STEIN and R. F. CARLINE
1981   Comparative bioenergetics of northern pike, muskellunge, and their F1
hybrid, tiger muskellunge. Presented at 43rd Midwest Fish and Wildlife
Conference.

Rates of food consumption, growth, and conversion efficiency were discussed
for the three fish, and peaked for pike 15 22.5–25.0 C. Compared with similar data collected by Casselman (1978), there was an indication of warm
water adaptation by Ohio stocks that were selectively bred for 25 years in
Ohio hatcheries.

1985   Assessing significance of physiological differences among three esocids with
a bioenergetics model. Canadian Journal of Fisheries and Aquatic Sciences
42:57–69.

To predict stocking success of esocids in Ohio waters with different thermal
regimes, the authors measured individual food consumption, conversion
efficiency, growth, and metabolic rate for Ohio stocks of pike, muskellunge,
and pike-muskellunge hybrid. The hybrid should outgrow both pike and
muskellunge in thermal regimes common to Ohio waters.

n.d.   Laboratory growth of northern pike, muskellunge, and their F1 hybrid, tiger
muskellunge. Unpublished MS. 15 pp.

Data on food consumption, conversion efficiency, growth, and digestive rate
at various temperatures are given for each species and their hybrid.

BEYERLE, G. B.
1970a   A study of two northern pike-bluegill populations. Michigan Department of
Natural Resources,Research Development Report 194; Institute for Fisheries
Research Report 1762.

Pike and bluegill populations were established and maintained for 3 years in
two small lakes closed to fishing. Growth of pike was slightly less than average for pike in Michigan. High densities of pike did not control an abundance
of bluegills.

1970b   Warmwater fish biology and population ecology. Management of an
impoundment containing a population of slow growing northern pike. Michigan Department of Conservation Project F-29-R-4, Job 6:1–6.

Fishing regulations on pike in Fletcher Floodwater were liberalized in 1963 in
an attempt to increase harvest and pike growth. 145% more pike were taken
from 1963–65 than during 3 previous years for which creel census data were
available and growth measured.

1971a   A study of two northern pike-bluegill populations. Transactions of the American Fisheries Society 100:69–73.

High densities of pike did not control the bluegill population.

1971b   Warmwater fish biology and population ecology. Food habits of predatory
fish in lakes. Michigan Department of Conservation Project F-29-R-5/Wk.Pl.
1/Job 1:1–10.

Shows correlation between size of predator to size of prey. Perches include
yellow perch and darters. Data were collected over 15 years.

1971c   Growth and survival rates of northern pike on various diets in lakes. Michigan Department of Natural Resources, Dingell-Johnson Project F-29-R-

4:55–58.

1971d   Management of an impoundment containing a population of slow growing northern pike. Michigan Department of Natural Resources, Dingell-Johnson Annual Progress Report 1969–1970, F-29-R-4:65–70.

1973a   Growth and survival of northern pike in two small lakes containing soft-rayed fishes as the principal source of food. Michigan Department of Natural Resources, Fisheries Research Report 1793:1–16.

Fingerling pike were stocked for 3 years in two small lakes, one containing only minnows and the other minnows and young coho salmon. The inclusion of salmon as a forage presumably increased the growth of larger pike to the extent that pike of age group II averaged 2.6 inches longer in the pike-minnow-salmon lake than in the pike-minnow lake.

1973b   Warmwater fish biology and population ecology. Comparative growth, survival, and vulnerability to angling of northern pike, muskellunge, and the hybrid tiger muskellunge stocked in a small lake. Michigan Department of Natural Resources Fisheries Research Report 1799. Dingell-Johnson Project F-29-R-7:1–11.

Pike, muskellunge, and pike-muskellunge hybrid fingerlings were stocked in equal numbers for 3 consecutive years in Daggett Lake. High survival of pike compensated for low survival of muskellunge, to produce a standing crop of esocids that closely approached carrying capacity.

1975   Marsh-reared northern pike surviving to anglers' creel. Michigan Department of Natural Resources, Annual Progress Report, Project F-35-R-1(2):61–64.

1978   Survival, growth, and vulnerability to angling of northern pike and walleyes stocked as fingerlings in small lakes with bluegills or minnows. American Fisheries Society, Special Publication 11:135–139.

For pike stocked as fingerlings in small lakes with bluegills, survival was high after 3 years for the initial plant but very low for the succeeding two plants. Growth was moderate through age 1 but slow thereafter, despite an abundance of edible size bluegills. Survival and growth were better when pike were stocked in lakes with minnows.

1980   Contribution to the anglers' creel of marsh-reared northern pike stocked as fingerlings in Long Lake, Barry County, Michigan. Michigan Department of Natural Resources, Fisheries Research Report 1876:1–22.

From 1973 to 1975 marsh-reared pike were stocked at the rate of 40 fingerlings per hectare per year. Survival to the anglers' creel varied from 15.8 to 36.3% (mean 23.7%). Harvest of each year class was essentially complete 4 years after stocking. Marsh-reared fish provided 65.1% of the total harvest from the 1973–75 year classes of pike.

1981   Comparative survival and growth of 8.9 and 17.8 cm (3.5 and 7.0 inch) tiger muskellunge planted in a small lake with forage fishes. Michigan Department of Natural Resources, Fisheries Research Report 1894:1–8.

1984   Survival and growth of early- and normal-plant tiger muskellunge stocked in a small lake with forage fish and largemouth bass. Michigan Department of Natural Resources, Fisheries Research Report 1923:1–11.

BEYERLE, G. B. and J. E. WILLIAMS

1965   Some observations of food selectivity by northern pike and bowfins in aquaria. Michigan Department of Conservation, Research and Development Report 28.

34

Pike selected minnows and chubsuckers over centrarchids and yellow perch. They showed no choice between centrarchids and yellow perch, but selected centrarchids over bullheads.

1968   Some observations of food selectivity by northern pike in aquaria. Transactions of the American Fisheries Society 97:28–31.

The optimum size of centrarchids eaten by 7- to 12-inch pike was 1.5 inches, and by 13- to 23-inch pike 2.5 inches. Pike selected minnows and chubsuckers over centrarchids and yellow perch. They showed no choice between centrarchids and yellow perch, but selected centrarchids over bullheads.

1972   Contributions of northern pike fingerlings raised in a managed marsh to the pike population of an adjacent lake. Michigan Department of Natural Resources, Research and Development Report 274:1–20.

Growth of both stocked and naturally raised pike was well above Michigan state average, indicating that the stocking rate of pike could be increased substantially with significant benefit to the fishery.

1973   Contribution of northern pike fingerlings raised in a managed marsh to the pike population of an adjacent lake. Progressive Fish-Culturist 35:99–103.

A yearly average of 4,827 fingerlings were stocked in Long Lake for 3 years. Contribution was determined by estimates of survival rate, yearly recruitment from natural reproduction, mortality, and angling harvest.

BEZRUKOVA, E. A.

1928   The development of the chondrocranium in *E. lucius*. Revue de Zoologie Russe 8(4):89–111.

BHUSHANA RAO, K. S. P.

1970   Low molecular weight proteins from the white muscles of codling (*Gadus callarias* L.) and pike (*Esox lucius*). Ph.D. thesis, University of Liege.

BHUSHANA RAO, K. S. P. and C. GERDAY

1973a   Low molecular weight proteins of pike (*Esox lucius*) white muscles. I. Extraction and purification-polymorphism. Comparative Biochemistry and Physiology 44B:931–937.

The white muscles of pike contain two low molecular weight proteins that were isolated by acetone fractionation, filtration on Sephadex G-75 and chromatography on DEAE-cellulose at pH 5.7. The purity of the two proteins was checked by starch gel electrophoresis. Regional gene duplication and tetraploidization seemed to explain very well the variable number of these proteins in different fish species.

1973b   Low molecular weight proteins of pike (*Esox lucius*) white muscles. II. Chemical and physical properties. Comparative Biochemistry and Physiology 44B:1113–1125.

The amino acid composition of the two low molecular weight proteins extracted from pike muscle were typical of this protein's family. The molecular weights were 11,525 and 11,740 respectively for components II and III. Their tryptic peptide maps showed large dissimilarities. The N-terminal groups were acetylated and alanine was the C-terminal residue in both proteins. For the two proteins 58% helicity was calculated from ORD data.

BIALOKOZ, W.

1974   Plodnosc wybranych gatunkow ryb z kilku jezior mazurskich przygotowanych do doswiadczalnego nawozenia. [Fecundity in chosen fish species from a few Mazurian lakes prepared for experimental fertilization.] Roczniki

35

Nauk Rolniczyck, Ser.H, 95(4):7–34.

Studies on the fecundity of pike and other species in five lakes from the region of Olsztyn.

BIALOKOZ, W. and T. KRZYWOSZ

1976a Dostepnosc ofiar i wybiorczosc pokarmowa szczupaka. [Prey availability and food selectivity of pike.] Gospodarka Rybna 18(6):13–15.

Food selectivity of pike as determined by prey availability.

1976b Ilosc pokarmu zjadanego przez szczupaka. [The food quantity consumed by pike]. Gosposarka rybna 28(10):18–19.

An attempt to define food rations and feed conversion rates in a pike population from Lake Dgal Wielki, Mazurian Lakeland.

1978 Racje pokarmowe i wspolczynnik pokarmowy szczupaka (*Esox lucius* L.) z jexiora Dgal Wielki. [Feed rations and the feed coefficient of the pike (*Esox lucius* L.) in Lake Dgal Wielki]. Roczniki Nauk Rolniczyck, Ser.H, 99(1):7–21.

Food digestion cycles, diurnal and annual rations and the feed coefficient in pike from Lake Dgal Wielki were determined. The feed coefficient ranged from 3.6 to 5.1 and was lowest in the lightest fish.

1979 Analiza skladu pokarmu, dostepnosci ofiar i wybiorczosci pokarmowej szczupaka (*Esox lucius*) z jeziora Dgal Wielki. [An analysis of the food conposition, availability of prey and food selectivity of the pike (*Esox lucius* L.) in Lake Dgal Wielki]. Roczniki Nauk Rolniczyck, Ser.H, 99(3):7–24.

Roach constitute the basic food component of pike due to the efficiency of pike in seizing this species of fish and its availability in its feeding ground. Pike adapt to change in the type of food available.

BICH, J. P. and C. G. SCALET

1977 Fishes of the little Missouri River, South Dakota. Proceedings of the South Dakota Academy of Science 56:163–177.

BIDGOOD, B. F.

1971 Ecology of walleyes *Stizostedion v. vitreum*, in the Richardson Lake—Lake Athabasca complex. Alberta Department of Lands and Forests, Fisheries Technical Report, 27 pp.

BIELEK, E.

1974 Die Entwicklung der Niere von Asche (*Thymallus thymallus* L.) und Hecht (*Esox lucius* L.). [The development of the kidney of the grayling (*Thymallus thymallus* L.) and the pike (*Esox lucius* L.)] Zoologische Jahrbuecher Abteilung fuer Anatomie und Ontogenie der Tiere 92:163–180.

1976 Observations of the ontogenesis of blood picture and haemopoietic organs in the pike (*Esox lucius* L.) Zoologische Jahrbuecher Abteilung fuer Anatomie und Ontogenie der Tiere 95:193–205.

1980 Elektronenmikroskopische Untersuchungen der Blutzellen der Teleostier. IV. Monocyten und Makrophagen. [Electron microscopical studies of blood cells in teleosts. IV. Monocytes and macrophages]. Zoologische Jahrbuecher Abteilung fuer Anatomie und Ontogenie der Tiere 103:498–509.

BIGGAR, H. P., ed.

1922 The works of Samuel de Champlain. Toronto, The Champlain Society, vol. 1. [1599–1607].

1925 The works of Samuel de Champlain. Toronto, The Champlain Society, vol. 2. [1608–1613]

1929   The works of Samuel de Champlain. Toronto, The Champlain Society, vol. 3, 416 pp. [1615–1618]

1932   The works of Samuel de Champlain. Toronto, The Champlain Society, vol. 4, 373 pp. [1608–1620]

BILLARD, R.

1978   Changes in structure and fertilizing ability of marine and freshwater fish spermatozoa diluted in media of various salinities. Aquaculture 14:187–198.

The spermatozoa of pike showed increased motility time and fertility ability in an extender with a salinity of 7 o/oo, as compared to fresh water.

1980   Effet de la densite initiale du peuplement sur la survie et la croissance du brochet (*Esox lucius* L.) eleve jusqu'au stade de brocheton (45 jours). [The effect of initial population density on the survival and growth of young pike (*Esox lucius* L.) reared as 45-day fingerlings.] *In* Pond fish farming. Symposium on fish production in ponds, Arbonne-la-Foret, France, 1980, pp. 309–316.

Just before the end of yolk sac resorption pike larvae were stocked in three similar 400 sq.m. ponds in three densities, 2.25 fish/sq.m., 3.75 fish/sq.m. and 5.0 fish/sq.m. Fingerlings from all three ponds had the same mean length and survival rate. Total biomass of pike was a direct function of the initial number stocked.

1982   On some patterns of reproduction physiology in male teleost fish. *In* Richter, C. J. J., and H. J. Goos (compilers), Reproductive physiology of fish. Center for Agricultural Publishing and Documentation, Wageningen, p. 192.

1983   Resume de quelques problemes poses par l'elevage du brochet et sa gestion dans divers milieux. *In* Billard, R., ed. Le brochet gestion dans le milieu naturel et elevage. Paris, Institute National de la Recherche Agronomique, pp. 321–334.

BILLARD, R., ed.

1980   La pisciculture en etang. Paris, Institute National de la Recherche Agronomique. 434 pp.

1983   Le brochet. Gestion dans le milieu naturel et elevage. Paris, Institute National de la Recherche Agronomique. 371 pp.

Contains 24 articles by several authors on reproduction of pike in the wild and in hatcheries, culture of fry, and management of pike populations.

BILLARD, R. and B. BRETON

1976   Sur quelques problemes de physiologie du sperme chez les poissons teleosteens. [On some problems of the sperm physiology in teleostean fishes]. *In* Hureau, J. C., and K. E. Banisters, eds. Acts of the 2nd European Ichthyological Congress, organized by the National Museum of Natural History, Paris, 1976, vol. 40, pp. 501–503.

BILLARD, R., M. DEBRUILLE, J. P. GERARD and G. DE MONTALEMBERT

1976   L'insemination artificielle du brochet. [Artificial insemination of pike.] Bulletin Francais de Pisciculture 262:30–34.

Procedures for holding mature adults, collecting eggs, and artificially fertilizing eggs are described. For example, the eggs were mixed with an equal volume of solution consisting of saline buffered at a pH of 9. One ml of sperm was then added for each liter of the composite egg solution.

BILLARD, R. and J. E. FLECHON

1969   Particularites de la piece intermediaire des spermatozoides de quelques pois-
        sons teleosteens. Journal of Microscopy 8(4):36.

BILLARD, R., W. C. MACKAY, and J. MARCEL

1983   Evolution de la gametogenese, du poids du corps et des gonades au cours du
        cycle reproducteur du brochet (*Esox lucius*). *In* Billard, R., ed., Le brochet
        gestion dans le milieu naturel et elevage. Paris, Institute National de la
        Recherche Agronomique, pp. 53–61.

BILLARD, R. and J. MARCEL

1980   Stimulation of spermiation and induction of ovulation in pike, *Esox lucius*.
        Aquaculture 21:181–195.

        Various types of hormonal treatments are discussed. Sperm obtained after
        hormonal treatment was of good quality.

BILLARD, R., J. MARCEL and G. DE MONTALEMBERT

1983   Stimulation de la spermiation chez le brochet (*Esox lucius*). *In* Billard, R.,
        ed., Le brochet gestion dans le milieu naturel et elevage. Paris, Institute
        National de la Recherche Agronomique, pp. 109–132.

        The number of spermatozoa produced during one annual reproductive cycle
        was measured on male pike in their first reproduction. The administration of
        various pituitary gonadotropin extracts considerably increased the number of
        spermatozoa emitted after a single injection.

BILLINGS, E.

1857   The Canadian naturalist and geologist. Montreal, John Lovell, vol. 1, 480 pp.
        A general description of the species of Esocidae in Canadian waters; refers to
        the northern pickerel, *Esox Boreus*.

BIMBER, D. L. and S. A. NICHOLSON

1981   Fluctuations in the muskellunge (*Esox masquinongy* Mitchell) population of
        Chautauqua Lake, New York. Environmental Biology of Fishes 6:207–211.

BJOERKLUND, I. and L. NORLING

1980   Inverkan an luftburet kvicksilver pa kvicksilverhalten i gaedda och i sediment
        runt en klor-alkalifabrik. [Mercury content of pike muscle and sediments near
        a chlor-alkali plant]. Vatten 36:54–62.

        The average content of mercury in muscle of pike was higher in
        Varmland/Kilsbergen than in Holland and Smaland.

BLACK, J. D. and L. O. WILLIAMSON

1947   Artificial hybrids between muskellunge and northern pike. Transactions of
        the Wisconsin Academy of Science, Arts, and Letters 38:299–314.

BLACK, R. D. C.

1981   Report of the committee of inquiry into angling in Northern Ireland. HMSO
        (Belfast)

BLACKMAN, B. G.

n.d.   Reproduction of northern pike, *Esox lucius* L., in inner Long Point Bay.
        Research Proposal. Ontario Ministry of Natural Resources, unpublished MS,
        5 pp.

BLAIR, F. W.

1957   Vertebrates of the United States. New York, McGraw-Hill. 819 pp.

BLANC, M., P. BANARESCU, J.-L. GAUDET and L.-C. HUREAU

1971   European inland water fish, a multilingual catalogue. Published by Food and
        Agriculture Organization of the United Nations.

Illustration of a pike and a map showing distribution in Europe.

BLAND, J. K. and D. BARDACK
1973   A Pleistocene pike *Esox* cf. *lucius* from the southern end of Lake Michigan. American Midland Naturalist 89:138–144.

    Description of a fossil fish, referable to *Esox lucius*. Age and locality of the fossil demonstrated the occurrence of pike during postglacial times within the present rate of the species.

BLASIUS, G.
1692   Miscellanea anatomica, hominis brutorumque variorum, fabrican diversam magna parte exhibentia. Amstelodami. 8 vol.

BLAXTER, J. H. S.
1969   Swimming speeds of fish. Food and Agriculture Organization of the United Nations, Fisheries Report 2(62):59–68.

1986   Development of sense organs and behaviour of teleost larvae with special reference to feeding and predator avoidance. Transactions of the American Fisheries Society 115:98–114.

BLIZNYUK, I. D.
1969   Experimental infection of fish with freely floating cercarii *Opisthorchis felineus* Riv. Vestnik Zoologii 3:76–79. [in Russian, English summary].

BLOT, J.
1968   Le squelette interne de la nageoire anale et ses relations avec le squelette axial. Comptes Rendus Hebdomadaires des Seances de l'Academie des Sciences (Paris) 266:1943–1946.

BODALY, R. A. and R. E. HECKY
1979   Post-impoundment increases in fish mercury levels in the Southern Indian Lake Reservoir, Manitoba. Manuscript Report, Canadian Fisheries and Marine Service 1531:1–19.

    Total mercury and methyl mercury concentrations were low in water samples and bank material in 1978. It was hypothesized that leaching of soils and shoreline erosion after impoundment may lead to increased fish mercury concentrations.

BODALY, R. A., R. E. HECKY and R. J. P. FUDGE
1984   Increases in fish mercury levels in lakes flooded by the Churchill River diversion, northern Manitoba. Canadian Journal of Fisheries and Aquatic Sciences 41:682–691.

    Increases in fish muscle mercury levels, occurring coincidentally with flooding, are documented for three lakes affected by the Churchill River diversion for which pre- and post-impoundment data were available. Because mercury levels in fish from nearby unflooded lakes have not shown recent increases, atmospheric fallout does not appear to be the cause of the problem.

BODALY, R. A. and L. F. W. LESACK,
1984   Response of a boreal northern pike (*Esox lucius*) population to lake impoundment: Wupaw Bay, Southern Indian Lake, Manitoba. Canadian Journal of Fisheries and Aquatic Sciences 41:706–714.

    A population of pike was monitored for 1 year prior to impoundment of the lake and 5 years after impoundment. Impoundment had a pronounced but transient effect on pike reproductive success but no discernible effect on growth, condition, or mortality of the adult pike population.

BODALY, R. A. and C. C. LINDSEY

1977   Pleistocene watershed exchanges and the fish fauna of the Peel River basin, Yukon Territory, Canada. Journal of the Fisheries Research Board of Canada 34:388–395.

Biochemical and morphological evidence suggests that races of pike now inhabiting the area originated either from the Yukon River system or developed in situ in unglaciated parts of the Peel River.

BODAMMER, J. E.

1974   The cellular organization and fine structure of the nasal epithelium in the teleost *Umbra limi* (Kirtland). Ph.D. thesis, University of Wisconsin.

BODDINGTON, M. J., B. A. MACKENZIE and A. S. W. DE FREITAS

1979   A respirometer to measure the uptake efficiency of waterborne contaminants in fish. Ecotoxicology and Environmental Safety 3:383–393.

BODNIEK, V. M.

1976   Feeding of pike in the reservoirs of the Daugava River. Trudy Muzeya Zoologii Latvia 15:114–126.

BODROVA, N. V. and B. V. KRAIUKHIN

1959   The sensitivity of fish species to electric current. Byulletin Instituta Biologiya Vodokhranilishcha 5:29–31.

Pike were more sensitive to alternating current than other species tested. Specific sensitivity is attributable to the various reactions of the nerve endings and central nervous system of different species.

1960a   The role of the lateral line in fish reaction to electric current. Byulletin Instituta Biologiya Vodokhranilishcha 8–9:50–52.

The dissection of both lateral nerves diminished fish sensitivity to electric current. Tension was increased from 14.5 to 41% to produce the initial reaction in dissected fish. Electronarcosis after sectioning occurred at the same tension as for normal fish.

1960b   The role of surface receptors of the body in the mechanics of the effect of electricity on fish. Byulleten Instituta Biologiya Vodokhranilishcha 3(6):266–272.

Pike were sensitive at 0.40 V and electronarcosis occurred at 2.67 V. Anesthetization of the body surface lowered sensitivity to the current.

1961a   Influence of the dissecting of lateral nerves on sensitivity of fish to alternating electric current. Byulletin Instituta Biologiya Vodokhranilishcha 10:51–53.

In pike, an increase in the voltage gradient was necessary to produce both an initial reaction and electronarcosis after the dissection. On the 12th day the effects of the operation lessened due to adaption of the body and partial regeneration of the nerves.

1961b   On the mechanism of the effect of electrical current on fish. Fiziolicheskii Zhurnal 47:913–917.

The threshold of sensitivity to alternating current and the voltage gradient at which near narcosis sets in were determined. Both normal fish and those whose lateral nerves had been dissected were tested. In pike the voltage gradient rose initially after dissection but decreased about 6 days later and then gradually returned to normal.

1963   Metabolic rate and sensitivity of fish to electric current. Materialy Biologii Gidrol. Volzh. Vodokhranilishcha, pp. 41–44.

Threshold figures were determined for intensity of current inducing initial

40

reaction and that for near narcosis at water temperatures 10–15 C and 20 C. A rise in temperature (and metabolic rate) lowered the threshold of initial reaction, while near narcosis required an increase in voltage gradient.

BOGDANOV, G. N. and S. V. STRELTSOVA,
1953   Seasonal change in fish respiration. Izvestiya Vsesoyuznogo Nauchno-Issledovatel'skogo Instituta Ozernogo i Rechnogo Rybnogo Khozvaistva 33:103–115.

BOGOSLOVSKAIA, E. I.
1960   The corpus luteum in the gonads of fishes. Nauchnye Doklady Vyssshei Shkoly Biologicheskie Nauki 1:21–26.
        A study of resorption of oocytes in pike. Large numbers of corpora lutea were considered indicative of unfavourable spawning conditions.

BOISAUBERT, J.-L. and J. DESSE
1975   Local accumulation of fish remains on the neolithic site La Saunerie at Auvernier Neuchatel, Switzerland; preliminary report. Bulletin de la Societe Neuchateloise des Sciences Naturelles 98:195–202.

BOLDYREFF, E. B.
1935   A microscopic study of the pancreas in fishes; especially those of the orders Haplomi and Cyprinodontes. Copeia 1935:23–34.
        The microscopic structure of the pancrease of *Esox* and a number of other fish is described. The pancreatic structure of *Esox* is compact, well-defined, rather large, and a distinctly independent organ located on the small intestine. Secretory alevoli are frequently found within the islands of Langerhans.

BOLOTOVA, T. G. and A. N. BURLAKOVA
1975   Productivity and spawning conditions of the pike and perch in Lake Gusi-noye, Buryat, ASSR. Izvestiya Gosudarstvennogo Nauchno-Issledovatel'-skogo Instituta Ozernogo i Rechnogo Rybnogo Khozvaistra 93:49–53.

BOND, W. A.
1974   Data on ciscoes, burbot and longnose suckers from Great Slave Lake, Northwest Territories, 1973. Canadian Fisheries and Marine Service, Data Report, Ser.CEN-D, 74–3:1–44.

BONIN, J. D. and J. R. SPOTILA
1978   Temperature tolerance of larval muskellunge (*Esox masquinongy* Mitchill) and F_1 hybrids reared under hatchery conditions. Comparative Biochemistry and Physiology 59A:245–248.
        Critical thermal maxima of larval muskellunge (32.8 C) and the pike-muskellunge hybrid (34.0 C) were determined. The hybrid had a higher temperature tolerance and developed faster. Both age and thermal history had important effects on the temperature tolerance of fry. Hybrid fry were better able to adjust to changing environmental conditions than were muskellunge fry.

BONNELL, B.
1967   The elements of the adhesive disc of echeneis and their homologies. Indian Science Congress Association Proceedings 54:469–470.

BOOTSMA, R.
1971   Hydrocephalus and red-disease in pike fry *Esox lucius* L. Journal of Fish Biology 3:417–419.
        Both diseases cause serious losses in Dutch pike culture. A lump on the head of fry was associated with an internal hydrocephalus. Haemorrhagic areas on

the trunk may be identical with redsore disease of pike.

1973   Infections with *Saprolegnia* in pike culture (*Esox lucius* L.). Aquaculture 2:385–394.

In Dutch pike hatcheries, egg fungus and fungal diseases of fry are caused exclusively by *Saprolignia* species. Malachite green oxalate appeared to be the best treatment.

BOOTSMA, R., P. DE KINKELIN and M. LEBERRE

1975   Transmission experiments with pike fry (*Esox lucius* L.) rhabdovirus. Journal of Fish Biology 7:269–276.

Experimental infection of fertilized pike eggs with "red-disease" virus produced 100% mortality in the fry. This mortality was associated with a disease that had previously been described as hydrocephalus internus, indicating that "red-disease" and hydrocephalus are different manifestations of the same disease. Experimental egg transmission of pike fry Rhabdovirus could be interrupted by disinfecting the eggs in a Wescodyne solution, suggesting that the virus was located on the egg surface.

BOOTSMA, R. and C. J. A. H. V. VAN VORSTENBOSCH

1973   Detection of a bullet-shaped virus in kidney sections of pike fry (*Esox lucius* L.) with red-disease. Netherlands Journal of Veterinary Science 98(2):86–90.

Electron microscopical examination of pike fry with red-disease revealed the presence of large numbers of bullet-shaped virus particles in kidney sections.

BORDES, G.

1979   Une science difficile pour un poisson d'Avenir: l'Esociculture. La Peche et les Poissons 411:35–38.

Magazine article on pike culture. Describes with illustrations the principal steps of artificial fertilization.

BORG, H., A. EDIN, K. HOLM and E. SKOLD

1981   Determination of metals in fish livers by flameless atomic absorption spectroscopy. Water Research 15:1291–1298.

BORGSTROM, R.

1970   Studies of the helminth fauna of Norway. Part 16. *Triaenophorus nodulosus* Cestoda in Bogstad Lake. Part 3. Occurrence in pike *Esox lucius*. Nytt Magasin for Zoologi 18:209–216.

1981   Bestanden av gjedde, *Esox lucius* L., i Arungen. NLVF - Arungenprosjektet 8:1–18.

BORISOVA, O. F., A. P. RAZJIVIN and V. I. ZAREGORODZEV

1974   Evidence for the quinacrine fluorescence on 3 at pairs of DNA. FEBS (Federation of European Biochemical Societies) Letters 46:239–242.

BORRONI, I. and E. GRIMALDI

1974   Ecology of *Diphyllobothrium latum* plerocercoids Cestoda Pseudophyllidea in host fish species of Lago Maggiore, Italy. Rivista di Parassitologia 35:261–276.

BORTKIEWICZ, K.

1967   Proby ustalenia norm przewozowych dla wylegu szczupaka, sielawy i siei. [An attempt to establish transportation standards for pike, vendace and whitefish hatchlings.] Gospodarka Rybna 18(4):4–5.

Experiments dealing with fish densities during transport.

42

BOUCHER, R. and E. MAGNIN

1977   Bioecologie du grand brochet, *Esox lucius* L. du lac Helene, territoire de la Baie James. Rapport scientifique 58, Service Environnement, Societe d'Energie de la Baie James, Montreal. 83 pp.

1979   Comportement et dynamique de la population des grands brochets *Esox lucius* L., du lac Helene, territoire de la Baie James. [Behaviour and dynamics of a population of northern pike, *Esox lucius* L., in Lac Helene, James Bay territory.] *In* Dube, J., and Y. Gravel, eds. Proceedings 10th Warmwater Workshop, Special Publication NE Division American Fisheries Society. Published by Quebec Ministere du Loisir, de la Chasse et de la Peche, Montreal, pp. 201–218.

        To evaluate the impact of the creation of a reservoir in James Bay region, the ecological requirements of pike were assessed for future considerations of fishery management. Pike represented 21% of the total fish population of Lac Helene. Activity patterns, habitat requirements, and distribution were considered.

BOUQUET, H. G. J.

1979   The management of pike stocks. Proceedings of the 1st British Freshwater Fish Conference. pp. 176–181.

BOUSSU, M. F.

1954   Statewide fisheries investigations. Lake fishery investigations. 1954. Silver Lake. South Dakota Department of Game, Fish and Parks, Dingell-Johnson Report F-1-R-4/Job 2/D1.

1959a   Statewide fisheries investigations. Southern lakes fishery investigations. 1957. Northern pike spawning area. South Dakota Department of Game, Fish and Parks, Dingell-Johnson Report F-1-R-7/Job 13/Q.

1959b   Statewide fisheries investigations. Southern lakes Fishery investigations. 1957. Northern pike spawning area. South Dakota Department of Game, Fish and Parks, Dingell-Johnson Report F-1-R-7/Job 14/Q.

1959c   Statewide fisheries investigations. Southern lakes fishery investigations. 1957. Northern pike spawning area. South Dakota Department of Game, Fish and Parks, Dingell-Johnson Report F-2-D-3/Q.

1961   Statewide fisheries investigations. Southern lakes fishery investigations. 1959. Northern pike spawning areas. South Dakota Department of Game, Fish and Parks, Dingell-Johnson Report F-1-R-9/Job 2/I.

BOWER, S. M. and P. T. K. WOO

1977a   *Cryptobia catostomi* incubation in plasma of susceptible and refractory fishes. Experimental Parasitology 43:63–68.

1977b   Morphology and host specificity of *Cryptobia catostomi* n.sp. (Protozoa, Kinetoplastida) from white sucker (*Catostomus commersoni*) in southern Ontario. Canadian Journal of Zoology 55:1082–1092.

BOYTSOV, M. P.

1974   The morphology of underyearling fishes in the zone affected by warm waters discharged from the Konakovo power station into Ivan'kovskoye Reservoir. Journal of Ichthyology 14:904–910.

BRACKEN, J. J.

1973   The age and growth of pike *Esox lucius* from four Irish trout rivers. Irish Fisheries Investigations, Ser. A (Freshwater), 12:1–15.

BRACKEN, J. J. and W. S. T. CHAMP
  1968   Age and growth of pike (*Esox lucius* L.) in five Irish limestone lakes. Ireland Department of Agriculture and Fisheries, Fishery Investigations, Series A.
  1971   Age and growth of pike (*Esox lucius* L.) in five Irish limestone lakes. Scientific Proceedings of the Dublin Society, Ser.B, 3:1–33.

BRACKEN, J. J. and M. P. KENNEDY
  1967   A key to the identification of the eggs and young stages of coarse fish in Irish waters. Scientific Proceedings of the Royal Dublin Society, Ser.B, 2:99–108.

BRAEKEVELT, C. R.
  1973   The fine structure of the pigment epithelial region in the eye of a teleost. Canadian Federation of Biological Societies, Proceedings 16:18.
  1974   Fine structure of the retinal pigment epithelium, Bruch's membrane, and choriocapillaris in the northern pike (*Esox lucius*). Journal of the Fisheries Research Board of Canada 31:1601–1605.
          Light and electron microscopy were used to study in detail the fine structure of the retinal pigment epithelium, Bruch's membrane, and choriocapillaris in adult pike. The pike eye differs morphologically from that described for most other vertebrates.
  1975   Photoreceptor fine structure in the northern pike (*Esox lucius*). Journal of the Fisheries Research Board of Canada 32:1711–1721.

BRAUM, E.
  1962   Erste Nahrungsaufnahme bei Blaufelchen (*Coregonus wartmanni* Bloch) und Hechtjungfischen (*Esox lucius* L.) des Bodensees. Naturwissenschaften 8:1–2.
  1963   Die ersten Beute Fang handlungen junger Blaufelchen (*Coregonus wartmanni* Bloch) und Hechte (*Esox lucius* L.). Zeitschrift fuer Tierpsychologie Beiheft 20:257–277.
          Immediately after hatch, larvae of pike remain nearly immobile and adhere to the substrate, while the yolk sac is absorbing. After yolk sac absorption, pike caught prey for the first time, especially Copepoda. Pike filled their swimbladders before the first feed. The capture of first prey was analysed by photography. Pike notice movement of the prey transverse to the longitude of their own bodies. Their posture before pushing forward depends on the movement direction of prey. While pushing forward the pike's head deviates to one side, determined by the chosen starting posture. The deviation is identical with the movement direction of the prey.
  1964   Experimentelle Untersuchungen Zur ersten Nahrungsaufnahme und Biologie an Jungfischen von Blaufelchen (*Coregonus wartmanni* Bloch), Weissfelchen (*Coregonus fera* Jurine) und Hechten (*Esox lucius* L.). Archiv fuer Hydrobiologie 28(Suppl.):183–244. [English summary]
  1967   The survival of fish larvae with reference to their feeding behaviour and the food supply. *In* Gerking, S. D., ed., The biological basis of freshwater fish production. IBP Symposium, Reading, 1966, pp. 113–131.

BRAUN, F.
  1974   The air bladder inflammation of the carp. Muenchener Beitraege zur Abwasser-Fischerei- und Flussbiologie 25:69–74.

BREDER, C. M.
  1926   Locomotion of fishes. Zoologica 4(5):159.

BREDER, C. M., Jr. and D. E. ROSEN

  1966   Modes of reproduction in fishes. Garden City, Natural History Press. 941 pp.

BREGAZZI, P. R.

  1978   Biology and management of perch (*Perca fluviatilis* L.) and pike (*Esox lucius*) in Slapton Ley, Devon. Ph.D. thesis, Exeter University.

BREGAZZI, P. R. and C. R. KENNEDY

  1980   The biology of pike, *Esox lucius* L., in a southern eutrophic lake. Journal of Fish Biology 17:91–112.

BRERETON, G. E. and J. M. FERRIER, eds.

  1981   Le menagier de Paris. Oxford.

          Information on purchasing, preparing, and eating freshwater fishes.

BRETT, J. R.

  1979   Environmental factors and growth. *In* Hoar, W. S., et al., eds., Fish physiology, vol. 8. New York, Academic Press, pp. 599–675.

BRIDGES, C. D. B.

  1969   Yellow corneas in fishes. Vision Research 9:435–436.

BRINKHUIZEN, D. C.

  1979   Preliminary notes on fish remains from archeological sites in the Netherlands. Palaeohistoria 21:83–90.

          Subfossil fish remains from 15 sites, 3500 B.C. to 1700 A.D.: 28 species. All freshwater types still extant in the Netherlands.

BRINKHURST, R. O.

  1969   Changes in the benthos of lakes Erie and Ontario. Buffalo Society of Natural History, Bulletin 25:45–71.

BRINLEY, F. J.

  1940   Development of the fish heart, brown trout (*Salmo fario*) and northern pike (*Esox lucius*). Lloydia 3:145–156.

BROFELDT, P.

  1917   Bidrag till kannedomen om fiskbestandet i vara sjoar. Finlands Fiskerier 4:172–212.

BROOK, G.

  1887   Note on the spawning of the pike. Fisheries Board of Scotland, Annual Report for 1887, pp. 347–349.

BROUGHTON, N. M. and K. A. M. FISHER

  1981   A comparison of three methods of pike (*Esox lucius* L.) removal from a lowland trout fishery. Fisheries Management 12:101–106.

          The seine netting, gill netting, and angling techniques used at Grafham Water for the removal of pike are described and assessed, and the effectiveness of the various methods compared. It was found that a combination of summer gill netting and seine netting was most effective, but it was concluded that angling was worthwhile during the autumn months.

BROWN, C. E.

  1915   Lake Wingra. Wisconsin Archeologist 14(3):1–117.

BROWN, C. J. D.

  1971   Fishes of Montana. Montana State University, 207 pp.

BROWN, E. H., Jr. and C. F. CLARK

  1965   Length-weight relationship of northern pike, *Esox lucius*, from East Harbor, Ohio. Transactions of the American Fisheries Society 94:404–405.

          Length-weight relationships were determined for the sexes separately.

45

Females averaged significantly heavier at the various lengths.

BROWN, E. R., W. C. DOLOWY, T. SINCLAIR, L. KEITH, S. GREENBERG, J. J. HAZDRA, P. BEAMER and O. CALLAGHAN

  1976   Enhancement of lymphosarcoma transmission in *Esox lucius* and its epi-demiologic relationship to pollution. Bibliotheca Haematologica 43:245–251. Variations of inoculation size and site, water temperature, and age of fish recipients affected rapidity of tumor appearance. Three water bodies of varying quality were examined to assess the relationship between contamination and tumor frequency.

BROWN, E. R., L. KEITH, J. J. HAZDRA and T. ARNDT

  1975   Tumors in fish caught in polluted waters; possible explanations. Bibliotheca Haematologica 40:47–57.

BROWN, E. R., L. KEITH, J. B. G. KWAPINSKI, J. HAZDRA and P. BEAMER

  1973   Frequency of tumors in fish populating a polluted water system. Proceedings of the American Association of Cancer Research 14:1.

BROWN, J. J.

  1876   The American angler's guide. 5th ed. New York, D. Appelton, 428 pp. Information on angling methods for various types of water bodies, tackle and baits, and other topics pertaining to sport fishing.

BROWN, J. R. and L. Y. CHOW

  1977   Heavy metal concentrations in Ontario fish. Bulletin of Environmental Con-tamination and Toxicology 17:190–195.

BROWN, L.

            Know your fish. London, A. & C. Black.

BRUCE, W. J. and R. F. PARSONS

  1979   Biology of the fishes of Ossokmanuan Reservoir, Labrador, 1976. Canadian Fisheries and Marine Service Report 836:1–32.

BRUEDERLIN, B. and B. H. WRIGHT

  1981   A creel census of Reed Lake, 1979. Manitoba Department of Natural Resources, Manuscript Report 81–25:1–70.
            Fork length, weight, and fin and scale samples were obtained from 270 pike collected on 26 randomly selected days during May to September 1979.

BRUEDERLIN, B. B.

  1982   A creel census of Goose Lake. Manitoba Department of Natural Resources, Manuscript Report 82–13:1–54.
            Results of a creel census and fish sampling program conducted for 22 ran-domly selected days from May to September, 1979.

BRUENKO, V. P.

  1976   The feeding of pike (*Esox lucius* L.) of the Kremenchug Reservoir during spawning. Gidrobiologicheskii Zhurnal 12:121–125.

BRUHL, L.

  1925   Was man durch Hechtaussetzung erreichen kann. Fischerei-Zeitung.
  1927a   Gefrashigkeit des Hechtes. Fischerei-Zeitung.
  1927b   Spat laichende Hechte. Fischerei-Zeitung 30.

BRUNNER, G. and H. REICHENBACK-KLINKE

  1961   Beitrag zur Fleckenseuche des Hechtes. Fischerei-Zeitung 86(10).

BRUYENKO, V. P.

  1976   Feeding habits of pike *Esox lucius* in the Kremenchug reservoir during the spawning period. Hydrobiological Journal 12:103–106.

BRY, C.
1980   Influence de la densite initiale de peuplement sur la survie et la croissance du brochet (*Esox lucius* L.) entre trois mois et un an d'age. [The effect of initial population density on the survival and growth of pike (*Esox lucius* stocked as 3-month fingerlings] *In* Billard, R., ed., Pond fish farming, Paris, Institute National de la Recherche Agronomique, pp. 317–323.

Consequences of overstocking pike fingerlings on number and biomass yields were examined. Three different densities were studied for nine months, each with the same food sources. Final number, survival rates, mean weight of pike, variability of individual weight, and net biomass were recorded. The results suggested that overstocking may cause poor yields.

BRY, C., R. BILLARD and G. DE MONTALEMBERT,
1978   Induction de la naturation ovocytaire et de l'ovulation par traitment hormonal chez le brochet (*Esox lucius*). [Induction of oocyte naturation and ovulation through hormonal treatment in pike (*Esox lucius*]. Bulletin Francais de Pisciculture 271:21–32. [in French]

BRY, C. and C. GILLET
1980a   Reduction of cannibalism in pike (*Esox lucius*) fry by isolation of full-sib families. Reproduction Nutrition Developpement 20:173–182.

1980b   Reduction du cannibalisme precoce chez le brochet (*Esox lucius*) par isolement des fratries. [Reduction of early cannibalism in pike (*Esox lucius*) obtained by isolating full-sib families]. Bulletin Francais de Pisciculture 277:142–153.

After 50 days of pond culture fewer pike fingerlings were recovered from the mixing of two full-sib families than from isolated families. Isolating full-sib families and using small, shallow ponds increased the recovery and growth rate of fingerlings.

BRY, C. and Y. SOUCHON
1982   Production of young northern pike families in small ponds: natural spawning versus fry stocking. Transactions of the American Fisheries Society 111:476–480.

Ponds were stocked with 5–10 fry/sq.m. in April-May, or with one female and two male pike in February. Comparable biomasses of juveniles were produced by both methods (41 and 52 kg/hectare respectively). Higher stocking densities may improve production in both methods, but natural spawning may be less difficult and expensive compared to fry stocking procedures.

BRY, C., Y. SOUCHON, G. NEVEU and L. TREBAOL
1983a   Production de familles de brochetons en petits etangs par reproduction naturelle amenagee: bilan de trois annees d'experimentation et comparaison avec la methode d'alevinage. *In* Billard, R., ed., Le brochet gestion dans le milieu naturel et elevage. Paris, Institute National de la Recherche Agronomique, pp. 63–73.

1983b   Production de familles de brochetons en petits etangs par reproduction naturelle amenages: Bilan de trois annees d'experimentation et comparaison avec la methode d'alevinage. [Production of young northern pike families in small ponds from managed natural spawning: Results from a three year experiment and comparison with the fry stocking method. Bulletin Francais de Pisciculture 288:46–56. [in French, English abstract]

The method of managed natural spawning (MNS) implies the stocking in mid-February of one pike female and two males. The production from MNS was compared with the results obtained when families of reared fry are stocked into ponds. Under the existing conditions, the MNS technique proved dependable, with minimal manpower, and little technical skill, sparing costs.

BRY, C., Y. SOUCHON and G. NEVEU

1984   Production of young northern pike in small ponds from managed natural spawning. Bulletin Francais de Pisciculture 293–294:59–64.
        Describes a method of producing young pike by managed natural spawning in a "protected" environment—small, drainable, grassy and shallow ponds, containing forage fish but no predator, and with a constant water level.

BRYAN, J. E.

1967   Northern pike production in Phalen Pond, Minnesota. Journal of the Minnesota Academy of Science 34:101–109.
        Physical, chemical, and biological conditions were related to the development and survival of eggs and young. Neither slow nor abnormal development increased egg mortality. Growth rate and production corresponded directly to quantity and distribution of plankton. Cladocera were selected over Rotifers, and low density of plankton triggered cannibalism.

BRYNILDSON, C.

1958   What's happening to northern pike spawning grounds? Wisconsin Conservation Bulletin 23(5):9–11.
        Shoreline improvements to lakes in southeastern Wisconsin have destroyed many pike spawning grounds. Those that remain must be preserved.

1970   Selective chemical fish eradication of Mill Creek, Richland County. Wisconsin Department of Natural Resources, Management Report 32.
        Antimycin was used as a fish eradicant, and along with other species, six pike ranging in length from 14–18 inches were removed.

BRYNILDSON, C., D. B. IVES and H. S. DRUCKENMILLER

1970   A two year creel census of Devils Lake, Sauk County. Wisconsin Department of Natural Resources, Management Report 35:1–11.
        The winter of 1969–70 was good for pike fishing, while the winter of 1968–69 was poor. Predation on trout is a significant problem.

BUBINAS, A. D.

1976   Feeding of asp and pike in the Kaunas hydro electric plant water reservoir in 1972. Lietuvos TSR Mokslu Akademijos Darbai, Serija C, Biologiuos Mokslai 2:133–142.
        The main food component of pike was the most common fish; species consumed varied with season. The young of commercial species were found in pike stomachs in smaller amounts. Recommends increasing the number of pike in the reservoir.

BUBINAS, A. P.

1976   Feeding of asp and pike in the Upper Dnieper. Rybnoe Khozyaistvo 3:84–93.

BUCK, O. D. and J. L. CRITES

1975   Impact of parasitic worms on Lake Erie fishes. Impact of the cestode parasite *Triaenophorus nodulosus* on Lake Erie fishes. Ohio Division of Wildlife, Project F-48-R-3:1–92.
        The parasite develops to the adult stage when infected white bass (*Roccus americana*) are eaten by pike.

48

BUCKE, D.

1971   The anatomy and histology of the alimentary tract of the carnivorous fish the pike *Esox lucius* L. Journal of Fish Biology 3:421–431.

The alimentary tract of pike is described in detail, and feeding habits are related to intestinal gut histology. The pancreas and liver are described briefly, the former being of an unusual compact type not often found in teleosts. The beta cells are seen in the periphery and alpha cells in the centre of the islets.

BUCKE, D., J. FINLAY, D. MCGREGOR and C. SEAGREAVE

1979   Infectious pancreatic necrosis (IPN) virus: its occurrence in captive and wild fish in England and Wales. Journal of Fish Disease 2:549–553.

BUDZYNSKA, H.

1956   Fish growth and food in Goplo Lake. The pike. Zoologica Poloniae 7(1):63–120.

BULGAKOVA, E. I.

1965   Reproductive patterns of fishes in the Sviyage Inlet of the Kuibyshev Reservoir. *In* Results of large-scale observations on the Sviyaga Bay fauna of the Juibyshev Reservoir during the periods of its formation. Kazan, Kazan University, pp. 152–161.

BULL, K. R., A. F. DEARSLEY and M. H. INSKIP

1981   Growth and mercury content of roach (*Rutilus rutilus* L.), perch (*Perca fluviatilis* L.) and pike (*Esox lucius* L.) living in sewage effluent. Environmental Pollution, Ser.25, 3:229–240.

Fish from the Rye Meads sewage lagoons in Hertfordshire, Great Britain, showed high growth rates, while their mercury content (positively correlated to size and age) indicated a slightly elevated mercury environment. Methylmercury represented a high proportion of the mercury found in all species.

BULLER, F.

1971   Pike. London, Pan Books. 287 pp.

1979   The Domesday Book of mammoth pike. London, Stanley Paul. 286 pp.

1981   Pike and the pike angler. London, Stanley Paul. 288 pp.

This book deals with natural history (breeding, growth, feeding habits, hybrids, and fossil pike), stories of "legendary monster pike", and advice on angling (rigs, tackles, methods).

BURDAK, V. D.

1972   A new species of *Conophorus* (Diptera, Bombyliidae) from the south-east Kazakhstan. Institute of Zoology, Academy of Sciences of the Kazakh SSR. [in Russian, English summary].

BURLAKOV, A. B. and N. E. LEBEDEVA

1976   Species specificity of gonadotropic hormones in fishes and mammals. Journal of Evolutionary Biochemistry and Physiology 12:180–182.

BURNAND, T.

1963   Pesca in acqua dolce. Milano, Mondadori. 160 pp.

Description, distribution in Italy, food, angling information.

BURROWS

1974   U.S. upper midwest *Rana pipiens* population decline. Smithsonian Institution, Center for Short Lived Phenomena, Event 157–74.

Aeromonas hydrophilla causes red leg in *Rana pipiens* and red fin in pike. Infected pike develop a reddish appearance on the undersides and within the body cavity. Mortality among adults can be 100%. Pike's spawning in pond habitats can be a major factor in the spread and perpetuation of the disease in *Rana pipiens*.

BUSNITA, T.

1969   The fauna of the impoundment lakes on the Danube, from source to mouth. Buletinui Institutului de Cercetari si Projectari Piscicole 28:57–61. [in Romanian, English summary].

BUSS, K.

1960   The muskellunge. Pennsylvania Fish Commission, Special Purpose Report, pp. 1–14.

1961a   A literature survey of the life history and culture of the northern pike. Pennsylvania Fish Commission, Benner Spring Fishery Research Station, Special Purpose Report, 58 pp.
        Reviews the change in attitude of fish managers towards pike, with references from 1875 to 1961. Policies changed from extermination to preservation as the pike became recognized as a "balancing mechanism" and as a desirable game fish. A summary of the known life history of the pike is given.

1961b   Record northern pike—fact or fiction. Pennsylvania Angler 30(10):6–8.

1963   Hybrid pike. Pennsylvania Angler 32(1):23.

1966a   Research and fish management. *In* J. M. Smith Division Reports to the Sportsman. Pennsylvania Angler 35(1):22–24.

1966b   The facts concerning the production and stocking of warmwater fishes. Pennsylvania Angler 35(6):5–8.

1968   On warmwater fishes, facts about production and stocking. Kentucky Happy Hunting Ground 24(3):26–28.

BUSS, K. and A. LARSEN

1961   The northern pike of Presque Isle Bay, Lake Erie. Pennsylvania Angler 30(9):4–6.
        Information on spawning, age, and growth.

BUSS, K., J. MEADE, III and D. R. GRAFF

1978   Reviewing the esocid hybrids. American Fisheries Society Special Publication 11:210–216.
        Artificial crosses of the larger pikes, although successful, produced only one with fertile progeny, the Amur pike (*Esox reichteri*) x pike. Crosses with smaller pickerel were generally unsuccessful or produced sterile young.

BUSS, K. and J. MILLER

1961   The age and growth of the northern pike. Pennsylvania Angler 30(3):6–7.
        Gives length-weight relationships of 540 pike from Pennsylvania waters and average calculated body lengths at each annulus, up to age 6.

1962   Part VI. The age and growth of the northern pike in Pennsylvania. *In* The age and growth of the fishes in Pennsylvania. Pennsylvania Fish Commission. pp. 11–12.

1967   Interspecific hybridization of esocids: hatching success, pattern development, and fertility of some F1 hybrids. U.S. Department of the Interior, Fish and Wildlife Service, Bureau of Sport Fisheries and Wildlife, Technical Paper 14:1–30.
        Five esocids were used as parent species to make 20 reciprocal crosses. Young were maintained from 1 to 4 years. Fertility of six reciprocal hybrids was established.

n.d.   Identifying the common fishes of Pennsylvania. Pennsylvania Fish Commission Pamphlet, 16 pp.

BUTLER, E. P.

1919   Notes on the presence of larval trematodes in eyes of certain fishes of Douglas Lake, Michigan. Michigan Academy of Science, 21st Annual Report, p. 116.

BUTLER, G. E.

1949   The lakes and lake fisheries of Manitoba. Transactions of the American Fisheries Society 79:18–29.

Mentions several lakes that have a pike sport fishery.

BUYNAK, G. L. and H. W. MOHN, JR.

1979   Larval development of the northern pike (*Esox lucius*) and muskellunge (*Esox masquinongy*) from northeast Pennsylvania. Proceedings of the Pennsylvania Academy of Science 53:69–73.

Pike eggs hatched 10 days after fertilization at a mean temperature of 10.9 C. Newly hatched larvae were 7.9–8.5 mm TL. Transformation to the postlarval phase occurred by 13.2 mm and to the late postlarval phase by 19.1 mm.

BYCZKOWAKA-SMYK, W.

1959   The respiratory surface of the gills in teleosts. Part IV. The respiratory surface of the gills in the pike (*Esox lucius* L.), stone-perch and burbot. Acta Biologica Cracaviensis 2(2).

Macroscopically the gills of pike differed considerably from those of other fish, the gill arches being much longer. This influenced the number of branchial lamellae. The number of lamellae on each arch is detailed. The length of the branchial lamellae of pike in relation to the dimensions of the gill arch was rather small. Because of the number of branchial lamellae, the number of respiratory plates in pike is many times larger than that of other fish. The vascularization of the gills of pike is the same as that of other teleosts.

BYKOV, N. E.

1974   Some of the characteristics of pike reproduction in the Saratov reservoir. Izvestiya Gosudarstvennogo Nauchno-Issledovatel'skogo Instituta Ozernogo i Rechnogo Rybnogo Khozvaistva 95:86–97.

Spawning efficiency of pike depended upon water level fluctuations, which resulted in mortality of deposited eggs.

BYZOV, A. L., Y. A. TRIFONOV, L. M. CHAILAHIAN and K. W. GOLUBTZOV

1977   Amplication of graded potentials in horizontal cells of the retina. Vision Research 17:265–273.

BYZOV, A. L., Y. A. TRIFONOV and L. M. CHAILAKHYAN

1973   Effect of polarization of horizontal cells of the pike retina on spread of the electrical potentials. Neurophysiology 4:72–77.

CACUTT, L.

1979   British freshwater fishes. The story of their evolution. London, Croom Helm. 202 pp.

A rambling general account of the pike for the angler, including classification, history, description, lore, growth, food, related species, angling methods. Some of the information is outdated, wrong, or doubtful. Many errors and typographical errors.

CAHN, A. R.

1927   An ecological study of southern Wisconsin fishes. Illinois Biological Monograms 2:1–151.

CAINE, L. S.

1949a   North American freshwater sport fish. New York, A. S. Barnes. 212 pp.

1949b   Northern pike *Esox lucius*. Heddon Fish Flashes 136:1–5.

Angler's notes on struggle between pike and fisherman, "tall tales", appearance, range, lures, and tackle. Mentions common names, record size, flavour, food, and methods.

CAKAY, E.

1958   Onemocnenie st'uk pasomnicami. Csl. Rybarstvi 1958:98–99.

CALDERON-ANDREU, E.-G.

1955   Acclimatation du brochet en Espagne. International Association of Theoretical and Applied Limnology Proceedings 12:536–542.

CALDERONI, P.

1965   Contribution to the study of growth of the pike (*Esox lucius* L.) living in the Trasimeno Lake. Rivista di Idrobiologica 4(1/2):3–15. [in Italian, English summary].

A study of gonad maturation, sex ratio, and growth of 179 pike. Mature gonads were found in 1-year-old fish. Female to male sex ratio was about 2:1. Growth of both sexes was similar up to the 4th year, reaching about 40 cm. Females reached about 70 cm at the 8th year.

CALDERONI, P., G. GIOVINAZZO, M. MEARELLI and L. VOLPI

1980   Contribution to knowledge of *Esox lucius* L. from the Trasimeno Lake. Rivista di Idrobiologica 19(2):347–359. [in Italian, English abstract].
Information on age, growth, sex ratio for a sample of 250 specimens.

CALENIUS, G.

1980   Parasites of fish in Finland. 5. Observations on protozoans of the genera *Trichophrya*, *Chilodonella*, and *Ichthyophthirius*. Acta Academiae Aboensis, Ser. B, Mathematica et Physica Matematik Naturvetenskaper Teknik 40(5):1–8.

CALENIUS, G. and G. BYLUND

1980   Parasites of fish in Finland. 4. Ciliates of the genus *Apiosoma*. Acta Academiae Aboensis, Ser, B, Mathematica et Physica Matematik Naturvetenskaper Teknik 40(4):1–12.

CALL, R. E.

1899.   Ichthyologia Ohiensis, etc., by Rafinesque, Constantine. A verbatim et literatim reprint of the original. Cleveland, Burrows. 175 pp.

CAMERON, G. S.

1948   An unusual maskinonge from Little Vermilion Lake, Ontario. Canadian Journal of Research, Ser.D, 26:223–229.

Description of the pike-muskellunge hybrid. All six hybrid specimens appeared to be sterile.

CAMERON, J. N.

1973   Oxygen dissociation and content of blood from Alaskan burbot (*Lota lota*), pike (*Esox lucius*) and grayling (*Thymallus articus*). Comparative Biochemistry and Physiology 46:491–496.

Oxygen dissociation curves of whole blood were determined for pike from interior Alaska. Temperature was either 5, 10, or 15 C, and the carbon dioxide tensions were in the physiological range of 0 to 7.0 torr. *P*50 values ranged from 2.7 to 7.3 for pike.

1974   Coronary blood supply in teleost fish. American Zoologist 13:1297. [Abstract]

Studied blood supply to myocardium in pike, using radioactive microspheres, rubidium[86] indicator-dilution technique, and microscopy. Made injections upstream and downstream from ventricle, followed by histological examination.

1975   Morphometric and flow indicator studies of the teleost heart. Canadian Journal of Zoology 53:691–698.

Calculations of probable limits for oxygen uptake of the ventricle, based on data in this study and in literature.

CAMP, R. R.

1951   Reel sport: pike, pickerel and musky. Colliers Magazine, July 1951, pp. 30–31, 60–61.

CAMPBELL, A. D.

1973   Acquisition of a parasite fauna by an experimental salmon stock. Parasitology 67(2).

CANESTRINI, R.

1886   Nota sui pesci mastruosi. Atti della Societa Scienze Padova 9:117–125.

CAPLAN, D. L.

1982   An experimental study of interactions between young of the year pike (*Esox lucius*) and muskellunge (*Esox masquinongy*). M.Sc. thesis, University of Wisconsin-Madison. 55 pp.

CARBINE, W. F.

1938   The pike: a prized and spurned fish. Michigan Conservationist 7(12):6–8.

Included are a description of pike and information on distribution, spawning, age and growth, habitat, food, importance to man, management, and angling.

1941   Observations on the life history of the northern pike (*Esox lucius*) at Houghton Lake, Michigan. Progressive Fish-Culturist 55:42–43.

Brief account with information on growth, sex ratio, and spawning.

1942a   Observations on the life history of the northern pike, *Esox lucius*, in Houghton Lake, Michigan. Transactions of the American Fisheries Society 71:149–164.

Surveyed sex ratio and average length of spawners caught in weirs during upstream migrations in 1939 and 1940. Assessed numbers and length of young leaving spawning grounds.

1942b   Northern pike experiments conducted at the Drayton Plains Hatchery from 1937–39. Michigan Institute of Fisheries, Research Report 761:1–15.

1942c   Sphaeriid clams attached to the mouth of young pike. Copeia 1942:187.

Three affected fingerlings were found in drainage ditches that flow into

Houghton Lake, Michigan. The clams were securely clamped on the jaws, and the jaws of one pike were clamped together. Fingernail clams have not been found in the stomachs of young pike and the circumstances surrounding the attachment were unknown.

1944   Egg production of the northern pike, *Esox lucius* L., and the percentage survival of eggs and young on the spawning grounds. Michigan Academy of Science, Arts, and Letters 29:123–137.

Pike captured during migration at Houghton Lake, Michigan, from 1939–1942 provided information on the size of mature eggs, relative number and total volume of mature and immature eggs, and the number of females spawning each year. Relationship between production and size and condition of the female was studied. Ovum diameter showed that all eggs to be spawned in one season form a single size group.

1945   Growth potential of the northern pike (*Esox lucius*). Michigan Academy of Science, Arts, and Letters 30:205–220.

Growth of pike reared in hatchery ponds was extremely variable. The largest fish at the end of the summer had grown an average of 2.6 mm and 2.69 g per day. The tremendous growth made by some during their first summer was not maintained throughout their retention in ponds for two more years.

CARBINE, W. F. and V. C. APPLEGATE

1948   The movement and growth of marked pike (*Esox lucius* L.) in Houghton Lake and the Muskegon River. Papers of the Michigan Academy of Science, Arts, and Letters 32:215–238.

This study of life history and habits began in 1937. Observations were made on the migration to and from the spawning ground, spawning habits, feeding, growth, and movements of young and adult pike.

CARBINE, W. F. and D. S. SHETTER

1944   Examples of the use of two-way fish weirs in Michigan. Transactions of the American Fisheries Society 73:70–89.

In 1939 and 1940, pike and yellow pikeperch (*Stizostedion vitreum*) comprised only 3.0% of the upstream and downstream migration of the Muskegon River.

CARDOT, J. and J. RIPPLINGER

1967   Action of adrenaline cardiovasc and noradrenaline epinephrine cardiovasc norepinephrine cardiovasc on washed heart of the pike *Esox lucius* and the carp *Cyprinus carpio*. Journal of Physiology 59:339–403.

CARL, C. G. and W. A. CLEMENS

1948   The fresh-water fishes of British Columbia. British Columbia Provincial Museum, Handbook 5:1–132.

CARL, C. G., W. A. CLEMENS and C. C. LINDSEY

1959   The freshwater fishes of British Columbia. 3rd ed. British Columbia Provincial Museum, Handbook 5:1–192.

CARLANDER, K. D.

1942   An investigation of Lake of the Woods, Minnesota, with particular reference to the commercial fisheries. Minnesota Bureau of Fisheries Research, Investigational Report 42:1–534.

1943   Length-weight relationship of Minnesota fishes. Minnesota Bureau of Fisheries Research, Investigational Report 17:1–23.

1944   Notes on the coefficient of condition, K, of Minnesota fishes. Minnesota Bureau of Fisheries Research, Investigational Report 41:1–40.

1947   Some trends in the commercial fisheries of Lake of the Woods, Minnesota. Transactions of the American Fisheries Society 77:13–25.
        The catch of pike declined about 70% in the previous 30 years.

1948   Some changes in the fish population of Lake of the Woods, Minnesota, 1910–1945. Copeia 1948:271–274.
        Pike is listed as one of the species netted from 1939 to 1945.

1949   Project No. 39. Yellow pike-perch management. Progressive Report of Iowa Cooperative Wildlife and Fisheries Research Units 1949 (January-March):44–57.

1950   Handbook of freshwater fishery biology. Dubuque, W. C. Brown. 281 pp.

1952   Vital statistics on the pike family. Field and Stream 56(10):74–76.

1953   Handbook of freshwater fishery biology with the first supplement. Dubuque, W. C. Brown. 429 pp.

1955   The standing crop of fish in lakes. Journal of the Fisheries Research Board of Canada 12:543–570.
        An analysis was made, primarily by regression methods, of the published estimates of standing crops of fish in lakes and ponds, to determine whether certain environmental factors may affect standing crop.

1956   Late spring may mean good pike fishing. Iowa Conservationist 15(4):25–32.

1957   Disturbance of predator-prey balance as a management technique. Transactions of the American Fisheries Society 87:34–38.
        Stocking of 5 pike per acre increased the weight of the predator population by about 10%. In the first 6 weeks of the next fishing season, over 20% of the stocked pike were caught by anglers.

1969   Handbook of freshwater fishery biology. Life history data on freshwater fishes of the United States and Canada, exclusive of the Perciformes. Ames, Iowa State University Press, vol. 1, 752 pp.

CARLANDER, K. D., J. S. CAMPBELL and R. J. MUNCY

1978a   Inventory of percid and esocid habitat in North America. Journal Paper No. J- of the Iowa Agriculture and Home Economics Experiment Station, Project 2002.

1978b   Inventory of percid and esocid habitat in North America. American Fisheries Society Special Publication 11:27–38.
        Distribution patterns of introduced and native populations revealed major concentrations of coolwater habitat around the Great Lakes. Habitats reported, as a percentage of total freshwater area of North America, were 54% for northern pike. Figures varied widely between regional groupings.

CARLANDER, K. D. and E. CLEARY

1949   The daily activity patterns of some freshwater fishes. American Midland Naturalist 41:447–452.

CARLANDER, K. D. and J. G. ERICKSON

1953   Some population estimates of young northern pike reared in a marsh. 15th Midwest Wildlife Conference, Chicago, 1953. 3 pp. [mimeo.].
        Numbered jaw tags were placed on 1,146 pike to 1) estimate the population, 2) determine the percentage that come out of the marsh before freeze-up, 3) determine the contribution to future angling, and 4) study movements after release in Clear Lake.

CARLANDER, K. D., J. L. FORNEY and W. PEARCY
   1951   Clear Lake investigations. Quarterly Report of the Iowa Cooperative Wildlife
          and Fisheries Research Units 17(1):37–43.
CARLANDER, K. D. and L. E. HINER
   1943a Preliminary report on fisheries investigations, Leech Lake, Cass County.
          Minnesota Bureau of Fisheries Research, 18 pp. [typewritten].
   1943b Fisheries investigation and management report for Lake Vermilion, St. Louis
          County. Minnesota Bureau of Fisheries Research, Investigational Report
          54:1–175.
CARLANDER, K. D. and J. W. PARSONS
   1949   Project No. 39. Yellow pike-perch management. Iowa Cooperative Wildlife
          and Fisheries Research Units, Progress Report 1949:49–52.
CARLANDER, K. D. and R. RIDENHOUR
   1955   Dispersal of stocked northern pike in Clear Lake, Iowa. Progressive Fish-
          Culturist 17:186–189.
          Tagged, stocked pike moved to all parts of Clear Lake within 6 months, even
          if stocked at one end. Movement is extensive and general, but fish stocked in
          some areas do not get to the other end of the lake in the same abundance. A
          longer time between stocking and capture might eliminate even this slight
          difference.
CARLANDER, K. D. and L. L. SMITH, Jr.
   1945   Some factors to consider in the choice between standard, fork, or total lengths
          in fishery investigations. Copeia 1945:7–12.
          For pike in Minnesota multiply SL by 1.078 to get fork length; if 200–499
          mm SL, multiply by 1.141 to get total length, if over 500 mm SL, multiply by
          1.033.
CARLANDER, K. D. and G. SPRUGEL
   1955   Fishes of Little Wall Lake, Iowa, prior to dredging. Proceedings of the Iowa
          Academy of Science 62:555–566.
CARLINE, R. F.
   1979   Evaluation of stocking northern pike in Ohio lakes. Ohio Department of
          Natural Resources, Federal Aid Project F-57-R-1:1–28.
          Existing data were analysed to develop some generalizations about lakes that
          support large and small pike populations. Computer simulations of growth
          and suggestions for improving assessment are given.
CARLSON, R. M. and R. CAPLE
   1980   An evaluation of the possible detrimental effects by the introduction of
          organic and second-order organics on commercial and sport fishing in Lake
          Superior. Minnesota Sea Grant Program, Research Report MSGP-RR-
          1:1–49.
          The study developed two approaches to the analysis of a complex matrix of
          chlororganics: one an "indicator analysis" as a monitor of the total problem,
          and the second the development of a fast yet sensitive method to analyze for
          various phenols.
CARLSSON, S.
   1978   A model for the turnover of ^{137}Cs and potassium in pike (*Esox lucius*).
          Health Physics 35:549–554.
          The model, quantitatively based on existing data on the food of pike and its
          concentrations of ^{137}Cs and potassium, was applied to calculate the biological

half-time of the elements in pike from Lake Uklesjon and estimated as 1.3 yr and 0.55 yr respectively, for a pike weighing 500 g and at a water temperatore of 8 to 10 C.

CARLSSON, S. and K. LIDEN

1977   Observed accumulation coefficients of cesium-137 and potassium in some fish and plant species in the littoral zone of an oligotrophic lake. Ekologiya 6:27–31.

CARLSTROM, D. and J. E. GLAS

1959   The size and shape of the apatite crystallites in bone as determined from line broadening measurements on oriented specimens. Biochimica et Biophysica Acta 35:46–53.

CARPENTER, R. G. and H. R. SIEGLER

1947   A sportsman's guide to the fresh-water fishes of New Hampshire. New Hampshire Fish and Game Commission. 87 pp.

CARTER, E. R.

1955   Harvest and movement of game fishes in Kentucky Lake and its tailwaters. Kentucky Department of Fish and Wildlife Resources, Fish Bulletin 15:1–15.

CARUFEL, L. H.

1958   Tentative checklist of fishes of North Dakota. North Dakota Outdoors 21(5):10–11, 16.

CASEY, N., M. MULCAHY and W. O'CONNELL

1975   Leukocyte characteristics and phytohemagglutinin-stimulated response in healthy and lymphoma-bearing pike *Esox lucius* L. Bibliotheca Haematologica 43:456.
        Abstract of a study of epizootic lymphoma in Irish pike.

CASPARS, H. and H. MANN

1961   Bodenfauna und Fischbestand in der Hamburger Alster. Ein quantitativokologischer Vergleich in einem Stradtgewasser. Abhandlungen des Naturwissenschaftlichen Vereins zu Hamburg 5:89–110.

CASSELMAN, J. M.

1967   Age and growth of northern pike, *Esox lucius* Linnaeus, of the upper St. Lawrence River. M.S. thesis, University of Guelph. 219 pp.
        The age and growth of pike was studied using the scale method and mark-recapture. The work describes a detailed method for recognizing annuli and pseudoannuli on the scales of pike. Scale checks were categorized. There were 11 types of annuli and 4 types of pseudoannuli. The occurrence of these changes with age of the fish. Time of annulus formation on scales is also detailed. Back-calculation of body size from scales was performed.

1969   Management aspects of northern pike recruitment—External sex determination and sex ratios of northern pike (*Esox lucius*). Presented at 31st Midwest Fish and Wildlife Conference, Minnesota, 1969.
        A method for externally sexing pike, which involves the urogenital pore. Seasonal efficiency of the method was discussed. Seasonal change in sex ratios was presented, indicating a natural seasonal activity cycle. Sex ratio on the spawning grounds was given.

1972   Metabolism and dissolved oxygen requirements of northern pike *Esox lucius*; a literature review. University of Toronto, unpublished MS. 31 pp.
        Considers impact of oxygen requirement on growth and survival.

1973   A limnological survey of Liverpool Creek, Pickering Township, Ontario County, Ontario. Conducted Spring 1973 for Runnymede Development, Toronto. 36 pp.

A study of a small warmwater stream of low flow. Pike spawning was negligible during April and May 1973. However, pike spawning was documented in the mouth of the stream in Frenchman's Bay. Naturally deposited eggs were collected and densities were measured.

1974a   External sex determination of northern pike, *Esox lucius* Linnaeus. Transactions of the American Fisheries Society 103:343–347.

Methods of externally sexing fish are reviewed. The spontaneous passage of reproductive products was examined on a seasonal basis, and a reliable method for externally sexing pike using the appearance of the urogenital region is described. The method applies to immature as well as mature pike, regardless of season. Accuracy of the method was tested throughout the year.

1974b   Analysis of hard tissue of pike *Esox lucius* L. with special reference to age and growth. *In* Bagenal, T. B., ed., Ageing of fish—Proceedings of an international symposium, Reading, 1973. England, Unwin, pp. 13–27.

Appositional growth of cleithra was examined, using tetracycline antibiotic. The chemical and physical nature of the zonation used in age and growth determination was analysed. The opaque zone in the cleithrum (flat bone of the pectoral girdle) is deposited at a rapid rate. The translucent zone forms much more slowly. Standardized terminology for the description of optically different zones in fish calcified tissue is presented. Specific gravity, ash residue, and protein content of whole and sectioned parts of cleithra are examined in relation to age and growth. Electron microprobe X-ray analysis was used to document differential mineralization of the optically different zones. The importance of protein growth in bone growth is emphasized.

1975   Sex ratios of northern pike, *Esox lucius* Linnaeus. Transactions of the American Fisheries Society 104:60–63.

Seasonal change in sex ratio of pike was examined from fish captured by netting, electrofishing, and angling. Regardless of the method or region of capture, sex ratio showed similar seasonal cycles. Males were relatively more abundant during spring and autumn, when the sex ratios were approximately equal; females were more abundant in summer and winter (1.5–2 times). The sexes appeared to have biannual peaks of availability that were related to activity and were independent of locality and method of capture.

1978a   Calcified tissue and body growth of northern pike, *Esox lucius* Linnaeus. Ph.D. thesis, University of Toronto. 782 pp.

Calcified tissue and body growth were studied quantitatively and qualitatively. Studies were conducted in the natural environment using tagged individuals. In the laboratory, fish were reared under controlled conditions. Chemical analyses were conducted on the soft and calcified tissue of these fish. The study describes the physiological processes and body growth, both somatic and reproductive. Environmental conditions such as temperature, light, and nutrition were monitored and manipulated in this study.

1978b   Effects of environmental factors on growth, survival, activity, and exploitation of northern pike. American Fisheries Society Special Publication 11:114–128.

Examines growth at various temperatures and describes the optimum temperature for growth (19 C, weight; 21 C, length) for subadult pike determined under both laboratory and natural conditions. The upper incipient lethal is 29.4 C. Examines the effect of day length on survival. Describes environmental requirements of pike, a typical "coolwater" fish. Details the effect of critically low winter oxygen on behaviour and catch per unit effort.

1979 The esocid cleithrum as an indicator calcified structure. *In* Dube, J., and Y. Gravel, eds., Proceedings 10th Warmwater Workshop, Special Publication NE Division of the American Fisheries Society. Published by Quebec Ministere du Loisir, de la Chasse et de la Peche, Montreal, pp. 249–272.

Basic data heretofore obtained only from examining whole fish can be extracted from cleithra. For fisheries managers working with esocids, the cleithrum provides age data, as well as a rapid and inexpensive method of obtaining many important biological characteristics. A preliminary presentation of the cleithral method of determining age of esocids and estimating growth.

1980 Identification of pike and muskellunge from cleithra. Muskies, Inc., May 1980, pp. 10–12.

Criteria are presented and illustrated.

1982 Length x girth-weight relationships for 10 Ontario sport fish. Calculated using 1980 and 1981 data supplied by the Ontario Federation of Anglers and Hunters from the Molson Big Fish Contest. Ontario Ministry of Natural Resources, unpublished MS.

The relationship between length x girth-weight was constructed from two years of trophy fish data; 95% confidence limits were included.

1983a Age and growth assessment of fish from their calcified structures—techniques and tools. *In* Prince, E. D., and L. M. Pulos, eds., Proceedings of the international workshop on age determination of oceanic pelagic fishes: tunas, billfishes, and sharks. NOAA Technical Report NMFS 8, pp. 1–17.

A general presentation of age and growth determination procedures that includes specific data involving the seasonal dynamics of qualitative growth of cleithra and scales and quantitative linear growth of the body, cleithra, and scales.

1983b Growth of four Ontario fishes—northern pike, walleye, lake whitefish, and lake trout. *In* The identification of overexploitation. Ontario Ministry of Natural Resources, Strategic Planning for Ontario Fisheries, Policy Development Report, SPOF Working Group No. 15. 84 pp.

Growth of pike is described by reviewing published literature on age and growth. Mean size at age from the scale method, the 95% confidence limits, and extremes demarcate the scope for growth. The von Bertalanffy growth model was applied to the average size at age data. Growth standards are illustrated and presented in table form.

CASSELMAN, J. M. and E. J. CROSSMAN

1986 Size, age, and growth of trophy muskellunge and muskellunge-northern pike hybrids—The Cleithrum Project, 1979–1983. *In* Hall, G., ed., Managing muskies. American Fisheries Society Special Publication 15, pp. 93–110.

Describes the age distribution, size, and growth of a large sample of trophy pike-muskellunge hybrids. Data were obtained from taxidermists, and involved an indicator calcified structure, the cleithrum.

CASSELMAN, J. M., E. J. CROSSMAN, P. E. IHSSEN, J. D. REIST and H. E. BOOKE
  1986   Identification of muskellunge, northern pike, and their hybrids. *In* Hall, G.,
          ed., Managing muskies. American Fisheries Society Special Publication 15,
          pp. 14–46.
          Details various methods of identifying pike, muskellunge, and their hybrids.
          Involves colour pattern, morphometrics, meristics, specific osteological
          characteristics such as tooth shape and dentition, scale pattern and shape, ver-
          tebral centra, electrophoresis, and karyotype. A thorough review of existing
          methods, with new procedures.

CASSELMAN, J. M. and H. H. HARVEY
  1973   Fish traps of clear plastic. Progressive Fish-Culturist 35:218–220.
          Description of a trap originally designed to capture small pike in shallow
          water.
  1975   Selective fish mortality resulting from low winter oxygen. International
          Association of Theoretical and Applied Limnology Proceedings
          19:2418–2429.
          Describes selective mortality associated with partial winterkill of several pike
          populations, indicating that pike that survived were significantly smaller,
          younger, slower growing than those that winterkilled. Significantly more
          males survived and females succumbed.

CASSERIUS, J.
  1552   De Vocis Auditusque Organis. Ferrariae, 1601–1600.
          Two figures of the ear of the pike, one showing the organ *in situ* and the other
          dissected.

CATAUDALLE, S. and P. MELOTTI
  n.d.   L'acquacoltura negli ambienti lacustri. [Aquaculture in the lacustrine
          environment]. *In* Aquaculture. Part 2. Scientific and technological develop-
          ment of culture systems. Published by Istituto de Tecnica e Propaganda
          Agraria, Italy, pp. 76–82. [in Italian]
          The culture of fish seed in lakes for repopulation purposes is discussed, con-
          sidering rearing of pike in particular.

CAVENDER, T.
  1969   An oligocene mudminnow (family Umbridae) from Oregon with remarks on
          relationships within the Esocoidei. University of Michigan Museum of Zool-
          ogy, Occasional Paper 660:1–33.

CAVENDER, T. M., J. G. LUNDBERG and R. L. WILSON
  1970   Two new fossil records of the genus *Esox* (Teleostei Salmoniformes) in North
          America. Northwest Science 44:176–183.

CECILIA, A.
  1973   El lucio y su pesca. I to IV. Caza y Pesca 371–375, various pages.
          A series of magazine articles on the distribution and angling of pike in several
          reservoirs and rivers of Spain.

CERNOHOUS, L.
  1974   Diet tests on walleye, northern pike and muskellunge. North Dakota Bureau
          of Sport Fisheries and Wildlife, Division of Fish Hatcheries, Valley City
          National Fish Hatchery. [mimeograph].

CERVINKA, S. and O. PECHA
  1975   Hematologicke hodnoty a celkova bilkovina v krevnim seru stiky obecne
          Esox lucius L. z rybnicniho chovu v obdobi po vyteru. [Hematological values

and total protein in the blood serum of pond-farmed pike (*Esox lucius* L.). Zivocisna vyroba 20:861−866.

CHABAN, R.

1973   Les carnassiens et leur peche. Les poissons blancs et leur peche. Le brochet. *In* La peche au Maroc, pp. 141−142.

In Morocco the numbers and mean weight of pike caught was greater than in most other countries. The size of these fish is detailed. The history of intro-duction is reviewed. In 1969−61 pike matured asychronously; eggs of females, especially the larger ones, matured in early summer when males were no longer producing milt. This was considered to occur because of high water temperatures. Egg collection was detrimentally affected, and produc-tion decreased. Angling techniques and gear are discussed.

CHAIKOVSKAYA, A. V., E. T. USKOVA and S. I. DAVIDENKO

1981   Comparative study of the chemical nature of the mucous substance of marine and fresh water fish. Vestnik Ceskoslovenske Spolecnosti Zoologicke 5:57−61.

CHAMBERS, E. D. T.

1896   The pike. *In* The ouananiche and its Canadian environment, pp. 283−288.

CHAMBERS, K. J.

1963   Lake of the Woods survey, northern sector—1963. Ontario Department of Lands and Forests, Preliminary Report, 65 pp.

Tables include: creel census, percent live release of catch, age-length-weight, stomach analyses, indices of fish abundance by gill and trap netting, and com-mercial catch from 1950 to 1963.

CHAMPEAU, A., A. GREGOIRE and G. BRUN

1978   The fish population of the artificial lakes of Verdon, France. Annales de Lim-nologie 14:245−272.

CHAPLEAU, D. and G. THELLEN

1979   Amenagement de frayers de grande brochet, *Esox lucius* L., au Quebec. [Management of northern pike, *Esox lucius* L., spawning ground in Quebec]. *In* Dube, J., and H. Gravel, eds., Proceedings 10th Warmwater Workshop, Special Publication NE Division of the American Fisheries Society. Pub-lished by Quebec Ministere du Loisir, de la Chasse, et de la Peche, Montreal.

Results of management of spawning grounds to prevent the disappearance of important spawning grounds in regions heavily used by sport fishermen, and to improve the production of young pike by regularizing the water level dur-ing incubation of eggs and rearing of young.

CHAPMAN, C. A. and W. C. MACKAY

1984a   Versatility in habitat use by a top aquatic predator, *Esox lucius* L. Journal of Fish Biology 25:109−115.

The habitat selected by pike was evaluated using radio location and ultrasonic telemetry. The authors propose that the versatility in range of habitats is an important feature of the behaviour of top predators.

1984b   Direct observation of habitat utilization by northern pike. Copeia 1984:255−258.

Concludes that there is an ecological segregation between the size classes of pike; suggests that it is due to different trophic relationships and different pre-dator avoidance strategies used by the two size classes.

CHAPMAN, D. W.
1967   Production in fish populations. *In* Gerking, S. D., ed., The biological basis of freswhater fish production. IBP Symposium, Reading, 1966. pp. 3–29.

CHAPPELL, L. H.
1967   On the occurrence of blood flukes (Sanguinicolidae: Trematoda) in British freshwater fish. Journal of Natural History 1:163–167.

CHAPPELL, L. H. and R. W. OWEN
1969   A reference list of parasite species recorded in freshwater fish from Great Britain and Ireland. Journal of Natural History 3:197–216.

CHARBONNEAU, S. M., I. C. MUNRO, E. A. NERA, R. F. WILLES, T. KUIPER-GOODMAN, F. IVERSON, C. A. MOODIE, D. R. STOLTZ and F. A. J. ARMSTRONG
1974   Subacute toxicity of methyl mercury in the adult cat. Toxicology and Applied Pharmacology 27:569–581.

CHATELAIN, R. and G. MASSE
1979   L'exploitation du grand brochet, *Esox lucius* L., dans la province de Quebec. [Exploitation of northern pike, *Esox lucius* L., in the province of Quebec]. *In* Dube, J., and Y. Gravel, eds., Proceedings 10th Warmwater Workshop, Special Publication NE Division of the American Fisheries Society. Published by Quebec Ministere du Loisir, de la Chasse, et de la Peche, Montreal, pp. 9–25. Analysis of certain parks and lakes included—exploitation, use of creel census to establish quotas, and the application of a mathematical model to the determination of optimum rate of exploitation.

CHAUDERON, L.
1969   Pisciculture en etangs des poissons de repeuplement pour les cours d'eau de la deuxieme categorie. Club halieutique interdepartmental.

CHAUVEHEID, A. and R. BILLARD
1983   Incubation et eclosion des oeufs de brochet et resorption vitelline des larves. *In* Billard, R., ed., Le brochet gestion dans le milieu naturel et elevage. Paris, Institute National de la Recherche Agronomique, pp. 163–176.
Reviews the necessary water quality and temperature conditions, precautions to take when planning a hatchery, and the organization of a hatchery.

CHENEY, A. N.
1885   Does transplanting affect the food or game qualities of certain fishes? Transactions of the American Fisheries Society 14:55–58.
Compares growth of pike stocked in various bodies of water with growth of fish from the parent waters. Refers to pike as a freshwater shark and says that after stocked, "there commences a warfare of survival of the one with the largest mouth".

1893   The pike. Forest and Stream 40(15):319.

1896   Mascalonge, pike, pickerel and pike perch. New York Commissioner of Fisheries, Game and Forests, 1st Annual Report, 1895, pp. 121–124.

1897   Mascalonge, pike, pickerel and pike-perch. Forest and Stream, May 1897, p. 29

1898   The pikes. Forest and Stream 50(17):330–331.

CHENEY, W. L.
1971   Life history investigations of northern pike in the Tanana River drainage. Alaska Department of Fish and Game, Annual Progress Report vol. 12, Study R-III:1–24.

1972   Life history investigations of northern pike in the Tanana River drainages. Alaska Department of Fish and Game, Annual Progress Report, vol. 13, Study R-III:1−30.

Information on age, seasonal migration, growth, and creel census. Comparative meristics of three Tanana drainage pike populations show significant differences among these groups.

CHERNIKOVA, V. V.

1966   Pokazatel'krovi u presnovodnykh ryb po sezonam. [Seasonal blood characteristics of fresh water fishes]. Report Summaries of the All-Union Conference on the Ecology and Physiology of Fishes, Moscow, pp. 88−90.

Blood characteristics of pike were characterized by significant seasonal changes.

CHERNYSHEVA, N. B.

1976   Morphological characteristics of and certain problems of the biology of the genus *Apiosoma infusoria peritricha* from the young of predatory fishes. Parazitologiya 10:170−177.

CHICEWICZ, M. and I. MANKOWSKA

1970   Embryonic development of pike (*Esox lucius* L.). Roczniki Nauk Rolniczych Ser.H, 92:27−52. [in Polish]

A description of pike embryonal development, embracing egg construction, its fertilization, and all stages of embryo development, until hatching.

CHICIAK, M.

1947   Klucz do oznaczania ryb. [Key to fish species.] Ksiegarnia Akademicka, 31 pp.

CHIHULY, M. B.

1979   Biology of the northern pike, *Esox lucius* Linnaeus, in the Wood River Lakes system of Alaska, with emphasis on Lake Aleknagik. M.S. thesis, University of Alaska, 122 pp.

Basic biological information about pike, focused on population structure, habitat, movement, and food habits.

CHIKOVA, V. M.

1966   The state of spawning associations flocks of fishes, and their propagation in Cheremshansk and Suskansk bays of the Kujbyshev reservoir. Trudy Instituta Biologii Vnutrennikh Vod Akademii Nauk 10(3):29−45. [in Russian]

CHIMITS, P.

1947   Note sur le repeuplement artificiel du brochet. Bulletin Francais de Pisciculture 146.

1951   Quelques observations sur la fraye du brochet et le transport des oeufs embryonnes. Bulletin Francais du Pisciculture 161:135−143.

1956   Le brochet. Bulletin Francais de Pisciculture 180:81−96

CHINNIAH, V. C. and W. THRELFALL

1978   Metazoan parasites of fish from the Smallwood Reservoir, Labrador, Canada. Journal of Fish Biology 13:203−213.

Pike were one of eight species examined for metazoan parasites. No differences were recorded in the parasite burden of male and female fish. There was no correlation between the number of parasite species per infected pike and host age. Food items of the fish examined were also noted.

CHIZHOVA, T. P.

1956   Diphllobothriasis in the Kalingrad district. Doklady Akademii Nauk SSSR 108:370–371.

CHODOROWSKA, W.

1973   Nutritional requirements of carnivorous fish fry during the first year of their cultivation in a pond. Annales de l'Association Canadienne Francaise pour l'Avancement des Sciences 40:147.

CHODOROWSKA, W. and A. CHODOROWSKI

1969   Les besoins nutritifs des alevins de certains poissons carnassiers. International Association of Theoretical and Applied Limnology Proceedings 17:1082–1089.

1975   Substitution of dietary elements in the young of carnivorous fishes. International Association of Theoretical and Applied Limnology Proceedings 19:2555–2562.

CHODOROWSKI, A.

1973a   Ecological problems inherent in the cultivation of mixed carnivorous fish in pisciculture. Annales de l'Association Canadienne Francaise pour l'Avancement des Sciences 40:147.

1973b   Quelques problemes ecologiques concernant l'elevage combine des carnassiers en pisciculture de repeuplement. Annales de la Station Biologique de Besse-en-Chandesse 7:235–272.

1975   Formation of B1 modal populations among the young of carnivorous fishes. International Association of Theoretical and Applied Limnology Proceedings 19:2546–2555.

1976   Rapports nutritifs entre les alevins de poissons carnassiers eleves en pisciculture de repeuplement. [Nutritive relations between carnivorous young fishes reared in restocking fish ponds]. In: Acts of the 2nd European Ichthyological Congress, Paris, 1976.

CHODYNIECKI, A., M. KURPIOS, M. PROTASOWICKI and J. JURAN

1974   Badania nad obecnoscia rteci w wybranych narzadach szczupaka -Esox lucius L. Jeziora Dabie. [Studies on mercury content in selected organs of pike - Esox lucius L. Lake Dabie.] Polish Academy of Science, Commercial Technology and Food Chemistry, Gdansk.

CHOLMONDLEY-PENNEL, H.

1865   The book of the pike. London, Robert Hardwicke.

CHOURROUT, D.

1982   Gynogenesis caused by ultra violet irradiation of salmonid sperm. Journal of Experimental Zoology 223:175–182.

CHOYNOWSKI, J.

1936   Na marginesie metod technicznych polowu szczupaka. Wedka do wleczenia czy normalny zestaw reczny jako narzedzie polowu sportowego na wielkich wodach nizinnych. [Comments on pike fishing methods. Rod or normal set for sport catches of pike in lowland waters.] Wiadomosci Wedkarskie 4(6):62–75 and (7):77–79.

CHRISTENSEN, K. E.

1959   Evaluation of fish management procedures. Test of the effects of increased size limits on black bass and northern pike. Michigan Department of Conservation, Dingell-Johnson Report F-12-R-1, Job 3.

1960a   Evaluation of fish management procedures. Test of the effects of protective regulations for northern pike. Michigan Department of Conservation, Dingell-Johnson Report F-12-R-2, Job 1.

1960b   Evaluation of fish management procedures. Test of the effects of increased size limits on black bass and northern pike. Michigan Department of Conservation, Dingell-Johnson Report F-12-R-2, Job 3.

1961a   Evaluation of fish management procedures. Test of the effects of protective regulations for northern pike. Michigan Department of Conservation, Dingell-Johnson Report F-12-R-3, Job 1.

1961b   Evaluation of fish management procedures. Test of the effects of increased size limits on black bass and northern pike. Michigan Department of Conservation, Dingell-Johnson Report F-12-R-3, Job 3.

1961c   Evaluation of fish management procedures. Test of the effects of several management practices on a group of lakes. Michigan Department of Conservation, Dingell-Johnson Report F-12-R-3, Job 5.

1962a   Evaluation of fish management procedures. Tests of the effects of protective regulations for northern pike. Michigan Department of Conservation, Dingell-Johnson Report F-12-R-4, Job 1.

1962b   Evaluation of fish management procedures. Tests of the effects of increased size limits on black bass and northern pike. Michigan Department of Conservation, Dingell-Johnson Report F-12-R-4, Job 3.

1962c   Evaluation of fish management procedures. Test of the effects of several management practices on a group of lakes. Michigan Department of Conservation, Dingell-Johnson Report F-12-R-4, Job 5.

CHRISTENSEN, K. E. and J. E. WILLIAMS

1969   Status of the northern pike population in Fletcher Floodwater, Alpena and Montmorency counties, 1948 and 1955–1956. Michigan Department of Conservation, Institute of Fisheries Research, Report 1576:1–13.

CHRISTENSON, L. M.

1957   Some characteristics of the fish populations in backwater areas of the Upper Mississippi River. M.S. thesis, University of Minnesota. 125 pp.

CHRISTENSON, L. M. and L. L. SMITH

1965   Characteristics of fish populations in upper Mississippi River backwater areas. U.S. Bureau of Sport Fisheries and Wildlife, Circular 212:1–53.

CHRISTIANSEN, D. G.

1976   Feeding and behavior of northern pike (*Esox lucius* Linnaeus). M.Sc. thesis, University of Alberta. 302 pp.
        The growth, feeding, and predatory and social behavior of pike in Kakisa Lake, Northwest Territories, were examined during the summers of 1973 and 1974. Food deprivation increased aggressiveness and decreased activity and social tolerance of pike.

CHUBB, J. C.

1963a   Seasonal occurrence and maturation of *Triaenophorus nodulosus* (Pallas, 1781) (Cestode: Pseudophyllidae) in the pike *Esox lucius* L. of Llyn Tegid. Parasitology 53:419–433.

1963b   Observations on the occurrence of the plerocercoids of *Triaenophorus nodulosus* (Pallas, 1781) (Cestoda:Pseudophyllidea) in the perch, *Perca fluviatilis* L. of Llyn Tegid (Bala Lake), Merionethshire. Parasitology 54:481–492.

Mature plerocercoids form the reservoir of infection for the definitive host of *T. nodulosus*, the pike.

1963c   On the characteristization of the parasite fauna of the fish of Llyn Tegid. Proceedings of the Zoological Society of London 141:609–621.

The relationship of the parasite fauna to the environment is discussed. It is proposed that the parasites of pike are the eutrophic element of the parasite fauna.

1968   Tapeworms of the genus *Diphyllobothrium* in the British Isles. Parasitology 58(4):22.

CHUMAKOV, K. A.

1963   Povedenie ryb pri navodnenii. [Behavior of fish during a flood]. Prioroda 52(10):91.

During August floods on the Ugra River it was noted that small fish abandoned the river channel in favour of floodplain shallows, in which the supply of food was more abundant. Larger carnivores such as pike soon followed this displacement of their prey.

CHURCHILL, W. and H. SNOW

1964   Characteristics of the sport fishery in some northern Wisconsin lakes. Wisconsin Conservation Department, Technical Bulletin 32:1–46.

Outlines conclusions for the guidance of anglers, managers, and planners in Wisconsin, on the assumption that the findings on these lakes are generally true throughout the northern United States.

CHURCHILL, W. S.

1961   Warm water fishery research. Five Lakes studies. Study of a newly established northern pike population in Escanaba Lake. Wisconsin Conservation Department, Dingell-Johnson Report F-61-R-1/Wk.Pl.4/Job G.

1962   Warm water fishery research. Five Lakes studies. Study of a newly established northern pike population in Escanaba Lake. Wisconsin Conservation Department, Dingell-Johnson Report F-61-R-2/Wk.Pl.5/Job G.

CIEPIELEWSKI, W.

1970   Wzrost jednolatkow szczupaka (*Esox lucius* L.) w jeziorach przyduchowych. [Growth of one-year pike (*Esox lucius* L.) in winterkill lakes]. Roczniki Nauk Rolniczych Ser.H, 92:53–66.

Significant variability of body length within a population of one-year-old pike inhabiting similar conditions.

1973   Eksperymentalnie powiekszone poglowie ryb w stawowym jeziorze Warniak. 3. Biomasa i produkcja szczupaka *Esox lucius* L. [Experimentally increased fish stock in the pond type Lake Warniak, Poland. Part 3. Biomass and production of pike *Esox lucius* L.] Ekologia Polska 21:445–463.

1981   Population of pike (*Esox lucius* L.) in pond type Lake Warniak in 1969–1978. Ecologia Polska 29:35–51. [in English, Polish summary]

Information on maximum and minimum catches, mean weight, and average age of individuals, population size, sex ratio, biomass, and production ranges.

CIHAR, J.

1955   Systematical and biological notes on the pike (*Esox lucius* L.). Universitas Carolina, Biologica 1:1–18.

Measurements were made on 68 pike 113–421 mm in length to determine what proportional relations of the body change with change in size. In young

66

fish (113–220 mm) length increases faster than weight; the opposite occurs in older fish. The pike fed on fish and invertebrates.

1956   Contribution to the knowledge of the early development of the pike (*Esox lucius* L.). Universitas Carolina, Biologica, 2:1–12.
Postembryonic development of pike from hatching of the eggs to location and order of the appearance of the first scales is described in detail. A graph of the growth rate is included.

1961   Rust ryb ve Slapske udolni nadrzi v r. 1959. Sbornik Ceskoslovenske Akademie Zemedelskych Ved 6(4)

CIRCLE, H.

n.d.   Northern pike *Esox lucius* L. Heddon Fish Flashes mimeo release 54G.
Mentions the thrill of pike angling, reproduction, distribution, world record for weight, food, and suitable tackle.

CLARK, C. F.

1950   Observations on the spawning habits of the northern pike, *Esox lucius*, in northwestern Ohio. Copeia 1950:285–288.
Observations made at a hatchery pond, at Nettle Lake, and at several streams. Descriptions of migration, water conditions, bottom, numbers of adults, spawning activities, and attachment sites and hatching conditions of eggs.

1957   Observations on the growth of the northern pike, *Esox lucius* L., in East Harbor, Ohio. Unpublished MS, 9 pp.

1958   Northern pike, *Esox lucius* Linnaeus. Prepared for the U.S. National Academy of Science - National Research Council. Unpublished MS.
General information on taxonomy, common names, distribution, morphology, colouration, growth, maturity, life span, assocated species, fecundity, development, diseases and parasites, movement, predation, value and reproduction, presented in tabular form. Differences between pike populations from Canada and USA were considered.

1960   Lake St. Marys and its management. Ohio Department of Natural Resources, Division of Wildlife, p. 56.
An account of the introduction of pike into Lake St. Marys from 1951 through 1955; the success cannot yet be determined.

CLARK, C. F. and E. D. NOW

1954   Experimental propagation of northern pike at the St. Marys Fish Farm. Ohio Department of Natural Resources, Division of Wildlife, Fish Management Section Investigational Report 1:1–9.
Jar hatchery experiments involved varying fertilization and processing methods. Breeders were raised at this farm and from two natural locations in Ohio.

1955   Operation northern pike. Ohio Conservation Bulletin 19(3):4–5, 26–28.
Artificial propagation in Ohio involved trapping and stripping breeders, various fertilization and incubation techniques, problems threatening egg and fry survival, and maintenance. Description of hatching process and natural propagation.

CLARK, C. F. and F. STEINBACH

1959   Observations on the age and growth of the northern pike, *Esox lucius* L., in East Harbor, Ohio. Ohio Journal of Science 59(3):129–134.
Scale samples from 688 pike were taken in March in the years 1951 to 1953. Growth was calculated on the assumption of direct proportion between scale

measurements and lengths of the fish at time of annulus formation. Information on growth rates, calculated annual increments, calculated growth, and life span is provided.

CLARK, E. R. and J. A. L. FRASER
  1983 The survival and growth of six species of freshwater fish in tapwater and diluted and undiluted effluent from sewage percolating filters. Journal of Fish Biology 22:431–445.

CLARK, G.
  1955 Game fish in Canada. Ottawa, Canadian Government Travel Bureau. 28 pp.

CLARK, J. (1)
  1908 An annotated list of Cornish fishes. Zoologist, Ser.4, 12:13–29.
         The pike was introduced into a pond near Truro, but it died out or was exterminated many years ago.

CLARK, J. (2)
  1972a Northern pike behavior. U.S. Marine and Fisheries Service, End of Segment Report, Project 6–11-D, Segment 14, Job 1: 1–24.
          Pike feeding, cannibalistic, and aggressive behaviors were investigated, described, and were shown to be specialized and adaptive.
  1972b Suitability of various non-piscivorous diets for fingerling northern pike. U.S. Marine and Fisheries Service, Project Completion Report, Project 6–11-D, Segment 14, Job 3: 1–6.
          Report of an attempt to provide pike with a non-piscivorous diet that could be easily provided.

CLARK, J. H.
  1974 Variability of northern pike pond culture production. M.S. thesis, Colorado State University. 40 pp.
  1975 Management evaluation of stocked northern pike in Colorado's small plains reservoirs. Ph.D. thesis, Colorado State University. 74 pp.
         Two size groups (50 mm and 377 mm) were stocked into 22 reservoirs, the smaller pike at a density of 62/ha and larger at 25/ha. Success rate and costs were compared and factors influencing success evaluated. Few statistical differences were seen in resident fish populations and sizes of individuals before and within a year of stocking.

CLARK, T. L.
  1975 Rearing of walleye and tiger muskellunge at the Corry/Union City Fish Cultural Stations in 1975. Proceedings 7th Interstate Musky Workshop, La Crosse, 1975, pp. 60–67 [mimeo].
         Describes the rearing facilities and techniques used at the Corry and Union City hatcheries.

CLARKE, C. H. D.
  1940 A biological investigation of the Thelon Game Sanctuary. Bulletin of the National Museum of Canada, Fishes, 96:112–117.

CLEARY, R. E.
  1956 The distribution of the fishes of Iowa. In Harlan, J. R., and E. B. Speaker, eds., Iowa fish and fishing, 3rd ed. Iowa Conservation Commission, pp. 267–324.

CLEERE, W. F., S. BREE and M. P. COUGHLAN
  1976 Urate oxidase and xanthine dehydrogenase activities in liver extracts from

68

fish caught in Irish waters. Comparative Biochemistry and Physiology 54B:117.

CLEMENS, W. A., R. V. BOUGHTON and J. A. RATTENBURY

    1945   A preliminary report on a fisheries survey of Teslin Lake, B.C. British Columbia Provincial Fisheries Department, Report for 1944, pp. 70–75.

CLEMENS, W. A., J. R. DYMOND and N. K. BIGELOW

    1924   Food studies of Lake Nipigon fishes. University of Toronto Studies, Biology Series No. 25, Publication of the Ontario Fisheries Research Laboratory 25:101–165.

           Ten species of fish were found in the 23 stomachs that contained food. Relatively small numbers of pike were taken in commercial gill nets and marketed, but demand was increasing.

CLERX, J. P. M.

    1978   Studies on pike fry rhabdovirus and the immunoglobulin of pike (*Esox lucius*). Ph.D. thesis, University of Utrecht.

CLERX, J. P. M., A. CASTEL, J. F. BOL and G. J. GERWIG

    1980   Isolation and characterization of the immunoglobulin of pike *Esox lucius*. Veterinary Immunology and Immunopathology 1:125–144.

CLINTON, D.

    1815   Some remarks on the fishes of the western waters of the State of New York in a letter to S. L. Mitchell, M.D. Transactions of the Literature and Philosophy Society of New York (1814) 1:493–501.

           "Pike or pickerel, weighing from three to twelve pounds, are taken in great numbers in the lakes, and as high up as the whirlpool, in the Niagara River; their bodies are long, and nearly round; their flesh somewhat soft, but fat, and much esteemed when boiled; they are not good when dried or salted."

COAD, B. W.

    1978   Poisonous and venomous fresh water fishes of Iran. Pahlavi Medical Journal 9:388–407.

COBLE, D.

    1973   Influence of appearance of prey and satiation of predator in food selection by northern pike (*Esox lucius*). Journal of the Fisheries Research Board of Canada 30:317–320.

           Pike were put in tanks with fantail and regular-tail goldfish (*Carassius auratus*) or with goldfish of different colors. Physical appearance of prey did not affect feeding. In plastic pools four species of fish were exposed to predation by pike that were satiated or deprived of food for either 2 or 4 weeks. Pike always selected carp (*Cyprinus carpio*) and fathead minnow (*Pimephales promelas*) over green sunfish (*Lepomis cyanellus*) and bluegill (*Lepomis macrochirus*).

COCKERELL, T. D. A.

    1913   Observations on fish scales. U.S. Bureau of Fisheries, Bulletin 32:1–174.

           Used individuals from Toledo, Ohio, to describe superficial characteristics of scales.

COHEN-SOLAL, L., M. LE LOUS, J. C. ALLAIN and F. MEUNIER

    1981   Absence of maturation of collagen cross links in fish skin. Federation of European Biochemical Societies, Letters 123:282–284.

COLAS, H.

    1937   Das vorstrecken der Hechte. Fischerei Zeitung 40:517–521.

    1938   Das vorstrecken der Hechte. Fischerei Zeitung 41:473–475.

COLE, W. D.

    1967   Statewide fisheries survey. Determination of conditions under which north-
            ern pike spawn naturally in Kansas reservoirs. Kansas Forestry, Fish and
            Game Commission, Dingell-Johnson Report F-15-R-2/Wk.Pl.C/Job 3:1–10.

COLORADO DIVISION OF WILDLIFE

    1974   The strategy of today, for wildlife tomorrow. Volume 1: A strategic plan for
            the comprehensive management of Colorado's wildlife resource. Colorado
            Division of Wildlife, Report FW-10-R:1–46.
            Outline of projected supply and demand for angling coolwater species,
            including pike.

CONNECTICUT BOARD OF FISHERIES AND GAME

    1959   A fishery survey of the lakes and ponds of Connecticut. Connecticut Board
            of Fisheries and Game, Lake and Pond Survey Unit, Report 1, Project F-4-
            R:1–395.

CONSEIL SUPERIEUR DE LA PECHE

    1976   Results des experimentations faites a Chauvineau en 1976. Region piscicole
            de Poitiers. [Results of experiments conducted at Chauvineau in 1976, fish
            culture region of Poitiers]. Bulletin d'Information Conseil Superieur de la
            Peche 105:91–104.

COOK, K. D.

    1978   Non-native predator fish development. Evaluation of non-native fish intro-
            ductions (northern pike). Oklahoma Department of Wildlife Conservation,
            Project F-21-D-13/Job 2:1–11.
            The project monitored survival, growth, reproduction, and fisherman harvest
            of pike fingerlings introduced into four Oklahoma lakes. Each year for 3
            years, fingerlings were stocked at various rates. Very little survival was
            found at any lake.

COOK, M.

    1985a   Where are the pike in Eleven Mile? Colorado Outdoors 34(3):6–8.

    1985b   How to debone a pike. Colorado Outdoors 34(4):10–11.

COOK, M. F. and E. P. BERGERSEN

    n.d.   Movements of northern pike in Eleven Mile Reservoir, Colorado. Colorado
            State University, unpublished MS, 11 pp.
            Movements and habitat selected by pike were observed by using ultrasonic
            telemetry from May 1983 to October 1984.

COOPER, G. P.

    1941   A biological survey of lakes and ponds of the Androscoggin and Kennebec
            River drainage systems in Maine. Maine Department of Inland Fish and
            Game, Fisheries Survey Report 4:7–238.

    1951   Estimation of fish populations in Michigan lakes. Transactions of the Ameri-
            can Fisheries Society 81:4–16.
            Fish population estimates, using trap nets in the Petersen mark-and-recapture
            procedure were made in 1948–50 on Sugarloaf Lake in Washtenaw County
            and during 1950 on Fife Lake in Grand Traverse County. Pike is listed as an
            important fish species.

COOPER, G. P. and W. C. LATTA

1954   Further studies on the fish population and exploitation by angling in Sugarloaf Lake, Washtenaw County, Michigan. Papers of the Michigan Academy of Science, Arts, and Letters 39:209–223.

A continuation of the study conducted in 1949–51.

COOPER, G. P. and R. N. SCHAFER

1954   Studies on the population of legal-size fish in Whitmore Lake, Washtenaw and Livingstone Counties, Michigan. Transactions of the North American Wildlife Conference 19:239–258.

COOPER, G. P. and G. N. WASHBURN

1949   Relation of dissolved oxygen to winter mortality of fish in Michigan lakes. Transactions of the American Fisheries Society 76:23–33.

A study of the effect of different degrees of oxygen depletion on the extent of mortality and survival of several common species of fishes in 11 lakes. There was a high survival rate of pike even in lakes where the oxygen was reduced to 0.3 or 0.2 ppm.

COOPER, J. L.

1971   The northern pike in Fort Peck Reservoir, Montana. Proceedings of the Montana Academy of Science 31:53–61.

COPE, E. D.

1864   Partial catalogue of the cold-blooded vertebrata of Michigan. Proceedings of the Academy of Natural Science, Philadelphia, 16:276–285.

1865   Partial catalogue of the cold-blooded vertebrata of Michigan. Part 2. Proceedings of the Academy of Natural Science, Philadelphia, 17:78–88.

1869   Supplementary synopsis of the Esoces of middle North America. Transactions of the American Philosophical Society 13:407–410.

A definition and description of each of six species of *Esox* that were considered to exist in North America at that time.

1870   Partial synopsis of the fresh-water fishes of North Carolina. Proceedings of the American Philosophical Society 9:448–495.

1877   Partial synopsis of the freshwater fishes of North Carolina. 2nd ed. Reprint of an article first published in Proceedings of the American Philosophical Society, June 1870.

COPELAND, J.

1975   Diet and nutrition of northern pike and tiger musky - visceral fat content on various diets and 'green' liver problems. Proceedings 7th Interstate Musky Workshop, La Crosse, 1975, pp. 36–40. [mimeo.]

COPLAND, W. O.

1956   Notes on the food and parasites of pike (*Esox lucius*) in Loch Lomond. Glasgow Naturalist 17:230–235.

A report of the stomach contents of 102 pike; the food of small pike (<20 cm) is considered separately from that of large pike (>20 cm). Pike were found to be infected with two species of parasitic helminth.

CORBIN, G. B.

1873   Voracity of pike. Zoologist, Ser 2, 8:3617.

Describes two incidents of cannibalism in adult pike. Each predator attempted to consume an animal similar to its own size.

CORDIER, G.

1959   Research on the concentration of cardiac glycogen in fresh-water fish. Comparison with marine fish. Comptes Rendus des Seances de la Societe de Biologie et de ses Filiales 153:435–437.

CORKUM, L. D. and P. J. MCCART

1981   A review of the fisheries of the Mackenzie Delta and nearshore Beaufort Sea, Canada. Canadian Manuscript Report, Fisheries and Aquatic Sciences 1613:1–55.

CORNELL, J. H.

1968   How fish reproduce. Wildlife North Dakota 32(10):8–9, (11):20–22.

COSTEA, E. and V. CURE

1971   Hydrobiological and ichthyological studies on the coastal lakes Tasaul and Gargalic in view of their use for fish management. Buletinul de Cercetari Piscicole 30:117–151.

COULLOUDON, J.

1960   Etiquetage d'esocides au moyen d'injections de latex liquide colore. Quebec Ministere du Chasse et des Pecheries, Journal du Bord 3(66):558–560
        Explains a method of marking muskellunge and pike with red- and blue-coloured latex injections.

COURTEMANCHE, A.

1954   The natural fecundity of the pike of Lake Munroe. Ephemerides of the Quebec Biological Bureau 1:29–30.
        A pond on the edge of Lake Munroe was calculated to contain a minimum of two million pike fry.

COWARD, T. A.

1914   Faunal survey of Rostherne Mere. II. Vertebrata. Manchester Memoir 68.

COX, P.

1899   Fresh water fishes and batrachia of the peninsula of Gaspe, P.Q., and their distribution in the Maritime provinces of Canada. Transactions of the Royal Society of Canada Ser.2, 5:141–151.

CRABTREE, J. E.

1969   Region 1A fisheries studies. Walleye and northern pike study. Texas Parks and Wildlife Department, Dingell-Johnson Project F-7-R-17, Job 17:1–12.
        Results regarding stocked pike in Greenbelt Lake, Texas, includes length and weight, stomach content analysis, and spawning success.

CRAGG-HINE, D.

1966   Age determination in coarse fish. *In* Jones, J. W., and P. H. Tombleson, eds. Proceedings of the 2nd British Coarse Fish Conference, Liverpool, 1965, pp. 3–6.

CRAIG, J. F. and C. KIPLING

1983   Reproduction effort versus the environment; case histories of Windermere perch, *Perca fluviatilis* L. and pike, *Esox lucius* L. Journal of Fish Biology 22:713–727.
        The theoretical limits of net reproduction rates for pike were estimated from the upper and lower limits of fecundity, growth, mortality, age of maturity, and biomass of parental stock observed in Windermere, over 40 years.

CRAIK, J. C. A.

1982   Levels of phosphoprotein in the eggs and ovaries of some fish species. Comparative Biochemistry and Physiology 72B:507–510.

CREICHTON, J. G. A.

1892   The landlocked salmon or Wananishe. *In* American game fishes. Their habits, habitat, and peculiarities; how, when and where to angle for them, pp. 81–110.

CROOKS, S.

1972   Water level fluctuations and yellow pickerel, northern pike and lake whitefish in Lac Seul. Ontario Ministry of Natural Resources, Internal Report, 33 pp.

An investigation was begun in 1968 to determine whether yearly water level fluctuations of Lac Seul were effecting a reported decrease in abundance of several species of fish, including pike. No relationships were found.

CROSS, F. B.

1967   Handbook of fishes of Kansas. University of Kansas, Museum of Natural History, Miscellaneous Publication 45. 357 pp.

A pond on the edge of Lake Munroe was calculated to contain a minimum of two million pike fry.

CROSSMAN, E. J.

1959   Hook in stomach of living pike. Ontario Department of Lands and Forests News Release 12(1).

A pike lived and had a gut filled with food in spite of a rusted hook which passed through the intestinal wall and was imbedded in the liver.

1960   Variation in number and asymmetry in branchiostegal rays in the family Esocidae. Canadian Journal of Zoology 38:363–375.

Counts of the number of branchiostegal rays on each hyoid segment may prove more useful as distinguishing characteristics than total counts now in use.

1962a   Black-spot parasite in fishes. Royal Ontario Museum, Department of Ichthyology and Herpetology, Information Leaflet, 4 pp.

Lists some common parasites infecting the pike.

1962b   Predator-prey relationships in pikes (Esocidae). Journal of the Fisheries Research Board of Canada 19:979–980.

In pike the selection of prey corresponded closely to relative abundance or availability of the prey species.

1965   Hybridization in the family Esocidae. Journal of the Fisheries Research Board of Canada 22:1261–1292.

1971   Pike. Related forms and history. Appendix 2. *In* Buller, F. Pike. London, Macdonald, pp. 292–307.

Provides general information on the various species which, with the pike, comprise the suborder Esocoidei and compares the pike in the Old and New Worlds.

1978   Taxonomy and distribution of North American esocids. American Fisheries Society Special Publication 11:13–26.

Changes in taxonomic concepts of the family and species are traced. The present distribution of each species is given in detail, and suggestions are made concerning their distributions in the past and future.

1979a   Piking in North America. Pike Angler's Club, Magazine No. 5:7–9.

Compares the popularity of pike angling to muskellunge angling and the nature of organizations devoted to each.

1979b   The record of the age of your pike. Pike Angler's Club, Magazine No. 5:9–11.

Description and appraisal of the various methods using bony parts to determine age. Advice on handling, mounting, and magnification of scales.

1984   Problems in pike encountered by anglers - black spot and red sore or red disease. Muskies Canada Newsletter 6(9):12–16.

Discussion of *Lymphosarcoma*, trematode metacercaria, and bacterial diseases of the pike and their effects on angled pike. This same item appeared verbatim in: 1985. Pikelines No. 28:29–30.

CROSSMAN, E. J. and K. BUSS

1965   Hybridization in the family Esocidae. Journal of the Fisheries Research Board of Canada 22:1261–1292.

Of 11 possible hybrids of species in the family Esocidae, six were known from nature, and they are reviewed. The occurrence of a seventh is recorded. Of 22 possible reciprocal combinations of these species, five were previously known, five are still unknown, and 12 are newly described.

CROSSMAN, E. J. and J. M. CASSELMAN

1969   Identification of northern pike and muskellunge from axial skeletons, scales, and epipleurals. Journal of the Fisheries Research Board of Canada 26:175–178.

Grooves and knobs on the vertebrae, ratio of length and width of scales, and ratio of lengths of rami of epipleural bones were used to separate pike and muskellunge in mutilated specimens, stomach contents, and archaeological material.

CROSSMAN, E. J. and C. R. HARINGTON

1970   Pleistocene pike, *Esox lucius*, and *Esox* sp., from the Yukon Territory and Ontario. Canadian Journal of Earth Sciences 7:1130–1138.

Two fish dentaries from Pleistocene deposits in the Old Crow area are referable to pike. They provide the first definite fossil record of the species for North America.

CROSSMAN, E. J. and J. W. MEADE

1977   Artificial hybrids between Amur pike *Esox reicherti* and North American esocids. Journal of the Fisheries Research Board of Canada 34:2338–2343.

Artificial hybrids between *Esox reicherti*, the only species in the family Esocidae that does not occur naturally in North America, and North American esocids were developed. Five of a possible 10 crosses are described in detail.

CRUEA, D. D.

1969   Some chemical and physical characteristics of fish sperm. Transactions of the American Fisheries Society 98:785–788.

The concentration of some elements and compounds found in the seminal fluids of various fishes were determined by atomic absorption spectrophotmetry and ultra-microbiochemical analyses. Histological studies showed the presence of several types of abnormalities. These abnormalities were categorized as primary or secondary on the basis of possible detriment to reproductive function, as observed with bovine spermatozoa.

CSANDA, D.

1981   Gigantic Great Lakes pike. In-Fisherman 39:79–84.

Angler's advice on locating pike in summer and fall, techniques, and gear.

CSANDA, D. and T. PORTINCASO

1981   Moose Country pike. In-Fisherman 35:98–109.

A technique for catching pike in spring, based on behaviour patterns.

CSENGO, N.
1914   Acsuka fejvazarol. Allattani Kozlemenyek 13:107–127.

CUERRIER, J. L. and A. COURTEMANCHE
1954   Fish diets and growth. Ephemerides of the Quebec Biology Bureau 1(1).

CUERRIER, J. P.
1962   Inventaire biologique des poissons et des pecheries de la region du lac Saint-Pierre. Le Naturaliste Canadien 89(6–7):193–214.

CUERRIER, J. P., F. E. J. FRY and G. PREFONTAINE
1946   Preliminary list of the fishes of the region of Montreal and Lake St. Peter. Le Naturaliste Canadien 73:17–32.

CUERRIER, J. P. and J. C. WARD
1952   Analysis of creel census cards received from Prairie National Parks during 1951 angling season. Canadian Wildlife Service, Game Fish Creel Census, 19 pp.
1953   Game fish creel census, 1952 season. Canada's Prairie National Parks. Canadian Wildlife Service, Game Fish Creel Census, 18 pp.
1954   Analysis of creel census cards received from Prairie National Parks during 1953 angling season. Canadian Wildlife Service, Game Fish Creel Census.

CULL, J. L.
1934   The 'lunge, pike and pickerel. Rod and Gun in Canada 35(10):27–28.

CUNNINGHAM, C. R., J. F. CRAIG and W. C. MACKAY
1983   Some experiments with an automatic grid antenna radio system for tracking freshwater fish. In Pincock, D. G., ed., Proceedings of the 4th International Conference on Wildlife biotelemetry, 1983. Halifax, Applied Microelectronics Institute and Technical University of Nova Scotia, pp. 135–149.

CUPPY, W.
        The pike. In How to become extinct. Chicago, University of Chicago Press, pp. 31–32.

CUVIER, G.
1910   Vorlesungen uber vergleichende Anatomie. Uebers von J. F. Meckel, Teil III, Verdauungsorgane.

CUVIER, M. B. and M. A. VALENCIENNES
1846   Histoire naturelle des poissons. Vol. 18. Paris, P. Bertrand. 505 pp.

CVANCARA, V. and C. PONTO
1981   Current references in fish research. Vol. 6. University of Wisconsin-Eau Claire, 204 pp.
        Contains 3,490 titles of papers published in over 300 different scientific journals in 1981.

CVANCARA, V. A.
1969   Distribution of liver allantoinase and allantoicase activity in fresh-water teleosts. Comparative Biochemistry and Physiology 29:631–638.
1977   Current references in fish research. Vol. 2. University of Wisconsin-Eau Claire. 108 pp.
1978   Current references in fish research. Vol. 3. University of Wisconsin-Eau Claire, 122 pp.
        Titles of fish papers published during 1977 in more than 130 different scientific journals.
1979   Current references in fish research. Vol. 4. University of Wisconsin-Eau Claire, 150 pp.

75

Nearly 3,000 titles taken from over 300 different scientific journals published during 1979.

1980   Current references in fish research. Vol. 5. University of Wisconsin-Eau Claire, 166 pp.

Titles were taken from over 300 different scientific journals published in 1980.

CVANCARA, V. A. and W. HUANG

1978   Tissue alkaline phosphatase EC-3.1.3.1 activitiy in selected fresh water teleosts. Comparative Biochemistry and Physiology. B. Comparative Biochemistry 60:221–224.

Liver alkaline phosphatase activity expressed in gram of protein was 16.26 for pike.

CVANCARA, V. A. and L. P. PAULUS

1976   Current references in fish research. University of Wisconsin-Eau Claire, 78 pp.

Over 1,100 titles of fish research published in 144 different scientific journals during 1976.

CVANCARA, V. A., S. F. STIEBER and B. A. CVANCARA

1977   Summer temperature tolerance of selected species of Mississippi River acclimated young of the year fishes. Comparative Biochemistry and Physiology. A. Comparative Physiology 56:81–85.

Under the experimental conditions described, LD (50) values for pike were 30.8 C.

CZAPIK, A.

1961   Szczupak (*Esox lucius* L.). [The pike (*Esox lucius* L.).] Wszechswiat 11:282.

Possibilities of breeding juvenile pike in an aquarium.

CZAPLICKI, J.

1964   Sportowy polow szczupaka. [Sport catches of pike.] Wiadomosci Wedkarskie 3:12–15.

Comments on fish behaviour and proper methods of pike catches.

CZELZUGA, B.

1977   Carotenoids in fish. Part 18. Carotenoids in the brain of some fishes. Folia Histochemica et Cytochemica 15:343–346.

1978   Karotenoidy u ryb. 9. *Esox lucius* (L.). [Carotenoids in fish. 9. *Esox lucius* (L.)]. Roczniki Nauk Rolniczyck 99:55–62.

Extracts were separated by column and thin-layer chromatography. Carotenoids from the eggs, skin, gills, muscles, liver, and intestines were identified. Astaxanthin was the dominant carotenoid in all parts of the body (48.5–94.7%).

76

DABROWSKI, J.

    1961   Badania nad unaczynieniem powierzchni skrzelowych szczupaka i karpia. [Research on the vascularity of the surface of pike and carp gills.] Zeszyty Naukowe Wyzszej Szkoly Rolniczej w Olsztynie 11(106):97–126.

           Morphology of the blood system in gills.

DABROWSKI, K. R.

    1982   The influence of light intensity on feeding of fish larvae and fry. 1. *Coregonus pollan* (Thompson) and *Esox lucius* (L.). Zoologische Jahrbuecher Abteilung fuer Systematik Dekologie und Geographie der Tiere 86:341–351.

DABROWSKI, T. and M. SALACKI

    1964   Badania technologiczne nad wielkoscia masy jajnikow szczupaka jako surowca rybnego. [Technological studies on the weight of pike ovaries treated as raw material.] Zeszyty Naukowe Wyzszej Szkoly Rolniczej w Olsztynie 18(3):305–314.

           Studies and observations on the obtained mass of pike eggs during pike filleting, and an estimation of its possible use on a national scale.

    1965   Wydajnosc ikry szczupaka z jezior woj olsztynakiego. [Pike fecundity in lakes of Olsztyn district.] Gospodarka Rybna 17(2):18–19.

           Observations on the amount of eggs obtained during pike filleting and an estimation of the amount of eggs it would be possible to obtain on a national scale for consumption purposes.

DAHL, J.

    1961   Alder og vaskst hos danske og svenske brakvandsgedder. Et bidrag til distussionem om genetableringen og den danske bestand of brakvandsgedder efter saltvands katastrofen: 1951. Ferskvandesgedder efter saltvands katastrofen i 1951. Ferskvandsfisk 59(2):34–38.

DALL, W. H.

    1870   The food fishes of Alaska. Report of the U.S. Commissioner of Agriculture for 1870, pp. 375–392.

DAMURAT, J.

    n.d.   Embryonic development of trout (*Salmo trutta* L.), pike, (*Esox lucius* L.) and roach (*Rutilus rutilus* L.) in waterless environment. [Translated from Polish]. U.S. Department of Commerce, Clearinghouse for Federal Scientific and Technical Information, Springfield, VA.

DANIL'CHENKO, O. P.

    1982   A comparison of the reaction of fish embryos and prolarvae to certain natural factors and synthesized compounds. Journal of Ichthyology 22:123–134.

           Pike was one of four species studied. The reaction of embryos and prolarvae to solutions of natural compounds was of an adaptive nature, while their reaction to synthesized compounds showed merely tolerance.

DANIL'CHENKO, O. P. and N. S. STROGANOV

    1975   Evaluation of toxicity to the early onotogeny of fishes of substances discharged into a body of water. Journal of Ichthyology 15:311–319.

           The effect of several antiseptics on the embryonic and early postembryonic development of several freshwater teleost fishes, including pike, was investigated. The degree of toxicity of the substances was assessed from their influence on the early development of these fishes.

DANILENKO, T. P.

1983   The reproductive cycle of the pike *Esox lucius* L. in the Kanev Reservoir. Hydrobiological Journal 18(4):21–27.

Data on sexual maturation of male and female pike from various zones of the Kanev Reservoir are presented.

DAUPHIN, R.

1983   Sur un exemple de grossissement de brochetons dans une Federation departementale d'Association de Peche et de Pisciculture. *In* Billard, R., ed., Le brochet gestion dans le milieu naturel et elevage. Paris, Institute National de la Recherche Agronomique, pp. 209–213.

Fry are reared in small ponds 2,200 to 4,500 sq.m. Number of fry released varies from 8 to 13 individuals/sq.m. and number of juveniles recovered varies between 5 and 20% after 7 to 11 weeks of rearing.

DAVIES, E.

1966   The parasites of the coarse fishes of the River Lugg. *In* Jones, J. W., and P. H. Tombleson, eds., Proceedings 2nd British Coarse Fish Conference, Liverpool, 1965, pp. 94–101.

DAVIES, E. H.

1967   Myxosporidian infections in the fish of the River Lugg. Proceedings 3rd British Coarse Fish Conference, pp. 18–19.

1968   Rhaphidascarid infections in the fish of the River Lugg, a tributary of the River Wye, Herefordshire, England. Parasitology 58:22–23.

DAVIS, H. S.

1953   Culture and diseases of game fishes. Berkeley, University of California Press. 332 pp.

DAVIS, J.

1983   Early-season northerns! Angler and Hunter, March 1983, pp. 4–6.

DAVISON, R. S. D.

1966   Research and the Angling Association. *In* Jones, J. W., and P. H. Tombleson, eds. Proceedings of the 2nd British Coarse Fish Conference, Liverpool, 1965, pp. 115–119.

DAVISSON, M. T.

1972   Karyotypes of the Teleost family Esocidae. Journal of the Fisheries Research Board of Canada 29:579–582.

Representatives of all five surviving species of Esocidae were found to have karyotypes consisting of 50 acrocentric chromosomes. The karyotype similarity suggests a cytological basis for the ease of hybridization and shows that speciation can occur without karyotypic change. Evolutionary implications are discussed.

DAWE, C. J.

1970   Neoplasma of blood cell origin in poikilothermic animals; a status summary. Bibliothetica Haematologica 36:634–637.

DAWE, C. J., W. G. BANFIELD, R. SONSTEGARD, C. W. LEE and H. J. MICHELITCH

1977   Cylindroid lamella particle complexes and nucleoid intracytoplasmic bodies in lymphoma cells of northern pike *Esox lucius*. Progress in Experimental Tumor Research 20:166–180.

Two types of intracytoplasmic structures not previously described in this neoplasm were found in neoplastic cells from a Canadian specimen of malignant lymphoma.

DAWE, C. J., D. G. SCARPELLI and S. R. WELLINGS, eds.
  1976   Progress in experimental tumor research. Tumors in Aquatic Animals Sym-
          posium, Cork, 1974. Basel, Karger, vol. 20, 438 pp.

DAWSON, L.
  1959   Summary of northern pike production, Valentine Fisheries Station. Nebraska
          Game, Forest, and Parks Commission, 4 pp. [mimeo.]

DAWSON, V. K. and P. A. GILDERHUS
  1979   Ethyl-P-aminobenzoate (Benzocaine): efficacy as an anesthetic for five
          species of freshwater fish. U.S. Fish and Wildlife Service, Investigations in
          Fish Control 87:1–5.

DAY, F.
  1884   The fishes of Great Britain and Ireland, vol. 2. London, Williams and Nor-
          gate. 388 pp.

DEALTRY, J. T.
  1970   A summer overturn and its effects on the fish fauna of an old Yorkshire clay-
          pit pond. Naturalist 915:121–125.

DEAN, B. C.
  1957   Watershed surveys and management plans. Reconnaissance impoundment
          survey—Switzer Lake, Lake County and Lost Lake, Crawford County.
          Michigan Department of Conservation, Dingell-Johnson Report F-4-R-5/Job
          5/A:1–3.

DEAN, E. L.
  1975   Aquatic ecology and fisheries in Reindeer Lake. Saskatchewan Department
          of Tourism and Renewable Resources, Churchill River Study, Final Report
          10.
          Data on pike captured with gill nets, seines, and fishing rods included: distri-
          bution and abundance, length, weight, age (assessed by scales and otolith),
          and growth, catch distribution in standard "gangs", and food habits (deter-
          mined by 181 stomachs).

DEAN, T.
  1982   Big reservoir pike. In-Fisherman 41:130–147.
          Attributes good pike angling in Oahe Reservoir to water level fluctuations,
          creating good spawning grounds; location; and bays. Advice to anglers on
          presentation.

DE BEER, G. R.
  1937   The development of the vertebrate skull. Oxford University Press, 152 pp.
          Notes on works of early authora.

DE BOISSET, L.
  1948   Poissons des rivieres de France. Librairie des Champs-Elysees, 1:1–237.

DEBONT, A. F.
  1967   Some aspects of age and growth of fish in temperate and tropical waters. In
          Gerking, S. D., ed., The biological basis of freshwater fish production. IBP
          Symposium, Reading, 1966, pp. 67–88.

DECHTIAR, A. O.
  1972a   Systematic status of Tetraonchus loftusi n. sp. (Monogenoidea: Tetraonchi-
          dae) and comparative studies of T. monenteron (Wagener, 1857) Diesing,
          1858, and T. variabilis Mizelle and Webb, 1953. Canadian Journal of Zool-
          ogy 50:1489–1495.
          Pike is a host species for T. monenteron. The parasite was studied from

specimens of pike taken from lakes Superior and Huron.

1972b   Parasites of fish from Lake of the Woods, Ontario. Journal of the Fisheries Research Board of Canada 29:275–283.

Results of a survey of the parasite fauna of fish from Lake of the Woods and adjacent lakes; 23 pike were examined, 23 were infected.

DECKER, D. J., R. A. HOWARD, JR. and W. H. EVERHART

1978   Identifying members of the pike family found in New York. New York State College of Agriculture and Life Sciences, Cornell University, Conservation Circular 16:1–7.

A brief description of distribution, growth, spawning, and feeding habits.

DE FREITAS, A. S. W., M. A. J. GIDNEY, A. E. MCKINNON and R. J. NORSTROM

1977   Factors affecting whole body retention of methyl mercury in fish. In Drucker, H., and R. E. Wildung, eds., Implications of metals in the environment. 15th Annual Hanford Life Sciences Symposium, Washington. Symposium Series 42:441–451.

DE FREITAS, A. S. W., S. U. QADRI and B. E. CASE

1974   Origins and fate of mercury compounds in fish. Proceedings of the International Conference on Transport of Persistent Chemicals in Aquatic Ecosystems, Ottawa, 1974.

Comparison of the mercury distribution in tissues from laboratory exposed fish with similar data from field studies suggest that environmentally contaminated fish may obtain most of their body burden of methyl mercury by direct uptake from water.

DE JAGER, S., M. E. SMIT-ONEL, J. J. VIDELER, B. J. M. VAN GILS and E. M. UFFINK

1976   The respiratory area of the gills of some teleost fishes in relation to their mode of life. Bijdragen tot de Dierkunde 46:199–205.

DE KAY, J. E.

1842.   Fishes. Part 4. In Zoology of New-York, or the New York fauna. New York Geology Survey, pp. 1–415.

Mere mention of external features of pike in this early paper.

DE KINKELIN, P., B. GALIMARD and R. BOOTSMA

1973   Isolation and identification of the causative agent of "red disease" of pike (Esox lucius L. 1766). Nature 241(5390):465–467.

Work is described which demonstrates that "red disease" of pike is caused by a rhabdovirus.

DEL CAMPILLO, C. and P. A. PELLITERO

1973   Ichthypathologic problems in Spain with special reference to trout raising and methods for their control. Annali della Facolta di Veterinaria di Leon 19:65–80.

DE LIGNY, W. and B. L. VERBOOM

1968   Bloedgroepenonderzoek bij snoek. [Research on bloodgroups of northern pike]. Visserij 21:177–179. [in Dutch]

DEMCENKO, I.

1970   Vyrascivanije scuki v prudovych chozjajstvach Ukrainy. Trudy Belorusskogo Nauchno-Issledovatel'skogo Instituta Rybnogo Chozjajstva 8:275–282.

DEMCENKO, I. F.

1961   Do pitannja rozvadennja scuki u stavsch. Kijev, Naukova praci 14:100–103.

1962   Biotechnika razvedenija scuki v stavach. Lvov, Knizkovo-zurnalne vidav-nictvo, pp. 64–101.

1963   Stiki pludek pomaha zvysovat vyrobu kapra. Cs. rybarstvi 3:40.

DEMCHENKO, I.

1959   Fingerlings of *Esox lucius* in carp fattening ponds. Rybovodstvi i Rhbolovstvo 4:14–15.

The simultaneous breeding of 2-year-old carp (*Cyprinus carpio*) and commercial fingerlings of pike in drainable fattening ponds permits food resources of ponds to be utilized more fully and gives an additional yield of 40–60 kg/ha of commercial pike fingerlings.

DEMCHENKO, I. F.

1963   On sexual differences in the pike (*Esox lucius* L.). Problems of Ichthyology 3:190–193.

Describes a method of differentiating sex from the urogenital and anal openings, with less than 3% error.

DEMEL, K.

1933   Wykaz bezkregowcow i ryb Baltyku naszego. [Invertebrates and fishes of the Baltic Sea.] Faun. Musei Zool. Pol. 2(13):121–136.

A review of species, their habitats and behaviour, as well as the distribution of invertebrates and fishes in the Baltic Sea.

DE MONTALEMBERT, G., C. BRY and R. BILLARD

1978   Control of reproduction in northern pike. American Fisheries Society Special Publication 11:217–225.

Describes several attempts to control gamete availability in pike, including precocious induction of ovulation, high doses of progesterone to induce increase of sperm release, and cryopreservation of diluted sperm.

DE MONTALEMBERT, G., B. JALABERT and C. BRY

1978   Precocious induction of maturation and ovulation in northern pike (*Esox lucius*). Annales de Biologie Animale Biochimie Biophysique 18:969–975.

The efficiency of partially purified salmon gonadotrophin and human chorionic gonadotrophin administered alone or in association with a progestagen was investigated in submature females using the germinal vesicle in non-peripheral position as the criterion for initial oocyte stage.

DE MONTALEMBERT, G., J. MARCEL and R. BILLARD

1980   Spermiation in pike. 1. Quantitative evolution of sperm release during the reproduction period. Bulletin Francais de Pisciculture 276:90–103.

DENCE, W. A.

1938   An unusual feeding incident in the great northern pike (*Esox lucius*). Copeia 1938:96.

An account of a 25-inch pike that died trying to swallow a 7-inch rock bass (*Ambloplites rupestris*).

DERBACK, B.

1947   The adverse effect of cold weather upon the successful reproduction of pickerel, *Stizostedion vitreum*, at Heming Lake, Manitoba, in 1947. Canadian Fish Culturist 3:22–23.

Pike spawn in Heming Creek, which is marshy, deep, meandering, and arises in a muskeg lake from which fish are blocked by a beaver dam.

81

DERKSEN, A. J.

1978   A report on the results of experimental gillnetting in Cedar Lake in August 1972, and prospects for a commercial fishery with particular reference to northern pike. Manitoba Department of Northern Affairs, unpublished MS.
Experimental gill-netting was conducted to determine if large quantities of pike >5 lb could be taken for export to Europe. Mercury levels of pike 5–7 lb exceeded 1.00 ppm, therefore a fishery could not be developed.

DES CLERS, S. and J. ALLARDI

1983   Efficacite de la reproduction naturelle et des repeuplements dans la Seine au niveau de Montereau. *In* Billard, R., ed., Le brochet gestion dans le milieu natureal et elevage. Paris, Institute National de la Recherche Agronomique, pp. 297–303.
Results of 8 years of mark-recapture and laboratory experiments concerning reproduction and water quality, temperature, thermal shock.

DEUFEL, J.

1964   Cancerous pike in Ireland. Irish Naturalists' Journal 14:312–315.

DEVILLERS, C.

1947   Explanations in vitro de blastodermes de poissons, (*Salmo, Esox*). Experientia 3:71–74.

DEVILLERS, C. and J. CORSIN

1968   Les os dermique craniens des Poissons et des Amphibiens; points de vue embryologiques sur les "territoires osseux" et les "fusions". *In* Orvig, T., ed., Current problems of lower vertebrate phylogeny. Stockholm, Almquist and Wiksell, pp. 413–428.

DEVITSINA, G. V. and T. A. BELOUSOVA

1978   On the participation of the trigemal system in odor reception in fish. Journal of Ichthyology 18:114–120.
The trigeminal system of the pike reacts to stimulation of the olfactory lining by solutions of different chemical substances. Responses recorded in the maxillary branch of the trigeminal nerve demonstrate a clear correlation with similar responses in the olfactory tract.

DEVITSINA, G. V. and G. A. MALYUKINA

1977   The functional organization of the olfactory organ in macrosomatic and microsomatic fishes. Journal of Ichthyology 17:432–440.
The olfactory organ is a slowly adapting system. The character of the oxmatic response does not depend on the type of stimulus and is species-specific and governed by the functional state of the fish. The intensity of the response is dependent on the type and dose of the stimulus.

DEVITSYNA, G. V.

1973   Certain morphological and functional properties of the olfactory bulb of pike and burbot. Vestnik Moskovskogo Universiteta Seriya 6, Biologiya Pochvovedenie 28:10–18.

1977   Comparative morphology of the olfactory analyzer in fish. Journal of Ichthyology 17:116–125.
Species-specific traits were noted in the olfactory receptor, and features of the olfactory bulb were correlated with development of its sensitivity.

DEXTER, R. W. and D. B. MCCARRAHER

1967   Clam shrimps as pests in fish-rearing ponds. Progressive Fish-Culturist 29:105–107.

Clam shrimp *Cyzicus mexicanus* become so numerous in rearing ponds as to clog the outlet screens. Of approximately 800 pike stomachs examined during 6 years, none contained clam shrimp; thus they do not contribute to fish production as do fairy shrimp.

DIANA, J. S.

1979a   An energy budget for northern pike (*Esox lucius*) in Lac Ste. Anne, Alberta. Ph.D. thesis, University of Alberta. 160 pp.

The annual energy budget was estimated for pike in Lac Ste. Anne by a combination of field and laboratory experiments. Pike were sampled between March 1976 and September 1978. Age groups 0 to 4 fish were used, sampled at five intervals over the year. Maintenance requirements were estimated from controlled experiments. Activity patterns were measured using ultrasonic telemetry. Daily rations were estimated from stomach contents. The annual allocation of energy to growth, maintenance, and reproduction was estimated from these data. Ration predicted from energy budgets and observed ration were usually in good agreement.

1979b   Northern pike activity patterns. Underwater Telemetry Newsletter 9(2):1–3.

1979c   The feeding pattern and daily ration of a top carnivore, the northern pike (*Esox lucius*). Canadian Journal of Zoology 57:2121–2127.

Food habits, digestive rates, and daily ration were determined for 1,290 pike collected from Lac Ste. Anne, Alberta. Data on major species consumed and caloric value of each species was studied. Variations in gastric evacuations with season and daily ration with sex and season are given.

1980   Diel activity pattern and swimming speeds of northern pike (*Esox lucius*) in Lac Ste. Anne, Alberta. Canadian Journal of Fisheries and Aquatic Sciences 37:1454–1458.

Movements of six pike were monitored for 5–51 days by ultrasonic transmitters implanted surgically. The pike were inactive during 80% of the 889 5-min intervals monitored during summer and winter. No regular diel changes in activity were noted, except that pike were inactive at night. Swimming velocities calculated from gross displacements were maximum, 42 cm/s (0.91 body lengths (BL)/s); average, 23.1 cm/s (0.45 BL/s).

1981   Latitudinal variations in the growth of northern pike. Presented at 43rd Midwest Fish and Wildlife Conference.

Differences in annual growth, age of first maturation, timing and magnitude of body and gonad production were examined for pike from four lakes in Michigan varying in latitude and ice cover duration.

1982   An experimental analysis of the metabolic rate and food utilization of northern pike. Comparative Biochemistry and Physiology. A. Comparative Physiology 71:395–399.

Metabolism of pike was determined by oxygen consumption and ration experiments for an energy budget analysis. Energy gain or depletion from the body was due to changes in amount of whole body tissue or body protein rather than specific utilization or storage of lipid. Conversion and assimilation efficiencies were also determined.

1983a   An energy budget for northern pike (*Esox lucius*). Canadian Journal of Zoology 61:1968–1975.

Allocation of energy by pike to maintenance, growth, and reproduction was estimated by a combination of laboratory and field techniques. Parameters were fitted to a bioenergetics model to determine the energy budgets of pike from Lac Ste. Anne, Alberta.

1983b   Growth, maturation and production of northern pike in three Michigan lakes. Transactions of the American Fisheries Society 112:38–46.

Differences in age at first maturation and timing and magnitude of body and gonad growth were examined for pike from lakes that varied in latitude, ice-free season, and total mortality.

DIANA, J. S. and W. C. MACKAY

1979   Timing and magnitude of energy deposition and loss in the body, liver and gonads of northern pike (*Esox lucius*). Journal of the Fisheries Research Board of Canada 36:481–487.

Pike were sampled periodically from Lac Ste. Anne, Alberta, between March 1976 and September 1978. The yearly cycle of production and depletion was determined for individual 3-year-old fish.

DIANA, J. S., W. C. MACKAY and M. EHRMAN

1977   Movements and habitat preference of northern pike (*Esox lucius*) in Lac Ste. Anne, Alberta. Transactions of the American Fisheries Society 106:560–565. Movements of nine pike in Lac Ste. Anne, Alberta, were monitored for 5 to 47 days using ultrasonic transmitters implanted in the fishes' stomachs. None established well-defined home ranges. Pike were usually found within 300 m of shore and in water <4 m deep. No major differences were found in the extent of movement or in habitat selection between summer and winter. Daily movements were from 0 to 4,000 m, but most <1,000 m.

DIANGELO, S.

1960   Watershed surveys and management plans. Northern pike spawning surveys and development plans. Michigan Department of Conservation, Dingell-Johnson Report F-4-R-7/Job H:1–10.

1961   Pike marsh production 1961. Michigan Department of Conservation, unpublished MS. 2 pp.

1962   Fish population control planning. Community pike-spawning marshes. Michigan Department of Conservation, Dingell-Johnson Report F-25-R-1/Job 1:1–9.

DIANGELO, S. and J. E. WILLIAMS

1962   Ponds for pike. Michigan Conservationist 31(3):2–7.

DICK, M. M.

1964   Fishes of the western North Atlantic. Suborder Esocoidea. Memoir of the Sears Foundation for Marine Research 1:550–560.

DICKINSON, W. E.

1960   Handbook of Wisconsin fishes. Milwaukee Public Museum, Popular Science Handbook Ser. 8:1–86.

DICONSTANZO, C. J. and R. L. RIDENHOUR

1957   Angler harvest in the summers of 1953 to 1956 at Clear Lake, Iowa. Proceedings of the Iowa Academy of Science 64:621–628.

DIES,

1927   Die Hechtkrankheit im Worthersee (in Karnten). Allgemeine Fischerei-Zeitung 52.

DIPLOCK, A. T. and G. A. D. HASLEWOOD

1967   The ubiquinone content of animal tissues. A survey of the occurrence of ubiquinone in vertebrates. Biochemical Journal 104:1004–1010.

DI PRISCO, G. L., G. MATERAZZI and G. CHIEFFI

1970   *In vitro* steroidogenesis in testicular tissue of the fresh water teleost *Esox lucius*. General and Comparative Endocrinology 14:595–598.

DISLER, N. N.

1967   Development of pike (*Esox lucius*) lateral-line sense organs. *In* Morpho-ecological studies of fish development, Moscow, Nauka, pp. 148–162.

DISSELHORST, R.

1904   Ausfuhrapparat und Anhangsdrusen der mannlichen Geschlechts organe. *In* Oppel-Lehrbach der Verleichenden Mikrokopischen Anatomie der Wirbel-liere 12:1–386.

DIUZHIKOV, A.

1959   On pike concentration in the tail-water of the Volga Hydroelectric Station. Rybnoe Khozyaistvo 3:15–16

        In the fall of 1956 pike began to descend from Kuibyshev Reservoir and con-tinued coming in great numbers for 2 years. By 1958 pike concentration reached 70–90% by weight of catch. It was felt necessary to control the number of pike to prevent the loss of valuable migratory species.

DOAN, K. H.

1948   Studies of jackfish in Heming Lake. Fisheries Research Board of Canada.

1964   Climate, hydrology, and freshwater fisheries. Manitoba Department of Mines and Natural Resources, Fisheries Branch, Manuscript Report. 35 pp.

n.d.   Control of the pike-whitefish tapeworm in central Canada. Proceedings of the 7th Pacific Science Congress 4:539–548.

DOBBEN, W. H. VAN

1952   The food of the cormorant in the Netherlands. Ardea 40(1/2):1–63.

DOBIE, J.

1966   Food and feeding habits of the walleye, *Stizostedion v. vitreum*, and associ-ated game and forage fishes in Lake Vermilion, Minnesota, with special refer-ence to the tullibee, *Coregonus (Leucichthys) artedi*. Minnesota Fisheries Investigations 4:39–71.

        Pike are rather scarce in Lake Vermilion and only 31 adults containing food were taken during three summers of netting. Fish made up 90.3% of the total volume of food eaten. Most of the time the pike taken had eaten fairly large fish and were not in direct competition with the walleyes for small *Perca flavescens*.

n.d.   Investigation into the food habits of the walleye, *Stizostedion v. vitreum* and associated forage fish. Unpublished MS.

DOBIE, J. and J. B. MOYLE

1962   Methods used for investigating productivity of fish-rearing ponds in Min-nesota. Minnesota Department of Conservation, Fisheries Research Unit, Special Publication 5:1–62.

DOBLER, E.

1977   Correlation between the feeding time of the pike (*Esox lucius*) and the disper-sion of a school of *Leucaspius dileneatus*. Oecologia 27:93–96.

        The pike eats *Leucaspius* predominantly when there is little light (50–75% of its prey at <1 Lux). It can be supposed that the pike is optically superior to its prey at low illumination levels and profits from this advantage when catching its prey.

DOCKRAY, G. J.

1974a   A secretin-like factor in intestinal extracts of pike *Esox lucius*. General and Comparative Endocrinology 22:390. [Abstract]

1974b   Extraction of a secretinlike factor from the intestines of pike (*Esox lucius*). General and Comparative Endocrinology 23:340–347.
A secretin-like factor was extracted from the intestines of pike with acetic acid, and was partially purified. It was concluded that a secretin-like factor exists in the intestines of teleost fish and that its biological properties are different from those of porcine secretin.

1975   Comparative studies on secretin. General and Comparative Endocrinology 25:203–210.

DOGIEL, V. A., G. K. DETRUSHEVSKI and I. I. POLYANSKI, eds.

1961   Parasitology of fishes, trans. by Z. Kobatz. Edinburgh, Oliver and Boyd. 384 pp.

DOLININ, V. A.

1973   The rate of basal metabolism in fish. Journal of Ichthyology 13:430–438.
Gives values for basal metabolism at different temperatures in pike. Discusses rhythmic fluctuations, measures indicators of respiratory function.

1974   Environmental dependence of the main parameters of the respiratory function in fishes differing in their activity and oxygen requirement. Journal of Ichthyology 14:122–132.
Determined main parameters of respiratory function in pike on reduction of oxygen concentration from 12 to 0.2–0.4 mg/l in water at temperatures of 5, 10, 15, and 20 C.

1975a   Main parameters of the respiratory function in fishes during alteration in respiratory activity. Journal of Ichthyology 15:124–132.
The dependence of ventilation volume, coefficient of uptake of oxygen from the water and frequency of respiratory movements on the degree of motor activity, assessed on the rate of respiratory metabolism, was determined at different temperatures and oxygen concentrations. A method of indirect assessment of the maximum possible values of the rate of respiratory metabolism and the maximum continuous swimming speed of fishes is proposed.

1975b   Mechanisms of ensuring gas exchange in fish. Journal of Ichthyology 15:649–657.
The absolute values and the character of change in the basic parameters of the respiratory function of pike with change of oxygen concentration and motor activity of the fish under conditions of constant, artificially-fixed volume of ventilation were determined.

1976   The regulatory mechanism of the respiratory rhythm in fish. Journal of Ichthyology 16:176–178.
An attempt to elucidate the regulatory features of the respiratory rhythm in two species of fish, differing in degree of mobility.

DOLLFUS, R. F.

1968   Les trematodes de l'histoire naturelle des helminthes de Felix Dujardin (1845). Museum National d'Histoire Naturelle (Paris), Mem. Ser. A, Zoologie 54(3):119–196.

DOLZHENKO, M. P. and V. P. VLASOV

1961   Measures for increasing fish productivity and improving the species composition of fish in some small lakes in the Altai district. Rybnoe Khozyaistvo

13/14:46–48.

For increasing the productivity of Lake Srostinsk it was necessary to raise the water level and stock it with *Abramis brama* and pike.

DOMANEVSKII, L. N.

1958   Commercial-biological characteristics of the pike of Tsimlyanskoe Reservoir. Izvestiya Gosudarstvennogo Nauchno-Issledovatel-skogo Instituta Ozernogo i Rechnogo Rybnogo Khozvaistva USSR 45:201–212.

1959   On the role of the pike in formation of the fish fauna of Tsimlyanskoe Reservoir. Rybnoe Khozyaistvo 4.

1962   Dosupnyi razmer zhertv dlya shchuki. [Size of prey accessible to pike]. Byulleten' Instituta Biologii Vodokhranilishcha 12:50–53.

This paper establishes the relationship between the sizes of pike and the sizes of various fish species devoured by them. Because the predator population is generally made up of older fish, no freshwater fish is able to avoid being directly affected by the pike population.

1963   Metodik ucheta shchuki *Esox lucius* L. Tsimlyanskogo vodokranilishcha. [A method for computing the numbers of pike *Esox lucius* L. in the Tsimlyan Reservoir]. Voprosy Ikhtiologii 2:513–521.

DOMANEVSKY, L. N.

1959   Some features of the biology of pike in Tsimlyansk reservoir. Trudy 6 Soveshch, po probleme biologii vnutrennikh vodnany, pp. 415–418.

There is a tendency towards a decrease in numbers of pike which will continue because spawning conditions will not improve, growth rate will drop, and fishery on the spawning grounds will certainly not cease.

1963   Growth characteristics of the pike (*Esox lucius* L.). Zoologicheskiy Zhurnal 42:1539–1545.

The growth of pike within its distribution range varies considerably and is influenced by the geographical position of the water body and its hydrological and biological peculiarities.

1964   Some features of the interspecific relationships between pike and the dominant fish species in Tsimlyansk reservoir. Zoologicheskii Zhurnal 43:71–79.

DOMBECK, M. P.

1979   Movement and behaviour of the muskellunge determined by radio-telemetry. Wisconsin Department of Natural Resources, Technical Bulletin 113:1–19.

DOMURAT, J.

1958   Rozwoj embrionalny szczupaka (*Esox lucius* L.) w oleju parafinowym. [Embryonal development of pike (*Esox lucius* L.) in paraffin oil] Polskie Archiwum Hydrobiologii 5:7–18. [in Polish, French summary].

Pike eggs fertilized in water and transferred to paraffin oil developed and gave 20% hatched larvae.

1966   Embryonic development of trout (*Salmo trutta* L.), pike (*Esox lucius* L.) and roach (*Rutilus rutilus* L.) in waterless environment. Polskie Archiwum Hydrobiologii 3(16):166–173.

DONAIRE, J. A.

1976   El lucio, coloso de los embalses. Trofeo 78:59–61.

A popular article that describes the habits of pike in relation to angling in Spanish reservoirs.

DONALDSON, E. M.

1977   Bibliography of fish reproduction 1963–1974. Part 2 of 3 parts—Teleostei, Clupea to Ompok. Canada Fisheries and Marine Service, Technical Report 732.

DONETZ, J. E.

1982   An evaluation of the current status of northern pike (*Esox lucius*) in Lake of the Woods, Ontario. Ontario Ministry of Natural Resources, Lake of the Woods -Rainy Lake Fisheries Assessment Unit Report 1982–03:1–76.

As of 1982 pike was considered to be the second most important game and commercial fish species in Lake of the Woods. Studies indicated that while populations in some areas of the lake were stable, others were stressed due to overfishing. The effects of stress on the population and the fisheries were discussed.

DOORNBOS, G.

1979   Winter food habits of smew (*Mergus albellus* L.) on Lake Yssel, the Netherlands: species and size selection in relation to fish stocks. Ardea 67:42–48.

DORIER, A.

1938   A propos de l'oeuf et de l'alevin de brochet. Bulletin Francais de Pisciculture 10(110):61–73.

1939   Sur la nature et l'origine des mouvements rhythmiques de l'oeuf de brochet. Comptes Rendus de la Societe de Biologie 130:991–992.

DORNESCU, G. T. and D. MISCALENCU

1968a   Etude comparative des branchies de quelques especes de l'ordre Clupeiformes. Gegenbaurs Morphologisches Jahrbuch 112:261–276.

1968b   Celetrei tipure de branhii alt Teleosteenilor. Analele Universitatii Bucuresti Seria Stiintele Naturii 17:11–20. [French summary]

DORSON, M., P. DE KINKELIN and C. MICHEL

1983   Pathologie du brochet. *In* Billard, R., ed., Le brochet gestion dans le milieu naturel et elevage. Paris, Institute National de la Recherche Agronomique, pp. 245–250.

DOUBREUIL, E.

1871   Note sur le brochet. Annales de la Societie Horticulture Histoire Naturel de Herault Ser.2, 2:29–30.

DOUDOROFF, P. and D. L. SHUMWAY

1970   Dissolved oxygen requirements of freshwater fishes. Food and Agricultural Organization of the United Nations, Fisheries Technical Paper 86:1–291.

DOVING, K. B., M. DUBOIS-DAUPHIN, A. HOLLEY and F. JOURDAN

1977   Functional anatomy of the olfactory organ of fish and the ciliary mechanism of water transport. Acta Zoologica 58:245–256.

DOXTATER, G.

1967   Experimental predator-prey relations in small ponds. Progressive Fish-Culturist 29:102–104.

An attempt to rate various predator species in their ability to suppress populations of bluegill *Lepomis macrochirus*.

DOYLE, J.

1968   Pike investigations. Inland Fisheries Bulletin (Eire) 4:9–10.

DRAGANIK, B. and J. A. SZCZERBOWSKI

1963   Wplyw odlowow elektrycznym agregatem pradotworczym na liczebnosc drapieznych ryb w potoku Kosno. [The influence of catches by means of an electric shocker on the number of predatory fish in Kosno Stream.] Zeszyty Naukowe Wyzszej Szkoly Rolniczej w Olsztynie 16(1):73–77.

Catches were made in order to remove pike, eel, perch, burbot and dace from a stretch of a river.

DRAIGHIN, P. A.

1958   Izvestia Vsesoyuznogo Nauchno Issledov-atelskogo Institute Ozernogo i Rechnogo Rybnogo Khozyaistra. [Communications of the All-State Research Institute of the Lake and River Fisheries]. Leningrad 46:1–105.

Considers the scales of many species, including pike, and illustrates them.

DRAKENBERG, T., M. SWAERD, A. CAVE and J. PARELLO

1985   Metal-ion binding to parvalbumin. A ^{113}Cd-n.m.r. study of the binding of different ianthanide ions. Biochemical Journal 227:711–717.

^{113}Cd-n.m.r. studies were used to investigate the binding of lanthanide ions to parvalbumins. It was shown that lanthanide ions with a smaller ionic radius bind sequential to Cd^{2+} saturated parvalbumin, whereas those with a larger ionic radius bind with similar affinity to both the Cd site and the Ef site.

DRIESCH, A. VON DEN

1982   Fischreste aus der slawisch-deutschen Furstenburg auf dem Weinberg in Hit-zacker (Elbe). Neue Ausgrabungen und Forschungen in Niedersachsen 15:395–423.

Fish remains from the 11th-13th centuries were 47.9% pike. Notes large average size of specimens and infers size reduction in Elbe fishes.

DRILHON, A., J. M. FINE and E. MAGNIN

1961   Etude des proteines seriques d'*Esox lucius* et d'*Esox masquinongy*. [Study of the serum proteins of *Esox lucius* and *Esox masquinongy*] Comptes Rendus Seances de la Societe de Biologie et des ses Filiales 155:451–453.

DRIMMELEN, D. E. VAN

1950   Kunstmatige teelt van snoek en het doorkweken van snoekbroed. Visserijnieuws 2(12)

1969   Northern pike culture, a summary of literature data, results of research of the Organization and experience with culture techniques. Special Report for the Organization for Improvement of Inland Fisheries, Utrecht. 242 pp.

DRYDEN, R. L. and C. S. JESSOP

1974   Impact analysis of the Dempster highway on the physical environment and fish resources of Frog Creek. Environment Canada, Resource Management Branch, Central Region Technical Report CEN/T-74–5:1–59.

The impact of improper culvert design and effects on the hydrology and fish biology of Frog Creek are discussed. Fish migration discharge design, as required by Environment Canada, is defined.

DUBE, J. and Y. GRAVEL

1980   Les grands brochets n'aiment pas l'obscurite des tuyaux. Eau Quebec 13:164–180.

DUBE, J. and Y. GRAVEL, ed.

1979   Proceedings of the 10th warm water workshop. Special Publication, NE Division of the American Fisheries Society. Montreal, Ministere du Loisir, de la Chasse et de la Peche, Direction de la Recherche faunique. 285 pp.

Works of biologists in fields of research and management dealing mainly with management techniques and population dynamics of esocids in North Amer-ica.

DUBRAVIUS, J.

1547   De piscinis ad Antonium Fuggerum. Vratislaviae, Andreas Vinglerus. [Modern edition: Schmidtova, A., ed., in Sbornik Filologicky CSAV 1, Suppl.1(1953):11–45.].

Work actually written in 1525, describes experiences in pond construction, and management and culture of pike.

DUERRE, D. C.

1966a   Statewide fisheries investigations. Tagging studies on five North Dakota impoundments and one natural lake. North Dakota State Game and Fish Department, Dingell-Johnson Report F-2-R-12/Job 9.

1966b   Statewide fisheries investigations. Tagging studies on five North Dakota impoundments and one natural lake. North Dakota State Game and Fish Department, Dingell-Johnson Report F-2-R-13/Job 9.

DUFOUR, D. and D. BARRETTE

1967   Polymorphisme des lipoproteines et des glycoproteines seriques chez la truite. [Polymorphism of serum lipoproteins and glycoproteins in the trout]. Le Naturaliste Canadien 94:305–308. [English summary]

Three serum proteins of pike have antigenic determinants common with the serum protein of rainbow trout *Salmo gairdneri*.

DUKRAVETS, G. M. and Y. A. BIRYUKOV

1976   Ichthyofauna of the Nura River basin in the central Kazakh, USSR. Journal of Ichthyology 16:271–276.

Brief mention of where pike were found.

DULMA, A.

1973   On the fish fauna of Mongolia. Mitteilungen aus dem Zoologischen Museum in Berlin 49:49–67.

DUMONT, P., R. FORTIN and H. FOURNIER

1979   Certain aspects of the reproduction of upper Richelieu and Missisquoi Bay northern pike, *Esox lucius* L. *In* Dube, J., and Y. Gravel, eds., Proceedings 10th Warmwater Workshop, Special Publication NE Division of the American Fisheries Society. Montreal, Quebec Ministere du Loisir, de la Chasse et de la Peche, pp. 231–248.

Studied the relation between spring water levels and 1) spawning ground availability and utilization, 2) egg deposition, hatching and early development, and 3) year class strength.

DUNBAR, M. J. and H. H. HILDEBRAND

1952   Contribution to the study of the fishes of Ungava Bay. Journal of the Fisheries Research Board of Canada 9:83–128.

Gives distribution of pike in northern Canada; occasionally taken in brackish water.

DUNHAM, D. K.

1956   How old is that fish? Wisconsin Conservation Bulletin 21(7):11–13.

DUNNING, D. J., J. T. EVANS and M. J. TARBY

Baseline biological studies preparatory to the assessment of winter naviations: Fisheries data base on the St. Lawrence River. Research Foundation of State University of New York, Project 210–6141.

A study of the fisheries, which included a winter creel survey and an assessment of characteristics of the fish community, concluded that if lowered water levels or increased turbidity resulted from extended winter navigation, fish growth and recruitment might be adversely affected.

DUNNING, D. J., Q. ROSS and J. GLADDEN

1982   Evaluation of minimum size limits for St. Lawrence River northern pike. North American Journal of Fisheries Management 2:171–175.

The imposition of a 660-mm minimum size limit resulted in a greater decline in total population size than that predicted under a 508-mm limit over a 50-year period. A decrease in yield was caused by an increase in the harvest of older females and a subsequent decrease in egg production.

DUNST, R.

1966   Statewide fishery research. Cox Hollow Lake. Annual changes in several parameters of a reservoir fish population. Wisconsin Conservation Department, Dingell-Johnson Report F-083-R-01/Wk.Pl.03/Job B/PT3.

DUNST, R. C.

1969   Cox Hollow Lake. The first eight years of impoundment. Wisconsin Department of Natural Resources, Research Report 47:1–19.

Development of the fishery was studied from 1958 to 1966 in Cox Hollow Lake, a new impoundment in southwestern Wisconsin. The three main species of fish, including pike, showed initial rapid population expansion and superior growth, followed by a tremendous decline in both population size and growth.

DUNSTAN, T. C. and J. F. HARPER

1975   Food habits of bald eagles in north central Minnesota. Journal of Wildlife Management 39:140–143.

DUPLINSKY, P. D.

1982   Sperm motility of northern pike and chain pickerel at various pH values. Transactions of the American Fisheries Society 111:768–771.

Sperm activity was observed at pH 3.9, 4.5, 5.4, 6.0, 6.4, 6.9, 7.4, and 7.9. Pike sperm showed a strong trend towards increased activity time with increasing pH. Minimum motility occurred at pH 5.4 (28 seconds) and maximum motility at pH 7.9 (67 seconds). Substantial variation in sperm motility time between the two pike tested did not occur.

DURAND, J.-P. and J.-M. GAS

1976   Quelques aspects de la reproduction du brochet (*Esox lucius* L., 1766) dans la Seine au niveau de Montereau. Croissance et comportement des alevins, dans diverses conditions experimentales. Memoires ISARA. 108 pp.

D'URBAN, W. S. M.

1859   Observations on the natural history of the valley of the River Rouge, and surrounding townships in the counties of Argenteuill and Ottawa. Canadian National Geologist 4:252–276.

DUSHAUSKENE-DUZH, N. F., G. G. POLIKARPOV and B. I. STYRO

1969   Coefficients of the accumulation of strontium-90 in some fish. Radiobiologiya 9(1):113–115.

DYER, W. J.

1952   Amines in fish muscle. VI. Trimethylamine oxide content of fish and marine invertebrates. Journal of the Fisheries Research Board of Canada 8:314–324.

Original determinations of the trimethylamine oxide content of 60 species of fish, including pike.

DYK, V.
　　n.d.　　Nove smery v umelem chovu stiky. Zvlastni Otisk Ze, Zemedelskeho Archivu 9:31.

DYKOVA, I. and J. LOM
　　1978　　Histopathological changes in fish gills infected with myxosporidian parasites of the genus *Henneguya*. Journal of Fish Biology 12:197–202.
　　　　　　H. psorospermica developed in the artery of pike. Describes infection process from vegetative stage to final stages.

DYMOND, J. R.
　　1922　　A provisional list of the fishes of Lake Erie. University of Toronto Studies in Biology Series 20, Publication of the Ontario Fisheries Research Laboratory 4:55–73.
　　　　　　Reported that pike are still of considerable commercial importance in Lake Erie, although less abundant than formerly.

　　1923　　A provisional list of the fishes of Lake Nipigon. Publication of the Ontario Fisheries Research Laboratory 12:33–38.
　　　　　　Pike were common in small bays along shore and were occasionally taken in fishermen's nets.

　　1926　　The fishes of Lake Nipigon. Publication of the Ontario Fisheries Research Laboratory 27:1–108.
　　　　　　A description of the pike, and brief information on its distribution.

　　1936　　Some fresh-water fishes of British Columbia. Royal Ontario Museum of Zoology, Contribution 9:60–73.
　　　　　　Reported that pike were native to the waters of the northern British Columbia tributary to the Arctic Ocean, but not found in the waters of the northern British Columbia tributary to the Pacific Ocean.

　　1937　　New records of Ontario fishes. Copeia 1937:59.
　　　　　　Reported pike from the Moose River, 1 mile above Moosonee.

　　1939　　The fishes of the Ottawa region. Royal Ontario Museum of Zoology, Contribution 15:1–43.
　　　　　　Described the ecological conditions and geological history of the region with a short note on distribution and commercial importance of pike. Catch in pounds is listed by year and area.

　　1947　　A list of the freshwater fishes of Canada east of the Rocky Mountains with keys. Royal Ontario Museum of Zoology, Miscellaneous Publication 1:1–36.
　　　　　　Reports that pike were found from Labrador to the Yukon south to northern British Columbia and the Great Lakes, also in northern Asia and Europe. Found in lakes as well as in quiet, weedy ponds and streams.

　　1964　　A history of ichthyology in Canada. Copeia 1964:2–33.
　　　　　　A brief review of the range of pike and of published descriptions of hybrids.

DYMOND, J. R. and J. L. HART
　　1927　　The fishes of Lake Abitibi (Ontario) and adjacent waters. Publication of the Ontario Fisheries Research Laboratory 28:1–19.
　　　　　　Pike is one of the commonest species of the lake and is of commercial importance.

DYMOND, J. R., J. L. HART and A. L. PRITCHARD
　　1929　　The fishes of the Canadian waters of Lake Ontario. University of Toronto Studies in Biology Series 33, Publication of the Ontario Fisheries Research Laboratory 37:1–35.

Information on distribution and commercial catch.

DYMOND, J. R. and W. B. SCOTT

1941   Fishes of Patricia portion of the Kenora district, Ontario. Copeia 1941:244.
         Pike were very common in suitable lakes throughout the area.

DZHUMALIYEV, M. K.

1977   The morphology and trophic characteristics of the swim bladder in some ord-
         ers of fish. Journal of Ichthyology 17:284–292.

DZIEKONSKA, J.

1954   Charakter zywienia sie doroslego szczupaka (*Esox lucius* L.), okonia (*Perca
         fluviatilis* L.) i sandacza (*Lucioperca lucioperca* L.) w jeziorach. [The feed-
         ing characteristics of a mature pike (*Esox lucius* L.), perch (*Perca fluviatilis*
         L.) and perch-pike (*Lucioperca lucioperca* L.) in lakes]. Polskie Archiwum
         Hydrobiologii 2:165–183.

EALES, J. G.

1969   A comparative study of purines responsible for silvering in several freshwater fishes. Journal of the Fisheries Research Board of Canada 26:1939–1942.

The major purines occurring in silvery deposition were analysed by paper chromatography and ultraviolet-spectrophotometry.

EATON, J. G., J. M. MCKIM and G. W. HOLCOMBE

1978   Metal toxicity to embryos and larvae of seven freshwater fish species. I. Cadmium. Bulletin of Environmental Contamination and Toxicology 19:95–103.

All species were killed or their growth retarded by concentrations ranging from about 4 to 12 ug Cd/liter. The larvae were consistently more sensitive than the embryos.

ECKROAT, L. R.

1969   Genetic analysis in brook trout (*Salvelinus fontinalis* Mitchill) plus some interspecific comparisons of lens proteins of Salmonidae and Esocidae. Ph.D. thesis, Pennsylvania State University.

Lens protein patterns of species of Esocidae and Salmonidae were compared by acrylamide gel and starch gel electrophoresis to assess lens proteins as a method of taxonomic comparisons.

1974   Interspecific comparisons of lens proteins of Esocidae. Copeia 1974: 977–978.

Comparison of the six species of Esocidae using acrylamide gel and starch gel electrophoresis indicated that the patterns produced by *Esox lucius, E. masquinongy, E. reicherti* were practically identical.

ECOLE, R. A.

1979   Recherches sur les etangs. Contribution a l'etude du brochet (*Esox lucius* L. 1758). Croissance et populations. [Research on ponds. Contribution to the study of pike (*Esox lucius* L. 1758). Growth and population]. Rennis, Institute Nationale de la Recherche Agronomique, Ecologie Hydrobiologique.

ECONOMON, P.

1960   Furunculosis in northern pike. Transactions of the American Fisheries Society 89:240.

Describes lesions on two pike found dead in a spawning pond.

EDDY, S.

1938   Classification of Minnesota lakes for fish propagation. Progressive Fish-Culturist 41:9–13.

Describes two typical pike lakes and one typical pike and bass lake. Lakes were classified by determining physical conditions, area of each bottom type within certain depths, temperature, oxygen, carbon dioxide, carbonates, total dissolved solids, and minerals.

1941a   Muskellunge and muskie hybrids. Minnesota Conservation Volunteer 3(14):41–44.

1941b   Do muskellunge and pickerel interbreed. Progressive Fish-Culturist 48:25–27.

Compares scalation on the check of pike with that of muskellunge and pickerel.

1944   Hybridization between northern pike (*Esox lucius*) and muskellunge (*Esox masquinongy*). Proceedings of the Minnesota Academy of Science 12:38–43.

1954   Pike—or pickerel? Minnesota Conservation Volunteer 17(99):1–8.

1957 How to know the freshwater fishes. Dubuque, Wm. C. Brown. 253 pp.

EDDY, S. and K. CARLANDER

1939 Growth of Minnesota fishes. Minnesota Conservation Volunteer 69:8–10.

1942 Growth rate studies of Minnesota fish. Minnesota Department of Conservation, Bureau of Fisheries Research, Investigational Report 28:1–64.

EDDY, S. and K. D. CARLANDER

1939 The growth rate of wall-eye pike (*Stizostedion vitreum* (Mitchill)) in various lakes of Minnesota. Proceedings of the Minnesota Academy of Science 7:44–48.

1940 The effect of environmental factors upon the growth rates of Minnesota fishes. Proceedings of the Minnesota Academy of Science 8:14–19.

EDDY, S. and T. SURBER

1943 Northern fishes. Minneapolis, University of Minnesota Press. 276 pp.
Contains first description of mutant pike.

1947 Northern fishes with special reference to the upper Mississippi Valley. 2nd ed. Minneapolis, University of Minnesota Press. 276 pp.
Key to family, family discussion, species discussion of pike, and silver pike illustrated.

1960 Northern fishes with special reference to the upper Mississippi Valley. Rev. ed. Newton Centre, Massachusetts, C. T. Brantford. 276 pp.

EDDY, S., R. C. TASKER and J. C. UNDERHILL

1972 Fishes of the Red River, Rainy River, and Lake of the Woods, Minnesota, with comments on the distribution of species in the Nelson River drainage. Bell Museum of Natural History, University of Minnesota, Occasional Papers 11:1–24.
Brief description of distribution.

EDDY, S. and J. C. UNDERHILL

1974 Northern fishes. Minneapolis, University of Minnesota Press. 414 pp.

1978 How to know the freshwater fishes. 3rd ed. The Pictured Key Nature Series, Wm. C. Brown. 215 pp.

EGERMAN, F. F.

1936 Material on the ichthyofauna of the Kuchurgan Liman (Dniester River Basin) collected in 1922–1925. Tr. Chern. Azv. Nauchn-Prom. 2:1–88. [in Russian]

EGGELING, H. VON

1908 Dunndarmerelief und Ernahrung bei Knockenfischen. Zeitschrift fuer Naturwissenschaftlich 43:486–488.

EGGERS, J.

1983 67 lbs 3 oz! The pike of the century? Coarse Angler.

1984 Russen in Amerika. [Russians in America]. Voor en door de Visser 19(12):16–19. [in Dutch]

EIGENMANN, C. H.

1894 Results of explorations in western Canada and the northwestern United States. Bulletin of the U.S. Fish Commissioner 14(1895):101–132.

EINSELE, E.

1964 Uber die Wirkung von Unterwassersprengungen auf Fische und Fischbestande. Osterreichische Fischerei 17:121–132.

EINSELE, W.

1952   Zur Frage der Abhangigkeit des Laichreifeeintrittes und der Laichablage bei Fischen von Wassertemperatur und Witterung. Osterreichische Fischerei 5.

1958   Biotechnische Hinweise zur Frage der Erbrutung Hechten und zur Frage des Transportes und Aussetzens von Hechtsezlingen. Osterreichische Fischerei 11.

EISLER, R.

1957   Some effects of artificial light on salmon eggs and larvae. Transactions of the American Fisheries Society 87:151–162.
        Cites work of Haempel and Lechler (1931) who found that eggs of pike were especially sensitive to light and easily destroyed.

EKBAUM, E.

1937   On the maturation and the hatching of the eggs of the cestode *Triaenophorus crassus* Forel from Canadian fish. Journal of Parasitology 23:293–295.
        Observations of *T. crassus* taken from pike at several localities in Ontario and Manitoba at various times of the year.

EKSTROM, V. C.

1835   Die Fische in dem Scheeren von Morko; aus dem Schwedischen ubersetzt und mit einigen Anmerkungen versechen von Dr. F. C. H. Creplin, Berlin. 269 pp.

EL-BASTAVIZI, A. M. and G. A. SMIRNOVA

1972   Change in the phospholipids of frozen pike during storage. Fishing Industry 3:57–59.

ELKINS, W. A.

1937   A fish yield study for certain lakes in the Chequamegon National Forest. Transactions of the American Fisheries Society 66:306–312.
        Brief information on distribution, angling, size.

ELLIS, J. E. and E. N. PICKERING

1973   The catching efficiencies of a 21.3-meter (headrope) standard wing trawl and a 21.3-meter electrical wing trawl in the Saginaw Bay area of Lake Huron. Transactions of the American Fisheries Society 102:116–120.
        Gives number and size of pike captured by both methods.

ELROD, J. H. and T. J. HASSLER

1969   Estimates of some vital statistics of northern pike, walleye, and sauger populations in Lake Sharpe, South Dakota. Bureau of Sport Fisheries and Wildlife, Technical Paper 30:1–17.

ELSER, H. J.

1961   Record Maryland fish. Maryland Conservationist 38(2):15–17.

ELSTER, H.-J. and H. MANN

1950   Experimentelle Beitrage zur Kenntnis der Physiologie der Befruchtung bei fischen. Archiv fuer Fischereiwissenschaft 2:49–73.

EMBODY, G. C.

1910   The ecology, habits and growth of the pike, *Esox lucius*. Ph.D. thesis, Cornell University, 84 pp.

1915   The farm fishpond. Cornell Reading Courses, Country Life Ser. 3:213–252.

1918   Artificial hybrids between pike and pickerel. Journal of Heredity 9:253–256.

ENDRES, A.

1969   Un vivier naturel dans une anse de la Marne en aval de Meaux. Les marais de Lesches. Bulletin philologique et historique (jusqu'a 1610) de comites travaux historiques et scientifiques 1:184–204.

Pike spawning habitat is described. The history of the spawning areas is detailed, including conflicts over water use and local poaching. In the 1960's continued fishing and poaching life of the area was threatened by the establishment of a pike hatchery to supply fry to regional fish pond operations, the plan to dam the river for a recreational lake, the increase in pollutants from the upper Marne, and the plan to dam it for a recreational lake.

ENGASHEV, V. G.
   1965   Seasonal dynamics of the invasion of pikes by the nematode *Raphidascaris acus*. Trudy Uzbekskogo nauchno-Issledovatel'skogo Instituta Veterinarii 16:199–202. [in Russian]

ENGELBRECHT, H.
   1958   Untersuchungen uber den Parasitenbefall der Nutzfische im Greifswalder Bodden und Kleinen Haff. [Investigations on the occurrence of parasites in commercial fishes in the Griefswalder Bodden and the Kleine Haff]. Zeitschrift fuer Fischerei und deren Hilfswissenschaften 7:481–511.

EPLER, P. and K. BIENIARZ
   1978   Breeding fish oocytes in vitro as a method for investigating the hormonal mechanism of their reproduction. Roczniki Nauk Rolniczyck, Ser. H, Rybactwo 98:175–193.

ERGENS, R.
   1964   Vysledky vyzkumu zdravotniho stavu stiky (*Esox lucius*) v Lipenske udolni nadrzi. Zprava CSAV, pp. 1–27.

   1966   Results of parasitological investigations on the health of *Esox lucius* L. in Lipno reservoir. Folia Parasitologica 13:222–236.

   1971   The species of the genus *Tetraonchus* Diesing, 1858 (Monogenoida) recovered from fishes of Mongolia. Folia Parasitologica 18:139–148. [in Czechoslovakian]

ERICKSON, G.
   1978   In pursuit of lunker northerns. Fins and Feathers Fishing Annual, 1978:20–24.

ERIKSON, G.
   1978   The search for the elusive northern. Fins and Feathers, May 1978.

ERIKSSON, L.-O. and S. ULVELAND
   1977   Long-term telemetric system for gill strokes of fish. Aquilo Ser Zoologica 17:61–64.

The system is based on ultrasonic transmission and allows continuous measurement of opercular rate of free-swimming fish kept in tanks or ponds for periods of up to one year.

ERLINGE, S.
   1968   Food studies on captive otters *Lutra lutra* L. Oikos 19:259–270.

The food habits of otters in the field are discussed in the light of feeding experiments carried out on captive otters.

   1969   Food habits of the otter *Lutra lutra* L. and the mink *Mustela vison* Schreber in a trout water in southern Sweden. Oikos 20:1–7.

The differences in food habits were primarily due to different adaptations of the two predators but to some extent to competition.

ESCHMEYER, R. W.

 1935 Analysis of the game-fish catch in a Michigan lake. Transactions of the American Fisheries Society 65:207–223.

 1936 A second season of creel census on Fife Lake. Transactions of the American Fisheries Society 66:324–334.

    Catch statistics given include size, number, catch per hour, weather conditions, comparison of winter fishing.

 1938 Summary of a four year creel census on Fife Lake, Michigan. Transactions of the American Fisheries Society 68:354–358.

ESLAMI, A. H., M. ANWAR and S. KHATIBY

 1972 Incidence and intensity of helminthoses in pike (*Esox lucius*) of Caspian Sea (Northern Iran). Riv. It. Piscis. Ittiop. 7:11–13.

    Three species of helminths were found in 78.9% of the 109 pike examined; one in the body cavity, and two in the alimentary canal.

EUROPEAN INLAND FISHERIES ADVISORY COMMITTEE

 1968 Report on extreme pH values and inland fisheries. European Inland Fisheries Advisory Committee Working Party on Water Quality Criteria for European Freshwater Fish, Technical Paper 4:1–24.

EVANS, H.

 1966 River authorities and freshwater fishery research. *In* Jones, J. W., and P. H. Tombleson, eds. Proceedings of the 2nd British Coarse Fish Conference, Liverpool, 1965, pp. 111–114.

EVERHART, W. H.

 1950 Fishes of Maine. Maine Department of Inland Fisheries and Game. 53 pp.

EVERMANN, B. W.

 1898 Key to the species of *Lucius*. Recreation 9:207.

 1902 Pike, pickerel, mascalonge. Forest and Stream 59:193.

    An attempt to correct misconceptions that might have arisen as a result of previous articles. Includes a key for identification of the species.

 1905 Report on inquiry respecting food-fishes and fishing grounds. Report of the U.S. Commissioner of Fisheries for 1904, pp. 81–162.

 1916 The fishes of Kentucky and Tennessee: a distributional catalogue of the known species. Bulletin of the Bureau of Fisheries 35(858):295–368.

EVERMANN, B. W. and E. L. GOLDSBOROUGH

 1901 Notes on the fishes and mollusks of Lake Chautauqua, New York. New York Forest, Fish, and Game Commission, 6th Annual Report (1900), pp. 357–366.

 1902 Notes on the fishes and mollusks of Lake Chautauqua, New York. Report of the U.S. Commissioner of Fish and Fisheries 27:169–176.

 1907a The fishes of Alaska. U.S. Bureau of Fisheries, Document 624:1–360.

 1907b A checklist of the freshwater fishes of Canada. Proceedings of the Biological Society of Washington 20:89–120.

    Under each species is given all the Canadian localities from which it has been recorded, together with references to the publications in which such records were made.

EVERMANN, B. W. and W. C. KENDALL

 1896 An annotated list of the fishes known from the state of Vermont. Report of the U.S. Fish Commissioner for 1894, pp. 579–604.

 1902a Notes on the fishes of Lake Ontario. Report of the U.S. Commissioner of Fish and Fisheries for 1901, pp. 209–216.

1902b   An annotated list of the fishes known to occur in Lake Champlain and its tri-
            butary waters. Report of the U.S. Commissioner of Fish and Fisheries for
            1901, pp. 217–225.

1902c   An annotated list of the fishes known to occur in the St. Lawrence River.
            Report of the U.S. Commissioner of Fish and Fisheries for 1901, pp.
            227–240.

EVSIN, V. N.

1969   The pike of lakes Knent, Yavr. Doklady Otdelov i Komissii
            Geograficheskogo Obshchestv SSSR 9:138–148.

FABRI, Z. J.

1984   Activity pattern of the thyroid gland and distribution of its hormones in tissues of fishes characterized by different ecology. Voprosy Ikhtiologii 24:340–343.

Regularities in iodine and thyroid homeostasis have been revealed in pike. The highest contents of total and hormonal iodine were found in the tissues of pike. Maximum iodine concentrations were recorded in the liver, kidneys, spleen and blood, and minimum values in the cerebrum.

FABRICIUS, E.

1950   Heterogeneous stimulus summation in the release of spawning activities in fish. Report Institute of Freshwater Research Drottningholm 31:57–99.

Discusses some phenomena that help explain the relationship between time of spawning and water temperature.

FABRICIUS, E. and K.-J. GUSTAFSON

1958   Some new observations on the spawning behaviour of the pike, *Esox lucius* L. Report Institute of Freshwater Research Drottningholm 39:23–54.

Spawning activities viewed in the field and in aquaria were recorded on film. Slow motion pictures were analysed to provide a detailed account of the spawning act. Aggressive behaviour, courtship, and responses from ripe and unripe females were observed.

1959   Gaddans och abborrens lekbeteende. Svensk Fiskeri Tidskrift 68:6–13.

FAGERSTROM, T., B. ASELL and A. JERNELOV

1974   Model for accumulation of methyl mercury in northern pike *Esox lucius*. Oikos 25:14–20.

The correspondence between the calculated concentration of methyl mercury in lateral muscle tissue and empirically observed values is acceptable though the calculated values in the lower weight range are somewhat high.

FAGERSTROM, T., R. KURTEN and B. ASELL

1975   Statistical parameters as criteria in model evaluation: kinetics of mercury accumulation in pike *Esox lucius*. Oikos 26:109–116.

Analysed mercury accumulation by means of computer simulations. Showed that patterns of temporal variations of processes at the individual level were reflected in statistical parameters at the population level.

FAGO, D.

1971a   Statewide fishery research. Factors influencing success of northern pike production in managed spawning and rearing marshes. Wisconsin Division of Forestry, Wildlife, and Recreation, Project F-83-R-6:1–15.

Gives production of fingerlings from stocked pike in two Wisconsin marshes. Fingerlings from one marsh were tagged and released. Also, two lakes were stocked with fingerlings.

1971b   Statewide fishery research. Factors influencing success of northern pike production in managed spawning and rearing areas. Wisconsin Conservation Department, Project F-83-R-7:1–3.

The Pleasant Lake managed spawning marsh produced 1,218 fingerlings in 1970 from previously stocked pike. The fingerlings were tagged and released into the lake.

1973   The northern's finicky spawning needs. Wisconsin Conservation Bulletin 38(2):18–19.

1983   Distribution and relative abundance of fishes in Wisconsin. Black, Trempealeau, and Buffalo river basins. Wisconsin Department of Natural Resources, Technical Bulletin 140:1–120.

1985   Distribution and relative abundance of fishes in Wisconsin. V. Grant and Platte, Coon and Bad Axe, and LaCrosse river basins. Wisconsin Department of Natural Resources, Technical Bulletin 152:1–112.

Includes numerous tables, distribution maps of the species, and discussion of many aspects of fish distribution in the three basins.

FAGO, D. M.

1977   Northern pike production in managed spawning and rearing marshes. Wisconsin Department of Natural Resources, Technical Bulletin 96:1–30.

Two marshes were stocked with spawning pike to determine factors that influence production. Average length, weight, fecundity, stocking rate, and ratio of the fish are provided. Influential factors were spawning stock, aquatic vegetation, egg survival, food supply, and physical and chemical factors. A Fortran program was developed to analyse stomach contents, zooplankton, and benthic samples.

FALCON, J.

1979a   L'organe pineal du brochet (*Esox lucius* L.). I. Etude anatomique et cytoloogique. [The pineal organ of the pike, *Esox lucius* L. I. A light and electron microscopic study.] Annales de Biologie Animale Biochimie Biophysique 19:445–465.

Detailed description of the pineal organ with some discussion as to the possible functions of specific components.

1979b   The pineal organ of the pike, *Esox lucius* L. II. An electron microscopic study of photoreceptor cell differentiation and regression and variations of the photoreceptive potential in different pineal regions. Annales de Biologie Animale Biochimie Biophysique 19:661–688.

FALCON, J., M. T. JUILLARD and J. P. COLLIN

1980a   The pineal organ of the pike *Esox lucius*. 4. Endogenous serotonin and mono amine oxidase activity of a histochemical ultracytochemical and pharmacological study. Reproduction Nutrition Developpement 20:139–154.

1980b   The pineal organ of the pike *Esox lucius*. 5. Radioautographic study of in vivo and in vitro incorporation of indoleaminergic precursors. Reproduction Nutrition Developpement 20:991–1010.

FALCON, J. and H. MEISSL

1980   Structure and function of the pineal organ of the pike *Esox lucius*. Pfluegers Archiv European Journal of Physiology 384 (Suppl.).

1981   The photosensory function of the pineal organ of the pike *Esox lucius*; correlation between structure and function. Journal of Comparative Physiology, A, Sensory Neural and Behavioral Physiology, 144:127–138.

FALCON, J. and J. P. MOCQUARD

1979   The pineal organ of the pike (*Esox lucius* L.). III. Intrapineal pathways for conduction of photosensory messages. Annales de Biologie Animale Biochimie Biophysique 14:1043–1062.

FALCONER, H.

1868   Miscellaneous notes on Indian zoology. II. Note on an Indian species of *Esox*. *In* Murcheson, C., ed., Palaeontological memoirs and notes of the late Hugh Falconer, vol. 1:589–590.

FALK, M. R. and L. W. DAHLKE

1974   Data on the lake and round whitefish, lake cisco, northern pike and Arctic grayling from Great Bear Lake, N.W.T. Canada Department of the Environment, Data Report CEN/D-74–1:1–52.

Creel census program was conducted from 1971 to 1973. Data and summaries on length, weight, age, growth, sex, and maturity of pike are presented.

FALK, M. R. and D. V. GILLMAN

1975a   Mortality data for angled Arctic grayling and northern pike from the Great Slave Lake area, Northwest Territories. Canada Department of the Environment, Data Report Series CEN/D-75–1:1–24.

Results of this study provide data on which possible regulation changes such as mandatory barbless hooks, fly-fishing only restriction, or minimum size limits may be based.

1975b   Data on the lake and round whitefish, lake cisco, northern pike, Arctic grayling and longnose sucker from the east arm of Great Slave Lake, N.W.T., 1971–74. Canada Department of the Environment, Data Report Series CEN/D-75–2:1–95.

Data on length, weight, age, growth, sex, and maturity are summarized in tabular and graphical form.

1980   Status of the Arctic grayling and northern pike sport fisheries in the Brabant Island-Beaver Lake area of the Mackenzie River, Northwest Territories. Canadian Manuscript Report of Fisheries and Aquatic Sciences 1553:53.

FALK, M. R., D. V. GILLMAN and L. W. DAHLKE

1974   1973 creel census data from sport fishing lodges on Great Bear and Great Slave Lake, Northwest Territories. Canada Department of the Environment Data Report Series CEN/D-74–5:1–28.

Data on numbers of fish caught, released, and retained, and average weight. Maps show areas fished.

FALKUS, H. and F. BULLER

1975   Falkus & Buller's freshwater fishing. London, MacDonald & James.

FARABEE, G. B.

1970   Factors influencing the vulnerability of largemouth bass to angling and the comparative learning ability of selected fishes. M.A. thesis, University of Missouri. 94 pp.

Selected species, including pike, differed in degree of development of a conditioned response.

FARRAN, G. P.

1946   Local Irish names of fishes. Irish Naturalists' Journal 8:9–12.

FAUBERT, N., M. DUBREUIL, L.-R. SEGUIN and D. ROY

1979   Propagation du grand brochet, *Esox lucius* L., au futur reservoir de LG 2, Baie James avec ou sans amenagement approprie. [Propagation of northern pike, *Esox lucius* L., in a future reservoir LG 2, James Bay, with or without appropriate management] *In* Dube, J., and Y. Gravel, eds., Proceedings 10th Warmwater Workshop, Montreal, 1977. Special Publication NE Division of the American Fisheries Society, Quebec Ministere du Loisir, de la Chasse et de la Peche, pp. 219–230.

A program to study repercussions on activity of fish made by the future dam and reservoir will determine whether existing populations of pike are adequate to ensure natural propagation. A description of the reservoir is given, with growth rates and activity patterns that may be expected of the pike when the reservoir is filled.

FEDAK, V. S., A. P. KOVAL and V. F. PROKOPENKO

1973   Die Messung der Schleimschicht bei Fischen. Gidrobiologicheskii Zhurnal 9(4):100–102. [in Russian].

FEDIN, S. P.

1958   Znachenie shchuki v bor'be s malotsennoi i sornoi rybol. [The importance of the pike in the struggle with inferior and mud fish]. Rybnoe Khoziaistvo 3:25–27.

       Information on distribution, sexual maturity, spawning, growth rate, food, and interaction with mud fish.

FEDYAKHINA, R. F.

1980   Biology of pike from Lake Lacha. Voprosy Ikhtiologii 20:59–64.

FELDT, W. and M. MELTZER

1978   Concentration factors of the elements cobalt, manganese, iron, zinc and silver for fish. Archiv fuer Fischereiwissenschaft 29(1–2):105.

FELLEGY, J.

1975   Interview with the Kiels: big northern specialists. Fins and Feathers January 1975.

FERGUSON, A. and F. M. MASON

1981   Allozyme evidence for reproductively isolated sympatric populations of brown trout *Salmo trutta* in Lough Melvin, Ireland. Journal of Fish Biology 18:629–642.

FERNANDEZ ROMAN, E.

1982   El lucio en Europa. Caza y Pesca 477:612–614.

       This popular article summarizes the angling of pike in several European countries and records of the bigger examples caught.

FERREIRA, J. T., H. J. SCHOOBEE and G. L. SMIT

1984   The anaesthetic potency of benzocaine-hydrochloride in three freshwater fish species. South African Journal of Zoology 19:46.

FETTERROLF, C. M., Jr.

1952   A population study of the fishes of Wintergreen Lake, Kalamazoo County, Michigan; with notes on movement and effect of netting on condition. M.S. thesis, Michigan State College. 127 pp.

FICKLING, N.

1982a   Pike fishing in the 80's. Enfield, England, Beekay. 222 pp.

1982b   The identification of pike by means of characteristic marks. Fisheries Management 13:79–82.

       The markings of pike were found to be specific to individual fish. The subsequent recapture of pike after two years of growth indicated that the markings could be used for the positive identification of specific pike.

FIEBIGER, J.

1927   Zur hechtenseuche im Worthersee. Osterreichische Fischerei-Zeitung 24.

FILATOV, D. P.

1935   Udalenie i peresodka zachatka glaza u embriona shchuki. Arkhiv for Anatomii, Gistologii, i Embriologii 14:45–50, 116–121.

FILIPSSON, O.

    1966   Gaddexplosition i nydamt kraft-verksmagasin. Svensk Fiskeri Tidskrift 75:142–143.

    1972   Sotvattenslaboratoriets provfiske- och provtagningsmetoder. Information fran Sotvattenslaboratoriet, Drottningholm 16:1–24.
            Use of metapterygoid for aging.

FILOSOFOVA-LYZLOVA, E. M.

    1972   Isoenzymes of aspartate and alanine amino transferase of somatic muscles of some lower vertebrates. Biochemistry 37(3, part 1):408–413.

FIMREITE, N. and L. M. REYNOLDS

    1973   Mercury contamination of fish in northwestern Ontario. Journal of Wildlife Management 37:62–68.
            Mercury levels were determined in lateral musculature of fish taken upstream and downstream from a chlorine plant and from lakes not contaminated from any known source. Maximum levels in pike were 27.8, 50–60 miles downstream from the plant.

FINNELL, L.

    1984   Statewide fish research. Northern pike studies. Northern pike life history and competition with salmonids. Colorado Division of Wildlife, Job Progress Report F-34:1–20.

    1985   Statewide fish research. Northern pike studies. Northern pike life history and competition with salmonids. Colorado Division of Wildlife, Job Final Report F-34:1–65.

FINNELL, L. M.

    1983   Statewide fish research. Northern pike studies. Colorado Divison of Wildlife, Job Progress Report F-34:1–29.

FISCHTHAL, J. H.

    1947   Parasites of northwest Wisconsin fishes. 1. The 1944 survey. Transactions of the Wisconsin Academy of Science 37:157–220.

    1950   Parasites of northwest Wisconsin fishes. 2. The 1945 survey. Transactions of the Wisconsin Academy of Science 40:87–113.

    1952   Parasites of northwest Wisconsin fishes. 3. The 1946 survey. Transactions of the Wisconsin Academy of Science 41:17–58.

FISH, M. P.

    1932   Contributions to the early life histories of sixty-two species of fishes from Lake Erie and its tributary waters. U.S. Department of Commerce, Bureau of Fisheries, Bulletin 47:293–398.

FITZMAURICE, P.

    1978   Resume of pike research in Irish waters and scientific data related to pike angling. Report of the Pike Committee to Bord Failte Eireann, April 30, 1978. Appendix IV. Irish Tourist Board - Bord Failte.

    1983   Some aspects of the biology and management of pike (*Esox lucius* L.) stocks in Irish fisheries. Journal of Life Science pp. 161–173.

FITZPATRICK, D. A. and K. F. MCGEENEY

    1975   Comparative immunology of vertebrate urate oxidase EC-1.7.3.3. Comparative Biochemistry and Physiology, B, Comparative Biochemistry 51:37–40.

FLEGEL, E.

    1965   Hechtsufzucht. Deutscher Angelsport 17:194–195.

FLEROVA, G. I., V. I. MARTEM'YANOV and R. A. ZAPRUDNOVA

1980   Electrolyte content in the blood serum of fresh water fishes. Biologicheskie Nauki 3:46–51.

FLICK, W. A.

1977   Some observations on age, growth, food habits, and vulnerability of large brook brout *Salvelinus fontinalis* from four Canadian lakes. Le Naturaliste Canadien 104:353–360.

FLICKINGER, S. A. and J. H. CLARK

1978   Management evaluation of stocked northern pike in Colorado's small irrigation reservoirs. American Fisheries Society Special Publication 11:284–291. Pike of 50 mm and 377 mm were stocked into several small irrigation reservoirs. Out of 18 introductions of 50-mm pike and 4 of 377-mm pike, 2 and 4 respectively resulted in populations of a density that would attract fishermen.

FLOURENS, P.

1957   Recherches experimentales sur les proprietes et les fonctions du systeme dans les animaux vertebres. *In* Brown, M. E., ed. The physiology of fishes. New York, Academic Press, vol. 2, p. 43.

FOCANT, B. and F. HURIAUX

1976   Light chains of carp and pike skeletal muscle myosins. Isolation and characterization of the most anodic light chain on alkaline pH electrophoresis. FEBS (Federation of European Biochemical Societies) Letters 65:16–19. This work dealt with 1) isolation of a light chain, the fast-moving component in alkaline urea gel, and 2) their characterization by molecular weight determination, ultraviolet absorption, and amino acid analysis.

FOCANT, B., F. HURIAUX and I. A. JOHNSTON

1976   Subunit composition of fish myofibrils: The light chains of myosin. International Journal of Biochemistry 7:129.

FOGLE, N. E.

1961   Report of fisheries investigations during the second year of impoundment of Oahe Reservoir, South Dakota, 1959. South Dakota Department of Game, Fish and Parks, Dingell-Johnson Project F-1-R-9(Jobs 12–14):1–43.

1963a   Report of fisheries investigations during the fourth year of impoundment of Oahe Reservoir, South Dakota, 1961. South Dakota Department of Game, Fish and Parks, Dingell-Johnson Project F-1-R-11(Jobs 10–12):1–43.

1963b   Report of fisheries investigations during the fourth year of impoundment of Oahe Reservoir, South Dakota, 1962. [The title is "fourth year", but the report apparently refers to the fifth year of impoundment.] South Dakota Department of Game, Fish and Parks, Dingell-Johnson Project F-1-R-12(Jobs 10–12):1–43.

1965   Report of fisheries investigations during the third year of impoundment of Oahe Reservoir, South Dakota, 1960. South Dakota Department of Game, Fish and Parks, Dingell-Johnson Project F-1-R-10(Jobs 9–12):1–57.

FOLEY, J. O.

1925   The spermatogenesis of *Umbra limi* with special reference to the behavior of the spermatogonial chromosomes and the first maturation division. Ph.D. thesis, University of Wisconsin.

FOOD AND AGRICULTURE ORGANIZATION OF THE UNITED NATIONS

1959   Current bibliography for aquatic sciences and fisheries. Rome, Biology Branch, Fisheries Division.

1977   Yearbook fisheries statistics; catches and landings, 1976. Rome, Food and Agriculture Organization of the United Nations, vol. 42.

1981   Report of the 11th session of the European Inland Fisheries Advisory Commission. Stavanger, Norway, May 28-June 3, 1980. Food and Agriculture Organization of the United Nations, Fisheries Report 248:1–56.

FORBES, S. A.

1878   The food of illinois fishes. Illinois State Laboratory of Natural History 1(2):71–87.

1888   Notes on the food of the fishes of the Mississippi Valley. Transactions of the American Fisheries Society 17:37–66.

Pike are almost wholly piscivorous, only a single specimen out of the 37 examined having taken dragonflies; 20 had taken gizzard shad *Dorosoma cepedianum*, which made nearly half of the food of the entire group.

1890   Studies of the food of freshwater fishes. Illinois Laboratory of Natural History 2.

FORBES, S. A. and R. E. RICHARDSON

1908   The fishes of Illinois. *In* Natural history survey of Illinois, State Laboratory of Natural History, pp. 205–209.

1920   The fishes of Illinois. 2nd ed. State Department of Registration and Education, Division of Natural History Survey. 357 pp.

Gives world-wide distribution.

FORELLE, F.

1857   On the classification of fishes. With particular reference to the fishes of Canada. Article 43. *In* Billings, E., ed., The Canadian naturalist and geologist, Montreal, J. Lovell, vol. 1, pp. 275–283.

FORNEY, J. L.

1967   Utility of a small spawning impoundment for increasing northern pike production. New York State Division of Fish and Game, Project F-17-R-11/Wk.Pl.02/JobA:1–3.

Upstream migrating pike were captured in a trap net during the spawning runs in 1964–66. Adults were transferred to the impoundment, and spawned in early April. Fewer young were produced in 1966 than in 1964 or 1965, but the average size was larger. Yield in weight was 49.4 lb in 1964, 23.5 lb in 1965, and 44.2 lb in 1966.

1968   Production of young northern pike in a regulated marsh. New York Fish and Game Journal 15:143–154.

From 1964 to 1967 the production and survival of young pike were studied in an experimental marsh on Oneida Lake. Recoveries during subsequent spawning runs suggested that few pike survived that were less than 65 mm long when they left the marsh.

1977   Evidence of inter- and intraspecific competition as factors regulating walleye (*Stizostedion vitreum vitreum*) biomass in Oneida Lake, New York. Journal of the Fisheries Research Board of Canada 34:1812–1820.

Reviews the events that led to the decline of the pike population. Reduction of wetlands, canalization, and less identifiable cultural changes nearly eliminated the American eel *Anguilla rostrata* and esocids, while the walleye *Stizostedion vitreum* population flourished, possibly due to reduced interspecific competition.

FORTIN, P.

1864   Continuation of the list of fish of the Gulf and River St. Lawrence. *In* Annual report of Pierre Fortin, Esq., commanding the expedition for the protection of the fisheries in the Gulf of St. Lawrence during the season of 1863, pp. 60–72.

FORTIN, R., P. DUMONT and H. FOURNIER

1983   La reproduction du grand brochet (*Esox lucius* L.) dans certains plans d'eau du sud du Quebec. *In* Billard, R., ed., Le brochet gestion dans le milieu naturel et elevage. Paris, Institute National de la Recherche Agronomique, pp. 39–51.

        Spawning activity, egg deposition, and growth of young-of-the-year were studied in relation to water temperatures and water levels.

FORTIN, R., P. DUMONT, H. FOURNIER, C. CADIEUX and D. VILLENEUVE

1982   Reproduction et force des classes d'age du Grand Brochet (*Esox lucius* L.) dans le Haut-Richelieu et la baie Missisquoi. Canadian Journal of Zoology 60:227–240.

        Pike were caught on the spawning grounds in April 1975–78; habitat, water depth, and temperature are described. Water temperature influenced the length of spawning and incubation periods. Factors that may determine year class strength are discussed.

FORTUNATOVA, K. R.

1955   Metodika izucenia pitania khishchykh ryb. [Methods of studying the feeding of predatory fishes]. Trudy Soveshchanii Ikhtiologicheskoi Komissii Akademii Nauk SSSR 6:62–84.

FORTUNATOVA, K. R. and O. A. POPOVA

1973   Pitanie i pishchev'ie vzaimootnoshenniia khishchnykh ryb v del'te Volgi. [The interrelation of nutrition and food in predatory fish in the Volga Delta.] Moscow, Publishing House "Science". 298 pp.

FOURNIER, H.

1980   Quelques aspects de la biologie du grand brochet (*Esox lucius* L.) dans une portion de la riviere Richelieu comprise entre la frontiere canado-americaine et St. Paul-de-l'Ile-aux-Noix. B.Sp.Sc. thesis, l'Universite du Quebec a Montreal. 143 pp.

FOWLER, H. W.

1913   Some local fish-eating birds. Cassinia 27:6–16.

1915   Fishes from eastern Canada. Proceedings of the Academy of Natural Science, Philadelphia. pp. 515–519.

1918a   Fishes from the middle Atlantic states and Virginia. Occasional Papers of the Museum of Zoology, University of Michigan, 56:1–19.

1918b   A review of the fishes described in Cope's partial catalogue of the cold-blooded vertebrata of Michigan. Occasional Papers of the Museum of Zoology, University of Michigan, 60:1–51.

1919   A list of the fishes of Pennsylvania. Proceedings of the Biological Society of Washington 32:49–73.

1935   Notes on South Carolina freshwater fishes. Charleston Museum, Contribution 7:1–28.

1945   A study of the fishes of the southern piedmont and coastal plain. Academy of Natural Science, Philadelphia, Monograph 7:1–408.

1948   Fishes of the Nueltin Lake expedition Keewatin 1947, Part I, Taxonomy. Proceedings of the Academy of Natural Science, Philadelphia, 100:141–152.

FOX, D. L.
1957   The pigments of fishes. *In* Brown, M. E., ed., The physiology of fishes, New York, Academic Press, vol. 2, pp. 367–385.

FRANCO, J. M.
1973   Residual levels of chlorinated pesticides in some Spanish species and their relation with the environment. Investigacion Pesquera 37:115–145.

FRANCOIS, Y.
1966   Structure et developpement de la vertebre de *Salmo* et des teleosteens. Archives de Zoologie Experimentale et Generale 107:287–328.

FRANK, S. and J. VOSTRADOVSKY
1961   Die ersten Erkenntnisse bezuglich der Anderungen, der Entwicklung und des Wachstums der Hechte und Plotzen in der Talsperre von Lipno. Sbornik KVM Ceske Budejovice 3:147–158.

FRANKENNE, F., L. JOASSIN, J. CLOSSET and C. GERDAY
1971   The isolation and sequence of three high molecular weight trypsic peptides of pike parvalbumin. Archives Internationales de Physiologie et de Biochimie 79:831–832.

FRANKENNE, F., L. JOASSIN and C. GERDAY
1973   The amino-acid sequence of the pike (*Esox lucius*) parvalbumin. FEBS (Federation of the European Biochemical Societies) Letters 35:145–147.

FRANKLIN, D. R.
1959   Some phases of the early life history of the northern pike, *Esox lucius* L. with special reference to the factors influencing the numerical strength of year classes. Ph.D. thesis, University of Minnesota. 127 pp.

1960   Notes on the early growth and allometry of the northern pike. Copeia 1960:143–144.

FRANKLIN, D. R. and L. L. SMITH, Jr.
1960a   Unitized system of water-level and fish population control structures for spawning sloughs. Progressive Fish-Culturist 22:138–140.

1960b   Note on the development of scale patterns in the northern pike, *Esox lucius* L. Transactions of the American Fisheries Society 89:85.

1960c   Notes on the early growth and allometry of the northern pike *Esox lucius* L. Copeia 1960:143–144.
        An analysis was made of allometric growth, using 90 fish between 25 and 115 mm.

1963   Early life history of the northern pike, *Esox lucius* L., with special reference to the factors influencing the numerical strength of year classes. Transactions of the American Fisheries Society 92:91–110.
        Determined the relationship of adult pike abundance to the strength of resulting year classes, the existence and chronology of critical survival periods, and the nature and origin of the mortality mechanisms involved.

FREEMAN, R. B.
1980   British natural history books, 1495–1900: a handlist. London, Dawson. 437 pp.
        This publication lists 4,206 titles, including books on the fauna and flora of the British Isles, Ireland, the Channel Islands, and Heligoland. Most of those pertaining to fish will include something on pike.

FRESHWATER BIOLOGICAL ASSOCIATION

1961   Twenty-ninth annual report for the year ended 31 March 1961. Freshwater
        Biological Association, Ambleside, Westmoreland. 88 pp.

FREY, D. G.

1964   Remains of animals in Quaternary Lake and bog sediments and their interpre-
        tation. Archiv fuer Hydrobiologie Beithefte 2:1–114.

FROLOVA, E. N. and T. V. SHCHERBINA

1975   A new species of the genus *Azygia*. Parazitologiya 9:489–493.

FROST, G. A.

1926   A comparative study of the otoliths. IV. Haplomi. Annals and Magazine of
        Natural History 18(9).

FROST, S., R. I. COLLINSON and M. P. THOMAS

1978   Fish deaths at Elton Reservoir. International Journal of Environmental Stu-
        dies 12:133.

FROST, W. and C. KIPLING

1967   Windermere's wave of change. The Coarse Fish Conference. Fishing, July
        1967, pp. 15–16.
        Information on sex ratio, age structure, growth, and interspecific relation-
        ships.

FROST, W. E.

1946   On the food relationships of fish in Windermere. 13th Biologisch Jaarboek,
        Dodonaea 1946:216–231.

1954   The food of pike, *Esox lucius* L., in Windermere. Journal of Animal Ecology
        23:339–360.
        The stomach contents of 3,060 specimens 1.05–105 cm long, collected by gill
        net, seine, and hand-net, were examined. Diet varied with size classes and
        season. Abundance and availability rather than selection determined the
        species eaten by pike. The effects of pike predation on the size and structure
        of prey populations are discussed.

1963   The pike—its age, growth and predatory habits. *In* Proceedings of the 1st
        British Coarse Fish Conference, Liverpool, 1963, pp. 35–39.
        Size data were obtained from pike gill netted from Lake Windermere, and age
        and growth information were determined from opercular bones. Two
        diagrams show age and its relationship to length and weight.

1977   The food of char *Salvelinus willughbii* in Windermere. Journal of Fish Biol-
        ogy 11:531–547.
        Brief notes on diet of pike fry. Concluded that char and pike do not compete
        for food in this lake.

FROST, W. E. and C. KIPLING

1959   The determination of the age and growth of pike (*Esox lucius* L.) from scales
        and opercular bones. Journal du Conseil International pour l'Exploration de
        la Mer 24:314–341.
        Both methods were examined critically and tested for validity. An equation
        that related fish length and length of the anterior part of the scale for Winder-
        mere pike is given.

1961   Some observations on the growth of pike, *Esox lucius*, in Windermere. Inter-
        national Association of Theoretical and Applied Limnology Proceedings
        14:776–781.
        Used opercular bones to determine age and growth of pike. Walford plots

were used as a method of detecting whether or not annuli were missing on any particular bone.

1965   Some observations on the age and growth of pike (*Esox lucius* L.) in Windermere. Salmon and Trout Magazine, January 1965, pp. 21–27.
       Information on the opercular bone method of assessing age and growth, age, and mean length and weight of males and females caught in the 1946–47 season, and growth of pike in other British and Irish waters compared to those of Lake Windermere.

1967   A study of reproduction, early life, weight-length relationship and growth of pike, *Esox lucius* L., in Windermere. Journal of Animal Ecology 36:651–693.
       Pike were sampled from 1944 to 1965 by gill nets. Age and growth were determined from opercular bones, and growth was described by the von Bertalanffy equation. Changes in ovaries and testes throughout the year and the effects of water temperature on hatching time and growth rates were recorded. Behaviour of fry in aquaria and characteristics of the spawning area are described.

1968a Removal of pike (*Esox lucius*) from Windermere and some of its effect on the population dynamics of that fish. Proceedings of the 3rd British Coarse Fish Conference, Liverpool, 1967, pp. 53–56.
       About 8,000 pike were removed since 1944 by annual gill netting. Determined effects on abundance, size, growth rate, number of prey, and angling. Calculated age and growth from opercular bones.

1968b Experiments on the effect of temperature on the growth of young pike, *Esox lucius* L. Salmon and Trout Magazine 184:170–178.
       Years in which growth of pike was better were years that had above average temperature in summer and early autumn. It seems that the warmer the water, the better the growth of pike at any age.

1970   A study of the mortality, population numbers, production and food consumption of pike, *Esox lucius* L., in Windermere from 1944–1962. Journal of Animal Ecology 39:115–157.
       A total of 7,751 pike were caught in fine flax gill nets each winter from 1944–45 to 1964–65, and tagged every year from 1949 to 1965. Information on mortality rate, estimated population of adult pike, population density, production, food consumption, and year class strengths.

FRY, F. E. J.
1947   Effects of the environment on animal activity. University of Toronto Studies in Biology 55, Ontario Fisheries Research Laboratory Publication 68:1–62.
       A graph shows the relation between temperature and oxygen consumption.

1955   Size, catch and population studies of lake trout, smallmouth bass, and northern pike in Manitoulin Island waters. Unpublished MS. 5 pp.

1960   Requirements for the aquatic habitat. Pulp, Paper and Paperboard Industrial Waste Conference, Chicago, 1959.
       Mentions pike in a histogram depicting temperature preference of various stream fishes in relation to stream temperatures associated with "good fish faunas".

FRY, F. E. J. and V. B. CHAPMAN
1948   The lake trout fishery in Algonquin Park from 1936–1945. Transactions of the American Fisheries Society 75:19–35.

110

Pike were captured in a limited region in the northwest corner of the park.

FRY, F. E. J. and J. P. CUERRIER

1941   Liste des poissons des lacs et des rivieres du Haut Saint-Laurent et de la region de Montreal. Quebec Ministere de la Chasse et de la Peche, Rapport de la Station Biologique de Montreal et de la Station Biologique du Parc des Laurentides, 2(App. 3):82–99.

FUHRMANN, O.

1934a   Le brochet. Sa nourriture et sa croissance. Bulletin suisse Peche et Piscicul-ture 3:33–37.

1934b   Alevins de brochets monstrueux. Bulletin suisse Peche et Pisciculture 7–8:123–126.

FUIMAN, L.

1982   Esocidae. In Auer, N. A., ed., Identification of larval fishes of the Great Lakes basin with emphasis on the Lake Michigan drainage. Great Lakes Fishery Commission, Special Publication 82–3:1–744 pp.
        Key to larval esocids, including pike, and descriptions from egg to 50.5 mm TL. Illustrations 7.9 to 50.5 m TL.

GABEL, J. A.

1974   Species and age composition of trap net catches in Lake Oahe, South Dakota, 1963–1967. U.S. Fish and Wildlife Service, Technical Paper 71–82:1–21.

GABELHOUSE, D. W., Jr.

1981   Use of relative stock (RSD) and catch rate for stock assessment. Proceedings of the 43rd Midwest Fish and Wildlife Conference, 1981.

A "quality" size subdivision system was developed to include minimum "preferred", "memorable", and "trophy" sizes. The approximate length ranges and proposed lengths estimated as percentages of world record lengths are as follows: for minimum Stock (10.5–13.7, 14 inches), Quality (18.9–21.5, 21 inches), Preferred (23.7–28.9, 26 inches), Memorable (31.0–33.6, 32 inches), and Trophy (38.9–42.0, 40 inches).

GABOURY, M. N.

1982   Fish stock assessment of Burntwood Lake, 1980. Manitoba Department of Natural Resources, Manuscript Report 82–15:1–80.

Pike were smaller than in other northern lakes but relatively numerous. Pike populations appeared healthy and could withstand more consistent and intensive exploitation.

GABOURY, M. N. and J. W. POTALAS

1982   The fisheries of Cross, Pipestone and Walker lakes, and effects of hydro-electric development. Manitoba Department of Natural Resources, Manuscript Report 82–14:1–198.

Assesses the fish stocks of the lakes and describes impacts of the current water level regime as regulated by the Jenpeg hydro-electric impoundment.

GABRIELSON, I. N. and F. LAMONTE

1950   The fisherman's encyclopedia. 2nd ed. Harrisburg, Stackpole and Hech. 698 pp.

GAGE, S. H.

1942   Zymogen granules in the fishes. Transactions of the American Fisheries Society 72:263–266.

All American fishes except *Amphioxus* and the Cyclostomata have a pancreas in which there is an abundance of zymogen granules. These are the precursors of the digestive ferment of pancreatic juice. Mingled with the exocrine pancreatic tissue is the islet or internal secreting endocrine tissue, with minute particles that are especially large in pike.

GAJDUSEK, J. and V. RUBCOV

1983   Investigations on the microstructure of egg membranes in pike, *Esox lucius*. Folia Zoologica 32:145–152.

GALAT, D. L.

1973   Normal embryonic development of the muskellunge (*Esox masquinongy*). Transactions of the American Fisheries Society 102:384–391.

GALINA, N. V., E. F. MARTINSON and V. I. REDIKSON

1958   On the biotechnique in artificial breeding of pike. Rybnoe Khoziaistvo 2:26–28.

Gives recommendations for collecting, fertilizing, transporting, and incubating pike eggs.

GAMMON, J. R.

1965   Device for collecting eggs of muskellunge, northern pike, and other scatter-spawning species. Progressive Fish-Culturist 27:78.

Describes the construction of a tray that reduces the difficulty of collecting eggs of fish species that scatter their eggs.

GARADI, P.
1978   Csukaevadek tavi elonevelesenek tapasztalatai a Temperaltvizu Halszaporito Gazdasagban. Halaszat 24:94–95.

GARDNER, J. A.
1926   Report on the respiratory exchange in freshwater fish, with suggestions as to further investigations. Fishery Investigations, Ministry of Agriculture, Fish, and Food (Great Britain), Ser. 1, Sea Fish, 3:1–17.
        Two pike were placed in a tub of water at 11 C. The water temperature was slowly raised to 27 C, at which the pike became more active and respiration deeper. At 30 C, movements became convulsive and both fish turned over.

GARDNER, J. A. and G. KING
1923   On the respiratory exchange in fresh water fish. Part 4. On pike. Biochemical Journal 17:170–173.

GARRARD, J.
1886   The game fishes of the west. The mascalonge of the Mississippi system. The American Angler, pp. 12–14.
        Discussed the discrepancy over identification and naming of esocids, including pike. Argued that scientific names were not correctly descriptive.

GASBARINO, P.
1985   Trophy northern pike. Angler & Hunter 10(1):20–22.

GASOWSKIEY, M.
1962   Krablouste i ryby (Cyclostome et Pisces). Klucze do oznaczania kregowcow Polski Czesc. 1. Polska Akademia Nauk, Zaklad Zoologiesystematycznejwkrakowie, pp. 1–240.

GAY, M.
1975   The beginner's guide to pike angling. London, Pelham.
1978   Pike from pits and lakes. *In* Guttfield, F., ed., The big fish scheme. London, Benn.

GEE, A. S.
1978   The distribution and growth of coarse fish in gravel-pit lakes in south-east England. Freshwater Biology 8:385.

GEE, J. H., K. MACHNIAK and S. M. CHALANCHUK
1974   Adjustment of buoyancy and excess internal pressure of swimbladder gases in some North American freshwater fishes. Journal of the Fisheries Research Board of Canada 31:1139–1141.
        Young-of-the-year pike taken from inlet streams of large lakes became significantly more buoyant in current than in still water.

GEE, J. H., R. F. TALLMAN and H. J. SMART
1978   Reactions of some great plains fishes to progressive hypoxia. Canadian Journal of Zoology 56:1962–1966.
        Fish were examined in progressive hypoxia to see if they used dissolved oxygen in the surface film. Pike were active only when breathing the surface film.

GEIGER, W., H. J. MENG and C. RUHLE
1975   Effects of simulated pumped storage operation on northern pike fry. Schweizerische Zeitschrift fuer Hydrobiologie 37:225–234.
        An examination of the effects on pike fry of periodic, simulated water level

fluctuations produced by pumped-storage operations. Daily fluctuations of 10 cm caused a significant increase in the daily mortality rate. Waves reduced the detrimental effect of water level fluctuations, at least during the adhesive phase of fry.

GELINEO, S.

1969   Hamoglobinkonzentration im Blut. Bulletin de l'Academie Serbe des Sciences Classe des Sciences Mathematiques et Naturelles 46(12):25–67.

GENGERKE, T.

1977   Commercial fisheries investigations. Northern pike investigations. Iowa Conservation Commission, Project Completion Report, Project 2–225-R:1–42.

Data on life history characteristics, population size, length-weight relationships, condition factors, age and growth, fecundity, and movement were collected from pike from the Mississippi River, 1974–77. Concentrations of dieldrin, DDE, heptochlor epoxide, chlordane, mercury and PCB's in pike flesh were less than FDA tolerance levels. Recommendations for returning pike to the commercial fishery are presented.

GENINA, N. V.

1958   Iskusstvennoje razvedenije scuki i vozmoznost'jejo transportirovki. Naucnaja konferencija po izuceniju vodojemov Pribaltiki 6:104–105.

GENINA, N. V., E. F. MARTINSEN and V. Y. REDIKSON

1958   O biotekhnike iskusstvennogo razvedaniya shchuki. [On biological methods of the pike.] Rybnoye Khozyaystvo 34(2):26–28.

Detailed description of a method of artificial breeding of pike. Incubation lasted 8 days at temperatures of 12–13 C.

GENSCH, R.

1979   Results and information on the rearing of fish brood in illuminated cage in the VEB Inland Fishery, Frankfurt. Zeitschrift fuer Binnenfischerei 26(2):38–41.

Results of rearing pike and other species in 2x2x2 m cages with artificial light to attract zooplankton.

GEOFFROY, C. J.

1735   Suite de l'examen chimique des chairs des animaux, ou de quelques-unes de leurs parties, etc. Memoirs de l'Academie de Science, Paris, 1732:17–30.

GEORGE, C. J.

1980   The fishes of the Adirondack Park. New York Department of Environmental Conservation. 93 pp.

Changes in the distribution of pike in the park since 1930 were reviewed, along with feeding and reproductive habits. The North American angling record from 1940 was mentioned.

GEORGES, D.

1964   Evolution morphologique et histologique des organes adhesifs du brochet (*Esox lucius* L.). Travaux Laboratoire d'Hydrobiologie et de Pisciculture de l'University de Grenoble 56:7–16.

GEORGESCAULD, D and H. DUCLOHIER

1969   Transient fluorescence signals from pyrene labeled pike nerves during action; potential possible implications for membrane fluidity changes. Biochemistry and Biophysical Research Communications 85:1186–1191.

114

GERDAY, C.

1976   The primary structure of the parvalbumin II of pike (*Esox lucius*). European Journal of Biochemistry 70:305.

GERKING, S. D.

1945   The distribution of the fishes of Indiana. Investigations of Indiana Lakes and Streams 3(1):1–137.

1955   Key to the fishes of Indiana. Investigations of Indiana Lakes and Streams 4(2):1–86.

1959   The restricted movements of fish populations. Biological Reviews 34:221–242.

GESNER

1558   Tigurini Historiae Animalium.

First to mention Emperor's pike captured 1497 in lake in Wurtemburg. A copper ring around the gill region with the inscription saying that it had been placed in the lake by Emperior Frederick II 1230, 267 years earlier. The fish was 19 feet long, 250 lb. An oil painting hangs in the castle of Lautern, Swabia. The skeleton, in the cathedral at Mannheim, consists of vertebra of more than one individual.

GIANOTTI, F. S. and G. GIOVINAZZO

1975   Four years of fishery, 1972–1975, in Lake Trasimeno. Rivista di Idrobiologica 14:283–329.

GIANOTTI, F. S., G. GIOVINAZZO and L. GORI

1975   Four years of fishery, 1968–1971, in Lake Trasimeno. Rivista di Idrobiologica 14:209–262.

GIBB, B., I. BECKER and M. KRAEMER

1974   Immunobiological studies in the antigenic character of indigenous fishes. Part 4. Gel chromatographic and sedimentation analytic findings. Biologisches Zentralblatt 93:537–544.

GIBBINSON, J.

1974   Pike. London, Osprey.

GIBBS, J.

1976   King of the weedbeds. Outdoor Life 158(5):66–67, 114, 116, 118.

Colourful portrayal depicting struggle with angler, past records of size, enormous appetite, and hunting behaviour. Advice on angling strategy and lures, based on feeding habits and preferred locations.

GIBSON, M. B. and J. W. MACPHERSON

1954   *Esox lucius* x *Esox masquinongy* hybrids. University of Toronto, Department of Zoology, Ontario Fisheries Research Laboratory Report. 3 pp.

GIBSON, R. J. and C. E. HUGHES

1969   Investigation of the angling potential in the Spruce Woods Provincial Park. Manitoba Department of Mines and Natural Resources, MS Report 69–10:1–28.

Pike were found in four of the six ox-bow lakes studied. If encouraged, fish immigration from Assiniboine River could provide angling and make use of the excellent nursery areas in the lakes. Pike stocking on a "put and take" basis in Muckie Manitou Lake was considered.

GIERALTOWSKI, M.

1938   Sprawa zarybiania wod otwartych szczupakiem. [Stocking of open waters with pike.] Przeglad Rybacki 11:193–195.

GIHR, M.

1957   Zur Entwicklung des Hechtes. [On the development of the pike]. Revue Suisse de Zoologie 64:356–470.

   Describes morphology of embryo and post-embryonic stage during which it attaches itself to a nearby object. Towards the end of this stage, it begins filling its air bladder, and with much effort rises to the surface. Describes morphology for each successive stadium of the free phase.

1958   Vom Hechtei zum Vollhecht. Osterreichische Fischerei-Zeitung 11(8).

GILDERHUS, P. A., B. L. BERGER and R. E. LENNON

1969   Field trials of antimycin A as a fish toxicant. U.S. Fish and Wildlife Service, Investigations in Fish Control 27:1–21.

GILDERHUS, P. A., B. L. BERGER, J. B. SILLS and P. D. HARMAN

1973   The efficacy of quinaldine sulfate as an anesthetic for freshwater fish. U.S. Fish and Wildlife Service, Investigations in Fish Control 49:1–9.

   The efficacy of the anesthetic was little affected by water temperature, but the compound lowers the pH of some soft waters to below 6, the point at which it becomes ineffective as an anesthetic. All fish retained some reflex action, thus some large fish were difficult to handle.

GILES, N.

1984   Development of the overhead fright response in wild and predator-naive three-spined sticklebacks, *Gasterosteus aculeatus* L. Animal Behaviour 32:276.

GILL, T., ed.

1898   "Report in part" of Samuel L. Mitchill, M. D., on the fishes of New York. Washington.

GILL, T. N.

1896   The families of synentognathous fishes and their nomenclature. Proceedings of the U.S. National Museum 18:167–178.

GILLEN, A. L., R. A. STEIN and R. F. CARLINE

1981   Predation by pellet-reared tiger muskellunge on minnows and bluegills in experimental systems. Transactions of the American Fisheries Society 110:197–209.

   Pike-muskellunge hybrids were size-selective in their choice of prey. In both aquaria and ponds they switched more rapidly to minnows than to bluegill.

GILTAY, C. M.

1832   Commentatio de *Esoce lucio* neurologue descripto et cum religuis vertebratis animalibus comparata. Lugduni Batavorum.

1833   Commentatio ad quaestionem..."Quaeritur descripto neurologica *Esocis lucii*...cum reliquis vertebratis animalibus...comparata". Annales Academie Lugduno Batavae.

GIRARD, C. F.

1854   Observations upon the American species of the genus *Esox*. Proceedings of the Academy of Natural Science, Philadelphia, 6:386.

   The "large number of species" was separated into two groups depending upon cheek scalation. The maskallonge (*E. nobilior*) and those with naked cheeks and opercular apparatus were called pikes, and *E. reticulatus* and those with scaled cheeks and operculars were called pickerels.

116

GIRSA, I. I.

1969　Reaction to light in some freshwater fishes in the course of early development and in altered physiological states. Problems of Ichthyology 9:126–135.

GLASS, R. L., T. P. KRICK and A. E. ECKHARDT

1974　New series of fatty acids in northern pike (*Esox lucius*). Lipids 9:1004–1008.

GLASS, R. L., T. P. KRICK, D. L. OLSON and P. L. THORSON

1977　The occurrence and distribution of furan fatty-acids in spawning male fresh water fish. Lipids 12:828–836.

GLAZUNOVA, G. A.

1974　The content of fibrinogen and the activity of fibrin stabilizing factor in various vertebrates. Zhurnal Evolyutsionnoi Biokhimii i Fiziologii 10:303–304.

GODDARD, J. A. and L. C. REDMOND

1978　Northern pike, tiger muskellunge, and walleye populations in Stockton Lake, Missouri: a management evaluation. American Fisheries Society Special Publication 11:313–319.

　　　A three-stage filling coupled with spring releases of pike fry and fingerlings into Stockton Lake for three successive years resulted in good survival, exceptional growth, and a quality fishery. With a minimum size limit of 762 mm, harvest averaged 1.5 kg/hectare.

GODFREY, J., Jr.

1945　Muskies unlimited. Outdoors 13(8):10–11, 36.

GOEDDE, L. E. and D. W. COBLE

1981　Effects of angling on a previously fished and an unfished warmwater fish community in two Wisconsin lakes. Transactions of the American Fisheries Society 110:594–603.

　　　Population structure and other vital statistics were determined for the pike population in Allen Lake (fished) and Mid Lake (unfished) for two successive 3-year periods. Population statistics in Mid Lake changed after angling.

GOEDMAKERS, A. and B. L. VERBOOM

1974　Studies on the maturation and fecundity of the pike, *Esox lucius* L. Aquaculture 4:3–12.

GOETHBERG, A.

1976　Bioassay technique using fish for effluent tests. 4. FAO/SIDA training course on aquatic pollution in relation to production of living resources. Food and Agriculture Organization of the United Nations, TF-INT—173(SWE) Suppl. 1:68–78.

GOLD, J. R., W. J. KAREL and M. R. STRAND

1980　Chromosome formulae of North American fishes. Progressive Fish-Culturist 42:10–23.

GOLDSPINK, C. R. and J. W. BANKS

1975　A description of the Tjeukemeer fishery together with a note upon the yield statistics between 1964 and 1970. Journal of Fish Biology 7:687–708.

　　　Pike data include: monthly catches, total catch, some catches by individual fishermen in other Frisian lakes, and winter monthly catch by seine and gill net.

GOLDWALD, D. S.

1967　Die Behandlung mit Methylenblau bie Saprolegniabefall von Hechteiern. Deutsche Fischerei Zeitung 14:161–164.

GOODE, G. B.
   1884   Natural history of useful aquatic animals. The Fisheries and Fishery Industry of the U.S., Section 1:1–895.

GORDON, D., N. A. CROLL and M. E. RAU
   1978   Les parasites des animaux sauvage du Quebec. 1. Les parasites des poissons et des mamiferes de la region de Schefferville. [Parasites of wild animals in Quebec. 1. Parasites of fish and mammals in the Schefferville region]. Le Naturaliste Canadian 105:55.

          Five species of fish (including pike) were examined during June-September 1976. The parasites identified are listed in a table.

GORDON, W. J.
          Our country's fishes and how to know them. London, Simpkin, Marshall, Hamilton, Kent. 152 pp.

GOROVAIA, S. L.
   1969   Concerning the structure of the olfactory organ in some fish. Vestsi. Akad. Navuk. Belarus. SSR Ser. Siyalagichnykh Navuk 5:117–119.

GORSLINE, T.
   1981   Ontario's great northern pike. Ontario Out of Doors 13(3):32–33, 62, 67–68.
          Summary of recent large catches, good locations, suitable angling methods.

GOSLINE, W. A.
   1960   Contribution toward a classification of modern Isospondylous fishes. Bulletin of the British Museum (Natural History), Zoology, 6(6).
          Considerable discussion of the systematic position and phylogeny of esocids as revealed by caudal skeleton.

GOSSELIN-REY, C., G. HAMOIR and R. K. SCOPES
   1968   Localization of creatine kinase in the starch-gel and moving-boundary electrophoretic patterns of fish muscle. Journal of the Fisheries Research Board of Canada 25:2711–2714.
          Figure shows starch-gel patterns of white muscle extracts stained for creatine kinase. Gives migration after 4-hr electrophoresis at 20 v/cm in the cold, using a discontinuous system at pH 8.4.

GOTHBERG, A.
   1977   Depleting a lake of fish for decontamination. Proceedings 20th Limnological Congress, Copenhagen, 1977. 306 pp.
          Tagged pike with low mercury concentrations were put into a lake to study quantitative changes in mercury content of muscle and liver tissues.

GOTTBERG, G.
   1917a   On the growth of pike in the Aland Islands. Suomen kalatalous 4:191–211. [in Swedish].
   1917b   Om gaddens tillvaxt i Alands skargard. Finlands Fisherier 4:223–243.
   1922   On the migrations of pike in the Aland Islands. Fiskeritidskrift Finland 30:1–6. [in Swedish].

GOTTWALD, S.
   1956   Zwalczanie plesni na ikrze sielawy i szczupaka przy pomocy zieleni malachitowej. [Malachite green for the prevention of mould development upon pike and vendace eggs.] Unpublished manuscript, 22 pp.
          Use of malachite green and a practical method of its application for eggs incubated in jars.

1958a Zagadnienie dalszego obnizania strat ikry szczupakow i sielawy. [Problem of decreasing the losses of pike and vendace eggs.] Gospodarka Rybna 10(3):26–27.
    Errors and mishandlings during artificial fertilization of eggs and their transport. Periods of high susceptibility of eggs to external factors.

1958b Zwalczanie plesni na ikrze sielawy i szczupaka przy pomocy zieleni malachitowej. [Combating fungus on eggs of *Coregonus albula* L. and pike by means of malachite green.] Roczniki Nauk Rolniczych, Ser. B, 73(2):295–311.
    Studies on the treatment of mould occurring on eggs of pike and vendace during incubation. Eggs were washed in a solution of malachite green. Description of the procedure, apparatus, solutions used, and the results of treatment.

1960 Z biologii zaplodnienia i rozwoju ikry szczupaka. [Biology of pike fertilization and egg development.] Gospodarka Rybna 12(2):26–28.
    Proper methods of fertilizing pike eggs in artificial conditions and their biological background. Estimations of the period during which eggs can be kept in closed jars.

1966a New methods applied during incubation and hatching of pike hatch. Gospodarka Rybna 18(4):6–7.

1966b Zastosowanie blekitu metylenowego do zwalczania plesni na ikrze szczupaka. [The application of methylene blue for combating fungus on pike eggs.] Gospodarka Rybna 18(10):8–10.

1970 Experimentelle Apparaturen zur Herstellung von Sauerstoffgradienten. [Apparatus for creating a gradient in oxygen concentration]. Archiv fuer Hydrobiologie Beithefte 68:143–150.

GOTTWALD, S., Z. KLEBUKOWSKA and A. WINNICKI

1965 Masowa smiertelnosc ikry szczupaka. [Mass mortality of pike eggs.] Gospodarka Rybna 17(9):8–9.
    Mass mortality of eggs and significant deformation of pike embryos in a hatchery caused by an environmental factors during the early stage of embryo development.

GOTTWALD, S. and Z. PLACZKOWSKI

1958 Proby polepszania wynikow inkubacji ikry szczupaka. [Attempts to improve factors connected with the incubation of pike eggs.] Gospodarka Rybna 10(8–9):21–22.
    Experimental study of the negative effect of long-term egg transport. High losses due to improper and prolonged storage of eggs in closed transporters.

GOTTWALD, S. and A. WINNICKI

1966 Observations on the abnormal development of fish egg aerola. Zeitschrift fuer Fischerei und deren Hilfswissenschaften 14(1/2):101–110. [in German].

GOUBIER, J. and Y. SOUCHON

1982 Controle de l'epoque de reproduction du brochet par retard de maturation. [Delay of the spawning period in pike]. Bulletin Francais de Pisciculture 286:247–254.
    By keeping brood fish at a low temperature during winter and early spring, spawning was delayed by 1–2 months. Production of pike fingerlings obtained from such breeders were comparable to those of control lots, but a better growth was observed.

119

GOULD, W. R., III and W. H. IRWIN

1965   The suitabilities and relative resistances of twelve species of fish as bioassay animals for oil-refinery effluents. Proceedings of the Southeast Association of Game and Fish Commissioners 16:333–348.

GRABDA, J.

1971   Pasozyty kragloustych i ryb. Katalog fauny pasozytniczej Polski. [Parasites of Cyclostomata and fish. The catalogue of parasitic fauna of Poland.] Vol. 2, 304 pp.

GRABDA-KAZUBSKA, B. and L. EJSYMONT

1969   Studies on morphology, variability and systematic status of *Echinorhynchus borealis* Linstow, 1901 (Acanthocephala, Echinorhynchidae). Acta Parasitologica Polonica 17(1/19):65–87.

GRAFF, D. R.

1968   The successful feeding of a dry diet to esocids. Progressive Fish-Culturist 30:152.
       Reports success in converting pike to dry food after starting them on 1) trout starter, 2) daphnia, and 3) graded daphnia followed by sucker fry.

1972   Observations on interactions between juveniles of *Esox lucius* and *Esox masquinongy*. M.Ed. thesis, Pennsylvania State University. 72 pp.
       A study of the competition between young pike and young muskellunge, including behaviour, feeding, postures (threat, alarm, submission), and relative survival.

1978   Intensive culture of esocids: the current state of the art. American Fisheries Society Special Publication 11:195–201.
       Discusses use of artificial diet, hatchery design, techniques, and pathology in culture of pike and pike-muskellunge hybrids.

GRAFF, D. R. and L. SORENSON

1969   The successful feeding of a dry diet to esocids. Pennsylvania Fish Commission, unpublished MS. 13 pp.
       Of several hatchery diets, only commercial trout food was readily accepted by pike in both experimental and production situations. Pike accustomed to a diet of daphnia and graded sucker fry converted to trout food and were maintained on it for several months.

1970   The successful feeding of a dry diet to esocids. Progressive Fish-Culturist 32:31–35.

GRASSE, P. P.

1958   Traite de zoologie, anatomie, systematique, biologie. Tome 13, Agnathes et poissons, anatomie, ethologie, systematique. Paris, Libraries de l'Academie de Medecine.

GRAVEL, Y. and J. DUBE

1979   Plan de conservation du grand brochet, *Esox lucius* L., au lac Saint-Louis, Quebec. *In* Dube, J., and Y. Gravel, eds., Proceedings 10th Warmwater Workshop, Special Publication NE Division of the American Fisheries Society. Quebec Ministere du Loisir, de la Chasse et de la Peche, Montreal, pp. 27–59.
       Pike populations in Lake St-Louis have decreased because of the destruction of spawning grounds. Work has begun on physical improvement on the one remaining excellent habitat, with encouraging results.

120

1980 Les conditions hydriques et le role de la vegetation dans une frayere a grands brochets *Esox lucius* Linne. Eau Quebec 13:229–230.

The effects of degradation and elimination of numerous spawning areas and habitat modification by regulation of water levels are discussed. Importance of vegetation in spawning habitats are noted and solutions to the problem are made. Observations are made on migration-stimulation factors for young pike related to self-defence against cannibalism.

GRAY, T. E.

1850 Fishes. *In* Rae, J., ed., Narrative of an expedition to the shores of the Arctic Sea, 1846–1847. London, T. W. Boone, pp. 204–205.

GREELEY, J. R.

1934 Fishes of the Raquette watershed with annotated list. Section 2. *In* A biological survey of the Raquette Watershed. New York State Conservation Department, Supplement to the 23rd Annual Report (1933), Biological Survey 8, pp. 53–108.

1938 Fishes of the area with annotated list. Section 2. *In* A biological survey of the Allegheny and Chemung watersheds. New York Conservation Department, Supplement to the 27th Annual Report (1937), Biological Survey 12, 287 pp.

1939a A biological survey of the freshwaters of Long Island. New York Conservation Department, Supplement to the 28th Annual Report (1938).

1939b Fishes of the watershed with annotated list. New York Conservation Department, Supplement to the 29th Annual Report (1939).

1940 Fishes of the watershed with annotated list. Part 2. *In* A biological survey of the Lake Ontario watershed. New York Conservation Department, Supplement to the 29th Annual Report (1939). 261 pp.

GREELEY, J. R. and S. C. BISHOP

1932 Fishes of the Upper Hudson watershed. Section 2. New York Conservation Department, Supplement to the 22nd Annual Report (1932), pp. 64–101.

GREEN, D. M., Jr.

1978 Fisheries investigations of Canadarago Lake. New York State Department of Environmental Conservation, Dingell-Johnson Project F-29-R, Job Ia:1–36.

Attempted to establish size, age, and species composition of the fish community, to be used as a baseline for assessing longterm changes in population structure following nutrient reduction.

GREEN, R.

1976 Breeding behavior of ospreys *Pandion haliaetus* in Scotland. Ibis 118:475–490.

Study at Loch Garten illustrated seasonal and diurnal changes in proportions of pike and trout in catch. Species composition of catch varied with prevailing weather conditions.

GREENBANK, J.

1950 The length-weight relationship of some upper Mississippi River fishes. Upper Mississippi River Conservation Committee, unpublished MS. 12 pp.

Gives a length-weight regression for pike.

1954 Sport fisheries survey, Katmai National Monument. U.S. Department of the Interior, National Parks Service, Administration Report. 31 pp.

1957 Creel census on the upper Mississippi River. U.S. Fish and Wildlife Service, Special Scientific Report Fisheries 202.

GREENE, C. W.

1935   The distribution of Wisconsin fishes. Wisconsin Conservation Commission. 235 pp.

Map of distribution in Wisconsin.

GREGORY, R. W., A. A. ELSER and T. LENHART

1984   Utilization of surface coal mine wastewater for construction of a northern pike spawning/rearing marsh. U.S. Fish and Wildlife Service, Office of Biological Services, Report 84/03:1–44.

This report illustrates potential problem areas in the planning, construction, and operation of such a project and stimulates ideas for developing other innovative uses of wastewater for fish and wildlife habitat enhancement.

GREGORY, R. W. and T. G. POWELL

1969   Warm-water fisheries investigations. Northern pike introduction. Colorado Game, Fish and Parks Department, Dingell-Johnson Report F-034-R-04, Job 03:1–7.

GREGORY, W. K.

1933   Fish skulls: a study of the evolution of natural mechanisms. Transactions of the American Philosophy Society 23:1–481.

GRENHOLM, A.

1923   Studien uber die Flossenmuskulatur der Teleostier. Uppsala Universitets Arsskrift, pp. 55–57.

GRIER, H. J. and J. R. LINTON

1977   Ultrastructural identification of the Sertoli cell in the testis of the northern pike, *Esox lucius*. American Journal of Anatomy 149:283–288.

GRIFFIN, P. J.

1953   The nature of bacteria pathogenic to fish. Transactions of the American Fisheries Society 83:241–253.

A review of published material; mentions *Pseudomonas hydropyila* from organs and blood of pike with "red sore" disease.

GRIMALDI, E.

1972   Lago Maggiore: effects of exploitation and introductions on the salmonid community. Journal of the Fisheries Research Board of Canada 29:777–785.

1974   Dependence of visceral infestation of perch *Perca fluviatilis* by larvae of *Diphyllobothrium latum* Cestoda Pseudophyllidaea on the phenomenon of re-infestation. Bollettino di Zoologia 41:497.

GRIMAS, U. and N.-A. NILSSON

1965   On the food chain in some north Swedish river reservoirs. Report Institute of Freshwater Research Drottningholm 46:31–48.

Stomach contents of pike from six reservoirs were tabulated.

GRIMM, M. P.

1980   De samenstelling van de snoekpopulatie in view Nederlandse wateren. [The composition of northern pike populations in four waters in the Netherlands.] Annual Report Organisatie ter Verbetering van de Binnenvisseri 1978/79:57–81.

1981a   The composition of northern pike (*Esox lucius* L.) populations in four shallow waters in the Netherlands, with special reference to factors influencing 0+ pike biomass. Fisheries Management 12(2):61–76.

Populations were sampled during a 4–5 year period, using mark-recapture methods. Factors influencing 0+ pike biomass were intraspecific predation and amount of aquatic vegetation.

1981b   Intraspecific predation as a principal factor controlling the biomass of north-
         ern pike (*Esox lucius*). Fisheries Management 12(2):77–79.
         Intraspecific predation plays a major role in the regulation of numbers of
         small pike <41 cm fork length. In four "natural" waters the biomasses of
         these pike, especially of the 0+ class, were negatively correlated with those of
         larger pike.

1982a   Regulation of biomass of small (<41 cm) northern pike (*Esox lucius* L.) with
         special reference to the contributions of individuals stocked as fingerlings
         (4–6 cm). *In* Documents presented at the Symposium on Stock Enhancement
         in the Management of Freshwater Fisheries, Budapest, 1982. vol. 1, pp.
         1–18.
         The composition and abundance of four pike populations were monitored
         from 1974 to 1982. Stocked pike did not contribute extra biomass to the
         population.

1982b   The evaluation of the stocking of pike fingerlings. Hydrobiological Bulletin
         16:285–286.
         In order to evaluate the stocking of artificially propagated pike fingerlings the
         composition and abundance of populations in four shallow waters were moni-
         tored during a 5–8 year period.

1983a   Regulation de la biomasse de brochet (*Esox lucius* L.) de petite taille (<41
         cm) et efficacite de l'introduction d'individus de 4–6 cm. *In* Billard, R., ed.,
         Le brochet gestion dans le milieu naturel et elevage. Paris, Institute National
         de la Recherche Agronomique, pp. 253–270.
         The composition and abundance of four pike populations were determined
         from 1974–82. The biomasses of the 0+ class and those of classes <35–41
         cm were negatively correlated by exponential function with the biomasses of
         larger fish.

1983b   Regulation of biomasses of small (<41 cm) northern pike (*Esox lucius* L.)
         with special reference to the contribution of individuals stocked as fingerlings
         (4–6 cm). Fisheries Management 14(3):115–134.

GRIMM, M. P., and R. G. RIEMENS,
1975   Het evaluatienoderzoerk van pootsnoek. Report Organisatie ter Verbetering
         van de Binnenvisseruk. pp. 71–89.

GROCHOWALSKI, J.
1954   Produkcja szczupaka handlowego z wycieru. [Production of market pike
         from larvae.] Gospodarka Rybna 6(2):19.
         Spring stocking of ponds with pike in order to clear the ponds of weed fish.
         This method gives pike of 150–200 g individual weight in autumn.

GRODZINSKI, Z.
1971   Anatomia i embriologia ryb. [Anatomy and embryology of fishes.] Warsaw,
         PWRiL. 316 pp.

GROEBNER, J. F.
1960   Appraisal of the sport fishery catch in a bass-panfish lake of southern Min-
         nesota; Lake Francis, LeSueur County, 1952–1957. Minnesota Department
         of Conservation, Investigational Report 225:1–17.
         Annual loss of catchable-size pike was estimated as 0.769. Pike catch
         declined over the years studied, although the average size taken by summer
         angling remained about the same.

1964   Contributions to fishing harvest from known numbers of northern pike finger-
        lings. Minnesota Department of Conservation, Investigational Report
        280:1–24.
        Fingerling production, abundance of two-year or older pike, exploitation and
        mortality rates in a 456-acre lake were estimated from 1957–60. The effect
        of population density on mortality rate, condition factor, harvest, and number
        of pike caught per man hour of fishing are discussed.

GROEN, C. L. and T. A. SCHROEDER
1978   Effects of water level management on walleye and other coolwater fishes in
        Kansas reservoirs. American Fisheries Society Publication 11:278–283.
        Discusses water level conditions affecting the following aspects of pike popu-
        lation: recruitment, reproduction, stocking success, growth, and size.

GROSS, G. W. and G. W. KREUTZBERG
1978   Rapid axoplasmic transport in the olfactory nerve of the pike. 1. Basic
        parameters for proteins and amino acids. Brain Research 139:65–76.
        The maximum transport velocity for protein was determined at two tempera-
        tures. Intact nerves revealed only wavefronts of radioactivity, whereas remo-
        val of the cell bodies 4 hours after isotope application produced characteristic
        peak and saddle regions that demonstrated a loss of material by the peak dur-
        ing transport. Studies also conducted on the olfactory of another species sug-
        gest that axoplasmic transport in C-fibres is independent of fibre length. Free
        amino acid V-max is identical to the protein V-max. The pike olfactory sys-
        tem presents evidence that a common, temperature correlatable V-max may
        exist in all nerves.

GROSS, G. W. and D. G. WEISS
1977   Sub cellular fractionation of rapidly transported axonal material in olfactory
        nerve evidence for a size dependent molecule separation during transport.
        Neuroscience Letters 5(1–2):15–20.

GRUPCHEVA, G. I.
1966   Investigation of *Myxosporidia* of fish from the Bulgarian sector of the
        Danube. Godishnik na Sofiiskiya Universitet Biologisheski Fakultet Kniga i
        Zoologiya Fiziologiya i Biokhimiya na Zhivotnite 60:147–165.

GUERIN, F.
1984   Exploitation modalities in aquaculture of zooplankton produced in stabiliza-
        tion lagoons. Cent. Natl. Mach. Agric. Genie Rural Eaux For. Montpellier
        (France), 178 pp.
        Experiments on zooplankton calorization through aquaculture processes have
        been worked out and young pike have been intensively cultured.

GUEST, W. C.
1977   Technique for collecting and incubating eggs of the fathead minnow. Pro-
        gressive Fish-Culturist 39:188.

GUIBERT, F.
1972   Fishing in Mont-Tremblant Park 1967 season. Quebec Service du Faune,
        Rapport 6:105–131.

GUILFORD, H. G.
1965   New species of Myxosporidia from Green Bay (Lake Michigan). Transac-
        tions of the American Microscopical Society 84:566–572.

GULIDOV, M. V.

  1969a   Embryonic development of the pike (*Esox lucius* L.) when incubated under different oxygen conditions. Problems of Ichthyology 9:841–851.

  An account of experimental data on the effect of oxygen conditions on the development of pike. Upper and lower threshold concentrations were established. There is a pattern in the variation in mortality of eggs and number hatched when oxygen is varied and qualitative development of embryos is established.

  1969b   Survival and certain features of development of pike (*Esox lucius* L.) embryos at different oxygen conditions of incubation. Doklady Biological Sciences 189(1–6):811–813.

GULIN, V. V. and G. P. RUDENKO

  1974   Procedure for assessment of fish production in lakes. Journal of Ichthyology 13:813–823.

  Data on biomass and production of 34 pike caught in Lake Demenets in July 1961, using gill nets and polychlorpinene.

GULISH, W. J.

  1970   Bluegill predation by three fish species. Indiana Academy of Science 139–147.

  Pike were less effective as bluegill predators than were largemouth bass (*Micropterus salmoides*), but more effective than white catfish (*Ictalurus catus*).

GUNTHER, A.

  1866   Catalogue of the Physostomi, containing the families Salmonidae, Percopsidae, Galaxidae, Mormyridae, Gymnarchidae, Esocidae, Umbridae, Scombresocidae, Cyprinodontidae, in the collection of the British Museum. London, vol. 6, 368 pp.

GUROVA, G. V., S. K. KRASNOV and N. D. MAZMANIDI

  1970   The effect of certain halides of phosphorus on fish during ontogeny, trans. by R. M. Howland. Voprosy Vodnoi Toksikologii, an SSSR, "Nauka", Moscow, pp. 136–141.

GUTIERREZ-CALDERON, E.

  1952   El lucio. [The pike.] Madrid 8(44):113–132.

  A brief account of the life history of the pike and of its introduction from France to Spain in 1949.

  1954   El lucio en Espana. Caza y Pesca 140:490–493.

  1955   Acclimatation du brochet en Espagne. International Association of Theoretical and Applied Limnology Proceedings 12:536–542.

  Presents the results of culture experiments with pike in Spain. Shows the results of its sexual precocity and rate of growth in relation to the high temperature of Spanish waters.

  1957   Seccion de biologie de las aguas continentales. [The section of the biology of continental streams.] Anales del Instituto Forestal de Investigaciones y Experiencias Madrid 29:147–181.

  The major part of this section is devoted to a study of the feeding of pike and trout (*Salmo irideus*).

  1969   El lucio (Su biologia y aprovechamiento) Folleto Informativo 2, Ministere Agriculture S.P.C.C. y PN, Madrid. 87 pp.

  A booklet on several aspects of pike biology and experiences with pike reproduction in a hatchery in Spain. Shows records of big pike caught in Spanish rivers and a list of restocking done from 1949 to 1960.

GUTIERREZ-CALDERON, E. and E. SCAPARDINI-ANDREU
1950   Aclimatation del lucio en Espana. [Introduction of pike in Spain.] Madrid 6(36):725–728.
       Pike introduced from France for release in the Tagus, thrived and reproduced when 11 months old.

GYURKO, S. and Z. I. NAGY
1971   Distribution structure and trophic relationships of the fish population of the upper course of the Muresh River. Studii se Cercetari Piscicole Institutul de Cercetari si Proiectari Alimentare 4:311–348.

HAAKH, T.
1929   Studien uber Alter und Wachstum der Bodenseefische. Archiv fuer Hydro-
        biologie 20:214–295.

HAAS, R. L.
1943   A list of fishes of McHenry County, Illinois. Copeia 1943:162.
        One specimen was found in the Fox River drainage.

HABEKOVIC, D.
1979   Krvna svojstva stuke (*Esox lucius* L.). [The blood properties of the pike
        (*Esox lucius* L.).] Ribar. Jugosl. 34(4):73–77.

HADLEY, W. F.
1970   Radio tracking investigation of the movement of carp (*Cyprinus carpio*) and
        pike (*Esox lucius*) in Cedar Creek, Anoka County, Minnesota. American
        Society of Ichthyologists and Herpetologists, 50th Annual Meeting, New
        Orleans, 1970.

HAEGEMAN, J.
1979   Coloring a northern pike. American Taxidermist Magazine 13(1):4–6.
        Step-by-step instructions for painting a pike for mounting.

HAEMPEL, O. and H. LECHLER
1931   Uber die Wirkung von ultravioletter Bestrahlung auf Fischeier und Fischbrut.
        Zeitschrift fur Vergleichende Physiologie 14:265–272.

HAEN, P. J. and F. J. O'ROURKE
1969a   Comparative electrophoretic studies of soluble eye lens proteins of some Irish
        freshwater fishes. Proceedings of the Royal Irish Academy, Section B, Bio-
        logical, Geological and Chemical Science, 68(4):67–75.
1969b   Comparative electrophoretic studies of the water-soluble muscle proteins of
        some Irish freshwater fishes. Proceedings of the Royal Irish Academy, Sec-
        tion B, Biological, Geological and Chemical Science, 68(7):101–110.

HAFFNER, C.
1912   Der Hecht in Aquarium. Blattchen Aquarien und Terrarien Kunde
        23:206–208.

HAGENOW, K F., VON
1860   Fisch un Vogel. Arch. Ver. Freunde Naturgesch. Mecklenburg 14:453–454.

HAGENSON, I. and J. F. O'CONNOR
1979   A fisheries inventory of Obukowin and Aikens lakes, 1978. Manitoba
        Department of Natural Resources, Fisheries Manuscript Report 79–75:1–54.
        Aikens Lake Lodge has had no major adverse effect on the pike population of
        Obukowin Lake.

HAIDER, G. and U. PAGGA
1983   Untersuchengen an Rheinfischen im Bereich des BASF. [Investigations on
        Rhine fishes in the area of BASF]. Verhandlungen Geseilschaft Oekol
        10:293–297.

HAIME, J.
1874   A history of fish culture in Europe from its earlier records to 1854. Report of
        the U.S. Commissioner of Fish and Fisheries 1871–72(App. D):463–492.

HAKANSON, L.
1980   The quantitative impact of pH, bioproduction and Hg-contamination on the
        Hg content of fish. Environmental Pollution 1:285–304.

HAKKARI, L. and P. BAGGE

1983　The densities of pike yearlings in Lake Saimaa. *In* Hirvonen, L., ed., Saimaan tutkimus, vol. 2, pp. 137–140. [in Finnish].

HAKKILA, K. and A. NIEMI

1973　Effects of oil and emulsifiers on eggs and larvae of northern pike (*Esox lucius*) in brackish water. Aqua Fennica: 44–59.

　　　The experiment was conducted in brackish water (salinity 5.8%). Not all substances studied increased the mortality of eggs, but all increased the occurrence of abnormal larvae. High temperatures increased the toxicity of emulsifiers. The resistance of larvae varied greatly at different stages of development.

HAKKINEN, I.

1978　Diet of the osprey *Pandion haliaetus* in Finland. Ornis Scandinavica 9:111–116.

HAKOKONGAS, M.

1971　On the biology of pike, *Esox lucius* L., in different seasons. M.S. thesis, University of Oulu. 50 pp. [in Finnish].

HALKETT, A.

1898　Report of the expedition to Hudson Bay and Cumberland Gulf in the steamship "Diana" under the command of Wm. Wakeham. Report Canadian Department of Marine Fisheries, Sessional Papers, 32(9):80–83.

1913　Checklist of the fishes of the Dominion of Canada and Newfoundland. King's Printer, Ottawa. 138 pp.

HALL, D. J. and E. E. WERNER

1977　Seasonal distribution and abundance of fishes in the littoral zone of a Michigan lake. Transactions of the American Fisheries Society 106:545–555.

　　　A team of divers performed seven censuses from May to October 1976. There was little habitat segregation in spring when temperatures rose and food was abundant; during summer species distributions and abundances were quite constant, considerable habitat segregation was apparent.

HALLET, C.

1977　Contribution a l'etude du regime alimentaire du martin-pecheur (*Alcedo atthis*) dans la vallee de la Lesse. [Contribution to the study of the diet of the kingfisher (*Alcedo atthis*) in the Lesse Valley.] Aves 14:128–144.

　　　Pike were practically non-existent in pellets.

HALLOCK, C.

1877　The sportsman's gazetteer and general guide. The game animals, birds and fishes of North America; their habits and various methods of capture. New York, Forest and Stream Publication. 688 pp.

1886　Esox at sea! The American Angler 9(8).

　　　Reports two 1859 sightings of pike at sea, one incident being several miles from land. Two were seen off Australia, and several were seen off Java.

HALME, E.

1957　Gaddmarkningar utforda av Timmero spinnfiskeklubb r. f. [Pike tagging by Timmero spinfishing club.] Fiskeritidskrift for Finland, Ny Ser., 1:8–15.

1958　Pike taggings performed by Timmero spinnfiskeklubb rf. Suomen kalastuslehti 2:35–41. [in Finnish].

HALME, E. and S. HURME

1952   Studies on fishing waters, fishes and fishery in the sea areas off Helsinki. Helsinki. 157 pp. [in Finnish].

HALME, E. and E. KORHONEN

1960   Migrations of pike in our coastal waters. Kalamies 4:1–12. [in Finnish].

HALNON, L.

1960   Fishery investigations of Lake Champlain and other waters. To collect management information on larger Vermont lakes and to appraise new and existing regulations. Vermont Fish and Game Department, Project F-1-R-8/Job 5:1–27.

HALNON, L. C.

1959   Fisheries investigations of Lake Champlain and other waters. Investigation of the effect of a season for shooting northern pike during spawning. Vermont Fish and Game Department, Project F-1-R-7/Job 2:1–14.
        Shooting pressure had little effect on reproductive intensity or success, probably due to weather conditions and water turbidity. Throughout the summer the number of yearlings in the shooting area and a nearby refuge were similar.

HALVORSEN, O.

1968   Studies of the helminth fauna of Norway. XII. *Axygia lucii* (Muller, 1776) (Digenea, Azygiidae) in pike (*Esox lucius* L.) from Bogstad Lake, and a note on its occurrence in lake and river habitats. Nytt Magasin for Zoologi 16:29–38.
        Infections were found in 91% of the pike from Bogstad Lake. Gives information on intensity, seasonality, size of *A. lucii*, size of pike infected. There appears to be a second intermediate host in the life cycle of *A. lucii*.

HALVORSEN, O. and K. ANDERSEN

1973   Parasites in fresh water environments. Fauna 26:165–189.

HAMACKOVA, J., J. KOURIL and S. CHABERA

1977   Prehled metod odchovu pludku stiky obecne *Esox lucius* L. [Methods of rearing technologies of pike fry.] Buletin Vyzkumy Ustav Rybarsky a Hydrobiologicky Vodnany 13(2):25–31.

HAMACKOVA, J., Z. SVOBODOVA and J. KOURIL

1975   Hematologicke hodnoty stiky obecne (*Esox lucius* L.) z rybnicniho chovu v predvyterovem obdobi. [Hematological values of pond-farmed pike (*Esox lucius* L.) in the pre-spawning period]. Zivocisna vyroba 20:851–860.

HAMER, C.

1975   Big northerns run deep. Fins and Feathers, April 1975, pp. 18–20.
        An account of angling a 16-lb and an 18-lb pike in a lake close to St. Paul.

HAMES, R.

1970   Northern pike spawning area investigations (1965–1966). Connecticut Board of Fisheries and Game, Project Completion Reports (unpublished). 4 pp.

HAMPTON, J. F.

1948   Fighting pike. Salmon and Trout Magazine 123:108.

HANKINSON, T. L.

1908   A biological survey of Walnut Lake, Michigan. Michigan State Board Geological Survey Report 1907:157–288.

1916   Results of the Shiras expeditions to Whitefish Point, Michigan: fishes. Michigan Geological and Biological Survey, Publication 20, Biology Series, 4:111–170.

1920   Report on investigations of the fish of the Galien River, Berrien County, Michigan. University of Michigan, Museum of Zoology, Occasional Papers, 89:1–141.

1929   Fishes of North Dakota. Papers of the Michigan Academy of Science, Arts and Letters 10:438–460.

HANNERZ, L.
1968   Experimental investigations on the accumulation of mercury in water organisms. Report Institute of Freshwater Research Drottningholm 48:120–176.

HANNON, M. R., Y. A. GREICHUS, R. L. APPLEGATE and A. C. FOX
1970   Ecological distribution of pesticides in Lake Poinsett, South Dakota. Transactions of the American Fisheries Society 99:496–500.
        Concentrations of pesticides were determined on six samples of pike by gas chromatograph and thin-layer chromatography. Higher fat content of fish was correlated with higher insectide levels. Residue levels increased with age. No significant difference was found between sexes, or between fall and spring collections.

HANSEN, J. P.
1983   Raubfische angeln—Hecht, Barsch, Zander. [Fishing predators—pike, perch, pike-perch.] Munich, BLV Verlagsgesellschaft.
        A guide for sport fishing.

1985   Tag sommargaddan pa metgrej. Fiske Journalen 7–8(July-August):16–17.

HANSON, A.
1966   Differences in the value of N-acetyl histidine in freshwater and marine teleosts. Comptes Rendus des Seances de la Societe de Biologie 160:265–268.

HANSON, H.
1958   Operation fish rescue. Progressive Fish-Culturist 20:186–188.
        Method of rescuing pike from freeze-out lakes. In one winter season 52,699 pike weighing 20,861 lb were taken from a 1,549-acre lake.

HARAM, O. J.
1966   Echo sounding in freshwater fishery research. *In* Jones, J. W., and P. H. Tombleson, eds., Proceedings of the 2nd British Coarse Fish Conference, Liverpool, 1965, pp. 120–125.

HARKA, A.
        Growth rate of pike in River Tisje. Halazzati 27:83

HARKNESS, W. J. K.
1936a   Biological study of Lake Nipissing. North Bay Nugget, February 14, 1936, Article No. 4.

1936b   Biological study of Lake Nipissing. North Bay Nugget, April 9, 1936, Article No. 12.

1936c   Biological study of Lake Nipissing. Nipissing's pike, maskinonge are observed by biologist. North Bay Nugget, April 17, 1936, Article No. 13.

HARKNESS, W. J. K. and J. L. HART
1927   The fishes of Long Lake, Ontario. Publication of the Ontario Fisheries Research Laboratory 29:21–31.
        The pike is common, especially in the shallow water at the north and south ends of the lake, and in bays.

130

HARLAN, J. R. and E. B. SPEAKER
1956   Iowa fish and fishing. 3rd ed. Iowa Conservation Commission. 377 pp.
HARPER, F.
1948   Fishes of the Nueltin Lake expedition, Keewatin 1947. Part 2—Historical
         and field notes. Proceedings of the Academy of Natural Science, Philadel-
         phia, 100:153–184.
1961   Field and historical notes on freshwater fishes of the Ungava Peninsula and
         on certain marine fishes of the north shore of the Gulf of St. Lawrence. Jour-
         nal of the Elisha Mitchell Scientific Society 77:312–342.
         Lists the occurrences of pike on the peninsula prior to 1961. The earliest
         record of pike mentioned was a reference to Cartwright (1792), from
         Sandwich Bay and White Bear River.
HARRINGTON, R. W., Jr.
1947   The breeding behavior of the bridled shiner, *Notropis bifrenatus*. Copeia
         1947:186.
         Bridled shiner is an important forage fish for the early stages of pike.
HARRIS, A. J.
1980   Pike attacking adult moorhen. British Birds. 73(3):159.
HARRIS, J. E.
1938   The role of the fins in the equilibrium of the swimming fish. Journal of
         Experimental Biology 15.
HARRISON, A. C.
1959   Progress report of fish populations, Humboldt study area. Iowa Conservation
         Commission, Quarterly Biology Report 11(2):24–29.
         Gives information on stocking, susceptibility to electrofishing, angling suc-
         cess, and growth.
HARRISON, E. J.
1978   Comparative ecologic life histories of sympatric populations of *Esox lucius*
         and *Esox masquinongy* of the upper Niagara River and its local watershed.
         Ph.D. thesis, State University of New York at Buffalo. 303 pp.
         Collected 623 pike during 1975 and 1976. Investigated length-weight rela-
         tionship, age and growth and mortality. Determined population estimate and
         movement patterns by mark-recapture studies.
HARRISON, E. J. and W. F. HADLEY
1978   Ecologic separation of sympatric muskellunge and northern pike. American
         Fisheries Society Special Publication 11:129–134.
         With the exception of a few one-year-old fish, no muskellunge were found in
         tributaries of the upper Niagara River during 1975–77, but 97% of pike were
         collected in tributaries. Differential adaptation to river current may be an
         important factor in coexistence.
1979   A comparison of the use of cleithra to the use of scales for age and growth
         studies. Transactions of the American Fisheries Society 108:452–456.
1982   Possible effects of black-spot disease on northern pike. Transactions of the
         American Fisheries Society 111:106–109.
         Of the 623 Niagara River pike examined, 22% were diseased. Attempts to
         identify the causative digenic trematode were unsuccessful. Suggests that
         retarded growth and increased mortality were related to infection.
1983   Biology of the northern pike in the upper Niagara River watershed. New
         York Fish and Game Journal 30:57–63.

Several life-history parameters of pike in the upper Niagara River watershed were determined and compared with similar data for other populations. Information on length-weight, age at maturity, and survival.

HARRISON, H. M., C. O'FARRELL and T. E. MOEN
　　1961　Progress report, renovation of the Winnebago River, Iowa. Iowa Conservation Commission, Quarterly Biology Report 13:32–37.
　　　　　Two years after eradication of the fish population and restocking, fry stocking of pike established a good seed stock population.

HARRISON, J. S.
　　1963　Northern pike survive. New Mexico Wildlife 8(6):10.

HART, J. L.
　　1931　On the daily movements of the coregonine fishes. Canadian Field-Naturalist 45(1):8–9.
　　　　　Between September 10 and 14, 1925, gill nets captured equal numbers of pike during day and night sets.

HART, P. J. B. and B. CONNELLAN
　　1979　On pike predation in a fishery. Proceedings of the 1st British Freshwater Fisheries Conference, Liverpool, pp. 182–195.
　　　　　A progress report on the development of a computer model as a management tool to determine the best levels of angling mortality and densities of pike and prey.
　　1984　Cost of prey capture, growth rate and ration size in pike, *Esox lucius* L., as functions of prey weight. Journal of Fish Biology 25:279–292.

HART, P. J. B. and T. J. PITCHER
　　1969a　Field trials of fish marking using a jet inoculator. Journal of Fish Biology 1:383–385.
　　　　　Pike 210–940 mm marked with Durazol Blue on body and fins retained a mark of average quality for 4 months in the field. The mark can be applied easily and quickly with minimal damage to the fish.
　　1969b　Population densities and growth of five species of fish in the River Nene, Northamptonshire. Journal of the Institute of Fisheries Management 4:69–86.

HARTLEY, P. H. T.
　　1940　The food of coarse fish. Freshwater Biological Association of the British Empire, Scientific Publication 3:1–33.
　　1947a　The coarse fishes of Britain. Freshwater Biological Association, Scientific Publication 12:1–40.
　　1947b　The natural history of some British freshwater fishes. Proceedings of the Zoological Society of London 117:129–206.
　　1948　Food and feeding relationships in a community of freshwater fishes. Journal of Animal Ecology 17:1–14.
　　　　　A total of 62 pike were examined to determine feeding habits. Adult pike were found to feed only upon fish while juveniles ate both fish and invertebrates.

HARTMANN, J.
　　1977　Fischereiliche Veranderungen in Kulturbedingt eutrophierenden Seen. Schweizerische Zeitschrift fuer Hydrologie 39:243–254.
　　1978　Growth of fishes during oligotrophic, mesotrophic and eutrophic status of Lake Constance. Schweizerische Zeitschrift fuer Hydrologie 40:32–39.

HARVEY, H. H.

    1980   Widespread and diverse changes in the biota of North American lakes and rivers coincident with acidification. *In* Drablos, D., and T. Tollan, eds., Proceedings International Conference, Norway, 1980, pp. 93–98.

HARVEY, H. H. and J. F. COOMBS

    1971   Physical and chemical limnology of the lakes of Manitoulin Island. Journal of the Fisheries Research Board of Canada 28:1883–1897.

             Winterkills of pike were observed in three lakes on Manitoulin Island from 1965 to 1970, but the presence of older age-classes of fish in most lakes suggested that extensive winterkills were not common.

HASANEN, E. and J. K. MIETTINEN

    1963   Caesium-137 content of freshwater fish in Finland. Nature 200:1018–1019.

             Especially high radiocaesium values were found in analyses of pike caught in 1961–63.

HASANEN, E. and V. SJOBLOM

    1968   Kalojen elohopeapitoisuus Suomessa vuonna 1967. [Mercury content of fish in Finland in 1967.] Suomen Kalatalous 36, Finlands Fiskerier, 24 pp.

             The mercury content of pike (white muscle, fresh weight) varied from 0.03 to 5.8 mg/kg, and similar levels have been found in burbot *Lota lota* and perch *Perca fluviatilis*. As a result, the wood conversion industry has stopped using fungicides that contain mercury, and the chlorine-alkali industry has been required to build protection and cleaning plants.

HASHIMOTO, Y.

    1975   Nutritional requirements of warm water fish. Proceedings of the 9th International Congress of Nutrition, Mexico, 1972. Vol. 3, Foods for the expanding world, pp. 158–175.

HASSELROT, T. B.

    1968   Report on current field investigations concerning the mercury content in fish, bottom sediment, and water. Report Institute of Freshwater Research Drottningholm 48:102–111.

             Great differences in mercury content can exist in pike caught upstream and downstream from a cellulose mill.

HASSELROT, T. B. and A. GOTHBERG

    1974   The ways of transport of mercury to fish. Proceedings of the International Conference on Transport of Persistent Chemicals in Aquatic Ecosystems, Ottawa, 1974.

             Pike from a lake unaffected by phenyl mercury were tagged and moved into a heavily contaminated lake. After a year, mercury values in the muscular tissue had greatly increased. It is concluded that important factors in the concentration of mercury are food and intake through the gills.

HASSINGER, R. and D. WOODS

    1974   Statewide fisheries research. Evaluation of Fintrol as a fish toxicant in deep softwater lakes. Minnesota Division of Game and Fish, Project F-26-R-5/SPI.

             Fintrol application during fall turnover successfully rehabilitated four trout lakes. Treatment was lethal for all target species of fish.

HASSLER, T. J.

    1969   Biology of the northern pike in Oahe Reservoir, 1959 through 1965. U.S. Bureau of Sport Fisheries and Wildlife, Technical Paper 29:1–13.

133

Variations in length, weight, and maturity of pike were associated with sex and year class. Females were larger and more numerous than males.

1970   Environmental influences on early development and year-class strength of northern pike in lakes Oahe and Sharpe, South Dakota. Transactions of the American Fisheries Society 99:369–375.

Mortalities between 97 and 100% during early embryonic stages were associated with sudden drops in water temperature below 10 C, prolonged temperatures near 5 C, and silt deposition of 1.0 mm per day. These factors, as well as dropping water levels, result in small year classes. Large year classes were related to stable or rising water levels and temperature, flooded vegetation, and calm weather.

1982   Effect of temperature on survival of northern pike embryos and yolk-sac larvae. Progressive Fish-Culturist 44:174–178.

Embryos and larvae were incubated at constant temperatures 3–24 C. The hatching range, optimum range, lethal temperatures, and maximum hatch temperatures were studied. The effects of embryo age and type of temperature change (shock or tempered) on test results were recorded. Management implications were discussed.

HATFIELD, C. T., J. N. STEIN, M. R. FALK, C. S. JESSOP and D. N. SHEPHERD

1972   Fish resources of the Mackenzie River valley. Canada Department of the Environment, Fisheries Service, Interim Report 1, 2:1–289.

Data on pike: length-weight relationship, length-frequency distribution, fork lengths by age class (age assessed by scales and otoliths), sex ratio, stomach contents analysis, catch summary, and heavy metal and chlorinated hydrocarbon concentrations in specimens.

HATTULA, M. L., J. JANATUINEN, J. SARKKA and J. PAASIVIRTA

1978   A five-year study of the chlorinated hydrocarbons in the fish of a Finnish lake ecosystem. Environmental Pollution 15:121–140.

In pike no statistically significant differences were observed in the concentrations of chlorinated hydrocarbons between the five limnologically different areas of Lake Paijanne, and the five research years.

HAWDY, P. W.

Life history and propagation of northern pike. Alchesay National Fish Hatchery, Whiteriver, Arizona.

HAZZARD, A. S.

Pennsylvania fishes. Pennsylvania Fish Commission, 32 pp.

1935   A preliminary study of an exceptionally productive trout water, Fish Lake, Utah. Transactions of the American Fisheries Society 65:122–128.

1945   Warm-water fish management. Wisconsin Conservation Bulletin 10(10): 12–15.

HAZZARD, A. S. and R. W. ESCHMEYER

1936   A comparison of summer and winter fishing in Michigan lakes. Transactions of the American Fisheries Society 66:87–97.

Winter fishing is not generally harmful to summer fishing in Michigan, although a closed period during the spawning season seems justifiable in "pike" lake such as Houghton Lake.

HAZZARD, A. S. and D. S. SHETTER

1939   Results from experimental plantings of legal-sized brook trout (*Salvelinus fontinalis*) and rainbow trout (*Salmo irideus*). Transactions of the American

134

Fisheries Society 68:196–210.

HEADLAM, M.

1939   Winter in prospect and retrospect. Salmon and Trout Magazine 97:304–308.

HEADRICK, M. R., M. S. BEVELHIMER, R. F. CARLINE and R. A. STEIN

1981   Evaluation of fish management techniques. Evaluation of stocking northern pike in Ohio lakes. Ohio Department of Natural Resources, Federal Aid Project F-57-R-3.

Pike in Lake Logan grew rapidly, but survival and harvest were poor. Population density was at or below the bottom of the range for natural populations. Most year classes were decimated within the first year after stocking. Data on diet, consumption rate, growth, survival, and optimal temperatures are given.

HEADRICK, M. R. and R. F. CARLINE

1980   Evaluation of fish management techniques. Evaluation of stocking northern pike in Ohio lakes. Ohio Department of Natural Resources, Federal Aid Project F-57-R-2:1–17.

Field sampling was done from October 1979 to March 1980. Computer simulations of growth indicated that pike must feed at more than 75% of the maximum rate to grow in typical Ohio lakes. Overwinter growth may account for 61–76% of the weight attained in the first two years. Radiotelemetry indicated that pike in Lake Logan spent most of the summer where the thermocline meets the lake bottom.

HEALEY, M. C.

1972   Bioenergetics of a sand goby (*Gobius minutus*) population. Journal of the Fisheries Research Board of Canada 29:187–194.

Pike are included in a table showing energy budgets for fish on restricted rations.

HEALY, A.

1956a   Pike (*Esox lucius* L.) in three Irish lakes. Scientific Proceedings of the Royal Dublin Society 27(N.S.):51–63.

A study based on scales, measurements, weights, stomach contents and some ovaries of pike collected 1950–54. Gives information on age, growth, maturity, condition, sex ratios, food, and reproduction.

1956b   Fishes of Lough Rea, Co. Galway, Ireland. 2. Pike and rudd with general conclusions. Salmon and Trout Magazine 148:246–249.

Summarizes the general biology of pike. Growth is discussed particularly.

HEALY, J. A. and M. F. MULCAHY

1979   Polymorphic tetrameric superoxide dismutase in the pike *Esox lucius* L. (Pisces: Esocidae). Comparative Biochemistry and Physiology 62b:563–566.

Heart muscle extracts of pike from Lake Malaren in Sweden exhibited two electrophoretic types of superoxide dismutase, one of which was identified as the cytoplasmic enzyme (s-SOD) and the other as the mitochondrial form (m-SOD). Individual analysis of 51 pike indicated that S-SOD was invariant while m-SOD displayed a pattern of variation that was explicable by a single-locus polymorphism. The observed m-SOD phenotype patterns suggested that the enzyme is a tetramer. This interpretation is supported by in vitro molecular hybridization studies.

1980   A biochemical genetic analysis of populations of the northern pike, *Esox lucius* L., from Europe and North America. Journal of Fish Biology 17:317–324.

Genetic variation as identified by starch gel electrophoresis and enzyme staining was studied in seven populations of pike: northern US, Canada, Swedish
fresh water, Swedish Baltic, the Netherlands, England, and Ireland. Mean
heterozygosity was estimated to be 0.019. This is discussed in terms of the
structure and possible origins of pike populations.

HEARD, W. R., R. L. WALLACE and W. L. HARTMAN
  1969   Distributions of fishes in fresh water of Katmai National Monument, Alaska,
          and their zoogeographical implications. U.S. Fish and Wildlife Service, Spe-
          cial Scientific Report, Fisheries 590:1–20.

HEARTWELL, C. and L. HESS
  1977   Small impoundment investigation. Literature review of large esocids
          (muskellunge, northern pike, hybrid tiger muskellunge). West Virginia
          Department of Natural Resources, Dingell Johnson Project F-23-R-1:1–40.

HEDERSTROM, H.
  1959   Observations on the age of fishes. Report Institute of Freshwater Research
          Drottningholm 40:161–164.
          A repudiation of "Heibrun's pike" which was claimed to have a length of 565
          cm, a weight of 148 kg, and an age of 267 years - especially its age.

HEESE, L. W. and B. A. NEWCOMB
  1982   On estimating the abundance of fish in the upper channelized Missouri River.
          North American Journal of Fisheries Management 2:80–83.
          Population estimates and 95% confidence limits were obtained by
          electrofishing during winters of 1979–80 and 1980–81 in two 16 km study
          areas.

HEGEMANN, M.
  1958a   Beitrage zur Biologie des Hechtes im Brackwasserbegiet des Briefswalder
          Boddens. Zeitschrift fuer Fischerei und deren Hilfswissenschaften
          7:459–476.
          The paper deals with the nutrition, the beginning of sexual maturity, the
          spawning season, growth in length and weight of pike from the Greifswald
          Bodden (shallow bay on the Baltic).
  1958b   Ein Vorkommen von *Henneguya creplini* Gurley 1894 beim Hecht. [*Henne-
          guya creplini* Gurley 1894 found in the pike]. Zeitschrift fuer Fischerei und
          deren Hilfswissenschaften 7:513–515.
  1964   Der Hecht. Stuttgart, Ziemsen-Verlag Wittenberg. 76 pp.

HEINRICH, D.
  1980   Die Fische. *In* H. Hinz, ed., Untersuchung einer Siedlungskammer in Osthol-
          stein. Vol. 4. Neumunster.
  1981   Contributions to the history of the fish fauna of Schleswig-Holstein, West
          Germany. Zoologischer Anzeiger 207:181–200.

HELDER, T.
  1980   Effects of 2,3,7,8 - tetrachlorodibenzo-p-dioxin (TCDD) on early life stages
          of the pike (*Esox lucius* L.). Science of the Total Environment 14:255–264.
          Freshly fertilized pike eggs were exposed to TCDD at concentrations of 0.1,
          1.0, and 10 ppt (ng/liter) for 96 hours. At all concentrations egg development
          was retarded by 23%; growth of fry was retarded for a long period after expo-
          sure.

HELFMAN, G. S.

1979   Fish attraction to floating objects in lakes. *In* Johnson, D. L., and R. A. Stein, eds., Response of fish to habitat structure in standing waters. North Central Division, American Fisheries Society Special Publication 6:49–57.

HELLAWELL, J.

1966   Coarse fish in a salmon river. *In* Jones, J. W., and P. H. Tombleson, eds., Proceedings of the 2nd British Coarse Fish Conference, Liverpool, 1965, pp. 43–48.

HELM, W. T.

1958   Notes on the ecology of panfish in Lake Wingra with special reference to the yellow bass. Ph.D. thesis, University of Wisconsin.

HELMS, D.

1976   Commercial fisheries investigations. Northern pike investigations. Iowa State Conservation Commission Project 2–225-R:1–18.
       Vital statistics of pike populations in four selected pools of the Mississippi River were determined to appraise suitability of the species as a commercial food-fish. Also examined a questionnaire on commercial fishing, chemical pollutants in pike flesh, and weight change due to food-fishing processing.

HELMS, D. R.

1966   1965 annual survey of the Coralville Reservoir fish population. Iowa Conservation Commission Quarterly Biology Report 18(2):27–32.
       An annual survey is conducted to maintain a continuous inventory and antici-pate population changes. Pike 13–17 inches were common in both pools and tailwaters.

1975   Progress report on the first year study of northern pike in the Mississippi River. Iowa Conservation Commission Fishery Investigation Project 2–225-R-1.
       A study was conducted in pools of the river bordering Iowa to determine the suitability of pike as a commercial food-fish.

HELSTROM, N.

1978   The growth and feeding of northern pike in Tvarminne. M.S. thesis, University of Helsinki. 67 pp. [in Finnish]

HENDERSON, N. E. and R. E. PETER

1969   Distribution of fishes of southern Alberta. Journal of the Fisheries Research Board of Canada 26:325–338.
       A map shows locations where pike were found.

HENEGAR, D.

1960a Fisheries—1959. North Dakota Outdoors, Jan. 1960, pp. 9–10, 18.

1960b Trolling still good. North Dakota Outdoors, May 1960, pp. 15, 20.

1969   Annual report. Fisheries Division. North Dakota Outdoors 31(7):28–34.

HENLEY, D. T. and R. L. APPLEGATE

1982   Seasonal distribution of esocids in a power plant cooling reservoir. Progressive Fish-Culturist 44:40–41.
       Ultrasonic transmitters were implanted in ten esocids. One muskellunge and two pike survived, were released, and then tracked from July 1979 to July 1980. They were found to be seasonally distributed in areas where temperatures were most favourable for survival and growth.

HENSHALL, J. A.

    1919   Bass, pike, perch and other game fishes of America. new ed. Cincinnati, Stewart and Kidd. 410 pp.

HERBERT, H. W.

    1851   Frank Forester's fish and fishing of the United States and British provinces of North America. 3rd ed. New York, Stringer and Townsend. 359 pp.

HEROLD, R. C.

    1971a   The development and mature structure of dentine in the pike *Esox lucius* analyzed by microradiography. Archives of Oral Biology 16:29–41.

    1971b   Osteodentinogenesis. An ultrastructural study of tooth formation in the pike *Esox lucius*. Zeitschrift fuer Zellforschung und Mikroskopische Anatomie Abteilung Histochemie 112:1–14.

HEROLD, R. C. and L. LANDINO

    1970   The development and mature structure of dentine in the pike *Esox lucius* analyzed by bright field microscopy, phase microscopy and polarization microscopy. Archives of Oral Biology 15:747–760.

HEROLD, R. C. B.

    1974   Ultrastructure of odontogenesis in the pike *Esox lucius*. Role of dental epithelium and formation of enameloid layer. Journal of Ultrastructure Research 48:435–454.

           Ultrastructure of dentine, enameloid layer, inner dental epithelium, and outer dental epithelium were investigated by electron microscopy.

    1975   Scanning electron microscopy of enameloid and dentin in fish teeth. Archives of Oral Biology 20:635–640.

HESS, L.

    1980a   Small impoundment investigation. Evaluation of existing small impoundment esocid populations. West Virginia, Performance Report. Dingell-Johnson Project F-23-R-4, Job IV-2:1–15.

    1980b   Small impoundment investigation. Establishment and evaluation of suitability of one or more strains as trophy fishes. West Virginia Performance Report. Dingell-Johnson Project F-23-R-4, Job IV-3:15–24.

    1980c   Small impoundment investigation. Preparation of esocid bulletin. West Virginia Performance report. Dingell-Johnson Project F-23-R-4, Job IV-4:24–25.

HESS, L. and C. HEARTWELL

    1977   Small impoundment investigation. Esocid literature review. West Virginia Department of Natural Resources, Project F-23-R-1, Job N-1:1–42.

           Evaluation and comparison of the suitability of pike, muskellunge, and pike-muskellunge hybrid as small impoundment sport fishes. Describes extensive and intensive culture and reviews production.

    1979   Literature review of large esocids (muskellunge, northern pike, hybrid tiger muskellunge). *In* Dube, J., and Y. Gravel, eds., Proceedings of the 10th Warmwater Workshop, Special Publication NE Division of the American Fisheries Society. Montreal, Quebec Ministere du Loisir, de la Chasse et de la Peche. 285 pp.

           The pike-muskellunge hybrid is difficult to sample; grows rapidly, particularly in new impoundments; returns better to the angler than the muskellunge; and is readily accepted by a growing segment of anglers as a valued trophy.

138

HESSEN, D. O.

1985   Introduction of pike *Esox lucius* to a small pond: Effects on planktivorous
        fish, zooplankton and phytoplankton. Fauna (Blindern) 36(4):119–124.
        The introduction of several small pike strongly reduced the number of smelt
        Osmerus eperlanus, resulting in a strong increase of cladocera and a decrease
        of rotifera. The algal biomass, which started to increase in early summer, was
        strongly reduced as the cladocerans increased.

HESSER, R. B.

1978   Management implications of hybrid esocids in Pennsylvania. American
        Fisheries Society Special Publication 11:302–307.

HESSLE, C.

1934   Markningsforsok ned Gadda, I. Ostergotlands Skargard Aren, 1928, Och
        1930. Stockholm, Mitteilungen der Anstalt fur Binnenfischerei bei
        Drottningholm.

HEUSCHMANN, O.

1940   Die Hechtzucht. *In* Handbuch der Binnenfischerei Mitteleuropas 6:750–787.

1957   Die Hechtartigen ordnung Haplomi (Esociformes). *In* Demoll, R., and H. N.
        Maier, eds., Handbuch der Binnenfischerei Mitteleuropas, Band III, 8:1–13.

HICKLEY, P. and A. SUTTON

1984   A standard growth curve for pike. Fisheries Management 15:29–30.
        Standard length for age values and corresponding standard growth curve for
        pike from six British waters.

HICKS, D.

1972a   Great northern pike introductions. Introductions. Oklahoma Department of
        Wildlife Conservation, Project F-22-R-5/Job 1:1–4.
        Information (numbers, size or age, and date) on pike stocking and survival in
        some Oklahoma lakes.

1972b   Great northern pike introductions. Fry sampling. Oklahoma Department of
        Wildlife Conservation, Project F-22-R-5/Job 2:1–3.
        Four lakes were sampled with electrofishing gear and a fry scoop to ascertain
        the presence of natural reproduction.

1972c   Great northern pike introductions. Gonadal inspection. Oklahoma Depart-
        ment of Wildlife Conservation, Project F-22-R-5/Job 3:1–7.
        In 1971 and 1972, 19 adult pike were collected with various nets and an
        electrofishing boat. The presence of ripeness was noted for males and
        females. Gonadal examination and egg enumeration were made for one
        female specimen.

HICKS, D. E., K. COOK and P. MAUCK

1970   Great northern pike introductions. Introductions. Oklahoma Department of
        Wildlife Conservation, Project F-22-R-3/Job 1:1–3.

HILDEN, W., R. HUDD and H. LEHTONEN

1982   The effects of environmental changes on the fisheries and fish stocks in the
        Archipelago Sea and the Finnish part of the Gulf of Bothnia. Aqua Finnica
        12:47–58.

HILE, R.

1931   Investigations of Indiana lakes. 2. Rate of growth of fishes of Indiana. Indi-
        ana Department of Conservation, Publication 107:7–55.

HILGENDORF, F. M.

1872   Ueber ben Bau der Oberkinnlade beim Hecht (*Esox lucius*). Dresden, Sitzber. Ges. Isis, pp. 230–231.

1880   Hornbekleidung der Kiefer bei Teuthis. Berlin, Sitzber. Ges. Naturf. Freunde, p. 121

HILL, K.

1974   The northern pike population in Brown's Lake, Iowa, following a winterkill. Iowa Fisheries Research Technical Series 74–1:1–32.
Population size, life history, seasonal food habits, length-weight relationships, body condition factors, body scale relationships, growth rates, and fecundity of pike from Brown's Lake were determined for 1970–72.

HILL, W. J.

1969   Statewide fisheries investigations. Fish tagging studies. North Dakota Game and Fish Department, Project F-2-R-16, Job 9:1–22.
This program continued in 1968 for its eighth consecutive year. Examined pike movement in two lakes, and the degree of tag loss.

HILL, W. J. and A. H. WIPPERMAN

1978   Northcentral Montana fisheries study. Inventory and survey of waters in the western half of region four. Montana Department of Fish and Game, Job Progress Report, 20 pp.
Pike populations were studied in two reservoirs and one lake in relation to age and growth, harvest, movement, and reproduction.

HINER, L. E.

1961   Propagation of northern pike. Transactions of the American Fisheries Society 90:298–302.
Eggs are incubated in Downing-type jars and the fry are stocked in hatchery ponds at the rate of 100,000 per acre. Filtered water is used for incubation, and ponds are fertilized 2 weeks prior to stocking. Average yield from ponds during 1959 and 1960 was 35,000 fingerlings per acre.

HINKS, D.

1943   The fishes of Manitoba. Manitoba Department of Mines and Natural Resources. 102 pp.

1957   The fishes of Manitoba. Manitoba Department of Mines and Natural Resources. 117 pp.

HINTON, D. E., E. R. WALKER, C. A. PINKSTAFF and E. M. ZUCHELKOWSKI

1984   Morphological survey of teleost organs important in carcinogenesis with attention to fixation. *In* Hoover, K. L., ed., Use of small fish species in carcinogenicity testing. Bethesda, National Institute of Health. pp. 291–320.
Key features of the gross and microscopic anatomy of teleost liver, digestive tract, kidney, and skin were reviewed from the world literature. New findings were obtained from light as well as scanning and transmission electron micrographs of tissues from seven freshwater fish species, including pike.

HINTZE, A.

1894   Gaddan sasom forellfiskare. Tidskrift Jagare Fiskeri 2:110.

HIRAKI, S., M. F. MULCAHY and L. DMOCHOWSKI

1978   Particle filament complex in tumor cells of northern pike *Esox lucius*. Texas Reports on Biology and Medicine 36:111–120.

HIRN, M.

1938   Die kunstliche Erbrutung des Hechtes. Allgemeine Fischerei-Zeitung
        6:55–58.

HOCHMAN, L.

1954   Fruchtbarkeit und Ernahrungszustand der Hechte aus den Tiechen. Acta
        Universatis Agriculturae Brno, A 3:557–567.

1964   Plodnost a stav vyzivenosti stik z rybniku. [Fecundity of pike.] Acta Univer-
        sitatis Agriculturae Brno.

HOFER, B.

1901   Ueber Missbildungen beim Hecht. Allgemeine Fischerei-Zeitung 26:14–15.

HOFFMAN, G. L.

1967   Fish and parasite check-list. In Parasites of North American freshwater
        fishes. Berkeley, University of California Press.

HOFFMANN, R., C. PFEIL-PUTZIEN and M. VOGT

1978   Cytolochemical studies on blood cells of three teleosts (carp—*Cyprinus car-
        pio* L., rainbow trout—*Salmo gairdneri* Richardson, and pike—*Esox lucius*
        L.). Berliner und Muenchener Tieraerztliche Wochenschrift 91(17):
        345–350.

HOFFMANN, R., P. WONDRAK and W. GROTH

1980   Seasonal anatomical variations in the testes of European pike, *Esox lucius* L.
        Journal of Fish Biology 16:475–482.
        The seasonal development of the testes in European pike was examined using
        wild fish and biopsies from pike housed in tanks. The size of the tubules and
        the different cell types were measured and their histological appearance
        described. Four stages of development were distinguished.

HOFMANN, J.

1965   Die Aufzucht der Hechtsetzlinge. Allgemeine Fischerei-Zeitung
        90(15):449–451.

HOGSTROM, G.

1944   Gaddklackning i invallningsdammar. Svensk Fiskerei Tidskrift 53:131.

HOKANSON, K. E. F.

1977   Temperature requirements of some percids and adaptations to the seasonal
        temperature cycle. Journal of the Fisheries Research Board of Canada
        34:1524–1550.
        Information on the temperature requirements of pike. Temperature
        classification, lethal temperature, physiological optimum, and the temperature
        range for reproduction are provided in table form.

HOKANSON, K. E. F., J. H. MCCORMICK and B. R. JONES

1973   Temperature requirements for embryos and larvae of the northern pike, *Esox
        lucius* (Linnaeus). Transactions of the American Fisheries Society
        102:89–100.
        The optimum temperature, median, upper, and lower tolerance limits for nor-
        mal and total hatches were recorded. The effects of embryo age on tolerance
        limits, growth, and mortality rates were evaluated. Recommendations were
        made for routine thermal bioassays for fish eggs.

HOKE, R. A., M. J. NORROCKY and B. L. PRATER

1975   Fish survey in the lower Portage River, Ohio. Ohio Journal of Science
        79:95–96.

141

HOLAK, H., B. JARZAB, A. BALDYS and B. WITALA

1979   Badania aktywnosci hipokalcemicznej ekstraktow z okolicy przegrody osierdziowo-otrzewnowej szczupaka. [Hypocalcemic activity of the intersep-tum separating pericardial and penfoneol cavities in the pike.] Zoologica Poloniae 2:291–296.

HOLCIK, J.

1966   The fishes of the River Hornad (East Slovakia) with regard to valley water reservoir building. Biology Works Science Commission Special Biology Slo-vakia Academy of Science 12/1(4):1–116.
Suggested that death of pike in a reservoir was due to metal, mining and metallurgy that pollute the river with waste water.

1968   Life history of the pike—*Esox lucius* L. 1758, in the Klicava Reservoir. Vestnik Ceskoslovenske Spolecnosti Zoologicke 132:166–180.
Deals with the life history of the pike in a reservoir (spawning, activity, mor-tality, age and growth). The decrease of pike abundance is related to unfavourable spawning conditions. Discusses the reasons for the fall in pike growth in relation to decrease of availability of different food components.

1970   Abundance, ichthyomass and production of fish populations in three types of water-bodies in Czechoslovakia (man-made lake, trout lake, arm of the Danube River). Ichthyologia 2:37–52.

1977   Changes in fish community of Klicava Reservoir with particular reference to Eurasian perch *Perca fluviatilis* 1957–1972. Journal of the Fisheries Research Board of Canada 34:1734–1747.
Changes in the fauna occurred after the 1955 filling of the 60-ha mesotrophic reservoir in Czechoslovakia. Lithophils were replaced by phytophils and then by ecologically more plastic species. Fish biomass increased in the first 12 years from 65 to 236 kg/ha but after 1967 dropped to 170 kg/ha. Pike was considered to have played a role in the decline of fish biomass in the reser-voir.

HOLCIK, J. and I. BASTL

1973   Ichthyocenoses of two arms of the Danube with regard to changes in species composition and population density in relation to the fluctuation of the water level in the main stream. Biological Works, Edition of the Scientific Commit-tee for Special Biology and of the Scientific Committee for General Biology of the Slovak Academy of Sciences XIX/1, 106 pp. [in Czech.]

1976   Ecological effects of water level fluctuation upon the fish populations in the Danube River floodplain in Czechoslovakia. Acta Scientiarum Naturalium Academiae Scientiarum Bohemoslovacae Brno 10(9):1–46.
Species composition, abundance, and ichthyomass of the fish communities in the Danube River arm of Zofin were investigated twice a year from 1969 to 1973. Water levels were positively correlated with the number of species and the ichthyomass of the arm. The importance of the floodplain for the fish communities was discussed.

HOLCIK, J. and J. MIHALIK

1968   Fresh-water fishes. Feltham, England, Spring Books. 128 pp.

HOLCIK, J. and K. PIVNICKA

1972   The density and production of fish populations in the Klicava Reservoir (Czechoslovakia) and their changes during the period 1957–1970. Interna-tional Revue der Gesamten Hydrobiologie 57:883–894.

Observations concerning species composition, ichthyomass, total and available production, harvestable yield and balance of fish populations (including pike) in a 67-ha reservoir in central Bohemia.

HOLDEN, A. V.

1973   International cooperative study of organo-chlorine and mercury residues in wildlife 1969–1971. Pesticides Monitoring Journal 7:37–52.

HOLLAND, L. E. and M. L. HUSTON

1984   Relationship of young-of-the-year northern pike to aquatic vegetation types in backwaters of the upper Mississippi River. North American Journal of Fisheries Management 4:514–522.

An evaluation of the impacts of potential loss of backwaters on available fish nursery habitats. Although preference for habitats with submerged vegetation was seemingly not related to food, the overall production of young was clearly best in these habitats.

HOLLER, P.

1935   Funktionelle Analyse des Hechtschadels. Morphol. Jahrb. 76:279–320.

HOLT, P. C., ed.

1972   The distributional history of the biota of the southern Appalachians. Part III: Vertebrates. Proceedings of a symposium sponsored by Virginia Polytechnic Institute, State University, Blacksburg, 1970. Association of Southeastern Biologists.

HOOGLAND, R., D. MORRIS and N. TINBERGEN

1957   The spines of sticklebacks (*Gasterosteus* and *Pygosteus*) as means of defence against predators (*Perca* and *Esox*). Behaviour 10:205–236.

A description of the predatory behaviour of pike is given. Analysis of the experiments shows that (1) sticklebacks are rejected when, after being snapped up, their spines hurt the predator's mouth; (2) after very few experiences pike become negatively conditioned to the sight of sticklebacks and avoid them before they have made contact.

HOOPER, F. F.

1951   Limnological features of a Minnesota seepage lake. American Midland Naturalist 46:462–481.

HOPKE, W.

1909   Hechte in Karpfenteichen. Fischerei Zeitung

1931   Das Wachstum des Junghechtes. Berlin, Mitteilungen der Fischerei Vereines.

1938   Kunstliche Erwarmung des Speisewassers in Hechtbrautanstalten. Fischerei Zeitung Neudam 41:319–321.

HORLER, A., M. E. JARVIS and R. A. C. JOHNSTON

1985   Creel census study on Fox, Marsh and Tagish lakes in the Yukon Territory 1983. Canadian Manuscript Report Fisheries and Aquatic Science 1803:1–53.

Data were compiled from 1,103 anglers to determine catch, effort, and angler origin. Catch per unit effort values are presented for each species by lake. Age, size, sex composition data,age-size, and size frequency are presented.

HOROSZEWICZ, L.

1964   Pokarm ryb drapieznych w Wille. [Food of predatory fishes in Vistula River.] Roczniki Nauk Rolniczyck 84:293–314.

Differentiation of food consumption in various river stretches, annual cycles of food change, and feeding differences of particular fish species.

143

HORTON, A., B. C. WORSSAM and J. B. WHITTOW

1981   The Wallingford fan gravel. Philosophical Transactions of the Royal Society of London, B, Biological Sciences 293(1064):215–255.

HORVATH, L.

1983   Elevage et production du brochet (*Esox lucius* L.) en Hongrie. *In* Billard, R., ed., Le brochet gestion dans le milieu naturel et elevage. Paris, Institute National de la Recherche Agronomique. 371 pp.
        Describes methods used to obtain stocking material for natural waters where pike is an important sport fish.

HOTTELL, H. E.

1976   Growth rate and food habits of the northern pike (*Esox lucius*) and the chain pickerel x northern pike hybrid (*E. niger* x *E. lucius*) in two North Georgia reservoirs. M.S. thesis, University of Georgia. 72 pp.
        Results of stocking (1) pike in stages of sac fry, fingerling, and subadult in a 338-ha reservoir; and (2) 50–75 mm hybrids in a 97-ha reservoir.

HOWARD, H. C. and R. E. THOMAS

1970   Behavior of northern pike fry as related to pond culture. Progressive Fish-Culturist 32:224–226.
        Behaviour of fry has significant implications in pond culture. Ponds stocked with eyed eggs and newly hatched fry are more productive than ponds stocked with 1- to 3-day-old fry. Success requires flooded vegetation to which newly hatched fry can attach.

HUBBS, CARL L.

1920   A comparative study of the bones forming the opercular series of fishes. Journal of Morphology 33:61–71.
        Describes branchiostegals of the order Haplomi.

1921   A note on unilateral reactions of the melanophores of the head in fishes. American Naturalist 55(638):286–288.

1922   Variations in the number of vertebrae and other meristic characters of fishes correlated with the temperature of water during development. American Naturalist 56(645):360–372.
        Results of this experiment using two fish species were similar to those obtained for pike.

1924   Studies of the fishes of the order Cyprinodontes. Miscellaneous Publication, Museum of Zoology, University of Michigan 13:1–31.

1926   A check-list of the fishes of the Great Lakes and tributary waters with nomenclatorial notes and analytical keys. Miscellaneous Publication, Museum of Zoology, University of Michigan 15:1–77.

1929   The fishes. *In* Christy, B. H., ed., The book of Huron Mountain. The Huron Mountain Club.

1955   Hybridization between fish species in nature. Systematic Zoology 4(1):1–20.
        Mentions two other esocids that crossbreed with pike. General discussion of role of environmental factors.

1979   List of the fishes of California. Papers of the California Academy of Science 133:1–51.

HUBBS, CARL L. and D. E. S. BROWN

1929   Materials for a distributional study of Ontario fishes. Transactions of the Royal Canadian Institute 17(1):1–56.

144

Habitat description of collection stations. List of species with note of general locality and station numbers.

HUBBS, CARL L. and C. W. GREENE
1928   Further notes on the fishes of the Great Lakes and tributary waters. Papers of the Michigan Academy of Science, Arts and Letters 8:371–392.

HUBBS, CARL L. and K. F. LAGLER
1939   Keys for the identification of the fishes of the Great Lakes and tributary waters. Ann Arbor, published by the authors. 37 pp.

1941   Guide to the fishes of the Great Lakes and tributary waters. Bulletin of the Cranbrook Institute of Science 18:1–100.

1949   Fishes of Isle Royale, Lake Superior, Michigan. Papers of the Michigan Academy of Science, Arts and Letters 33:73–133.
Information on theory of how pike were introduced, present distribution in Isle Royale lakes, and types of water bodies they inhabit.

1957   List of fishes of the Great Lakes and tributary waters. Michigan Fisheries 1:1–6.

1958   Fishes of the Great Lakes region. Ann Arbor, University of Michigan Press. 213 pp.

HUBBS, CARL L. and A. M. WHITE
1923   A list of fishes from Cass Lake, northern Minnesota. Copeia 1923:103–104.
Collected fish during summer of 1921 and followed sequence of species and numbers adopted by Surber.

HUBBS, CLARK
1972   A checklist of Texas freshwater fishes. Texas Parks and Wildlife Department, Technical Series 11:1–11.
Successful introduction of pike as a game species.

HUBER, E. H. and H. R. KITTEL
1961   A creel census of a Minnesota northern pike-centrarchid lake, Linwood Lake, Anoka County, 1951–1957. Investigative Report 227:1–11.
No significant trends were observed in fishing pressure and harvest from December 1, 1951, to March 31, 1957. Fishing success seemed to be affected mostly by relative strength of the year class being exploited.

HUBERT, W. A.
1980   Tiger muskie dynamics and ecology in public fishing lakes. Iowa Cooperative Fishery Research Unit, Project 2378.
Outlines a proposed research project.

HUBLEY, R. C., Jr.
1961   Incidence of lamprey scarring on fish on upper Mississippi River, 1956–58. Transactions of the American Fisheries Society 90:83–85.
During 3 years of fishing surveys, more than one-third of all fish scarred were pike.

HUCHSON, D. R. and J. M. SHEPPARD
1963   Some scuba observations for the fresh-water angler. Ontario Fish and Wildlife Review 2(2):15–19.
Pike were very wary. They were usually found singly, and never with more than two in a group in larger bodies of water. Most pike were seen near dense weed beds. They showed a wide range of flight and a tendency to return to the original location.

145

HUDD, R., M. HILDEN, L. URHO, M.-B. AXELL and L.-A. JAFS

1984   Fishery investigations (in 1980–1982) of the Kyronjoki River estuary and its influence area in the Northern Quark of the Baltic Sea. National Board of Waters, Report 242:1–275.

HUET, M.

1948   Esociculture; la production de brochetons. Bulletin Francais de Pisciculture 148:121–124.

1960   Traite de pisciculture. Brussels, De Wyngaert. 369 pp.

1970   Traite de pisciculture, 4th ed. Brussels, De Wyngaert. 718 pp.

1972a   Textbook of fish culture. Breeding and cultivation of fish. London, Fishing News (Books). 436 pp.

1972b   Elevage et maturation de geniteurs brochets en petits etangs. International Association of Theoretical and Applied Limnology Proceedings 18: 1128–1134.

       During a period of several years, at least 15 female pike out of 18 matured sexually. They produced 250,000 to 350,000 eggs. Temperature was regulated between 9 and 10 C.

1976   Reproduction, incubation et alevinage du brochet. European Inland Fisheries Advisory Committee Technical Paper 25:147–163.

HUET, M., A. LELEK, J. LIBOSVARSKY and M. PENAZ

1969   Contribution a l'identification des zones piscicoles de quelques cours d'eau de Moravie (Tcheoslavaquie). International Association of Theoretical and Applied Limnology Proceedings 17(2):1103–1111.

HUET, M. and J. A. TIMMERMANS

1958   Esociculture. Production de brochetons de sept semaines. Station de Recherches Eaux Forets Groenendaal, Travaux Ser. D, 24:1–10.

1959   Production de brochetons de sept semaines. Bulletin d'Information Conseil Superieur de la Peche 1:15–21.

HUGGHINS, E. J.

1959   Parasites of fishes of South Dakota. South Dakota Department of Game, Fish, and Parks, Bulletin 484:1–73.

HUGGINS, A. K., G. SKUTSCH and E. BALDWIN

1969   Ornithine-urea cycle enzymes in teleostean fish. Comparative Biochemistry and Physiology 28:771–776.

HUGGLER, T.

1975   Big pike through the ice: tripping the flags. Fins and Feathers, December 1975.

HUGHES, T.

       Pike. *In* Miller, K., ed., Writing in England Today, the last fifteen years, pp. 125–126.

       A poem about pike.

HUISMAN, E. A.

1975   Hatchery and nursery operations. European Inland Fisheries Advisory Committee Technical Paper 25:101–110.

HUISMAN, E. A., J. H. KOEMAN and P. V. I. M. WOLFF

1971   An investigation into the influence of DDT and other chlorinated hydrocarbons on the fertility of the pike. Organization for the Improvement of the Freshwater Fishery, Annual Report, April 1970 - March 31, 1971. pp. 69–86.

146

HUNER, J. V.

1983   The northern pike - a cosmopolitan species. Farm Pond Harvest 17(3):12–14, 29.

HUNER, J. V. and O. V. LINDQUIST

1983   How Finland stocks her rivers and lakes. Fish Farming International 10(4):10–11.

The production and stocking of fry and fingerlings of high value species is an important part of Finland's fisheries program. Pike is a species of particular importance.

HUNN, J. B.

1972a   Blood chemistry values for some fishes of the upper Mississippi River. Journal of the Minnesota Academy of Science 38:19–21.

Plasma concentrations of sodium, potassium, calcium magnesium, chloride, inorganic phosphate, glucose, lactic acid, total carbon dioxide, whole blood pH, and hematocrit were determined for nine species of fish, including pike. All pike sampled were ripe males.

1972b   Concentrations of some inorganic constituents in gallbladder bile from some freshwater fishes. Copeia 1972:860–861.

The pike sampled for this study were mature males captured from the wild.

HUNN, J. B., R. A. SCHOETTGER and E. W. WHEALDON

1968   Observations on the handling and maintenance of bioassay fish. Progressive Fish-Culturist 30:164–167.

Ten-day pre-test holding period, using pond-reared or field-collected fish (including pike) involved preparation of *Daphnia* for food, diet, and feeding schedule, and hematological examination.

HUNT, B. P. and W. F. CARBINE

1951   Food of young pike, *Esox lucius* L., and associated fishes in Peterson's Ditches, Houghton Lake, Michigan. Transactions of the American Fisheries Society 80:67–83.

Stomach contents of 551 pike (11–152 mm in length) were examined. Food organisms were listed and changes in diet with increased size were recorded. Competition for food, predation, cannibalism, as mortality factors in young pike are discussed.

HUNT, R. L.

1965   Food of northern pike in a Wisconsin trout stream. Transactions of the American Fisheries Society 94:95–97.

Stomachs of 91 pike were analysed. Only one item was present in each of the 24 stomachs containing food. Seven food species were represented, and 88% of the diet was fish.

HUNTER, G. W., III and J. S. RANKIN

1941   Parasites of northern pike and pickerel. Transactions of the American Fisheries Society 69:268–272.

The parasitic fauna of pike from a Connecticut lake was investigated. Two species of trematodes, two of tapeworms, one each of roundworms, spiny-headed worms, protozoa, and parasitic crustacea are reported.

HUNTER, J. G.

1968   Fishes and fisheries. *In* Beals, C. S., ed., Science, History and Hudson Bay. Canada Department of Energy, Mines and Resources, vol. 1, 502 pp.

HUNTER, M.

1907   Voracious pike. Canadian wilds. Columbus, A. R. Harding, pp. 220–224.
Reminiscences of a Hudson's Bay officer with 40 years of experience at various posts from 1863 to 1903; tells about the Hudson Bay Company, northern Indians, and their modes of hunting and trapping.

HUNTINGFORD, F. A.

1976   The relationship between anti-predator behaviour and aggression among conspecifics in the three-spined stickleback, *Gasterosteus aculeatus*. Animal Behaviour 24:245–260.

1982   Do interspecific and intraspecific aggression vary in relation to predation pressure in sticklebacks. Animal Behaviour 30:909–916.

HURLEY, D. A. and W. J. CHRISTIE

1977   Depreciation of the warmwater fish community in the Bay of Quinte, Lake Ontario. Journal of the Fisheries Research Board of Canada 34:1849–1860.
The sequence of species shifts since the 1930's is interpreted in terms of climatic changes and the influences of man. Eutrophication, high fishing intensity, and low water levels were considered responsible for the decline of the pike population. Decrease in piscivores increased the instability of the community.

HURUM, H. J.

A history of the fish hook. London, A & C. Black.

HUTCHINSON, H. G.

1904   Pike. *In* Fishing. London. Vol. 2.

HUVER, C. W.

1960   Occurrence of a northern pike in Fisher's Island Sound. New York Fish and Game Journal 12(1):113.
In August 1959 anglers caught a pike 17 miles east of the mouth of the Connecticut River. It is suggested that the pike was a stray, which came downstream from the Connecticut River to Long Island Sound and followed the less saline inshore waters to Fisher's Island Sound.

HYSLOP, E. J.

1980   Stomach contents analysis: a review of methods and their application. Journal of Fish Biology 17:411–429.

148

IGNAT`EVA, G. M.

1974a   Dependence of egg cleavage rate on temperature in the carp, pike, and peled. Ontogenez 5:27–32.

1974b   Relative duration of the same periods of early embryogenesis in teleosts. Ontogenez 5:427–436.

IGNAT`EVA, G. M. and N. N. ROTT

1970   Time relationships between processes occurring before the start of gastrulation in teleosts. Doklady Akademii NAUK SSSR, Seriya Biologiya 190:484–487.

IGNATIEVA, G. M.

1976a   Regularities of early embryogenesis in teleosts as revealed by studies of the temporal pattern of development. Part 1. The duration of the mitotic cycle and its phases during synchronous cleavage divisions. Wilhelm Roux's Archives of Development Biology 179:301–312.

1976b   Regularities of early embryogenesis in teleosts as revealed by studies of the temporal pattern of development. Part 2. Relative duration of corresponding periods of development in different species. Wilhelm Roux's Archives of Development Biology 179:313–325.

IGNATIEVA, G. M. and N. N. ROTT

1970   The temporal pattern of interphase prolongation and nuclear activities during early embryogenesis in Teleosti. Wilhelm Roux's Archives of Development Biology 165:103–109.

IL`YENKO, A. I.

1970   Concentration of strontium-90 and caesium-137 by freshwater fishes. Journal of Ichthyology 10:860–862.
    A study of the movement of artificial radioisotopes from the food into the body under natural conditions. It is considered that the bulk of the radioisotope enters from food and not from the environment.

1972   Some features of caesium-137 concentration in fish populations of a body of fresh water. Journal of Ichthyology 12:149–153.
    Pike were caught in 1969–70 in a body of water in which caseium-137 content was artificially modified nonperiodically. A study was made of seasonal variation in the content of this radioisotope in the muscle of pike; it did not coincide with the variation of its content in the water.

INCE, B. W.

1979   Metabolic effects of partial pancreatectomy in the northern pike, *Esox lucius* L. Journal of Fish Biology 14:193–198.
    A 70% pancreatectomy did not cause the development of a diabetic state in pike over a one-month period.

INCE, B. W. and A. THORPE

1975   Hormonal and metabolite effects on plasma free fatty-acids in the northern pike *Esox lucius*. General and Comparative Endocrinology 27:144–152.
    The effects of intraarterial injections of bovine and codfish insulin, glucagon, adrenalin, noradrenalin, glucose, and amino acids on plasma free fatty acid (FFA) levels were studied in the pike, which were cannulated to permit serial blood sampling.

1976a   The effects of starvation and force-feeding on the metabolism of northern pike, *Esox lucius* L. Journal of Fish Biology 8:79–88.
    Pike are well adapted for periods of prolonged starvation and hepatic and

149

extra-hepatic lipid and glycogen stores serve for metabolic needs during food shortage. The endocrine basis for these changes in the tissue and blood constituents is discussed.

1976b   The in vivo metabolism of ^{14}C-glucose and ^{14}C-glycine in insulin-treated northern pike (*Esox lucius* L.). General and Comparative Endocrinology 28:481.

1978   The effects of insulin on plasma amino acid levels in the northern pike *Esox lucius* L. Journal of Fish Biology 12:503–506.
The data support the hypothesis that insulin plays a major role in the regulation of protein metabolism in pike.

INLAND FISHERIES TRUST
The validity of scale reading. Iontaobhas Iascaigh Intire Ioncorportha Balnagowan, Mobhi Boreen, Glasnevin, Dublin 9. 7 pp.

1972   Annual report 1971/72. 22nd Annual General Meeting of the Inland Fisheries Trust Incorporated, 1972. 96 pp.
Over 45,000 pike weighing almost 23 tons were removed from lakes and rivers being developed as trout fisheries.

1973   Pike fisheries. Annual Report of the Inland Fisheries Trust Incorporated 1972/73.

1977   Development of brown trout lakes. Pike removal. Annual Report Inland Fisheries Trust Incorporated, pp. 8–10.

INSKIP, P. D.
1980   Annual and seasonal variability in growth of sympatric muskellunge (*Esox masquinongy* Mitchill) and northern pike (*Esox lucius* Linnaeus). M.S. thesis, University of Wisconsin. 119 pp.

1982a   Northern pike (*Esox lucius* Linnaeus). Unpublished MS. 50 pp.
Extensive compilation consisting of brief summaries of present published knowledge of biological requirements as they apply to habitat use. Includes habitat suitability index models based on these data.

1982b   Habitat suitability index models: northern pike. U.S. Fish and Wildlife Service, FWS/OBS-82/10.17:1–40.
Presents models intended for use in impact assessment and habitat management activities. Literature concerning the habitat requirements and preference of pike is reviewed and then synthesized into HSI models, which are scaled to produce an index between 0 (unsuitable habitat) and 1 (optimal habitat).

INSKIP, P. D. and J. J. MAGNUSON
1983   Changes in fish populations over an 80-year period: Big Pine Lake, Wisconsin. Transactions of the American Fisheries Society 112:378–389.

IOWA CONSERVATION COMMISSION
1961   Calculated total lengths at each annulus for various species of fish taken from De Soto Bend, September 25–29, 1961. Unpublished MS, 13 pp.

IVANOV, M. E.
1956   Yaitsevye obolochki ryb, ikh sravnitel'naya morfologiya i ekologicheskoe snachenie. [Fish egg membranes, their comparative morphology and ecological significance]. Vestnik Leningradskogo Universiteta 21:79–90.

IVANOV, N. M.
1978   Innervatsiya mochevyvodyashchikh putej kostistykh ryb. [Innervation of the urinary tract of bony fishes]. Journal of Ichthyology 18:341–346.

Study of the fine structure and histochemistry of nervous apparatus of urinary paths of bony fishes, including pike.

IVANOVA, M. N.

On the speed of digestion of food by young pike. Biologiya Vnutrennykh vod Informatsionii Byulleten 48:42–45.

1959   Diet of pike of the Rybinsk Reservoir. *In* Akatova, N. A., et al., eds., Transactions of the 6th Conference on the Biology of Inland Waters, 1957. Translated from Russian by Israel Program for Scientific Translations. pp. 326–332.

Pike older than one year fed exclusively on fish between 10 and 600 mm. The majority of pike fed on fish whose body length was <100 mm. Low-value fish comprised 70.3% of their diet.

1963   O pitanii khishchnykh ryb v pervye chetyre goda sushchestvovaniya Gor'kovskogo vodokhranilishcha. [Observations on the feeding of predaceous fishes during the first four years of the existence of the Gor'Kovoe Reservoir.] Trudy Instituta Biologii Vodokhranilishcha Akademii Nauk SSSR 5:81–86.

Immature pike fed on fish, frogs, and invertebrates. Adults fed exclusively on fish.

1966   Age-dependent and local changes in the food composition of pike in the Rybinsk Reservoir. Trudy Instituta Biologii Vnutrennikh Vod Akademii Nauk SSSR 10:111–118.

1968   Pishchevye ratsiony i kormovye koeffitsienty khishchnykh ryb v rybinskom vodokhranilishche. [Nutritive rations and food coefficients of predatory fishes in Rybinsk Reservoir]. Trudy Instituta Biologii Vnutrennikh Vod Akademii Nauk SSSR 17(20):189–198.

Information on digestion rates throughout the year, daily and yearly food ration of fingerlings, yearlings, juveniles, and adults, and food coefficients of juveniles and adults. The effects of predators on the valuable and low value species were studied.

1969   The behavior of predatory fish during feeding. Problems of Ichthyology 9:574–577.

Mature pike are solitary predators that feed mainly during the hours of darkness. They may hunt temporarily in schools, particularly when food is abundant. Pike change their method of hunting, depending on conditions, or if behaviour of the prey changes.

1970   On age and local changes of food of the pike in the Rybinsk Reservoir. Memorial University, St. John's, Library Bulletin 4(6):9–11.

Young pike fed almost exclusively on underyearlings of several species, especially perch *Perca fluviatilis* and roach *Rutilus rutilus*. For large size pike, the main influence on the composition of food came from different factors, especially the place of feeding. Sexually mature specimens fed both in the shoreline zone (in spring) and in the open water (in fall).

IVANOVA, M. N. and A. N. LOPATKO

1979   Determining diet in predatory fishes. Journal of Ichthyology 19(4):157–160. Observations on the feeding of pike were obtained using different gear. Estimations of food ration size were made from the gear type used.

1983   Feeding behaviour of pike *Esox lucius* (Esocidae), larvae from the progeny of a single pair of spawners. Journal of Ichthyology 23:171–173.

A study of the feeding behaviour and nature of food of pike larvae. The ability of individual larvae to catch and hold prey differ. Maintenance of young pike with equal concentrations of prey determined the quanitative difference in the progeny of a single female.

IVANOVA, M. N., A. N. LOPATKO and L. V. MALTSEVA

    1982   Rations and food coefficients of young pike *Esox lucius* L. in the Rybinsk Reservoir. Voprosy Ikhtiologii 22:233–239.

IVLEV, V. S.

    1939a   The energy balance of growing larvae of *Silurus glanis*. Doklady Akademii Nauk SSSR 25:87–89.

    1939b   The effect of fasting on the conversion of energy in fish growth. Dkolady Akademii Nauk SSSR 25:90–92.

    1954   The relation of metabolic rate to size in fish. Fiziologicheskii Zhurnal SSSR Imeni I. M. Sechenova 40:717–721.

    1961   Experimental ecology of the feeding of fishes. Newhaven, Yale University Press.

IZYUMOV, N. A.

    1959   The formation of the parasitic fauna of fish in the Rybinsk Reservoir. Byulleten' Instituta Biologii Vodokhranilishch Akademii Nauk SSSR 4:38–40.

Changes in the parasitic fauna of fish in the Rybinsk reservoir were observed over 8–9 years. *Henneguya oviperda*, a specific parasite of female pike gonads, is reported for the first time in the reservoir.

JACOB, B.
1969   Natural marshes vs. controlled spawning ponds. Michigan Department of Natural Resources.

JACOBSHAGEN, E.
1913   Untersuchungen uber des Darmsystem der Fische und Dipnoer. Jena Zeitschrift fuer Naturwissenschaftlich 49:521–524.

JACOBSSON, S. and T. JARVI
1976   Anti-predator behavior of 2-year-old hatchery reared Atlantic salmon *Salmo salar* and a description of the predatory behavior of burbot *Lota lota*. Zoologisk Revy 38(3):57–70.

JAEGAR, T., H. DAUSTER and A. KIWUS
1980   Aufzucht von Hechtsetzlingen in erfeuchteten Netzgehegen. [Rearing of young pike in illuminated net cages]. Fischerei Teichwirt 31:323–326.
        This east European rearing method concentrates zooplankton by phototaxis, making it more available to the larvae. German experiments are described, including cage construction, optimal stocking density and diseases.

JAKUBOWSKI, M.
1965   Cutaneous sense organs of fishes. II. The lateral-line organs in the burbot (*Lota lota* L.) and pike (*Esox lucius* L.). Acta Biologica Cracoviensia, Series Zoologia 8:87–100.

JAKUBOWSKI, M., W. BYCZKOWSKA-SMYK and Y. MIKHALEV
1969   Vascularization and size of the respiratory surfaces in the Antarctic white-blooded fish *Chaenichthys rugosus* Regan (Percoidei, Chaenichthyidae). Zoologica Poloniae 19:303–317.
        Area of capillaries per 1 g of body weight for pike 105–222 g: gills - 1593 mm, skin - 52 mm, skin and fins together - 77 mm. Surface ratio of gill vessels to skin vessels - 30.6:1; including fins - 21.2:1.

JALABERT, B.
1976   In vitro oocyte maturation and ovulation in rainbow trout (*Salmo gairdneri*), northern pike (*Esox lucius*), and goldfish (*Carassius auratus*). Journal of the Fisheries Research Board of Canada 33:974–988.
        The efficiency of various steroids in initiating maturation was studied. Some mediators likely to act on ovulation have been identified.

JALABERT, B. and B. BRETON
1974   In-vitro maturation of pike *Esox lucius* oocytes. General and Comparative Endocrinology 22:391. [Abstract]
        The gonadotropic steroid most effective in initiation of maturation was 20 beta-dihydro, 17 alpha-hydroxyprogesterone. The presence of hydrocortisone enhanced the effect of gonadotropic extracts.

JAMSON, G. C.
1973   Michigan's 1972 sport fishery. Michigan Department of Natural Resources, Surveys and Statistical Services Report 122:1–6.

JANEC-SUSLOWSKA, W.
1957   Osteologia szczupaka. [Pike osteology.] Warsaw, PWN. 99 pp.

JANISCH, J. L.
1976   Fish management at Starve Hollow Lake 1970–1975. Indiana Department of Natural Resources, pp. 1–10.
        Fall drawdowns, addition of structure, a 14-inch size limit on largemouth bass *Micropterus salmoides*, and supplemental stockings of channel catfish

Ictalurus punctatus and pike were used in an effort to improve the fishery of Starve Hollow Lake.

JANISZEWSKI, M.

1934   Szczupak na wedce. [Pike angling.] Przeglad Rybacki 7(5):172–181.
        Details of pike biology of use for anglers.

1938a   Szczupak na wedce. [Pike angling.] Wiadomosci Wedkarskie 3(3):34–35.
        Details of pike biology for use of anglers.

1938b   Szczupak na wedce. Dokonczenie. [Pike angling. Last part.] Wiadomesci
        Wedkarskie 3(4):41–42.

JANKE

1925   Zahmung eines freilebenden Hechtes. Blattchen Aquarien und Terrarien
        Kunde

JARA, Z.

1968   Polish general parasitology during the period of 1964–1967. Monografie
        Parazytologiczne 6:57–90.

JARDINE, A.

1898   Pike and perch, illustrated. London. Pike, pp. 1–143.

JARVENPA, O.

1962   Save wetlands for northern pike. Conservation Volunteer 25(146):8–12.
        Categorizes pike spawning areas into five different types, and describes
        Minnesota's efforts to acquire, improve, and manage natural spawning and
        rearing areas.

JARVENPA, O. M.

1962   Northern pike spawning area management in Minnesota. Minnesota Depart-
        ment of Conservation, Annual Progress Report, 4 pp.

1963   Northern pike production from controlled spawning areas and shallow lakes
        in Minnesota. Minnesota Department of Conservation, Annual Progress
        Report. 4 pp.

JARVENPA, O. M. and W. KIRSCH

1969   Propagation of pike in multi-purpose lake management. Journal of the Min-
        nesota Academy of Science 36:52–55.

JARVENPAA, T., M. TILLANDER and J. K. MIETTINEN

1970   Methylmercury: half-time of elimination in flounder, pike and eel. Suomen
        Kemistilehti B 43:439–442.

JARVI, T. H.

1931   Tagged pikes. Suomen Kalastuslehti 11:183–191. [in Finnish]

JASINSKI, A.

1965   The vascularization of the air bladder in fishes. Part II. Sevruga (*Acipenser
        stellatus*), grayling (*Thymallus thymallus* L.), pike (*Esox lucius* L.), and
        umbra (*Umbra krameri* Walbaum). Acta Biologica Cracoviensia, Series
        Zoologia 8:200–210.
        Physical description of air bladder, its associated organs and blood systems.
        Two figures accompany the text on pike.

1977a   Intraendothelial canaliculi in choroidal capillaries of pike, *Esox lucius*
        (Teleostei). Bulletin de l'Academie Polonaise des Sciences, Serie des Sci-
        ences Biologiques 25:452–454.

1977b   Endothelial to perivascular cell junctions. Bulletin de l'Academie Polonaise
        des Sciences, Serie des Sciences Biologiques 25:455–458.

JASKOWSKI, J.

1962   Materialy do znajomosci ichtiofauny Warty i jej doplywow. [Materials on
the ichthyofauna in the Warta River and its tributaries.] Fragmenta Faunistica
9(28):449–499.
Faunistic and physiographic review of fishes in the Warta River and its main
tributaries.

JEFIMOVA, A. J.

1949   Scuka Ob - Irtyskogo basiejna. Izv. VNIORKh 28

JENKINS, J. T.

1954   The fishes of the British Isles both freshwater and salt. London, Frederick
Warne. 408 pp.

JENKINS, R. E., E. A. LACHNER and F. J. SCHWARTZ

1972   Fishes of the central Appalachian drainagees: their distribution and dispersal.
In The distributional history of the biota of the southern Appalachians. Part
III: Vertebrates. A symposium sponsored by Virginia Polytechnic Institute
and State University and the Association of Southeastern Biologists.
Blacksburg, Virginia, 1970.

JENKINS, R. M.

1968   The influence of some environmental factors on standing crop and harvest of
fishes in US reservoirs. Reservoir Fishery Resources Symposium, Georgia,
1967. pp. 298–321.

1969   The influence of engineering design and operation and other environmental
factors on reservoir fishery resources. Water Resources Bulletin 6:110–119.
The apparent effect of selected reservoir environmental variables on fish
standing crop in 140 large impoundments was explored through partial correlation and multiple regression analyses. Partial correlation revealed a nega-
tive effect of water level fluctuation on pike.

1970   Large reservoirs - management possibilities. Proceedings of the Annual
Midwest Fish and Game Commission 36:82–89.
Suggests controlled water level fluctuation and improved substrate to enhance
spawning and survival of pike.

1973   Reservoir management prognosis: migraines or miracles. Proceedings of the
27th Annual Congress Southeastern Association of Game and Fish Commissioners, pp. 374–385.

1982   The morphoedaphic index and reservoir fish production. Transactions of the
American Fisheries Society 111:133–140.

JENKINS, R. M. and D. I. MORAIS

1971   Reservoir sport fishing effort and harvest in relation to environmental variables. American Fisheries Society Special Publication 8:371–384.

JENNINGS, J. T.

1954   The fishes of the British Isles both freshwater and salt. London, Frederick
Warne. 408 pp.

JENNINGS, T. L. and F. FRANK

1965   Results of an experimental muskellunge-silver northern pike cross. Iowa
Conservation Commission, Quarterly Biology Report 17(4):1–3.
Apparently a cross between a male muskellunge and a female silver northern
pike could occur in the wild and produce healthy, rapidly growing individuals. Hybrids could be distinguished from purebreds in most instances since
none of the hybrids examined had all of the characteristics of either parent.

JESSOP, C. S., T. R. PORTER, M. BLOUW and R. SOPUCK
  1973   Fish resources of the Mackenzie River Valley. Special report, an intensive
          study of the fish resources of two main stem tributaries. Department of the
          Environment, Fishery Service, Winnipeg. 148 pp.

JESTER, D. B.
  1977   Effects of color, mesh size, fishing in seasonal concentrations and baiting on
          catch rates of fishes in gill nets. Transactions of the American Fisheries
          Society 106:43.
          Gives catch rates of several species, including pike, in 16 replications of
          baited and unbaited white experimental gill nets.

JOASSIN, L., F. FRANKENNE and C. GERDAY
  1971   Cleavage of pike parvalbumin II by cyanogen bromide. Archives Interna-
          tionales de Physiologie et de Biochimie 79:834–835.

JOHAL, M. S.
  1978   Further notes on the growth of pike, *Esox lucius*, from Czechoslovakia
          (Pisces, Esocidae). Vestnik Ceskoslovenske Spolecnosti Zoologicke
          44:105–115.
          Growth rate of pike was studied from the scales of 270 specimens collected
          during 1956–1976. Pike of seven year classes were recorded.

JOHANSSON, N. and J. E. KIHLSTROM
  1975   Pikes (*Esox lucius* L.) shown to be affected by low pH values during first
          weeks after hatching. Environmental Research 9:12–17.
          Newly hatched pike sac fry from artificially fertilized eggs were reared for
          eight days in water solutions with different pH values. At pH 6.8 the mortal-
          ity was 17%, 26% at pH 5.0, and 97% at pH 4.2.

JOHNELS, A. G., M. OLSSON and T. WESTERMARK
  1968   *Esox lucius* and some other organisms as indicators of mercury contamination
          in Swedish lakes and rivers. Bulletin de l'Office International des Epizooties
          69:1439–1452.

JOHNELS, A. G. and T. WESTERMARK
  1969   Mercury contamination of the environment in Sweden. *In* Chemical Fallout;
          Current research on persistent pesticides. Publication of Rochester University
          Conference on Toxicity; Selected Water Resources Abstracts 3(23):40.

JOHNELS, A. G., T. WESTERMARK, W. BERG, P.I. PERSSON and B. SJOSTRAND
  1967   Pike (*Esox lucius* L.) and some other aquatic organisms in Sweden as indica-
          tors of mercury contamination in the environment. Oikos 18:323–333.
          Activation analysis of mercury content in axial musclature of pike was used
          to estimate the level of mercury in the water environment. The concentration
          factor from water to pike was 3000 or more. The relation between mercury
          content and weight and age of fish specimens is discussed.

JOHNSON, F. H.
  1957   Northern pike year-class strength and spring water levels. Transactions of the
          American Fisheries Society 86:285–293.
          A high spring water level during spawning and a small decline in the levels
          during egg incubation represent good conditions for the production of a
          strong pike year class.

JOHNSON, F. H. and J. B. MOYLE
  1969   Management of a large shallow winterkill lake in Minnesota for the produc-
          tion of pike (*Esox lucius*). Transactions of the American Fisheries Society

156

98:691–697.

Management of a large shallow winterkill lake for production of fingerling and yearling pike is described. Pike are removed from the lake in winter by attracting them to traps through which a flow of aerated water is directed from large capacity pumps. Trapping is done in the lake and in the outlet.

JOHNSON, F. H. and A. R. PETERSON

1955   Comparative harvest of northern pike by summer angling and winter dark-house spearing from Ball Club Lake, Itasca County, Minnesota. Minnesota Department of Conservation, Investigational Report 164:1–11.

Concludes that neither angling nor spearing appear to detrimentally affect the pike population of this lightly fished lake. The entire population was better harvested by a combination of angling and spearing than would have been done by angling alone.

JOHNSON, L.

1960   Studies of the behaviour and nutrition of the pike (*Esox lucius* L.). Ph.D. thesis, University of Leeds. 181 pp.

1966a   Temperature of maximum density of freshwater and its effect on circulation in Great Bear Lake. Journal of the Fisheries Research Board of Canada 23:963–973.

1966b   Experimental determination of food consumption of pike, *Esox lucius*, for growth and maintenance. Journal of the Fisheries Research Board of Canada 23:1495–1505.

Under simulated field conditions changes occurred in growth and seasonal maintenance requirements, which were partially independent of temperature. Values are given for maintenance requirements, maintenance coefficient, coefficient of utilization, and efficiency of utilization. Pike were found to have low maintenance requirements and high values for conversion of food to pike substance.

1966c   Consumption of food by the resident population of pike, *Esox lucius*, in Lake Windermere. Journal of the Fisheries Research Board of Canada 23:1523–1535.

The annual food consumption, production, and yield of pike were determined. Prior to heavy exploitation in 1944, the biomass was estimated to be 8182 kg with an annual consumption of 22.124 kg. After 10 years of fishing, the biomass had been reduced by 47%, and consumption 25%. Results are discussed in terms of cropping the annual production of the lake.

1973   Stock and recruitment in some unexploited Canadian Arctic lakes. Journal du Conseil International pour l'Exploration de la Mer 164:219–227.

1981   The thermodynamic origin of ecosystems. Canadian Journal of Fisheries and Aquatic Sciences 38:571–590.

JOHNSON, L. D.

1958   Pond culture of muskellunge in Wisconsin. Wisconsin Conservation Department Technical Bulletin 17:1–54.

Figure 1 shows dates and temperatures at which pike spawn, eggs hatch, and fry swim.

1959   Story of a thousand stomachs. Wisconsin Conservation Bulletin 24(3):7–9.

Analysed stomachs of pike caught by Wisconsin anglers 1956–58 to determine quantity, size, and type of food. Advice on bait, method, and time of day best suited for fishing.

1961a   Warm water fishery research. Muskellunge studies. Stomach analysis of pond and lake muskellunge and northern pike. Wisconsin Conservation Department, Dingell-Johnson Report F-61-R-1/Wk.Pl. 1/Job B:8–13.

1961b   Warm water fishery research. Muskellunge studies. Muskellunge age and growth studies. Wisconsin Conservation Department, Dingell-Johnson Report F-61-R-1/Wk.Pl. 1/Job C.

1962a   Warm water fishery research. Muskellunge studies. Behavior. Wisconsin Conservation Department, Dingell-Johnson Report F-61-R-2/Wk.Pl. 1:Job A:1–4.

1962b   Warm water fishery research. Muskellunge studies. Stomach analysis of muskellunge and northern pike. Wisconsin Conservation Department, Dingell-Johnson Report F-61-R-2/Wk.Pl. 1/Job B:4–7.

1962c   Warm water fishery research. Muskellunge studies. Biological inventory of muskellunge habitat. Wisconsin Conservation Department, Dingell-Johnson Report F-61-R-2/Wk.Pl. 1/Job D.

1965   Statewide fishery research. Muskellunge studies. Feeding habits of muskellunge. Wisconsin Conservation Department, Dingell-Johnson Report F-83-R-01/Wk.Pl. 02, Job B. 6 pp.

1969   Food of angler-caught northern pike in Murphy Flowage. Wisconsin Department of Natural Resources Technical Bulletin 42:1–26.
Stomach content analysis showed that pike fed on bluegills, perch, minnows, and crappies. Although bluegills were the predominant prey species, pike took perch more frequently than bluegills in proportion to their abundance. Pike tended to feed continuously during daylight hours on small forage fishes. Information on the success of various baits is provided.

1971   Statewide fishery research. Development of improved muskellunge stocking procedures. Wisconsin Conservation Department, Report F-83-R-7/Wk.Pl. 29/Job 5:1–14.

1978   Evaluation of esocid stocking program in Wisconsin. American Fisheries Society Special Publication 11:298–301.
Pike survived in the range of 0 to 60% over short term intervals. Despite high variations, the stocked fingerlings added to the lake populations. Pike x muskellunge survived at values up to 85%.

1981   Comparison of muskellunge (*Esox masquinongy*) populations in a stocked lake and unstocked lake in Wisconsin, with notes on the occurrence of northern pike (*Esox lucius*). Wisconsin Department of Natural Resources Research Report 110:1–17.
Briefly discusses the apparent effects of the establishment of a large pike population in lakes inhabited by muskellunge.

n.d.   Stomach analysis of pond and lake muskellunge and northern pike. Warm water Research. Wisconsin Conservation Department, Dingell-Johnson Project F-61-R-1, Job 1b:1–5.

JOHNSON, L. D. and H. LAUGHLIN

1955   The musky story. Wisconsin Conservation Bulletin 20(5):5–11.

JOHNSON, M. G., J. H. LEACH, C. K. MINNS and C. H. OLVER

1977   Limnological characteristics of Ontario lakes in relation to associations of walleye (*Stizostedion vitreum vitreum*), northern pike (*Esox lucius*), lake trout (*Salvelinus namaycush*) and smallmouth bass (*Micropterus dolomieui*). Journal of the Fisheries Research Board of Canada 34:1592–1601.

Lake depth and area were important in distinguishing lake types by discriminant analysis. Low frequency of walleye in small lakes may be partially caused by an unsuccessful coexistence with pike.

JOHNSON, M. K.

1960   More northerns for Iowa waters. Iowa Conservationist 19(6):41–45.

JOHNSON, M. W., W. J. SCIDMORE, J. H. KUEHN and C. R. BURROWS

1957   Status of the northern pike fishery in Minnesota. Minnesota Department of Conservation, Investigational Report 178:1–10.

For 5 years creel census was conducted on representative lakes to determine sport fishing harvest. Of the 52 lakes, 32 had pike and were fished by summer angling and dark house spearing, as well as winter angling in some. Gives information on harvest, catch per unit effort, weight, and sex ratios.

JOHNSON, R. E.

1945   Ever hooked a hybrid. Minnesota Conservationist (Volunteer) 8(49):18–22.

1949   Maintenance of natural population balance. Proceedings of the International Association of Game Commissioners 38:35–42.

JOHNSON, R. P.

1971   Limnology and fishery biology of Black Lake, northern Saskatchewan. Saskatchewan Department of Natural Resources, Fish and Wildlife Branch, Fisheries Report 9:1–47.

Information on distribution in the lake, habitat, angler success, growth, age, and stomach contents.

JOHNSON, T. and K. MUELLER

1978   Migration of juvenile pike *Esox lucius* from a coastal stream to the northern part of the Bothnian Sea. Aquilo Ser. Zoologica 18:57–61.

JOLLIE, M.

1975   Development of the head skeleton and pectoral girdle in *Esox*. Journal of Morphology 147:61–88.

The variations of the latero-sensory canal system, its associated bones, and other skeletal elements of pike and *E. americanus* were studied, using aspects of regression or specialization. The relationship between dermal and chondral bone was examined.

JONES, A. N.

1972   Notes on the origin of the freshwater fish of west Wales. Nature in Wales 13(1):2–10.

JONES, D. R., J. W. KICENIUK and O. S. BAMFORD

1974   Evaluation of the swimming performance of several fish species from the Mackenzie River. Journal of the Fisheries Research Board of Canada 31:1641–1647.

JONES, F. R. H.

1963   The reaction of fish to moving backgrounds. Journal of Experimental Biology 40:437–446.

An apparatus is described to study the response of fish to moving backgrounds. Pike followed a moving background equivalent to a water current of 0.03 cm/sec. Pike were the best and most consistent performers among the fresh-water species.

JONES, J. A.

1973   The ecology of the mud minnow, *Umbra limi*, in Fish Lake (Anoka County, Minnesota). Ph.D. thesis, Iowa State University. 115 pp.

JONES, R. H.
  1982   Old-world tactics + Ontario fish = Trophies. Ontario Out of Doors, August 1982, p. 26.
          Review of Buller's book on pike angling. Gives some information on Buller's theory of the pike's feeding strategy and some "old world" fishing tips. A shortened list of record pike from around the world is included.

JORDAN, D. S.
  1877a   Review of Rafinesque's Memoirs on North American fishes. Bulletin of the U.S. National Museum 9:3–53.
  1877b   Notes on Cottidae, Etheostomatidae, Percidae, Centrarchidae, Aphododeridae, Umbridae, Esocidae, Dorysomatidae, Cyprinidae, Catostomidae, and Hyodontidae with revisions of the genera and descriptions of new or little known species. Bulletin of the U.S. National Museum 10:5–120.
  1880   Notes on certain typical specimens of American fishes in the British Museum and in the Museum d'Histoire Naturelle at Paris. Proceedings of the U.S. National Museum 2:218–226.
  1882   Report on the fishes of Ohio. In Zoology and Botany, Part 1, Zoology. Ohio Geological Survey 4:1–1020.
          Information on synonomy, description, diagnosis, habits and habitat.
  1885   Nematognathi, Seyphopheri, Teleocephali, Gymnoti, Haplomi. In Kingsley, J. S., ed., The standard natural history, vol. 3. Boston.
  1888   The distribution of fresh-water fishes. Transactions of the American Fisheries Society 17:4–24.
          "The Behring Strait has evidently proved no serious obstacle to diffusion; and it is not unlikely that much of the close resemblance of the fresh-water faunae of northern Europe, Asia and North America is due to this fact."
  1890   Report of explorations made during 1888 in Virginia North Carolina and Tennessee and in western Indiana, etc. Bulletin of the U.S. Fishery Commission 1888, 8:97–173.
  1905a   A guide to the study of fishes. Vol. 2. London, Archibald Constable.
  1905b   A guide to the study of fishes. Vol. 2. New York, Henry Holt. 427 pp.
  1907   Fishes. New York, Henry Holt. 789 pp.
  1918   Name of the pickerel. Copeia, No. 16.
          Jordan expressed doubt that the Esox estor of American waters was identical with the European Esox lucius.
  1925   Fishes. Rev. ed. New York, D. Appleton. 773 pp.
  1929   A manual of the vertebrate animals of the northern United States. 13th ed. Chicago, Jansen, McClurg. 446 pp.

JORDAN, D. S. and B. W. EVERMANN
  1896   The fishes of North and Middle America Bulletin of the U.S. Museum, 47, Part 1.
  1902   American food and game fishes. New York, Doubleday, Page. 572 pp.
  1917   The genera of fishes. Leland Stanford Jr. University Publications, University Series, Stanford University. 161 pp.

JORDAN, D. S., B. W. EVERMANN and H. W. CLARK
  1930   Check list of the fishes and fishlike vertebrates of North and Middle America north of the northern boundary of Venzuela and Colombia. Report of the U.S. Commissioners of Fisheries for 1928, Appendix 10, Document 1055. 670 pp.

JORDAN, D. S. and C. H. GILBERT

  1882   A synopsis of the fishes of North America. U.S. National Museum Bulletin 16. 1018 pp.

JORDAN, M. and Z. SREBRO

  1956   Rozwoj jaj niektorych gatunkow ryb zaplodnionych plemnikami zatrutymi iperytem azotowym. [Development of fish eggs fertilized by spermatozoa poisoned with nitrogen mustard.] Folia Biologica 4(1):35–44.
  Disturbances in the development of fish eggs, including pike, fertilized with a sperm treated with nitrogen mustard, depending on the concentration of this compound.

JUDAY, C. and C. L. SCHLOEMER

  1936   Growth of game fishes in Wisconsin. 4th report. Notes from Limnology Laboratory, Wisconsin Geological and Natural History Survey. 26 pp.

  1938   Growth of game fish in Wisconsin waters. 5th report. Notes from Limnology Laboratory, Wisconsin Geological and Natural History Survey. 26 pp.

JUNE, F. C.

  1970   Atresia and year-class abundance of northern pike, *Esox lucius*, in two Missouri River impoundments. Journal of the Fisheries Research Board of Canada 27:587–591.
  Widespread atresia in pike ovaries was associated with low year class abundance in 1966–68 in lakes Oahe and Sharpe. Fluctuations in water temperature and levels that apparently interrupted spawning could be related to the condition.

  1971   The reproductive biology of northern pike, *Esox lucius*, in Lake Oahe, an upper Missouri River storage reservoir. American Fisheries Society Special Publication 8:53–71.
  The ova and ovaries of 1,433 females collected from 1964 to 1973 were examined and descriptions of different maturity stages are provided. Annual variations in size of mature ova and fecundity are discussed. Information on spawning, average age and length at sexual maturity, and sex ratio are provided.

  1976   Changes in young-of-the-year fish stocks during and after filling of Lake Oahe, an upper Missouri River storage reservoir, 1966–74. U.S. Fish and Wildlife Service Technical Paper 87:1–25.

  1977   Reproductive patterns in 17 species of warmwater fishes in a Missouri River reservoir. Environmental Biology of Fishes 2:285–296.
  Timing of ovarian maturation and spawning of pike in Lake Oahe was estimated from changes in mean ovary indices (ratios of ovary weight to fish length).

JURKOWSKI, M. K.

  1976   Sklad kwasow tluszczowych w lipidach ikry szczupaka (*Esox lucius* L.) z Zatoki Puckiej i jezior okolic Lipusza. [The fatty acids composition in egg lipids of pike, *Esox lucius* L. from the Puck Bay and lakes near Lipusz.] Acta Ichthyologica et Piscatoria, Academy of Agriculture, Szczecin 6(2):9–15.
  Analysis of lipids made on the basis of thin-layer chromatography, and analysis of fatty acids and their methyl esters made with gas chromatography.

JUSZCZYK, D.

  1975   Studies on the morphology of gonadal blood vessels in certain bony fishes. Zoologica Poloniae 24:393–454.

KACZYNSKI, C.

1976   Polowy szczupaka w Zalewie Zegrzynskim. [Catches of pike in Zegrzynski dam reservoir.] Gospodarka Rybna 28(2):8–10.

Commercial and recreational catches of pike in 1965–74.

KAJ, J.

1958   Siec tarlisk ochronnych w dorzeczu Warty. [A network of protected spawning grounds in the Warta River basin.] Ochrona Przyrody 25:96–110.

A project of introducing full protection of spawning grounds in 35 areas of the Warts River basin. It was assumed that the project will improve ichthyological relations in the basin. Eight spawning grounds were selected for pike, based on their mass use by the species.

KAJ, J. and B. WLOSZCZYNSKI

1957   Dojrzewanie plciowe i plodnosc ikrzyc szczupaka z dorzecza z dorzecza Warty jako podstawy do normowania wymiarow ochronnych. [The sexual maturity and prolificity of female pikes from the Warta Basin as a basis for regulating protective standard dimensions.] Poznanskie Towarzystwo Przyjaciol Nauk Wydzial Matematyczno-Przyrodniczy, Prace Komisja Nauk Rolniczych i Leshych 3(5):179–208.

Pike stocks in western Poland are diminishing in spite of an extensive artificial rearing program. The authors recommend that the size limit be increased from 30 cm total length to 40 cm, at which size the optimal relative prolificity occurs.

KAJAVA, R.

n.d.   The growth and mortality of northern pike in Tvarminne. M.S. thesis, University of Helsinki. 113 pp. [in Finnish]

KALABINSKI, E.

1909   Przewodnik do okreslania ryb krajowych. [Manual of the classification of local fishes.] Wydawnictwa E. Wende i S-ka, 29 pp.

KALGANOV, V. M.

1949   On alternation of teeth in pike. Priroda 8:70.

KALLIO, D. M., P. R. GARANT and C. MINKIN

1971   Evidence of coated membranes in the ruffled border of the osteoclast. Journal of Ultrastructure Research 37:169–177.

KAMPS, L. R., R. CARR and H. MILLER

1972   Total mercury-monomethylmercury content of several species of fish. Bulletin of Environmental Contamination and Toxicology 8:273–279.

Shows the total mercury versus monomethylmercury content in the edible portion of five species of fish. Mercury content ranged from 0.04 to 2.60 ppm. The proportion of methylmercury to total mercury ranged from 67 to 125%. Mercury in the edible portion of pike is essentially all monomethylmercury.

KAMYSHNAYA, M. S. and E. A. TSEPHIN

1973   A contribution to the ecology of pike *Esox lucius* L. in the lower Umba River. Journal of Ichthyology 13:929–933.

A study of the ecology of pike inhabiting a river along which young salmon migrate to the sea.

KANGUR, A.

1968   On the seasonal character and specific peculiarities of the ATP-ASE activity of the muscular tissue of fishes. Eesti nvs Teaduste Akadeemia Toimetised Bioloogia 17:44–54.

KANNEGIETER, J.
1938   Kunstliche Erwarmung des Speisewassers in Hechtbrutanstalten. Fischerei Zeitung 41:350–352.

KAPCZYNSKA, A. and T. PENCZAK
1969   Wzrost szczupaka *Esox lucius* L., w rzekach Wyzyny Lodzkiej i terenow przyleglych. [Growth of pike, *Esox lucius* L., in rivers of Lodz upland and adjacent areas.] Przeglad Zoologiczny 13:66–72.
        Data on pike growth based on direct scale readings.

KARAMIAN, A. I.
1949   Evolution of the functional relationships of the cerebellum and of the cerebral hemispheres. 1. On the functional relations of the cerebellum and of the anterior part of the brain in bony fishes. Fiziologicheskii Zhurnal 35:167–181.

KARDASHEV, A. V. and A. R. SHAMUN
1984   Biological valve of cannery as dependent on port-mortem state and frozen and cold storage of raw fish. *In* Bykov, V. P., ed., Fishery technology. VNIRO, Moscow, pp. 57–59.
        Report of a considerable decrease in canned fish biological value which resulted from frozen and particularly from long-term cold storage of raw material. The highest biological value was recorded in cannery products prepared of raw fish at the rigor mortis state.

KARLSSON, S. and K. LIDEN
1977   Nablyudaemye koehffitsienty nakopleniya tseziya-137 i kaliya v nekotorykh vidakh ryb i rastenij litorali oligotrofnogo ozera. [Observed coefficients of Cs.SUP—137 and K accumulation in some fishes and aquatic plants from the ologitrophic lake littoral.] Ehkologiya 6:27–31.
        Coefficient was 3055 in pike.

KARPOVICH, I. Y.
1968   Development of fisheries in the Khanty-Mansi National Okrug. Problemy Severa 13:199–207.

KARVELIS, E. G.
1964   The true pikes. U.S. Fish and Wildlife Service, Fishery Leaflet 569:1–11.
        Briefly describes pike and its habitat, distribution, spawning, food, growth, and its value as a sport and commercial fish.

KARZINKIN, G. S.
1935   Toward knowledge of the fishery productivity of waters. Report 4. Duration of passage of food and its assimilation by young pike (*Esox lucius* L.) Trudy Limnologicheskogo St. V. Kosine, 20, M.
1939   Contribution to the fish productivity of fresh waters. 7. Growth of the one-summer old pikes as influenced by some of the natural food. Proceedings Kossino Limnological Station of the Hydrometerological Service USSR 22:219–240.
        Growth and feeding of young pike was studied in aquaria. Dry weight and protein content were determined and consumption assimilation was estimated. When fed upon *Daphnia pulex* and *Cyclops*, pike growth was retarded and weight decreased. *Cyclops* and small *D. pulex* are an acceptable food for only the first 20–30 days after hatch. Pike cannot exist on this food.

1952   Foundations of the biological productivity of waters. Moscow, Pishcheprom-
        izdat.
KASANSKY, B. N., R. I. BALASHOV and L. A. BELOGOLOVAYA
1972   Renewal of aboriginal fish populations after some extremal treatments of the
        lakes in the northwest of the USSR. International Association of Theoretical
        and Applied Limnology Proceedings 18:1207–1211.
KASANSKY, W. J.
1929   Die kreuzung von *Esox lucius* L. mit den Arten der Cyprinidae und Percidae.
        Zoologischer Anzeiger 90:168–175.
KASHIN, S. M., L. K. MALININ and G. N. ORLOVSKY
1976   The speed of predation and prey during the rushing movement. Biologiya
        Vnutrennykh vod Informatsionii Byulleten 30:29–32.
KASHIN, S. M., L. K. MALININ, G. N. ORLOVSKY and A. G. PODDUBNY
1977   Behaviour of some fishes during hunting. Zoologicheskii Zhurnal
        56:1328–1339.
        Kinograms during hunting were studied. The peculiarities of approachment,
        rush and catching the prey are described.
KAUKORANTA, E. and E. A. LIND
1975   The pike, *Esox lucius* L., in the estuary of the Oulujoko River. I. Ecology.
        Ichtyol. Fenn. Borealis 1975(1–2):1–40.
        The study area was a 3-km section between the sea and the Merikoski power
        station. Two hundred pike caught in gill nets were measured, weighed,
        tagged, sexed, and released, with 55% recaptured by 1975. Information on
        exploitation rate, growth, time of milt and roe flow, temperature during
        spawning, length, weight, locomotor activity, methyl mercury concentrations,
        and homing behaviour is provided.
KAUSHIK, S. J., K. DABROWSKI and P. LUQUET
1985   Experimental studies on some trophic relationships in juvenile pike, *Esox
        lucius* L. Journal of Fish Biology 25:171–180.
        A postprandial increase in ammonia nitrogen excretion and oxygen consump-
        tion rates was observed in juvenile pike fed a natural diet or an artificial dry
        diet. 50% of ingesta was evacuated within 5 to 6 hours in pike of 25 mg body
        weight and 9 to 10 hours in those weighing 150 mg. Daily nitrogen excretion
        rates were related to body weight. Respiratory quotient and energy retention
        efficiency were affected by the nature of the diet ingested by pike. Parame-
        ters of the energy balance were related to energy intake.
KAVANAGH
1978   Report of pike committee to Bord Failte Eireann. Ireland Tourism.
KEARN, G. C.
1966   The adhesive mechanism of the monogenean parasite *Tetraonchus monen-
        teron* from the gills of the pike (*Esox lucius*). Parasitology 56:505–510.
KEAST, A.
1970   Food specializations and bioenergetic interrelations in the fish faunas of some
        small Ontario waterways. *In* Steele, J. H., ed., Marine food chains. Edin-
        burgh, Oliver and Boyd, pp. 377–411.
1978   Trophic and spatial interrelationships in the fish species of an Ontario tem-
        perate lake. Environmental Biology of Fishes 3:7–31.
        Brief note on: distribution, description of mouth area, pharyngeal pads, rela-
        tive abundance in habitat types, and food volume.

1979   Patterns of predation in generalist feeders. *In* Clepper, H., ed., Predator-prey systems in fisheries management. Washington, Sport Fishing Institute, pp. 243–255.

KEAST, A. and D. WEBB

1966   Mouth and body form relative to feeding ecology in the fish fauna of a small lake, Lake Opinicon, Ontario. Journal of the Fisheries Research Board of Canada 23:1845–1874.

Describes mouth and body form of pike, and concludes that pike are greatly specialized for a piscivorous way of life.

KEDLEC, J.

1952   Selected bibliography on food habits of the pike. University of Michigan, unpublished MS, 5 pp.

An annotated bibliography.

KELEHER, J. J.

1961   Comparison of largest Great Slave Lake fish with North American records. Journal of the Fisheries Research Board of Canada 18:417–421.

The largest Great Slave Lake pike was 30.0 lb caught on August 17, 1958. North American pike appear not to exceed 50 lb.

1963   The movement of tagged Great Slave Lake fish. Journal of the Fisheries Research Board of Canada 20:319–326.

KELENYI, G.

1972   Phylogenesis of the azurophil leukocyte granules in vertebrates. Experientia 28:1094–1096.

KELSEY, P. M.

1968   Pickerel, pike or muskie? Conservationist 22:41.

Describes characteristics for the angler to differentiate among the species.

KELSO, J. R., H. R. MACCRIMMON and D. J. ECOBICHON

1970   Seasonal insecticide residue changes in tissues of fish from the Grand River, Ontario. Transactions of the American Fisheries Society 99:423–426.

KEMPF, C. and B. SITTLER

1977   Mercury and organo chlorine pollution in the Rhine River Basin; its effects upon bird and fish populations. Terre Vie 31:661–668.

KEMPINGER, J. J.

1966a   Statewide fishery research. Five Lakes studies. Evaluation of maintenance stocking of game fish species. Wisconsin Conservation Department, Dingell-Johnson Report F-83-R-1/Wk.Pl. 5/Job D.

1966b   Statewide fishery research. Five Lakes studies. Evaluation of a 22 inch size limit on northern pike. Wisconsin Conservation Department, Dingell-Johnson Report F-83-R-1/Wk.Pl. 5/Job F.

1967a   Statewide fishery research. Northern highland research project. Evaluation of game fish stocking. Wisconsin Conservation Department, Dingell-Johnson Report F-83-R-2/Wk.Pl. 4/Job B:5–12.

1967b   Statewide fishery research. Northern highland research project. Evaluation of a 22-inch minimum size limit on northern pike in Escanaba Lake. Wisconsin Conservation Department, Dingell-Johnson Report F-83-R-2/Wk.Pl. 4/Job D.

1972   Statewide fishery research. Evaluation of a 22-inch minimum size limit on northern pike in Escanaba Lake. Wisconsin Conservation Department F-83-R-7/Job 2:1–6.

Some statistics on the pike population during the 6 years of no size limits (prior to 1964), in spring 1971, and during the 8 years of restrictive size limits (1964–71).

KEMPINGER, J. J. and R. F. CARLINE

1977   Dynamics of the walleye (*Stizostedion vitreum vitreum*) population in Escanaba Lake, Wisconsin, 1955–1972. Journal of the Fisheries Research Board of Canada 34:1800–1811.

1978a   Dynamics of the northern pike populations and changes that occurred with a minimum size limit in Escanaba Lake, Wisconsin. American Fisheries Society Special Publication 11:382–389.

        A 56-cm minimum length limit was applied in 1964 and removed 9 years later. This paper gives information on changes in yield, catch per unit effort, growth rate, and mortality rate.

1978b   Changes in population density, growth, and harvest of northern pike in Escanaba Lake. Wisconsin Department of Natural Resources Technical Bulletin 104:1–17.

        Changes were related to the implementation of a 22-inch size limit which was imposed in the last 9 years of a 14-year study. Population densities and mortality rates increased. Growth rates, condition factors, and fishing pressure declined. No change was noted in the number of 22-inch pike harvested.

KEMPINGER, J. J. and W. S. CHURCHILL

1970   Statewide fishery research. Estimate of abundance and exploitation of the fish population of Escanaba Lake, Wisconsin. Wisconsin Conservation Department, Dingell-Johnson Report F-83-R-5/Wk.Pl. 21/Job 7/Fin:1–50.

KEMPINGER, J. J., W. S. CHURCHILL, G. R. PRIEGEL and L. M. CHRISTENSON

1975   Estimate of abundance, harvest, and exploitation of the fish population of Escanaba Lake, Wisconsin, 1946–69. Wisconsin Department of Natural Resources Technical Bulletin 84:1–30.

        Results were obtained from a compulsory creel census program on the 293-acre lake. Each year anglers fished an average of 65 hours/acre, catching 20 lb/acre at a rate of 0.84 fish per hours. The highest exploitation rate was for pike (.46).

KENDALL, A. W., Jr. and J. B. MARLIAVE, eds.

1985   Descriptions of early life history stages of selected fishes: from the 3rd International Symposium on the early life history of fishes and 8th annual larval fish conference. Canadian Technical Report of Fisheries and Aquatic Sciences 1359:1–82.

KENDALL, R. L., ed.

1978   Selected coolwater fishes of North America. Proceedings of a symposium, St. Paul, 1978. American Fisheries Society Special Publication 11. 437 pp.

KENDALL, W. C.

1895   Notes on the fresh-water fishes of Washington County, Maine. Bulletin of the U.S. Fish Commission 14:43–54.

1909   The fishes of Labrador. Proceedings of the Portland Society of Natural History 13:207–243.

1918   The Rangeley lakes, Maine, with special reference to the habits of the fishes, fish culture, and angling. Bulletin of the Bureau of Fisheries, vol. 35, Document 861, pp. 487–594.

1919   The pikes; their geographical distribution, habits, culture, and commercial importance. Report of the U.S. Fishery Commission, 1917(app. 5):1–45.

1920   An annotated list of a collection of fishes made by F. Harper in the Athabasca region in 1920. Contributions to Canadian Biology, new ser. 1(23):419–439.

KENDLE, E. R. and L. A. MORRIS

1965   Device for holding objects in the stomachs of fish. Transactions of the American Fisheries Society 94:193–194.

1972   A gastric battery for fish. Progressive Fish-Culturist 34:216.
        The feasibility of a small battery using the gastric juices in a fish's stomach as the electrolyte was investigated as a power source for miniaturized fish-tracking ultrasonic transmitters. After such a battery had been in the stomach of a pike for 226 days, it was not visibly eroded and still produced as much power as when installed in the fish.

KENNEDY, M.

1965   Spawning of pike in four Irish lakes in 1965. Unpublished MS.

1969   Irish pike investigations. Spawning and early life history. Irish Fishery Investigations, Series A (Freshwater), 5:4–33.
        A study of spawning conditions, description of pike eggs, the incubation period, and development of the larvae until absorption of the yolk sac.

KENNEDY, M. and P. FITZMAURICE

1969   Factors affecting the growth of coarse fish. Proceedings of the 4th British Coarse Fish Converence, pp. 42–49.

KENNEDY, W. A.

1946   Food, age, sex and maturity of jackfish in Kakisa and Tathlina lakes. Fisheries Research Board of Canada, unpublished MS.

1947   Some information on the minimum adult stock of fish needed to provide adequate natural spawning. Canadian Fish Culturist 2:14–15.
        Merely mentions that pike in Tathlina Lake and the adjoining muskeg waters were not affected by the winterkill of 1942–43.

1954   Growth, maturity and mortality in the relatively unexploited lake trout, *Cristivomer namaycush*, of Great Slave Lake. Journal of the Fisheries Research Board of Canada 11:827–852.
        Pike is listed as one of the species fished commercially

KENNEDY, W. A. and W. M. SPRULES

1967   Goldeye in Canada. Fisheries Research Board of Canada Bulletin 161:1–45.
        Pike is listed as a predator of goldeye.

KEPLER, P.

1973   Population studies of northern pike and whitefish in the Minto Flats complex with emphasis on the Chatanika River. Alaska Department of Fish and Game, Sport Fishery Division 14:59–81.

KERNEHAM, R. J.

1976   A bibliography of early life stages of fishes. Ichthyological Associates, Bulletin 14:1–190.

KERR, T.

1942   A comparative study of some teleost pituitaries. Proceedings of the Zoological Society of London (A)112:37–56.

KETOLA, H. G.

1978   Nutritional requirements and feeding of selected coolwater fishes: A review. Progressive Fish-Culturist 40:127–132.

KETZ, H. A., G. ASSMANN and H. WITT
  1960   The sodium, potassium and glucose contents of serum and erythrocytes in birds and fish. Acta Biologica et Medica Germanica 4:598–605.

KIERMEIR, A.
  1939   On the blood sugar of freshwater fish. Zeitschrift fur Vergleichende Physiologie 27:460–491.

KILARSKI, W.
  1966   Budowa siateczki sarkoplazmatycznej w miesniach szkieletowych ryb. 3. Szczupak (*Esox lucius* L.). [Organization of the sarcoplasmik reticulum in skeletal muscles of fishes. III. Pike (*Esox lucius* L.).] Bulletin de l'Academie Polonaise des Sciences 14:575–580.

KIME, D. E.
  1978   The hepatic catabolism of cortisol in teleost fish. Adrenal origin of hoxotestosterone precursors. General and Comparative Endocrinology 35:322.

KIME, D. E. and E. A. HEWS
  1978   In vitro biosynthesis of 11 beta-hydroxy and 11 oxotestosterone by testes of the pike (*Esox lucius*) and the perch (*Perca fluviatilis*). General and Comparative Endocrinology 36:604–608.

KING, F. A.
  1959   Call him pike, "jack" or luce. Pennsylvania Angler 28(7):4–7.

KIPLING, C.
  1965   Pike in Windermere. Mitteilungen Internationale Vereinigung fuer Theoretische und Angewandte Limnologie 13:197–198.
          Describes exhibit showing results of work in progress on Lake Windermere pike.
  1972   The commercial fisheries of Windermere. Transactions of the Cumberland and Westmorland Antiquarian and Archaeological Society 72:156–204.
          A historic study of the fisheries in Windermere to the present.
  1975   The effects of variation in growth on the gill net selection of a population of pike. European Inland Fisheries Advisory Committee Technical Paper 23(suppl. 1, vol. 1):80–89.
          A simple model to provide information on the effects of gill net selection on a population of pike is described. The model is designed to give successive annual estimates of the number of pike that were caught, died, and survived each year.
  1976   Year class strengths of perch and pike in Windermere. Report of the Freshwater Biological Association 44:68–75.
          Perch <150 mm are the main food of pike. Pike year class strengths are closely correlated with temperature conditions for the first few months of life.
  1983a   Changes in the growth of pike (*Esox lucius*) in Windermere. Journal of Animal Ecology 52:647–657.
          Pike were sampled in Windermere every year from 1944 to 1982. Lengths-for-age of 11,775 fish were determined from the opercular bones. Three periods of different growth were identified and are described.
  1983b   Changes in the population of pike (*Esox lucius*) in Windermere from 1944 to 1981. Journal of Animal Ecology 52:989–999.
          From October 1944 to March 1982, 13,195 pike were caught in Lake Windermere in gill nets set in winter. Estimates of numbers of adult pike are given for each basin. Temperature, food supply, and cannibalism were identified as

168

important factors in causing changes in numbers, biomass, and growth.

KIPLING, C. and W. E. FROST

1969   Variations in the fecundity of pike *Esox lucius* L. in Windermere. Journal of Fish Biology 1:221–237.

Egg counts were made during four consecutive winters, and the mean number of eggs per gram of total fish weight was estimated. The mean egg number showed a steady increase after the second winter, possibly due to a previous decrease in population density. Variation between individuals in any years was considerable. No association between temperature, growth, and food supply and the number of eggs per gram of total fish weight was seen.

1970   A study of the mortality, population numbers, year class strengths, production and food consumption of pike *Esox lucius* L., in Windermere from 1944 to 1962. Journal of Animal Ecology 39:115–157.

The age and growth of 7,751 pike caught in gill nets, traps, and seines were determined. Pike were tagged every year from 1949–65 and up to 70% of tagged fish were recaptured. Age was determined using the opercular bone. Year class strengths were correlated to temperatures during the first year of life. Sex ratio and biomass were calculated.

1972   Certain effects of an annual removal of pike (*Esox lucius*) from Windermere. International Association of Theoretical and Applied Limnology Proceedings 18:1122–1127.

Since netting started in 1944 the number of pike has not changed appreciably, but the population is younger. The paper describes the effects of the removal of pike on other species.

KIPLING, C. and E. D. LE CREN

1975   Experiences in Windermere with estimating population numbers by tag recapture methods. European Inland Fisheries Advisory Committee Technical Paper 23(suppl. 1, vol. 2):611–619.

1984   Mark-recapture experiments on fish in Windermere, 1943–1982. Journal of Fish Biology 24:395–414.

A total of 4,696 pike were tagged and were recaptured up to 12 years later. The experiments provided useful information on movement and growth.

KIRSIPUU, A.

1964a   On protein fractions and their sexual differences in blood serum of some food-fishes of the Estonian S.S.R. Eesti NSV Teaduste Akadeemia Toimetised Bioloogie 13:45–54.

1964b   On seasonal changes in blood serum protein fractions of fishes. Eesti NSV Teaduste Akadeemia Toimetised Bioloogia 13:278–284.

1975   Blood serum lipoproteins and glycoproteins in the pike *Esox lucius*; results of a paper electrophoretic investigation. Eesti NSV Teaduste Akadeemia Toimetised Bioloogia 24:68–71.

KIRTLAND, J. P.

1844   Descriptions of the fishes of Lake Erie, the Ohio River and their tributaries. Boston Journal of Natural History 4:231–234.

1854   Revision of the species belonging to the genus *Esox*, inhabiting Lake Erie and the River Ohio. Annals of Science 2(3):78–79.

KISTELSKI, B.

1933   Szczupak w stawach karpiowatych. [Pike in carp ponds.] Przeglad Rybacki 6(5):164–166.

Practical suggestions on the culture of pike in carp ponds as an additional stock.

KLAASSEN, H. E. and S. D. CRAWFORD

1973   Scanning electron microscopy of fish scales. Presented at 35th Midwest Wildlife Conference, St. Louis, 1973.

KLAVERKAMP, J. F., D. A. HODGINS and A. LUTZ

1983   Selenite toxicity and mercury-selenium interactions in juvenile fish. Archives of Environmental Contamination and Toxicology 12:405–413.

        Acute lethal toxicities of selenium and the effects of selenium on mercury accumulation were determined in freshwater fish species. Selenite concentrations required to produce 50% mortality were approximately 11 mg SE/l in pike.

KLEBERT, E.

1904   Jakie stawy zarybiec szczupakiem? [What ponds should be stocked with pike?] Okolnik Rybacki 68:11–12.

        Suggestions on stocking of small farm ponds with pike.

KLEERKOPER, H.

1969   Olfaction in fishes. Bloomington, Indiana University Press.

KLEINERT, S. J.

1967a   Statewide fishery research. Factors influencing success of northern pike reproduction in natural and artificial areas. Wisconsin Conservation Department, Dingell-Johnson Report F-83-R-2/Wk.Pl. 6/Job C.

1967b   Statewide fishery research. Evaluation of northern pike stocking. Wisconsin Conservation Department, Dingell-Johnson Report F-83-R-2/Wk.Pl. 6/Job B.

1970   Production of northern pike in a managed marsh, Lake Ripley, Wisconsin. Wisconsin Department of Natural Resources Research Report 49:1–19.

        The number of pike produced in Perrys Marsh was too small to significantly improve the pike fishery of Lake Ripley. It was concluded that Perrys Marsh was poorly suited as a managed production area for pike due in part to low zooplankton food levels in the marsh.

KLEINERT, S. J., P. E. DEBURSE and T. L. WIRTH

1968   Occurrence and significance of DDT and dieldrin residues in Wisconsin fish. Wisconsin Department of Natural Resources Technical Bulletin 41:1–43.

KLEINERT, S. J. and D. F. MRAZ

1965a   Statewide fishery research. Delafield studies. Northern pike studies. Survival of stocked northern pike fingerlings. Wisconsin Conservation Department, Dingell-Johnson Report F-83-R-1/Wk.Pl. 10/Job A.

1965b   Statewide fishery research. Delafield studies. Northern pike studies. Northern pike incubation study. Wisconsin Conservation Department, Dingell-Johnson Report F-83-R-1/Wk.Pl. 9/Job A.

1965c   Statewide fishery research. Delafield studies. Northern pike studies. Survival and growth of northern pike in ponds. Wisconsin Conservation Department, Dingell-Johnson Report F-83-R-1/Wk.Pl. 9/Job B.

1965d   Statewide fishery research. Delafield studies. Northern pike studies. Evaluation of an artificial rearing area for northern pike. Wisconsin Conservation Department, Dingell-Johnson Report F-83-R-1/Wk.Pl. 9/Job C.

1965e   Statewide fishery research. Delafield studies. Northern pike studies. Natural spawning area study. Wisconsin Conservation Department, Dingell-Johnson Report F-83-R-1/Wk.Pl. 8/Job A/FIN.

1966   Life history of the grass pickerel, (*Esox americanus vermiculatus*) in southeastern Wisconsin. Wisconsin Conservation Department Technical Bulletin 37:1–39.

KLESSEN, O.

1961   Hechtbesatz und Hechtwirtschaft. Deutsche Fischerei-Zeitung 8:356–358.

KLUPP, R.

1978   Die production von Hechtsetzlingen in Karpfenteichen. [The production of pike fingerlings in carp ponds.] Fischerei Teichwirt 20:144–148.

        The possibiligy of using pike fingerlings as the second species in carp farming ponds is discussed. Various aspects of pike behaviour, including cannibalism, must be considered. Indications of stocking and stock density are given.

KLUYTMANS, J. H. F. M.

1971   Onderzoek naar de vetzuursamenstelling en het vermogen tot biosynthese van vetzuren bij de snoek (*Esox lucius* L.). Thesis, University of Utrecht.

KLUYTMANS, J. H. F. M. and D. I. ZANDEE

1973a   Lipid metabolism in the northern pike (*Esox lucius* L.) I. The fatty acid composition of the northern pike (*Esox lucius* L.). Comparative Biochemistry and Physiology 44:451–458.

        The fatty acid composition of the total lipids from the pike was studied by standard gas-chromatographic methods, in combination with hydrogenation, i. r. spectroscopy and periodate-permanganate oxidation of semi-preparative collected peaks. Many different positional isomers appeared to be present in the unsaturated fatty acids. The presence of many of the quantitative important acids was in accordance with a biosynthesis starting from linoleic or alpha-linolenic acid.

1973b   Lipid metabolism in the northern pike (*Esox lucius* L.). II. The composition of the total lipids and of the fatty acids isolated from lipid classes and some tissues of the northern pike. Comparative Biochemistry and Physiology 44:459–466.

        The percentage composition of lipid classes of total lipids from the pike is given. The total lipids consisted mainly of polar lipids (51%), cholesterol (13%), and triglycerides (27%). The fatty acid composition of these lipid classes was studied. The fatty acid composition of the testis lipids differed considerably from those of lipids isolated from other organs in containing a very high concentration of long chain polyunsaturated fatty acids.

1974   Lipid metabolism in the northern pike (*Esox lucius* L.). 3. In vivo incorporation of 1–14 C-acetate in the lipids. Comparative Biochemistry and Physiology 48:641–649.

        The specific radioactivity of the total lipids isolated from different organs of the pike after injection of Na-a-14-C-acetate showed the highest values in the liver and the gills. In the liver, radioactivity was found mainly in the fatty acids, while in the gills the greater part was present in the unsaponifiable lipids. The percentage incorporation of radioactivity in lipid classes did not change significantly from 2 to 24 hours after injection, but decreased in phospholipids and increased in triglycerides during shorter incubation times.

KLYSZEJKO, B.

1973   Zmiany osmotyczne surowicy krwi szczupaka *Esox lucius* L. w przebiegu procesu adaptacyjnego do zwiekszonej koncentracji zasolenia wody. [Osmotic changes in the blood serum of the pike *Esox lucius* L. during the process of adaptation to the increased salinity of water.] Acta Ichthyologica et Piscatoria 3(1):125–137.

Studies on 850 pike from natural environments of varying salinity.

KMIOTECK, S. and J. M. HELM

1961   Observations on the effects of electric shock on eggs and sperm in spawning northern pike. Wisconsin Conservation Department, Investigational Memo 6:1.

KNAUTHE, K.

1902   Varietaten des Hechtes. Zoologische Garten 43:405.

KNOWELDEN, M.

1984   A passion for pike, the legendary monster. Scanorama, July-August, 1984, pp. 90–95.

KOBEC, G. F., V. S. ZAVJALOVA and M. L. KOMAROVA

1969   Der Einflus des Fischschleimes auf die turbulente Reibung. Bionika 3:80–84. [in Russian]

KOBES, R.

1982   Big jerks - big pike. In-Fisherman 45:72–83.

Describes equipment and technique for fishing pike with "jerkbait".

KOCH, H.

1970   Hechtaufzug auf der Insel Reichenau. Allgemeine Fischerei-Zeitung 95(15):505.

KOCH, W., O. BANK and G. JENS

1976   Fischzucht, Lehrbuch fur Zuchter und Teichwirte. 4th ed. Hamburg, Paul Parey. 264 pp.

KOGTEVA, E. P.

1961   Fish parasites from Pskov Chud water reserve. In Petruschevskii, ed., Parasites and diseases of fish. Jerusalem, Israel Program for Scientific Translations. 338 pp.

KOIVUSAARI, J.

1976   Chlorinated hydrocarbons and total mercury in the prey of the white-tailed eagle Haliaeetus albicilia in the Quarken Straits of the Gulf of Bothnia, Finland. Bulletin of Environmental Contamination and Toxicology 15:235–241.

KOKES, J.

1977   Prispevek ke studiu potravy stiky obecne. [A contribution to the study of the food eaten by the pike.] Vertebratologicke zpravy, pp. 26–28.

KOLGANOV, D. I.

1968   How the pike changes its teeth. Rybovodstvo i rybolovstvo, no. 4.

KOLI, L. and M. SOIKKELI

1974   Fish prey of breeding Caspian terns in Finland. Annales Zoologici Fennici 11:304–308.

KOMAROVA, M. L.

1969   Uber die chemische Zusammensetzung des Schleines des Hechtes und der Quappe. Bionika 3:84–90. [in Russian]

KONFAL, E.

1971   Valvula bauhini and the large intestine in Esox lucius. Biologia 26:427–430.

KONOBEEVA, V. K., A. G. KONOBEEV and A. G. PODDUBNYI

1980   The mechanism of massing on young perch Perca fluviatilis in the open part of lake type reservoirs using Rybinsk Reservoir Russian-SFSR USSR as an example. Voprosy Ikhtiologii 20:258–271.

KONONOV, V. A.

1957   Conditions and efficiency of reproduction of fishes in the Kakhovka reservoir in its first year. Transactions of the 6th Conference on the Biology of Inland Waters, 1957, pp. 428–435.

The numbers of young of valuable predators are low. Therefore, their importance as biological regulators of numbers of trash fishes should be markedly strengthened.

KONOVALOV, P. M. and T. V. LUGAVAYA

1968   The results of experiments in the artificial rearing of pike at the Krememenchug spawning and fish rearing establishment. Rybnoe Khozyaistvo Respublikanskii Mezhvedomstvennyi Tematicheskii Nauchnyk Sbornik 6(6):50–61.

KONRAD

1962   Volksmundliche Fischnamen. Allgemeine Fischerei-Zeitung 87:517–518.

KORHONEN, M.

1961   Haukikalat. *In* Pitkanen, H., ed., Suuri kalakirja. Helsinki, pp. 136–148.

KOROVINA, V. M., A. I. LYUBITSKAYA and E. A. DOROFEEVA

1965   The effect of visible light and darkness on rate of formation of skeletal cartilage elements in teleost fishes. Voprosy Ikhtiologii 5:503–510.

Pike was one of the species used in an experiment to incubate eggs under varying illumination. The degree of illumination had a significant effect on development of the skeletal cartilage; however, an approximation of natural light yielded optimal conditions.

KOROVINA, V. M. and N. E. VASIL'EVA

1976   Anatomic and histological data on phylogenetic links of salmonoid fishes. Arkhiv Anatomii Gistologii i Embriologii 70:66–73.

KORULCZYK, T. and L. KOZLOWSKA

1970   Kiedy lowic szczupaka. [When to catch pike.] Gospodarka Rybna 22(11):19–21.

National pike catches in the period 1958–1968. Distribution of catches in an annual cycle. Intensification of pike catches with traps and set gear in autumn.

KORWIN-KOSSAKOWSKI, M.

1976   Plodnosc i wzrost szczupaka (*Esox lucius* Linnaeus 1758) z jeziora Warniak. [The fecundity and the growth of pike *Esox lucius* from the Warniak Lake, Poland.] Roczniki Nauk Rolniczyck, Series H, Rybactwo 94(2):43–61.

Estimation of absolute and relative fecundity and growth of pike. Relationship between absolute fecundity, relative fecundity, and age, body weight and length in the first year of life, also egg size, based on linear and multiple regression analysis.

KORZHUEV, P. A.

1958   Ekologo-fiziologicheskie osobennosti nekotorykh vidov ryb. Trudy Soveshchanii Ikhtiologicheskoi Komissii Akademii Nauk SSSR 8:364–371.

KORZHUEV, P. A. and T. N. GLAZOVA

1968   Comparative physiological characteristics of the blood and hematopoietic organs of fish and aquatic mammals. Fiziologiya Osnovy Ekologii vodnykh Zhivotnykh Seriya Biologii Morya Vyp 15:131–146.

KORZYNEK, W.

1956   O tarle szczupaka glebinowego. [On pike spawning.] Gospodarka Rybna 8(3):23–24.

Catches of adult pike by the use of fyke nets placed at a depth of 3.5 to 8 m from April 30 to June 3.

1960   O ochronie szczupaka. [Pike protection.] Wiadomosci Wedkarskie 1:9–10. Practical suggestions on better protection of pike by the use of proper angling methods.

1962   Szczupak olbrzym. [A giant pike.] Gospodarka Rybna 14(3):32. Description of record-size (24–34 kg) pike caught by fishermen.

KOSHELEV, B. W.

1961   Changes in the sexual cycles of fishes with a single annual spawning, associated with changes in environmental conditions. Voprosy Ikhtiologii 1:716–724.

KOSHEVA, A. F.

1957   The formation of the parasitofauna of fish in the Kutuluk Basin. *In* Petrushevskii, G. K., ed., Parasites and diseases of fish. Jerusalem, Israel Program for Scientific Translations, pp. 120–126.

KOSHINSKY, G. D.

1969   The Lac la Ronge and Hunter Bay creel census, 1969. Saskatchewan Department of Natural Resources, MS Report, 24 pp.

1972   An evaluation of two tags with northern pike (*Esox lucius*). Journal of the Fisheries Research Board of Canada 29:469–476.

In a 4-year study of pike, barb-anchored spaghetti dart tags were retained longer than monofilament-attached preopercular disc tags. Tagging mortality, condition, growth, dispersal, and angling vulerability were compared in fish bearing each tag type.

1979   Northern pike at Lac La Ronge. Part 1. Biology of northern pike. Part 2. Dynamics and exploitation of the northern pike population. Saskatchewan Department of Tourism and Renewable Resources, Fisheries Laboratory Technical Report 79–80:1–303.

Data on fisheries, reproduction, length-weight relationships, migration habits, environmental factors, habitat, food and feeding, age, growth, tagging results, annual mortality of fish and eggs, age of maturity, population size, parasitism, predator-prey relationships, and fishing regulations. Recommendations were given for stiffer fishing regulations and additional research.

KOSSWIG, C.

1969   New contributions to zoogeography of fresh water fish of Asia Minor, based on collections made between 1964–1967. Israel Journal of Zoology 18(2/3):249–254.

KOSTER, W. J.

1957   Guide to the fishes of New Mexico. University of New Mexico Press. 116 pp.

KOSTOMAROV, B.

1961   Die Fischzucht. Berlin, VEB Deutscher Landwirtschaftsverlag. 375 pp.

KOSTOMAROVA, A. A.

1959   Biologicheskoe znachenie etapa smeshannogo pitaniya dlya razvitiya lichinok shchuki. [Biological importance of the phase of mixed nourishment for the development of the larvae of the pike (*Esox lucius*).] Rybnoe Khozyaistvo 8:25–27.

A study of dietary needs of pike larvae from time of hatch until 2 days after they become mobile.

174

1961   Zhachenie etapa smeshannogo pitaniya dlya vyzhivaemosti lichinok shchuki. [The significance of the stage of mixed feeding for the survival of *Esox lucius* L. larvae.] Trudy Soveshchanii Ikhtiologicheskoi Komissii Akademi Nauk SSSR 13:344–347.

Availability of food from the time they transferred to live food appeared necessary to the normal morphological, anatomical, and physiological development of the larvae. Those which fed only on the yolk sac failed to develop physically, lost the ability to react to water currents, and starved after three days following resorption.

KOTLYAREVSKAYA, N. V.

1966   The effect of the hatching enzyme on the envelope capsule of the pike egg. Doklady Akademii Nauk SSSR 169:485–488.

The strength of the egg membrane was studied. Comparably high residual strength of the pike egg envelope (minimum 25–60 g) after it has been weakened by the enzyme indicates that the movement of the embryo plays an important role in hatch of pike. The chemical action of the hatching enzyme was studied. The egg envelope does not contain acid mucopolysaccharides, which agrees with the observations obtained with other types of fish, and the changes observed cannot be ascribed to hyaluronidase activity.

1969   The hatching process in the pike (*Esox lucius* L.). Problems of Ichthyology 9:85–94.

The development of the embryo before, and its morpho-physiological state during, hatching was investigated. The functional states of the hatching and adhesive glands were examined, attentuation of the egg membranes by hatching gland secretion, and embryo movement were important elements in the hatching process.

KOURIL, J.

1975   Dospivani, pohlavni cyklus a plodnost stiky obecne (*Esox lucius* L.) chovane v rybnicich. [Maturation, sexual cycles and fertility of pike reared in fishponds.] Buletin Vyzkumy Ustav Rybarsky a Hydrobiologicky Vodnany, 69 pp.

KOURIL, J. and J. HAMACKOVA

1975   Plodnost stiky obecne (*Esox lucius* L.) z rybnicniho chovu. [Fecundity of pond-reared pike (*Esox lucius* L.).] Zivocisna vyroba 20:841–850.

1977   Rocni pohlavni cyklus stiky obecne chovane v rybnicich. [The annual sexual cycle of pond farmed pike *Esox lucius* L.] Buletin Vyzkumy Ustav Rybarsky a Hydrobiologicky Vodnany 13:8–16.

Describes and illustrates the annual morphological and histological changes in gonads of both sexes of farmed pike, third age group.

1978   Doporucena technologie: Odchov pludku stiky obecne (*Esox lucius* L.). [Recommended technology: rearing of pike fry.] Buletin Vyzkumy Ustav Rybarsky a Hydrobiologicky Vodnany. 11 pp.

KOURIL, J., J. HAMACKOVA and Z. SVOBODOVA

1976   Exterierova a kondicni ukazatele stiky obecne (*Esox lucius* L.) z rybnicniho chovu v predvyterovem obdobi. [Conformation and condition indices of pond-farmed pike (*Esox lucius* L.) in the pre-spawning period.] Buletin Vyzkumy Ustav Rybarsky a Hydrobiologicky Vodnany 12(3):3–8.

KOVAL, N. V.

1969   Experimental use of neutral red dye to tag young fish. Hydrobiological Journal 5(6):95–99.

KOVAL, V. P.

1969   Trematodes of the genus *Phyllodistomum braun* 1899 from the fishes of Ukr. SSR. Vesnik Kiivs'kogo Universiteta, Seriya Biologii 11:167–174.

KOZHOV, M.

1963   Lake Baikal and its life. The Hague, Junk. 344 pp.

KOZICKA, J.

1953   Pasozyty ryb w jeziorze Tajty. [Fish parasites in Lake Tajty.] Roczniki Nauk Rolniczych, Ser. D, 67:171–186.

1971   Cestode larvae of the family Dilepididae parasitizing fresh water fish in Poland. Acta Parasitologica Polonica 19:81–93.

KOZMIN, A. K.

1952   On the biology of the pike in the Kama River and catches of it in the stretch between the Vishera and the Chosovaya. Izvestiya Yestestvenno-nauchn, Instituta pri Molotovsk Universitete 13(4–5).

1980   The biology of the pike, *Esox lucius*, from Lake Lacha. Journal of Ichthyology 20:44–48.

    Data on the size-age and sexual composition of the population, the nature of spawning, rate of growth and sexual maturation, the condition and feeding of the pike in Lake Lacha are given. With the aim of increasing the abundance of this species, it is proposed to halve pike catches during the spring period, to regulate recreational fishing and to restrict the commercial catch to 20–25 tons a year.

KRAUSE, R.

1923   Mikroshopische Anatomie des Wirbeltiere. IV. Teleostier Plagiostomen, Ziplostomen und Leptokardier. Berlin, Walter de Gruyter, pp. 609–681.

KRAWKOW, N. P.

1913   Uber die Wirkung von Giften auf die Gefasse isolierter Fischkiemen. Pfluegers Archiv fuer die Gesamte Physiologie des Menschen und der Tiere 151:583–603.

KREUTZBERG, G. W. and G. W. GROSS

1977   General morphology and axonal ultrastructure of the olfactory nerve of the pike *Esox lucius*. Cell Tissue Research 181:443–457.

KREUZER, R. O. and J. G. SIVAK

1984   Spherical aberration of the fish lens: interspecies variation and age. Journal of Comparative Physiology, A. Sensory Neural and Behavioral Physiology 154:415–422.

KRIEGSMANN, F.

1970   Jungfischaufzucht mit Zooplankton. Arbeiten des Deutschen Fischerei-Verbandes 14:27–31.

KRISTOFFERSSON, R. and S. BROBERG

1972   Effect of temperature acclimation on some blood constituents of the pike (*Esox lucius* L.). Annales Zoologici Fennici 8:427–433.

    The haemoglobin, haematocrit, serum total proteins, protein fractions, and free amino acids were investigated in brackish-water pike acclimated to water temperatures of 16 C and 6 C for 4 weeks without food. The mean weight losses in the two groups were 10.3 and 5.3% of the respective initial weights.

Four weeks of fasting at a water temperature of 16 C as well as a sudden drop in temperature to 6 C decreased both Her and the Hb values. Total proteins remained unchanged in all experimental groups. Changes in serum electro-pherograms are described.

KRISTOFFERSSON, R., S. BROBERG and A. OIKARI

1972   Effect of temperature change on some blood constituents and osmotic balance in the pike (*Esox lucius* L.) in brackish water. Annales Zoologici Fennici 9:212–218.

Pike were acclimated to water temperatures of 6 C and 16 C for 16 days without food. The temperatures were then reversed for 12 hours. A clear change was seen in plasma potassium and inorganic phosphate levels at both temperatures and in plasma and muscle tissue water contents of pike transferred from 6 C to 16 C.

1973   Physiological effects of a sublethal concentration of phenol in the pike (*Esox lucius* L.) in pure brackish water. Annales Zoologici Fennici 10:392–397.

The effect of phenol on pike living in brackish water of relatively stable salin-ity, 5–6%, was studied in continuous-flow aquarium experiments. The highest concentration for survival for at least one week was 5 ppm of phenol at a water temperature of 10 C. After one week of exposure, the test fish were still in good condition, as judged from their external appearance. No differences could be demonstrated between the control and phenol-affected groups in blood haemoglobin, haematocrit, total plasma protein, and various ions. The total amount of plasma free amino acids was slightly increased in the phenol-affected group. No clearly destructive histopathological changes in the gill lamellae or liver structures of the phenol-affected group could be detected.

KRISTOFFERSSON, R., S. BROBERG, A. OIKARI and M. PEKKARINEN

1974   Effect of a sublethal concentration of phenol on some blood plasma enzyme activities in the pike (*Esox lucius* L.) in brackish water. Annales Zoologici Fennici 11:220–223.

In pike kept for 8 days in brackish water (about 6% S) containing about 5 ppm phenol at 10 C, the activities of the plasma enzymes lactate dehydro-genase, glutamate-oxaloacetate transaminase, and glutamate-pyruvate tran-saminase were found to be significantly elevated. The activity of cho-linesterase remained unchanged.

KRITSCHER, E.

1975   The fish of the Neusiedler Lake and their parasites. Part 2. Parasitic Copepoda and Branchiura. Annalen des Naturhistorischen Museums in Wien 79:589–596.

KROHN, D. C.

1968a   Evaluation of northern pike stocking. Wisconsin Department of Natural Resources, Dingell-Johnson Report F-83-R-3, Job 6-B.

1968b   Factors influencing success of northern pike reproduction in natural and artificial spawning areas. Wisconsin Department of Natural Resources, Dingell-Johnson Project F-83-R-3, Job 6C.

1969   Summary of northern pike stocking investigations in Wisconsin. Wisconsin Department of Natural Resources Research Report 44:1–35.

Various stocking efforts in 19 lakes in Wisconsin, Minnesota, and Iowa were evaluated, and recommendations for future stocking provided.

177

KRUGLOVA, E. E.

1971a   Biochemical characterization of the synaptosomes of the brain in a series of vertebrates.   Journal   of   Evolutionary   Biochemistry   and   Physiology 6:381–383.

1971b   Biochemical characteristics of brain synaptosomes in vertebrates. Neuroscience 16:105–108.

KRULL, J. N.

1968   Some observations concerning fish found in the Montezuma National Wildlife Refuge. New York Fish and Game Journal 15:201–202.

KRUPNER, V. and C. PEKAR

1965   Rozmnozovani stiky obecno Lipenske Udolninadrzi. Buletin Vyzkumy Ustav Rybarsky a Hydrobiologicky Vodnany 5:103–149.

KRUTZBERG, G. W. and G. W. GROSS

1977   General morphology and axonal ultrastructure of the olfactory nerve of the pike, *Esox lucius*. Cell Tissue Research 181:443.

KUEHN, J. H.

1949   Statewide average total length in inches at each year. Minnesota Fisheries Research Laboratory, Supplement to Investigational Report 51.

KUHNE, E. R.

1939   A guide to the fishes of Tennessee and the mid-south. Tennessee Department of Conservation, Division of Game Fish. 124 pp.

        Pike have been established in several smaller lakes of middle Tennessee by artificial introduction.

KULAKOVSKAYA, O. P.

1976   Parasitic fauna of *Umbra umbra crameri*. Vestnik Zoologie 4:82–84.

KULEMIN, A. A., I. I. MAKKOVEYEVE and M. I. SOLOPOVA

1971   Age composition, growth rate and condition of the pike (*Esox lucius* (L.)) of Lake Pleshcheyevo. Journal of Ichthyology 11:31–36.

        Increase in the weight of pike in this body of water is most intensive after 5 years of age, and it should therefore be regarded as irrational to catch younger specimens. The low numbers of the pike in Lake Pleshcheyevo make it essential to increase its protection.

KULIKOV, N. V.

1970   Radio sensitivity of the eggs of *Esox lucius* during fertilization and early division. Radiobiologiya 10:768–770.

KULIKOV, N. V. and V. G. KULIKOVA

1977   Accumulation of strontium-90 and cesium-137 in some freshwater fish under natural conditions. Ekologiya 5:45–49.

KULIKOV, N. V., V. G. KULIKOVA and S. A. LYUBIMOVA

1971   Excretion of strontium 90 and cesium 137 with fish eggs during spawning. Ekologiya 2(4):12–16.

        A quantitative determination of the excretion of Sr90, Cs137, Ca, Mn, and K from female pike with their eggs during spawning under natural conditions. The coefficients of discrimination of Sr90 relative to Ca and Mg and of Cs137 relative to K upon uptake of these elements from the aquatic environment into the fishes and their excretion from the fishes with eggs are presented.

KULMATYCKI, W.

1929   O "chorobie szczupakow".   [Pike disease.]   Przeglad Zoologiczny 2(2):61–66.

Hypotheses on possible causes of a "pike disease". Outline of management methods to be used in order to increase lake productivity and preserve decreasing stocks of pike.

KUPCHINSKAYA, E. S.

1985   Pike, *Esox lucius*, of Ust-Ilimskoe Reservoir. Journal of Ichthyology 25:133–141.

The distribution of pike in Ust'-Ilimskoe Reservoir was studied, along with growth, feeding, ration, and condition.

KUPERMAN, B. I. and V. V. KUZ'MINA

1984   Ultrastructure of the intestinal epithelium of pike *Esox lucius* (Esocidae). Journal of Ichthyology 3:34–42.

KUPERMAN, B. I. and R. E. SHUL'MAN

1972   Experimental study of the effect of temperature on some pike parasites. Vestnik Leningradskogo Universiteta Biologiya 27:5–15.

The change of temperature had different effects on *Triaenophorus nodulosus*, *T. crassus*, and *Ergasilus sieboldi* was investigated. Temperature affects the parasites indirectly, as it changes the physiological state of the host, and this in turn affects the parasites.

KURSIPUU, A.

1971   Some physiological processes and environmental conditions affecting the protein composition of the blood serum in fish. Rapports et Proces-Verbaux des Reunions Commission Internationale pour l'Exploration Scientifique de la Mer 161:154–157.

KUSHNARENKO, A. I.

1978   The minimal commercial size and natural mortality of the north Caspian roach *Rutilus rutilus caspicus*. Voprosy Ikhtiologii 18:1000–1009.

Data on consumption of roach by pike in USSR.

KUZ'MINA, V. V.

1977   Characteristics of membrane digestion in fresh water bony fishes. Voprosy Ikhtiologii 17:111–119.

Method of gradual alpha-amylase desorption from gut section showed seasonal changes in relation to activities of enzyme adsorbed by intestinal mucosa and unsorbed enzyme.

1981   Nutritive adaptation of digestive enzymes in fresh water Teleostei. Zhurnal Obshchei Biologii 42:258–265.

1984   Temperature effects on the pH activity of phosphates from fish intestine. Voprosy Ikhtiologii 24:151–157.

A study was made of temperature effect on pH activity of phosphatases from the intestinal mucous of pike. The maximum phosphatase activity was observed in the region of pH 5.0 and 9.0–10.0 both at 20 and 0 C. Temperature fall led to a considerable decrease in the enzymatic activity at the physiological pH and produced a slighter effect at the optimum pH. The pH activity of the alkaline phosphatase was found to be related to the ecological features of the species.

KUZ'MINA, V. V. and I. L. GOLOVANOVA

1980   The effect of pH and the amylolytic activity of the intestinal mucosa in some species of freshwater teleosts. Journal of Ichthyology 20(3):157–162.

The pH optimum of the amylolytic enzymes corresponds to the pH values of the gut of the fish. The nature of pH dependence is variable, depending mainly on the type of feeding and membership of a given ecological group and also on the functional state of the organism.

KUZ'MINA, V. V. and E. N. MOROZOVA

1977   Effects of temperature on alpha amylase activity of freshwater teleosts. Journal of Ichthyology 17:778–785.

        The study showed differences in: enzyme activity between ecological groups, rate of reaction with temperature rise, relative alpha amylase activity at low and active temperatures, and temperature optima in predatory and non-predatory fishes. Little specific discussion of these regarding pike.

KUZ'MINA, V. V. and L. P. ZHILINA

1974   The ratio of glycogen concentrations in the liver and muscles of some freshwater teleost fishes. Journal of Ichthyology 13:623–627.

        Data on seasonal variations of glycogen content in liver, red muscle, and white muscle tissues.

KUZNETSOV, V. A.

1972   The growth pattern of the larvae and young of some freshwater fish at different stages of development. Journal of Ichthyology 12:433–442.

        Five growth periods have been established for larvae and young at different stages of growth, four of which apply to pike. The periods are characterized by corresponding growth rate indices and are related to specific features of nutrition.

1975   Intrapopulational differentiation of fishes in rivers with regulated flow. Ekologiya 6(4):61–69.

1977   Analysis of ecological groups of fishes according to the concept of S. G. Kryzhanovskii. Zoologicheskii Zhurnal 56:1503–1510.

1980   Fluctuation in the abundance of commercial fishes influenced by regulated river discharge (as exemplified by Kuybyshev Reservoir). Journal of Ichthyology 20(5):32–38.

LAARMAN, P. W.

   1964a   Research and management of the sport fisheries of Michigan—age and growth, Michigan fishes. Michigan Department of Conservation, Dingell Johnson Project F-27-R-2/Wk.Pl. 8/Job 1:1–11.

   1964b   Length of common Michigan sport fishes. Michigan Fisherman 1964(5):2 pp.

LAFRANCE, J.-M.

   1974   Etude de la reproduction du brochet (*Esox lucius* L.) dans la frayere Pelissier lac McGregor, comte de Papineau, 1974. Quebec Ministere du Tourisme, de la Chasse et de la Peche, unpublished MS. 67 pp.

   1975   Frayere de grand brochet Pelissier, lac McGregor. Operations, donnees recueillies et compilations sommaires. Quebec Ministere du Tourisme, de la Chasse et de la Peche, unpublished MS. 66 pp.

   1976   Brochet du nord. Frayere Pelissier, lac McGregor. Operations, donnees recueillies et compilations sommaires. Quebec Ministere du Tourism, de la Chasse et de la Peche, unpublished MS. 38 pp.

LAGLER, K. F.

   1939   Ohio fish management progress report. Ohio Conservation Bulletin 3(1):16–19.

   1956   The pike, *Esox lucius* Linnaeus, in relation to waterfowl on the Seney National Wildlife Refuge, Michigan. Journal of Wildlife Management 20(2):114–124.
   creation of a favourable habitat for pike and waterfowl from 1936 to 1942 and the resulting increase in pike population is described. The life history, growth, and distribution of pike are discussed. Food and population size of the pike were analysed, and duckling mortality calculated. Recommendations for reducing duckling mortality by controlling pike populations are given.

LAGLER, K. F., J. E. BARDACH and R. R. MILLER

   1962   Ichthyology. New York, John Wiley. 380 pp.

LAGOM, T.

   1962   The fishes of the lakes Rauta and Liekovesi. Kalataloudellisen tutkimustoimiston monistettuja julkaisuja 20:29–32.

LAIRD, M.

   1961   Parasites from northern Canada - 2. Haematozoa of fishes. Canadian Journal of Zoology 39:541–548.
   Parasites were present in thin blood films from only 6 of 188 fishes of 11 species, collected in the Northwest Territories and northern Quebec. The haemoflagellate *Crypobia gurneyorum* is recorded from North America for the first time, from pike.

LAMBERT, A.

   1978   Oncomiracidium of *Tetraonchus monenteron* Monogenea Tetraonchidae, parasite of *Esox lucius* Teleostei. Annales de Parasitologie Humaine et Comparee 53:117–119.

LANDHURST, R. S.

   1978   A creel census on Shawano Lake, 1977–78, with emphasis on northern pike. Wisconsin Department of Natural Resources, Fish Management Report 121:1–19.
   In an attempt to assess the effects of liberal regulations on pike, a stratified random creel census was conducted from June 6, 1977, to June 5, 1978. Information on angling pressure, harvest rate.

181

LANDNER, L., K. LONDSTROEM, M. KARLSSON, J. NORDIN and L. SOERENSEN
  1977   Bioaccumulation in fish of chlorinated phenols from kraft pulp mill bleachery effluents. Bulletin of Environmental Contamination and Toxicology 18:663–673.

LANGFORD, T. E.
  1966   Fishery biology as applied by a river board. *In* Jones, J. W., and P. H. Tombleson, eds., Proceedings of the 2nd British Coarse Fish Conference, Liverpool, 1965, pp. 12–28.

LANGLOIS, T. H.
  1927   Artificial propagation of pike perch, yellow perch and pikes. Report of the U.S. Bureau of Fish for 1927, Appendix 1: 1–27.
  1954   The western end of Lake Erie and its ecology. Ann Arbor, J. W. Edward. 479 pp.

LANOISELEE, B.
  1984   Fertilisation organique en aquaculture: Utilisation du lisier de porc pour l'alevinage de poissons d'etang. [Organic fertilization in aquaculture: utilization of pig liquid manure for pond fish rearing.] Paris, Institut National Agronomique. 252 pp.

LANTZ, A. W. and D. G. IREDALE
  1966   Sweet cured freshwater fish slices. Trade News 18(10–11):8–9.
          The method of sweet curing fish to produce a ham or bacon type product with good texture and flavour is described.
  1971   A practical method for drying freshwater fish. Journal of the Fisheries Research Board of Canada 28:1061–1062.
          A method and equipment suitable for drying fish, including pike, in remote areas are described. Results of different preparation methods are compared.

LAPITSKII, I. I.
  1958   Formirovanie stad i sostoyanie zapasov osnovnykh promyslovykh ryb Tsimlyanskoso vodokhranilishcha. [Formation of populations and condition of the stocks of the main commercial fishes of Tsimlyan Reservoir.] Izvestiya Vsesoyuznogo Nauchno-Issledovatel-skogo Instituta Ozernogo i Rechnogo Rybnogo Khozyaistva 45:90–110.
          Water level fluctuations have interferred with pike recruitment. Stocks are not stable. Pike, along with several species, is commercially harvested.

LAPKIN, V. V., A. G. PODDUBNYY and A. M. SVIRSKIY
  1983   Thermoadaptive properties of fishes from temperate latitudes. Journal of Ichthyology 23(2):45–54.

LARIONOV, Y. P.
  1969   Ichthyofauna of the Dolgan Lake and its significance in trade. Trudy Yakutsk Otdeleniya Sibirskogo Nauchno-Issledovatel'skogo Instituta Rybnogo Khozyaistva 3:205–216.

LARSEN, A.
  1944   Om Abomer og Gedder og deres Yagleforhold ved Bornholms Kyster. Flora og Fauna 50:4–8.

LARSEN, K.
  1943   Svers aftkastning og gedde og aborne. Lystfisheritidskrift 55(414): 4513–4516.
  1945   Geddens stilling i det dansk fisheri. Sportsfiskeren 20(6):97–99.

1951a   Om geddens (*Esox lucius* L.) føde i vandløb. [On the food of pike (*Esox lucius* L.) in streams.] Sportsfiskeren 26(2):3–11.

1951b   Nogle fiskeribiologiske betragtninger over gedden i vore ferske. Naturens Verden 35:182–192.

1961   The fish population of a peat pit as determined by rotenone poisoning. Meddelelser Komm. Havundersøgelser 3:117–132.

1962   Ferskvandsfiskene i Thy og Vester-Hanherred. [The fishes of the inland waters of Thy and Vester-Hanherred.] Flora og Fauna 68(3):121–129.

1966   Studies on the biology of Danish stream fishes. I. The food of pike (*Esox lucius* L.) in trout streams. Meddelelser fra Danmarks Fiskeri-og Havundersøgelser, NY Ser, 4:271–326.

> Stomach contents of 895 pike were examined. Gives information on feeding biology of pike, frequency of food species and empty stomachs. Crustaceans were found most frequently, followed by fish, nymphs and larvae of insects, *Annelida*, frogs and lampreys.

LARUE, G. R.

1926   Studies of the trematode family Strigeidae (Holostomidae). Transactions of the American Microscopical Society 45:282–288.

LASSLEBEN

1960   Pike breeding. Der Fischwirt 3:79–81.

> Information on temperature conditions, mortality, and criteria of Swedish method for middle European pike breeding from fertilization procedure to hatching.

LATTA, W. C.

1971   The northern pike in Michigan: a commentary on regulations for fishing. Michigan Department of Natural Resources, Research Development Report 241:1–36.

> The effects of various fishing regulations on northern pike in Michigan were evaluated with a model of a typical population. The apparently valid observation that pike are decreasing in abundance in Michigan is probably a result of destruction of their spawning marshes rather than overexploitation through lax regulations.

1972   The northern pike in Michigan: a simulation of regulations for fishing. Michigan Academician 5:153–170.

> The effects of winter spearing on spring spawning stock and summer harvest, and the combination of regulations which would provide the optimum harvest are discussed. Shoreline habitat destruction is considered responsible for the population decline, rather than overfishing.

LAVROVA, Y. A. and Y. V. NATOCHIN

1974   Cation concentration in the blood of some Baikal fishes and the ion regulating function of the kidney. Journal of Ichthyology 13:764–769.

> Shows differences in cation concentration between fishes of different families. Descriptions of cation processing in kidney tubules and reaction of kidneys from magnesium chloride solution injection.

LAWLER, G. H.

1950   Trammel netting for pike at Heming Lake. Fisheries Research Board of Canada, unpublished MS. 4 pp.

> Trammel nets were especially effective in summer, fished parallel to shore along the edges of vegetation in sandy, marshy areas.

1953   Preliminary report on the activity patterns of four species of fish from Heming Lake, Manitoba. Fisheries Research Board of Canada, Biological Station Manuscript Report 542:1–10.
       Analysis of gill-net catches at various times of the day indicates that pike are more active during night and the hour immediately preceding and following than during the daytime.

1959   Biology and control of the pike-whitefish parasitic worm, *Triaenophorus crassus*, in Canada. Fisheries Research Board of Canada, Progress Reports of the Biological Station and Technological Unit, 1:31–37.
       Outlines the life history of the parasite and possible ways of controlling it, including the destruction of the adult host. A review of the Heming Lake experiment is given.

1960a A history of an intensive fishery on Heming Lake, Manitoba. Presented at 22nd Midwest Fish and Wildlife Conference. 4 pp.

1960b A mutant pike, *Esox lucius*. Journal of the Fisheries Research Board of Canada 17:647–654.
       A striking variant of the pike, differing from the normal pike in colour and in some morphological measurements, comprised 0.2% of the pike population of Heming Lake, Manitoba.

1961a Heming Lake experiment. Fisheries Research Board of Canada, Progress Reports of the Biological Station and Technological Unit, 2:48–50.

1961b Silver pike: another fish to watch for. Fisheries Research Board of Canada, Fishing 2(3):8–10.
       Describes the appearance of the mutant pike and compares the relative abundance, anatomy, food, and hardiness with a common pike. Areas where silver pike are known to occur are listed. Silver pike have been hatchery reared in Manitoba.

1961c Silver pike: a fish to watch for—and to report. Wildlife Crusader 7(4):6.
       General information on the colour variant of the silver pike found in Heming Lake, Manitoba, in 1952. Notes on other accounts of this form.

1963   Using the trammel net in Canadian waters. Canadian Fisherman 50(8):4 pp.
       The trammel net could be useful in management studies of fish such as pike that inhabit shallow water because of its mobility and high yield per effort. It is not strictly a lethal gear so could be used to trap fish for removal to other areas or for tagging. It might be useful in commercial fisheries.

1964a Further evidence of hardiness of "silver" pike. Journal of the Fisheries Research Board of Canada 21:651–652.
       Describes the capture, handling, and surgery of a 38-cm silver pike. It survived with help for 30 days after many traumatic experiences under septic conditions, including the removal of the small intestine.

1964b A northern pike, *Esox lucius*, with an accessory fin. Journal of the Fisheries Research Board of Canada 21:1547.
       The pike was found in 1963 in Heming Lake, Manitoba, with the extra fin on the ventral surface of the head. The location, malformation of the branchiostegal rays, anatomy, and appearance of the fin are described. Two figures illustrate the text.

1965   The food of the pike *Esox lucius* in Heming Lake, Manitoba. Journal of the Fisheries Research Board of Canada 22:1357–1377.
       The stomach contents of 29,477 pike captured mainly in gill nets between

1950 and 1962 were examined. Food consisted mainly of fish and some invertebrates. Seasonal variation in food content and annual variation in the degree of feeding were studied. The possible effects of the pike on prey species are discussed.

1966a Pugheadedness in perch, *Perca flavescens*, and pike, *Esox lucius*, of Heming Lake, Manitoba. Journal of the Fisheries Research Board of Canada 23:1807–1808.

Description of this anomaly and a table listing the frequency of occurrence in 1964–65 are provided. Genetic and environmental factors are considered to be responsible for the upraising of the median portion of the cranium, resulting in pugheadedness.

1966b A second record of an accessory fin on *Esox lucius*. Journal of the Fisheries Research Board of Canada 23:1969.

An accessory fin was observed on a pike, on the ventral surface of the body between the pectoral and pelvic fins.

1969a Aspects of the biology of *Triaenophorus nodulosus* in yellow perch *Perca flavescens* in Heming Lake, Manitoba. Journal of the Fisheries Research Board of Canada 26:821–831.

The infection level in perch declined when average size of the pike was reduced through intensive fishing.

1969b Activity periods of some fishes in Heming Lake, Canada. Journal of the Fisheries Research Board of Canada 26:3266–3267.

The catch of pike in shallow water was highest during the hours of darkness. After sunrise catch per unit effort declined sharply and then slowly increased until a peak was reached soon after sunset. In deeper water the catch rose sharply just after sunrise, declined until late afternoon, and then increased slightly with approaching darkness.

1969c Occurrence of *Triaenophorus* spp. in Lake Malaren fishes. Report Institute Freshwater Research Drottningholm 49:120–128.

In pike, *Triaenophorus nodulosus* was more abundant than *T. crassus*.

1970 Parasites of coregonid fishes. *In* Lindsey, C. C. and C. S. Woods, eds., Biology of coregonid fishes. University of Manitoba Press, pp. 279–309.

1978 Review and a look ahead. American Fisheries Society Special Publication 11:436–437.

Summary speech of a symposium; mentions that pike is a commercially important species and that trophy-size pike are still to be found. For these reasons, the species needs effective management.

n.d. Dynamics of fish production in a small, heavily exploited lake. Fisheries Research Board of Canada, unpublished MS.

Results of preliminary analysis of data collected during a study of the exploitation of the fish population of a small lake.

LAWLER, G. H. and W. B. SCOTT
1954 Notes on geographical distribution and the hosts of the cestode genus *Triaenophorus* in North America. Journal of the Fisheries Research Board of Canada 11:884–893.

Describes the role of pike in the parasitic life cycle of *Triaenophorus* species.

LAWLER, G. H. and N. H. F. WATSON
1958 Limnological studies of Heming Lake, Manitoba, and two adjacent lakes. Journal of the Fisheries Research Board of Canada 15:203–218.

Pike were present in all three lakes, and dominant in Heming Lake.

LAYCOCK, G.

1966   New nurseries for pike. Field and Stream 70(11):10–12, 14, 16.
        Water level controls on once-drained marshes provide better than original
        spawning habitat. The marshes are stocked with breeder pike, two males and
        one female per acre.

LEACH, G. C.

1927   Artificial propagation of pike perch, yellow perch and pikes. U.S. Depart-
        ment of Commerce, Bureau of Fisheries Document 1018, Appendix 1, pp.
        1–27.
        Description of pike and information concerning distribution, weight, food,
        spawning habits, and growth rate.

LEALOS, J. M. and G. G. BEVER

1982   The Flambeau Flowage fishery. Wisconsin Department of Natural Resources,
        Fish Management Report 110:1–17.

LEBEDEV, V. D.

1960   Presnovodnaia chetvertichnaia ikhtiofauna Evropeiskoi chasti SSSR. [Quater-
        nary fresh-water fishes of the European part of the USSR.] Izd-vo Mosk.
        Univ. 401 pp.

1961   Effect of fisheries on the biological characteristics of fishes (based on
        archaeological data). Trudy Soveshchanii Ikhtiologicheskoi Komissii Aka-
        demii Nauk SSSR 13:173–179.
        Analysis of fish fossils from archaeological finds permitted a determination of
        the character of fish fauna before the effects of intensive commercial activity.
        Average size of pike was larger in the early settlements than it is at present.

LEBEDEVA, N. E. and Y. L. CHERNYAKOV

1978   The chemical signal of danger in the predator prey system among fishes.
        Zhurnal Evolyutsionnoi Biokhimii i Fiziologii 14:392–397.

LEBEDEVA, O. A. and M. M. MESHKOV

1968   Changes in the time of organ anlage and the duration of embryogensis in
        Osmerus eperlanus eperlanus m. spirinchus and Esox lucius under the effect
        of temperature changes. In Emelianov, S. V., ed., The tempo of individual
        development of animals and its changes during evolution. Moscow, Nauka.
        The embryological development of pike was studied at seven temperatures,
        ranging from 2 to 20 C.

LE CREN, E. D., T. B. BAGENAL and C. KIPLING

1975   Experiences with fish sampling methods in Windermere. European Inland
        Fisheries Advisory Committee Technical Paper 23(Suppl. 1):58–65.

LE CREN, E. D., C. KIPLING and J. C. MCCORMACK

1971   Changes in the fish populations in Windermere. Presented at Symposium on
        Salmonids and Coregonids in Oligotrophic Lakes.
        A successful net fishery for pike operated for several centuries until 1922.
        The Freshwater Biological Association has gill netted pike from 1944 to the
        present; large pike have been reduced but young pike are more numerous.

1972   Windermere: effects of exploitation and eutrophication on the salmonid com-
        munity. Journal of the Fisheries Research Board of Canada 29:819–832.

1977   A study of the numbers, biomass, and year class strengths of perch Perca
        fluviatilis in Windermere from 1941–1966. Journal of Animal Ecology
        46:281–307.

LECYK, M.

1965   Effect of temperature on the rate of embryonic development of *Esox lucius*.
        Zoologica Poloniae 15:101–110.
        Observations were carried out for 3 years proving that the longest period of
        embryonic development of pike coincides with a mean temperature of about 8
        C (optimal temperature). Above and below this, the number of day-degrees
        that elapse between fertilization and mass hatching decreases, being one-half
        lower at 18.5 C than at the optimal temperature. Action of an enzyme upon
        the egg membrane is suggested.

LEEUWEN, J. L. VAN and M. MULLER

1983   The recording and interpretation of pressures in prey-sucking fish. *In*
        Leeuwen, J. L. van, Optimum prey capture techniques in fish. The Nether-
        lands, L. H. Wageninger. pp. 111–162.

LEFEBRE, P.

1977   Les esocides rencontres dans le district des Trois-Rivieres. Ministere du
        Tourisme, de la Chasse et de la Peche, unpublished MS. 7 pp.

LEGENDRE, V.

1952   Les brochets du Quebec: les ogres de nos eaux. [The pike of Quebec: the
        ogres of our waters.] Quebec Department of Fish and Game, Office of Biol-
        ogy, unpublished MS. 42 pp.

1954   Les poissons d'eau douce. Tome 1. Clef des poissons de peche sportive et
        commerciale de la province de Quebec. [The freshwater fishes. Vol. 1. Key
        to game and commercial fishes of the province of Quebec.] Montreal, Societe
        Canadienne Ecologie. 180 pp.

LEHNHERR, H. R.

1981   Bericht ueber die Schweizerische Bodenseefischerei im Jahre 1980. Fanger-
        traege im Bodensee-Obersee. [Report on the Swiss Lake Constance fisheries
        in 1980. Yields in Bodensee-Obersee.] Fischwirt 31(5):33–34.

LEHTONEN, H.

1972   The results of fish-tagging in Helsinki sea area. Report Helsinki Water Con-
        servation Laboratory 4(9):1–111. [in Finnish, English summary]
        Pike have intermediate salinity requirements. Salinity is good at 3–10 m./l,
        medium at 2–3 ml/l, and poor at 1–2 ml/l.

1973   Migrations of the northern pike in our coastal waters. Suomen kalastuslehti
        80:101–105. [in Finnish]

1978   Fishing of freshwater fishes in Finnish Baltic Sea area in 1976. Suomen kala-
        talous 48:25–40. [in Finnish, English summary]

1979   Pike in coastal waters. Kalamies 6:1–4. [in Finnish]

1981   The profitability of northern pike stockings. Kalamies 4:1–3. [in Finnish]

LEHTONEN, H., P. BOHLING and M. HILDEN

1983   Fish resources in the northern part of the Archipelago Sea. Acta Zoologica
        30:1–131.

LEHTONEN, H. and M. HILDEN

1980   The influence of pollution on fisheries and fish stocks in the Finnish part of
        the Gulf of Finland. Finnish Marine Research 247:110–123.

LEHTONEN, H. and M. PETTERSSON

1973   Alustavia tuloksia jatkokasvatetuilla hauenpoikasilla suoritetuista istutuksista
        Helsingin merialueella. [Preliminary results on the profitability of stockings

carried out with pike fingerlings in the sea area off Helsinki.] Suomen Kalastuslehti 7:181–183.

LEHTONEN, H. and K. SALOJARVI
1981   Subsistence and recreational fisheries in Finland in 1978. Suomen Kalatalous 50:30–72. [in Finnish, English summary]

LEINERTE, M. P., D. R. VADZIS, Z. K. KALNINYA and Y. Y. SLOKA
1974   Study of the strontium-90 isotope balance in a Latvian lake. Ekologiya 5(5):77–79.

LEKANDER, B.
1949   The sensory line system and the canal bones in the head of some Ostariophysi. Acta Zoologica 30:1–131.

LELEK, A.
1978   Die Fischbesiedelung des noerdlichen Oberrheins und des suedlichen Mittelrheins. [The colonization of the northern upper Rhine and the southern central Rhine.] Natur und Museum. Bericht der Senckenbergischen Naturforschenden Gesellschaft 108:1–9.

1980   Threatened freshwater fishes of Europe. European Committee for the Conservation of Nature and Natural Resources, Nature and Environment Series 18:1–269.
        General information on the distribution, ecology, and distinguishing characteristics of pike. Conservation measures to help prevent continued decline in European pike are listed. Includes a map showing worldwide distribution

LE LOUARN, H.
1983   Production de brochet. Amelioration de la production naturelle ou repeuplement. In Billard, R., ed., Le brochet gestion dans le milieu naturel et elevage. Paris, Institute National de la Recherche Agronomique, pp. 305–318.
        Discusses whether it is better to improve natural environments or to stock, and when.

LEMAIRE, O.
1974   Installation de vidange favorisant le recuperation des brochetons. Piscic. fr. 38:37–40.

LEMMETYINEN, R. and J. MANKKI
1975   The three-spined stickleback Gasterosteus aculeatus in the food chains of the northern Baltic. Merentutkimuslaitoksen Julkaisu Havsforskningsinstitutets Skrift 239:155–161.

LENKIEWICZ, D.
1939   Zmniejszyc produkcje szczupaka. [To decrease pike production.] Przeglad Rybacki 12(4):160–164.

LEONARD, N. A.
1952   The pike is no piker. Rod and Gun, August 1952, pp. 11–12, 42.
        Tells of angling techniques, method of cleaning and cooking.

LEONARD, V. J.
1963   An investigation into the feeding habits of the pike in Loch Kinellan. Report Rugby School Natural History Society 96:9–12.

LEONG, T. S. and J. C. HOLMES
1981   Communities of metazoan parasites in open water fishes of Cold Lake, Alberta. Journal of Fish Biology 18:693–714.
        Communities of metazoan parasites in ten species of fishes, including pike, from Cold Lake, Alberta, are described and compared. Relative abundances

in the overall community of parasites in the lake were estimated using data on abundance in each host species, plus estimates of the relative abundance of the host species.

LEOPOLD, M. and B. DABROWSKI

1975   General premises and selected elements of a method of estimating fish stocks and populations in Polish lakes. European Inland Fisheries Advisory Committee Technical Paper 23(Suppl 1):722–727.

LEOPOLD, M., T. KORULCZYK, W. NOWAK and L. SWIERZOWSKA

1975a   Effectiveness of gill net catches as a tool for the estimation of fish populations in Polish lakes. European Inland Fisheries Advisory Committee Technical Paper 23(Suppl. 1):90–95.

1975b   Effectiveness of catches from various types of trap net for the estimation of fish populations in Polish lakes. European Inland Fisheries Advisory Committee 23(Suppl. 1):519–529.

LEOPOLD, M., T. KORULCZYK, L. SWIERZOWSKA and W. NOWAK

1975a   Effectiveness of seine catches for the estimation of fish populations in Polish lakes. European Inland Fisheries Advisory Committee Technical Paper 23(Suppl. 1):49–57.

1975b   Effectiveness of trammel-net catches as a tool for the estimation of fish populations in Polish lakes. European Inland Fisheries Advisory Committee Technical Paper 23(Suppl. 1):117–121.

LEPAN, S. R.

1985   Spawning and early life history of muskellunge and northern pike in the St. Lawrence River. M.S. thesis, State University of New York. 84 pp.

LEREBOULLET, A.

1853   Recherches d'embryologie comparee sur le developpement du Brochet, de la Perche et de l'Ecrevisse. Paris. pp. 4–445.

1854   Embryogenies des vertebres et des animaux articules—Quelques propositions sur l'embryologie des poissons, particulierement du brochet et de la perche, et sur l'embryogenie de l'ecrevisse. Comptes Rendus de l'Academie de Science, Paris 38:970–980.

1861   Recherches sur les monstruosites du brochet observees dans l'oeuf et sur leur mode de production. Annales des Sciences Naturelles (Zoologie) 4(16):359–368.

LEREBOULLET, D. A.

1854   Resume d'un travail d'embryologie comparee sur le developpement du brochet, de la perche et de l'ecrevisse. Annales des Sciences Naturelles Zoologie 4(1):237–289.

1862a   Recherches d'embryologie comparee sur le developpement du brochet, de la perche et de l'ecrevisse. Memoires Savans Etrang., Paris 17:447–805.

1862b   Experiences relatives a la production artificielle des monstruosities dans l'oeuf du brochet. Comptes Rendus de l'Academie de Science, Paris 54:761–762.

LEROUX, D.

1984   An assessment of the fish stocks in Rocky Lake, 1981. Manitoba Department of Natural Resources, Manuscript Report 84–20:45 pp.
Pike have decreased in abundance and are demonstrating characteristic responses to exploitation.

LESLIE, J. K. and J. F. GORRIE
  1983   Early development and growth of the Ontario muskellunge, *Esox masquinongy*, of Stony Lake, Ontario. Unpublished manuscript. 36 pp.
  1985   Distinguishing features for separating protolarvae of three species of esocids. *In* Kendall, A. W., Jr., and J. B. Marliave, eds. Descriptions of early life history stages of selected fishes. Canadian Technical Report of Fisheries and Aquatic Sciences 1359, pp. 1–19.
          Provides developmental characteristics and illustrations to aid in the taxonomic separation of the protolarval phase of *Esox americanus vermiculatus, E. masquinongy*, and *E. lucius*.

LESUEUR, C. A.
  1818   Descriptions of several new species of North American fishes. Journal of the Academy of Natural Science, Philadelphia, 1:413–417.
  1821   Observations on several genera and species of fishes belonging to the natural family of Esoces. Journal of the Academy of Natural Science, Philadelphia, 2:124–138.

LETENDRE, G. C., C. P. SCHNEIDER and N. F. EHLINGER
  1972   Net damage and subsequent mortality from furunculosis in smallmouth bass. New York Fish and Game Journal 19(1):71–82.

LETICHEVSKY, M. A.
  1946   Fish fertility in the southern part of Aral Sea. Zoologicheskii Zhurnal 25:351–356.

LEVI, G.
  1939   Etudes sur le developpement des dents chez les Teleosteens. II. Developpement des dents pourvues de dentine, trabeculaire (*Esox, Sphyraena*). Archives d'Anatomie Microscopique 32:201–221.

LEVIN, A. A.
  1970   A comprehensive appraisal of the effects of cooling water discharge on aquatic ecosystems. Battelle Memorial Institute, Columbus.

LEVINE, J. S. and E. F. MACNICHOL
  1982   Color vision in fishes. Scientific American 246(2):140–149.

LEWINGTON, J.
  1973a   Not even a well-trained salmon. The Financial Post. August 25, 1973.
          Report of a study to determine swimming speed against currents, specifically through culverts necessitated by highway and pipeline construction. Pike rank about 27.3 inches per second, and will revive quickly after apparent exhaustion.
  1973b   Now they're quizzing the fish. The Financial Post, August 25, 1973.
          Environmental studies on proposed Mackenzie Valley gas pipeline.

LEWIS, S. A.
  1975   Great northern pike introductions. Oklahoma Department of Wildlife Conservation, Project F-22-R/Job 4:1–32.
          This study of pike in Oklahoma lakes was conducted from 1967 to 1973. Survival of introductions, age and growth, fecundity, sexual maturity, and reproduction observations.

LEYCK, M.
  1965   Effect of temperature on the rate of embryonic development of *Esox lucius*. Zoologica Poloniae 15:101–110.

LEYDIG
  1879   Ueber die Hautdecke und Hautsennesorgane der Fische. Halle.
LIEDER, U.
  1953   Chromosomenstudien an Knochenfischen. I. Die Chromosomen des Hechtes (*Esox lucius* L.) in den embryonalen Mitosen. Zeitschrift fuer Fischerei 2:417–419.
  1956   Ergebnisse und Probleme der Chromosomenforschung bei unseren Nutzfischen. Albrecht-Thaer-Archiv 1:274–297.
  1959   Die Chromosomenverhaltnisse von *Esox lucius* L., *Perca fluviatilis* L. und *Lucioperca lucioperca* L. Arkiv for Zoologie 12(9):123–126.
LIEPOLT, R. and E. PESCHECK
  1958   Oriented breeding studies with spawning stock of pike from Neusiedler Lake. Wass und Abwasser, Beitrage zur Gewasserforschung, pp. 298–301. [in German]
LILLELUND, K.
  1957   Versuche zur Bestimmung de Verdauungsgeschwindigkeit fur der Brut von Hecht (*Esox lucius* L.), kleiner Marane (*Coregonus albula* L.) and grosser Marane (*Coregonus holsatus* (Thienemann)). Kurze Mitteilungen aus dem Institut fuer Fischerei Biologie Hamburg 7:29–39.
  1958   Versuche zur Anfutterung von Hechtbrut in einer auf dem Landeingebauten Vorstreckanlage. [Studies on feeding pike fry at a "stretching" station in the country.] Fischwirt 8:281–284.
  1967   Versuche zur Erbrutung der Eier vom Hecht, *Esox lucius* L., in Abhangigkeit von Temperatur und Licht. [Experiments on the incubation of the eggs of the pike (*Esox lucius* L.) in relationship to temperature and light]. Archiv fur Fischereiwissenschaft 17:95–113. [in German, English summary]
         Eggs of pike collected from mature fish from several lakes were reared at constant temperatures ranging from 3.7 to 24 C. Duration of development was studied in relation to temperature. Number of day-degrees was examined. Hatching rate within the range of 9–15 was not influenced by temperature. Fluctuating temperature decreased the rate of hatch. The influence of light was also examined. Larvae from eggs exposed to temperatures above 18 C at a very early embryonic stage demonstrated a decrease in vitality.
LINCOLN, R. P.
  1953   The pike family. Harrisburg, Stackpole. 274 pp.
LIND, E. A.
  1960   Ascending and succeeding of pike in small ditches. Luonnon tutkija 64:155–156. [in Finnish]
  1974   Seasonal variation in weight and activity of the freshwater fishes *Perca fluviatilis* and *Esox lucius* L. Nordic Council Arct. Med. Res. Rep. 10:65–66.
LIND, E. A. and E. KAUKORANTA
  1975a   Oulujoen suiston hauki, *Esox lucius* L. I. Ekologia. Universitaet Oulu. 40 pp.
  1975b   The pike, *Esox lucius* L., in the estuary of the Oulujoki River. II. Population. Ichthyologica Fennici Borealis 1975(3–4):41–66.
         Information on population density, sex ratio, fish and gonad production, number of eggs spawned, survival rate for eggs and mature fish, exploitation and natural mortality rates, food consumption, and the annual catch from brackish and freshwater areas is presented.

LINDBERG, G. U.

1936   Materials for the fish fauna of the maritime province of the Soviet far-east. Scientific results of the far-eastern hydro-faunistic expedition in 1927. Trudiu, Academii Nauk 3:

1974   Fishes of the world. New York, John Wiley. 545 pp.

LINDEBORG, R. G.

1941   Records of fishes from the Quetico Provincial Park of Ontario, with comments on the growth of yellow pike-perch. Copeia 3:159–161.
        Pike are very common throughout the region, especially in the shallow, weedy bays.

LINDNER, A.

1976   Al Lindner's pike challenge. In'Fisherman, Segment 1, Study Report 4, Unit 1, pp. 1–3.
        Author was given a hypothetical angling situation and provided his analysis of how to locate best angling and his suggestions for bait to be used.

LINDNER, B.

1978   Top baits and lures for northerns. Fins and Feathers Fishing Annual, 1978, pp. 12–16, 18–19.

LINDNER, R. and J. ZERNOV

1975   Al Lindner's challenge. In'Fisherman, Segment 1, Study Report 3, Unit 3, pp. 20–21.

LINDROTH, A.

1942   Sauerstoffverbrauch der Fische. II. Verschiedene Entwicklungs-und Altersstadian vom Lachs und Hecht. Zeitschrift fur Vergleichende Physiologie 29:583–594.

1944   Gaddklackningsproblem. Svensk Fiskerei Tidskrift 53:181–184.

1946   Zur Biologie der Befruchtung und Entwicklung beim Hecht. Report Institute Freshwater Research Drottningholm 24:1–73.

1947   Time of activity of freshwater fish spermatozoa in relation to temperature. Zoologica Bidrag fran Uppsala 25:165–168.

LINDSEY, A. J.

1970   Goofy muskie and pike. Fur-Fish-Game, June 1970, pp. 24–26.

LINDSEY, C. C., K. PATALAS, R. A. BODALY and C. P. ARCHIBALD

1981   Glaciation and the physical, chemical and biological limnology of Yukon lakes. Canadian Technical Report Fisheries and Aquatic Science 966:1–37.

LINDSTEDT, P.

1914   Untersuchungen uber Respiration und Stoffwechsel von Kaltblutern. [Studies on the respiration and metabolism of cold-blooded animals.] Zeitschrift fuer Fischerei und deren Hilfswissenschaften 14:193–245.

LINHART, O.

1984a   Evaluation of pike and wels sperm. Buletin Vyzkumy Ustav Rybarsky a Hydrobiologicky Vodnany 20(2):22–33.
        The sperm of pike was milky in consistency and colour and its density was thin to very thin. The largest pike sperm volume of 0.53 ml per fish was obtained from lower-weight males (721 g). The time of stepwise mass movement was 28–33 s and the total sperm movement time was 66–80 s. The average sperm concentrations were higher in heavier individuals. The absolute number of spermatozoa per male was at its highest level in the lighter males; the same applies to the relative number.

1984b   Spermatocrit - method for timely determination of fish sperm concentration.
         Buletin Vyzkumy Ustav Rybarsky a Hydrobiologicky Vodnany 20(3):15–21.
         A direct linear dependence was recorded between the relative spermatocrit
         value and the number of spermatozoa in pike (r = 0.98). Depending on the
         length of time elapsing from sperm collection, there is a distortion of sperma-
         tocrit values; it is therefore recommended to determine spermatocrit values
         immediately at the site of sperm collection.

LINKO, R. R., J. KAITARANTA, P. RANTAMAKI and L. ERONEN
   1974   Occurrence of DDT and PCB compounds in Baltic herring and pike from the
           Turku Archipelago. Environmental Pollution 7:193–207.
           Pike muscle contained on average only 0.04 ppm DDT compounds and 0.05
           ppm PCBs on a fresh weight basis. Chlorinated hydrocarbons were found to
           accumulate in the liver and ovary of the pike and, to a lesser degree, in the
           testis and kidney.

LINKO, R. R. and K. TERHO
   1977   Occurrence of methyl mercury in pike and Baltic herring from the Turku
           Archipelago. Environmental Pollution 14:227–235.
           Methyl mercury was measured in pike from seven different areas in the Turku
           Archipelago. Although there was considerable variability, pike muscle con-
           tained an average of 0.25 mg/Hg/kg on a fresh tissue basis. In different tis-
           sues the level of methyl mercury decreased in the following order: muscle
           tissue greater than liver, liver greater than or equal to kidney, kidney much
           greater than gonads.

LINSS, W.
   1969a   Elektronenmikroskopische Untersuchungen am Oseophagus des Hechtes
           (*Esox lucius* L.). II. Die Feinstruktur der Becherzellen. Anatomischer
           Anzeiger 125:73–87.
   1969b   Licht- und elektronenmikroskopische Befunde an den Tubuli der Niere des
           Hechtes. Anatomischer Anzeiger 124:88–104.
   1969c   Elektronenmikroskopische Untersuchungen am Oesophagus des Hechtes
           (*Esox lucius* L.). III. Die Feinstruktur der indifferenten Zellen des Epithels.
           Anatomischer Anzeiger 125:113–127.
   1969d   Uber die Feinstruktur der Einkornezellen im Osophagusepithel von *Esox*
           lucius L. Anatomischer Anzeiger 125:537–540.

LINSS, W. and G. GEYER
   1968   Elektronenmikroskopische Untersuchungen am Oesophagus des Hechtes
           (*Esox lucius*). I. Die Feinstruktur der Einkonzellen. [Electron microscopic
           investigations of the esophagus of the pike *Esox lucius*. I. The ultrastructure
           of the single granular cell.] Anatomischer Anzeiger 123:423–438.

LINZEL, W., H. PFEIFFER and I. ZIPPEL
   1939   Investigation on trimethylamine. IV. Report on the occurrence of trimethy-
           lamine oxide in the muscle of freshwater fish. Biochemische Zeitschrift
           301:29–36.

LIPSIT, J. H.
   1976a   Diet of northern pike, *Esox lucius* L., in inner Long Point Bay. Research pro-
           posal. Ontario Ministry of Natural Resources, unpublished MS. 5 pp.
   1976b   The biology of the northern pike, *Esox lucius*, Linnaeus. A critical literature
           review. Ontario Ministry of Natural Resources, unpublished MS. 26 pp.
           A literature review and brief symopsis of the biology of pike.

1977   Diet, age and growth, and management of northern pike, *Esox lucius* L., in inner Long Point Bay, Lake Erie. University of Western Ontario, unpublished MS. 26 pp.

The stomach contents of 74 pre-spawning pike were examined and their diet analysed. Recommendations for an increase in the commercial harvest of pike and elimination of size restrictions were made.

LIVINGSTONE, D. A.

1951   The freshwater fishes of Nova Scotia. Proceedings of the Nova Scotia Institute of Science 23(1):1–90.

LJUNGBERG, O.

1963   Report of fish diseases and inspection of fish products in Sweden. Bulletin de l'Office International des Epizooties 59:111–120.

1976   Epizootiological and experimental studies of skin tumors in northern pike (*Esox lucius* L.) in the Baltic Sea. Progress in Experimental Tumor Research 20:156–165.

In certain coastal brackish waters of the Baltic Sea, there is a high frequency of skin tumours (sarcoma). The Baltic pike sarcoma did not occur before 1950. It is reported that some of these parts of the Baltic are heavily polluted. Transmission of the sarcoma to young pike was achieved by inoculation. The chromosomes of the tumour were studied.

1977   Tumorer hos gadda pa den svenska oslersjokusten. [Tumors in pike on the Swedish Baltic coast.] Scandanavian symposium on water pollution/fish diseases, Copenhagen, 1977. Nordisk Veterinaermedicin 29(12 Suppl. 1):15–16. [in Swedish]

LJUNGBERG, O. and J. LANGE

1968   Skin tumors of northern pike (*Esox lucius* L.). I. Sarcoma in a Baltic pike population. Bulletin de l'Office International des Epizooties 69:1007–1022.

LOCASCIO, N. J.

1969   A study of multiple molecular forms of enzymes in species of Salmonidae and Esocidae. Ph.D. thesis, Pennsylvania State University.

Zone electrophoresis and histochemical staining were used to study a variety of enzyme systems, including G-6-PD and 6-PGD, esterases, and achromatic oxidase in a variety of species, including pike. The genetic basis and molecular structure of the last three enzymes were deduced.

LOCASCIO, N. J. T. and J. E. WRIGHT, Jr.

1973   A study of achromatic regions in species of Salmonidae and Esocidae. Comparative Biochemistry and Physiology 45B(1):13–16.

LOCKHART, W. L., J. F. UTHE, A. R. KENNEY and P. M. MEHRLE

1972   Methylmercury in northern pike (*Esox lucius*): distribution, elimination, and some biochemical characteristics of contaminated fish. Journal of the Fisheries Research Board of Canada 29:1519–1523.

Contaminated pike were captured from Clay Lake, Ontario, and released in Heming Lake, Manitoba, an area relatively free of mercury. Distribution and concentration of mercury in various body tissues of recaptured fish were studied. Biochemical profiles of blood serum constituents of fish from each lake (including transplanted ones) were compared.

1973   Studies on methyl mercury in northern pike (*Esox lucius* L.). *In* Hemphill, D. D., ed. Trace substances in environmental health. A Symposium, University of Missouri, 1972, pp. 115–118.

194

In November 1970, pike heavily contaminated with methyl mercury were captured from Clay Lake, Ontario, and released in Heming Lake, Manitoba, a site relatively free of mercury. Muscle biopsy samples revealed that over 70% of the original mercury was still present in October 1971, although concentrations were reduced by weight gains. Distributions of total and methyl mercury among various body tissues were essentially unchanged. Blood sera differences were examined.

LOEFFLER, C. A.

1971   Water exchange in the pike egg. Journal of Experimental Biology 55:797–811.
        The amount and rate of exchangeable water was determined in all analogues and normally developing egg embryos. Essentially the entire water content of both was exchanged with an isotopic medium, but the pattern and rate of exchange differed between the two.

LOEFFLER, H.

1977   Biological evaluation of fishing data in the Grosse Lauter, a trout brook in the Swabian Alb, West Germany. Beitraege zur Naturkundlichen Forschung in Suedwestdeutschland 36:81–90.

LOFTS, B. and A. J. MARSHALL

1957   Cyclical changes in the distribution of the testis lipids of a teleost fish, *Esox lucius*. Quarterly Journal of Microscopical Science 98:79–88.
        Cyclic changes in the distribution of testis lipids were examined and found comparable with those occurring in birds. Cholesterol was examined in relation to spermatogenesis, and the development of "lobule boundary cells" was examined in relation to season and temperature. The only period of true inactivity is at the height of spermatogenesis during midwinter and early spring.

LOM, J.

1970   Some aspects of the host parasite relation in Myxosporidians of the genus *Henneguya*. Journal of Parasitology 56(Sec. II, Pt. 2):442.

1973   Experimental infections of freshwater fishes with blood flagellates. Journal of Protozoology 20:537.

LOPINOT, A.

        What fish is this? Illinois Department of Conservation, 24 pp.

1958   How fast do Illinois fish grow? Outdoors in Illinois 5(4):8–10.

LOPINOT, A. C.

n.d.   Illinois fish conservation teachers' manual. Illinois Division of Conservation Education. 69 pp.
        Explains that pike are distinguished from muskellunge by the scalation of the cheek.

LOW, A. P.

1895a   List of principal food fishes of the Labrador peninsula, with short notes on their distribution. Geological Survey of Canada, Annual Report, new ser., vol. 8, app. 3, pp. 5–31.

1895b   Report on explorations in the Labrador Peninsula along the East Main, Koksoak, Hamilton, Manicuagan, and portions of other rivers in 1892, 1893, 1894, and 1895. Geological Survey of Canada, Annual Report, new ser., vol. 8, app. 3, pp. 329–332.

LUBITSKAYA, A. I. and E. A. DOROFEEVA

1961   Vliyanie vidimogo svetaul-trafioletovykh luchei i temperatury na matameriu tela ryb. Soomshch 2. Vliyania ul'trafioletovykh luchei na vyzhivanie i metameriu tela *Esox lucius* L. i *Acerina cernua* L. [Effect of visible light, ultraviolet rays and temperatures of metamerism of fish bodies. Report 2. Effect of ultraviolet rays on survival and metamerism of the body in *Esox lucius* and *Acerina cernua* L.] Zoologicheskii Zhurnal 40:1046–1057.

LUCAS, J.

1953   Want a big pike or muskellunge? Sports Afield, November, pp. 86–89.

1960   Big pike and muskellunge. Sports Afield, November, pp. 104–106.

1963   Let's stop misnaming fish! Sports Afield, December, pp. 70–72.
        Discusses the various common names used for pike in different regions of North America.

LUCCHETTA, J. C.

1983   Utilisation de sites naturels pour le groississement d'alevins de brochet produits an ecloseries. [The use of natural sites for the growth of hatchery-produced pike fry.] *In* Billard, R., ed., Le brochet gestion dans le milieu naturel. Paris, Institute National de la Recherche Agronomique, pp. 199–208. Describes an experiment showing how natural sites such as inundated prairies, copse, and woods can be used for the economical production of pike fry.

LUCE, W. M.

1933   A survey of the fishery of the Kaskaskia River. Illinois Natural History Survey Bulletin, vol. 20, art. 2.

LUGOVAYA, T. V.

1967   Nutrition of pike in the Upper Dnepr. Rybnoe Khozyaistvo 3:84–93.

1971a   The ration of pike in the Kremenchug Reservoir. Hydrobiological Journal 7:112–115.

1971b   Feeding habits of pike in the Kremenchug Reservoir. Rybnoe Khozyaistvo 12:104–110.
        The annual ration of pike from this reservoir and food utilization coefficients for different life stages were studied and modelled.

1973   Fishery significance of the pike in the Kremenchug Reservoir. Rybnoe Khozyaistvo 16:77–80.

LUKOWICZ, M. VON

1972   Die Heranzucht von Hechtbesatzmaterial in Teichen. Allgemeine Fischerei-Zeitung 97:320–321.

1983   Production et elevage du brochet en Republique federale allemande. *In* Billard, R., ed., Le brochet gestion dans le milieu naturel et elevage. Paris, Institute National de la Recherche Agronomique, pp. 225–234.
        Pike are produced for restocking only at the swimming fry, 4–9 cm, and 20–30 cm stages. Older fish for angling are imported.

LUNDSTROM, D. L.

n.d.   The life history of the northern pike, *Esox lucius* (Linnaeus).
        Discussion of following topics: description, distribution, reproduction, habitat, food, habits, enemies, and relative importance.

LUPO DI PRISCO, C., G. MATERAZZI and G. CHIEFFI

1970   In vitro steroidogenesis in the testicular tissue of the fresh water teleost *Esox lucius*. General and Comparative Endocrinology 14:595–598.

LUQUET, P. and J. F. LUQUET

1983   Appreciation du niveau d'ingestion et de la vitesse du transit alimentaire chez l'alevin de brochet nourri avec un aliment compose. *In* Billard, R., ed., Le brochet gestion dans le milieu naturel et elevage. Paris, Institute National de la Recherche Agronomique, pp. 233–243.

Food intake and the rate of food transit were studied, based on the kinetics of the accumulation of an inert marker (chrome oxide) incorporated into the food at a rate of 1%.

LUSK, S.

1981   Development of the fish population in the Musov Reservoir in the first year after filling. Folia Zoologica 30:249–261.

After the first year of the reservoir's existence, pike was one of six important species produced.

LUSTIG, V. and J. A. KELLEN

1971   Species, organ and subcellular specificity of alkaline phosphatases as determined by amino acid inhibition studies. Comparative Biochemistry and Physiology 39B:305–310.

LUX, F. E.

1960   Notes on first-year growth of several species of Minnesota fish. Progressive Fish-Culturist 22:81–82.

Information about growth of pike seined on 15 dates during May to October, 1954.

LUX, F. E. and L. L. SMITH, Jr.

1960   Some factors influencing seasonal changes in angler catch in a Minnesota lake. Transactions of the American Fisheries Society 89:67–79.

Pike was one of the species used to determine the relationship between angler success and food availability and selectivity. Angling success was inversely related to food availability and food intake, but changes in physical and chemical factors did not appear to be related to rate of angler take.

LYAKHNOVICH, V. P., T. I. NEKHAYEVA and T. M. SHEVTSOVA

1973   Effectiveness of the utilization of food resources by food fish in bodies of water in the Belorussian forest region (Polesye). Journal of Ichthyology 13:112–120.

Food requirements were determined from the rate of weight increase, metabolic rate, and composition of the contents of fish intestines.

LYNCH, T. M.

1957   Northern pike (*Esox lucius*). Colorado Progress Report, Exotic Fish Study, Project 1A:1–8.

Briefly describes the introduction of pike into two Colorado reservoirs in 1956 for harvest by anglers. Bonny Reservoir was stocked with 52 adult fish and 700,000 fry. Fry reached an average size of 11.9 inches by fall, and stocked adults had reproduced in the next spring. Of 50,000 fry planted in North Sterling Reservoir, none were seen in 1957.

LYSLOVA, E. M., T. P. SEREBRENIKOVA and N. A. VERZHBINSKAYA

1975   Isozymes of aspartate amino transferase EC-2.6.1.1 and glycogen phosphorylase EC-2.4.1.1 in muscle of lower vertebrates. *In* Markert, C. L., ed., Isozymes. II. Physiological function. Third International Conference, New Haven, 1974, pp. 547–566.

LYUBITSKAYA, A. I.

1961   Effect of visible light, ultraviolet rays and temperature on body metamerism of fish. I. Effect of different parts of the visible spectrum, darkness and temperature on survival and body metamerism of fish. Zoologicheskii Zhurnal 40:397–407.

Visible light had an effect on the rate of growth in the fish and on the process of tissue differentiation. The absence of all visible and thermal parts of the spectrum caused an increase or decrease in the number of metameres or the formation of deformities. In pike, darkness suppressed the activity of the hatching gland.

MACAN, T. T.

Some observations on the growth of pike, *Esox lucius* in Windermere. International Association of Theoretical and Applied Limnology Proceedings 14.

1970   Biological studies of the English lakes. New York, American Elsevier. 260 pp.

MACDONALD, P. D. M. and PITCHER, T. J.

1979   Age groups from size frequency data; a versatile and efficient method of analyzing distribution mixtures. Journal of the Fisheries Research Board of Canada 36:987–1001.

Study involved interactive computer program and aging of subsample by biological methods. Showed that several published methods gave no better advantages.

MACFIE, J. A.

n.d.   The pike, citizen of the northern world. Ontario Department of Lands and Forests News Release 19(26):4–5.

General information for anglers on various aspects of the biology and distribution in Ontario.

MACHNIAK, K.

1975   The effects of hydroelectric development on the biology of northern fishes (reproduction and population dynamics). II. Northern pike *Esox lucius* (Linnaeus). A literature review and bibliography. Environment Canada, Fisheries and Marine Service Technical Report 528:1–82.

MACHO

1922   Von der Gefrashigkeit des Hechtes. Osterr. Fischerei-Zeitung

MACHON, A., M. J. NORTH, N. C. PRICE and D. E. WELLS

1984   Dietary accumulation of the mothproofing agent Evlan WA New and its tissue distribution in the northern pike *Esox lucius*. Environmental Pollution, Series A, Ecological and Biological 33:295.

MACINS, V.

1972   The fisheries of Lake of the Woods. Ontario Ministry of Natural Resources, 44 pp.

Brief information on harvest, reproduction, food, migration, growth, and habitat.

MACK, G. L., S. M. CORCORAN, S. D. GIBBS, W. H. GUTENMANN, J. A. RECKAHN and D. J. LISK

1964   The DDT content of some fishes and surface waters of New York State. New York Fish and Game Journal 11:148–153.

DDT content of pike captured November 1963 in edible flesh - 0.2 ppm, testes - 3.7 ppm. visceral fat - 4.2 ppm.

MACKAY, H. H.

1931   The maskinonge and its conservation. Ontario Department of Game and Fish, Fish Culture Bulletin 1:1–11.

Description, including a diagram, of how to distinguish between muskellunge and pike.

1959   Northern pike. Sylva 15(6):3–11.

1963   Fishes of Ontario. Toronto, Bryant Press. 300 pp.

MACKAY, W. C.

1967   Plasma glucose levels in the northern pike, *Esox lucius* and the white sucker,

199

Catostomus commersonii, and renal glucose reabsorption in the white sucker. M.S. thesis, University of Alberta. 70 pp.

MACKAY, W. C. and D. D. BEATTY

    1968   Plasma glucose levels of the white sucker *Catostomus commersonii* and the northern pike *Esox lucius*. Canadian Journal of Zoology 46:797–803.

            Plasma glucose of females was more variable than that of males sampled at the same time. At certain times of the year, males had a significantly lower concentration than females. Plasma glucose levels were higher and more variable in fish caught by gill net or held in the laboratory than those of fish sampled from trap nets.

MACKAY, W. C. and J. F. CRAIG

    1983   A comparison of four systems for studying the activity of pike, *Esox lucius* L. and perch, *Perca fluviatilis* L. and *P. flavescens* (Mitchill). *In* Pincock, D. G., ed., Proceedings 4th International Conference on Wildlife Biotelemetry, Halifax, 1983, pp. 22–30.

MACKENTHUN, K. M.

    1948   Age-length and length-weight relationship of southern area lake fishes. Wisconsin Conservation Department, Fishery Biology Investigational Report 586(rev.):1–7.

MACKENTHUN, K. M. and E. F. HERMAN

    1948   A heavy mortality of fishes resulting from the decomposition of algae in the Yahara River, Wisconsin. Transactions of the American Fisheries Society 75:175–180.

            Pike were observed among the many thousands of dead fish. Death was attributed primarily to the depletion of oxygen by the decomposing algal mass, and secondly to toxic substances liberated into the water.

MACKENZIE, R. A.

    1930   Observations on the movement of the pike (*Esox lucius*). Canadian Field-Naturalist 14(6):130–133.

MACKINTOSH, A.

    1806   The Driffield Angler. London, Gainsborough.

MACLEAN, J. and J. J. MAGNUSON

    1977   Species interaction in percid communities. Journal of the Fisheries Research Board of Canada 34:1941–1951.

MACLEOD, R. D.

    1956   Key to the names of British fishes, mammals, amphibians and reptiles. London, Sir Isaac Pitman & Sons.

MACOUN, J.

    1888   List of fishes known to occur in the Mackenzie Basin, submitted by Prof. Macoun. Canada Parliament, Senate Select Committee, 1888:264–265.

MADIGAN, P.

    1978   The pugnacious northern pike. Angler and Hunter in Ontario 3(2):33–34.

            General fishing information on lure types, angling stretegy, habits, and habitats.

MAFTEI, D. V.

    1963   Contributions a l'etude des variations morphologiques et de la biologie de la croissance du brochet (*Esox lucius* L.) du Delta du Danube. Analele Universitatii Bucuresti Seria Stintele Naturii Biologie 38:139–154.

MAGNIN, E.

1964   Premier inventaire ichthyologique du Lac et de la Riviere Waswanipi. Naturaliste Canadien 91(11):273–308.

        Pike were present in this 1963 inventory.

MAGNIN, E., E. MURAWSKA and V. LEGENDRE

1973   Croissance de onze especes de poissons de la region de Waswanipi (centre-ouest du Quebec). Quebec Ministere du Tourisme, de la Chasse et de la Peche, Service de la Faune du Quebec Travaux en Cours, Rapport 8:13–42.

MAGNUSON, J. J. and D. J. KARLEN

1970   Visual observation of fish beneath the ice in a winterkill lake. Journal of the Fisheries Research Board of Canada 27:1059–1068.

        Vertical distribution and behaviour of five adult pike were compared with the levels of dissolved oxygen, free carbon dioxide, hydrogen sulfide, and water temperature. A combination of little locomotory activity and a position immediately beneath the ice apparently favoured the survival of pike.

MAGNUSON, J. J. and B. PETROSKY

1973   Behavioral responses of northern pike, yellow perch, and bluegill to oxygen concentrations under simulated winterkill conditions. Copeia 1973: 124–133. Critically low winter oxygens and natural conditions were simulated in the laboratory. The behaviour of pike, perch, and bluegill was examined. For pike maximum ventilation rates occurred at 0.5 mg/l dissolved oxygen. Locomotor activity was greatest at 0.25 mg/l. Pike moved to the bottom of the ice sheet at 0.5 mg/l. Of the species studied, pike were the best adapted for survival in winterkill lakes.

MAIER, H. N.

1914   Der Hecht,seine wirtschaftliche Bedeutung und Zucht. Blattchen Aquarien und Terrarien Kunde.

MAITLAND, P. S.

1969   The reproduction and fecundity of the powan, *Coregonus clupeoides* Lacepede, in Loch Lomond, Scotland. Proceedings of the Royal Society of Edinburgh 70:233–264.

        Pike prey extensively upon adult powan in certain parts of Loch Lomond.

MAKHOTIN, Y. M.

1977   The spawning efficiency of fishes in Kuybyshev Reservoir and factors determining it. Journal of Ichthyology 17:24–35.

        The pike spawns only in shallow areas. Consequently, even with a very slight reduction in water level, their eggs dry up almost completely. Abundant year-classes are very rare and the numbers of this species have been strongly reduced. Spawning begins at a temperature of 4 C.

MAKKOVJEVA, I. I.

1957   Pitanije molodi scuki Rybinskogo vodochranilisca. Voprosy Ichthyologii 7

MAKOWECKI, R.

1973a   The trophy pike, *Esox lucius* of Seibert Lake. M.S. thesis, University of Alberta. 239 pp.

        The pike population was small and average size of individuals large. Factors most responsible for pike growth were low pike production, type and associations of vegetation, and an abundant whitefish *Coregonus clupeaformis* forage base. The management of a trophy pike fishery is discussed.

1973b   The trophy pike of Seibert Lake (condensed version). Alberta Lands and
        Forests Fisheries Research Report 10:1–46.

        The purpose of the study was to determine the various factors (including the
        human factor) that affect the trophy fishery resource and to suggest manage-
        ment practices that will best maintain or enhance this resource.

MAKOWSKI, M. L.

1966   Jesienne szczupaki wod biezacych. [Autumn pike in flowing waters.] Wia-
        domosci Wedkarskie 10:13.

        Angling catches of pike in rivers.

MAKSIMOVA, E. M.

1969   Effect of intracellular polarization of horizontal cells on ganglion cell activity
        in the fish retina. Neuroscience Translations 11:114–120.

MAKSIMOVA, E. M. and V. V. MAKSIMOV

1972   Changes in direct current input resistance in horizontal cells of fish retina dur-
        ing excitation. Neurophysiology 3:160–165.

MAKSUNOV, V. A.

1956   The morphology and biology of the pike in the Farkhadsk Reservoir. Izv. old
        est. Nauk A. N. Tadzhukislon SSSR, no 15.

1972   Age composition and growth of reservoir fish in Northern Tadzhikistan.
        Journal of Ichthyology 12:652–666.

        The introduction of Mysidae into these reservoirs in 1963–1965 led to an
        increase in the productivity of the benthos and to marked improvement in the
        nutrition of the fish. Pike of younger age groups predominate in catches.
        None of the pike investigated were more than 6+ years old.

MALCOLM, J.

1975   Development of the head skeleton and pectoral girdle in *Esox*. Journal of
        Morphology 147:61–88.

MALININ, L. K.

1969   Uchastki obitaniya i instinkt vozvroskcheniya ryb. [Home range and homing
        instinct of fish.] Zoologicheskii Zhurnal 48:381–391. (Fisheries Research
        Board of Canada Translation Series 2050).

        Place and site of the home range depend mainly on forage resources. Most
        fishes with restricted movements are characterized by the homing instinct
        during both reproductive and non-reproductive periods. A fish population
        consists of mobile and sedentary components; i.e., the territorial conservatism
        can be regarded as a relative phenomenon.

1970   Use of ultrasonic transmitters for tagging bream and pike. Report I. Reaction
        of fish to net webbing. Biologiya Vnutrennykh vod Informatsionii Byulleten
        7:64–69. (Fisheries Research Board of Canada Translation 1818:1–8).

1971a   Application of the ultrasound transmitter for marking of *Abramis brama* and
        Esox lucius. II. Fish behaviour at the mouth of rivers. Biologiya Vnutren-
        nykh vod Informatsionii Byulleten 8:75–78.

        Pike movement (displacement) was limited. The maximum activity was
        recorded in the morning from 6 to 8 a.m. and in the evening from 5 to 7 p.m.
        During the remainder of the day and night the fish were relatively inactive.
        Under natural conditions, maximum mobility occurred over a light range of
        100–0.01 lux. At the time of the decrease in activity after the evening max-
        imum and in the period of the morning increase, the illumination at a depth of
        0.5 m was approximately 0.01 lux.

202

1971b   Home range and actual paths of fish in the river pool of the Rybinsk reservoir. Biologiya Vnutrennykh vod Informatsionii Byulleten 22:158–166. (Fisheries Research Board of Canada Translation Series 2282).

The movement of pike in relation to water depth and location is reported. Lengthy tracking showed that pike sense changes in wind direction. Their "hunting" area was no greater than 500 m in diameter. Pike had three maximums in motor activity: evening, daytime, and morning maximum. The daytime peak was considerably smaller than the morning and evening peaks, and occurred about midday. At night, the activity of pike was minimal, particularly during heavy cloudiness. On moonlight nights, a slight increase in activity was sometimes noted.

MALLEY, M. W. and S. M. BROWN

1983   Some factors influencing the number, size and distribution of pike in Lough Erne. Proceedings of the 3rd British Freshwater Fisheries Conference, pp. 126–137.

Compares the number of pike over 250 mm in commercially fished areas with those in non-commercial or sanctuary areas. Numbers and sizes of pike associated with different types of vegetation were also studied.

MALMBERG, G.

1970   *Gyrodactylus* species on Finnish, Norwegian, and Swedish edible fish. Nytt Magasin for Zoologi 18:102–103.

MALONEY, J. and D. SCHUPP

1977   Use of winter rescue northern pike in maintenance stocking. Minnesota Department of Natural Resources, Section of Fisheries Investigational Report 345:1–29.

The stocking of 0-age pike taken in winter rescue operations in central Minnesota resulted in high returns of stocked fish to anglers, but the relative contribution to the sport fishery was high only in Horse Shoe Lake where the abundance of resident pike was low. Guidelines for stocking winter rescue young-of-year and yearling pike are presented.

MALYUKINA, G. A., G. V. DEVITSYNA and E. A. MARUSOV

1974   Communication on the basis of chemoreception in fishes. Zhurnal Obshchei Biologii 35:70–79.

MALYUKINA, G. A., N. G. DMITRIEVA, E. A. MARUSOV and G. V. YURKEVICH

1977   Olfaction and its role in fish behaviour. *In* Poznanin, L. P., ed., Ichthyology. New York, Amerind, pp. 38–87.

MA MANZUDU, B.

1984   The food of the perch (*Perca fluviatilis* L.) and of the pike (*Esox lucius* L.) in the Ourthe Canal at Chanzhe-Poulseur (Belgium). Cahiers Ethol. Appl. 4:261–270.

A numerical method is applied to analyse the stomach contents of 23 pike. The pike is essentially piscivorous as soon as it reaches 15 cm long.

MANN, H.

1958   Fleckenseuche bei Hechten. Der Fischwirt 8.

MANN, K.

1982   Pike in a mixed fishery. Salmon and Trout Magazine 223:56–58.

MANN, R. H. K.

1971a   On the coarse fish of the Dorset Stour. Proceedings of the 5th British Coarse Fish Conference, Liverpool, 1971, pp. 129–134.

The maximum age and ultimate length were reported. Growth rate was similar to other British populations.

1971b   The populations, growth and production of fish in four small streams in southern England. Journal of Animal Ecology 40:155–190.

1975a   Production of pike in the River Frome, Dorest. *In* Proceedings of the 7th British Coarse Fish Conference, pp. 109–113.

1975b   Quantitative fish sampling in two hard water rivers in southern England. European Inland Fisheries Advisory Committee Technical Paper 23(suppl. 1, vol. 1):194–200.

1976   Observations on the age, growth, reproduction, and food of the pike *Esox lucius* (L.) in two rivers in southern England. Journal of Fish Biology 8:179–197.

Information on age and growth as determined from opercula, spawning, condition, age at maturity, and food.

1980   The numbers and production of pike (*Esox lucius*) in two Dorset rivers. Journal of Animal Ecology 49:899–915.

The following data were determined for River Frome and River Stour: numbers by mark-recapture methods, population densities, growth, and mean annual production. Discusses simulation studies on effects of various levels of fishing mortality.

1982   The annual food consumption and prey preferences of pike (*Esox lucius*) in the River Frome, Dorset. Journal of Animal Ecology 51:81–95.

The annual maintenance coefficient and efficiency of food utilization were estimated from feeding experiments in flowing water channels using four adults, size range 624–1010 g. Variations in diet are explained and possible diets for both young and larger pike listed. It is suggested that removal of large pike from game fisheries may not always result in increased numbers of salmonids.

1985   A pike management strategy for a trout fishery. Journal of Fish Biology 27(Suppl. A):227–234.

The efficiency of pike removal from a chalkstream trout fishery, by an angling society using electrofishing, was estimated over five successive autumns using mark-recapture methods.

MANN, R. H. K. and W. R. C. BEAUMONT

1980   The collection, identification, and reconstruction of lengths of fish prey from their remains in pike stomachs. Fisheries Management 11:169–172.

A simplified Seaburg sampler was used to obtain stomach contents from anaesthetized pike. Well-digested remains of fish prey were identified from pharyngeal bones or the skeletal structure of the caudal region. The original lengths of the prey were estimated from linear relationships between fish length and size of the caudal fin, or size of the pharyngeal bone.

MANN, R. H. K. and T. PENCZAK

1984   The efficiency of a new electrofishing technique in determining fish numbers in a large river in central Poland. Journal of Fish Biology 24:173–185.

MANOHAR, S. V.

1970   Postmortem glycolytic and other biochemical changes in white muscle of white sucker (*Catostomus catostomus*) and northern pike (*Esox lucius*) at 0 C. Journal of the Fisheries Research Board of Canada 27:1997–2002.

Higher glycogen content in the posterior portion of pike muscle as compared

204

with that in the anterior portion may partly explain the apparent high glycogen content in the muscle of this fish after several days of storage.

MANOHAR, S. V. and H. BOESE

1971   Postmortem changes in the glycogen phosphorylase activity of the muscle of white sucker (*Catostomus commersoni*) and northern pike (*Esox lucius*). Journal of the Fisheries Research Board of Canada 28:1325–1326.

Phosphorylase "a" activity decreased during 7 days storage at 0 C, while the total amount of phosphorylase "a" + phosphorylase "b" remained constant during the same period. The reduced "a" activity may explain slow degradation of glycogen during storage of pike.

MANSUETI, R.

1954   A partial bibliography of fish eggs, larvae and juveniles with particular reference to migratory and estuarine species of the Atlantic coast and supplemented by a check list and references to the early development of fish and fish-like chordates of Maryland waters. Maryland Department of Research Education, unpublished MS, 55 pp.

MANTEIFEL, B. P., I. I. GIRSA, T. S. LESHCHEVA and D. S. PAVLOV

1965   Sutochnye ritmy pitaniya i dvigatel'noi aktivnosti nekotorykh presnovodnykh kishchnykh ryb. [Diel rhythms of feeding and of the motor activity of freshwater predacious fishes.] *In* Pitanie khishchnykh ryb i ikh vzaimootnosheniya s kormovymi organizmami. [The feeding of predacious fishes and their relationships with food organisms.] Moscow, Nauka, pp. 3–81.

An examination of diel feeding rhythms of predacious fishes of Rybinsk Reservoir, including pike, as well as their food. Considers the influence of temperature and amount of food on the digestive rate, dynamics of underwater illumination over 24 hours and at various depths, feeding intensity, and behaviour of both predator and prey.

MANTEIFEL, B. P., ed.

1965   Pitanie khishchnykh ryb i ikh vzaimootnosheniya s kormovymi organizmami. [Feeding in predatory fishes and their relations to the food organisms.] Moscow, Nauka. 196 p.

MARCEL, J., G. DE MONTALEMBERT and R. BILLARD

1980   Influence de la temperature de stabulation appliquee apres traitement d'hypophysation' sur le rendement de l'ovulation et la fecondabilite des ovules chez le brochet (*Esox lucius*). [Influence of rearing temperature after "hypophysation" on ovulation performance and egg fertility in the pike (*Esox lucius*).] Revue Canadienne de Biologie 39:225–232.

At the 10 and 13 C temperature regimes, yield of ovulation and fertility were not affected. Yield was significantly decreased at 15 C and fertility was decreased in one experiment at 15 C but not in another. Thermal requirements during oocyte maturation and ovulation appear stricter than other periods of the sexual cycle.

1983   Donnees experimentales sur la gestion et l'insemination artificielle des gametes du brochet (*Esox lucius*). *In* Billard, R., ed., Le brochet gestion dans le milieu naturel et elevage. Paris, Institute National de la Recherche Agronomique, pp. 133–151.

Reports the development and use of an insemination diluent for pike, having a pH of 9 and an osmotic pressure of 250–300 mOsmol.

MAREAN, J. B.

1976   The influences of physical, chemical, and biological characteristics of wet-
        lands on their use by northern pike. M.S. thesis, State University of New
        York. 174 pp.
        Evaluates and compares importance as spawning areas several marshes in
        Jefferson County, New York. Measures environmental variables likely to
        affect this use and correlates these data with spawning data.

MARGOLIS, L.

1951   "Red sore" disease of pike in Mont Tremblant Park district. Canadian Fish
        Culturist 10:30–32.
        First record in Canada, outside Ontario, of this septacemic disease, caused by
        Pseudomonas hydrophila, with description, location on fishes, and distribu-
        tion in Quebec.

1952   Aerobic bacteria in the intestines and slime of the pike (*Esox lucius*) in Lake
        Munroe, Quebec. Revue Canadienne de Biologie 11(1):20–48.

MARION, R.

1976   How to find lunker pike in big wilderness lakes. Fins and Feathers,
        November 1976.

MARITA, N. M.

1959   The distribution of *Diphyllobothrium* and *Opisthoreis* infections in Moldavian
        S.S.R. Meditsinskaya Parazitologiya 28:590–591.

MARKIEWICZ, F.

1960   Development of blood vessels in branchial arches of the pike (*Esox lucius* L.).
        Acta Biologica Cracoviensia, Series Zoologia, 3:163–172.

1967   Przypadek schorzenia pecherza plawnego u szczupaka. [A case of swim
        bladder disease in pike.] Gospodarka Rybna 18(5):9.
        A swim-bladder disease was noted in pike bred in carp ponds.

MARKING, L. L.

1967   Investigations in fish control. 12. Toxicity of MS-222 to selected fishes. U.S.
        Bureau of Sport Fisheries and Wildlife Resource Publication 18:1–10.

1969a   Toxicity of methylpentynol to selected fishes. U.S. Bureau of Sport Fisheries
        and Wildlife, Investigations in Fish Control 30:1–7.

1969b   Toxicity of quinaldine to selected fishes. U.S. Bureau of Sport Fisheries and
        Wildlife, Investigations in Fish Control 23:1–10.

1970   Juglone (5-hydroxy-1, 4-naphthoquinone) as a fish toxicant. Transactions of
        the American Fisheries Society 99:510–514.
        Gives the 96-hour LC50 values obtained from static bioassays at 12 C for
        several species, including pike.

MARKOV, V. I.

1962   O znachenii aktivnykh termal-nkh ploshchadok v zhizni pozvonochnykh (no
        primere Kamchatki). [The importance of thermally active areas in the life of
        vertebrates (based on Kamchatka).] Voprosy ekologii 6:97–98.

MARLBOROUGH, D.

1969   Further London fish records to 1968. London Nature 48:76–85.

MARSHALL, S.

1950   Wyprawa glowy szczupaka. [How to prepare pike head.] Wiadomosci Wed-
        karskie 8–9:13–15.
        How to prepare a pike head as an angling souvenir.

206

MARSHALL, T. L. and R. P. JOHNSON

1971   History and results of fish introductions in Saskatchewan 1900–1969.
        Saskatchewan Department of Natural Resources, Fisheries Report 8:1–32.
        Pike is one of the 30 species that has been introduced into fresh and saline
        waters since 1900. Stocking of eggs and sac fry has been minimally success-
        ful, fingerlings and adults more successful.

MARSHALL, W. S. and N. C. GILBERT

1905   Notes on the food and parasites of some freshwater fishes from the lakes at
        Madison, Wisconsin. U.S. Commission for Fish and Fisheries, Appendix to
        Report for 1904, pp. 513–522.

MARSTON, R. B.

1889   "Cross line" and "otter" fishing and monster pike in Ireland. American
        Angler 25(16):240.
        Letter discussing the problems of spearing fish, and the old legends of giant
        pike.

MARS-VALLETT, A. E.

1968   Le brochet. Betes et Nature 57:13–15.

MARTEM'YANOV, V. I. and R. A. ZAPRUDNOVA

1982   Dynamics of electrolyte concentration in the blood plasma, erythrocytes and
        muscular tissue of freshwater fish under stress. Biologicheskie Nauki
        10:44–49.
        Blood plasma, erythrocyte, and muscle Na, K, and Ca were examined in rela-
        tion to capture, transport, and maintenance conditions. Fluctuations in elec-
        trolytes were greatest shortly after capture.

MARTIN, N. V. and D. C. SCOTT

1959   Use of tricaine methanesulfonate (M.S. 222) in the transport of live fish. Pro-
        gressive Fish-Culturist 21:183–184.

MARTYNIAK, A., J. TERLECKI and J. A. SZCZERBOWSKI

1976   Odzywianie sie szczupaka, klenia i mietusa w rzekach zlewiska Lyny. [Food
        of pike, chub and burbot in the Lyna River system.] Roczniki Nauk Rol-
        niczych, Ser. H, 97(2):63–78.
        Assessment of food composition and pressure of the species under study upon
        the ichthyofauna.

MARTYSHEV, F. G.

1983   Pond fisheries. Rotterdam, A. A. Balkema.

MARX, M.

1978   Study on the zooplankton of Lake Marica. Travaux du Museum d'Histoire
        Naturelle 'Gregore Antipa' 19:169–170.

MARZAL, M.

1958   El lucio, incognita de la pesca. Caza y Pesca 18:231–233.
        This article is perhaps the first published in a sport magazine in Spain that
        describes in detail the general biology of pike.

1967   Algunos comentarios sobre el lucio y su Pesca. Caza y Pesca 299:873–881.
        Summarizes some aspects of pike biology and methods of angling; also
        describes its value as a game and food fish and future potential.

MASON, J. W. and G. D. WEGNER

1970   Wild river fish populations (Pine, Popple and Pike rivers). Wisconsin Depart-
        ment of Natural Resources Research Report 58

MASSARO, E. J. and C. L. MARKERT

1968   Isozyme patterns of salmonid fishes, evidence for multiple cistrons for lactate dehydrogenase polypeptides. Journal of Experimental Zoology 168:223–238.

MASSE, G.

1979   Identification des vrais et des faux annuli sur les ecailles du grand brochet, *Esox lucius* L., et sa croissance dans le fleuve Saint-Laurent, pres de Montreal, Quebec. M.S. thesis, University du Quebec a Montreal. Rapport Technique 06–32, 1–186.

MAST, H.

1919   Eizahlen bei Hecht, Barsch und Bachseibling. Allgemeine Fischerei Zeitung 44(20):194–195.

MATHER, F.

1881   Fishes which can live in both salt and fresh water. Transactions of the American Fish Culture Association, 10th Annual Meeting, pp. 65–75.
        Reports of pike being found in brackish and even salt waters of Maryland, and in the Caspian Sea.

1898   Fresh water angling—no. VI: pickerel, pike and mascalonge. Forest and Stream 50(21):410–412.

MATHERS, R. A. and P. H. JOHANSEN

1985   The effects of feeding ecology on mercury accumulation in walleye (*Stizostedion vitreum*) and pike (*Esox lucius*) in Lake Simcoe. Canadian Journal of Zoology 63:2006–2012.
        A study of the accumulation of mercury, as related to age of the pike, species composition of the prey consumed, size of the prey.

MATHERS, R. A. S.

1984   The effects of feeding ecology on mercury accumulation in walleye (*Stizostedion vitreum*) and pike (*Esox lucius*) in Lake Simcoe, Ontario. M.S. thesis, Queen's University.

MATSKASI, I.

1969   Helminthological investigations of fish in Lake Halaton. II. (Monogenoidea). Annales Instituti Biologici (Tihany) Hungaricae Academiae Scientiarum 35:135–139.

MATVEEVA, R. P.

1955   The nutrition of the young pike in the spawning cultivation establishment in 1953. Voprosy Iktiologii 5:61–70.
        Stomachs of young pike from a spawning-culture establishment in the Volga Delta were examined. Young pike go through four alimentary stages. Feeding progresses from copepods and Cladocera to assorted young fish, and is almost exclusively carnivorous at lengths >34 mm. Index of intestinal filling correlated with the dimensions of the pike and its prey and on daily variation in nutrition are also used. Young pike do not feed at night.

MATVEIEV, B.

1929   Die Entwicklung der vorderen Wirbel und des Weber'schen Apparates bei Cyprinidae. Zoologische Jahrbucher 51:463.

MAUCK, W. L.

1970   Vulnerability of various fishes to northern pike predation. M.A. thesis, University of Missouri. 186 pp.

MAUCK, W. L. and D. W. COBLE

1971   Vulnerability of some fishes to northern pike (*Esox lucius*) predation. Journal of the Fisheries Research Board of Canada 28:957–969.

Compares the vulnerability to predation of several species of fish. Variables included water turbidity and availability of cover.

MAVRINSKAYA, L. F.

1956   Motor nerve endings of the skeletal muscles of the lower vertebrates. Doklady Akademii Nauk SSSR 106:347–349.

MAWDESLEY-THOMAS, L. E. and J. S. LEAHY

1967   Organichlorine pesticide residues in pike. Progressive Fish-Culturist 29(1):64.

Used gas liquid chromatography to analyse organichlorine pesticide residues in muscle and fat of pike. Higher concentrations were invariably found in larger fish.

MAY, S. P.

1858   The handbook of Toronto, containing its climate, geology, natural history, educational institutions, courts of law, municipal arrangements, etc., etc. Toronto, Lovell and Gibson, pp. 62–63.

MAYERHOFER, F.

1909   Farbwechselversuche am Hechte (*Esox lucius* L.). Archiv fuer Entwicklungsmechanik der Organismen 28:546–560.

MCALLISTER, D. E.

1959   Fish remains from a 600-year-old St. Lawrence River Iroquois site. National Museum of Canada, Contributions to Zoology, Bulletin 172:33–38.

Various fish skull remains were determined to be a species of *Esox*, either *Esox masquinongy* or *Esox lucius*.

1962a   Fish remains from Ontario sites 700 to 2500 years old. National Museum of Canada, Natural History Paper 17:1–6.

A 56-mm maxillary found in the Goessens site belongs to either *Esox lucius* or *Esox masquinongy*.

1962b   Fishes of the 1960 "Salvelinus" program from western arctic Canada. National Museum of Canada, Bulletin 185:22–23.

1963   Fish remains from a 600-year-old Yukon archaeological site. Canadian Field-Naturalist 77:232.

An incomplete right dentary, 50 mm long, bearing one tooth is identifiable as pike.

1968   The evolution of branchiostegals and associated opercular, gular and hyoid bones and the classification of Teleostome fishes, living and fossil. National Museum of Canada, Bulletin 221:1–239.

1975   Fish collections from the Otish Mountain Region, central Quebec. Syllogeus 8:1–12.

MCALLISTER, D. E. and B. W. COAD

1974   Fishes of Canada's National Capital Region. Canada Department of the Environment, Fisheries and Marine Service Miscellaneous Special Publication 24:1–200.

MCALLISTER, D. E. and E. J. CROSSMAN

1973   A guide to the freshwater sport fishes of Canada. National Museums of Canada, National Museum of Natural Science, Natural History Series 1:1–89.

Information to help the angler identify fish. Figure and brief text describe habits, distribution, and maximum size.

MCALLISTER, D. E. and D. ST-ONGE

1981   Postglacial fossil fishes from Coppermine River, Northwest Territories. Canadian Field-Naturalist 95:203–205.

MCCABE, B. C.

1943   An analysis of the distribution of fishes in the streams of western Massachusetts. Copeia 1943:85–89.
        Pike have been introduced into one drainage system.

1958   *Esox niger* LeSueur; tabular treatment of the life history and ecology of the chain pickerel. Massachusetts, Springfield College, 45 pp.

MCCARRAHER, B.

1956   What about northern pike? Outdoor Nebraska, Spring 1956.

1958a   A hole in the ice. Outdoor Nebraska, February 7–8.

1958b   Operation northern pike. Outdoor Nebraska, April 18–19.
        Describes techniques used for stripping and incubating eggs, rearing and stocking the fry.

1960   Northern pike population studies. Nebraska Game, Forestation and Parks Commission, Dingell-Johnson Project F-4-R, Job 6:1–15.
        Study concentrated on 10 lakes and impoundments in the Sandhill region, with productive pike spawning and rearing areas. Comparative growth rates, age, angler harvest, sex ratio, and waterfowl predation are discussed. The presence of pike indicates that the species is adaptable to moderately euryhaline waters.

MCCARRAHER, D. B.

1955   The status and value of the northern pike (*Esox lucius*) in North America sport fishery. Presented at 17th Midwest Wildlife Conference, Purdue University, 1955. 5 pp.

1957a   The status of the northern pike in Nebraska's Sandhill Lake Region. Transactions 2nd Annual Conference, Central Mountain and Plains Section, Wildlife Society, 8 pp.
        Describes the Sandhill Lakes and gives physical, chemical, and biological characteristics of a pike lake. Life history, breeding habits, distribution, numbers, age, growth, management and harvest are discussed.

1957b   The fishery of an alkaline sandhill lake, Nebraska. Presented 19th Annual Midwest Wildlife Conference, Milwaukee, 1957. 6 pp.
        Describes the physical, chemical, and biological characteristics of the lake. Information on life history, behaviour, food, growth, and management of pike in the lake is given, and an estimation of the lake's standing crop is made.

1957c   The natural propagation of northern pike in small drainable ponds. Progressive Fish-Culturist 19:185–187.
        The use of ripe pike spawners in hatchery ponds, at a rate of five females per acre, shows promise as an economical and efficient method of production. Fry should be cropped when 2 inches in length.

1959a   Northern pike. Outdoor Nebraska, July 26–27.
        Describes unpredictable nature of artificial propagation and stocking, stressing that the production of a good population depends on favourable natural conditions. Creation of adjoining marsh areas on lakes lacking such spawning sites has often improved fishing and perhaps should supplement stocking.

1959b   The northern pike-bluegill combination in north-central Nebraska farm ponds. Progressive Fish-Culturist 21:188–189.

Two new farm ponds 5.5 and 7.1 surface acres stocked with pike fingerlings and adult bluegills at 5.1 and 36.1. Natural pike reproduction has occurred in both ponds. Bluegills are the predominant forage for all year classes of pike.

1959c   Phyllopod shrimp populations of the Big Alkali Lake drainage, Nebraska, and their relationship to young pike (*Esox lucius*). American Midland Naturalist 61:509–510.

Adult pike use the entire drainage basin for spawning, while shrimp populations occurred in 60% of the pools in the basin. Fingerlings fed on shrimp if available and had a greater average size than those in pools with no shrimp.

1960   Pike hybrids (*Esox lucius* x *E. vermiculatus*) in a sandhill lake, Nebraska. Transactions of the American Fisheries Society 89:82–83.

A description of four fish captured in 1958–59, believed to be the first recorded description of this cross.

1961a   Sandhill lakes survey. Nebraska Game, Forestation and Parks Commission, Job Completion Report F-4-R, 1954–61:1–83.

1961b   Extension of the range of northern pike, *Esox lucius*. Transactions of the American Fisheries Society 90:227–228.

In 1955, 26 states and provinces had resident pike populations. This paper documents extensions of the range during the following 5 years.

1962   Northern pike, *Esox lucius*, in alkaline lakes of Nebraska. Transactions of the American Fisheries Society 91:326–329.

Pike were introduced successfully where mean annual total alkalinity did not exceed 1,000 ppm. Information on dissolved oxygen content, growth rate variation, reproduction, and survival, spawning habitat, forage fish.

1963   Production of northern pike in natural rearing ponds in Nebraska. Progressive Fish-Culturist 25:165.

Brief discussion on harvest variability, rearing period, and economic feasibility. Ponds were considered to be an auxillary production tool, and a summary of pond production between 1955–62 for the Valentine Hatchery is included.

1971   Survival of some freshwater fishes in the alkaline eutrophic waters of Nebraska. Journal of the Fisheries Research Board of Canada 28:1811–1814.

Fourteen species of freshwater fish were held in cages in 13 lakes and ponds where carbonate alkalinity ranged from slightly alkaline to strongly alkaline. Pike was among the most tolerant species.

1977   Nebraska's sandhills lakes. Nebraska Game and Parks Commission, Project F-54-R:1–67.

MCCARRAHER, D. B. and R. E. THOMAS

1972   Ecological significance of vegetation to northern pike, *Esox lucius*, spawning. Transactions of the American Fisheries Society 101:560–563.

An evaluation of pike spawning success in six Nebraska sandhill lakes in relation to preferred type of aquatic vegetation. Water quality, spring water levels and temperature, and the species of submergent aquatic vegetation present within individual lakes all influence pike spawning success in the sandhill region.

MCCAULEY, R. W. and J. M. CASSELMAN

1981   The final preferendum as an index of the temperature for optimum growth in fish. *In* Tiews, K., ed., Proceedings of the world symposium on aquaculture

211

in heated effluents and recirculation systems, Stavenger, 1980. Berlin, Heenemann Verlagsgesellschaft, vol. 2, pp. 81–93.

An extensive literature review indicating that the final preferendum is usually several degrees above the optimum temperature for growth. The final preferendum for sub-adult pike is 23–24 C, while the optimum temperature for growth is 20 C.

MCCAY, C. M.

1931   Phosphorus distribution, sugar, and haemoglobin in the blood of fish, eels, and turtles. Journal of Biological Chemistry 90:497–505.

MCCLANE, A. J.

1954   The American angler. Field and Stream Outdoor Series. New York, Henry Holt, 207 pp.

1961   The pike family. Field and Stream, June 1961, pp. 40–43, 47, 89–92.

1976   Pike on the fly. Field and Stream 81(1):180–182, 184, 186.

MCCLENDON, E. W.

1976   Conflicts and compatibilities associated with regulating the Missouri River main stem reservoir system to enhance the fishery resource. In Orsborn, J. F., and C. H. Allman, eds., Instream flow needs. American Fisheries Society, vol. 2, pp. 148–157.

During the past decade special operations were scheduled for one or more reservoirs each year to enhance spawning of fish species, including pike.

MCCORMACK, J.

1965   Populations of fish in the English lake district. International Association of Theoretical and Applied Limnology Proceedings 13:198

MCCORMACK, J. C.

1970   Observations on the food of perch *Perca fluviatilis* in Windermere. Journal of Animal Ecology 39:255–267.

Brief comment on the effect of intensive pike fishery on perch and char.

MCCORMICK, L. M.

1892   Descriptive list of the fishes of Lorain County, Ohio. Oberlin College, Laboratory Bulletin 2:1–33.

MCCRIMMON, H. R.

1956   Fishing in Lake Simcoe. Ontario Department of Lands and Forests, 137 pp.

MCCRIMMON, H. R. and E. SKOBE

1970   The fisheries of Lake Simcoe. Ontario Department of Lands and Forests, 140 pp.

MCDONALD, D. B.

1969   Post-tagging mortality of pike, perch, walleye and rainbow trout following dart tag application. Alberta Fish and Wildlife Division, Management Report 7:1–11.

MCFADDEN, J. T.

1964   Trout, walleye, musky and pike. Michigan Conservation Bulletin 33(3):14–16.

MCFARLANE, G. A. and W. G. FRANZIN

1980   An examination of Cd, Cu, and Hg concentrations in livers of northern pike, *Esox lucius*, and white sucker, *Catostomus commersoni*, from five lakes near a base metal smelter at Flin Flon, Manitoba. Canadian Journal of Fisheries and Aquatic Sciences 37:1573–1578.

Concentrations of cadmium, copper, and mercury increased with age in pike livers, but the relationships of metal concentration to fish age were not consistent with the degree of water contamination. Calcium concentration of lake waters appeared to affect liver metal concentrations.

MCGOVERN, S. P.

1983a Development of a fisheries management plan for Lac Seul, northwestern Ontario. M.S. thesis, University of Manitoba. 159 pp.

Among the suggestions are: reduce harvest limits on pike for non-resident anglers on Lac Seul only, divert non-resident pike angling to water bodies near Lac Seul capable of sustaining additional pressure.

1983b An annotated bibliography on: the effects of water level fluctuations on walleye, northern pike, and lake whitefish. University of Manitoba, Natural Resources Institute, unpublished MS, 22 pp.

MCKENZIE, R. A.

1930 Observations on the movements of the pike (*Esox lucius*). Canadian Field-Naturalist 44:130–133.

Tagging of 61 pike in Lake Nipigon during July and August of 1926 was considered successful in 88% of the fish. Of the recaptured fish, 80% were found near the original capture site so the fish appeared to have a particular retreat.

MCKIM, J. M., J. W. ARTHUR and T. W. THORSLUND

1975 Toxicity of a linear alkylate sulfonate detergent to larvae of four species of freshwater fish. Bulletin of Environmental Contamination and Toxicology 14:1–7.

A report of a study to determine the 96-hr LC50 for linear alkylate sulfonate on the 30-day standing crop of larvae of four species, including pike.

MCKIM, J. M., J. G. EATON and G. W. HOLCOMBE

1978 Metal toxicity to embryos and larvae of eight freshwater fishes. 2. Copper. Bulletin of Environmental Contamination and Toxicology 19:608.

Fish larvae and early juveniles were more sensitive to copper than were embryos. Embryo survival was affected only at the higher concentrations tested. Pike larvae seemed to be considerably more resistant than other species.

MCKNIGHT, T. C. and S. L. SERNS

1974 Food habits of coho salmon (*Oncorhynchus kisutch*) in an inland Wisconsin lake. Transactions of the American Fisheries Society 103:126–130.

MCLEOD, H.

1964 Lake St. Lawrence fish and wildlife report. April 1964. Ontario Department of Lands and Forests, unpublished MS. 56 pp.

MCNAMARA, F.

1937 Breeding and food habits of the pikes (*Esox lucius* and *Esox vermiculatus*). Transactions of the American Fisheries Society 66:372–373.

Breeding times, localities, and behaviour before and during spawning were observed in a marsh adjacent to Lake Chemung during April from 1933–36. Stomach contents were also examined.

MCPHAIL, J. D. and C. C. LINDSEY

1970 Freshwater fishes of northwestern Canada and Alaska. Fisheries Research Board of Canada Bulletin 173:1–381.

M'DONNELL, R.

1864 On the system of the "lateral line" in fishes. Transactions of the Royal Irish Academy 24:161.

Briefly discusses scale shape, nerve fibres in lateral line follicles, and the cephalic portion of the pike system.

MEAD, C. W.

1915   Pike-fishing incidents. Copeia 22:35–36.
        Stories of pike fishing in the Adirondack Mountains.

MEADE, J. and D. R. GRAFF

1978   Reviewing the esocid hybrids. American Fisheries Society Special Publication 11:210–216.
        Crosses of the larger pikes produced only one with fertile progeny, the Amur pike x pike. Crosses of pike with muskellunge and Amur pike produced hybrids that appear to have great potential as a sport fish—relatively easy to rear, use artificial foods, grow fast, prized by anglers.

MEADE, J. W., W. F. KRISE and T. ORT

1983   Effect of temperature on production of tiger muskellunge in intensive culture. Aquaculture 32:157–164.
        Juvenile hybrids were reared at constant temperatures in the range 14–28 C. Information is given on growth, production, and feed conversion efficiency.

MECKLENBURG, C. VON

1974   The development of saccus vasculosus in two teleosts. Acta Zoologica 55:137–148.
        Examines the development and differentiation of the ventro-caudal part of the diencephalon, the saccus infundbuli.

MEDFORD, B. A.

1976   Annual cycle in condition and nutrient composition of northern pike (*Esox lucius* L.). M.S. thesis, University of Alberta. 61 pp.
        Pike were sampled at regular intervals from Lac Ste. Anne, Alberta, between May 1973 and July 1974. Condition and protein and lipid content (on a percentage basis) of liver, gonad, and muscle were measured. Somatic body weight (condition) and total protein and total lipid content of liver and gonad were calculated for a pike 50 cm FL to elucidate seasonal changes in these parameters. Since the pike examined did not have any large fat storage depots, it appears that the changes in somatic body weight observed were due to the catabolism of whole muscle tissue.

MEDFORD, B. A. and W. C. MACKAY

1978   Protein and lipid content of gonads, liver and muscle of northern pike (*Esox lucius*) in relation to gonad growth. Journal of the Fisheries Research Board of Canada 35(2):213–219.
        Pike were sampled at regular intervals from Lac Ste. Anne, Alberta, between May 1973 and July 1974. The weight, protein, and lipid content of gonads, liver, and somatic tissue were determined. From changes seen throughout the year, the deposition of nutrients into gonads and the areas of possible nutrient storage were assessed.

MEDVEDKIN, V. N., Y. V. MITIN and E. A. PERMYAKOV

1984   Semisynthesis of pike parvalbumin. III. Fragment 74–108. *In* 16th Meeting of the Federation of European Biochemical Societies, Moscow, 1984. Abstracts published by Federation of European Biochemical Societies, Amsterdam. p. 328.
        Parvalbumins have an invariant pair of amino acid residues Arg and Glu between domains. They are localized inside the molecule and form an ion

214

bond. Isolation of the EF-domain by trypsinolysis disrupts this structure. A semisynthetic fragment 74-108 of pike parvalbumin III was prepared to clarify the role of the Arg residue in forming the secondary structure of the EF-domain. Native protein was modified with BOC-azide and cleaved with trypsin.

MEEK, A.
1916   The migrations of fish. London.

MEEK, S. E.
1899   Notes on a collection of fishes and amphibians from Muskoka and Gull lakes. Field Columbian Museum Publication 41, Zoology Series, 1(17):307–311.

MEEK, S. E. and H. W. CLARK
1902   Notes on a collection of cold-blooded vertebrates from Ontario. Field Columbian Museum Publication 67, Zoology Series 3(7):131–140.

MEEK, S. E. and R. G. NEWLAND
1886   A review of the species of the genus *Esox*. Proceedings of the Academy of Natural Science, Philadelphia, 3(1885):367–375.
        Key, synonymy, origin of each description, and notes on habitat for each species.

MEIEN, V. A.
1926   Growth of the pike, *Esox lucius* L. Revue Suisse de Zoologie 6(2):33–41.
        A synopsis of growth of pike in the USSR, both historic and current.

MEIER, W.
1981   Viral hemorrhagic septicemia in non-salmonid fishes. Bulletin of the European Association of Fish Pathologists 1:15–17.

MEIER, W. and P. E. V. JORGENSEN
1979a   Isolation of VHS virus from pike fry (*Esox lucius*) with hemorrhagic symptoms. *In* Fish diseases, 3rd Session on Cooperative Programme of Research on Aquaculture, Munich, 1979.
        Pike fry were infected with VHS virus. Infected pike suffered losses of close to 100%, while only 6% of the pike control group died. Virus was readily isolated from fish belonging to the artificially infected group, but not from non-infected controls. It was not known whether pike at later stages of development are susceptible to the disease, or if they become carriers of the virus.
1979b   Egtved virus: characteristics of a virus strain isolated from pike fry (*Esox lucius* L.) Nordisk Veterinaermedicin 31:484–485.
        A viral disease outbreak occurred in a hatchery in Hallwilersee, Switzerland. The symptoms are described. Viral pathogenieity is compared to that of a freshly isolated Egtved strain; both caused identical symptoms in pike fry, with losses close to 100%. Details of the serological differentiation between Egtved virus and rhabdovirus disease are given.

MELANCON, C.
1958   Les poissons de nos eaux, 3rd ed. Quebec Societe de Zoologie, 254 pp.

MELLEN, I.
1927   The natural and artificial foods of fishes. Transactions of the American Fisheries Society 57:120–137.

MELLORS, P. J. and R. W. OWEN
1980   Some observations on the biology of a gasterostome digenetic fluke *Rhipidocotyle campanula* of fish in the Riva-aire, Yorkshire. Parasitology 81(2).

MEL'NIKOV, V. N. and E. T. PREL
1981   Some peculiarities of the effect of an electric field on fish. Journal of Ichthyology 21:144–151.

MENDIS, A. S.
1956   A limnological comparison of four lakes in central Saskatchewan. Saskatchewan Department of Natural Resources, Fish report 2:1–23.
        Pike were collected in all four lakes. Gives information on catch per unit effort, abundance, and food.

MERRILEES, M. J.
1972   Relationship between the lateral line sensory system and the cardioid scale pits in the family Esocidae (Salmoniformes). Ph.D. thesis, University of Toronto. 195 pp.
        General study of the number and histological structure of pits in all esocid fishes, emphasizing the smaller species but including the situation in pike.

MERRILEES, M. J. and E. J. CROSSMAN
1973   Surface pits in the family Esocidae. I. Structure and types of surface pits. Journal of Morphology 141:307–320.
        Histology of lateral line pits and neural structures in smaller esocid species. The condition in pike is mentioned.
1974   Species and geographic variability of surface pits in the Esocidae. Copeia 1974:893–909.
        The lateral line system of the pike consists of shallow pits with neuromasts. Unlike smaller esocid species, there are no pits without sensory structures. Geographic variation in number of sensory pits in the pike is presented.

MESZAROS, F.
1969   Helminthological investigations of fish in Lake Balaton. II. Parasitic nematodes from fish in the lake. Annales Instituti Biologici (Tihany) Hungaricae Academiae Scientiarum 35:141–144.

MEYER, F. P. and J. A. ROBINSON
1973   Branchiomycosis: a new fungal disease of North American fishes. Progressive Fish-Culturist 35:74–77.

MEYER, M. C.
1954   The larger animal parasites of the freshwater fishes of Maine. Maine Department of Inland Fisheries, Bulletin of the Fisheries Research Division 1:1–92.

MEYER, P., ed.
1901   L'histoire de Guillaume Marechal. 3 vol. Paris.
        A pike was bestowed as a prize to a knight who had gained the admiration of all by his valour and skill in a tournament in the spring of 1177.

MEZHNIN, F. I.
1980   The evolution of the suprarenal body in the phylogeny of Cyclostomata and Pisces. Journal of Ichthyology 20(4):80–93.

MEZQUITA, J., R. BARTRONS, G. PONS and J. CARRERAS
1981   Phylogeny and ontogeny of the phosphoglycerate mutases. 2. Characterization of phosphoglycerate mutase isozymes from vertebrates by their thermal lability and sensitivity to the sulfhydryl group reagents. Comparative Biochemistry and Physiology 70:247–256.

MICHAELIS, A.
1911   The artificial culture and hatching of pike. Transactions of the American Fisheries Society 40:429–432.

MICHAJLOW, W.

1933   Les Stades larvaires de *Triaenophorus nodulosus* (Pallas). I. Le coracidium. Annales de Parasitologie Humaine et Comparee 11:339–358.

MICHAJLOW, W. and I. WITA

1976   Effect of VAPAM - a pesticide of the carbamate group - on *Ergasilus sieboldi* Nordmann (Copepoda) a parasite of the pike and on *Paradistigma triangulatum* Wita (Euglenoidina) a parasite of this copepod. Bulletin de l'Academie Polonaise des Sciences, Serie des Sciences Biologiques 24:113–116.

The reaction of the pike parasite *E. sieboldi*, and of its hyperparasite *P. triangulatum*, to the following VAPAM concentrations was tested: 1000, 100, 10, 1, 0.1, and 0.01 ppm. It was found that the hyperparasite population has less chance of survival than *E. siboldi*. It is, therefore, probable that low contamination of water with VAPAM may result in an enhanced ergasilosis as observed in many water bodies in Poland.

MIDTTUN. B.

1980   Ultrastructure of atrial and ventricular myocardium in the pike *Esox lucius* L. and mackerel *Scomber scomburus* L. (Pisces). Cell and Tissue Research 211:41–50.

The differences and similarities between the heart tissues of the two species are described considering the muscle cell description, sarcolemma, sarcomere, sarcoplasmic reticulum, sarcolemmal cisternae, intercalated discs, nexuses, heart granules, and junctional processes.

1981   Ultrastructure of atrial and ventricular endocardium and cardiac capillary endothelium of the pike. Tissue Cell 13:747–756.

The endocardium of the pike consists of an attenuated squamose endothelium, a sparse population of subendothelial cells, and varying amounts of collagen. Fibroblasts are not found in the endocardium, and the collagen is probably produced by the endothelium. Capillary and endocardial endothelium differ structurally in several aspects. The structure data thus indicate that capillary endothelia mainly have a transport function, while the endocardial endothelium is also largely concerned in protein synthesis.

1983   Ventricular myocardium of the pike *Esox lucius* L. (Teleostei) ultrastructure of the junctional region. Zoologischer Anzeiger 210(5/6):271–281.

MIETTINEN. V., E. BLANKENSTEIN, K. RISSANEN. M. TILLANDER and J. K. MIETTINEN

1970   Preliminary study on the distribution and effects of two chemical forms of methyl mercury in pike and rainbow trout. *In* FAO Technical Conference on Marine Pollution and its Effects on Living Resources and Fishing, Rome, 1970. 12 pp.

The highest mercury concentrations of all fish species are reported in pike. Experiments were conducted to determine whether methylmercury is more toxic in the free ionic form than when bound to SH-groups of protein, as it is in the food chain; to determine the approximate dose of methylmercury that is lethal to pike and to find the pathological changes and the gross distribution of labelled methylmercury in the fish. With fast dosing the LD50/30D value is approximately 50 mg Hg/kg. From what remained absorbed after the first day, an approximate biological half-life of 110 + or - 20 days was observed.

MIETTINEN, V., Y. OHMOMO, M. VALTONEN, E. BLANKENSTEIN, K. RISSANEN, M. TILLANDER and J. K. MIETTINEN
   1969   Preliminary notes on the distribution and effects of two chemical forms of methyl mercury on pike. *In* 5th Radioactivity in Scandinavia Symposium, University of Helsinki.

MIGDALSKI, E. C.
   1962   Angler's guide to the freshwater sport fishes of North America. New York, Ronald Press. 431 pp.

MILHALIK, J.
   1963   Novy zpusob odchov stiky v plevoucich kolebkach. Ceskoslovenska Rybarstvi 1:4–5.

MILLER, C. T., Z. ZAWIDZKA, E. NAGY and S. M. CHARBONNEAU
   1979   Indicators of genetic toxicity in leukocytes and granulocytic precursors after chronic methyl mercury ingestion by cats. Bulletin of Environmental Contamination and Toxicology 21:296–303.

MILLER, J. and K. BUSS
   1962   Distinguishing the pikes of Pennsylvania. Pennsylvania Angler May 1962, pp. 6–7.

   n.d.   The age and growth of northern pike in Pennsylvania. *In* Miller, J., and K. Buss, eds., The age and growth of the fishes in Pennsylvania. Pennsylvania Fish Commission, Conservation Education Division. 2 pp.
           Provides anglers with information on variability in growth rate and age in Pennsylvania populations. Gives figures for mean length x weight, age x length, and lists good fishing areas.

MILLER, J. G.
   1954   A survey of the sport fishing at the north end of Cayuga Lake. M.S. thesis, Cornell University.
           Pike in the north end appeared to be faster growing than those from other areas of the lake, probably because of more abundant food supply and a longer growing season, due to earlier warming of the shallow water.

MILLER, R. B.
   1943   Studies on cestodes of the genus *Triaenophorus* from fish of Lesser Slave Lake, Alberta. I. Introduction and the life of *Triaenophorus crassus* Forel and *T. nodulosus* Pallas in the definitive host *Esox lucius*. Canadian Journal of Research 21:160–170.
           Outlines the life cycle of each parasite and the role played by pike as the host. Information on attachment, reproduction, infection period, and host age specificity is given.

   1944   Suggestions for experiments in the control of the pike-whitefish tapeworm, *Triaenophorus crassus*. Alberta Department of Lands and Mines, Report of the Fisheries Branch.

   1946   Northwest fisheries survey. Chapter 4. Great Bear Lake. Fisheries Research Board of Canada Bulletin 72:31–44.

   1948   A note on the movement of the pike, *Esox lucius*. Copeia 1948:62.

   1949   Preliminary biological surveys of Alberta watersheds, 1947–1949. Alberta Department of Lands and Forests. 139 pp.

   1950a   The Square Lake experiment: an attempt to control *Triaenophorus crassus* by poisoning pike. Canadian Fish Culturist 7:3–18.
           Concludes that the use of rotenone is impracticable because of the cost, and

218

because pike will rapidly repopulate the depleted areas.

1950b   A critique of the need and use of poisons in fisheries research and management. Canadian Fish Culturist 8:30–33.
         Because of the high cost of repeated poisonings with rotenone, suggests setting nets along shore and using rotenone to drive fish into them.

1952   A review of the *Triaenophorus* problem in Canadian lakes. Fisheries Research Board of Canada Bulletin 95:1–42.

MILLER, R. B. and W. A. KENNEDY
1948   Pike (*Esox lucius*) from four northern Canadian lakes. Journal of the Fisheries Research Board of Canada 8:190–199.
         Scale samples and length and weight measurements were used to calculate rate of growth. Northern fish live 5 years longer but never attain as large a size. The relationship between length and weight is independent of rate of growth. Males and females grow at the same rate but females appear to live longer than males.

MILLER, R. B. and M. J. PAETZ
1959   The effects of power, irrigation, and stock water developments on the fisheries of the South Saskatchewan River. Canadian Fish Culturist 25:13–26.
         The large reservoirs have developed valuable commercial and sport fisheries for pike. The small reservoirs which acquired a coarse fish fauna at the time of their construction have provided good pike angling.

MILLER, R. B. and R. C. THOMAS
1956   Alberta's pothole trout fisheries. Transactions of the American Fisheries Society 86:261–268.
         Trout grow poorly in lakes with a small pike population, and do not survive at all where there is a well-established pike population.

MILLER, R. B. and H. B. WATKINS
1946   An experiment in the control of the cestode, *Triaenophorus crassus* Forel. Canadian Journal of Research D 24(6).
         Describes an unsuccessful attempt to kill the coracidia of this parasite of pike by increased pH.

MILLER, T. B.
1971   Rock Island County surface water resources. Illinois Department of Conservation, Division of Fisheries. 59 pp.

MILLS, D. H.
1964   The ecology of the young stages of the Atlantic salmon in the River Bran, Rosshire. Freshwater Salmon Fisheries Research, Scotland, 32:1–58.

MILNER, J. W.
1876   Nomenclature of the pike family. Forest and Stream 1876(7):163.

MINAKOWSKI, W.
1962   Aminokwasy podczas rozwoju ikry szczupaka (*Esox lucius*L.). [Amino-acids during the development of the pike (*Esox lucius* L.) eggs.] Zeszyty Naukowe Wyzszej Szkoly Rolniczej w Olsztynie 12(1):41–48.
         Studies on free amino acids with the use of ion-phorasis and chromatography.

MINAKOWSKI, W. and Z. NOWICKA
1962   Total content of L-ascorbic acid during the embryonal development of the common pike (*Esox lucius* L.) eggs. Zeszyty Naukowe Wyzsz, Szkoly Rolniczej Olsztyn 12:49–54.

MINOR, J. D.

1976   Analysis of meristic characters of northern pike, *Esox lucius* for longitudingal and latitudinal clines in Canada. University of Toronto, unpublished MS, n.p.

MISHRA, T. N. and J. C. CHUBB

1969   The parasite fauna of the fish of the Shropshire Union Canal, Cheshire. Journal of Zoology 157(part 2):213–224.

MISIK, V.

1964   Estimation of the quantitative occurrence and standing crop of mudminnow (*Umbra krameri*) and pike (*Esox lucius*) in the canals of the Zitny Ostrov in Slovakia. Vistnik Ceskoslovenske Spolecnosti Zoologicke 28:357–368.
Sections of the canals were blocked off and fish were caught by electrofishing. Pike reacted well to electric current, and their visibility once at the surface made them easy to collect. The numbers and weights of both species caught from each locality are listed.

MISRA, P. M.

1966   Some observations on the morphology and food habits of northern pike *Esox lucius*. Proceedings of the Indian Science Congress 53(4):35.

MISSISSIPPI RIVER WORK UNIT

1978   Pool 8 northern pike spawning study. Summary report. *In* Mississippi River Work Unit Annual Report 1977–1978, Wisconsin Department of Natural Resources, pp. 31–44.

MITCHILL, S. L.

1815   Fishes of New York described and arranged. Transactions of the Literary and Philosophy Society of New York 1:355–492.

MITENEV, V. K.

1975   Two new species of parasites from fishes *Myxobilatus schulmani* new species and *Apiosoma longiciliaris* new species of the Kola Peninsula water bodies, Russian-SFSR, USSR. Parazitologiya 9:459–461.

MITZNER, L.

1971   Sport fishery harvest at Red Haw Lake and Red Rock Reservoir, 1971. Iowa State Conservation Commission, Job Completion Report 5–71–3.

MOCZARSKI, K. M. and I. KOSCIUSZKI

1983   Properties of pike *Esox lucius* L. milt and its cryopreservation. Polskie Archiwum Hydrobiologii 30:69–78.
Non-injected males as compared with those injected with a carp pituitary homogenate, yielded more milt of heavier consistency. The greatest milt volume obtained per ejaculation was 4.0 cm. The percentage of spawn fertilization with thawed milt was 79.94%, similar to that obtained from fresh non-frozen milt, 78.41%.

MOEN, T. and D. HENEGAR

1971   Movement and recovery of tagged northern pike in Lake Oahe, South and North Dakota, 1964–68. American Fisheries Special Publication 8:85–93.
During 1964–68, recovery of 2,019 out of 6,958 tagged pike provided information on angler harvest, angling mortality, and fish movement. Direction and distance of movement varied with season, sex, and tagging location.

MOEN, T. and M. LINDQUIST

1954   The northern pike hatch at the Clear Lake (Iowa) hatchery. Progressive Fish-Culturist 16:89–90.
An account of methods used, and results of, the first year's hatch of pike.

220

MOEN, T. E.

1953   Summary of hatchery studies at Spirit and Clear Lake hatcheries, spring of 1953. Iowa State Conservation Commission Quarterly Biology Report 5(2):70–76.

1955   Summary of hatchery studies, spring, 1955. Iowa State Conservation Commission Quarterly Biology Report 6(4):15–17.

MOHL-HANSEN, U.

1954   Marrow-split bones in interglacial deposits in Jutland. Saertryk af Aarboger for Nordisk Oldkyndighed og Historie, pp. 101–126.

MOILANEN, R., H. PYYSALO, K. WICKSTROM and R. LINKO

1982   Time trends of chlordane, DDT, and PCB concentrations in pike (*Esox lucius*) and Baltic herring (*Clupea harengus*), in the Turku Archipelago, Northern Baltic Sea for the period 1971–1982. Bulletin of Environmental Contamination and Toxicology 29:334–340.
        Data on time trends and concentrations in muscle and liver tissues.

MOLNAR, G. and E. TAMASSY

1970   Study of the haemoglobin content of a single erythrocyte (M index) in various cultured fish species. Journal of Fish Biology 2:167–171.
        Investigations of the erythrocyte count, haemoglobin content, and M index of seven fish species, including pike, were performed under equivalent environmental conditions in the same period of the year. It is concluded that M index values are useful as one parameter differentiating between fish with distinctly different food habits.

MOLNAR, G., E. TAMASSY and I. TOLG

1967   The gastric digestion of living, predatory fish. *In* Gerking, S. D., ed., The biological basis of freshwater fish production. IBP Symposium, Reading, 1966. pp. 135–149.

MOLNAR, G. and I. TOLG

1963   Versuche zum erkennen der mechanischen magentatigkeit einiger susswasserraubfische. Archiv fur Fischereiwissenschaft 14(1/2):33–39.
        Studies were conducted on the mechanical functioning of the stomach of several predatory fishes by taking X-ray photographs of artificially-stuffed stomachs every 5 to 6 hours.

MOLNAR, K.

1976   Data on the developmental cycle of *Philometra obturans*, Nematode, Philometridae. Acta Veterinaria Academiae Scientianum Hungaricae 26:183–188.

1980   Recent observations on the developmental cycle of *Philometra obturans*, Nematoda, Philometridae. Parasitologia Hungarica 13:65–66.

MONGEAU, J., A. COURTEMANCHE, G. MASSE and B. VINCENT

1974   Cartes de repartition geographique des especes de poissons au sud du Quebec, d'apres les inventaires ichthyologiques effectues de 1963 a 1972. Faune du Quebec, Special Report 4, n.p.

MONGEAU, J.-R.

1954   Valeur alimentaire comparative des larves aquatiques d'insectes et des poissons pour la croissance du brochets (*Esox lucius* L.). Annales de l'Association Canadienne Francaise pour l'Avancement des Sciences 20:80–85.

1955a   Comportement alimentaire du brochet commun, *Esox lucius* L., dans deux lacs du Parc du Mont-Tremblant, province de Quebec. M.S. Thesis, University of Montreal. 137 pp.

        Tables of food organisms consumed are provided, indicating the type and numbers of food items eaten and size of pike feeding. Conditions affecting food consumption were studied. Alleged voracity of pike was studied experimentally in an aquarium; results indicated an exaggeration of this assumption.

1955b   Valeur alimentaire comparative des larves aquatiques d'insectes et des poissons pour le croissance du brochets (*Esox lucius* L.) de moins d'un an. Annales de l'Association Canadienne Francaise pour l'Avancement des Sciences 21:96–101.

1960   Croissance du brochet commun, *Esox lucius* L., dans deux lacs du Parc du Mont-Tremblant, province de Quebec. Ph.D. thesis, University of Montreal. 150 pp.

        Variations related to both physical and biological conditions are given. Effects of availability of food for the young and breeding ponds in nature are analysed. The principal factors influencing growth are discussed, as well as the way in which these factors act on the level of the individuals and the populations.

1976   La dynamique de la population de grands brochets *Esox lucius* L., du lac Imp, Parc du Mont-Tremblant. Quebec Ministere du Tourisme, de la Chasse et de la Peche, Service Amenagement Faune, Rapport Technique. 76 pp.

1979   Dossiers des poissons du Bassin Versant de la Baie Missisquoi et de la Riviere Richelieu. Quebec Ministere du Tourisme de la Chasse et de la Peche, Rapport Technique. 251 pp.

MONGEAU, J.-R., J. LECLERC and J. BRISEBOIS

1980   La repartition geographique des poissons, les ensemencements, la peche sportive et commerciale, les frayeres et la bathymetrie du Fleuve Saint-Laurent dans le Bassin de la Prairie et les Rapides de Lachine. Quebec Ministere du Tourisme de la Chasse et de la Peche, Rapport Technique 06–29:1–145.

MONOD, T.

1968   Le complexe urophore des poissons Teleosteens. Memoires de l'Institut Fond Afrique Noire 81:1–705.

MONTEN, E.

1948   Undersokningar ovar gaddynglets biologi soch nagra darmed sammanhangande problem. Sodra Sveriges Fiskeriforening 1:1–38.

1949   Research on the northern spawning grounds in northern Straken in 1948 and 1949 on fry production and the hazards to the fry. Sodra Sveriges Fiskeriforening 2:20–101.

MONTPETIT, A. N.

1897   Les poissons de'eau douce du Canada. Montreal, C. O. Beauchemin, 552 pp.

MOODY, R. C., J. M. HELLAND and R. A. STEIN

1983   Escape tactics used by bluegills and fathead minnows to avoid predation by tiger muskellunge. Environmental Biology of Fishes 8:61–65.

        Quantified behavioural interaction between pike x muskellunge hybrids and fathead minnows *Pimephales promelas* and bluegills *Lepomis macrochirus* to explain why esocids prefer cylindrical,soft-rayed prey over compressed, spiny-rayed prey.

MOORE, J. W. and D. J. SUTHERLAND
    1980   Mercury concentrations in fish inhabiting two polluted lakes in northern Canada. Water Research 14:903–908.

MOORE, W. G.
    1942a   Limnological conditions in ice-covered lakes, especially as related to winter-kill of fish. Ecological Monographs 15:342–392.
    1942b   Field studies on the oxygen requirements of certain fresh-water fishes. Ecology 23:319–329.
            Describes field studies on the delimitation of summer and winter oxygen thresholds and approximate lethal oxygen concentrations.

MORALES, A.
    1980   Los peces fosiles del Yacimiento Achelense de Aridos 1 (Arganda, Madrid). Ocupaciones Achelenses en al Valle del Jarama, Diputacion Prov. de Madrid, pp. 93–104.
            Remains of seven species of fish from the Asheulian deposit of Aridos near Madrid are described and illustrated. The discovery of one pike vertebra, a species supposedly forming the Spanish ichthyofauna and the chronology of its extinction are discussed.

MORAVEC, F.
    1977   A new nematode parasite *Esocinema bohemicum*, new genus, new species Skrjabillanidae, of the European pike. Folia Parasitologica 24:86–90.
    1978a   Redescription of the nematode *Philometra obturans* with a key to the philometrid nematodes parasitic in European freshwater fishes. Folia Parasitologica 25:115–124.
            A redescription of *P. obturans*, based on specimens from pike from the Elbe basin in Czechoslovakia. Gravid, subgravid and mature females from the blood system, as well as males and mature females found for the first time in the host's eye, are described.
    1978b   The development of the nematode *Philometra obturans* in the intermediate host. Folia Parasitologica 25:303–315.
    1979   Occurrence of the endoparasitic helminths in pike (*Esox lucius* L.) from the Macha Lake fish pond system. Vestnik Ceskoslovenske Spolecnosti Zoologicke 43:174–193.

MORAVEC, F. and I. DYKOVA
    1978   On the biology of the nematode *Philometra obturans* in the fish pond system of Macha Lake, Czechoslovakia. Folia Parasitologica 25:231–240.
            A description is given of the occurrence of the nematode *P. obturans* in pike from the Macha Lake fishpond system in Czechoslovakia. By contrast to other philometrid nematodes, this pathogenic, specific parasite of pike does not exhibit clear-cut seasonal changes in its maturation, and gravid females are recovered throughout the year. The natural reservoir hosts of the larvae are mainly perch *Perca fluviatilis*. Differences in an affinity of *P. obturans* for the various size groups of pike are influenced mainly by the growth changes in the composition of food of these hosts. The development and circulation of *P. obturans* in the environment, and the problem of reservoir hosts of this nematode are discussed.

MORAWSKA, B.
    1968   Ryby i rybactwo w Wisle pod Wloclawkiem. [Fishes and fisheries in the Vistula River near Wloclawek.] Zeszyty Naukowe Szkoly Glownej

Gospodarstwa Wiejskiego w Warszawie, Ser. Zootechnika, 7(3):23–56.
Biological and fishery studies undertaken as a result of constructing a small dam upon the Vistula River.

MOREAU, G. and L. LEGENDRE
1979   Relation between habitat and fish communities - experiment for definition of numerical method for northern rivers. Hydrobiologia 67:81–88.

MORGAN, N. C.
1972   Productivity studies at Loch Leven, a shallow nutrient-rich lowland lake. *In* Productivity problems of fresh waters. Proceedings of the International Biological Programme, Poland, 1970, pp. 183–205.

MORIN, R., J. DODSON and G. POWER
1980   Estuarine fish communities of the eastern James - Hudson Bay coast. Environmental Biology of Fishes 5:135–141.

MORRE, J. and J. BARRET
1963   Potassium content of various fisheries products with a view to measuring the radioactivity of food. Revue des Travaux de l'Institut des Peches Maritimes 27:235–240.

MORRIS, J., L. MORRIS and L. WITT
1972   The fishes of Nebraska Nebraska Game and Parks Commission, Dingell-Johnson Project F-4-R:1–98.

MORRIS, J. W.
1972   Fishery inventory and investigations. Monitor survival of northern pike produced in an experimental artificial spawning marsh. Nebraska Game and Parks Commission, Project F-4-R-17, Job 1:1–4.
        The artificial spawning marsh at Bluestem Lake was stocked with 47 adult pike, then was drained. Notes survival of the estimated 14,680 young pike that were released into the lake.
1973   Monitor survival of northern pike produced in an experimental artificial spawning marsh. Monitor survival of hatchery-reared northern pike stocked in three Salt Creek watershed reservoirs. Nebraska Game and Parks Commission, Dingell Johnson Project F-4-R-18, Job IX-b and IX-c:16–19.
        Report of a study of the success of two culture methods. All young were released in May, and summer surveys revealed that pike were present later in 3 of the 4 study lakes. Continuing evaluation of these management tools was recommended.
1974   Northern pike investigations in southeast Nebraska reservoirs. Nebraska Game and Parks Commission, Dingell-Johnson Project F-4-R-19, Job 9-b and 9-C:1–4.
        Evaluated the stocking of hatchery reared pike and pike reared in artificial spawning marshes as management tools for maintaining populations.

MORRIS, R. L. and L. G. JOHNSON
1971   Dieldrin levels in fish from Iowa streams. Pesticides Monitoring Journal 5:12–16.

MORRISON, B.
1976   The coarse fish of the lake of Menleith, recently developed as a trout fishery. Fisheries Management 7(4):89.

MORROW, J. E.
1964   Populations of pike, *Esox lucius*, in Alaska and north-eastern North America. Copeia 1964:235–236.

224

Meristic characters of 83 pike from the Tanana and Yukon rivers were compared in an attempt to establish whether Alaskan pike differed from those in northeastern North America. Statistically significant differences occurred between mean values of some counts, but the author suggested that these differences were no greater than what could be expected, since the two populations were so widely separated.

MORSTROM, R. J., A. E. MCKINNON, A. S. W. DE FREITAS and D. R. MILLER

1975   Pathway definition of pesticide and mercury uptake by fish. *In* Environmental quality and safety supplement, vol. 1, Pesticides. International Union of Pure and Applied Chemistry, Third International Congress, Helsinki, 1974, pp. 811–816.

MOSINDY, T.

1980   The ecology of northern pike, *Esox lucius* (Linnaeus), in Savanne Lake, Ontario. M.S. thesis, Lakehead University. 159 pp.

A study of important aspects of the life history and population dynamics of pike in Savanne Lake, Ontario, during 1977 and 1978. Feeding relationships involving pike and walleye *Stizostedion vitreum vitreum* and the initial impact of an open water sport fishery on these unexploited populations were also examined.

MOSKALENKO, B. K.

1956   Vliyanie mnogoletnikh kolebanii urovnya reko Obi na rost, plodovitost i razmnozhenie nekotorykh ryb. [The effect of perennial fluctuations in the level of the River Ob on the growth, fecundity and reproduction of some fish.] Zoologicheskii Zhurnal 35:746–752.

MOSSIER, J. N.

1971   The effect of salinity on the eggs and sac fry of the fathead minnow (*Pimephales promelas promelas*), northern pike (*Esox lucius*) and the walleye (*Stizostedion vitreum vitreum*). Ph.D. thesis, North Dakota State University.

MOULTON, J.

1975   Establish northern pike in Bantam Lake. Connecticut Research Project Performance Report F-39-R-1:1–13.

MOULTON, J. C.

1978   Establish northern pike in Bantam Lake. Evaluation of northern pike spawning areas/Population estimates/Preparation of final report. Connecticut Department of the Environment, Project F-36-D, F-39-R:1–36.

Data on the impact of the introduction of pike on the white perch population and the ability of pike to establish a self-sustaining population. Specific areas of the evaluation include: population estimates, calculation of age and growth parameters, operation of an experimental spawning marsh.

MOYLE, J. B.

1949a   Fish-population concepts and management of Minnesota lakes for sport fishing. Transactions of the North American Wildlife Conference 14:283–394.

1949b   Gill nets for sampling fish populations in Minnesota waters. Transactions of the American Fisheries Society 79:195–204.

Data from 31 series of gill net catches were used to assess the reliability of standard experimental gill nets for estimating comparative size of populations. A table showing error of means of series of net catches at the 80% probability level is included.

225

1955   Sport fishing trends in Minnesota. Progressive Fish-Culturist 17:136–137.
        In 1894–97, pike comprised 3.20% of the catch from seven Minnesota lakes, whereas in 1952, pike constituted 14.6% of the catch from six similar lakes.

MOYLE, J. B. and C. R. BURROWS
1954   Manual of instructions for lake survey. Minnesota Bureau of Fisheries, Fish Research Unit Special Publication 1:1–70.

MOYLE, J. B. and W. D. CLOTHIER
1959   Effects of management and winter oxygen levels on the fish population of a prairie lake. Transactions of the American Fisheries Society 88:178–185.
        Pike were tolerant of low oxygen and survived well when levels fell to nearly 1 ppm. Even with low winter oxygen levels, pike maintained themselves without stocking.

MOYLE, J. B. and D. R. FRANKLIN
1955   Quantitative creel census on 12 Minnesota lakes. Transactions of the American Fisheries Society 85:28–38.
        Pike comprised 6.9% of the total catch for a one-year period, 28.2% of the total weight, and an average of 10.2 pounds per acre from the four lakes from which the take was principally of large predaceous fishes.

MOYLE, J. B., J. H. KUEHN and C. R. BURROWS
1948   Fish population and catch data from Minnesota lakes. Transactions of the American Fisheries Society 78:163–175.
        Pike is the most widespread and, from the viewpoint of fishery management, the most valuable predatory fish in Minnesota. Pike are an effective check on populations of yellow perch *Perca flavescens*.

MOYLE, J. B. and R. LOUND
1960   Confidence limits associated with means and medians of series of net catches. Transactions of the American Fisheries Society 89:53–58.

MRAZ, D. F.
1961   Warm water fishery research. Delafield studies. Northern pike propagation studies. Stock ponds with northern pike and carp. Wisconsin Conservation Department, Dingell-Johnson Report F-61-R-1/Wk.Pl. 11/Job 1.
1962a   Warm water fishery research. Delafield studies. Northern pike propagation studies. Stock ponds with northern pike fry, adult carp and muskie fingerlings. Wisconsin Conservation Department, Dingell-Johnson Project F-61-R-2/Wk.Pl. 12/Job A:18–19
1962b   Warm water fishery research. Delafield studies. Northern pike exploitation studies. Tag northern pike. Wisconsin Conservation Department, Dingell-Johnson Report F-61-R-2/Wk.Pl. 13/Job A.
1963   Warm water fishery research. Delafield studies. Northern pike propagation studies. Stock ponds with northern pike and carp. Wisconsin Conservation Department, Dingell-Johnson Report F-61-R-1/Wk.Pl. 11/Job A.

MUENCH, B.
1963   Length-weight relationship of eighteen species of fish in northeastern Illinois. Illinois Department of Conservation, unpublished MS.
1964   The northern pike in Illinois. Illinois Department of Conservation, Fish Management Leaflet 29.

MUHLEN, M. VON ZUR
1903   Der Hecht, sein Nutzen Schaden. Grunes Korrespondenzbl.

MUIR, B. S.

1957   Bay of Quinte sport fishery survey. Ontario Department of Lands and Forests, Progress Report.

1961   Estimates of mortalities and population size for the Nogies Creek maskinonge (*Esox masquinongy* Mitchill). Ph.D. thesis, University of Toronto. 129 pp.

MULCAHY, M.

1970   Hemic neoplasms in cold blooded animals; lymphosarcoma in the pike *Esox lucius*. Comparative Leukemia Research 1969. Bibliotheca Haematologica 36:644–645.

        General information on pike lymphosarcoma.

MULCAHY, M. F.

1963   Lymphosarcoma in the pike, *Esox lucius* L. (Pisces; Esocidae) in Ireland. Proceedings of the Royal Irish Academy, vol. 63, section B(7):103–129.

        Description of location and macroscopic appearance of tumours on 13 pike. Examination of histological sections showed all tumours to be lymphosarcomas. One pike had lymphocytosis associated with the neoplastic condition. Attempts to isolate the virus from tumours of two pike failed.

1969   Serum protein changes in UDN-infected Atlantic salmon. A possible method of diagnosis. Journal of Fish Biology 1:333–338.

        Describes the range of variation of serum protein level and electrophoretic pattern in healthy and diseased fish. Comparing the blood from five healthy and cancerous pike, the mean serum protein level of healthy pike was 4.68g% and 3.24g% in pike with lymphosarcoma. The serum electrophoretic pattern varied only slightly between the two.

1970a   Blood values in the pike *Esox lucius* L. Journal of Fish Biology 2:203–209.

        The ranges and mean values of haematocrit, red cell, white cell and differential cell counts, red/white cell ratio, red cell fragilities, haemoglobin levels and serum protein concentrations of adult pike were measured, and the serum electrophoretic patterns on cellulose acetate and polyacrylamide gel are described and discussed.

1970b   The thymus glands and lymphosarcoma in the pike. *Esox lucius* (L.) in Ireland. Comparative Leukaemia Research. Bibliotheca Haematologica 36:600–609.

        Histology of the thymus gland was examined in healthy pike, in 11 pike with spontaneous lymphosarcoma, in 2 pike that were injected with ultrafiltered tumour homogenate, and in 5 controls. Discusses the role of thymus gland in lymphosarcoma development.

1975   Fish blood changes associated with disease; a hematological study of pike lymphoma and salmon ulcerative dermal necrosis. *In* Ribelin, W. E., and G. Migaki, eds., The pathology of fishes. Madison, University of Wisconsin Press, pp. 925–944.

1976   Epizootiological studies of lymphomas in northern pike in Ireland. Progress in Experimental Tumor Research 20:129–140.

        Discussion of incidence and distribution of lymphoma-bearing pike, age and sex ratio of neoplastic pike, and annual and seasonal incidence.

MULCAHY, M. F. and A. O'LEARY

1970   Cell-free transmission of lymphosarcoma in the northern pike *Esox lucius* L. (Pisces: Esocidae), summary trans. by R. B. Howland. Experientia 26:891.

In the pike, a lymphosarcoma could be transmitted using cell-free filtrate and therewith the virus etiology demonstrated.

MULCAHY, M. F. and F. J. O'ROURKE

1964a   Lymphosarcoma in the pike *Esox lucius* L. in Ireland. Life Sciences 3:719–721.

1964b   Cancerous pike in Ireland. Irish Naturalists' Journal 14:312–315.

MULCAHY, M. F., A. SAVAGE and N. CASEY

1983   The leucocytes of the pike *Esox lucius* L. Irish Fisheries Investigations, Ser. A, 23:81–86.

MULCAHY, M. F., G. WINQUIST and C. J. DAWE

1970   The neoplastic cell type in lymphoreticular neoplasms of the northern pike, *Esox lucius* L. Cancer Research 30:2712–2717.
        Morphological characteristics of lymphoreticular tumour cells are described. The study was based on light microscopy of sections and imprints subjected to selected staining and histochemical procedures and on electron microscopy of thin sections.

MULLAN, J.

1960   Walleyes, muskies and northerns. Massachusetts Wildlife 11(4):17–19.

MULLER, H.

1954   On pike breeding. Deutche Fischerei Zeitung 1:101–102.

1959   Hechtbesatz in Binnengewassern. [Pike stocking in inland waters.] Deutsche Fischerei Zeitung 6(3):69–73.

1966   A practical classification of the lakes of northern Germany and its limnological basis. International Association of Theoretical and Applied Limnology Proceedings 16:1145–1160.

MULLER, K.

1982   Jungfischwanderungen   zur   Bottensee.   Archiv   fuer   Hydrobiologie 95(1/4):271–282.

MUNRO, A. L. S., J. LIVERSIDGE and K. G. R. ELSON

1976   The distribution and prevalence of infectious pancreatic necrosis virus in wild fish in Loch Awe. Proceedings of the Royal Society of Edinburgh, Section B, 75:223–232.

MUNRO, C. W.

1921   A preliminary study of the digestive secretions of pickerel and perch. Wisconsin Academy of Science, Arts and Letters 20(269):273.

MUNRO, W. R.

1957   The pike of Loch Choin. Scottish Home Department, Freshwater and Salmon Fisheries Research 16:1–16.
        Fish population of the lake was destroyed by rotenone in October 1955; this permitted determination of abundance, food, sex ratio, and age at maturity. Length-weight relationships, growth rates, and ages (from scales) are given.

MUNTYAN, S. P.

1978   Some observations on the reproduction and embryonic development of five species of fish kept in experimental radioactive water bodies. Journal of Ichthyology 18:1033–1038.
        Data on the activity of the muscles and bones of spawners.

MURCHISON, C., ed.

1868   Paleontological memoirs and notes of the late Hugh Falconer, A.M., M.D., 2 vols. London, Robert Hardwicke.

MUSACCHIA, X. J., B. J. SULLIVAN and C. G. WILBER

    1957   A comparison of liver and muscle lipids in Arctic fishes. Copeia 1957:10–12. Compares blackfish *Dallia pectoralis* liver cholesterol content, liver phospho-lipid, and total fatty acid values with those of pike.

MYERS, B. J.

    1979   The great pike. Ontario Out of Doors, April 1979, p. 47. Stories of angling for pike.

MYERS, G. S.

    1958a   Trends in the evolution of teleostean fishes. Standord Ichthyological Bulletin 7(3):27–30.

    1958b   Nomenclator of certain terms used for higher categories of fishes. Stanford Ichthyological Bulletin 7(3):31–40.

NAGIBINA, L. F.
   1961   Parasitofauna of fish of "Novoe Vygozero" (New Vygozero Lake). *In* Petrushevskii, G. K., ed. Parasites and diseases of fish. Jerusalem, Israel Program for Scientific Translations, pp. 127–140.

NANSEN, C.
   1973   The tiger muskie. Field and Stream 78(6):52, 53, 92, 94, 98.

NASH, C. W.
   1913   Fishes. *In* Natural History of Toronto region, Ontario, Canada, pp. 249–271.

NATIONAL GEOGRAPHIC SOCIETY
   1965   Wondrous world of fishes. Washington, National Geographic Society, Natural Science Library. 367 pp.

NAWRATIL, O.
   1954   On the biology of the pike in the Lakes Neusiedl and Atter in Austria. Oesterreichische Zoologische Zeitschrift 4(415):489–529.
         The pike is one of the fastest growing fishes of middle Europe (average length and weight in the 4th year 78 cm, 3650 g). The coefficient of condition for pike is given and length-weight relations are tabulated.

NEBOL'SINA, T. K.
   1956   Nerest ryb v kultuchnoi zone i avandel'te r. Volgi. [Fish spawning in the bayou area and in the sea off the Volga Delta.] Rybnoe Khozyaistvo 12:53–55.

NECKHAM, A.
   1863   De natura rerum libri duo. *In* Wright, T., ed., Chronicles and memorials of Great Britain and Ireland during the Middle Ages (Rolls Series), 34. London. Refers to fish and fishing in the Middle Ages; mentions pike.

NECRASOV, O.
   1968   Sur la variabilite intraspecifique du volume de l'encephale et de la moelle au cours de la croissance chez les poissons. Revue Roumaine de Biologie, Serie de Zoologie, 13:433–439.

NEEDHAM, J. G.
   1920   Clean waters for New York State. Cornell Rural School Leaflet 13:153–182.
   1922   A biological reconnaissance of Lake George. A biological survey of Lake George, New York. New York State Conservation Commission, pp. 8–36.

NEEDHAM, W.
   1720   Descriptio anatomica Lucii et Alosae. *In* Valentini, M. B., ed., Amphitheatrum zootomicum. Frankfurt, pp. 122–123.

NEILL, S. R. ST. J. and J. M. CULLEN
   1974   Experiments on whether schooling by their prey affects the hunting behavior of cephalopods and fish predators. Journal of Zoology (London) 172:549–569.
         The effect of prey group size on hunting success was tested and found to decrease with increasing prey density. Increasing prey numbers appeared to cause frequent performance of acts not related to hunting in ambush predators, including pike, therefore reducing the hunting success rate.

NELLEN, W.
   1965   Beitrage zur Brackwasserokologie der Fische im Ostseeraum. [Contributions on brackish water ecology of fishes in the Baltic Sea area.] Kieler Meeresforschung 21:192–198.
         This analysis of the community of fishes living in brackish waters connected

230

with the Baltic was based on freshwater fishes found in the northern German lowland. The salinity tolerance of pike was examined.

NELSON, E. W.

1887   Fishes. *In* Henshaw, H. W., ed., Report upon natural history collections made in Alaska between the years 1877 and 1881 by E. W. Nelson. Washington, pp. 297–322.

NELSON, G. J.

1969   Infraorbital bones and their bearing on the phylogeny and geography of osteoglossamorph fishes. American Museum Novitates 2394:1–37.

1972   Cephalic sensory canals, pitlines, and the classification of esocoid fishes, with notes on galaxiids and other teleosts. American Museum Novitates 2492: 1–49.

NELSON, L. R.

1983   Northern Pike (*Esox lucius*) and white sucker (*Catostomus commersonii*) swimming performance and passage through a step and pool fishladder. M.S. thesis, University of Alberta. 174 pp.
        Biological and swimming performance data collected at Driedmeat Lake and Steele Lake, Alberta. Observed speed in various man-made situations, and noted preferred hours of activity.

NELSON, M. N. and A. D. HASLER

1942   The growth, food, distribution and relative abundance of the fishes of Lake Geneva, Wisconsin, in 1941. Transactions of the Wisconsin Academy of Science, Arts and Letters 34:137–148.

1943   Lake Geneva and its fishes. Wisconsin Conservation 8(7):17–22.

NELSON, W. R.

1974   Age, growth, and maturity of thirteen species of fish from Lake Oahe during the early years of impoundment, 1963–68. U.S. Fish and Wildlife Service Technical Paper 77:1–29.
        Describes the body-scale relation, calculated length, length-weight relation, age at maturity, and sex ratio of fish caught with trap net and bottom trawl. As growth rate decreased, age at sexual maturity increased. Inundation of new lands was associated with rapid growth, but increased average reservoir depth was associated with decreased fish growth.

1978   Implications of water management in Lake Oahe for the spawning success of coolwater fishes. American Fisheries Society Special Publication 11: 154–158.
        Reviews spawning requirements for pike and three other species, since population trends of these species are related to changes in quantity and quality of spawning habitats. Recommends that minimum spring stream flows be assured and critical reservoir spawning areas be protected and enhanced.

NETH, P. C.

1978   An analysis of the International Champlain-Richelieu Board proposal for water level regulation in Lake Champlain. New York State Department of Environmental Conservation, pp. 1–62.
        A loss of more than 22% of the wetlands in the basin would adversely affect pike spawning to a considerable degree.

NETSCH, N. F.

1975   Fishery resources along the route of the Trans-Alaska pipeline between Yukon River and Atigun Pass in north central Alaska. U.S. Fish and Wildlife

Service Resource Publication 124:1–45.

NEUMAN, W. F. and B. J. MULRYAN

1968   The discrepancy in the carbonate found in fish bone and blood. Calcified Tissue Research 2:237–241.

Just refers to the findings of Carlstrom and Glas (1959) for the bones of the Baltic pike.

NEUMAYER, L.

1895   Histologische untersuchungen uber den feineren Bau des centralnervensystems von *Esox lucius* mit Berucksichtigung vergleichend-Anatomischer verhaltnisse. Archiv fuer Mikrobiologie Anatomie 44(3):34–364.

NEUSCH, A.

1958   Augenentwicklung und Schlumpftermin bei Hecht und Forelle. Revue Suisse de Zoologie 65.

NEVEU, G. and C. BRY

1983   Ovulation spontanee de femelles brochets en petits etangs de maturation. *In* Billard, R., ed., Le brochet gestion dans le milieu naturel et elevage. Paris, Institute National de la Recherche Agronomique, pp. 77–74.

Spontaneous ovulations were obtained in female pike stocked into small ponds together with forage fish several months before reproduction. This method may supply the pike culturist with spontaneously ovulated females in a dependable and efficient way. Over 3 to 5 weeks, almost all the females ovulate with high ovulation and fertilization rates.

NEWBURG, H.

1973   Statewide fisheries research. Evaluation of potential use of pulsed direct current electrofishing gear in some fish management activities. Minnesota Division of Game and Fish, Project F-26-R-3/Wk.Pl. 15:1–19.

Unaltered and pulsed direct current boat-mounted electrofishing gear was evaluated for estimation of pike abundance in potential winter rescue areas.

NEWDICK, J.

1979   The complete freshwater fishes of the British Isles. London, A. & C. Black.

NEW YORK DEPARTMENT OF CONSERVATION

1969   Fish and Fishing in New York. Albany, Division of Conservation Education, 37 pp.

NICHOLS, J. T. and V. HEILNER

1920   World's record catches with rod and reel and otherwise of fifty N.A. popular fish and salt water fishes. Field and Stream, July 1920, pp. 268–269.

NICHOLSON, D.

1932   *Diphyllobothrium* infection in *Esox lucius*. Canadian Journal of Research 6:166–170.

The heaviest infections were in summer-caught, and small to medium-sized pike. Suggests the infection probably occurs annually in early summer and that the larvae die and disintegrate after a period of development

NIENSTEDT, W., I. NIENSTEDT and J. MANNISTO

1981   Metabolism of testosterone and progesterone by gastrointestinal tissues of the pike (*Esox lucius*). General and Comparative Endocrinology 43:148–156.

The two hormones were incubated with homogenates of liver and of esophageal, gastric, and intestinal mucose. The metabolism in the intestinal and hepatic samples was almost identical both qualitatively and quantitatively and more active than that in the esophageal and gastric samples.

232

NIGRELLI, R. F.

1947   Spontaneous neoplasma in fishes. 3. Lymphosarcoma in *Astyanax* and *Esox*.
        Zoologica 32:101–109.

1953   Tumors and other atypical cell growth in temperate freshwater fishes of North
        America. Transactions of the American Fisheries Society 83:262–296.
        Mentions Nigrelli's 1943 report of an adenoma in the kidney of a pike.

NIKANOROV, Y. I.

1962   Ob ulovakh shchuki v ozere Seliger. [On the catches of pike in Lake Seliger.]
        Izvestiya Gosudarstvennogo Nauchno-Issledovatel'skogo Instituta Ozernogo i
        Rechnogo Rybnogo Khozvaistva 15:53–54.
        As a result of intensive fishing, the supplies of pike sharply declined. Data
        for the catches of 1960 show that the spawning stock of pike was dominated
        by younger age groups. For increasing the abundance of pike, fish conserva-
        tion measures and artificial rearing are recommended.

NIKITINA, A. G.

1958   Growth and development of pike in L. Syamozero during the first year of life.
        Ich. Zap. Leningr. Gos. Ped.In-ta im. A. I. Gertsena, 143.

NIKOLSKI, G. W.

1957   Spezielle Fischkunde. VEB Deutscher Verlag Der Wissenschafter, Verling.
        632 pp.

NIKOL'SKII, G. V.

1961   Special ichthyology, 2nd ed. Israel Program for Scientific Translations,
        National Science Foundation and Smithsonian Institute. 538 pp.
        Lists characteristics of the Esociformes and discusses origin and taxonomic
        position. A chart shows growth rate in various reservoirs.

NIKOLSKII, G. V.

1969   Theory of fish population dynamics as the biological background for national
        exploitation and management of fishery resources. Edinburgh, Oliver &
        Boyd.

NIKOLSKY, G.

1946   Investigations on the subfossil freshwater fishes in the Soviet Union. Copeia
        1946:24–26.
        Reduction in mean length resulting from exploitation is marked among many
        of the species represented in the collections. Remains of many fish including
        pike in the Desna River included specimens much larger in size than are
        found in the same waters today. Distribution, growth rate, and even age com-
        position were different 2,000 years ago.

NIKOLSKY, G. V.

1963   The ecology of fishes, trans. by L. Birkett. London, Academic Press. 352 pp.

NIKOLYUKIN, N. I.

1935   Uber Kreuzungsversuche an Knochenfischen. Zoologischer Anzeiger
        112(11–12):305–318.

1963   Ein versuch zur Ausnutzung von Hybriden zwischen Hausen und Sterlet als
        wirtschriftsobjekt in Strauseen. Rybno Khozyaistvo 39(2):32–34.

NILSSON, D.

1921   Nagra insjofiskars alder och tillvaxt i Bottniska viken och Malaren.
        Meddelelser LantbrStyr., Stockholm, 231.

NILSSON, N.-A.

1967   Interactive segregation between fish species. *In* Gerking, S. D., ed., The biological basis of freshwater fish production. IBP Symposium, Reading, 1966,
pp. 295–313.

NISSINEN, T.

1965a   Gaddmarkningar i norra savolax. Meddelanden fran Byran for fiskeneko-
nomiska undersotningar 1:10–16.

1965b   Tagging of northern pike in northern Savo. Kalataloudellisen tutkimustoimiston tiedonantoja 1:9–15.

1971   Hauen kasvusta vaelluksista ja kalastuksesta Ouluvarvella suoritettujen mer-
kintakokeiden valossa. [The growth and migration of the pike and pike
fishing in Lake Oulujarvi in the light of marking tests.] Kalataloudellisen tut-
kimustoimiston tiedonantoja 1:6–16.

A total of 531 pike were aged, weighed, marked and released over two
winters. Recapture data provided information on seasonal fishing intensity
and migration.

NITSKANSKII, S. G.

1961   Pitanie i temp rosta shchuki, okunya i soma iz poimennykh oser r. Prut.
[Feeding and growth rate of pike, perch, and *Silurus* from the floodplain lakes
of the Prut River). Trudy Kishinevskogo Sel'skokhozyaistvennogo Instituta
25:187–192.

Analysis of commercial catches were done in connection with the use of the
flood plain for carp *Cyprinus carpio* rearing. Predaceous fish comprised 20%
of the catch. Feeding intensity and growth rate for these fish was considered
to be low.

NOGUSASHY, S.

1960   A comparative study of the chromosomes in fishes with particular considerations on taxonomy and evolution. Memoirs of the Hyogo University of Agriculture 3:1–62.

NOLAND, W. E.

1951   The hydrography, fish, and turtle population of Lake Wingra. Transactions of
the Wisconsin Academy of Science, Arts and Letters 40(2):5–58.

NOMURA, S., T. IBARAKI, H. HIROSE and S. SHIRAHATA

1972   Applications of back-pack cardiotelemeter for fishes. I. Heart rate and cardiac reflex in fishes during unrestrained swimming. Bulletin of the Japanese
Society of Scientific Fisheries 38:1105–1117.

NONNOTTE, G.

1981   Cutaneous respiration in six freshwater teleosts. Comparative Biochemistry
and Physiology, A, 70:541–543.

An investigation of the oxygen consumption of excised skin and normal
cutaneous oxygen uptake in situ. Uptake from the external medium was less
than cutaneous oxygen consumption in pike, so the skin is not an oxygen
exchanger for the benefit of other organs.

NORDQUIST, H.

1940   Preliminara resultat av gaddodlingsforsok. Skrifter Sodra Sveriges Fiskeriforening Lund 1939(2):39–49.

NORMAN, J. R.

1930   The emperor's pike: a fish story. Natural History Magazine 2(14):177–181.

Accounts in historical literature and paintings about a pike tagged and

234

released by Frederick the Second and recaptured 267 years later. Points out discrepancies in the literature.

NORRIS, T.

1864   American angler's book, new ed. Philadelphia, Porter and Coates. 701 pp.
         A 19th century book on angling which mentions giant pike in Europe.

NORTH, E.

1980   The effects of water temperature and flow upon angling success in the River Severn. Fisheries Management 11:1–9.

NOSAL, A.

1961   Opyt razvedenija scuki na Ukraine. Rybovod. Rybolov. 4(4):23–24.

NOWAK, W.

1971   Eksploatacja rybacka i poloxy szczupaka w jeziorze Dargin. [Fishing exploitation and catches of pike in Lake Dargin]. Roczniki Nauk Rolniczych, Seria H, Rybactwo, 93(4):87–102. [in Polish, English summary]
         An analysis of the number of pike in Lake Dargin carried out on the basis of catches by selected gear, 1953–62. The pike population dropped during the consecutive years, as shown by the increasing catches of pike >3 kg and by the decrease in effort needed to catch 1 kg of pike.

NUHI, A. and Y. KHORASANI

1981   Bacterial pollution indicators in the intestinal tract of various fish species living in Amir-Kolayeh Lagoon, Iran. Zentralblatt fuer Bakteriologie Parasitenkunde Infektionskrankheiten und Hygiene Zweite Naturwissenschaftliche Abteilung Mikrobiologie der Landwirtschaft der Technologie und des Unweltschutzes 136:566–571.

NUORTEVA, P., M. LODENIUS and S.-L. NUORTEVA

1979   Decrease in the mercury levels of *Esox lucius* (L.) and *Abramis farenus* (L.) (Teleostei) in the Hameenkyro watercourse after the phenylmercury ban in Finland. Aquilo 19:97–100.

NURNBERGER, P. K.

1930   The plant and animal food of the fishes of Big Sandy Lake. Transactions of the American Fisheries Society 60:253–259.
         A report of the food and parasites found in the stomachs and intestines of 52 pike, 62–620 mm in length.

NURSALL, J. R.

1973   Some behavioral interactions of spottail shiners (*Notropis hudsonius*), yellow perch (*Perca flavescens*), and northern pike (*Esox lucius*). Journal of the Fisheries Research Board of Canada 30:1161–1178.
         The species studied show a range of gregariousness from the solitary pike, the facultative schools of perch, to the obligate schooling of spottail shiners. Pike are described as lone, opportunistic predators whose hunting technique combines motionlessness, axial tracking, and lunging. Prey may be swallowed head first, tail first, or sideways.

NURSALL, J. R. and M. E. PINSENT

1969   Aggregations of spottail shiners and yellow perch. Journal of the Fisheries Research Board of Canada 26:1672–1676.
         Pike prey from below the aggregations.

NYBELIN, O.

1943   Vara fiskbar. [Our fishes.] Stockholm, Albert Bonniers. 83 pp.
         General text of Swedish fishes, which briefly discusses distribution,

taxonomy, life history, behaviour, food, and growth of the pike family.

NYBERG, P.

1979   Production and food consumption of perch *Perca fluviatilis* in two Swedish
forest lakes. Institute of Freshwater Research Drottningholm Report
58:140–157.

NYGREN, A., P. EDLUND, U. HIRSCH and L. AHSGREN

1968   Cytological studies in perch (*Perca fluviatilis* L.), pike (*Esox lucius* L.), pike-
perch (*Lucioperca lucioperca* L.) and ruff (*Acerina cernua* L.). Hereditas
59(2/3):518–524.
Chromosome number (2n = 50) was determined in adult pike from Sweden.
Polyploid mitosis was formed in the testis and kidney tissue and these cells
may contain over 1000 chromosomes. Bivalents are formed only during
meiosis and in polyploid meiotic cells bivalents alone are formed.

NYSTROM, M.

1979   Histological changes in some organs in pike with skin tumours. A preliminary study. Proceedings of the 9th Symposium of the Scandinavian Society
for Parasitology, Turku, 1979. Institute of Parasitology Abo Akademi, Finland.

1982   Skin tumours of pikes in the archipelagoes of southern Finland. Skargard
5(1):25–31. [in Swedish]

OATIS, P. H. and J. G. LINDENBERG

1979 The role of northern pike in Massachusetts inland sport fisheries. *In* Dube, J., and Y. Gravel, eds., Proceedings of the 10th Warmwater Workshop, Special Publication NE Division of the American Fisheries Society. Montreal, Quebec Ministere du Loisir, de la Chasse et de la Peche, pp. 195–200.

In addition to natural reproduction, pike have been stocked as yearlings to help satisfy angler demand. East of the Berkshires, the survival of pike fry or spawn appeared inhibited but suggests methods to assure consistent supplies of pike.

OBER, R. D.

1976 Food habits of northern pike, *Esox lucius* Linnaeus, black bullheads, *Ictalurus melas* (Rafinesque), and white bass, *Morone chrysops* (Rafinesque), in Lake Ashtabula, North Dakota. M.S. thesis, University of North Dakota. 95 pp.

OBERSZTYN, A.

1953 The resorption of the teeth of the pike (*Esox lucius*). Folia Morphologica 4(1):31–48.

The resorption of pike teeth can be differentiated by three periods: A preliminary one in which the author observed the appearance of free reticular cells in the osteodentin channels. In the second period osteoclasts lay at the walls of the hole that was formed by resorption of the middle part of the dentin by osteoclasts. In the third period the joint of the tooth with the bone is destroyed and the tooth stays loosely in the soft tissues.

OCVIRK, J.

1982 Slovenske kapitalne ribe. [The largest specimen of the Slovenian freshwater fish.] Ichthyos 2:31–34.

Gives lists of length, weight, date of catch, river, and fisherman for 17 Slovenian freshwater fish species caught from 1964 to 1982.

1984 Dinamika rasti Scuke (*Esox lucius* Linnaeus 1758) v Jezeru Vrana, Otok Cres. [Growth dynamics of pike (*Esox lucius* Linnaeus (1758)) in Lake Vrana, Island Cres.] Ichthyos 2:11–17.

The growth dynamics of pike in Lake Vrana was established on the basis of measurements of 206 pike caught from 1974 to 1978. The sex ratio, length, and weight of pike are shown and compared with growth dynamics of pike from Mrtva Tisa.

ODELL, T. T.

1931 Lakes of the Oswegatchie and Black River systems. *In* A biological survey of the Oswegatchie and Black River systems, Supplement to the 21st Annual Report 6:94–119.

1932 The depth distribution of certain species of fish in some of the lakes of New York. Transactions of the American Fisheries Society 62:331–335.

Fifty-eight pike were collected in 35 of 277 net sets. Of these, 51 were between 0 and 15 feet deep.

ODENING, K.

1974 On the species question in the trematode genus *Azygia* from European pike. Angewandte Parasitologie 15(1):5–10.

1976 The life cycle of *Azygia lucii* trematoda in East Germany Biologiske Zentralblatt 95(1):57–94.

ODENING, K. and I. BOCKHARDT
  1976   On the seasonal occurrence of *Azygia lucii* Trematoda in *Esox lucius* Pisces. Zoologischer Anzeiger 196:182–188.
          The transmission and infection by pike of various ages is discussed.
ODENWALL, E.
  1927   Fiskfaunan i Lappajarvi sjo. Acta Societatis pro Fauna et Flora Fennica 56(13):1–48.
OEHMCKE, A. and K. WALKER
  1969   Temperature control in northern pike and muskellunge egg hatching. Wisconsin Department of Natural Resources, Fish Management Report, unpublished MS.
OEHMCKE, A. A.
  1949   Muskellunge fingerling culture. Progressive Fish-Culturist 11:3–18.
          Compares muskellunge growth with that reported for pike by Carbine (1942), and concludes that they are similar, but after 141 mm, muskellunge reared in ponds grow faster than pike.
  1951   Muskellunge yearling culture and its application to lake management. Progressive Fish-Culturist 13:63–70.
OEHMCKE, A. A., L. JOHNSON, J. KLINGBIEL and C. WISTROM
  1965   The Wisconsin muskellunge, its life history, ecology, and management. Wisconsin Conservation Department Publication 225:1–12.
          Contrasts and compares various aspects of life history of muskellunge with that of pike.
O'GRADY, M. F.
  1983   An estimate of the standing crop of adult pike (*Esox lucius* L.) in Lough Sheelin, 1977–1979. Journal of Life Sciences, pp. 191–194.
OHLMER, W. and I. SCHWARTZKOPFF
  1959   Schwimmgeschwin dig keiten von Fischen aus stehenden Binnengewassern. Naturwissenschaften 46:362–363.
OHMONO, Y., V. MIETTINEN, E. BLANKENSTEIN, M. TILLANDER, K. RISSANEN and J. K. MIETTINEN
  1969   Studies on the distribution of 203 Hg-labelled methyl mercury and phenyl mercury in pike. 5th Radioactivity in Scandinavia Symposium, Helsinki.
OIKARI, A.
  1975a   Hydro mineral balance in some brackish water teleosts after thermal acclimation particularly at temperatures near zero. Annales Zoologici Fennici 12:215–229.
  1975b   Seasonal changes in plasma and muscle hydro mineral balance in three Baltic teleosts with special reference to the thermal response. Annales Zoologici Fennici 12:230–236.
  1978   Ionic and osmotic balance in the pike, *Esox lucius* L., in fresh and brackish water. Annales Zoologici Fennici 15:84–88.
          Plasma Na, Cl, and Mg concentrations are maintained at higher levels in brackish than in fresh water. Concentrations increased and blood glucose and tissue water concentrations decreased during 4-day exposure to a slightly hyperosmotic medium. Blood mean corpuscular haemoglobin concentration, a rough index of circulatory red cell volume, increased in pike exposed to slightly hyperosomatic and Mg supplemented brackish water.

238

OIKARI, A. and A. SOIVIO

1975   Influence of sampling methods and anesthetization on various hematological parameters of several teleosts. Aquaculture 6:171–180.

1977   Physiological condition of fish exposed to water containing pulp and paper industry wastes and sewage. *In* Alabaster, J. S., ed., Biological monitoring of inland fisheries. Proceedings of a symposium of the European Inland Fisheries Advisory Commission, Helsinki, 1976. London, Applied Science, pp. 89–96.

OLIPHAN, L. V.

1940   Diurnal rhythms in the respiration of fish larvae. Doklady Akademii Nauk SSSR 29:620–623.

OLIVA, O.

1956   K biologii stiky (*Esox lucius* L.). [To the biology of the pike (*Esox lucius* L.).] Vestnik Ceskoslovenske Zoologicke Spolecnosti 20:208–223.

A study of the biology of the pike in some experimental small natural ponds. Age was determined by the scale method. Gives body-scale relationship, time of annulus formation, back-calculated lengths, and sexual maturity.

1960   Jeste k. metode odhadu velikosti rybi osadky. [Some further remarks on the methods of estimating fish populations.] Vestnik Ceskoslovenske Zoologicke Spolecnosti 24:105–129.

The fish population of the River Labe was studied using mark-recapture and the Schnabel method. Pike was an important species in the study.

1965   The myodome in pike, *Esox lucius* Linnaeus. Vestnik Ceskoslovenske Zoologicke Spolecnosti 3:256–258.

Two myodomes or eye muscle canals occur in pike, the anterior (with two obliqui muscles) and the posterior (with rectus externus muscle only). The posterior myodome is closed by basioccipital bone.

OLIVA, O. and A. S. NAIKSATAM

1979   Note on growth of some fishes from the River Dunajec. Vestnik Ceskoslovenske Zoologicke Spolecnosti 43:278–282.

Growth from scales was studied in pike captured in a fish ladder of the Roznow Valley water reservoir.

OLSSON, G.

1975   Gaddans predation pa nyutsatt lax- och havsoringsmolt i Angermanalven. Fiskeriintendenten i nedre norra distriktet, Harnosand. 3 pp.

OLSSON, M.

1976   Mercury level as a function of size and age in northern pike 1 and 5 years after the mercury ban in Sweden. Ambio 5(2):73–76.

Pike were collected in 1968 and 1972 in Lake Marmen, downstream from a papermill. The correlation was studied between mercury levels and different size parameters of specimens, considering sex and age classes.

OLSSON, M. and S. JENSEN

1975   Pike as the test organism for mercury, DDT and PCB pollution. A study of the contamination in the Stockholm Archipelago. Institute of Freshwater Research Drottningholm Report 54:83–106.

Pike was shown to be a suitable organism for studying pollution patterns in areas contaminated by bioaccumulating substances. High levels of mercury, DDT, and PCB substances in pike from one of two island lakes in the prevailing wind direction from Stockholm indicate airborne fallout. Differences in

239

the degree of contamination may be explained by the level of biomass and rate of the water exchange in the lake.

OMAND, D. N.
1950   A population estimate based on catch-effort statistics. Canadian Fish-Culturist 6:15–19.

Pike were collected in O'Reilly Lake during a study of smallmouth bass *Micropterus dolomieu* planting.

OMAROV, O. P. and O. A. POPOVA
1985   Feeding behavior of pike, *Esox lucius*, and catfish, *Silurus glanis*, in the Arakum Reservoirs of Dagestan. Journal of Ichthyology 25:25–36.

The daily, monthly, and annual rations of pike were determined and the quantity of various organisms eaten by a single predator during the year was examined. Pike in the Arakum reservoirs mainly prey on low value species and are valuable components of the ecosystem.

O'NEILL, R. H.
1932   We looked for trout and caught pike. Rod and Gun in Canada.

ONTARIO DEPARTMENT OF LANDS AND FORESTS
1953   Some age and growth rates of Ontario northern pike (*Esox lucius*). Fish and Wildlife Management Report 10.

The scale method is considered to be accurate to within one or two years for Ontario pike. Growth rate varies in different waters.

OPUSZYNSKI, K.
1979   Podstawy biologii ryb. [Bases of fish biology.] Warsaw, PWRiL. 589 pp.

ORGAN, W.
1960   Manitoba pike are no pikers. Rod and Gun, June 1960, pp. 14–15.

ORLOVA, E. L.
1976   Feeding habits of predatory fishes in the outer delta of the Volga. Hydrobiological Journal 12(2):41–47.

ORLOVA, E. L. and G. K. AZHIGALIYEVA
1984   Food availability and growth of pike in the Volga Delta. Hydrobiological Journal 20:26–31.

Relationships are established for the annual ration and annual consumed amount of roach *Rutilus rutilus*, and also for an annual gain in weight and annual ration. The intensive roach consumption in spring enhances the pike growth in length, and the autumn feeding favours mainly gain in weight.

ORLOVA, E. L. and O. A. POPOVA
1976   The feeding of predatory fish, the sheatfish, *Silurus glanis*, and the pike, *Esox lucius*, in the Volga Delta following regulation of the discharge of the river. Journal of Ichthyology 16:75–87.

Over a period of 25 years spawning and feeding conditions of the predator changed because of changes in the hydrologic regime of the delta with regulation of the discharge of the river. A redistribution of the predators occurred, as well as a change in species composition of their prey, feeding rhythm, size of annual ration, and a decrease in abundance of pike.

ORME, L. E.
1978   The status of coolwater fish diets. American Fisheries Society Special Publication 11:167–171.

Seven diets were formulated specifically for coolwater fish and tested. Pike fry did not start on the dry feeds. Pike-muskellunge hybrids readily accepted all feeds with good survival and are fed them on a production scale.

ORSKA, J.

        Anomalies in the vertebral columns of the pike (*Esox lucius* L.). Acta Biologica Cracoviensia, Series Zoologia 5:327–345.

ORTENBURGER, A. I. and C. L. HUBBS

    1926   A report on the fishes of Oklahoma with descriptions of new genera and species. Proceedings of the Oklahoma Academy of Science 5:123–141.

OSBORN, T. C., D. B. ERNST and D. H. SCHUPP

    1981   The effects of water levels and other factors on walleye and northern pike reproduction and abundance in Rainy and Namakan reservoirs. Minnesota Department of Natural Resources, Investigational Report 374:1–46.

OSBORNE, P. J. and F. W. SHOTTON

    1968   The fauna of the channel deposit of early Saalian age at Brandon, Warwickshire. Philosophical Transactions of the Royal Society of London, B, Biological Sciences 254(796):417–424.

OSBURN, R. C.

    1901   The fishes of Ohio. Ohio Academy of Science Special Paper 4:1–105.

OTTE, E.

    1969   Mykobakterielle Infektionen bei Fischen-Erreger und ihre Beurteilung. Zeitschrift fuer Fischerei 17(5/7):515–546.

OTTERSTROM, C. V.

    1927   Geddespesten. Ferskvandsfiskbl. 25(6):13–16.

    1928   Die Hechtpest in Danemark. Allgemeine Fischerei-Zeitung 53(20):312–313.

OTTO, C.

    1979   The effects on a pike (*Esox lucius* L.) population of intensive fishing in a south Swedish lake. Journal of Fish Biology 15:461–468.

        During 7 years of intensive fishing, the average individual size of pike caught declined progressively until the last year of the study. Three phases could be identified: 1) a high proportion of large fish; 2) a high proportion of small fish; and 3) equal numbers of large and small fish. The growth of the different year classes in their first year of life increased from 180 to 220 mm.

OWMAN, C. and C. RUDEBERG

    1970   Light microscopic, fluorescence microscopic and electron microscopic studies on the pineal organ of the pike *Esox lucius* with special regard to 5-hydroxytryptamine. Zeitschrift fuer Zellforschung und Mikroskopische Anatomie 107:522–550.

PAASIVIRTA, J., J. SAERKKA, K. SURMA-AHO, T. HUMPPI, T. KUOKKANEN and
M. MARTTINEN
  1983   Food chain enrichment of organochlorine compounds and mercury in clean
          and polluted lakes of Finland. Chemosphere 12:239–252.
          Lakes polluted by pulp mill and urban wastes including chlorobleaching of
          pulp, semipolluted lakes, and reference lakes in nearly natural conditions in
          central Finland were studied for contents of mercury, methyl mercury, and
          organichlorine compounds in sediment, plankton, roach *Rutilus rutilus* and
          pike.

PAASIVIRTA, J., J. SAERKKAE, M. AHO, K. SURMA-AHO, J. TARHANEN and A. ROOS
  1981   Recent trends of biocides in pikes of the Lake Paeijaenne. Chemosphere
          10:405–414.
          Pike were sampled in May 1980 from three areas of the lake and analysed for
          their contents of total mercury, methyl mercury, hexachlorobenzene (HCB),
          DDE, PCB, and chlorophenolic residues. Results were compared to levels
          seen in 1970 from the same three areas.

PAETZ, M. J. and J. S. NELSON
  1970   The fishes of Alberta. Edmonton, Queen's Printer. 282 pp.

PAGEAU, G., Y. GRAVEL and V. LEGENDRE
  1979   Distribution and value of the Esocidae in Quebec waters. *In* Dube, J., and Y.
          Gravel, eds., Proceedings of the 10th Warmwater Workshop, Special Publica-
          tion NE Division of the American Fisheries Society. Montreal, Quebec Min-
          istere du Loisir, de la Chasse et de la Peche, pp. 1–7.
          Value of pike is described briefly in terms of sports fishing, commercial
          fishing, management, and regulations.

PAGEAU, G., Y. GRAVEL and L. LEVESQUE
  1971   The ichthyofauna and flora of Lake St. Louis on the St. Lawrence River near
          Montreal, Quebec; general features and recent changes. Proceedings of the
          14th Conference on Great Lakes Research, 1971. International Association
          for Great Lakes Research, pp. 79–89.
          Accelerated changes that occurred in the Great Lakes and St. Lawrence River
          over the past 30 years have affected Lake St. Louis. The major modifying
          agents have been pollution, Seaway construction, regional warming of the cli-
          mate, and the perturbation of biological competition. Increased fertility may
          have led to an increase in individuals and species, but game fish populations
          have shown a net reduction.

PALMIERI, J. R.
  1975   Physiological strains of the strigeoid trematode *Posthodiplostmum minimum*
          Trematoda Diplostomatidae. Journal of Parasitology 61:1107.

PALOHEIMO, J. E.
  1958   A method of estimating natural and fishing mortalities. Journal of the
          Fisheries Research Board of Canada 15:749–758.

PANCHENKO, S. E.
  1972   O nakoplenii pestitsidov v rybe. [On the accumulation of pesticides in fish.]
          Rybnoe Khozyaistvo 12:31–32.
          Accumulation of organichlorine and organophosphorus pesticides in fish liv-
          ing in Karpievskii Firth was studied. Accumulation occurs even if pesticide
          does not exceed 0.05 mg/l, and may lower reproductive capacity.

PAPAS, T. S., J. DAHLBERG and R. A. SONSTEGARD

 1976   Type C virus in lymphosarcoma in northern pike (*Esox lucius*). Nature
          261(5560):506–508.

          Outlines the method for detecting reverse transcriptase, an enzyme present in
          all known RNA tumour viruses. The enzyme was found in cancerous pike
          but not healthy ones. Due to the seasonal nature of the disease, a temperature
          profile of enzyme activity was done.

PAPAS, T. S., M. SHAFFER, T. PRY and R. A. SONSTEGARD

 1977   DNA polymerase in lymphosarcoma in northern pike (*Esox lucius*). Cancer
          Research 37:3214–3217.

          This study characterized the lymphosarcoma enzyme and compared its
          biochemical properties with those associated with neoplasia in mammals and
          birds.

PARAGAMIAN, V. L.

 1976   Population characteristics of northern pike in the Plover River, Wisconsin.
          Progressive Fish-Culturist 38:160–163.

          Population size, standing stock, growth, K-factors, total annual mortality, and
          survival of pike were determined.

PARISI, G.

 1968   Biochemistry of oxidative phenomena in the arteries. Quaderni di Anatomia
          Pratica 24:108–122.

PARSONS, R. F.

 n.d.   The limnology and fish biology of Ten Mile Lake, Labrador. Resource
          Development Branch, Newfoundland Region, Technical Report Series
          NEW/T-75-3.

          Pike was one of the seven species collected during the summer of 1974.
          Chemical and physical parameters of the lake were measured.

PASTUSZYNSKI, J.

 1966   Hodowla narybku szczupaka w stawach karpiowych. [Breeding of pike
          fingerlings in carp ponds]. Gospodarka rybna 18(4):11–13.

          Requirements for fish production in ponds, also autumn pike. Prospects for
          the development of such production.

PATERSON, R. J.

 1968   The pike population. *In* The lake trout of Swan Lake, Alberta. Alberta
          Recreation, Parks and Wildlife, Fisheries Research Report 2:88–96.

PATRIARCHE, M. H.

 1963   Research and management of sport fisheries of Michigan. Northern Michigan
          fish population investigations. Study of lakes subject to extreme oxygen
          depletion. Michigan Department of Conservation, Dingell-Johnson Report
          F-27-R-1/Wk.Pl. 6/Job 9.

 1966   Research and management of sport fisheries of Michigan. Study of lakes sub-
          ject to extreme oxygen depletion. Michigan Department of Conservation,
          Dingell-Johnson Project F-19-R-6 and F-27-R-4, Job No. 9(7/1/60–6/30/63)
          and 7(7/1/63–6/30/66).

          In 1959 pike were stocked in Grebe Lake to evaluate their survival potential
          under low oxygen conditions. Tested several techniques to prevent severe
          oxygen depletion beneath the ice in Lodge Lake.

 1968   Warmwater fish biology and population ecology. Artificial manipulation of a
          northern pike population in a lake. Michigan Department of Conservation,

Dingell-Johnson Project F-29-R-2, Job 7:1–7.

Calculated pike population and production in Grebe Lake, and tested the application of a mathematical model for maximum sustained production.

1971   Controlled harvest of northern pike in a lake closed to angling. Michigan Department of Natural Resources, Dingell-Johnson Project F-29-R-4, No. 7:71–72.

PATRIARCHE, M. H. and H. GOWING

1961   Northern Michigan fish population investigations. Study of lakes subject to extreme oxygen depletion. Michigan Department of Conservation, Dingell-Johnson Report F-19-R-1/Job 9.

1962a   Northern Michigan fish population investigations. Evaluation of population manipulation on angling success and growth. Michigan Department of Conservation, Dingell-Johnson Report F-19-R-2/Job 10.

1962b   Northern Michigan fish population investigations. Study of lakes subject to extreme oxygen depletion. Michigan Department of Conservation, Dingell-Johnson Report F-19-R-2/Job 9.

PATRIARCHE, M. H. and J. W. MERNA

1970   A resume of the winterkill problem. *In* Schneberger, E., ed., A symposium on the management of midwestern winterkill lakes. North Central Division, American Fisheries Society, Special Publication, pp. 7–17.

PATRICK, B. and R. HAAS

1971   Finpulling as a technique for marking muskellunge fingerlings. Progressive Fish-Culturist 33:116–118.

PATTERSON, R. R.

1971   Statewide fisheries investigations. Establishment of breeding populations of northern pike in Alamagordo, Ute, Conchas, and Elephant Butte reservoirs from fry and fingerling releases. New Mexico Department of Game and Fish, Project F-22-R-12/Wk.Pl. C/Job 4:1–3.

Stocking fry was 100% unsuccessful. Fingerling stocking did appear to have some merit.

PAUL, A.

1980   Knochenfunde aus dem mittelalterlich-neuzeitlichen Lubeck (Grabung Konigstrasse 59–63). Lubecker Schriften zur Archaeologie und Kulturgeschichte 2:7–104.

Excavated remains of three pike from earliest (12th century) stratum.

PAVLOV, D. S., A. D. MACHEK and S. N. KAPUSPIN

1981   Daytime distribution of fish in a river based on underwater observations. Voprosy Ikhtiologii 21:177–180.

PEACH, U. A. and V. A. REMOROV, eds.

1977   Motor and secretary function of gastrointestinal tract of fishes other than in digestion. Conference on the Ecology of Fish, 1967. Indian National Scientific Documentation Centre, New Delhi, pp. 339–350.

PEARCE, W. A.

1961   The upper St. Lawrence River ice fishery. New York Fish and Game Journal 8(1):32–36.

Pike was the primary species fished during the winters of 1958–59 and 1959–60. Gives information on fishing pressure, catch per unit effort, ratio of males to females. There was no indication of overharvest of pike.

PEARSE, A. S.

1922   Distribution and food of the fishes of Green Lake, Wisconsin, in summer.
Bulletin of the U.S. Bureau of Fisheries 37:253–272.

PEARSE, A. S. and H. ACHTENBERG

1918   Habits of yellow perch in Wisconsin lakes. Bulletin of the U.S. Bureau of
Fisheries 36:295–366.

PEARSON, J.

1980   Migration of northern pike into tributaries of an Indiana watershed. Indiana
Department of Natural Resources, Division of Fish and Wildlife, Fisheries
Section. 9 pp.
Determined the spawning areas and migratory routes of pike in the Elkhart
River and its tributaries. Management proposals concerning population sur-
veys, tagging, and stocking are listed.

PEARSON, W. D. and L. A. KRUMHOLZ

1984   Distribution and status of Ohio River fishes. Oak Ridge National Laboratory,
Oak Ridge, Tennessee. 401 pp.

PECHA, O.

1983   Methodes de production d'oeufs embryonnes et alevins a vesicule resorbee de
brochet (*Esox lucius* L.) a l'ecloserie de Tabor en Tchecoslavaquie. *In* Billard, R., ed., Le brochet gestion dans le milieu naturel et elevage. Paris, Institute National de la Recherche Agronomique. 371 pp.
Describes techniques used by the Tabor hatchery, which produces 20 million
eyed eggs annually and as many sac fry.

PECHKURENKOV, V. L. and G. L. POKROVSKAYA

1978   On the correspondence of data on the incubation of fish eggs in solution of
strontium-90—yttrium-90 of varying activity under laboratory conditions and
natural waters. Journal of Ichthyology 18:995–1002.
Dose load determined by levels of radionuclide accumulation by developing
egg, silting up of egg, and radionuclide accumulation in ooze; involved
correction coefficients for egg sizes.

PECHKURENKOV, V. L., I. A. SHEKHANOVA and I. G. TELYSHEVA

1972   The effect of chronic small dose irradiation on the embryonic development of
fishes and the validity of various assessment methods. Journal of Ichthyology
12:71–79.
Studied the effect of four radionuclides on pike and found that the
Kolmogorov-Smirnov test was best but were unable to establish the effect of
radionuclides in this study.

PECK, J. W.

1974   Migration, food habits, and predation on yearling coho salmon in a Lake
Michigan tributary and bay. Transactions of the American Fisheries Society
103:10–14.

PECKHAM, R.

1968   Spawning techniques for northern pike in Nebraska. *In* Proceedings of the
North Central Warmwater Fish Culture Workshop, Ames, pp. 18–20.

1970   Northern pike management in Pelican Lake, Cherry County. Nebraska Game
and Parks Commission, unpublished report, 9 pp.

PECKHAM, R. D.

1973   Annual progress report for Study G-III-E lake and stream investigations.
Evaluation of interior Alaska waters and sport fish with emphasis on managed

lakes. Alaska Department of Fish and Game, Division of Sport Fish, 14:18–47.

Harding Lake was test netted from June 8–21 to determine abundance of pike spawners in potential spawning habitat and to evaluate gill nets as a possible means of control. Only 11 pike were captured in 215 net hours; 8 were ripe males, 3 were spent females, indicating that spawning had occurred while the lake was still ice-covered. Also gives catch per net hour and stomach contents of 33 pike.

PECOR, C. H.

1978   Intensive culture of tiger muskellunge in Michigan during 1976 and 1977. American Fisheries Society Special Publication 11:202–209.

The pike-muskellunge hybrid was reared intensively on artificial diets during 1976 and 1977. Improved survival during 1977 was attributed to better egg quality and modifications of feeding techniques which resultsed in a lower incidence of cannibalism.

1979   Experimental intensive culture of tiger muskellunge in a water reuse system. Progressive Fish-Culturist 41:103–108.

PECZALSKA, A.

1953   Ryby slodkowodne Baltyku. [Freshwater fishes of the Baltic Sea.] Wydawnictwa Komunikacyjne, Warsaw. 94 pp.

1954   Ryby uzytkowe Baltyku. [Fishes of the Baltic Sea.] Panstwowe Zaklady Wydawnictw Szkolnych, Warsaw. 86 pp.

PEHRSON, T.

1944   The development of laterosensory canal bones in the skull of *Esox lucius*. Acta Zoologica 25:135–157.

The embryonic stages studied were between 8–40 mm long. Whole material was examined in transverse sections.

PENA, J. C.

1985   Annotated bibliography on northern pike in Europe. Unpublished MS, 17 pp.

n.d.   Introduccion y expansion del lucio (*Esox lucius* L. 1758) en la peninsula Iberica: Sintesis general y estudio de las poblaciones en la Cuenca del Esla. [Introduction and expansion of pike (*Esox lucius* L. 1758) in Iberian peninsula: General synthesis and populations study of pike in Esla basin]. Universidad de Leon, unpublished MS. n.p.

PENA, J. C., F. J. PURROY and J. DOMINGUEZ

n.d.   Alimentacion del lucio, *Esox lucius* L. 1758, en la Cuenca del Esla (Espana): Predacion sobre la trucha comun. [Food of pike, *E. lucius* L. 1758, in the Esla Basin (Spain): Predation on the brown trout.] Universidad de Leon, unpublished MS, n.p.

Stomachs of 505 pike were analysed during 1982–85. Diet variation in relation to pike length was: small size - invertebrates; medium size -invertebrates and fishes; big size - fish and some invertebrates; very big - fish.

PENAZ, M.

1963   Nekolik poznamek k umelemu chovu stiky. Ces. rybarstvi 4:55–56.

PENCZAK, T.

1966   Udzial ciernika i cierniczka w pokarmie ryb drapieznych. [Share of sticklebacks in the food of predatory fishes.] Kosmos 15(4):441–443.

Review of the literature on the share and availability of sticklebacks as prey for predatory species such as pike.

246

1969a   The ichthyofauna of the rivers of the Lodz Upland and adjacent areas. Part I. The hydrography and fishes of the Warta basin. Acta Hydrobiologica 11:69–118.

1969b   The ichthyofauna of the rivers of the Lodz Upland and adjacent areas. Part III. A review and character of species. Acta Hydrobiologica 11:339–360. [in Polish, English summary]

1970   Wyzsze kregowce w pokarmie ryb drapieznych. [Higher vertebrates in the food of predatory fishes.] Wszechswiat 1:19–20.
        Review of the literature on the share of higher invertebrates (amphibians and their larvae, reptiles, birds, mammals) in the food of local predatory fishes, such as pike.

1981   Ecological fish production in two small lowland rivers in Poland. Oecologica 48:107–111.

PENCZAK, T., M. ZALEWSKI and M. MOLINSKI
1976   Produkcja szczupaka, ploci i klenia w wybranym odcinku rzeki Pilicy (rejon brzany). [Production of pike, roach and chub in a selected fragment of Pilica River (Narbel region)]. Polish Archiwum Hydrobiologii 23:139–153.
        Material was collected monthly with the use of an aggregate producing rectified full-wave current. Production was calculated arithmetically and graphically.

PENN, G. H.
1950   Utilization of crayfishes by cold-blooded vertebrates in the eastern United States. American Midland Naturalist 44:643–658.

PENNANT, T.
1788   Introduction to the Arctic zoology. 2nd ed. London, 334 pp.

PENNEL, H. C.
1863   The pike family. In The angler-naturalist; a popular history of British fresh-water fish. London, pp. 181–209.

PENNELL, D. A.
1969   Parasite studies. University of Washington, Fisheries Research Institute, pp. 27–28.

PENNOCK, J. F., R. A. MORTON, D. E. M. LAWSON and D. L. LAIDMAN
1962   Quinones and related compounds in fish tissues. Biochemistry Journal 84:637–640.

PERGAMINUS, N.
1480   Dyalogus creaturarum moralizatus. Gouda, Gerard Leeuw.
        Alleged to contain the earliest known illustration of an angler fishing with a float; apparently was fishing for pike.

PERLOWSKA, R.
1969   The helminth parasites of fishes in the Zegrzynski Reservoir in 1963–1964. Acta Parasitologica Polonica 16(1/19):27–32.

PERMITIN, I. E.
1959   Age and rate of growth of pike in Rybinsk Reservoir. Trudy Instituta Biologii Vodokhranilishch 2:148–158.

PERMYAKOV, E. A., L. P. KALINICHENKO, V. N. MEDVEDKIN, E. A. BURSTEIN and C. GERDAY
1983   Sodium and potassium binding to parvalbumins measured by means of intrinsic protein fluorescence. Biochimica et Biophysica Acta 749:185–191.
        The binding of Na+ and K+ to pike parvalbumins (pI 4.2 and 5.0) results in a

rise of the tyrosine and phenylalanine fluorescence quantum yield for the pike protein.

PERRIER, H., J. P. DELCROIX, C. PERRIER and J. GRAS

1974   Disc electrophoresis of plasma proteins of fish physical and chemical characters; localization of fibrinogen transferrin and ceruloplasmin in the plasma of the rainbow trout *Salmo gairdneri*. Comparative Biochemistry and Physiology, B, Comparative Biochemistry 49:679–685

PERSSON, P. E.

1980   Sensory properties and analysis of two muddy odour compounds, geosmin and 2-methylisoborneol, in water and fish. Water Research 14:1113–1118.

PERSSON, P.-E., H. PENTTINEN and P. NUORTEVA

1978   DI-2 ethylhexyl phthalate in the vicinity of an industrial area in Finland. Environmental Pollution 16:163–166.

PERVOZVANSKIJ, V. Y.

1984   Biology of pike *Esox lucius* (Esocidae) from water bodies associated with the Kamennaya R. (the Kem' R. basin, the White Sea). Voprosy Ikhtiologii 24:54–68.

       Biological characteristics of pike from four Karelian lakes are based on the analysis of 623 individuals, 2–18 years old. Intensive fishery for pike and sport fishing resulted in the deterioration of the biological state of the population. Suggests raising the commercial size of pike up to 40 cm and to retain the pike fraction in the catches of 7–10%.

PETERKA, J. J.

1972   Effects of saline waters upon survival of fish eggs and larvae and upon the ecology of the fathead minnow in North Dakota. North Dakota Water Resources Research Institute, Completion Report WI-221–013–72:1–11.

       Pike eggs hatched well in water of 1300 microhmos, but poorly at 4000 micromhos. No sac fry survived in water of 6000 microhmos.

PETERKA, J. J. and J. S. KENT

1976   Dissolved oxygen, temperature, survival of young at fish spawning sites. U.S. Environmental Protection Agency, National Environmental Research Center, Ecological Research Series EPA 600/3–76–113:1–36.

       Fluctuations of dissolved oxygen concentrations and water temperatures in their natural spawning sites were measured during embryo through larva stages of pike. Dissolved oxygen concentrations from combined measurements 1 and 10 cm from the bottom ranged from 0.0–16.6 mg/l, and water temperatures from 2.5–23.0 C; average daily fluctuations were 3.0 mg/l and 1.6 C.

PETERKA, J. J. and L. L. SMITH, JR.

1970   Lake whitefish in the commercial fishery of Red Lakes, Minnesota. Transactions of the American Fisheries Society 99:28–43.

       Pike made up 3% of the average annual catch for the years 1949–1961.

PETERS, J. C., ed.

1964   Summary of calculated growth data on Montana fishes, 1948–61. Montana Fish and Game Department, Dingell-Johnson Job Completion Report F-23-R-6 (Jobs 1–2):1–76.

PETERS, L., D. CAVIS and J. ROBERTSON

1978   Is *Diphyllobothrium latum* currently present in northern Michigan? Journal of Parasitology 64:947–949.

248

PETERSON, J., M. TAYLOR and A. HANSON

    1980   Leslie population estimate for a large lake. Transactions of the American Fisheries Society 109:329–331.

           The accuracy of a population estimate made by the Leslie removal method was evaluated for adult pike in a 288-hectare lake. The Leslie estimate of 6,290 fish was within 1% of that obtained from direct enumeration.

PETIT, G. D.

    1973   Effects of dissolved oxygen on survival and behavior of selected fishes of western Lake Erie. Bulletin of the Ohio Biological Survey, N.S. 4(4):1–76.

           A 3-year study to determine oxygen tolerances of young-of-the-year pike.

PETLINA, A. P.

    1980   Discussion of problems of fish culture in Siberia-Russian-SFSR, USSR. Voprosy Ikhtiologii 20:762–764.

PETROSKY, B. R. and J. J. MAGNUSON

    1973   Behavioral responses of northern pike, yellow perch and bluegill to oxygen concentrations under simulated winterkill conditions. Copeia 1973:124–133.

           Maximum ventilation rates occurred at 0.5 mg/l dissolved oxygen for pike, locomotory activity was greatest at 0.25 mg/l, and they began to move towards the surface at 0.5 mg/l.

PETRUSHEVSKII, G. K., ed.

    1961   Parasites and diseases of fish. Jerusalem, Israel Program for Scientific Translations. 338 pp.

PETTERSEN, S.

    1980   Supersaturation in water from Norwegian hydroelectric power station. *In* Tiews, K., ed., Aquaculture in heated effluents and recirculation systems. Berlin, Heenemann Verlagsgesellschaft, pp. 95–101.

           Supersaturation of gases was the likely cause of pike deaths downstream from the Rygene power plant.

PFLIEGER, W. L.

    1971   A distributional study of Missouri fishes. University of Kansas Publications, Museum of Natural History 20:225–570.

PHENICIE, C. K. and J. R. LYONS

    1973   Tactical planning in fish and wildlife management and research. U.S. Fish and Wildlife Service Resource Publication 123:1–22.

           A step-down plan for a pike artificial spawning marsh study is outlined as one system for developing a tactical plan.

PHILLIPS, C. L.

    1971   Fishery investigations. Warm water studies - northern pike. Rhode Island Division of Fish and Game, Project F-20-R-12/Job 4:1–7.

           Forty-two hundred pike were stocked through the ice in Worden Pond, Rhode Island, in late December. The winter ice fishery resulted in the examination of 420 adult pike. The following were studied: age and growth on 180 pike, fecundity of 18 pike, and stomach contents of 118 pike.

    1972   Fishery investigations. Warm water studies - northern pike. Rhode Island Division of Fish and Game, Project F-20-R-13/Job 4:1–6.

           Twenty-six hundred yearling pike were stocked in three Rhode Island water bodies in early December. The winter ice fishery resulted in the examination of 306 adult pike. Studied age and growth, stomach contents, and sex ratio.

1980   Study of northern pike in the Connecticut River. Connecticut Department of Environmental Protection, Project F-41-R:1–23.

Pike in the Connecticut River demonstrated fast growth, high natural mortality, and a relatively short life span of 8.41 years. Yield models were used to evaluate the effect of various minimum length limits on yield in weight, numbers, and number of trophy sized pike.

PHILLIPS, G. R. and R. W. GREGORY

1979   Assimilation efficiency of dietary methylmercury by northern pike (*Esox lucius*). Journal of the Fisheries Research Board of Canada 36:1516–1519.

Pike retained an average of 19% of the methylmercury ingested. The total amount increased with time (up to 42 d), but concentration in the tissue decreased due to growth dilution. Dietary source was young-of-the-year carp *Cyprinus carpio*.

PHILLIPS, G. R., T. E. LENHART and R. W. GREGORY

1980   Relation between trophic position and mercury accumulation among fishes from the Tongue River Reservoir, Montana. Environmental Research 22:73–80.

PHILLIPS, R.

1974   Dry diet trials. *In* Proceedings of the 6th Interstate Muskellunge Workshop, Morehead, 1974, pp. 10–13.

Outlines the methods and results of rearing pike on a dry diet.

PICHU, E. C.

1966   Rybochozjajstvenno-biologiceskoje znacenije scuki, okunja, sudaka i nalima v Pskovsko-Cudskom ozere. Gidrob. i ryb. choz, Psk. Cud. oz 4:235–247.

PICOS, C. A., G. NASTASESCU and G. IGNAT

1969   Comparative researches on the oxygen consumption of some freshwater species of fishes. Communications in Animal Physiology, pp. 89–94.

PIENING, H.

1970   Nurseries for northerns. Wisconsin Conservation Bulletin 35(4):10–11.

Reports a study of physical and biological requirements for pike spawning and makes recommendations for semi-natural developments that closely resemble natural spawning marshes.

PIETERS, H., J. SPEUR and P. G. WASSENAAR-SCHOLTZ

1983   Total mercury contents in fish species from Dutch surface waters in relation to biological parameter and pollution level. International Council for the Exploration of the Sea, Copenhagen, 1983. ICES-CM-1983/E:1–19.

PIEZ, K. A.

The amino acid chemistry of some calcified tissues. Annals of the New York Academy of Science, pp. 256–268.

PIEZ, K. A. and J. GROSS

1960   The amino acid composition of some fish collagens: the relation between composition and structure. Journal of Biological Chemistry 235:995–998.

PIHU, E.

1961   Biology of pike in Lake Vortsjarv. Loodus Selts. Tallinn 53:195–217. [English summary]

PIKHU, E. K. and E. R. PIKHU

1969   Seasonal changes in the nutrition of pike, perch, and burbot in Lake Pskov-Chudskoe. *In* Hydrobiology and fish farming in the inland reservoirs of the Baltic region, Tallin, Valgus Press. pp. 212–213.

250

PINCHER, C.
1948   A study of fish. New York, Duell, Sloan and Pearce. 343 pp.

PIPPING, M.
1927   Erganzende Beobachtungen uber den Geruchsinn der Fische mit besonderer Berucksichtigung seiner Bedeutung fur das Aufsuchen des Futters. Comment. Biol. Helsingf. 2(10):1–10.

PIROZHNIKOV, P. L., A. F. KARPEVICH, A. I. ISAYEV and V. I. KARPOVA
1969   Biological principles for improving fisheries in inland waters. Problems in Ichthyology 9:744–751.

PITCHER, T. J.
1980   Some ecological consequences of fish school volumes. Freshwater Biology 10:539–544.

PITKYANEN, G. B. and Y. A. ZAITSEV
1974   Characteristics of the radiation conditions of development of eggs of freshwater fishes belonging to different ecological groups. Ekologiya 5(6):73–75.

PITMAN, C. R. S.
1961   Waterfowl predation in Canada by the northern pike (or jackfish), *Esox lucius* L. Bulletin of the British Ornithology Club, N 82.

PIWERNETZ, D.
1968a   Zur Entwicklung der Schwanzflossenanlage bei Hechtlarven. Zoologischer Anzeiger 181(3/4):199–203.
1968b   Regeneration und Missbildung bei Verletzung embryonaler Flossenanlagen bei Hechtlarven (*Esox lucius* L.). Zeitschrift fuer Fischerei, N.S. 16(3/4):279–300. [English summary]

PJATECKIJ, V. E. and J. N. O. SAVCENKO
1969   Uber den Einfluss des Schleimes auf den hydrodynamischen Widerstand des Fischen. Bionika, Kiev 3:90–96.

PLACK, P. A.
1964   Retinal in eggs, blood and liver. Exploratory Eye Research 3:383–387.

PLACK, P. A. and S. K. KON
1961   A comparative survey of the distribution of vitamin A aldehyde in eggs. Biochemistry Journal 81:561–570.

PLATONOVA, O. P.
1966   The food of predatory fishes in the Sviyaga Inlet of Kuibyshev Reservoir. Kazansk University, pp. 111–151.
        A study of the qualitative and quantitative composition of the food and feeding rates of various age and size groups of pike during different seasons and years. Materials were collected from ecologically different areas of the inlet.

PLISZKA, F.
1956   Fizjologia ryb. [Physiology of fishes.] Lodz, PWN. 239 pp.
1964   Biologia ryb. [Fish biology.] Warsaw, PWRiL. 334 pp.

PLISZKA, F. R.
1954   Spostrzezenia nad xyplwem warunkow rozrodu ryb jeziorowych na liczebnosc populacji ich statiow mlodocianych. [The effect of spawning conditions in lakes on young fish populations.] Polskie Archiwum Hydrobiologii 1(14):165–188.
        A study of conditions of spawning, relations between fry, the loss of fry at the earliest times of life, as well as the various stages between the larvae and the early predatory and non-predatory fry.

PODDUBNY, A. G.

1976   Ecological topography of fish populations in reservoirs. New Delhi, Amerind.

PODDUBNYI, A. G., L. K. MALININ and V. V. GAIDUK

1970   Experiment in telemetric observations under ice of the behaviour of wintering
fish. Biologiya Vnutrennykh Vod Informatsionii Byulleten 6:65–70.

POJMANSKA, T., B. GRABDA-KAZUBSKA, S. L. KAZUBSKI, JADWIGA and K. NIEWIA-
DOMSKA

1980   Parasite fauna of five fish species from the Konin Lake complex artificially
heated with thermal effluents and from Lake Goplo, Poland. Acta Parasitologica Polonica 27:319–358.

POLLOCK, K. H. and R. H. K. MANN

1983   Use of an age-dependent mark-recapture model in fisheries research. Canadian Journal of Fisheries and Aquatic Sciences 40:1449–1455.

An age-dependent generalization of the Jolly Seber mark-recapture model for
fish populations subject to birth and migration is illustrated using data from a
study on pike in Dorset, England. These data show strong evidence of differential survival with age. The average annual survival rate is estimated to
be 50% for pike aged 2 or more years and 34% for those aged 1 year.

POLYAK, S.

1957   The vertebrate visual system. Chicago, The University of Chicaco Press.

PONEDELKO, B. I.

1957   Factors in distribution and numbers of eggs and larvae of phytophilous fish of
Lake Il'men. In Akatova, N. A., et al., eds., Transactions of the 6th Conference on Biology of Inland Waters, pp. 177–181.

POPOVA, O. A.

1960   Nekotorye osobennosti ekologii shchuki i okunya v del'te Volgi. [Some
features of the ecology of the pike and perch in the Volga delta.] Voprosy
Ikhtiologii 15:55–70.

Information on growth rate, nutritional status, and fertility in the lower and
middle zones of the delta. Recommendations are made for the regulation of
the numbers of predatory fish in the different zones of the delta.

1961   O vozdeistvii shchuki i okunya na populyatsiyu nekotorykh ryb v del'te
Volgi. [Effect of pike and perch on the population of some fish in the Volga
Delta.] Trudy Soveshchanii Ikhtiologicheskoi Komissii Akademii Nauk
SSSR 13:283–289.

1962   Nekotorye osobennosti ekologii shchuki i okunya v del'te Volig. [Some
features of the ecology of the pike and perch in the Volga Delta.] Anales del
Instituto Forestal de Investigaciones y Experiencias Madrid.

1965   Ekologiya shchuki i okunya v del'te Volgi. [The ecology of pike and perch in
the Volga dalta.] In The food of predaceous fishes and their relationships
with their food organisms. Moscow, Nauka, pp. 91–172.

Changes in the ecology of the delta due to dams (1954–55), regulation of
water flow (1966), and a decrease in the water level of the Caspain Sea were
investigated. The differences in size, age, sex composition, spawning patterns, and survival rates of spawn and fry were recorded. The size-age structure of the pike population and the feeding relationship between pike and
perch are discussed.

1967   The 'predator-prey' relationship among fish. *In* Gerking, S. D., ed., The biological basis of freshwater fish production. IBP Symposium, Reading, 1966, pp. 359–376.

1971   Biological indices of the pike and perch in waters with different hydrologic regimes and feeding capacities. *In* Patterns of growth and maturation of fishes. Moscow, Nauka, pp. 102–153.

PORTER, L. R.

1977   Review of selected literature on muskellunge life history, ecology and management. Minnesota Department of Natural Resources, Division of Fish and Wildlife, Section Fisheries, Special Publication 119:1–81.

POTOPOVA, O. I.

1966   Some aspects of the reproduction and spawning grounds of Karelian pike. Trudy Karel'skogo Otdeleniya Gosudarstvennogo Nauchno-Issledovatel'-skoto Instituta Ozernogo i Rechnogo Rybnogo Khozyaistva 4(2):36–46. [in Russian]

POTVIN, C.

1973   Inventaire ichthyologique du bassin de la riviere des Envies. Decouverte de populations indigenes de maskinonge. Travaux en Cours, Service de la Faune du Quebec, Rapport 7:105–121.

POUPE, J.

1973   Note on growth of the pike, *Esox lucius* Linnaeus, 1758 in the central Bohemian inundation area of the River Labe. Vestnik Ceskoslovenske Spolecnosti Zoologicke 38:279–284.
          A study of the scales of pike captured mostly during seining operations in the Central Bohemian inundation area of the river Labe. The growth of pike there is faster; it is only a little slower than in Ireland and North America, where the largest increments were observed.

POUVREAU, M.

1980   Etude du cycle sexual femelle du brochet, *Esox lucius* L., et de quelques problemes lies a l'induction de la ponte. Dipl. Etudes Approf. Univ. Poitiers, Ecophysiologie Reproduction, 29 pp.

POUVREAU, M., G. MAISSE, B. JALABERT and B. BRETON

1983   Efficacite du controle de l'ovulation par traitement gonadotrope dans und population heterogene de brochet (*Esox lucius*): relation avec le stade ovocytaire et comparaison avec les resultats d'ovulations spontanees. *In* Billard, R., ed., Le brochet gestion deans le milieu naturel et elevage. Paris, Institute National de la Recherche Agronomique, pp. 85–95.
          A single injection of partially purified salmon gonadotropic hormone was given to 122 female pike. The best efficiency was observed when injections were performed at the stage of peripheral germinal vesicle, but the number of ova produced was lower than after spontaneous ovulation.

POWELL, T. G.

1972a   Warm water fisheries investigations. Northern pike introductions. Colorado Game, Fish and Parks Department, Fish Research Review Project F-34-R-7/Job 3:1–9.

1972b   Northern pike in Colorado. Fishery information leaflet number 19. Outdoor facts. Colorado Game, Fish and Parks Department, Report F-34-R:1–2.
          General information on size, appearance, spawning, early life, habitat management, and stocking to control sunfish populations.

1972c   Warmwater fisheries investigations. Northern pike introductions. Colorado Game, Fish and Parks Department, Report F-34-R-7/Job 3:1–9.
In 1971, 2,000 pike were stocked in Carbody Reservoir. Gill net catches were analysed by various statistical tests. Determined the effect of introductions on the fish population structure.

1973   Effect of northern pike introductions on an overabundant crappie population. Colorado Division of Wildlife, Special Report 31:1–6.
In 1969 subadult and fingerling pike were successfully planted in the Carbody Reservoir for crappie population control. Increased average size of age group III crappies and a levelling off of the abundance cycle resulted. Stocking recommendations for panfish control are provided.

PRAKKEN, R., J. BEKENDAM and G. A. PIETERS
1955   The chromosomes of *Esox lucius* L. Genetica 27:484–488.
Pike was found to have 48 rod-shaped chromosomes with completely terminal centromeres. In previous work done by Svardson and Wickbom (1939) the somatic number of chromosomes was found to be 18. Differences in methods used may explain the discrepancy of the results.

PRATT, H. S.
1935   A manual of land and fresh water vertebrate animals of the United States, 2nd ed. P. Blakiston's Son. 416 pp.

PRATT, K.
1975   Rearing tiger muskies on artificial diets. Proceedings of the 7th Interstate Musky Workshop, La Crosse, 1975, pp. 25–33.
Discusses rearing the pike-muskellunge hybrid at the Wolf Lake Hatchery, Michigan, in 1975. Artificial food was used during the 90-day rearing program with good success. Observations on survival rates, weight gains, water quality, behaviour, rearing problems and successes, and techniques are presented.

PRAVDA, O.
1973   On the influence of herbicides on some freshwater animals. Hydrobiologia 42:97–142. [in German, English abstract]
Toxicity of 14 herbicides was determined for 13 animal species, including pike. The organisms were divided into four groups according to their sensitivity to herbicides.

PRAVDINA, N. I. and M. A. CHEBOTAREVA
1971   Fatty-acids of the phospholipids from the vertebrate brain. Zhurnal Evolyutsionnoi Biokhimii i Fiziologii 7:30–39.

PRAVDINA, N. I., M. A. CHEBOTAREVA and E. E. KRUGLOVA
1974   Sphingomyelin fatty-acids in myelin and mitochondria in vertebrates. Zhurnal Evolyutsionnoi Biokhimii i Fiziologii 10:325–330.

PRAWOCHENSKI, R.
1976   Rybactwo. [Fisheries.] Warsaw, PWN. 172 pp.

PREBLE, E. A.
1908   A biological investigation of the Athabaska-MacKenzie region. U.S. Department of Agriculture, North American Fauna 27:1–574.

PREFONTAINE, G.
1941   Etude biologique des eaux de la plaine de Montreal Quebec Ministere de la Chasse et de la Peche, Rapport de la Station Biologique de Montreal et de la Station Biologique du Parc des Laurentides 1:34–66.

PREISSER, E.

1976   Investigations on the mass cultivation of zooplankton and its use for rearing artificially brooded edible fish together with a summary of previous experience in this field. Wissenschaftliche Zeitschrift der Universitaet Rostock Mathematisch-Naturwissenschaftliche Reihe 25:327–332.

PREUDHOMME, J.-C.

1965   Notes techniques explicatives se rapportant aux discussions du comite de la peche. Magazine Fishing Club du Moyen-Atlas, Revue Annuelle, pp. 13–18.

1976   Troubles sexuels resultant de l'acclimation chez les poissons, notamment brochet et truite arc-en-ciel. Pisciculture Francais 43:38–46.

PRIBYSLAVSKY, J. and Z. LUCKY

1967   Parasite fauna of the fish in the reservoir of Kninicky. II. Results of invesgiations of parasites of several prey fish. Acta Universitatis Agriculturae Facultas Veterinaria 36:137–145.

PRICE, C. E.

1969   Report on an unpublished manuscript: the first study of Danish freshwater monogenetic trematodes. Revista Iberica de Parasitologia 29(2/3):233–234.

PRICE, J. W.

1957   Embryonic development of the northern pike, *Esox lucius* Linn., at the St. Mary's Fish Farm, spring 1956. Ohio Department of Natural Resources, unpublished MS. 16 pp.

PRIEGEL, G. R.

1965   Statewide fishery research. Movement and harvest of stocked northern pike. Wisconsin Conservation Department, Dingell-Johnson Report F-83-R-1/Wk.Pl.16/Job A:1–4.

1967   Statewide fishery research. Lake Winnebago studies. Movement and harvest of stocked northern pike. Wisconsin Conservation Department, Dingell-Johnson Report F-83-R-2/Wk.Pl. 05/Job G.

1968a   Movement and harvest of tagged northern pike released in Lake Poygan and Big Lake Butte des Morts. Wisconsin Department of Natural Resources, Research Report Fisheries 29:1–7.
Describes an investigation of the movement and harvest of pike captured in Rush Lake during winter rescue operations and released into waters containing an excellent natural northern pike population.

1968b   Northerns, Swedish style. Wisconsin Conservation Bulletin, January-February 1968, pp. 18–19.

1969   Statewide fishery research. Factors influencing success of northern pike reproduction in natural and artificial spawning areas. Wisconsin Conservation Department, Project F-83-R-5/Job 15:1–4.
Two spawning marshes were stocked with brood fish, then they were drained to capture the fingerlings. In the artificial area, the fingerlings were tagged and released and recaptured in November to determine survival.

PRIEGEL, G. R. and D. C. KROHN

1971   Statewide fishery research. Northern pike spawning in Gilbert and Big Cedar Lakes, Washington County. Wisconsin Conservation Department, Project F-83-R-6:1–26.
Egg density associated with vegetation, condition of spawners, egg development and survival, movement of adult fish, average length of male and female

spawners. Spawning was observed from March 25 through the first week in April.

1973 Characteristics of a northern pike spawning population. Wisconsin Department of Natural Resources, Technical Bulletin 86:1–18.

The Gilbert Lake population was studied in 1968 and 1969 to describe characteristics of the spawning habitat, early life history, spawning population, and to determine the extent of angler harvest.

PRINCE, E. E.

1896 On the Esocidae of Canada. Report of the British Association for the Advancement of Science 66:688.

PRITCHARD, D. L., O. D. MAY and L. RIDER

1976 Stocking of predators in the predation stocking evaluation reservoirs. Presented at the 13th Annual Conference, Southeastern Association of Game and Fish Commissioners.

PRIVOLNEV, T. I.

1951 Transportation of live fish. Moscow, Pishchepromizdat. [in Russian]

1954 Physiological adaptations of fishes to new conditions of existence. Trudy Soveshchanii Ikhtiologicheskoi Komissii Akademi Nauk SSSR 3:40–49. (Trans. from Russian by Risheries Research Board of Canada Translation Series 422, 1963.)

1963 Threshold concentration of oxygen in water for fish at different temperatures. Doklady Akademii Nauk SSSR, Biological Science Section 151:439–440. (Trans. published by National Science Foundation, 1964.)

1964a Relationship of freshwater and diadromous fishes to different salinities. Izvestiya Gosudarstvennogo Nauchno-Issledovatel'skogo Instituta Ozernogo i Rechnogo Rybnogo Khozvaistva USSR 58:58–83. [English summary]

The tolerance of fishes to various concentrations of dissolved salt was studied experimentally. Seventeen species of fish were kept in aquaria at different salinities for 15–20 days. According to salinity tolerance, the fishes are divided into two groups. Group I includes fishes, such as pike, capable of withstanding a salinity not higher than 10–12%.

1964b On the respiratory coefficient of fishes. Izvestiya Gosudarstvennogo Nauchno-Issledovatel'skogo Instituta Ozernogo i Rechnogo Rybnogo Khozvaistva USSR 58:123–127.

PRIVOLNEV, T. I. and N. V. KOROLEVA

1953 Critical concentrations of oxygen for fish at different temperature in different seasons of the year. Doklady Akademii Nauk SSSR 89:175–176. [in Russian]

PROKOPENKO, L. I., A. S. ARTAMOSHIN and A. A. FROLOVA

1978 Distribution of diphyllobothriasis in the USSR and prevention of the formation of new foci of invasion. Part 2. The role of migration of the USSR population in the dissemination and importation of diphyllobothriasis. Meditsinskaya Parazitologiya i Parazitarnye Bolezni 47(2):10–14.

PRONINA, S. V.

1977a Changes in argyrophilic liver stroma in some fishes during infection with the pleurocercoids of *Triaenophorus nodulosus* and *Diphyllobothrium dendriticum* Cestoidea Pseudophyllidea. Parazitologiya 11:361–364.

1977b Cytochemical characteristics of labrocyte-like cells in the capsule of cestode plerocercoids *Triaenophorus nodulosus* and *Diphyllobothrium dendriticum*.

Arkhiv Anatomii Gistologii i Embriologii 73:108–112. [in Russian]

PRONINA, S. V., E. D. LOGACHEV and N. M. PRONIN

1981   Carbohydrate containing biopolymers of plerocercoid cestodes of the order Pseudophyllidea and capsules surrounding them. Izvestiya Sibirskogo Otdeleniya Akademii Nauk SSR, Seriya Biologo-Meditsinskikh Nauk 2:121–127.

PRONINA, S. V. and N. M. PRONIN

1982   The effect of cestode (*Trianophorus nodulosus*) infestation on the digestive tract of pike (*Esox lucius*). Journal of Ichthyology 22:105–113.
        Histological and histochemical structure of normal and cestode infested digestive tracts of pike were studied. Significant histopathological disturbances were observed not only at the places of contact between the parasite and the host, but also in the entire mucosa of the stomach and intestine.

PROROK, P.

1983   Early summer lunker pike. In-Fisherman 49:70–92.

PROTAL, J.

1947   Observations sur la pisciculture artificielle du brochet. Bulletin Francais de Pisciculture 147:61–70.

PROTASOWICKI, M. and A. OCIEPA

1978   Wplyw wieku, ciezaru i plci na zawartosc rteci w miesniach i wybranych narzadach szczupaka (*Esox lucius* L.). [Effect of age, weight and sex on the mercury content in the muscles and selected organs of northern pike (*Esox lucius* L.).] Zeszyty Naukowe Akademii Rolniczo, Szczecin, Ser. Rybactwo Morskie, 9(70):145–155.
        Average levels of mercury in muscles, kidney, liver, food tract, spleen, gills, and gonads.

PUCILOWSKA, A.

1969   Dynamics of infection with endoparasites of fishes in the Zergrzynski Reservoir. Acta Parasitologica Polonica 16(1/19):33–46.

PUPYRNIKOVA, A. V.

1953   Seasonal variation in feeding and growth of young pike. Trans. USSR Inst. Fish Ocean. VNIRO 24:338–345.
        During spring and summer, accumulation of body protein was accompanied by an increase in length and weight. Fat was accumulated in winter and only weight increased. Relative size of 24 hour food ration decreased as pike switched from plankton to predatory feeding and decreased again as the winter months approached. Duration of winter had no effect on survival rate.

PUTNAM, F. W.

1861   On the young of *Pomotis brythus* and *Esox*. Proceedings of the Boston Society of Natural History 7(3):34.

QADRI, S. U. and P. J. RUBEC
  1977   Age, growth and population density of brown bullhead, northern pike, walleye, sauger and yellow perch in a 3 mile section of the Ottawa River. Ottawa River Project Progress Report, 60 pp.
QUEBEC MINISTERE DES PECHERIES ET DE LA CHASSE
  1961   List of species known to occur in Verendrye Park. Journal de bord, de l'office de biologie, 4(76).
QUEBEC MINISTERE DU TOURISME, DE LA CHASSE, ET DE LA PECHE
  1966   Les poissons combative du Quebec. [Quebec sport fishes.] Province du Quebec. 41 pp.
QUEIRAZZA, G., E. SMEDILE and E. TIBALDI
  1969   On the transfer of some radioactive isotopes through a food chain in a river. Atti dell'Accademia Nazionale dei Lincei Rendiconti Classe di Scienze Fisiche Matematiche et Naturali 46:81–90.
QUIGLEY, D. T.
  1982   Ireland's specimen pike. Coarse Angler 6(6):22–24.
QUILLIER, R. and R. LABAT
  1977   Mise au point sur la reproduction des esocides; etude preliminarire. [Study on the reproduction of Esocidae; preliminary investigation.] Investigacion Pesquera 41:33–38. [in French]
          Various methods of controlling the reproduction of pike are considered: to have a supply of sexually mature specimens, to trigger spawning in the female, to reconstitute milt in the male. The use of heterologous gonadotropins to induce maturation and ovoposition is one possibility; hormonotherapy with delay steroids has allowed abundant milt to be obtained.
QVENILD, T.
  1981   The fisheries in Lake Randsfjorden, Norway, 1978–1980. Fauna 34: 116–122.

RAAT, A. J. P.
1987   Synopsis of the biological data on the northern pike *Esox lucius* Linnaeus 1758. Fisheries and Agricultural Organization Fisheries Synopsis 30(rev. 2). The most up-to-date synopsis of pike literature and biology.

RADCLIFFE, W.
1921   Fishing from the earliest times. London.
Has notes re pike and ponds in the Middle Ages.

RADFORTH, I.
1944   Some considerations on the distribution of fishes in Ontario. Contributions of the Royal Ontario Museum of Zoology 25:1–116.
Contains a brief note on the distribution of pike throughout the world.

RAFFIN, J. P. and C. LERAY
1980   Comparative study on amp deaminase EC-3.5.4.6 in gill muscle and blood of fish. Comparative Biochemistry and Physiology, B, Comparative Biochemistry 67:533–540.

RAGAN, J. E.
1970   Statewide fisheries investigations. Management surveys of the Missouri River and its mainstem reservoirs in North Dakota. North Dakota State Game and Fish Department, Project F-2-R-17, Job 1.
In 1975, 1,441 pike were tagged to study movement in two large reservoirs, Lake Oahe and Lake Sakakawea. Pike movements in Lake Oahe ranged from 59 miles upstream to 58 miles downstream. Lake Sakakawea pike moved upstream 13 miles and downstream 38 miles.

1975   Mortality and movement of adult walleye and pike. North Dakota Game and Fish Department, Dingell-Johnson Project F-2-R-23, Study 4, Jobs 4-A and 4-B.

RAHN, J.
1972   Hy produktion in Intensivanlagen. Zeitschrift fuer Binnenfischerei 19:124–127.

1978   Wasserzufuhr und Sauerstoffverhaeltnisse in Zuger Glaesern dei der Hechter-bruetung. [Water addition and oxygen ratio in Zuger glasses in pike rearing]. Zeitschrift fuer die Binnenfischerei der DDR 25(2):39–43.
The quantity of water flowing through the Zuger glasses and consequently the oxygen supply to the eggs is an important factor for the successful rearing of pike. At the Eldenburg breeding station a flow of 2.3–3.0 l/min from the 30 d.degree to 4–7 l/min for the 40 d.degree. The quantity of oxygen transported to the eggs was not fully used. The reasons for this and the necessary conditions for optimum oxygen use are discussed.

RAHN, M.
1975   New method tempts northern pike. Fins and Feathers, February 1975.
Describes a method of fishing for pike through the ice, using large, dead suckers and minnows.

RAJAD, M.
n.d.   Note sur l'introduction du brochet au Maroc. Morrocco Ministere de l'Agriculture, Service de la Peche, unpublished MS. 3 pp. [in French]
A history of the introduction of pike in Morocco is reviewed, and culture and artificial propagation are detailed. The methods of collection, fertilization, and culture of the eggs are explained. The fry are reared in nursery ponds for 4–6 weeks and are then stocked.

RAMANUJAM, S. G. M.

1966   The study of the development of the vertebral column in teleosts, as shown in the life history of the herring. Proceedings of the Zoological Society of London 3:365–414.

RANDOW, F. and H. A. SCHULZE

1971   Studies on the artificial radioactivity of fish in 1967 and 1968. Nahrung 15:81–89.

RANEY, E. C.

1955   Natural hybrids between two species of pickerel (*Esox*) in Stearns Pond, Massachusetts. *In*Supplement to fisheries report for some central, eastern, and western Massachusetts lakes, ponds, and reservoirs, 1951–1952. Massachusetts Bureau of Wildlife Resource Management, Division of Fish and Game. 447 pp.

1959   Some young fresh-water fishes of New York. New York State Conservationist, August-September 1959, pp. 22–28.
        Contains a brief and general description of spawning, distribution, size, growth, migration, and early life history of pike. The destruction of spawning habitat by shoreline construction is mentioned.

RANEY, E. C. and W. H. MASSMAN

1953   The fishes of the tidewater section of the Pamunkey River, Virginia. Journal of the Washington Academy of Science 43:424–432.

RATHBUN, R. and W. WAKEHAM

1897   Report of the joint commission relative to the preservation of the fisheries in waters contiguous to Canada and the United States. U.S. House Document 315, 54th Congress, Second Session, 1897, pp. 14–178.

RATHKE, M. H.

1824   Beitrage zur Geschichte der Thierwelt. Neuer Schrift Naturforschung Ges Danzig, Heft 1–4.

RAWSON, D. S.

1932   The pike of Waskesiu Lake, Saskatchewan. Transactions of the American Fisheries Society 62:323–330.
        The study was conducted because fishing pressure may have resulted in a marked decrease in angling success. The fish were examined during the spawning period, from May 12 to mid June 1932, for information on life history, growth rate, and population size.

1947a   Northwest Canadian fisheries survey. Fisheries Research Board of Canada, Bulletin 72:45–68.
        Mentions habitat, predatory habits, and parasites of pike in Great Slave Lake.

1947b   Northwest fisheries survey. Fisheries Research Board of Canada, Bulletin 72:69–85.
        Reports on parasites and domestic use of pike in Lake Athabasca.

1947c   Estimating the fish population of Great Slave Lake. Transactions of the American Fisheries Society 77:81–92.

1948   The failure of rainbow trout and initial success with the introduction of lake trout in Clear Lake, Riding Mountain Park, Manitoba. Transactions of the American Fisheries Society 75:323–335.
        Briefly mentions pike in the lake and the effects that changing water levels had on the population. Predation by pike was also considered partly responsible for the destruction of the rainbow trout *Salmo gairdneri* population.

1949   A check list of the fishes of Saskatchewan. Saskatchewan Department of
        Natural Resources and Industrial Development, Report of the Royal Commis-
        sion on Fisheries. 8 pp.

1951   Studies of the fish of Great Slave Lake. Journal of the Fisheries Research
        Board of Canada 8:207–240.

1957   Limnology and fisheries of five lakes in the Upper Churchill drainage,
        Saskatchewan. Saskatchewan Department of Natural Resources, Fish
        Branch, Fisheries Report 3:7–61.
        Pike are present in the lakes, grow rather slowly, and eat small fish, amphi-
        pods, and chiromids.

1959   Limnology and fisheries of Cree and Wollaston lakes in northern
        Saskatchewan. Saskatchewan Department of Natural Resources, Fisheries
        Report 4:5–73.
        Pike in Cree Lake eat a variety of fish and grow slowly.

1960a   Five lakes on the Churchill River near Stanley, Saskatchewan. Saskatchewan
        Department of Natural Resources, Fish Branch, Fisheries Report 5:1–38.
        Information on numbers caught in test nets, growth rate, food, parasites, and
        angling fishery.

1960b   A limnological comparison of twelve large lakes in northern Saskatchewan.
        Limnology and Oceanography 5:195–211.
        Pike inhabit all of the lakes, but are considerably more numerous in the south.

RAWSON, D. S. and F. M. ATTON
1953   Biological investigation and fisheries management at Lac la Ronge,
        Saskatchewan. Saskatchewan Department of Natural Resources, Fisheries
        Branch, pp. 7–39.

RAWSON, D. S. and J. E. MOORE
1944   The saline lakes of Saskatchewan. Canadian Journal of Research
        22:141–201.
        Pike is considered to be a dominant species throughout lakes with salinities
        <15,000 ppm.

RAY, J.
        Kansas and the great northern. Fish and Game 23(3):3–4.
        Popular account on experimental stocking, description of appearance, spawn-
        ing habits, and advice on angling and preparation for eating.

REAY, G. A.
1939   The nitrogen extractives of fish. Report of the Food Investigation Board
        1938:87–89.

REECE, M.
1963   Fish and fishing Meredith Press. 224 p.

REED, E. B.
1962   Limnology and fisheries of the Saskatchewan River in Saskatchewan.
        Saskatchewan Fisheries Report 6:1–48.
        Pike is classified as a species of secondary importance, but one of the chief
        angling species.

REED, G. B. and G. C. TONER
1941   Red sore disease of pike. Canadian Journal of Research 19:139–143.
        Common in pike in eastern Ontario waters, the disease is caused by infection
        with *Proteus hydrophilus*, which is also responsible for "red leg" disease in
        frogs and may cause "ulcer disease" in trout in a New York hatchery.

1942	*Proteus hydrophilus* infections of pike, trout and frogs. Canadian Journal of Research 20:161–166.

REGAN, C. T.

1911	The freshwater fishes of the British Isles. London, Methuen. 287 pp.

REGIER, H. A.

Changes in species composition of Great Lakes fish communities caused by man. Proceedings of the 44th North American Wildlife Conference, pp. 558–566.

REGIUS, K.

1921	Ein Hecht im Freilandbecken. Blattchen Aquarien und Terrarien Kunde.

REHBROUN

1965	Eine ambulante Hechterbrutungsanlage. Allgemeine Fischerei-Zeitung 90(5):130–132.

REICHENBACH, S. F. and H. H. KLINKE

1961	Beitrag zur Fleckenseuche des Hechtes. Allgemeine Fischerei-Zeitung 86:310–311.

REICHENBACH-KLINKE, H. H.

1966	Krankheiten und Schadigungen der Fische. Stuttgart, Gustav Fischer Verlag. 389 pp.

1970	Die wichtigsten Nutzfischarten der Donau und ihre mutmassliche Verteilung. [The main commercial fishes of the Danube and their supposed distribution.] Archiv fuer Hydrobiologie Suppl. 36(2/3):263–278.

About 4.4 million kg of fish are caught annually in the Danube. An attempt is made to show how this catch is distributed by individual species; pike is a predominant species.

1971	On a new disease of the skin of salmoids in central Europe. Rivista Italiana di Piscic. Ittiopatologia 6:17–18.

1974	The manifestation types of ulcerative dermal necrosis. Muench Beitraege zur Abwasser-Fischerei- und Flussbiologie 25:47–54.

REID, D. J.

1977	1977 spring pike spearing creel census. Ontario Ministry of Natural Resources, unpublished MS. 29 pp.

From March 21 till April 17, an estimated 1,108 pike were harvested, 75.4% of which were females.

REIFEL, C. W. and A. A. TRAVILL

1978a	Gross morphology of alimentary canal in 10 teleostean species. Anatomischer Anzeiger 144:441–449.

1978b	Structure and carbohydrate histochemistry of the stomach in eight species of teleosts. Journal of Morphology 158:155–168.

Esocids have the simplest looking stomachs, which consist of spindle-shaped expansions of the fore-gut. Presumably, their straightness and length allow an entire ingested fish to be accommodated easily.

REIGHARD, J.

1915	An ecological reconnaissance of the fishes of Douglas Lake, Cheboygan County, Michigan, in midsummer. U.S. Bureau of Fisheries Bulletin 33:215–249.

REIGHARD, J. E.

1914	A plea for the preservation of records concerning fish. Transactions of the American Fisheries Society 43:106–110.

REIST, J. D.

1978   Predation as a factor in maintaining the pelvic polymorphism in a central Alberta population of *Culaea inconstans* (Kirtland) (Pisces : Gasterosteidae). M.S. thesis, University of Alberta. 177 pp.

1980   Selective predation upon pelvic phenotypes of brook stickleback, *Culaea inconstans*, by northern pike, *Esox lucius*. Canadian Journal of Zoology 58:1245–1252.
Laboratory and field work assessed the importance of pike predation in maintaining pelvic skeletal phenotypes in a population of brook stickleback. Individuals possessing a pelvis and pelvic spines had a selective advantage over those lacking these parts. The advantage conferred by the spines depended upon relative size of predator to prey, and likely has no effect upon predation by larger pike.

1983a   Studies on the systematic significance of the external body morphometry of esocoid fishes. Ph.D. thesis, University of Toronto.

1983b   Behavioral variation in pelvic phenotypes of brook stickleback, *Culaea inconstans*, in response to predation by northern pike, *Esox lucius*. Environmental Biology of Fishes 8(3/4):255–267.
Populations of brook stickleback from Alberta and Saskatchewan exhibit phenotypic variation in expression of the pelvic skeleton and associated spines, from complete presence through intermediate forms to complete absence. Such variation influences predation by pike, which prefer the least spiny prey.

1985   An empirical evaluation of several univariate methods that adjust for size variation in morphometric data. Canadian Journal of Zoology 63:1429–1439.
An extensive set of morphological data collected from 300 pike from five geographic regions from both Europe and North America is examined to determine what analytical procedures should be used to reduce the effect of size variation.

REMBISZEWSKI, J. M. and H. ROLIK

1975   Katalog fauny Polski kraglouste i ryby. [Catalogue of the fauna of Poland Cyclostomata and Pisces.] Polish Academy of Sciences, Institute of Zoology. 252 pp.

REMOROV, V. A.

1966   Motor function in the stomach of the pike (*Esox lucius* L.) and the influence on it of transection of the vagus nerves. Fiziologicheskii Zhurnal SSSR Imeni I. M. Sechenova 51:613–620.

RENAULD, R.

1953   Le brochet. Ses moeurs.—Ses peches. Paris, Bornemann, p. 128.

REPERANT, J., M. LEMIRE, D. MICELI and J. PEYRICHOUX

1976   A radioautographic study of the visual system in freshwater teleosts following intraocular injection of tritiated fucose and proline. Brain Research 118:123–131.

REZNICHENKO, P. N.

1956a   O ritmakh dvizhenii embrionov nekotorykh kostistykh ryb. [On the movement rhythm of embroys of some bony fish (Teleostei).] *In* Soveshchanie po biologicheskim osnovam rybnogo khozyaistvo. Tezisy dokladov, pp. 35–36.

1956b   Protsess stanovleniya embrional'noi motoriki shchuki v khode ontogeneze. [Development process of the embryonic motor system of pike in the course of ontogeny.] *In* Tezisy dokladov na soveshchanii po izucheniy fiziologii ryb, pp. 57–59.

1958   Ontogenez embrional 'noi motoriki schuki. [The ontogenesis of the embryonic motor activity in the pike.] Trudy Soveshchanii Ikhtiologicheskoi Komissii Akademii Nauk SSSR 8:393–409.

Movements of the pike embryo were observed from fertilization to hatching. The effects of temperature, oxygen, and carbon dioxide were studied using kymography and time photography. Two stages of embryonic motor activity were identified, protoplasmic and neuromuscular activity.

REZNICHENKO, P. N., N. V. KOTLYAREVSKAYA and M. V. GULIDOV

1966   Demonstration of specific ecological features of pike spawn in relation to temperature by incubation at constant temperature. Proceedings of All-Union Congress on the Ecological Physiology of Fishes, Moscow.

1967   Survival rates of pike spawn incubated at constant temperature. *In* Morpho-ecological Analysis of the Development of Fishes. Moscow, Nauka.

RHODES, C. J. and W. BARKER

1953   Alaska's fish and wildlife. U.S. Fish and Wildlife Service, Circular 17:1–60.

RHUDE, L.

1980   Driedmeat Lake - northern pike tagging study. Alberta Department of Energy and Natural Resources.

RIBELIN, W. E. and G. MIGAKI, eds.

1975   The pathology of fishes. Madison, The University of Wisconsin Press.

RICHARD, A.

1979   Recherches sur les etangs. Contribution a l'etude du brochet (*Esox lucius* L. 1758). Croissance et population. Institute National de la Recherche Agronomique, Ecologie Hydrobiologique Rennes.

RICHARDS, B. and N. FICKLING

1979   Zander. London, A. & C. Black.

RICHARDSON, J.

1836   The fish. Part 3. Fauna Boreali-Americana; or the zoology of the northern parts of British America; containing descriptions of the objects of natural history collected on the late northern land expeditions under command of Sir John Franklin, R. N. London, R. Bently. 327 pp.

RICHARDSON, J. R.

1823   Notice of the fishes. *In* Franklin, J., ed., Narrative of a journey to the shores of the Polar Sea in the years 1819, 1820, 1821 and 1822. London, John Murray, pp. 705–728.

1836   Fishes. *In* Back, G., ed., Narrative of the Arctic Land Expedition of the mouth of the Great Fish River and along the shores of the Arctic Ocean in the years 1833, 1834, and 1835. London, John Murray, pp. 518–522.

RICHARDSON, L. R.

1935   The freshwater fishes of south eastern Quebec. Ph.D. thesis, McGill University.

1941   The parasites of the fishes of Lake Wakonichi, central northern Quebec. Transactions of the American Fisheries Society 71:286–289.

1944   Brief record of fishes from central northern Quebec. Copeia 1944:205–208.

RICKARDS, B.

1976   Pike fishing step by step. London, Cassells.

1978   Tarbet turns up trumps. Angler's Mail, April 12, 1978, pp. 8–9.
        Advice on suitable location and tackle for angling at Loch Lomond, Scotland,
        based on author's trip there. Photographs of trip.

1980   Pike killing: the big con. Coarse Fisherman, December 1980, pp. 32–33.
        An attempt to persuade anglers not to remove big pike.

1984   The great Irish folly. Coarse Fisherman, April 1984, pp. 42–43.
        Contains tables that record numbers and tonnage of pike killed by the Irish
        Inland Fisheries Trust.

RICKARDS, B. and R. WEBB
1971   Fishing for big pike. London, A. & C. Black.

RICKARDS, B. and K. WHITEHEAD
1976   Plugs and plug fishing. London, A. &. C. Black.
1977   Spinners, spoons and wobbled baits. London, A. & C. Black.

RICKER, W. E.
1975   Computation and interpretation of biological statistics of fish populations.
        Fisheries Research Board of Canada Bulletin 191:1–382.

RICKER, W. E., ed.
1968   Methods for assessment of fish production in fresh waters. Oxford,
        Blackwells. IBP Handbook No. 3. 313 pp.

RIDENHOUR, R. L.
1955   The northern pike, *Esox lucius* L., population of Clear Lake, Iowa. M.S.
        thesis, Iowa State University.

1957   Northern pike, *Esox lucius* L., population of Clear Lake, Iowa. Iowa State
        College Journal of Science 32:1–18.
        Gill nets, fyke nets, wire traps, and angling were used to collect 445 pike
        from 1941 to 1955 in Clear Lake and adjacent Ventura Marsh. Growth and
        condition of pike from the lake, marsh, and other systems were compared.
        Angler tag returns were used to estimate harvest. The lake was stocked in
        1953.

1960   Abundance, growth, and food of young game fish in Clear Lake, Iowa, 1949
        to 1957. Iowa State Journal of Science 35:1–23.

RIEHL, R. and K. J. GOETTING
1975   Structure and development of the micropyles in the oocytes of some freshwa-
        ter teleosts. Zoologischer Anzeiger 195:363–373.

RIEHL, R. and E. SCHULTE
1977   Vergleichende rasterelektronenmicroskopische Untersuchungen an den
        Mikropylen ausgewaehlter Suesswasser-Teleosteer. [Scanning electron
        microscopical investigations of the micropyles of selected freshwater teleost
        fishes]. Archiv fuer Fischereiwissenschaft 28(2–3):95–107.
        Criteria based on micropyles can be used for the identification of eggs. Pike
        eggs can be fertilized when their micropyles are clogged. This explains why
        egg envelopes must also be penetrable for sperm at other places.

1978   Bestimmungsschlussel der wichtigsten deutschen Susswasser-Teleosteer
        anhand ihrer Eier. [An identification key of the most important German
        freshwater teleost fishes by means of their eggs.] Archiv fuer Hydrobiologie
        83:200–212.

RIEMENS, R. G.
1977   Overleving van snoek die met de hengel is gevangen en meteen daarna is
        teruggezet. [Survival of northern pike capture by angling and released

265

immediately after capture.] Annual Report Organisatie ter Verbetering van de Binnenvisserij 1975/1976:67–83. [in Dutch, English summary]

1978   De invloed van geslikte enkele en drietandige haken op de overleving van de hengelgevangen snoek. [The influence of swallowed single and treble hooks on the survival of northern pike caught by angling.] Annual Report Organisatie ter Verbetering van de Binnenvisserij 1977/1978:60–68. [in Dutch, English summary]

RIPLEY, O.

1932   Muskies in the fall. Rod and Gun in Canada 34(4):13.

RISTIC, M.

1964   Nova saznanja u komplexu problems vestackog razmnozavanja stuke (*Esox lucius* L.). Ribarstvo Jugoslaviye 19(3):57–63.

RIVO

1976   Projekt 5.1. Onderzoek snoek. [Northern pike research.] Visserj 29:313.

RIZVANOV, R. A.

1971   The availability of food and spawning grounds for the Lake Ladoga pike-perch [*Lucioperca lucioperca* (L.)]. Journal of Ichthyology 11:624–630.
         Pike are one of the species consumed by young pike-perch.

RIZVI, S. S. H.

1969   Studies on the structure of the sucker and seasonal incidence of *Argulus foliaceus* (L., 1758) on some freshwater fishes (Branchiura, Argulidae). Crustaceans 17:200–206.
         A. foliaceus was found on pike from the eutrophic lake, Rostherne Mere. The fish showed infestations rates from 16 to 31.28% with an intensity of 1 to 10 parasites per infested host. The total of infested fish was high from July to September.

ROACH, L. S.

1948   In fishing circles. Ohio Conservation Bulletin 12(6):12–13.

ROBERTSON, D.

1886   The pike *Esox lucius* L. Transactions of the Natural History Society of Glasgow, N.S. 2:212–214.

ROBERTSON, M. R.

1969   An investigation of a spawning population of northern pike (*Esox lucius* Linnaeus) from Floatingstone Lake, Alberta. Alberta Fish and Wildlife Division, Research Report 5:1–57.

ROBINSON, G.

1941   Bait casting. A. S. Barnes. 66 pp.

ROGALSKI, J.

1937   Moj Pobyt w Wielkopolskim - Pomorskim Towarzystwie Rybackim w czasie produkcji ikry szczupaka. [My visit to Pomeranian Fishery Association during production of pike eggs.] Przeglad Rybacki 10(7):268–270.
         Methods of artificial fertilization of pike eggs.

ROGOWSKI, U. and F. W. TESCH

1961   Erste Nahrung fressfahig gewardener Fischbrut. Zeitschrift fuer Fischerei 9:735–747.

ROSEBOROUGH, D.

1957   Internal report on the age of pike in inner Long Point Bay. Ontario Department of Lands and Forests, unpublished MS.

ROSEN, D. E.

1974   Phylogeny and zoogeography of salmoniform fishes and relationships of *Lepidogalaxias salamandroides*. Bulletin of the American Museum of Natural History 153:267–325.

ROSENLUND, K.

1976   Catalogue of subfossil Danish vertebrates. Fishes. Kobenhavn.
        A report of pike remains found in Denmark.

ROSS, D. A.

1940   Jackfish investigations, Alberta. Winnipeg, Ducks Unlimited.

ROSS, M. J. and C. F. KLEINER

1982   Shielded-needle technique for surgical implanting radio-frequency transmitters in fish. Progressive Fish-Culturist 44:41–43.
        Describes a shielded-needle technique to guide an antenna of Teflon coated conductor wire along the intestine under the pelvid girdle. The method enables the transmitter to be positioned anywhere in the peritoneal cavity, thus reducing healing problems and the damage to vital organs that may occur when the transmitter is placed at the incision or anterior to it.

ROSS, M. J. and D. B. SINIFF

1980   Spatial distribution and temperature selection of fish near the thermal outfall of a power plant during fall, winter, and spring. Environmental Protection Agency Report EPA-600/3–80–009.

ROSS, M. J. and J. D. WINTER

1981   Winter movements of four fish species near a thermal plume in northern Minnesota. Transactions of the American Fisheries Society 110:14–18.
        During winter 1975, six pike were equipped with radio frequency transmitters to determine movements. Data on mean home range size, mean water depths at fish location, and average number of movements between heated and unheated areas per individual per week.

ROSSI, A., P. DAMIANI and E. DONATI

1973   Characterization of the principal fish species of Trasimeno Lake by protein electrophoretic patterns. Rivista di Idrobiologica 12:3–20.

ROST, G.

1914   Einhumische Fische: Hecht. Woehenschrift Aquarien und Terrarien Kunde 11:284–285.

ROSTLUND, E.

1952   Freshwater fish and fishing in native North America. University of California Publications in Geography 9:1–313.

ROTH, H.

1960   The propagation of pike and the development of fry. Schweizerische Fischerei-Zeitung 9:214–216, 10:239–243.

ROTH, H. and W. GEIGER

1972   Brienzersee, Thunersee, and Bielersee: effects of exploitation and eutrophication on the salmonid communities. Journal of the Fisheries Research Board of Canada 29:755–764.

ROTHSCHILD, B. J.

1961   Production and survival of eggs of the American smelt, *Osmerus mordax* (Mitchill). M.S. thesis, Cornell University. 41 pp.

ROUSSOW, G.
  1960   Cycle du parasite *Diphyllobothrium latum* (Linne). Journal de Bord de
          l'Office Biologie 3(52):398–401.
ROWLEY, L. B.
  1934   Lake Wingra and its borders in the seventies. *In* Sachse, N. D. A thousand
          ages. App. 1, pp. 109–114.
ROYAL ONTARIO MUSEUM
  1946   Pike, pickerel and maskinonge. Royal Ontario Museum of Zoology, mimeo-
          graphed circular no. 1:1–3.
          Discussion of the common names of the Esocidae and the various fish to
          which these names have been applied. An effort was made to define each
          species and apply an appropriate common name.
ROYER, L. M.
  1971   Comparative production of pike fingerlings from adult spawners and from fry
          planted in a controlled spawning marsh. Progressive Fish-Culturist
          33:153–155.
          Study was done over a 7-year period at Kenosee Lake, Saskatchewan.
          Stocked adult spawners produced 1000+ fingerlings/acre while the planted fry
          produced only 2 fingerlings/acre. Possible factors responsible for the low sur-
          vival of hatchery fry are discussed.
ROZANSKI, M.
  1913a   Czy nie nalezaloby zwrocic uwagi na szczupaka? [Should we not pay atten-
          tion to pike?] Okolnik Rybacki 30(3):46–48.
          Points out pike's value as a consumption and market product.
  1913b   W sprawie sztucznej hodowli szczupakow. [On artificial breeding of pike.]
          Okolnik Rybacki 30(8):161–165.
          Some sceptical comments on artificial farming of pike.
  1914   Szczupak (*Esox lucius*). [The pike (*Esox lucius*).] Okolnik Rybacki
          31(6):128–132.
          General data on pike biology. Role of pike in fishery management.
ROZNIAKOWSKI, J.
  1957   Zaplodnienie ikry szczupaka bezposrednio w sloju. [Fertilization of pike
          eggs directly in a jar.] Gospodarka Rybna 9(5):27.
          "Dry" method of artificial fertilization of pike eggs; 95% survival of the eggs
          was obtained.
ROZWADOWSKI, J.
  1904   Szczupak (*Esox lucius* - Der Hecht). [The pike (*Esox lucius* - Der Hecht).]
          Okolnik Rybacki 69:81–91.
          Morphometry, biology, distribution, pond farming, commercial and recrea-
          tional catches of pike.
RUBNER, M.
  1924   Aus dem Leben des Kaltbluters. I. Teil: Die Fische. [On the life of cold-
          blooded animals. 1. Fishes.] Biochemische Zeitschrift 148:222–267.
RUCKE
  1911   Die kunstliche Aufzucht der Hechtbrut. Fischerei Zeitung Neudamm
          14:199–200.
RUDAKOVSKIY, L. G., L. N. SOLODILOV, V. R. PROTAXOV and V. M. KRUMIN
  1970   The frightening of fish by an explosion. Journal of Ichthyology 10:555–557.
          Indications that pike may have been frightened by the explosive effect of

pneumatic emitters with chamber volumes of 0.7 and 3 liters and a gas deto-
nator with a chamber of 8 liters, whose main energy was concentrated in the
frequency band 20–150 cps, and also the detonation of hexogen charges
weighing between 1.5 and 35 g.

RUDD, J. W. M., A. FURUTANI and M. A. TURNER
  1980   Mercury methylation by fish intestinal contents. Applied Environmental
          Microbiology 40:777–782.

RUDEBERG, C.
  1969   Structure of the parapineal organ of the adult rainbow trout, *Salmo gairdneri*
          Richardson. Zeitschrift fuer Zellforschung und Microskopische Anatomie
          Abtetlung Histochemia 93:282–304.
  1971   Structure of the pineal organs of *Anguilla anguilla* and *Lebistes reticulatus*
          Teleostei. Zeitschrift fuer Zellforschung und Microsckopische Anatomie
          Abtetlung Histochemia 122:227–243.

RUDENKO, G. P.
  1971   Biomass and abundance in a roach-perch lake. Voprosy Ikhtiologii
          11:630–642.
          In July 1961 fish were collected by toxicant treatment on Lake Dements,
          USSR. Data given include biomass, production, abundance, and size-age and
          sex structure of the pike population.

RUDENKO, G. P. and Y. P. VOLKOV
  1974   The productivity of the fish populations in the mesotrophic Lake Rachkovo,
          the Velikaya River basin. Hydrobiological Journal 10:63–67.

RUDNICKI, A.
  1951   Ryby i ich zycie. [Fishes and their life.] Wiedze Powszechna. 72 pp.
  1965   Ryby wod polskich. Atlas. [Fishes of Polish waters. Atlas.] Panstwowe
          Zaklady Wydawnictw Szkolnych. 104 pp.

RUDNICKI, A., J. WALUGA and T. WALUS
  1971   Rybactwo jeziorowe. [Lake fisheries.] Warsaw, PWRiL. 391 pp.

RUDOLPHI, C. A.
  1802   Anatomisch-physiologische Abhandlungen. Ueber die Darmzotten, pp.
          39–108.

RULEWICZ, M.
  1974   Ze studiow nad rybolowstwen we wczesnosredniowiecznych miastach przy
          ujscie Odry. Archeologia Polski 19:387–475.
          Reference to 9th-13th century angling for pike, including the use of iron and
          brass spoons.

RUNDBERG, H.
  1977   Trends in harvests of pikeperch (*Stizostedion lucioperca*), Eurasian perch
          (*Perca fluviatilis*) and northern pike (*Esox lucius*) and associated environmen-
          tal changes in lakes Malaren and Hjalmaren 1914–74. Journal of the
          Fisheries Research Board of Canada 34:1720–1724.
          The fish communities in and the trophic states of lakes Malaren and Hjal-
          maren have changed gradually since the late 1700's. In both lakes, pike are
          important species in the recreational and commercial fishery.

RUNNSTROM, S.
  1949   Director's report for the year 1948. Institute of Freshwater Research
          Drottningholm, Report 29:5–28.

1950   Director's report for the year 1949. Institute of Freshwater Research Drottningholm, Report 31:5–18.

        Outlines results of several tagging methods, which were an attempt to assess the effectiveness of stocking in Sweden, and experiments on egg loss in nature. Notes the outcome of stocking the colour mutant.

1954   Director's annual report for the year 1953. Institute of Freshwater Research Drottningholm, Report 35:5–10.

RUPP, R. S.

1959   Variation in the life history of the American smelt in inland waters of Maine. Transactions of the American Fisheries Society 88:241–252.

RUTLEDGE, W. P. and S. G. CLARKE

1971   Fisheries studies. Region 1-A. Northern pike study. Texas Parks and Wildlife Department, Project F-7-R-20/Job 176:1–10.

        Data collected during 1971 indicated that the pike population in Greenbelt Lake, Texas, was rapidly declining. There were 91 pike captured, 52 tagged, 28 examined for stomach contents and gonadal development, and an absence of pike spawning during 1971.

RUTLEDGE, W. P. and J. A. PRENTICE

1973   Northern pike life history study. Texas Parks and Wildlife Department, Project F-7-R-21, Job 17b:1–30.

        To assess the 1967 introduction of pike into Texas lakes, a study was conducted from 1968 to 1971 on Greenbelt Lake, Donley County. Food and reproductive habits, growth patterns, seasonal distribution and movement, and parasitic observations were made.

RYCHECKY, F.

1966   Chov rocni nasady a rychleneho pludku stiky. Ces rybarstvi 4:53–54.

RYDER, R. A. and S. R. KERR

1978   The adult walleye in the percid community—a niche definition based on feeding behaviour and food specificity. American Fisheries Society Special Publication 11:39–51.

RYDER, R. A., S. R. KERR, K. H. LOFTUS and H. A. REGIER

1974   The morphoedaphic index, a fish yield estimator - review and evaluation. Journal of the Fisheries Research Board of Canada 31:663–688.

RYDER, R. A., W. B. SCOTT and E. J. CROSSMAN

1964   Fishes of northern Ontario, north of the Albany River. Royal Ontario Museum, Life Sciences Contribution 60:1–30.

        Gives distribution, habitat, and commercial importance of pike in the Patricia portion of Ontario.

SACHSE, N. D.
1965   A thousand ages. Regents of the University of Wisconsin, Madison. 151 pp.
SACKMAUEROVA, M., O. PAL'USOVA and A. SZOKOLAY
1977   Contribution to the study of drinking water. Danube water and biocenoses contamination with chlorinated insecticides. Water Research 11:551–556.
SAKOWICZ, L.
1939   Szczupak. Produkcja materialu zarybieniowego. [Pike. Production of stocking material.] Wydawnictwa Zw. Org. Rybacki R.P., Warsaw, Ser. B, Praktyczne Opracowania Techniczno-Gospodarcze 11:1–52.
        An outline of pike biology, methods of stocking, and breeding of pike fry.
SAKOWICZ, L. and W. URBANOWSKI
1933   Wasowa produkcja zaoczkowanej ikry szczupaka. [Mass production of eyed pike eggs.] Przeglad Rybacki 6(6):198–205.
        Practical suggestions on the method of incubating pike eggs in two types of Californian apparatus, together with the methods of egg transport.
SALMI, J.
1982   Food of northern pike, perch, pike-perch and burbot in our coastal waters. M.S. thesis, University of Helsinki. 97 pp. [in Finnish]
SALOJARVI, K., H. AUVINEN and E. IKONEN
1981   A plan for management of fishery in the watercourse of the River Oulujoki. Finnish Game and Fisheries Research Institute, Fisheries Division. Monestettuja julkaisuja 1:1–277.
1982   A plan for fisheries management in the lakes drained by the Oulujoki River. Hydrobiologia 86:211–218.
SALYER, J. C., II and K. F. LAGLER
1949   The eastern belted kingfisher, *Megaceryle alcyon alcyon* (Linnaeus), in relation to fish management. Transactions of the American Fisheries Society 76:97–117.
        The kingfisher eats pike, which are considered to be a liability in trout streams.
SAMOKHVALOVA, L. K.
1974   The biological characteristics of the pike. Trudy Atlanticheskogo Nauchno-Issledovatel'skogo Instituta Rybnogo Khozyaistva Okeanografii 46:148–153.
1976   Ratsiony in kormovye koehffitsienty khishchnykh rybrkurshskogo zaliva. [Diets and food coefficients in predatory fish from Kursiu Mariosh.] *In* Fedorov, S. S., et al., eds., Biological fishery investigations in the Atlantic Ocean. Kaliningrad, AtlantNIRO, 65:69–75.
        The annual rations and food coefficients in pike were calculated from the balance equation formula suggested by Vinberg. Food coefficients were found to increase with the predator age and to be significantly higher in males than in females.
SANDERSON, C. H. and Z. BEAN
1974   Tiger muskellunge culture. Artificial diet—concrete rearing units. Proceedings 6th Interstate Muskellunge Workshop, Morehead, Kentucky, 1974, pp. 19–20.
        Discusses a project to determine the practicability of training pike-muskellunge hybrids to accept pellet food. Data indicate some success.

271

SAUTER, S., K. S. BUXTON, K. J. MACEK and S. R. PETROCELLI

    1976   Effects of exposure to heavy metals on selected freshwater fish. U.S. Environmental Protection Agency, National Environmental Research Centre, Ecological Research Series, EPA 600/3–76–105:1–75.

SAUVADON, G.

    1868   Note sur le brochet. Bulletin de la Societe Acclim. Paris, 2, ser. 5.

SAVAGE, A. G.

    1983   The ultrastructure of the blood cells of the pike *Esox lucius* L. Journal of Morphology 178:187–206.

           The ultrastructure of pike peripheral blood cells, lymphocytes, thrombocytes, granulocytes, and monocytes is described.

SAZONOVA, Y. A.

    1979   The fecundity of the pike of Lake Pskov-Chud. *In* Fisheries development of reservoirs. Leningrad, State Institute for Lake and Rivers Fisheries, 26:48–51.

SBIKIN, Y. N.

    1974   External morphology of the brain in Acipenseridae. Journal of Ichthyology 13:797–800.

           Brief information on optic lobes of pike.

SCHAFERNA, K.

    1944   Aus der Pathologie der Susswasserfische. Archiv fuer Hydrobiologie 40:733–742.

SCHAPERCLAUS, W.

    1933   Lehrbuch der Teichwirtschaft. Berlin, Paul Parey. 289 pp. U.S. Fish and Wildlife Service Leaflet 311:1–260.

    1940   Studies on eggs and fry of marane, pike and trout. International Association of Theoretical and Applied Limnology Proceedings 9:215–251.

    1961   Lehrbuch der Teichwirt-schaft. Berlin, Paul Parey. 582 pp.

    1979   Fischkrankheiten, 4th ed. Berlin, Akademie Verlag.

SCHAUINSLAND

    1906   In O. Hertwing's Entwickelunglehre der wirbeltiere. Bd. iii, Teil 2, Kap. vi, 1906 Jena.

SCHINDLER

    1946   Concerning the development, habits and the culture of the pike. Allgemeine Fischerei-Zeitung 71(7/8):13–16, (9/10):1–6.

SCHLESINGER, D. A. and H. A. REGIER

    1983   Relationship between environmental temperature and yields of subarctic and temperate zone fish species. Canadian Journal of Fisheries and Aquatic Sciences 40:1829–1837.

SCHLUMPBERGER, W.

    1961   Besatz mit Hechtbrut oder vorgestreckten Hechten? Ein Beitrag zur Frage der Rentabilitat des Hechtbesatzes. Deutsche Fischerei Zeitung 8:259–261.

SCHMIDT, B.

    1913   Das Gegiss den *Cyclopterus lumpus* L. Zeitschrift fuer Natur-wissenschaftich-Medizinische Grundlagenforschung 49:313–372.

SCHMIDT, K. P.

    1946   On the zoogeography of the Holarctic region. Copeia 1966(3):144–152.

SCHMIDTT, H.

1980   Fisheries studies of a gravel pit lake used exclusively by sport fishermen. *In* Gravel pit lakes and nature conservation characteristics and usefulness. Akademie der Natursch. Landschaftspflege, Laufen/Salzach, pp. 243–257.

The results show the importance of gravel pits for private angling clubs, and conclusions are discussed. Activities leading to unnatural composition of the fish populations are shown.

SCHMITZ, W. R.

1953   Observations of the northern pike in Lake Mendota. University of Wisconsin, unpublished special report.

A report of spawning observations and collections of spontaneously laid eggs made in marshes of Lake Mendota in 1952.

SCHNAKENBECK, W.

1936   Uber den Zahnwechsel beim Hecht. Zoologischer Anzeiger 114(3/4):69–76.

SCHNEIDER, J. C.

1971   Characteristics of a population of warm-water fish in a southern Michigan lake, 1964–1969. Michigan Department of Natural Resources, Research Development Report 236:1–158.

The size of the fish populations was estimated each spring by means of mark-recapture techniques. Data on growth and food habits were also collected. Age structure, year class strength, and natural mortality rates of the fish populations were determined.

SCHNUTE, J. and D. FOURNIER

1980   A new approach to length-frequency analysis: growth structure. Canadian Journal of Fisheries and Aquatic Sciences 37:1337–1351.

SCHOENECKER, W.

1961   Summary of northern pike, *Esox lucius*, tagging in Watts Lake, Cherry County. Nebraska Game and Parks Commission Annual Report, 1961:34–37.

1970   Management of winterkill lakes in the sandhill region of Nebraska. *In* Schneberger, E., ed., A symposium on the management of midwestern Winterkill lakes. American Fisheries Society, North Central Division, Special Publication.

SCHOETTGER, R. A. and E. W. STEUCKE, Jr.

1970a   Quinaldine and MS-222 as spawning aids for northern pike, muskellunge, and walleyes. Progressive Fish-Culturist 32:199–201.

The study was done under field conditions using 10 to 20 ppm of quinaldine, or 100 to 150 ppm of MS-222. Both anesthetics act rapidly. Quinaldine could be tolerated for relatively long exposures but did not block reflex activity, while the reverse was true if MS-222 was used.

1970b   Synergic mixtures of MS-222 and quinaldine as anesthetics for rainbow trout and northern pike. Progressive Fish-Culturist 32:202–205.

Mixtures were found to be 3 to 5 times more effective, with a reduced chemical cost of 60% or more (ranges 20–60 ppm MS-222 and 5–20 ppm quinaldine). All reflex movement was blocked within 2 to 12 minutes, and anesthesia maintained for up to one hours.

SCHOLTZ, C.

1932   Experimentale Untersuchungen die Nahrungswertung des ein und zweisommerigen Hechtes. Zeitschrift fuer Fischerei 30:523–604.

SCHOOTS, A. F. M. and J. M. DENUCE

1981   Purification and characterization of hatching enzyme of the pike (*Esox lucius*). International Journal of Biochemistry 13:591–602.

A choriolytic enzyme was isolated from the hatching medium of pike. The molecular weight was 24,000, its isoelectric point was 6.5 and pH optimum about pH 8. The enzyme was a glycoprotein containing 2% carbohydrate. The molecule contained two disulphide bonds but no free cysteine. Enzyme was a zinc-metal-loprotease.

SCHOOTS, A. F. M., P. A. C. M. EVERTSE and J. M. DENUCE

1983   Ultrastructural changes in hatching-gland cells of pike embryos (*Esox lucius* L.) and evidence for their degeneration by apoptosis. Cell and Tissue Research 229:573–589.

SCHOOTS, A. F. M., B. J. A. JANSSEN and J. M. DENUCE

1981   Antigenicity of highly purified hatching enzyme from the pike, *Esox lucius*. Archives Internationales de Physiologie et de Biochimie 89:B75-B76.

The function and possible source of the proteolytic or hatching enzyme (HE) is discussed. The preparation of antibodies against pike hatching enzyme and some preliminary immunological studies are described.

SCHOOTS, A. F. M., R. J. G. OPSTELTEN and J. M. DENUCE

1982   Hatching in the pike *Esox lucius* L.: Evidence for a single hatching enzyme and its immunocytochemical localization in specialized hatching gland cells. Developmental Biology 89:48–55.

Antibodies against purified hatching enzyme (HE) have been used to examine different aspects of the presence of the enzyme in the ontogeny of pike. Immunochemical analysis indicates that the two proteolytic enzymes that occur in the hatching medium rise from a single protease. Immunofluorescence microscopy by means of anti-HE demonstrates that HE is localized in the so-called hatching gland cells. HE can be detected from the ten somite stage on. Discrete hatching gland remnant bodies phago-cytized by epidermal cells are observed in larval stages until 3–7 days after emergence of the embryo.

SCHOOTS, A. F. M., J. J. M. STIKKELBROECK, J. F. BEKHUIS and J. MANUEL DENUCE

1982   Hatching in teleostean fishes; fine structural changes in the egg envelope dur-ing enzymatic breakdown in vivo and in vitro. Journal of Ultrastructure Research 80:185–196.

During the hatching process distinct ultrastructural changes take place in the egg envelopes of pike. In the pike, with thin envelopes, a decrease in thick-ness of 30% is observed. The extent to which the ZRI is affected in vitro by hatching enzyme or Pronase depends on incubation time, temperature, and enzyme concentration. Total breakdown of the ZRI is possible, while the zona radiata externa remains intact.

SCHOPF, J. F.

1784   Der gemeine Hecht in Amerika. Naturforcher 20:26–31.

SCHREITMULLER, W.

1915   Junge Hechte (*Esox lucius* L.) im aquarium. Blattchen Aquarien und Ter-rarien Kunde 26:209–211.

SCHRYER, F. and W. D. COLE

1966   Statewide fisheries survey. Determinations of conditions under which north-ern pike spawn naturally in Kansas reservoirs. Kansas Forestry, Fish and

Game Commission, Dingell-Johnson Report F-15-R-1/Wk.Pl. C/Job 3:1–40.

SCHRYER, F. and V. EBERT
   1968   Statewide fisheries survey. Determination of conditions under which north-
           ern pike spawn naturally in Kansas reservoirs. Kansas Forestry, Fish and
           Game Commission, Dingell-Johnson Report F-15-R-3/Wk.Pl. C/Job
           3/PT3:1–17.

SCHRYER, F., V. W. EBERT and L. DOWLIN
   1971   Statewide fisheries survey. Determination of conditions under which north-
           ern pike spawn naturally in Kansas reservoirs. Kansas Forestry, Fish and
           Game Commission, Dingell-Johnson Report F-15-R-6/Wk.Pl. C/Job
           3/FIN:1–37.
           Presents complete records of stocking and a review of reproduction. Data on
           tag returns, growth, population dynamics, and other observations during 6
           years of pike study at two reservoirs.

SCHULTZ, F. H.
   1955   Investigation of the spawning of northern pike in Prince Albert National Park,
           Saskatchewan, 1953. Canadian Wildlife Service, Wildlife Management Bul-
           letin, ser. 3(4):1–21.
           The effects of beaver colonies on pike migration were studied to determine
           what action could improve spawning facilities. Dams were dynamited to free
           passageways and pike were trapped on the spawning run. Length, weight,
           age, sex, maturity, and stomach contents were determined.
   1956   Transfer of anaesthetized pike and yellow walleye. Canadian Fish Culturist
           18:1–5.
           Describes experiments to discover how long pike could be held on ice in an
           anaesthetized condition.

SCHUMANN, G. O.
   1963   Artificial light to attract young perch: a new method of augmenting the food
           supply of predaceous fish fry in hatcheries. Progressive Fish-Culturist
           25:171–174.

SCHUPP, D. H.
   1974   The fish population structure and angling harvest of Lake of the Woods, Min-
           nesota 1968–70. Minnesota Department of Natural Resources, Division of
           Fish and Wildlife, Fisheries Investigational Report 324:1–16.
           Gill nets were used for sampling; six species made up over 99% of the
           catches. Differences in seasonality of catches and in depth distribution
           among species were noted. Pike appeared able to sustain more intensive sport
           fishing.

SCHWALME, K.
   1984   The influence of burst exercise on the carbohydrate metabolism and blood
           acid-base status of northern pike (*Esox lucius* L.). M.S. thesis, University of
           Alberta. 49 pp.

SCHWALME, K. and W. C. MACKAY
   1985a   The influence of exercise-handling stress on blood lactate, acid-base, and
           plasma glucose status of northern pike (*Esox lucius* L.). Canadian Journal of
           Zoology 63:1125–1129.
           Capture by angling was used to exercise pike for the study. Glycogen in the
           white muscle and liver, lactate in the white muscle, liver, and blood, and glu-
           cose in the blood were measured from 0–96 hours after exercise.

1985b The influence of angling-induced exercise on the carbohydrate metabolism of northern pike (*Esox lucius* L.). Journal of Comparative Physiology B 156:67–75.

Changes in blood lactate, pH, PCO_2, and plasma bicarbonate, and glucose were measured during recovery from exercise-handling stress in chronically cannulated pike. Intraarterial infusion of a large quantity of sodium lactate elevated plasma glucose only slightly, indicating that postexercise hyperglycemia in pike is a response to stress and not simply a consequence of lactate removal by conversion into glucose.

SCHWALME, K., W. C. MACKAY and D. LINDNER

1985 Suitability of vertical slot and Denil fishways for passing north-temperate, nonsalmonid fish. Canadian Journal of Fisheries and Aquatic Sciences 42:1815–1822.

Although high water levels allowed most fish to surmount the weir, of those that chose the fishway, pike strongly preferred to ascend the Denil fishways. Plasma glucose and lactate measurements on pike revealed that ascending the Denil fishways was only moderately stressful for these fish.

SCHWARTZ, F. J.

1960a The pickerels. Maryland Conservationist 37(4):23–26.

A short article discussing esocids in Maryland and providing a simple key to help distinguish between species. General information on length, weight, spawning, and distribution.

1960b A bibliography of Maryland fisheries, including published and unpublished papers on the fisheries and related fields of tidewater Maryland. Chesapeake Biological Laboratory Contribution 144:1–35.

In 1956 pike were first introduced into Maryland in Deep Creek Lake, Garrett County, as a predator for yellow perch *Perca flavescens*.

1962 Artificial pike hybrids, *Esox americanus vermiculatus* x *E. lucius*. Transactions of the American Fisheries Society 91:229–230.

Two experimentally produced hybrids exhibited characteristics intermediate between the parent species, although the snout seemed shorter than found normally.

1972 World literature on fish hybrids with an analysis by family, species, and hybrid. Gulf Coast Research Laboratory Publication 3:1–328.

SCHWARTZ, F. J. and H. J. ELSER

1962 Additions to Maryland list: new record fish. Maryland Conservationist 39(2):26–27.

SCHWARTZ, J. J.

1974 Prevalence of pathogenic pseudomonad bacteria isolated from fish in a warm-water lake. Transactions of the American Fisheries Society 103:114–116.

SCHWARZ, S. S., V. G. ISTSCHENKO, L. A. DOBRINSKAYA, A. Z. AMSTISLAVSKII, I. N. BRUSYNINA, I. A. PARAKETZOV and A. S. YAKOLEVA

1968 Rate of growth and size of the fish brain. A contribution to the problem of species and intraspecific categories in different classes of vertebrates. Zoologicheskii Zhurnal 47:901–915. [in Russian, English summary]

SCIDMORE, W. J.

1955 Notes on the fish population structure of a typical rough fish-crappie lake of southern Minnesota. Minnesota Department of Conservation, Investigational Report 162:1–11.

276

1964   Use of yearling northern pike in the management of Minnesota fish lakes. Minnesota Division of Game and Fish, Investigational Report 227.

1970   Using winterkill to advantage. *In* A symposium on the management of midwestern winterkill lakes, 32nd Midwest Fish and Wildlife Conference, Winnipeg, pp. 47–52.

SCOTT, D. P.

1964   Thermal resistance of pike (*Esox lucius* L.), muskellunge (*E. masquinongy* Mitchill), and their F_1 hybrids. Journal of the Fisheries Research Board of Canada 21:1043–1049.

Comparison of thermal resistances indicates close similarity between the species. The hybrids tend to be more resistant to thermal stress at the average acclimation and test temperatures encountered in the experiments. The greatest difference between the hybrids and parents occurred at the lowest test temperatures.

1974   Mercury concentration of white muscle in relation to age, growth, and condition in four species of fishes from Clay Lake, Ontario. Journal of the Fisheries Research Board of Canada 31:1723–1729.

Studies of large samples from each of four areas of Clay Lake, a highly mercury-contaminated lake, confirmed previous findings that the larger the fish, the greater the white muscle mercury concentration, within species, within populations.

SCOTT, D. P. and F. A. J. ARMSTRONG

1972   Mercury concentration in relation to size in several species of freshwater fishes from Manitoba and northwestern Ontario. Journal of the Fisheries Research Board of Canada 29:1685–1690.

Approximately 20 specimens from several fishing areas were obtained by gill netting; the largest available size range was collected. Fork lengths and total weights were recorded. Mercury in the white muscle was determined.

SCOTT, W. B.

1954   Freshwater fishes of eastern Canada. Toronto, University of Toronto Press. 75 pp.

1958   A checklist of the freshwater fishes of Canada and Alaska. Royal Ontario Museum, Division of Zoology and Palaeontology. 30 pp.

1967   Freshwater fishes of eastern Canada, 2nd ed. Toronto, University of Toronto Press. 137 pp.

SCOTT, W. B. and E. J. CROSSMAN

1969   Checklist of Canadian freshwater fishes with keys for identification. Royal Ontario Museum, Life Sciences Miscellaneous Publication. 104 pp.

1973   Freshwater fishes of Canada. Fisheries Research Board of Canada Bulletin 184. 966 pp.

SEABURG, K. G.

1957   A stomach sampler for live fish. Progressive Fish-Culturist 19:137–139.

SEABURG, K. G. and J. B. MOYLE

1964   Feeding habits, digestive rates, and growth of some Minnesota warm-water fishes. Transactions of the American Fisheries Society 93:269–285.

Quality and quantity of food ingested, summer feeding habits, and digestion rates are reported for pike from two western Minnesota lakes, one of which had a dense population of centrarchid panfishes and the other a smaller population. Both lakes also had game and forage fishes.

SEAMAN, W.

1968   ID for fish. Colorado Outdoors.

SEDLAR, J.

1969   Die gegenwartige Beschaffenheit des Fisch bestandes im Einzugsgebiet des Flusses Nitra (Slowakei). Biologicke Prace 15(2):1–78. [in Slovakian, Russian and German summaries]

1971   Some data on the age and growth of *Stizostedion lucioperca* and *Esox lucius* found in the Lake Lion. Biologia 26:627–634.

SEGERSTRALE, C.

1948   Northern pike and perch in the coastal waters of southern Finland. Helsinki, Skargardsboken, pp. 401–441.

SEGUIN, R. L.

1967   *Salvelinus fontinalis* and other fish of the Quyon River, Pontiac County, Quebec. Quebec Service de la Faune Rapport 4:5–23.

1972   Work and activity report of the administrative district Outaouais Abitibi during 1967. Quebec Service de la Faune Rapport 6:77–91.

SEIDLITZ, H. J.

1979   Einseitiger Hechtfang auf der Edertalsperre und seine Folgen. Osterreichs Fischerei 32:6–10.

SEKUTOWICZ, S.

1938   Ryby. [Fishes.] Panstwowe Wydawnictwo Ksiazek Szkolnych. 48 pp.
        School atlas of most common fish species.

SELBIG, W.

1970   Chemical rehabilitation of chronic winterkill lakes. *In* A symposium on the management of midwestern winterkill lakes, 32nd Midwest Fish and Wildlife Conference, Winnipeg, pp. 27–30.

SELL, J.

1974   Przyczynki do plamicy szczupakow i wrzodzienicy lososiowatych. [Maculosis of pike and furunculosis of salmonids.] Gospodarka Rybna 26(10):16–17.
        Factors causing the disease. Description of clinical symptoms. Methods of prevention and cure.

SELL, R. J.

1952   A survey of the incidence of infestation of helminth parasites in the northern pike, *Esox lucius*, from northwestern Ohio. M.S. thesis, Bowling Green State University, 26 pp.

SENTEIN, P. and P. REBOULIN

1969   Origine mitochondriale du vitellus dans l'ovocyte d'*Esox lucius* L. Comptes Rendus Hebdomadaires des Seances d l'Academie des Sciences, Serie D, Sciences Naturelles 268:345–347.

SEPPANEN, P.

1970   The growth of fishes in the Helsinki Sea area. Water Conservation Laboratory Report 2(12):1–89. [in Finnish]

SEREBRINIKOVA, T. P. and E. M. LYZLOVA

1977   Some characteristics of the molecular evolution of glycogen phosphorylase and amino transferases in muscle tissue of vertebrates. Journal of Evolutionary Biochemistry and Physiology 13:106–113.

278

SERNS, S. L. and T. C. MCKNIGHT

1977   The occurrence of northern pike x grass pickerel hybrids and an exceptionally large grass pickerel in a northern Wisconsin stream. Copeia 1977:780–781.

Five hybrids were captured between 1970 and 1975 in Rice Creek, Vilas County, using 25-mm square mesh fyke nets. A table listing the characteristics of each species and the hybrid is given, along with a physical and chemical description of the creek.

SHAFI, M.

1969   Comparative studies of populations of perch (*Perca fluviatilis* L.) and pike (*Esox lucius* L.) in two Scottish lochs. Ph.D. thesis, University of Glasgow.

1974   Studies of populations of perch *Perca fluviatilis* and pike *Esox lucius* in two British lakes. Dacca University Studies, Part B, 22:33–37.

SHAFI, M. and P. S. MAITLAND

1971   Comparative aspects of the biology of pike, *Esox lucius* L., in two Scottish lochs. Proceedings of the Royal Society of Edinburgh, Section B (Biology) 71:41–60.

SHAMARADINA, I. P.

1954   Changes in the respiratory rate of fishes in the course of their development. Doklady Akademii Nauk SSR 98:689–692. [in Russian]

SHAMARDINA, I. P.

1957   The developmental stages of the pike. Trudy Instituta Morfologii Zhivotnykh Akademii Nauk SSSR 16:237–298.

SHANDON

1889   The matter of the big Irish pike. American Angler 15(25):898–899.

The author described large pike commonly found in Ireland in 1889, defended the use of the otter and cross line to remove pike from lakes with good trout fishing.

SHARONOV, I. V.

1961   The role of the pike in the formation of the fish fauna of the Kuibyshev reservoir. Rybnoe Khoziaistvo Respublikanskii Mezhvedomstvennyi Tematicheskii Nauchnyk Sbornik 12:30–33.

SHARP, R. W., L. H. BENNETT and E. C. SAEUGLING

1952   A preliminary report on the control of fungus in the eggs of the pike (*Esox lucius*) with malachite green. Progressive Fish-Culturist 14:30.

The experiments reported on here indicate that malachite green might be of much value in controlling fungus and reducing the labour in handling pike eggs.

SHCHERBUKHA, A. Y.

1971   The growth and condition of fishes of the northern Donets and its tributary, the Aydar, in the area affected by warm water discharged from Lugansk power station. Journal of Ichthyology 11:231–241.

Information on six species in the USSR, including pike. States minimum breeding sizes.

1974   Study of morphological variability in the pike from some Ukrainian rivers. Vestnik Zoologii 2:45–49.

SHENTIAKOV, V. A.

1963   The parameters of fish reactions in electric fields of alternating currents. Biological aspects of research in reservoirs. Trudy Instituta Biologii Vnutrennikh Vod Akademii Nauk SSSR 6–9:224–229

Considers the influence of temperature and electric conductivity of water on reactions of fish in electric fields. One parameter was kept constant and the other varied; changes in sensitivity to alternating current were observed.

SHENTYAKOVA, L. F.

1966   Some biological and topographical characteristics of fish scales. Gidrobiologicheskii Zhurnal 2(3):60–67.

1969   The technique of compiling monograms for reconstruction of the growth of fishes from their scales. Hydrobiological Journal 5(6):83–86.

SHERSTYUK, V. V.

1965   Nutrition of *Esox lucius* in the upper part of the Kremenchug reservoir. Gidrobiologicheskii Zhurnal 1(6):50–53.

SHERWOOD, F.

1978   Phenetic and cladistic lineages of the family Esocidae (Osteichthyes: Salmoniformes). University of Toronto, unpublished MS. 12 pp.
        A comparison of current theories of esocid phylogeny and evolution based on zoogeographical data and some meristics, with those derived from numerical taxonomy character analysis.

SHETTER, D. S.

1949   A brief history of the sea lamprey problem in Michigan waters. Transactions of the American Fisheries Society 76:160–176.

SHIELDS, J. T.

1956   Report of fisheries investigations during the third year of impoundment of Fort Randall Reservoir, South Dakota, 1955. South Dakota Department of Game, Fish and Parks, Dingell-Johnson Project F-1-R-5:1–91.

1957   Report of fisheries investigations during the fourth year of impoundment of Fort Randall Reservoir, South Dakota, 1956. South Dakota Department of Game, Fish and Parks, Dingell-Johnson Project F-1-R-6:1–60.

SHIKHSHABEKOV, M. M.

1978   Sexual cycles of catfish (*Silurus glanis* L.), pike (*Esox lucius* L.), perch *Perca fluviatilis* L.), and pikeperch (*Lucioperca lucioperca* L.). Journal of Ichthyology 18:457–468.
        The specificity of the sexual cycles and of the spawning ecology of four species from Dagestan waters is shown on the basis of material collected in 1967–1975.

SHILENKOVA, A. K.

1956   Materialy po biologii shchuki Irgiz-Turgaiskikh ozer. [Data on the biology of pike of the Irgiz-Turgai Lakes.] Sbornik Rabot po Ikhtiologii i Gidrobiologii 1:215–231.

SHILIN, Y. A.

1972   The reproductive system of fish from the middle Kolyma. Soviet Journal of Ecology 2:245–252.

SHKOL'NIK-YARROWS, E. G.

1975   Microscopic study of the comparative morphology of the retina. Neurophysiology 7:52–58.

SHKORBATOV, G. L.

1965a   Intraspecific variability in respect to oxyphilia among freshwater fishes. Gidrobiologicheskii Zhurnal 1(5):3–8. [in Russian]

1965b   Intraspecific variability in thermal tolerance among freshwater fishes. Kharkov Universytet Vestnik, Seriia Biologii, 1:123–126.

SHLYAPNIKOVA, R. L.

1961 The parasitofauna of Lake Vyrts'yarv fish. *In* Petrushevskii, G. K., ed. Parasites and diseases of fish. Jerusalem, Israel Program for Scientific Translations, pp. 226–274.

SHLYUMPBERGER, V.

1966 Opredelenie soleustoichivosti shchuki *Esox lucius* s pomoshch 'yu Na^{22}. [Determination of the salt tolerance of pike (*Esox lucius*) by means of Na^{22}.] *In* Ecology of aquatic organisms. Moscow, Nauka, pp. 161–167.

The rate of Na^{22} excretion was found to rise with increased salinity. After they were transferred from fresh to salt water, the excretion rate increased within 5–15 hours. On transfer from salt to fresh water, the Na^{22} excretion rate fell off within 10 hours.

SHODEEN, D.

1969 Spawning marsh area requirements. Presented at 31st Midwest Fish and Wildlife Conference, Minnesota, 1969.

SIBLEY, C. K.

1922 Notes on the adult fishes of Lake George, and their feeding habits. *In* A biological survey of Lake George. New York Conservation Commission, pp. 64–68.

SIBLEY, C. K. and V. RIMSKY-KORSAKOFF

1931 Food of certain fishes in the watershed. Section 4. *In* A biological survey of the St. Lawrence watershed. New York Conservation Department Biological Survey 1930, pp. 109–120.

SIEDELMAN, D. L., P. B. CUNNINGHAM and R. B. RUSSELL

1973 Life history studies of rainbow trout in the Kvichak drainage of Bristol Bay. Alaska Department of Fish and Game, Sport Fish Division, 14:1–50.

SIEFERT, R. E., W. A. SPOOR and R. F. SYRETT

1973 Effects of reduced oxygen concentrations on northern pike (*Esox lucius*) embryos and larvae. Journal of the Fisheries Research Board of Canada 30:849–852.

At 15 and 19 C, and at flows of 60 and 30 ml/min (velocities about 3.3 and 1.6 cm/min), 50% oxygen saturation was sufficient for survival and development of pike from fertilization until all surviving larvae fed. Oxygen tensions of about 33% saturation appeared inadequate for proper survival.

SILLS, J. B., J. L. ALLEN, P. D. HARMAN and C. W. LUHNING

1973 Residue of quinaldine in ten species of fish following anesthesia with quinaldine sulfate. U.S. Fish and Wildlife Service, Investigations in Fish Control 50:1–9.

The concentration and persistence of residues of the anesthetic quinaldine in five species of both coldwater and warmwater fishes were measured following treatment with the new formulation quinaldine sulfate. Pike were treated with 30 mg/l of quinaldine sulfate for 30 minutes at 7 and 12 C.

SIMONTACCHI, C., C. BOITI, N. BONALDO, P. COLOMBO BELEVEDERE and L. COLOMBO

1983 Hormonal induction of spawning, biosynthesis and plasma levels of ovarian steroids in pike (*Esox lucius*). *In* Billard, R., ed., Le brochet gestion dans le milieu naturel et elevage. Paris. Institute National de la Recherche Agronomique, pp. 97–107.

Three experiments have been worked out on pike females: induction and anticipation of spawning in capture females by hormonal injections; study of variations in plasma levels of ovarian steroids, according to the ovarian maturational condition; and in vitro biosynthesis of ovarian tissue with labelled pregnenolone or progesterone.

SIMONTACCHI, C., D. CASCIOTTI and C. BOITI

    1982   Plasma steroid profile during the spawning season of pike. *In* Richter, C. J. J., and H. J. Goos (compilers), Reproductive physiology of fish. Center for Agricultural Publishing and Documentation, Wageningen, Netherlands, p. 110.

            The aim of this work was to investigate plasma profiles of sex-steroid hormones in connection with gonadal maturation of female pike during the reproductive cycle.

SIMONTACCHI, C., D. CASCIOTTI, M. SILVESTRELLI and C. BOITI

    1981   Preliminary report on hormonally induced spawning of pike (*Esox lucius*). Abstracts of World Conference on Aquaculture, Venice, 1981. [Abstract]

SISOVA-KASATOCKINA, O. A. and A. J. DUBOVSKAJA

    1975   Proteinase activity in certain cestode species parasitizing vertebrates of different classes. Acta Parasitologica Polonica 23:389–393.

SJOBERG, G.

    1983   Gaddan i ett kraftverksmagasin-pbestandsstorlek och fodoval. [Northern pike in a river reservoir. Population size and food habits.] FAK informerar nr 16. National Board of Fisheries, Harnosand, Sweden. 28 pp. [in Swedish, English summary]

            Information on population size, standing crop, food, prey length, sport fishing, management.

SJOLANDER, E. and B. OHMAN

    1981   Gaddlek i kraftverksmagasin. Projektarbete pa fiskevardslinjen, Goteborgs Universitet. Unpublished MS. 8 pp.

SKIBINSKI, L.

    1910   Hodowla szczupaka w malych lesnych rzeczulkach. [Pike culture in small woodland streams.] Okolnik Rybacki 109:69.

            Culture of two-year-old pike in small enclosures in the rivers of Polesie lakeland.

SKRYABINA, E. S.

    1978   Morphological variability of thorny-headed worms of the genus *Neoechinorhynchus* Acanthocephala Neoechinorhynchidae from fishes of water bodies of the glacial province in USSR. Parazitologiya 12:512–522.

SKUBBE, G.

    1979   Erfolge und Misserfolge mit dem Hechtvorstreckkasten. Zeitschrift fuer Binnenfischerei 26(3):86.

SKURDAL, J.

    1981   A snub-nosed pike caught in Lake Tyrifhorden. Fauna 34(2):87.

SLAN

    1925   Der Hecht. Osterreichische Fischerei-Zeitung.

SLASTENENKO, E. P.

    1956   Una lista de los hibridos naturales de peces del Mundo. Revista Sociedad Mexicana de Historia Natural 17(1/4):63–84.

    1957   A list of natural fish hybrids of the world. Hidrobiologi, ser. B, 4(2–3):76–97.

SLOKA, J.

1977   Fish from 13th-14th century Riga. Latvijas psr Zinatnu Akademijas Vestis 6:100–107. [in Latvian]

SLOTERDIJK, H.

1979   Concentrations of PCB's, mercury and some other metals in lateral muscle of northern pike, *Esox lucius* L., in the province of Quebec. *In* Dube, J., and Y. Gravel, eds., Proceedings of the 10th Warmwater Workshop, Montebello. Quebec, Ministere du Loisir, de la Chasse et de la Peche, pp. 89–115.

Mercury, but not other heavy metals, is accumulated by pike to a much higher degree than by its prey species, possibly because mercury in biological systems is mainly in the organic form, for which intestinal and branchial absorption efficiency is high. PCB's are also bioconcentrated along the food chain. There is a significant regression between mercury concentration and the size or age of pike.

SMALL, H. B.

1883   Fishes of the Ottawa district. Transactions of the Ottawa Field Naturalists' Club 4:31–49.

SMIRNOV, A. A. and E. V. CHIRKOVSKAYA

1969   Phosphatidic-acid in vertebrate brains and a technique for determining them. Zhurnal Evolyutsionnoi Biokhimii i Fiziologii 5:255–260.

SMISEK, J.

1966a   Vyber generacnich stik pro umely vyter a odchov stikiho pludku. Metodiky UVTI-MZLH, Praha 19:1–19.

1966b   Odchov sticihoplodku. Oborova norma On 46 6836, UNM Praha. 8 pp.

1966c   Odchov sticiho pludku. Zivocisna vyroba 39:703–714.

1967a   Investigation of the possibility of a repeated spawning of brood pike. Buletin Vyzkumy Ustav Rybarsky a Hydrobiologicky Vodnany 3(1):18–24.

1967b   The fertilizability of pike spawn from different parts of the ovary. Buletin Vyzkumy Ustav Rybarsky a Hydrobiologicky Vodnany 3(2):34–36.

1968a   Feeding of pike fry by natural feeds and substitutes. Buletin Vyzkumy Ustav Rybarsky a Hydrobiologicky 4(1):3–7.

1968b   The intensity of the acceptance of food by pike fry in the course of 24 hours. Buletin Vyzkumy Ustav Rybarsky a Hydrobiologicky 4(3):14–18.

SMISEK, J. and J. HAVELKA

1964   Pruzkum zdravotniho stavu generacnich stik, lihnuti a odchov sticiho pludku. Buletin Vyzkumy Ustav Rybarsky a Hydrobiologicky. 69 pp.

SMITH, C. L.

1962   Some Pliocene fishes from Kansas, Oklahoma and Nebraska. Copeia 1962:505–520.

Record of two complete teeth found in the High Plains Pliocene deposits. The teeth appear to belong to a species of Esocidae, quite possibly *Esox lucius* L., due to the similarity in tooth shape.

SMITH, E. C., F. BERKES and J. A. SPENCE

1975   Mercury levels in fish in the La Grande River area, northern Quebec. Bulletin of Environmental Contamination and Toxicology 13:673–677.

SMITH, H. M.

1893   Report on a collection of fishes from the Albermarle region of North Carolina. Bulletin of the U.S. Fisheries Commission 11:185–200.

283

1896   A review of the history and results of the attempts to acclimatize fish and other water animals in the Pacific states. Bulletin of the U.S. Fisheries Commission 15:379–472.

In December 1891, 400 yearling pike were put in Lake Cuyamaca, near San Diego and 100 in Feather River, Butte County, all from Quincy, Illinois. In 1896 four fish under 8 inches were caught; two were females with well developed eggs.

1907   The fishes of North Carolina. North Carolina Geographic and Economic Survey 2:1–453.

SMITH, H. M. and T. A. BEAN
1899   Fishes known to inhabit the waters of the District of Columbia. Bulletin of the U.S. Fisheries Commission 18:179–187.

SMITH, H. M. and M.-M. SNELL
1891   Review of the fisheries of the Great Lakes in 1885. *In* Report of the U.S. Commission of Fish and Fisheries 1887(Part 15):1–333.

SMITH, L. L., D. R. FRANKLIN and R. H. KRAMER
1958   Investigations of year class formation in game fish. Determination of factors influencing year class strength in northern pike and largemouth bass. Minnesota Division of Game and Fish. Project F-12-R-3; F-12-R-02/Job 2:1–328.

SMITH, L. L., Jr.
1941   The northern pike, its past and future. Minnesota Conservation Volunteer 3(15):1–5.

SMITH, L. L., Jr. and N. L. MOE, Compilers
1944   Minnesota fish facts. Minnesota Department of Conservation Bulletin 7:1–31.

SMITH, L. L., Jr. and D. M. OSEID
1970   Toxic effects of hydrogen sulfide to juvenile fish and fish eggs. Scientific Journal Series 4(6):56.

Bioassays were conducted on eggs and fry of pike. Fry were much more sensitive to hydrogen sulfide than their eggs.

1974   Effect of hydrogen sulfide on development and survival of eight freshwater fish species. *In* Blaxter, J. H. S., ed., The early life history of fish. Berlin, Springer-Verlag. pp. 417–430.

SMITH, L. L. and D. M. OSEID
1972   Effects of hydrogen sulfide on fish eggs and fry. Water Research 6:711–720.

SMITH, M. W.
1950   The use of poisons to control undesirable fish in Canadian fresh waters. Canadian Fish Culturist 8:17–29.

Describes attempts to poison pike selectively, and by controlling the numbers of the host of *Traenophorus crassus*, to reduce its infestation in the valuable coregonids.

SMITH, O. W.
1922   The book of the pike. Cincinnati, Stewart Kidd. 197 pp.

SMITH-VANIZ, W. F.
1968   Freshwater fishes of Alabama. Agricultural Experimental Station, Auburn University. 211 pp.

SMITT, F. A.
1892   A history of Scandinavian fishes. The pike. Stockholm. vol. 2, pp. 997–1010.

SNIESZKO, S. F.
1952   Ulcer disease in brook trout (*Salvelinus fontinalis*): its economic importance, diagnosis, treatment and prevention. Progressive Fish-Culturist 14:43–49.

SNIESZKO, S. F. and G. L. BULLOCK
1968   Freshwater fish diseases caused by bacteria belonging to the genera *Aeromonas* and *Pseudomonas*. U.S. Department of the Interior, Report F.D.L.-11.

SNOW, H.
1958   Northern pike of Murphy Flowage. Wisconsin Conservation Bulletin 23(2):15–18.
        General information on how mortality of eggs and young due to natural causes and angling affect population size. Notes on average length-weight of various age groups.

SNOW, H. E.
        Results of stocking northern pike in a 180 acre Wisconsin impoundment. Presented at 30th Annual Midwest Fish and Wildlife Conference, Columbus.
1961   A comparison of the fish population in Murphy Flowage, Wisconsin, before and after a panfish removal program. Wisconsin Conservation Department, pp. 1–5.
1967a   Statewide fishery research. Murphy Flowage studies. Northern pike stocking in Murphy Flowage. Wisconsin Conservation Department, Dingell-Johnson Project F-83-R-2(Wk.Pl. 3)Job A:1–20.
1967b   Statewide fishery research. Northern pike stocking in Murphy Flowage. Wisconsin Conservation Department, Dingell-Johnson Project F-83-R-3(Wk.Pl. 3)Job A:1–7.
1967c   Statewide fishery research. Murphy Flowage studies. Standing crop and mortality estimates in Bucks Lake. Wisconsin Conservation Department, Dingell-Johnson Report F-83-R-2(Wk.Pl. 3)Job D.
1969a   Comparative growth of eight species of fish in thirteen northern Wisconsin lakes. Wisconsin Department of Natural Resources, Research Report 46:1–23.
1969b   Statewide fishery research. Northern pike of Murphy Flowage. Wisconsin Conservation Department. 113 pp.
1973   The constant northern. Wisconsin Conservation Bulletin, May-June 1973. 2 pp.
        A hypothetical pike population was used to describe mortality and food preference at various stages of the life history. Angling mortality was considered to have little or no effect on total mortality, so a size limit was considered unnecessary.
1974   Effects of stocking northern pike in Murphy Flowage. Wisconsin Department of Natural Resources, Technical Bulletin 79:1–20.
        The pike population was increased by stocking in an effort to control bluegill *Lepomis macrochirus* numbers and increase growth. After stocking, pike mortality increased and angler harvest declined, while the bluegill population was unaffected. Stocking considerations are discussed.
1978a   Responses of northern pike to exploitation in Murphy Flowage, Wisconsin. American Fisheries Society Special Publication 11:320–327.

This 15-year study was conducted under liberalized fishing condition. Complete creel census and annual population estimates were used to describe relationships between exploitation and other selected statistics.

1978b   A 15-year study of the harvest, exploitation, and mortality of fishes in Murphy Flowage, Wisconsin. Wisconsin Department of Natural Resources, Technical Bulletin 103:1–22.

Complete angling records were obtained through compulsory creel census from 1955 to 1970. Information on harvest, angler success, natural mortality, and exploitation rate are given as an annual average. A significant relationship between natural mortality and harvest rate for pike was found, since catch by anglers had little effect on total mortality.

1982   Hypothetical effects of fishing regulations in Murphy Flowage, Wisconsin. Wisconsin Department of Natural Resources, Technical Bulletin 131.

The hypothetical effects of bag, season, and size limits on pike were estimated using complete angling and harvest records. These were obtained through compulsory creel census over 15 years while no regulations were in effect. It was concluded that liberalized regulations within the range of fishing pressure seen were not a detriment to the fish populations.

n.d.   Responses of northern pike to exploitation in Murphy Flowage. Wisconsin Department of Natural Resources.

Conclusions from a 15-year study (1955–70) which included compulsory creel census, liberalized fishing conditions (no bag, season, or size limits) and annual population estimates. Discussion of three management techniques (pike stocking, panfish removal, and winter drawdown) and the impact of these techniques both directly and indirectly on the native pike population.

SNOW, H. E. and T. D. BEARD

1972   A ten-year study of native northern pike in Bucks Lake, Wisconsin, including evaluation of an 18.0 inch size limit. Wisconsin Department of Natural Resources, Technical Bulletin 56:1–20.

Pike was the only predator species present, and its growth rate was considered slow, both locally and regionally. Estimates for average and maximum standing crops, annual fishing pressure, and catch rates are given. The size limit was not considered biologically justified.

SOBOLVE, J. A.

1973   Rekomendacii po razvedeniju scuki v karpovych chozjajstvach. Trudy Belorusskogo Nauchno-Issledovatel'skogo Institute Rybnogo Chozjaj pp. 26–37.

SOIN, S. G.

1980   Type of development of salmoniform fishes and their taxonomic importance. Journal of Ichthyology 20:49–56.

SOIVOI, A. and A. OIKARI

1976   Haematological effects of stress on a teleost, *Esox lucius* L. Journal of Fish Biology 8:397–411.

Stress produced a haemoconcentration, elevated blood lactate, increased glucose concentrations, and altered the plasma electrolyte balance in two groups (brackish and freshwater) of the pike after one month's starvation. The blood glucose level of the freshwater pike was twice that of the brackish-water group, and the plasma sodium and magnesium concentrations in the brackish-water pike were significantly higher in freshwater pike. The plasma potassium and calcium concentrations in the two groups did not differ.

SOKOLOV, B. M.

1961   Fish scales as organs of vision. Byulleten Nauchno Trudy Ryazanskogo Otdela Vsesoyuznogo Nauchno Obshchestva Anatomov, Gistologiv, i Embriologiv 6:75–78.

A study of the anterior portions of scales situated in scale pouches of pike. Chromatophores in fish scales from different parts of the body were studied under the microscope. Fish possessing cycloid or ctenoid scales exhibited bipartition of the organ of vision—a feature characteristic of many invertebrates.

SOKOLOV, L. I.

1962   Litnee pitanie shchuki v srednem techenii Amura. [Summer diet of pike in the middle course of the Amur River.] Vestnik Moskovskogo Universiteta Seriya 6, Biologiya Pochvovedenie 3:44–48.

1971   A morphoecological characteristic of *Esox lucius* in the middle reaches of the Lena River. Byulleten Moskovskogo Obshchestva Ispytatelei Priorody Otdel Biologicheskii 76:100–104.

SOKOLOV, L. I. and E. A. TSEPKIN

1969   *Esox lucius* from the neolithic stage of the Lena River basin. Byulleten Moskovskogo Obshchestva Ispytatelei Prirody Otdel Biologicheskii 74:54–57.

SOLJAN, T.

1946   Fauna 1. Flora Jadrona, Knjiga I. Instituta za oceanografiju i Ribarstvo FNR Jugoslavije.

Reports pike from E. Ninni 1912 Catalogo die pesci del Mare Adriotico (Venezia 1913) as occurring in brackish water lagoons of Venice, but says may have been barracuda.

SOLMAN, V. E. F.

1940   Pike study, 1940, lower Saskatchewan Delta, Manitoba. Unpublished MS. 11 pp.

1945   The ecological relations of pike, *Esox lucius* L., and waterfowl. Ecology 26:157–170.

The consumption of waterfowl by adult pike in the Prairies was discussed. Data on growth of fry over summer, adult sex ratios, food habits, weight of food in stomachs, length-weight-sex ratio, and time and rate of digestion are given. Methods of controlling pike populations are also discussed.

1950   History and use of fish poisons in the United States. Canadian Fish Culturist 8:3–16.

Describes treatment of a lake in Vermont, in 1913, with copper sulphate to kill unwanted pike.

SOLONINOVA, L. N.

1975   The fecundity of the pike of Bokhtarma Reservoir. *In* Rybnye resursy vodoyemov Kazakhstana i ikh ispol'zovaniye. [Fish resources of the bodies of water of Kazakhstan and their utilization]. Kayna, Alma-Ata 9:109–113.

1976   Growth of the pike of Bukharma Reservoir. Hydrobiological Journal 12(6):47–54.

The pike grew faster in Bukhtarma reservoir than in some other waters. Differences were established in the growth of fish in different parts of the reservoir and in different years. There were no significant discrepancies in the growth of members of different year classes. Concludes that it is desirable to rear pike in Bukhtarma reservoir.

SOMMANI, E.
1969   Variazioni apportate all'ittio fauna italiana dall'attivita dell'uomo. Bollettino di Pesca Piscicoltura e Idrobiologia 22:149–166. [English summary]

SONSTEGARD, R., K. NIELSEN and L. A. MCDERMOTT
1970   Epizootiological evidence for a viral etiology of lymphosarcoma in *Esox*. International Association of Aquatic Animal Medicine, Guelph.

SONSTEGARD, R. A.
1975   Studies of the etiology and epizootiology of lymphosarcoma in northern pike (*Esox lucius*) and muskellunge (*Esox masquinongy*). Bibliotheca Haematologica 43:242–244.
        Describes the clinical course of lymphosarcoma from studies of tissues of tumour-bearing and normal specimens under the microscope and "transplantation trails" made by two routes of inoculation.

1976   Studies of the etiology and epizootiology of lymphosarcoma in *Esox (Esox lucius* L. and *Esox masquinongy*). Progress in Experimental Tumor Research 20:141–155.
        This comprehensive review of the disease includes the following: history, occurrence, modes of transmission, and experiments.

SONSTEGARD, R. A. and J. G. HNATH
1978   Lymphosarcoma in muskellunge and northern pike: guidelines for disease control. American Fisheries Society Special Publication 11:235–237.
        Epizootics of a malignant blood cancer affect feral populations of pike. Overall frequencies of occurrence of the disease in pike were found. Spontaneous regressions are common. Pike should be stocked as eggs or fry, not as adults, if the spread of lymphosarcoma is to be restricted.

SONSTEGARD, R. A. and J. F. LEATHERLAND
        Handbook for identification of tumors in Great Lakes fishes. Unpublished MS, 115 pp.
        Description of the gross pathology, histopathology, and etiologic agents of lymphosarcoma and epidermal hyperplasia in pike. Photographs of various lesions and growths are included.

SONSTEGARD, R. A. and T. S. PAPAS
1977   Descriptive and comparative studies of type C virus DNA polymerase of fish. Proceedings of the American Association for Cancer Research 18:202. [Abstract]
        Pike lymphosarcoma DNA polymerase was partially purified from particulate fractions banding at 1.15–1.16 gm/cc^3 from homogenates prepared from frozen necropsies of tumor-bearing pike. The enzyme behaves as a typical reverse transcriptase in that it prefers ribotemplates to deoxytemplates.

SOOT-RYEN, T.
1926   Bidrag til kjendskaben om Finmarkens ferskvandsfisker. [Freshwater fishes from Finland.] Tromso Museums Skrifter 48(2):1–48. [English summary]

SORENSON, L., K. BUSS and A. D. BRADFORD
1966   The artificial propagation of esocid fishes in Pennsylvania. Progressive Fish-Culturist 28:133–141.
        Spawning and egg incubation experiments included sperm collection

methods, spawning of females using blood-pressure instruments, and fungus prevention.

SOROKIN, V. N. and A. A. SOROKINA

1979   Morphometric description of the Baikal pike, *Esox lucius lucius*. Journal of Ichthyology 19:143–147.

Assesses morphometric and meristic characters of sexually mature specimens collected in 1963–64 and 1975. Compares results from both sexes, the two sampling periods, and different water bodies.

SOROKINA, A. A.

1977   Pitanie molodi ryb Selenginskogo rajona Bajkala. [Feeding of young fishes from the Selenga River area of Lake Baikal.] Novosibirsk, Nauka. 112 pp.

On the basis of data obtained in 1965–72 discusses qualitative and quantitative characteristics of feeding and food relationships in pike and other species in the period from hatching to the fry stage.

SOUCHON, Y.

1979   Cycle de developpement des gonades de brochet (*Esox lucius* L., 1758). Rapport Conseil Sup. Peche, pp. 1–35.

1980   Effet de la densite initiale du peuplement sur la survie et la croissance du brochet (*Esox lucius* L.) eleve jusqu'au stade de brocheton (45 jours). *In* Billard, R., ed., La pisciculture en Etang. Paris, Institute National de la Recherche Agronomique, pp. 309–317.

Survival rate and growth of young pike in three ponds were studied. The biomass of pike fingerlings was analysed in relation to the initial number of pike stocked and the food source.

1983   La reproduction du brochet (*Esox lucius* L., 1758) dans le milieu naturel; revue bibliographique. *In* Billard, R., ed., Le brochet gestion dans la milieu naturel et elevage. Paris, Institute National de la Recherche Agronomique, pp. 21–37.

Describes types of spawning habitat corresponding to three criteria: presence of substrates for adhesive eggs and prolarval fixation; presence of cover for postlarvae; adequate food. Reproductive success depends on a combination of external factors, such as temperature, light, and substrate.

SPANOVSKAYA, V. D.

1963   Pitanie shchuki-segoletka (*Esox lucius* L.). [Food of pike fingerlings (*Esox lucius* L.).] Zoologicheskii Zhurnal 42:1071–1079.

SPANOVSKAYA, V. D. and L. N. SOLONINOVA

1983a   The fecundity of pike, *Esox lucius* (Esocidae). Journal of Ichthyology 23(5):75–83.

The reproductive capacity of pike, evaluated by the value of relative fecundity (RF) was studied. This index varies considerably in females from the same generation. The change in relative fecundity depends on physiological and ecological factors. The egg-producing capacity of females increases during ontogeny; once an RF of more than 30 eggs/g is reached, physiological aging and natural mortality are accelerated. The value of RF also changed, depending on foraging and spawning conditions. The dynamics of the values of absolute and relative fecundity and the distribution series of the latter can be used together with other biological indices as indicators of the state of pike populations.

1983b   Fecundity of pike, *Esox lucius* (Esocidae), within its area of distribution. Voprosy Ikhtiologii 23:797–804.

The reproductivity ability of the pike was evaluated using the value of its relative fecundity (RF). The change in RF depended on physiological and ecological factors. Dynamics of the values of relative and absolute fecundity and the distribution series of the latter can be used together with other biological indices as indicators of the state of pike populations.

SPATARU, P.

1968   Relatii trofice la pestiicomplexului de balti Crapina Jijila (Zona in undabila a Dunarii). Analele Universitatii Bucuresti Stiintele Naturii 17:77–88. [French summary]

1969   Dynamics of nutrition in small fish from the Crapina-Jijila Fen Complex Danube floodplain. Comunicari de Zoologie 57–63.

SPECKERT, W., B. KENNEDY, S. L. DAISLEY and P. DAVIES

1981   Primary structure of protamine from the northern pike *Esox lucius*. European Journal of Biochemistry 136:283–289.

SPEIRS, J. M.

1952   An outline of fisheries research on the Great Lakes. Summary of Lake Superior fisheries literature. University of Toronto, Ontario Fisheries Research Laboratory, unpublished MS. 25 pp.

SPENCE, E. F.

1928   The pike fisher. London, A. & C. Black.

SPENCER, P. J.

1979   Fish that men gnawed upon. Interim 6:9–11.

Preliminary report on fish remains from Coppergate, York, obtained by large-scale wet sieving and flotation of 30 contexts including pit- and trench-fills, floor levels, and dump layers of 10th-13th centuries.

SPEYER, M. R.

1980   Mercury and selenium concentrations in fish, sediments and water of two northwestern Quebec lakes. Bulletin of Environmental Contamination and Toxicoloty 24:427–432.

SPOTSWOOD, L.

1985   Go deep for summer water-wolves. Angler & Hunter 9(10):34–35.

SPRAGUE, J. W.

1961   Report of fisheries investigations during the seventh year of impoundment of Fort Randall Reservoir, South Dakota, 1959. South Dakota Department of Game, Fish and Parks, Dingell-Johnson Report F-1-R-9(Jobs 5–8):1–49.

SPRULES, W. M.

1946   Food of jackfish in Saskatchewan River. Fisheries Research Board of Canada.

1947   A management program for goldeye (*Amphiodon alosoides* in Manitoba's marsh regions. Canadian Fish Culturist 2:9–11.

Describes a possible solution to the problem of winterkill in the marsh regions.

SROCZYNSKI, S.

1972   Elementy systemu naprowadzajacego ne ofiare w budowie glowy i funkcjach narzadu wzroku szczupaka *Esox lucius* L.) [Elements of visual perception system of pike *Esox lucius* L.]. Acta Ichthyologica et Piscatoria 2:77–90.

Studies carried out on pike 20–70 cm long.

1975   Die spharische Aberration der Augenlinse des Hechts (*Esox lucius* L.). Zoologische Jahrbuecher Abteilung fuer Allgemeine Zoologie und Physiologie der Tiere 79:547–558.

1976   Untersuchungen uber die Wachstumsgesetzmassigkeiten des Sehorgans beim Hecht (*Esox lucius* L.). [Investigations on the growth regularity of the organ of sight on pike (*Esox lucius* L.)]. Archiv fuer Fischereiwissenschaft 26(2/3):137–150.

Several parameters of the dioptical system, as well as of the whole eye, were measured for pike from 20 to 70 cm in length. The measurements were aimed at determining developmental tendencies of eyes as related to their functioning and structural proportions. Focal length of the crystalline lens was the most important of all measured parameters. Distance of binocular vision increases during ontogeneses proportionally to body length and exceeds the growth of focal length of the lens.

STAFFORD, J.

1904   Trematodes from Canadian fishes. Zoologischer Anzeiger 27:481–496.

STAINTON, M. P.

1971   Syringe procedure for transfer of nanogram quantities of mercury vapor for flameless atomic absorption spectrophotometry. Commercial Fisheries Abstracts 24(6):15. [Abstract]

Describes a method, using a syringe, for transferring nanogram quantities of mercury vapor (in equilibrium with reducing solution) for the cuvette in the determination of mercury by flameless atomic absorption spectrophotometry. The method was tested by analysing the mercury content of pike.

STAMMER, A.

1969   Comparative investigations on the ciliary ganglion of freshwater fishes. Acta Biologica Szeged. 15(1/4):101–109.

STAMMER, A., I. HORVATH, M. CSOKNYA and K. HALASY

1978a   Structural investigation into the oblong medulla of Tisza fishes. Tiscia 13:183.

1978b   The differences between the structures of swimming bladder in Tisza fishes. Tiscia 13:206.

STANGE, D.

1986a   Patience, persistence, and early-season northern pike. Part 1. In-Fisherman, Book 65:122–132.

Hints on how to angle for pike, and a trip to Manitoba.

1986b   One, two, three—presentation pike. Part 2. In-Fisherman, Book 65:137–156.

Introduces European fishing tackle and techniques.

STANGENBERG, M.

1966   Coarse fish research in Poland. Proceedings of the 2nd British Coarse Fish Conference, Liverpool, 2:72–86.

STARKS, E. C.

1904   A synopsis of characters of some of the fishes belonging to the order Haplomi. Woods Hole Biological Bulletin 7:254–262.

1916   The sesamoid articular, a bone in the mandible of fishes. Leland Stanford Jr. University Publication, University Series

1930   The primary shoulder girdle of the bony fishes. Stanford University Publications, University Series, Biological Sciences 6:147–239.

Description of the girdle of pike and the variations seen in these bones as the animal develops.

STARMACH, K.

1951a   Zycie ryb slodkowodnych. Zarys morfologii, fizjologii i biologii ryb slod-kowodnych. [Life of freshwater fishes. An outline of the morphology, physiology and biology of freshwater fishes.] Warsaw, PWRiL. 305 pp.

1951b   Ilosc krwi u ryb wiaze sie z ich trybem zycia. [Amount of blood in fishes is connected with their life biology.] Swzechswiat 10:316–317.
Variations in the amount of blood in various fishes, including pike, are connected with their ecological character.

STEFFENS, W.

1961   Flossenschadigungen beim Hecht (*Esox lucius*). [Fin damage in the pike (*Esox lucius*).] Biologisches Zentralblatt 80:79–84.
A specimen deficient in fin structure serves as a basis for a general discussion of the influences that may produce such anomalies.

1976   Hechtzucht. Zeitschrift fuer Binnenfischerei 23:327–343, 360–371.

STEIN, H.

1981   Light and electron optical studies of the spermatozoa of various teleost fish. Zeitschrift fuer Angewandte Zoologie 68:183–198.

STEIN, H. and H. BAYRLE

1978   Cryopreservation of the sperm of some freshwater teleosts. Annales de Biologie Animale Biochemie Biophysique 18:1073–1076.

STEIN, H. and H. ENZLER

1983   Beutelselektion und Futterverwertung beim Hecht. [Prey selection and food conversion of pike.] Fischwirt 33(9):61–62.
Gives the species preferred by pike. Small pike (<150 g) consumed an average of two fish per day, about 5% of their body weight. Food conversion rate was 3.15 to 3.38.

STEIN, R. A.

1979   Evaluation of stocking tiger muskies in Ohio lakes (1978 July to 1979 June). Ohio Department of Natural Resources, Project F-57-R-1, Study 4. [Abstract]

STEIN, R. A., R. F. CARLINE and R. S. HAYWARD

1981   Largemouth bass predation on stocked tiger muskellunge. Transactions of the American Fisheries Society 110:604–612.

1982   Evaluation of fish management techniques: evaluation of stocking tiger muskies into Ohio lakes. Ohio Department of Natural Resources, Project F-47-R-4, Study 4:1–82.
Michanisms influencing poor survival were investigated, and stocking procedures tested, to reduce short-term mortality of stocked hybrids. Survival was related to type and availability of prey, hybrid size, time of stocking, and availability of vegetation.

STELLA, E., L. FERRERO and F. G. MARGARITORA

1978   Alterations of the plankton in a much polluted lake in central Italy latium the volcanic Lake Nemi. International Association of Theoretical and Applied Limnology Proceedings 20:1049–1054.

STENSON, J. A. E.

1982   Fish impact on rotifer community structure. Hydrobiologia 87(1):17–20.

STEPANEK, M.
1968   Beitrage zur Bioakustik der Binnengewasser. 1. Die Reaktionen der Susswasserorganismen auf die von der Wasseroberflache kommenden Gerausche. Archiv fuer Hydrobiologie 6(3/4):397–422.

STERBA, G.
1963   Freshwater fishes of the world. New York, Viking Press. 878 pp.

STERNFELD, A.
1882   Uber die Struktur des Hechtzahnes. Archiv fuer Microbiologie Anat. 20.

STEUCKE, W.
1975   Survival of hatchery stocked fish in two North Dakota lakes. Proceedings 7th Interstate Musky Workshop, La Crosse, 1975, pp. 105–110.

STEWART, D.
1969   Some native freshwater fish. Canadian Audubon 31:100–103.

STIGER, H.
        A new world record, a 52 lb. 4 oz. northern. In-Fisherman 35:95–96.
        An account of the angling of a 52 lb 4 oz pike in Germany in 1971.

STIRLING, A. B.
1863   Notice of a pike, *Esox lucius* Linn., in whose stomach a water hen and water ouzel were found. Proceedings of the Royal Society of Edinburgh 1859–62(2):44–45.

STOCKWELL, G. A.
1875   Fishes and fishing of the Great Lakes. Maskinonge, pike, perch, gar pike and sturgeon. Forest and Stream 5:293, 327.

STONE, P.
1977   Huge pike breaks record. Oxford Mail, October 14, 1977, p. 12.

STONE, U. B.
1937   Growth habits and fecundity of the ciscoes of Irondequoit Bay, New York. Transactions of the American Fisheries Society 67:234–245.

STORER, D. H.
1848   Notes on a specimen of *Esox lucius* from Bellows Falls, Vermont. Proceedings of the Boston Society of Natural History 2:105–106.

STRATILS, A., V. TOMASEK, J. CLAMP and J. WILLIAMS
1985   Partial characterization of transferins of catfish (*Silurus glannis* L.) and pike (*Esox lucius* L.) Comparative Biochemistry 80:909–911.

STRAUB, M.
1984   Abklaerungen und erste Betriebserfahrungen mit Netzgehegen im Greifenses. [Experiences with illuminated net cages in Lake Griefensee.] Schriftenreihe Fisch., Bundesamt Umweltschultz 43:35–42.
        Growth of pike in illuminated net cages was compared to growth in ponds.

STREL'TSOVA, S. V.
1970   Adaptation of carp and rainbow trout to different oxygen contents of the water. Jerusalem, Israel Program for Scientific Translations, pp. 13–23.

STRICKER, J. D.
1969   Second start. Wisconsin Conservation Bulletin 34(3):10–11.

STROGANOV, N. S. and O. P. DANIL'CHENKO
1973   Effect of small concentration of antiseptics on embryonic fish development. Vestnik Moskovskogo Universiteta, Seriya VI, Biologiya Pochvovedenie 28(4):33–38.

STROGANOV, N. S. and V. G. KHOBOTJIEV
1968 Peculiar features of the hydrochemical regime in reservoirs and aqueous organisms. *In* Bogorov, B. G., and N. S. Stroganov, eds., Some problems of hydrobiology. Trudy Moskovskogy Obshchestva Ispytatelei Prirody, pp. 139–152.

STROGANOV, N. S. and I. A. LASHMANOVA
1968 Skin penetration in fresh water fishes. *In* Bogorov, B. G., and N. S. Stroganov, eds., Some problems of Hydrobiology. Trudy Moskovskogo Obshchestva Ispytatelei Prirody, pp. 159–169.

STROUD, R. H.
1955 Fisheries report for some central, eastern and western Massachusetts lakes, ponds and reservoirs, 1951–52. Division of Fish and Game, Massachusetts Bureau of Wildlife Research Management.

STROUD, R. H. and R. M. JENKINS
1961 Midwest fish facts. Sport Fishery Institute Bulletin 110:6–7.

STRZELECKI, J.
1929 Wobronie szczupaka. [In favour of pike.] Przeglad Rybacki 2(4):240–242. Decrease in pike catches and propositions for protection periods. Comments on artificial pike breeding.

STRZYZEWSKA, K.
1957 Stado tracego sie szczupaka (*Esox lucius* L.) na Zalewie Wislanym w roku 1953. [The stock of spawning pike (*Esox lucius* L.) in Firth of Vistula in 1953.] Prace Morskiego Instytutu Rybactwa w Gdyni 9:247–257. Studies on age and size at which pike commence spawning. Numerical ratio of sexes in the spawning population. Assessment of maturation and rate of growth.

STUCKY, N. P.
1973 Collection and identification of fish parasites. Job Progress Report, Project F-4-R-18, Job 15-a:59–70. This study investigated the level of parasitism in major fishing waters of Nebraska and evaluated its impact on utilization of harvested fish. A total of 881 from 24 localities had a 62% infection rate.

STUDNICKA, F. K.
1944 Die Entwicklung des Zahnbeins des Osteodentins.e Entwicklung des Hechtes. Internat. Cl. Sci. Math., Nat. et Med. Acad. Tcheque Sci. Bull 45:1–16. Pike teeth are made up of canalized osteodentine, very similar to Haversian canals of bone. The embryologic development of these is traced, with numerous figures and plates.

STUDNIKA, F. K.
1927 Les cytodesmes et les plasmodesmes du tissu cordial de l'*Esox lucius*. Comptes Rendus de la Societe de Biologie 96:1093–1906.

STURTEVANT, E. L.
1904 Was ein Hecht verzehrt. Blattchen Aquarien und Terrarien Kunde
1916 Gewichtszunahme des Hechtes. Schweizersiche Zeitschrift fuer Fischerei Zeitung

SUKHANOVA, G. I.
1979 O nereste i plodovitosti shchuki *Esox lucius* L. Vilyujskogo vodokhranilishcha. [On the spawning and fecundity of pike, *Esox lucius* L., in the Vilyujskoe Reservoir.] Voprosy Ikhtiologii 19:278–283.

294

Observations on spawning in the USSR in 1976. Related weight-length, age, egg diameter, and weight of gonads with fecundity.

SULLIVAN, M. G.

1985   Population regulation of northern pike (*Esox lucius* L.) in an unexploited lake in northern Saskatchewan. M.S. thesis, University of Alberta. 106 pp.
Since populations of pike in unexploited lakes exhibit stability in size and structure, four possible mechanisms for this regulation were investigated; food limitations, interspecific predation, spacing behaviour, and cannibalism. It was concluded that only cannibalism affected regulation in this population.

SUMARI, O.

1965   On the migration of northern pike (*Esox lucius* L.). Kalataloudellisen tut-kimustoimiston tiedonantoja 2:1–27. [in Finnish]

1971   Structure of the perch populations of some ponds in Finland. Annales Zoolo-gici Fennici 8:406–421.
One of the main factors affecting the perch population in the ponds studies was predation upon perch young by fish such as pike.

SUMARI, O. and K. WESTMAN

1969a   Northern pike. Kalamies 4:1–4. [in Finnish]

1969b   The management of northern pike (*Esox lucius*) populations. Suomen Kala-talous Finlands Fiskerier 43:1–24. [in Finnish, English summary]
Concludes that there is little biological justification for stocking newly hatched pike. Suggests management techniques, including the enlargement of breeding areas, stocking bigger young pike (3+ cm), use of fishing regula-tions, and the reduction of other fish populations having a harmful effect on the pike population.

SUNDARARAJ

1958   The seminal vesicles and their seasonal changes in the Indian catfish, *Heteropneustes*. Copeia 1958:289–297.
Notes that Disselhorst (1904) noticed seminal vesicles in large male pike dur-ing the spawning season.

SUNDBACK, K.

1971   Hauen suomu Ianmaaritykssessa. [Aging of northern pike from scales.] Ruo-men Kalastuslehti 1:9–10. [in Finnish]

SUOMINEN, H.

1980   The microflora of pike in relation to its environment. Lic. thesis, University of Helsinki.

SUPRYAGA, V. G. and A. A. MOZGOVOI

1974   Biological characteristics of *Raphidascaris acus* Anisakidae Ascaridata, a freshwater fish parasite. Parazitologiya 8:494–503.

SURBER, E. E.

1929   The utilization of sloughs in the upper Mississippi wildlife and fish refuge as fish ponds. Transactions of the American Fisheries Society 59:106–113.

SUSLOWSKA, W.

1971   A comparative study on the muscles of the head of *aspius aspius* (Linnaeus, 1758) and *Esox lucius* Linnaeus 1758. Acta Zoologica Cracoviensia 16:695–713.
A description of the structure and topographic relations of the muscles used in the process of food ingestion in pike, a typical flesh-eater.

SUSLOWSKA, W. and K. URBANOWICZ

1957 Badania porownaweze nad wybranymi elementami szkieletu szczupaka—
Esox lucius L., bolenia—*Aspius aspius* (L.) i karpia—*Cyprinus carpio* L.
Zeszyty Naukowe Uniwersytetu Lodz, ser. 2(3):71–93.

SVARDSON, G.

1944 Anordning for vard av gaddyngel i klackningsanstalt. Svensk Fiskerier
Tidskrift 53(4):58–62.

1945 En gaddler i siffror. Svensk Fiskeri Tidskrift 55:187–192.

1947 Gaddlekstudier. Skrifter Sodra Sveriges Fiskeriforening 2:34–59.

1949a Note on spawning habits of *Leuciscus erythrophthalmus* (L.), *Abramis brama*
(L.), and *Esox lucius* L. Institute of Freshwater Research Drottningholm,
Report 29:102–107.
In the spring of 1948, pike were trapped and put into aquaria to spawn under
controlled conditions. Prespawning and spawning behaviour were noted and
possible releasing mechanisms are described.

1949b Natural selection and egg number in fish. Institute of Freshwater Research
Drottningholm, Report 29:115–122.
Discusses the relationship between the number and size of eggs, survival, and
intraspecific competition. Factors considered are parental care, selection
pressure, altitude, latitude, and population status.

1964a Resultatlos gaddodling. Information fran Sotvattenslaboratoriet
Drottningholm 5:2.

1964b Resultatlos gaddodling. Svensk Fiskerier Tidskrift 73:1–8.

1964c Gaddan. Fiske 1964:8–38.

1966 P. M. angaends uppkomsten av rika arsklasser hos gaddan. Svensk Fiskerier
Tidskrift 75(5/6):65–66.

1976 Interspecific population dominance in fish communities of Scandinavian
lakes. Institute of Freshwater Research Drottningholm, Report 55:144–171.
The interactive relations of the best-known species are presented, with discussion of evolutionary trends, specific ecological niches, ecological subspecia-
tion, and non-genetic "interactive segregation". The effects of stress, dominance phenomena, and "buffer species" are included, along with some
management suggestions.

SVARDSON, G. and G. MOLIN

1968 Fiskets effekt pa gaddans storlek och numerar. Information fran Sotvattenslaboratoriet Drottningholm 1968(5):1–20.

1973 The impact of climate on Scandinavian populations of the sander, *Stizostedion lucioperca* (L.). Institute of Freshwater Research Drottningholm,
Report 53:112–139.

1981 The impact of eutrophication and climate on a warm water fish community.
Institute of Freshwater Research, Drottningholm, Report 59:142–151.

SVARDSON, G. and T. WICKBOM

1939 Notes on the chromosomes of some teleosts, *Esox lucius* L., *Lucioperca
lucioperca* L., and *Perca fluviatilis* L. Hereditas 25:472–476.
The diploid number of chromosomes in pike was found to be 18. There were
6 pairs of long chromosomes, among which 4 pairs were V-shaped. Somatic
pairing was found.

SVETOVIDOV, A. N.

1929   On the question of growth and age of the perch, roach and pike of Lake Krugloe. Zoologicheskii Zhurnal 9(3):

SVETOVIDOVA, A. A.

1960   Material on the ichthyofauna age composition and growth rate of fishes in the Lake Dalai-Nor (Peoples Republic of China). Academy of Science USSR 39(2).

          Pike is an important commercial species in the lake, and is more prevalent in the eastern portion.

SVOBODOVA, Z. and M. HEJTMANEK

1976   Total mercury content in the musculature of fishes from the River Ohre and its tributaries. Acta Veterinaria 45(1–2):45–49.

          Used flameless atomic absorption to determine amount of mercury in muscle of 110 fishes, including pike.

SWEETING, R. A.

1976   Studies on *Ligula intestinalis* (L.) effects on a roach population in a gravel pit. Journal of Fish Biology 9:515.

1977   Studies on *Ligula intestinalis*; some aspects of the pathology in the second intermediate host. Journal of Fish Biology 10:43–50.

          The effects of the plerocercoids of *Ligula intestinalis* were studied on a population of roach in a gravel pit. The incidence of the cestode fell from 92% in 0+ roach in April to 25% in January of the succeeding year. The fall in the number of parasitized fish was due to predation, mainly by pike.

SWIDERSKI, E.

1908   Znad Wisloka. [From the Wislok River.] Okolnik Rybacki 100:178–180.

          Protection size and periods for pike.

SWIFT, D. R.

1965   Effect of temperature on mortality and rate of development of the eggs of the pike (*Esox lucius* L.) and the perch (*Perca fluviatilis* L.). Nature 206(4983):528.

          Eggs were stripped from one female pike, fertilized, and placed in trays in constant environment aquaria at the same water temperature as that in which the fish were caught. Temperature controls were adjusted to various temperatures. Daily records were kept of the number of dead eggs or hatched alevins in each aquarium.

SWIRSKI, G.

1980   Untersuchungen uber die Entwickelung des Schultergurtels und des Skelets der Brustflosse des Hechts. Dorpat, Schnakenburg. 60 pp.

SYCH, R.

1971   Elementary teorii oznaczania wicku ryb wedlug lusek: problem wiarydognosci. [Elements of theory on age determination in fish by using scales: problem of likelihood.] Roczniki Nauk Rolniczyck 93:5–73.

SYCHEVA, V. N.

1965   Reaktsiya polvykh zhelez shchuki *Esox lucius* L. na izmenenie ekologicheskikh Uslovii. [Sex gland reaction in pike *Esox lucius* L. to a change in the ecologic environment.] Voprosy Ikhtiologii 5:296–301. [in Russian]

SYMINGTON, D. F.

          Fisheries resources of Saskatchewan. Saskatchewan Department of Natural Resources, Conservation Bulletin 4:1–24.

1959   The fish of Saskatchewan. Saskatchewan Department of Natural Resources, Conservation Bulletin 7:1–25.

SYROVATSKAYA, M. J.

1927   Materialy po plodovitosti ryb r. Dniepra. Trudy Gosudarstvennogo 3(1)

SYTCHEVSKAYA, E. C.

1974   The genus *Esox* from Tertiary deposits in USSR and Mongolia. *In* Kramarenko, N. N., ed., Transactions of the Joint Soviety-Mongolian Paleontological Expedition, Issue 1, Mesozoic and Cenozoic fauna and Biostratigraphy of the Mongolian People's Republic. 367 pp. [in Russian]

1976   The fossil esocoid fishes of the USSR and Mongolia. Academy of Science, USSR 156:1–101. [in Russian]

SZCZERBOWSKI, J. A.

1963   Presja szczupaka na mlodziez troci (*Salmo trutta m. lacustris* L.) a jeziora Wdzydze w potoku Trzebiocha. [The pressure of pike on young trouts (*Salmo trutta m. lacustris* L.) from the Lake Wdzydze in the stream Trzebiocha.] Zeszyty Naukowe Wyzszej Szkoly Rolniczej w Olsztynie 16(1):61–72.
        An attempt to estimate predation by pike on juvenile trout in new conditions. Relationship between predatory activities of pike and its size, age, and sex. Effectiveness of electric catches as a method of reducing pike density.

1965   Proba stosowania nowych rozwiazan przy wyleganiu szczupaka. [Attempts to introduce new methods in artificial pike hatching.] Gospodarka Rybna 17(5):7.

1969   Smiertelnosc wylegu szczupaka. [Mortality of pike hatchlings.] Gospodarka rybna 21(2):7.
        Time of stocking and condition of stocking material needed in order to increase the efficiency of pike stockings.

1972   Fishes in the Lyna River system. Polskie Archiwum Hydrobiologii 19:421–435.

SZCZERBOWSKI, J. A., A. MARTYNIAK and J. TERLECKI

1976   Wzrost szczupaka, krapia, jelca, klenia i ploci w rzebach zlewiska Lyny. [Growth of pike, white bream, dace, chub and roach in the Lyna River system.] Roczniki Nauk Rolniczych, Ser. H, 97(2):79–96.
        Rate of growth of most common river fish species in the catchment area of the Lyna River as a basis for estimating the size at which catches are most effective, both as regards stability of fish production and optical utilization of the existing production conditions.

SZLAMINSKA, M.

1980   A histochemical study of digestive enzymes in pike larvae. Fisheries Management 11(3):139–140.
        The morphological development of the digestive organs and the amylolytic, trypsin-like, pepsin-like and lipolytic types of enzymatic activity were determined in 18-day larvae and in adult pike. Larvae had fully functional digestive organs and with the exception of lipolytic activity, the presence and location of the enzymes were identical in larvae and adult. The results may indicate that pike larvae digest food in the initial period of development.

SZMANIA, D.

1973   Production of northern pike in a winterkill lake. M.A. thesis, University of Wisconsin-Milwaukee.

SZTRAMKO, L. and PAINE, J. R.

1982   Sport fishery data for the Canadian portion of Lake Erie and connecting waters, 1948–80. Ontario Ministry of Natural Resources, Lake Erie Fisheries Assessment Unit, Report 1982–3:1–88.

Entire report consists of tabulated information, with data on pike found throughout.

SZUBA, Z.

1971   Wstepne badonia nad asymetria czaszki szczupaka *Esox lucius* L. [An introductory study of pike (*Esox lucius* (L.) skull asymetry.] Zeszyty Naukawe Wyzszej Szkoly Rolniczej w Olsztynie 2(35):3–16.

Studies were made on 35 skulls of pike of both sexes.

TACK, E.
1972   The fish of the south Westphalian highland including the Moehne dam and Ruhr. Decheniana 125(1–2):63–77.

TACK, S. L.
1973   Distribution, abundance, and natural history of the Arctic grayling in the Tanana River drainage. Alaska Department of Fish and Game, Division of Sport Fish, 14:1–34.

TAGSTROM, B.
1940   Om forstrackning av gaddyngel. Svensk Fiskerier Tidskrift 49:31–38.

TAN, E. L. and T. WOOD
1969   Enzymes of the pentose phosphate cycle in muscles of rat, ox, frog, lobster, chicken, northern pike and carp and Ehrlich ascites cells. Comparative Biochemistry and Physiology 31:635–643.

TANDON, K. K. and O. OLIVA
1978   Further notes on the growth of pike, *Esox lucius* from Czechoslovakia (Osteichthys: Clupeiformes). Vestnik Ceskoslovenske Spolecnosti Zoologicke 42:69–76.
        Growth rate of pike collected during 1965–75 was studied from the scales of 87 specimens. Pike of 11+ years were recorded. Back-calculation was used for lengths at the formation of respective annuli.

TARNAVSKII, N. P.
1967   Biologija scuki Verchnego Dnepra. Rybnoe Khozyaistvo 3:61–69.

TAVERNER, E. and J. MOORE
1935   The angler's weekend book. London, Seely, Service. 512 pp.

TAYLOR, F.
1962   Angling in earnest. London, MacGibbon & Kee.

TEDLA, S. and C. H. FERNANDO
1969   Changes in the parasite fauna of the white perch, *Roccus americanus* (Gmelin), colonizing new habitats. Journal of Parasitology 55:1063–1066.

TELLER, S. and D. BARDACK
1974   New records of late Pleistocene vertebrates from the southern end of Lake Michigan. American Midland Naturalist 94(1):179–189.
        Fossils from LaPort Co., Indiana, included *Esox*. The fossil beds were from 5500 to 6300 years old. Evidence suggested that the fossils were deposited in a shallow lake or pond with a muddy bottom and weedy vegetation. Other Pleistocene vertebrate records from the Great Lakes drainage are discussed.

TEN KATE, J. H.
1973   Angular acceleration detection by the growing pike. Oto-Rhino-Laryngology 19:110–119.

TEN KATE, J. H. and J. W. KUIPER
1970   The viscosity of the pike's endolymph. Journal of Experimental Biology 53:495–500.

TEODORESCU, A.-C.
1970   Contribution to the study of the growth of the digestive tract in fish in relation to the diet. Studii si Cercetari de Biologie, Seria Zoologie, 22:493–499.

TEODORESCU-LEONTE, R.
1969   Considerations upon the actual fish population structure inside the Danube delta. Buletinui Institutului de Cercetari si Proiectari Piscicole 28(3):29–37. [in Romanian, English summary]

300

TEPLOVA, V. N. and V. P. TEPLOV

1953   The feeding of the pike in the upper Pechora basin. Voprosy Ikhtiologii 1.

TERESHENKOV, I. I.

1972   Replacement of teeth in the pike [*Esox lucius* (L.)]. Journal of Ichthyology 12:807–812.

TERLECKI, J.

1973   Plodnosc szczupaka - *Esox lucius* (Linnaeus 1758) z jeziora Sniardwy. [Fecundity of pike - *Esox lucius* (Linnaeus 1758) from Lake Sniardwy.] Roczniki Nauk Rolniczych 95(3):161–176.

       Ninety-six gonads of female pike from Sniardwy Lake were taken in 1968–70 and their absolute fecundity was determined. Dependence between absolute fecundity, body size, and age of the fish was traced. Fecundity of the pike from Sniardwy Lake was compared with that of pike from other waters.

TERSKOV, I. A., E. A. VAGANOV and V. V. SPIROV

1976   Microphotometric analysis of some freshwater fish scales. Izvestiya Sibirskogo Otdeleniya Akademii Nauk SSR, Seriya Biologo-Meditsinskikh Nauk 2:95–103.

TESARCIK, J. and J. MARES

1967   The case of pox of brook pike. Buletin Vyzkumy Ustav Rybarsky a Hydrobiologicky Vodnany 3(1):18.

THIENEMANN, A.

1950   Verbreitungsgeschichte der Susswasserwelt Europas. Versuch einer historischen Tiergeographie der Europaischen Binnengewasser. Schweizerbart'sche Verlagsbuchhandlung. Stuttgart, Erwin Nagele.

THOMPSON, D.

1979   Aging pike and muskie. Outdoor Canada, March/April 1979, pp. 45–47.

THOMPSON, E. S.

1898   A list of the fishes known to occur in Manitoba. Forest and Stream 51(11):214.

THOMPSON, G. J. and H. C. GILSON

1952   How to remove unwanted perch and pike. Journal of the British Waterworks Association 35:88–98.

THOMPSON, G. T. and T. B. BAGENAL

1973   Pike gill netting in Windermere. Fisheries Management 4:97–101.

THOMPSON, J. S.

1982   An epizootic of lymphoma in northern pike, *Esox lucius* L., from the Aland Islands of Finland. Journal of Fish Diseases 5:1–11.

       Macroscopic and microscopic inspection of 19 tumorous pike showed that this lymphoma was similar to those seen in North America, Ireland, and Sweden. It was classified as a stem cell lymphoma. Tumour cells cultured during several months at 4 C showed morphological features of differentiation and resembled plasma cells. No conclusive evidence of viruses in the lesion was obtained.

THOMPSON, P.-A. and W. THRELFALL

1978   The metazoan parasites of two species of fish from the Port-Cartier-Sept-Iles Park, Quebec. Naturaliste Canadien 105:429–431.

THOMPSON, W.

1883   A trouting trip to St. Ignace Island. *In* Orvis, C. F., and Cheney, A. N., ed., Fishing with the fly. pp. 97–117.

THOMPSON, Z.

1850   Description and drawings of a new species of *Esox*. Proceedings of the Boston Society of Natural History 3:55–163, 173, 305–306.

1853   History of Vermont, natural, civil and statistical. Part 1, Chapter 5, Fishes of Vermont. Burlington, published by the author, pp. 137–138.

THORPE, A.

1976   Studies on the role of insulin in teleost metabolism. *In* Grillo, T., et al., eds., The evolution of pancreatic islets. Symposium, Leningrad, 1975, pp. 271–284.

THORPE, A. and B. W. INCE

1974a   The effects of hormones, drugs and glucose loading on blood metabolites in the pike *Esox lucius*. General and Comparative Endocrinology 22:345–346. [Abstract]
        The levels of plasma glucose, amino acid nitrogen, and cholesterol were determined. A heart cannulation technique was used to permit serial blood sampling and the administration of hormones and drugs directly into the blood stream.

1974b   The effects of pancreatic hormones, catecholamines and glucose loading on blood metabolites in the northern pike (*Esox lucius* L.). General and Comparative Endocrinology 23:29–44.

1976   Plasma insulin levels in teleosts determined by a charcoal-separation radioimmunoassay technique. General and Comparative Endocrinology 30:332.

THORPE, L. M. and D. A. WEBSTER

        A fishery survey of important Connecticut waters. Connecticut Geology and Natural History Survey, Bulletin 63.

THREINEN, C. W.

        Impact of shore development on northern pike spawning. Wisconsin Department of Natural Resources.

1969   An evaluation of the effect and extent of habitat loss on northern pike populations and means of prevention of losses. Wisconsin Department of Natural Resources, Fish Management Bureau, Management Report 28:1–25.
        Attempts to assess whether recreational or other uses of inland surface fresh waters significantly affect the pike fishery, and what measures might alleviate the conflict.

THREINEN, C. W. and A. OEHMCKE

1950   The northern invades the musky's domain. Wisconsin Conservation Bulletin 15(9):10–12.
        Argues that fishery practices such as stocking the two species in the same water body favour pike survival due to its better start in life. Lists "invaded'"water bodies in Wisconsin.

THREINEN, C. W., C. A. WISTROM, B. APELGREN and H. E. SNOW

1966   The northern pike: its life history, ecology, and management. Wisconsin Conservation Department Publication 235:1–16.
        Topics of discussion include classification, distribution, description, habits, reproduction, growth, population, angling, and economic value.

THRELFALL, W. and G. HANEK

1970   Helminths from northern pike (*Esox lucius* L.) in Labrador. Journal of Parasitology 56:662.
        A list of helminths found in four pike from two localities.

302

THUEMLER, T. G.

1982   Winter creel census on Lake Noquebay, Marinette County. Wisconsin
        Department of Natural Resources, Fish Management Report 122:1–16.
        Between December 20, 1981, and April 15, 1982, 3,051 anglers were inter-
        viewed. They fished an estimated 32,142 hours. The harvest rate was 0.65
        fish/hour. Pike were the primary game fish taken.

TIMMERMANS, G. A.

1979   Culture of fry and fingerlings of pike, *Esox lucius*. European Inland Fisheries
        Advisory Committee Technical Paper 35(Suppl. 1):177–183.

TIMOSHINA, L. A.

1970   Changes brought about in the amino acid composition of fish muscles and
        blood by starvation. Journal of Ichthyology 10:342–347.
        Combined and free amino acids in pike muscle during the period of winter
        starvation were determined by paper chromatography. After winter starvation
        the concentration of most amino acids was reduced, with the exception of
        threonine. After a month of summer starvation combined amino acids were
        not significantly altered, but the concentration of free amino acids was per-
        ceptibly increased.

TINBERGEN, N.

1956   Spines, safe and advantages. Levende Natuur 59(2):25–33.

TODD, A.

1968   St. Lawrence River - Thousand Island Kemptville District, 1968 creel census
        report. Ontario Department of Lands and Forests.
        Information collected included the number of anglers, number of each species
        caught, total number of hours angled, residence of anglers, growth rates, and
        size range of angled fish, and other related data.

TOMCKO, C. M.

1982   Use of bluegill forage by tiger muskellunge, effects of predator experience,
        vegetation, and prey density. M.S. thesis, Ohio State University.

TOMCKO, C. M., R. A. STEIN and R. F. CARLINE

1984   Predation by tiger muskellunge on bluegill: effects of predator experience,
        vegetation, and prey density. Transactions of the American Fisheries Society
        113:588–594.
        Tested the effects of predator experience (using hybrids previously exposed
        to bluegill), vegetative cover, and bluegill density on the number of hybrids
        capturing prey. Few experienced or naive hybrids captured bluegills at low
        prey density, regardless of the presence or absence of vegetation. When blue-
        gill density was increased from 1 to 5 prey/sq.m. in ponds or to 40/sq.m. in
        aquaria, many hybrids captured bluegills.

TOMLIN, W. D.

1892   The pike. *In* American game fishes. Chicago, Rand, McNally, pp. 367–380.

TONER, E. D.

1959a   Predation by pike in three Irish lakes. Irish Department of Lands, Report of
        Sea Inland Fisheries 1959(app. 25):1–7.
        Predatory habits of pike have been known to seriously reduce trout and sal-
        mon stocks and the extent of this damage was estimated. Drastic thinning of
        pike stocks increased trout survival and improved trout angling.

1959b   Predator and prey relationships. Salmon and Trout Magazine May 1959, pp.
        104–110.

1966   Synopsis of biological data on the pike, *Esox lucius* Linnaeus 1758. Fish and Agricultural Organization Fisheries Synopsis 30:1–30.

TONER, E. D. and G. H. LAWLER

1969   Synopsis of biological data on the pike, *Esox lucius* Linnaeus 1758. Food and Agricultural Organization Fisheries Synopsis 30 (rev. 1):1–37.

TONER, G. C.

1943   Ecological and geographical distribution of fishes in eastern Ontario. M.A. thesis, University of Toronto. 91 pp.

         Notes on numbers of pike taken at 36 sites. General information on habitat and spawning.

n.d.   Conservation and Canada's game fish. Carling Conservation Club, 8 pp.

TONG, S. C., W. H. GUTENMANN, D. J. LISK, G. E. BURDICK and E. J. HARRIS

1972   Trace metals in New York state fish. New York Fish and Game Journal 19(2):123–131.

         Analysis of barium, cadmium, cobalt, nickel, silver, tin, vanadium, and zinc was performed by spark source mass spectrometry following dry ashing of samples

TONN, W. M. and J. J. MAGNUSON

1982   Patterns in the species composition and richness of fish assemblages in northern Wisconsin lakes. Ecology 63:1149–1166.

TOWARNICKI, R.

1962   O unaczynieniu przysadki mozgowej szczupaka (*Esox lucius* L.) i o znaczeniu tego narzadu u ryb w ogole. [The vascularization of the pituitary body of the pike (*Esox lucius* L.) and on the role of this organ in fishes.] Folia Morphologica 13:1–20.

         The vascularization of the various lobes of the pituitary, as well as the blood supply, are described.

1963   Anatomia rozpoznawcza kostnoszkieletowych ryb uzytkowych. Cz. I. Myologia makroskopowa szczupaka i karpia. [Basic anatomy of teleost fishes. Part I. Macroscopic myology of pike and carp.] Skrypty Wyzszej Szkoly Rolniczej w Olsztynie. 54 pp.

TOWNSEND, A. H. and P. P. KEPLER

1974   Population studies of northern pike and whitefish in the Minto Flats complex with emphasis on the Chatanika River. Alaska Department of Fish and Game, Project F-9–6(vol. 15):59–79.

TOWNSEND, D. C.

         Game fishing devices. London, A. & C. Black

TRAUTMAN, M. B.

1957   The fishes of Ohio. Ohio State University Press. 683 pp.

TRAUTMAN, M. B. and C. L. HUBBS

1936   When do pike shed their teeth? Transactions of the American Fisheries Society 65:261–266.

         Tooth analysis of 188 *Esox lucius*, 7 *E. masquinongy*, and 6 *E. niger* did not support the theory that pike shed their teeth in late summer.

1948   When do pike shed their teeth? Michigan Conservation 17(8):4, 5, 10.

TRDAN, R. J.

1981   Reproductive biology of *Lampsilis radiata siliquoidea* Pelecypoda, Unionidae. American Midland Naturalist 106:243–248.

TRESSLER, W. L., L. H. TIFFANY and W. P. SPENCER
  1940   Limnological studies of Buckeye Lake, Ohio. Ohio Journal of Science
          40:261–290.
TRETIAKOV, D.
  1936   Morfogenez zuba szczuki i sargana. Archives d'Anatomie d'Histologie et
          d'Embryologie 15
TRETJAKOFF, D. K. VON
  1941   Gattungsunterschiede des Hechtes und der Umbra. Comptes Rendus de
          l'Academie des Sciences de l'URSS 30:86–89.
TRIPLETT, J. R., D. A. CULVER and G. B. WATERFIELD
  1981   An annotated bibliography on the effects of water-level manipulation on lakes
          and reservoirs. Ohio Department of Natural Resources, Project F-57-R(Study
          8):1–50.
TROCHERIE, F. and C. BERCY
  1984   Ultrasonic tagging of pike (*Esox lucius* L.) and carp (*Cyprinus carpio* L.) in
          the Seine River near the Montereau power station. Cahiers de la Laboratorie
          Hydrobiologie Montereau 15:13–20.
          Transmitters were attached to six pike. All pike were tracked for 15 days
          after tagging and three for more than a month. The experiment indicated that
          the tagging technique used can provide useful information on movement of
          adult pike during the spawning period, but cannot be transposed to other
          species without testing.
TROCHERIE, F. and B. MIGEON
  1984   Effects of repeated thermal shocks (+4 C and +8 C) on survival and hatching
          of pike eggs (*Esox lucius* L.). Cahiers de la Laboratorie Hydrobiologie Mon-
          tereau 15:21–24.
          The highly significant results of this experiment indicated that the lack of
          reproduction success of pike on artificial spawning grounds placed in the
          discharge canal of the Montereau power station must be related to environ-
          mental factors other than the variations of thermal discharge of this plant.
TROFIMENKO, V. Y.
  1969   On the question of genesis of the helminthofauna of freshwater fishes of the
          Asiatic subarctic. Izvestiya Akademii Nauk SSSR, Seriya Biologicheskikh,
          6:912–918. [in Russian, English summary]
TRUMAN, E. B.
  1869   Observations on the development of the ovum of the pike. Monthly Micros-
          copy Journal 2:185–203.
          An account of collecting pike eggs, keeping them alive, and watching their
          development.
TSCHORTNER, U.
  1956   Untersuchungen uber den Einfluss einiger Milieufaktoren auf die Entwick-
          lung des Hechtes (*Esox lucius* L.). Archiv fuer Hydrobiologie 24:123–152.
TSEPKIN, E. A.
  1970   The history of the ichthyofauna of the Dniester. Byulleten Moskovskogo
          Obshchestva Ispytatelei Prirody Otdel Biologicheskii 75:127–132.
  1972   Fish from archaeological excavations of ancient Moscow. Byulleten
          Moskovskogo Obshchestva Ispytatelei Prirody Otdel Biolocheskii 77:80–84.
  1976   The history of the commercial ichthyofauna and fishing in the Lake Baikal
          basin. Byulleten Moskovoskogo Obshchestva Ispytatelei Prirody Otdel

Biologicheskii 81:65–73.

1977   The history of commercial ichthyofauna of the Klyazma River basin. Biolo-gicheskie Nauki 20(8):53–55. [in Russian]

1978   History of commercial ichthyofauna and fishing in the Irtysh Basin. Byul-leten Moskovskogo Obshchestva Ispytatelei Prirody Otdel Biologicheskii 83(2):81–87.

1980   History of commercial ichthyofauna and fishing in the middle course of the Angara River. Voprosy Ikhtiologii 20:543–545.

1981   Changes in species composition of the ichthyofauna fishes in the Oka Basin during the late Holocene. Byulleten Moskovskogo Obshchestva Ispytatelei Prirody Otdel Biologicheskii 86:51–55.

TSVETKOV, V. I.

1969   The sensitivity of some freshwater fishes to rapid pressure change. Problems in Ichthyology 9:706–711.

TUBB, R. A., F. A. COPES and C. JOHNSTON

1965   Fishes of the Sheyenne River of North Dakota. Proceedings of the North Dakota Academy of Science 19:120–128.

TURNER, L. J.

1984   Space and prey use by northern pike (*Esox lucius* L.) in two Alberta lakes. M.S. thesis, University of Alberta. 177 pp.

           Factors affecting the distribution and foraging rate of pike were assessed in two small, deep, north temperate lakes. Activity of both juvenile and adult pike was primarily confined to daylight hours. Water temperature, dissolved oxygen concentration, and the presence of vegetation influenced depth distri-bution of pike in both populations. Within the selected depth stratum, ecolog-ical interactions appeared to have been responsible for the finer resolution of microhabitat use, intraspecific predation pressure in juveniles and foraging strategies in adult pike.

TURNER, L. J. and W. C. MACKAY

1985   Use of visual census for estimating population size in northern pike (*Esox lucius*). Canadian Journal of Fisheries and Aquatic Sciences 42:1835–1840.

           Detailed underwater observation within a specified area was used to assess depth distribution, sample independence, and reaction of pike to the presence of the observer. Pike selected depths of <1 m, constant throughout the sum-mer months. Samples were 92% independent; reaction of pike to a diver con-tributed an estimated 4% error to the estimate.

TURNER, L. M.

1886   Contributions to the natural history of Alaska, May 1874 -August 1881. Washington.

TURNER, M. A. and A. L. SWICK

1983   The English-Wabigoon River system. 4. Interaction between mercury and selenium accumulated from waterborne and dietary sources by northern pike. Canadian Journal of Fisheries and Aquatic Sciences 40:2241–2250.

           Although selenium is a pollutant released by several industries, it is also an essential nutrient that protects mammals against mercury intoxication. Pike were held in water containing trace or elevated concentrations of selenium. It is inferred that selenium added to aquatic ecosystems and incorporated subse-quently in the food web would interfere with biomagnification of mercury.

TURRELL, W. J.

    1910   Ancient angling authors. London.

              Covers English angling literature in the 10th-18th centuries. Plate of a man pike fishing with a float. Tale of pike fearing bait, tench taking it, pike learning therefrom.

TYMOWSKI, J.

    1939   Szczupak i jego rola w gospodarce jeziorowej. [Pike and its role in lake fisheries.] Przeglad Rybacki 12(4):205–210.

              Comments and observations on food conversion rate in pike. Profitability of pike production.

    1951   Jeszcze w sprawie szczupaka. [More comments on pike.] Wiadomosci Wedkarskie 1–2:19–14.

              Increase of pike stocks through artificial stockings.

TYSZKIEWICZ, K.

    1969   Structure and vascularization of the skin of the pike (*Esox lucius* L.) Acta Biologica Cracoviensia, Series Zoologia, 12:68–79.

              Investigation of the structure and vascularization of the skin of pike was carried out on 10 specimens ranging in weight from 140 to 222 g. The epidermis was on the average 90 microns thick. The capillaries of the subepithelial network, expressed as the length per 1 sq.mm. of area, averaged 13.37 mm. The capillaries on the average were 9.4 microns in diameter.

UMINSKI, W.

1917   O rybach w rzekach, jeziorach i morzach. [About fishes in rivers, lakes, and seas.] Wydawnictwa imeni M. Brzezinskiego. 91 pp.

UNDERHILL, A. H.

1939   Cross between *Esox niger* and *E. lucius*. Copeia 1939:237.

Eggs of chain pickerel were artificially fertilized with the sperm of a pike. The resulting hybrids showed characteristics intermediate between the two species.

UNDERHILL, J. C. and J. B. MOYLE

1968   The fishes of Minnesota's Lake Superior region. Conservation Volunteer 31(177):29–53.

The pike is common in many lakes of the Lake Superior basin.

UNGUREANU, E. M., A. C. DRANGA and R. P. MARINOV

1970   Diphyllobothriasis in the Danube Delta. Journal of Parasitology 56:477–478.

UPPER MISSISSIPPI RIVER CONSERVATION COMMITTEE

1959   Supplemental report, fish technical subcommittee, proceedings of the 13th annual meeting. Unpublished MS, 147 pp.

URBANOWSKI, W.

1937   Z kampanii szczupakowej. [Pike campaign.] Przeglad Rybacki 10(8): 320–323.

Description of spring pike campaign, during which eyed eggs of pike were obtained.

U.S. BUREAU OF COMMERCIAL FISHERIES

1965   Missouri River reservoir commercial fishing investigations. A documentation of 1963–64 activities and findings. Unpublished MS, 74 pp.

U.S. FISH AND WILDLIFE SERVICE

1974   Report of the National Task Force for Public Fish Hatchery Policy. U.S. Fish and Wildlife Service, Washington, D.C. 295 pp.

During 1973, 515 state and federal hatcheries produced and stocked 17 million pike.

1976   Ecological studies for navigation season extension on the St. Lawrence River. U.S. Fish and Wildlife Service, Cortland, New York. 166 pp.

1981   Standards for the development of habitat suitability index models. U.S. Fish and Wildlife Service, Division of Ecology Service.

UTHE, J. F., E. ROBERTS, L. W. CLARKE and H. TSUYUKI

1966   Comparative electropherograms of representatives of the families Petromyzontidae, Esocidae, Centrarchidae, and Percidae. Journal of the Fisheries Research Board of Canada 23:1663–1671.

The starch gel electropherogram of muscle myogens and blood hemoglobins of representatives from the family Esocidae were found to be within the limits of species specificity, with some exceptions.

VALKEAJARVI, P.
  1983   On the migrations, growth and mortality of perch, pike, burbot, whitefish and roach according to the taggings in Lake Konnevesi, central Finland Tiedonantoja 33:83–109. [in Finnish, English summary]

VAN ENGEL, W. A.
  1940   The rate of growth of the northern pike, *Esox lucius* Linnaeus, in Wisconsin waters. Copeia 1940:177–188.
          Analysis of size data and scales from 515 angled pike. Age groups II, III, IV comprised 62% of the specimens. The ratio of standard to total length was 1:1–13. There was a positive correlation between rate of growth and range of latitude. Average length was 18 inches (15.9 inches S.L.) by end of the second year. Coefficient of condition was 0.6+, increasing with increase in age.

VAN LEEUWEN, J. L. and M. MULLER
  1983   The recording and interpretations of pressures in prey-sucking fish. Netherlands Journal of Zoology 33:425–475.

VAN LOON, J. C. and R. J. BEAMISH
  1977   Heavy-metal contamination by atmospheric fallout of several Flin Flon area lakes and the relation of fish populations. Journal of the Fisheries Research Board of Canada 34:899–906.
          High concentrations of zinc, copper, and cadmium were found in 31 lakes in the vicinity of the Flin Flon smelter. Pike populations did not appear to be adversely affected by the heavy metal concentrations.

VAN NOORDEN, S. and G. J. PATENT
  1978   Localization of pancreatic polypeptides (PP)-like immunoreactivity in the pancreatic islet of some teleost fishes. Cell Tissue Research 188:521.

VAN OOSTEN, J.
  1937   The age, growth, and sex ratio of the Lake Superior longjaw, *Leucichthys zenithicus* (Jordan and Evermann). Papers of the Michigan Academy of Science, Arts and Letters 22:691–711.
  1946   The pikes. U.S. Fish and Wildlife Service, Fishery Leaflet 166:1–6.
  1957   Exotics and hybrids in fish management. Proceedings 24th Annual Meeting, Association of Midwest Game and Fish Commissioners, 24:17–22.
  1960   The true pikes. U.S. Fish and Wildlife Service, Fishery Leaflet 496:1–9.
          Information on morphological characteristics, habitat, reproduction, and growth.

VARLEY, M. E.
  1967   British freshwater fishes. London, Fishing News (Books). 148 pp.

VASEY, F. W.
  1968   Fisheries management planning and research. Special fisheries and methods of management of impoundments. Introduction of northern pike. Missouri Conservation Commission, Dingell-Johnson Report F-1-R-17/Wk.Pl. 05/Job 10:1–7.
  1974   Life history of introduced northern pike in Thomas Hill Reservoir. Missouri Conservation Commission, Dingell-Johnson Project F-1-R-23, Study I-5, Job 2:1–14.
          Survival, growth rate, reproduction, feeding habits, and contribution to creel were investigated for stocked fish from 1967 through 1971.

VASHCHENKO, D. M.

1958a   Value of the pike in regulation of the composition of the ichthyofauna in Kakhovskoe Reservoir. Trudy Nauchno-Issledovatel'skogo Instituta Rybnogo Khozyaistva 2.

1958b   Toward the question on the role of the pike in suppression of the number of low-value and trash fish in reservoirs. Trudy Nauchno-Issledovatel'skogo Instituta Rybnogo Khozyaistva 11

1958c   The carp as food of pike during the first year after the filling of Kakhov reservoir. Zoologicheskii Zhurnal 37:1745–1748.

1962a   Vliyanie shchuki na zapasy sazana v Kremenchugskom vodokhranilishche. [The effect of pike on the carp stock of the Kremenchug Reservoir.] Zoologicheskii Zhurnal 41:1749–1751.

In Kremenchug water reservoir, at the sites of concentration of the sazan young, the pike is a dangerous predator. In other areas of the reservoir the pike is a beneficial predator which consumes fishes of little value and coarse fish.

1962b   Sravnitel 'naya otsenka roli khishchnykh ryb: shchuka, sudaka i okunya vodokhranishch. [Comparative appraisal of the role of predatory fish: *Esox*, *Lucioperca* and *Perca* in the formation of the fish fauna in the Dnieper reservoirs.] Voprosy Ekologii 5:22–23.

An analysis of the feeding of *Esox* in the Dnieper and its reservoirs showed that these fish fed on little-valued and waste fish. The *Esox* are valuable food fish, which in suitable numbers played a useful role in the formation of the fish fauna of the Dneiper and its reservoirs.

VASILIU, G. D. and C. SOCA

1968   Fauna vertebratica Romaniae. Romania, Muzeul Judetean Bacau. 296 pp. [in Romanian]

VASIL'YEV, V. P.

1980   Chromosome numbers in fish-like vertebrates and fish. Journal of Ichthyology 20:1–38.

Data for 1076 species, including pike. Presents data obtained by old and new methods separately.

VAUGHAN, G. E. and D. W. COBLE

1975   Sublethal effects of three ectoparasites on fish. Journal of Fish Biology 7:283–294.

Laboratory experiments were carried out in which fish with and without the parasites and with light or heavy infestations of the parasites were exposed to predation by pike.

VEILLEUX, C. M. and R. L. SEGUIN

1968   Transformations a la frayere de brochet (*Esox lucius*) au ruisseau Pelisser, comte de Papineau, et observations sur les brochetons. Annales de l'Association Canadienne Francaise pour l'Avancement des Sciences 35:91–92.

VELAZ DE MEDRANO, L.

1949   Nota informativa sobre el lucio. Montes 25:11–22.

Literature review on the life history of pike previous to introduction to the Iberian Peninsula.

VENDRELY, R. and C. VENDRELY

1950   On the absolute concentration of deoxyribose nucleic acid in the cell nuclei of several species of birds and fish. Comptes Rendus Hebdomadaires des Seances de l'Academie des Sciences 120:788–790.

VERHEIJEN, F. J.

1963   Alarm substance in some North American cyprinid fishes. Copeia 1963:174–176.

1969   Some aspects of the reactivity of fish to visual stimuli in the natural and in a controlled environment. Food and Agriculture Organization Fish Report 2(62):417–429.

VERHEIJEN, F. J. and H. J. REUTER

1969   The effect of alarm substance on predation among cyprinids. Animal Behaviour 17:551–554.

VERZHBINSKAYA, N. A., L. I. PERSHINA and V. G. LEONT'EV

1977   Proteins of mitochondrial membranes in lower vertebrates. Journal of Evolutionary Biochemistry and Physiology 13:118–124. [in Russian]

VESEY-FITZGERALD, B. and F. LAMONT, eds.

n.d.   Game fish of the world. New York, Harper and Brothers. 446 pp.

VESSEL, M. F. and S. EDDY

1941   A preliminary study of the egg production of certain Minnesota fishes. Minnesota Bureau of Fishery Research, Investigational Report 26:1–26.

VIBERT, R., ed.

1967   Fishing with electricity; its applications to biology and management. London, Fishing News (Books). 276 pp.
        Pike is mentioned briefly as an easy fish to catch using an electroshocker. The use of electricity to control unwanted pike populations during the spawning season is described.

VIENNA: ARCHIV

1965   Archivalien aus acht Jahrhunderten. Ausstellung des Archivs der Stadt Wien. Historisches Museum der Stadt Wien. 15. Sonderausstellung. Dec. 1964-Feb. 1965. Wien.
        Exhibition guidebook and catalogue; no text, but a plate - 1507 Feb. 24 fishery ordinance of Maximilian I, including coloured picture of pike.

VILHANEN, M., H. KOKKO and V.-M. KAIJOMAA

1982   Fishing, fishes and factors influencing them in Lake Pyhaselka. University of Joensuu, Publication of Karelian Institute 48:1–120.

VINCENT OF BEAUVAIS

1624   Speculum naturale. Vol. 1 of his Speculum quadruplex sive speculum maius. 4 vols. Duaci, Baltazaris Belleri. Reprinted Graz, Akademische, 1964–1965.

VINNIKOV, Y. A., V. I. GOVARDOVSKII and I. V. OSIPOVA

1965   Electron-microscopical study of the organ of gravitation, the utriculus, of the pike (Esox lucius). Biofizika 10:1003–1006.
        The utriculus contains a single type of receptor cell of a cylindrical form. The neurological supply is described. The peculiarities of the substructure of the organization of the utriculus of pike are characterized by retention of a series of primitive features that are characteristic of lateral line organs.

VIRBICKAS, J.

1972   Osobennosti razvitija molodi scuki v prudach. Voprosy razvedenija ryb i rakobraznych v vodojemach Litvy, Vil'njus, Mintis, pp. 167–182.

VLADYKOV, V. D.

1958   Liste des familles de poissons d'eau salee du Quebec, suivie d'une liste des especes capturees et leurs endroits de capture. Quebec Departement Pecheries, pp. 1–66.

VLADYKOV, V. D. and D. E. MCALLISTER

1961   Preliminary list of marine fishes of Quebec. Naturaliste Canadien 88(3):53–78.

VOIGT, V. E.

1935   Die fische aus der mitteleozanen Braunkohle des Geiseltales. Mit besonderer berucksichtigung der erhaltenen Weichteile. Nova Acta Leopoldina 2:21–146.

VOINO-YASENETSKII, A. V.

1958   Otrazhenie evolyutsionnoi zakonomernosti v epileptiformnoi reaktsii zhivotnykh na deistvie vysokogo partsial'nogo davleniya kisloroda. [Reflection of the evolutionary pattern in the epileptiform reaction of animals to the effect of a high partial pressure of oxygen.] Moscow.
        Investigated the effect of increased oxygen content on pike and found that the fish develop chaotic movements, which were ascribed to a breakdown in the upper levels of the central nervous system.

VOLCHUK, H. L.

1976   Distribution of radioactive materials in aquatic environments, with consideration of their carcinogenic potential in aquatic animals. Progress in Experimental Tumor Research 20:35–43.
        In the open ocean, naturally occurring radioisotopes are the predominant source of exposure to animals. In coastal areas, where releases of radioactivity have occurred due to operations of the nuclear power industry, fission or activation products predominate.

VOLKOVA, L. A.

1973   The effect of light intensity on the availability of food organisms to some fishes of Lake Baikal. Journal of Ichthyology 13:591–602.
        Determined threshold values of light intensity, the lowest values of light intensity for the commencement of active feeding and the maximum feeding rate. The role of vision in feeding was established.

VOLODIN, V. M.

1960   Effect of temperature on the embryonic development of the pike, the blue bream (*Abramis ballerus* L.) and the white bream (*Blicca bjoerkna* L.). Trudy Instituta Biologii Vodokhran. 3(6):231–237.

VONK, H. J.

1927   Die Verdauung bei den Fischen. Zeitschrift fur Vergleichende Physiologie 5:445–546.

1939   Die biologische Bedeutung des pH - optimums der Verdauungsenzyme bei den Vertebraten. Ergebnisse der Enzymforschung 8:55.

VOOREN, C. M.

1972   Ecological aspects of the introduction of fish species into natural habitats in Europe, with special reference to the Netherlands. A literature survey. Journal of Fish Biology 4:565–583.
        Revises the information existent on the 39 species of fishes that have been introduced into European waters during the last two centuries. Discusses the abiotic and biotic factors in relation to each species and the problems created

312

by the introductions, especially of piscivorous species.

VORONIN, F. N. and V. V. KRYLOV

1971   Fish of Lake Vygonovskoe and fishery. Part 2. Vestnik Zoologii 5(3):40–44.

VORONONKOVA, L. D.

1964   On fishing in the Tripol settlements (III—1st milennium B.C.). Problems in Ichthyology 4:599–602.

VOSTRADOVSKA, M.

1978   K potravni biologic stiky ceeche vodarenskhch nadrzice Zelivka a Hubenov. [On the trophic biology of pike in the water-supply reservoirs Zelivka and Hubenov.] Vertebratologicke Zpravy, pp. 74–80. [in Czechoslovakian, English summary]

       The food consumed by various sizes of pike in each reservoir and the dietary changes that have occurred since the filling of the Zelivka reservoir are discussed.

VOSTRADOVSKY, J.

1968a   Dynamika populace stiky obecne (*Esox lucius* L.) v udoltelem na hospodarskou tezby ryb. Zapiski Zpravy, pp. 39–68.

1968b   Dynamika populace stiky obecne (*Esox lucius* L.) v udolni nadrzi Lipno. Kand. disert. prace Hydrob. Laborator., pp. 1–110.

1969a   Znackovani, migrace a rust znackovanych stik v udolni nadrzi Lipno. [Tagging, migration, and growth of tagged pikes in the Lipno Dam Lake. Buletin Vyzkumy Ustav Rybarsky a Hydrobiologicky Vodnany 5(3):9–18. [English summary]

       Study of 459 pike marked with monofilament threads and acetate cellulose tags, including times and distances of recapture.

1969b   Vyvoj ulovku a pomer pohlavi stiky obecne (*Esox lucius* L.) v udolni nadrzi Lipno. [The development of catches and the sex ratio of pike in the Lipno dam lake.] Buletin Vyzkumy Ustav Rybarsky a Hydrobiologicky Vodnany 5(4):7–17.

       Compares catches of nets and anglers from 1958 in Czechoslovakia. Discussion of size selection by nets, effectiveness of angling, sex ratio of 2,465 pike, and change in harvest rate by nets and angling.

1969c   The mortality rate, survival, the biomass, and the abundance of the pike (*Esox lucius* L.) in the Lipno Valley Dam. Zivocisna vyroba 14(42):799–812. [English summary]

       Study of 2,522 Czechoslovakian specimens caught 1960 to 1967. Involved the application of Jackson's method and calculations of the recaptures of tags.

1970a   Vypocet delkoveho rustu ryb podle Sentjakove na prikoadu stiky obecne (*Esox lucius*) z Lipna. [The calculation of the growth nomogram according to Shentyuakova, using the example of pike (*Esox lucius* L.) from the Lipno Dam Lake.] Buletin Vyzkumy Ustav Rybarsky a Hydrobiologicky Vodnany 6(3):26–32.

       Considers the allometric relation between radius of the scale and length of the body. Compares calculated values with empirical values, showing high consistency in 257 pike.

1970b   Vztah delky a vahy, coeficient kondice a vztahy delek u stiky (*Esox lucius* L.) z Lipna. [Length and weight relationship, coefficient of condition and the relation of lengths in pike (*Esox lucius* L.) of the Lipno Dam.] Zivocisna Vyroba 16(43):497–508.

Determined the constant of the length-weight relationship by empirical or calculated weight values of 3,107 specimens.

1971   Potrava stiky obecne (*Esox lucius* L.) v udolni nadrzi Lipno. [The food of pike (*Esox lucius* L.) in the Lipno Reservoir.] Buletin Vyzkumy Ustav Rybarsky a Hydrobiologicky Vodnany 9:159–189.
Data on 941 specimens including: length of pike in relation to food types, lengths, and numbers of prey species, seasonal food variation, and economic value of prey.

1973   Rust stiky (*Esox lucius* L.) v udolni nadrzi Lipno. Buletin Vyzkumy Ustav Rybarsky a Hydrobiologicky Vodnany 10.

1975   Horizontal distribution of individually tagged fish in the Lipno Reservoir. European Inland Fisheries Advisory Committee, Technical Paper 23(Suppl. 1):651–655.

1977   The age and growth of pike (*Esox lucius* L.) in the artificial reservoir Lipno. Buletin Vyzkumy Ustav Rybarsky a Hydrobiologicky Vodnany 10:21–46.
Growth of pike was studied during the first 9 years of the existence of the lake. Age and growth were studied using scales and opercula. Growth rate was extremely rapid. Back-calculated size at age determined from scales was greater than from opercula.

1980   The biology (size, growth, food) of pike in three Czech reservoirs. *In* Sladecek, V., ed., Congress in Japan 1980; Proceedings. Stuttgart, Schweizerbartsche Verlagsbuchhandlung, pp. 1264–1269.
Study found that growth rates for males and females differed, food spectrum depended on species composition of most abundant species, and pike had bio-ameliorative function in these reservoirs.

1983   Techniques et methodes d'amenagement et d'elevage du brochet en Tchecoslovaquie. *In* Billard, R., ed., Le brochet gestion dans le milieu naturel et elevage. Paris, Institute National de la Recherche Agronomique. pp. 271–281.
Information on management, rearing, age, growth, food.

VOSTRADOVSKY, J. and M. VOSTRADOVSKA
1973   K uloze stiky (*Esox lucius* L.) v uvodni periode vyvoje ichthyofauny Lipenske udolni nadrze. [On the role of pike (*Esox lucius* L.) during the initial period of ichthyofauna development in the Lipno artificial lake.] Vysoka Skola Zemedelska v Brne Symposium, pp. 195–204.
Study indicates the effect of fishing methods on numbers and reproduction, age and growth, food, length-weight, sex ratio, and mortality. Gives recommendations for methods of increasing pike numbers.

VOTH, D. R. and O. R. LARSON
1968   Metazoan parasites of some fishes from Goose River, North Dakota. American Midland Naturalist 79:216–224.
During the summer and autumn of 1964, 105 fishes representing 10 species were collected from two sites along the Goose River in eastern North Dakota. Thirty genera or species of parasites were identified and all fish were affected.

VOUGA, M.
1939   Le role du brochet dans l'economie piscicole des lacs et des rivieres. L'esociculture. Bulletin Suisse Peche et Pisciculture 7:123–126.

314

VROLIK, A. J.

1873   Studien uber die Verknocherung und die Knochen des Schadels der Teleos-
        tier. Archives de Zoologie 1:219–290.

VUORINEN, P. and M. B. AXELL

1980   Effect of the water soluble fraction of crude oil on herring eggs and pike fry.
        International Council for the Exploration of the Sea 30:1–10.
        Growth of pike fry was significantly poorer in high oil concentrations than in
        the control. In the gills of pike fry exposed to oil, the secondary lamellae
        were bent and changes were observed in the lamella epithelium. The
        epithelium of the intestine was also damaged.

WACHS, B.

1982   Concentration of heavy metals in fishes from the river Danube. Zeitschrift fuer Wasser-Abwasser-Forschung 15(2):43–48. [in German, English abstract]
        From 1977 to 1980 the heavy metal content of fishes from the Bavarian Danube area was determined. The accumulation in fish comes from the water, not from the food.

WAGNER, W. C.

1972   Utilization of alewives by inshore piscivorous fishes in Lake Michigan. Transactions of the American Fisheries Society 101:55–63.
        Examined stomach contents of 405 pike during April-October of 1966–68 to determine their food habits when alewives were abundant and scarce. When alewives were abundant they provided 66% of the total weight of foods taken.

WAHL, D. H. and R. A. STEIN

1985   Evaluation of stocking northern pike, muskellunge, and tiger muskellunge into Ohio lakes: a comparative approach. Ohio Department of Natural Resources, Project F-57-R-7:1–38.
        Describes experiments in hatchery ponds, borrow pits, and reservoir systems to compare differences in survival, growth, and good habits. Growth and food habits were similar among all three; muskellunge survival was higher than for the other two species.

WAINIO, A.

1966a   Age assessment of pike scales. Ontario Department of Lands and Forests Report, 6 pp.
        Problems of aging Lake Huron pike from scales, including information of Michigan pike derived from Ph.D. thesis of J. E. Williams.

1966b   A study of pike (*Esox lucius*, Linnaeus) in two areas of Lake Huron. M.S. thesis, University of Toronto. 72 pp.
        Information on length and weight, lamprey predation, food, age at maturity, age composition.

1978   An obvious difference. Angler and Hunter in Ontario 3(5):26–27.
        Brief summary of morphological distinctions between pike and masquinongy. Notes on appetite and angling records.

WAJDOWICZ, Z.

1958   Zbiornik Goczalkowicki jako obiekt gospodarki rybackiej. Cz. II. Formowanie sie stada ryb w poczatkowym okresie istnienia zbiornika. [Goczalkowice dam reservoir as an object of fishery management. Part II. Formation of fish populations in the initial period after reservoir construction.] Biul. Polskiej Akademii Nauk, Zaklad Biologii Stawow 7:67–86.
        Changes taking place in fish stock of the Vistula River two years after construction of a dam in Goczalkowice.

1964   The development of ichthyofauna in dam reservoirs with small variations in water level. Acta Hydrobiologica 6:61–79.

1965   Szczupak w zbierniku Goczalkewickim. [Pike in Goczalkowice dam reservoir]. Acta Hydrobiologica 7:179–195.
        General characteristics and conditions of the development of pike in Goczalkowice dam reservoir.

WALECKI, A.
1864   Systematyczny przeglad ryb krajowych. Materialy do Fauny Ichtyologicznej
        Polski. [Systematic review of local fishes. Materials to the Ichthyological
        Fauna of Poland.] 115 pp.
1889   Przyczynek do naszej fauny ichtyjologicznej. [Comments on our ichthyologi-
        cal fauna.] Pamietn. Fizjogr.: 3–23.
        Addendum to the list of local fish species.
WALKER, C. E., R. F. BROWN and D. A. KATO
1974   Catalogue of fish and stream resources of Carmacks area. Environment
        Canada, Fisheries and Marine Service Report PAC/T-74–8:1–55.
WALKER, K. W.
1968   Temperature control in northern pike and muskellunge egg hatching.
        Proceedings of the North Central Warmwater Fish Culture Workshop, Ames,
        1968. Mimeographed report. 5 pp.
WALKER, R.
1953   Still water angling. London, MacGibbon and Kee. 232 pp.
        Mentions pike as a winter sport fish.
WALKER, S. J.
1931   Biological and oceanographic conditions in Hudson Bay. 2. Report on the
        Hudson Bay fisheries expedition of 1930. B. Investigations at Churchill,
        Manitoba. Contributions to Canadian Biology and Fisheries 6(23):472–474.
WALLS, G. L.
1942   The vertebrate eye. Cranbrook Institute of Science Bulletin. 785 pp.
WALTER, C. M., F. C. JUNE and H. G. BROWN
1973   Mercury in fish, sediments, and water in Lake Oahe, South Dakota. Journal
        of Water Pollution Control Federation 45:2203–2210.
        Analyses for total mercury content were made of fish, sediment, and water
        samples collected in several locations in Lake Oahe and its tailwaters. Mer-
        cury concentrations equal to or exceeding 0.5 mg/kg occurred in 30 of 225
        fish samples tested. Higher concentrations were found most frequently in
        predatory game fishes such as pike.
WALTER, H.
1912   Unser Hecht (*Esox lucius*) in Aquarium. Blattchen Aquarien und Terrarien
        Kunde 23:40–41.
WALTERS, V.
1953   The fishes collected by the Canadian Arctic Expedition, 1913–1918, with
        additional notes on the ichthyofauna of western arctic Canada. National
        Museum of Canada Bulletin 128:257–274.
1955   Fishes of western arctic America and eastern Siberia. Taxonomy and
        zoogeography. Bulletin of the American Museum of Natural History
        106(6):259–368.
WALTHER, J.
1882   Die Entwicklung der Deckknochen am Kopfskelett des Hechtes (*Esox lucius*).
        Zeitschrift fuer Naturwissenschaftlich 16:59–87.
WALTON, I. and C. COTTEN
1835   Observations of the luce or pike, with directions how to fish for him. [Fac-
        simile reprint of the first edition published in 1653.] *In* The Compleat Angler.
        London, J. Major, pp. 142–156.
        Observations on feeding habits and instructions on bait and cooking.

317

WARD, A. L.
1979   So fangt man Hechte. Hamburg, Paul Parey. 99 pp.
WARREN, C. E. and G. E. DAVIS
1967   Laboratory studies on the feeding, bioenergetics, and growth of fish. *In* Gerking, S. D., ed., The biological basis of freshwater fish production. IBP Symposium, Reading, 1966. Oxford, Blackwell Scientific Publications. pp. 175–214.
WASHBURN, F. L.
1886   Mortality of fish at Lake Mille Lac, Minnesota. American Naturalist 20:896–897.
Unexplained mortality in June and July of many species, including pike, attributed to an external parasite.
WATSON, R. A. and T. A. DICK
1980   Metazoan parasites of pike, *Esox lucius* Linnaeus, from Southern Indian Lake, Manitoba, Canada. Journal of Fish Biology 17(3):255–261.
Parasites were studied to reveal species composition, differences with host age, sex, and location and season of capture. Pike hosted 18 species of metazoan parasites, two of which made up over 84% of parasite numbers. Impoundments could greatly change pike parasite levels.
WEBB, P. W.
1978a   Fast-start performance and body form in seven species of teleost fish. Journal of Experimental Biology 74:211–226.
Normal three-stage kinematic patterns were observed. Duration of kinetic stages, maximum acceleration rates, maximum velocity and distance were recorded. Performance was determined at an acclimation and test temperature of 15 C.
1978b   Hydrodynamics: nonscrombroid fish. *In* Hoar, W. S., and D. J. Randall, eds., Fish physiology, vol. 7, Locomotion, pp. 190–239.
1980   Does schooling reduce fast-start response latencies in teleosts? Comparative Biochemistry and Physiology 65A(2):231–234.
1982   Avoidance responses of fathead minnow to strikes by four teleost predators. Journal of Comparative Physiology 147A(3):371–378.
Predator avoidance behaviour was analysed using stop-action video-tape recordings of predator-prey interactions. Response patterns, response thresholds, and the apparent looming thresholds of the minnows were recorded for attacks by the pike-muskellunge hybrid.
1983   Speed acceleration and manoevrability of two teleost fish. Journal of Experimental Biology 102:115–122.
1984a   Body and fin form and strike tactics of four teleost predators attacking fathead minnow (*Pimephalus promelas*) prey. Canadian Journal of Fisheries and Aquatic Sciences 41:157–165.
Piscivore locomotor tactics varied with body/fin morphology. Pike-muskellunge hybrids always used S-start fast starts, and sometimes overshot their prey. Speed and strike were greatest in the esocid than in the other three species studied. The esocid attacked at maximum speed.
1984b   Chase response latencies of some teleostean piscivores. Comparative and Biochemical Physiology 79A:45–48.
WEBB, P. W. and J. M. SKADSEN
1980   Strike tactics of *Esox*. Canadian Journal of Zoology 58:1462–1469.

Strike patterns of cultured pike-muskellunge hybrids on fathead minnow (*Pimephales promelas*) in an aquarium were observed on videotape. These tactics were expected if the predator is to maximize the probability of catching prey.

WEBB, R. and B. RICKARDS
1976   Fishing for big pike, 2nd ed. London, A. & C. Black.

WEBSTER, D. A.
1942   The life histories of some Connecticut fishes. A fishery survey of important Connecticut lakes. Geology and Natural History Survey of Connecticut, Bulletin 63:122–227.

WEBSTER, J., A. TRANDAHL and J. LEONARD
1978   Historical perspective of propagation and management of coolwater fishes in the United States. American Fisheries Society Special Publication 11:161–166.
Of 40 responding state agencies, 14 had pike production programs. Suggests money and personnel be allocated to management programs such as the use of pike in non-native areas as a predator to control overabundant forage fish, and producing the pike-muskellunge hybrid in a put-grow-and-take trophy fishery.

WEED, A. C.
1922   The distribution of pickerels. Copeia 115:21–23.
1927   Pike, pickerel and muskalonge. Field Museum of Natural History, Zoology Leaflet 9:153–204.

WEINFURTER, E.
1950   Die Oberpannonsiche Fischfauna vom Eichkogel bei Modling. Sitzungsberichte der Oesterreichische Akademie der Wissenschaften 159:37–50.

WEISEL, G. F.
1949   The seminal vesicles and testes of *Gillichthys*, a marine teleost. Copeia 1949:101–109.

WEISS, D. G.
1980   Rapid axonal transport of amino acids and peptides in the olfactory nerve of the pike *Esox lucius*. European Journal of Cell Biology 22:349.
1982   3–0 methyl-D glucose and beta alanine rapid axoplasmic transport of metabolically inert low molecular weight substances. Neuroscience Letters 31:241–246.

WEISS, D. G., G. W. GROSS and G. W. KREUTZBERG
1978a   Experiments concerning the mechanism of axoplasmic transport. Neuroscience Letters, Suppl. 1:S13.
1978b   Subcellular distribution of rapidly transported material in the olfactory nerve of the pike *Esox lucius*. Hoppe-Seyler's Zeitschrift fuer Physiologische Chemie 359:336.

WEISS, D. G., V. KRYGIER-BREVART, G. W. GROSS and G. W. KREUTZBERG
1978   Rapid axoplasmic transport of the olfactory nerve of the pike. II. Analysis of transported proteins by SDS gel electrophoresis. Brain Research 139:77–87.
In order to ascertain the balance of synthesis, transport, and turnover, an analysis of different regions of the olfactory system as well as of the peak and plateau regions from the characteristic isotope distribution profile was performed.

WEISS, J.

1979   Uber Vorkommen and ultrastruktur von Mastzellen im Hypothalamus der Knochenfische. [The occurrence and ultrastructure of the mast cells of the hypothalamus of bony fish.] Zeitschrift fuer Mikroskopisch-Anatomische Forschung 93:147–160.

WEITHMAN, A. S.

1975   Survival, growth, efficiency, preference and vulnerability to angling of Esocidae. M.S. thesis, University of Missouri. 97 pp.

Growth and survival were assessed by stocking ponds with pike, muskellunge, and pike-muskellunge hybrids separately and together, then draining the ponds several months later. Studied feeding and growth in tanks and vulnerability by offering uniform sizes and numbers of selected species.

WEITHMAN, A. S. and R. O. ANDERSON

1976   Angling vulnerability of Esocidae. Proceedings of the Annual Conference of the Southeast Association of Game and Fish Commissioners 30:99–102.

Five yearling pike, muskellunge, or their hybrid were stocked in duplicate 0.2-ha ponds. Two additional ponds were stocked with a combination of five fish of each of the three forms. In 58 hours of angling from April to September, pike were 3.1 and 4.2 times more vulnerable than the hybrid and muskellunge, respectively. No fish were caught in 19 hours of fishing from June 15 to August 13. Repeat catches accounted for 35.6% of the total catch; hooking mortality was 1.7%).

1977   Survival, growth, and prey of Esocidae in experimental systems. Transactions of the American Fisheries Society 106:424–430.

Data for pike, muskellunge, and their hybrid (including maintenance diets) suggest the hybrid is the most desirable form because of rapid growth rate, intermediate angling vulnerability, and ease of rearing in a hatchery compared to either parent species.

WELCH, H. E.

1968   Relationships between assimilation efficiencies and growth efficiencies for aquatic consumers. Ecology 49:755–759.

Energy budgets compiled from the literature.

WELCOMME, R. L.

1979   Preliminary record of international transfers of fish species. Food and Agriculture Organization Fisheries Circular 715:1–37.

Pike have been transferred from Ireland to the U.K., Spain to France, Madagascar to France, and Uganda to Israel.

WENT, A. E. J.

1957   The pike in Ireland. Irish Naturalists' Journal 12(7):1–5.

History of distribution through accounts in literature dating from the end of the 12th century.

1966   The status of various species of coarse fish in Irish waters. In Jones, J. W., and P. H. Tombleson, eds., Proceedings of the 2nd British Coarse Fish Conference, Liverpool, 1965, pp. 102–108.

WERNER, R. G. and N. H. RINGLER

1980   Population biology of esocids in the St. Lawrence River. Research proposal submitted to New York Sea Grant Institute.

A decline in the quality of the pike fishery was reported. This research proposed to help fill the need for information on esocids in the St. Lawrence

River and to relate that knowledge to future management of the fishery.

WESLOH, M. L. and D. E. OLSON

1962   The growth and harvest of stocked yearling northern pike, *Esox lucius* Linnaeus, in a Minnesota walleye lake. Minnesota Department of Conservation, Investigational Report 242:1–9.

The contribution of stocked yearling pike to the sport fishery of an 885-acre walleye lake was evaluated through the return of marked fish in a census of the anglers' catch. Of 5,133 pike stocked in December 1958, 44.1% were harvested in the course of two complete angling seasons.

WESSLER, E. and I. WERNER

1957   On the chemical composition of some mucous substances in fish. Acta Chemica Scandinavica 11:1240–1247.

WESTERS, H.

1978   Biological considerations in hatchery design for coolwater fishes. American Fisheries Society Special Publication 11:246–253.

A summary of oxygen consumption and ammonia production of the pike-muskellunge hybrid.

1979   Controlled fry and fingerling production in hatcheries. European Inland Fisheries Advisory Committee Technical Paper 35(suppl. 1):32–52.

Advantages of the intensive flow-through rearing method over the extensive pond method are described. Design and biological principles of the intensive method are discussed, considering water consumption and various fish culture management practices. Economic implications are not covered. A method for successful intensive rearing of pike-muskellunge hybrids is described with problem areas identified.

WESTMAN, J.

1961   Why fish bite and why they don't. Englewood Cliffs, Prentice-Hall. 211 pp.

WHANG-PENG, J., R. A. SONSTEGARD and C. J. DAWE

1976   Chromosomal characteristics of malignant lymphoma in northern pike (*Esox lucius*) from the United States. Cancer Research 36:3554–3560.

Chromosome analyses were performed on tumour cells and normal hematopoietic cells of specimens bearing malignant lymphomas.

WHEELER, A.

1969   Fish-life and pollution in the lower Thames: a review and preliminary report. Biological Conservation 2:25–30.

1977   The origin and distribution of the freshwater fishes of the British Isles. Journal of Biogeography 4:1–24.

1978   Why were there no fish remains at Star-Carr. Journal of Archaeological Science 5:85–90.

WHITE, W. J. and R. J. BEAMISH

1972   A simple fish tag suitable for long-term marking experiments. Journal of the Fisheries Research Board of Canada 29:339–341.

WHITEHOUSE, F. C.

1948   Sport fishing in Canada. Vancouver, published by the author. 188 pp.

WHITNEY, A. N.

1953   Southern Montana fisheries study. Sampling fish populations in reservoirs. Montana Fish and Game Department, Dingell-Johnson Report F-6-R-2/Job 01/B:1–4.

WHITWORTH, W. R., P. L. BERRIEN and W. T. KELLER
  1968   Freshwater fishes of Connecticut. Connecticut Geological and Natural History Survey, Bulletin 101:1–134.
WICH, K. and J. W. MULLAN
  1958   A compendium of the life history and ecology of the chain pickerel *Esox niger* (LeSueur). Massachusetts Division of Fish and Game, Fish Bulletin 22:1–27.
WICKLUND, R. B. and S. DIANGELO
  1959   Watershed surveys and management plans. Surveys and plans—northern pike spawning surveys and development plans. Michigan Department of Conservation, Dingel-Johnson Report F-4-R-5/Job 02/H:1–7.
WIEBE, A. H.
  1931   Notes in the exposure of several species of fish to sudden changes in the hydrogen-ion concentration of the water and to an atmosphere of pure oxygen. Transactions of the American Fisheries Society 61:216–224.
WIKTOR, J. and C. ZUKOWSKI
  1962   Szczupak w gospodarce zalewu Szczecinskiego a latach 1948–1957. [The pike in Szczecin first husbandry in the years 1948–1957.] Prace MIR 11/A, 421–441.
          Size of pike stock in Szczecinski Bay. Role of pike in biocenosis in the presence of another predator, pike-perch.
WILBER, C. G.
  1955   Lipids in the northern pike. Transactions of the American Fisheries Society 84:150–154.
          Blood and liver were analysed for fatty acids, sterols, and phospholipids. The pike is distinctive in having a rather high liver cholesterol—0.89% of fresh tissue. The other lipids are not unique; however, pike in general have consistently less fat in the liver than do marine fish.
WILDING, J. L.
  1939   The oxygen threshold for three species of fish. Ecology 20:253–263.
WILIMOVSKY, N. J.
  1954   List of fishes of Alaska. Stanford Ichthyological Bulletin 4:279–294.
WILKENS, H. and A. KOEHLER
  1977   The fish fauna of the lower and middle Elbe River, West Germany, the species used 1950–1975. ABH Verhandlungen Naturwiss ver Hamb. 20:185–222. [in German]
WILKONSKA, H. and H. ZUROMSKA
  1967   Obserwacje nad rozrodem szczupaka (*Esox lucius* L.) i ploci (Rutilus rutilus L.) w jeziorach Pojezierza Mazurskiego. [Observations of the spawning of pike (*Esox lucius* L.) and roach (*Rutilus rutilus* L.) in Mazury Lake district.] Roczniki Nauk Rolniczych 90:477–502.
          Utilization of spawning grounds by fishes; division of spawning areas into types; factors affecting terms of spawning.
WILLEMSE, J. J.
  1968   Helminth and sporozoan parasites of fishes in the Netherlands. Bulletin Zoologisch Museum Universiteit van Amsterdam 1(8):83–87.
  1969   The genus *Proteocephalus* in the Netherlands. Journal of Helminthology 43:207–222.

WILLEMSEN, J.

1955   De waarde van poot snoekjes voor uitzetting. [The biological value of pike fingerlings for stocking.] Visserij-Nieuws 7:150–151.

Between fingerlings of 5 and 10 cm, no difference could be shown concerning viability (survival in ponds without predators), predator resistance (survival in presence of predators) and in size after one growing season.

1958   Onderzoek ten behoeve van de pootsnoekproduktie. [Research on behalf of the production of pike-fingerlings.] Organisatie ter Verbetering van de Binnenvisserij, Utrecht, Jaarverslag 1958:58–65.

1965   Het voedsel van de snoek. [Food of pike.] Visserij-Nieuws 18:298–305.

The mean length of prey fish is small, even for large pike. Food conversion of pike was determined in concrete basins. Food conversion appeared not to be size dependent. With abundant feeding of prey, the conversion amounted to 3–5.5.

1967a   Research on the feeding of pike. Proceedings 3rd British Coarse Fish Conference 1967:33–36.

A summary of research in the Netherlands on food of pike and frequency of cannibalism.

1967b   Voedsel en groei van snoek. [Food and growth of pike.] Visserij-Nieuws 20:72–75.

A comparison of growth rate determined from scales collected at time of tagging and recapture. Gives growth rate of pike from two waters.

1978   Voedsel en groei van zoetwater-roofvis. [Food and growth of a freshwater predator.] Visserij-Nieuws 31:192–200. [in Dutch]

1979   Relatie tussen de lengte van paaisnoek en het voortplantingsresultaat. [Relation between length of pike and the spawning success.] RIVO-rapport ZS 79–2:1–12.

Within the range of 50–100 cm no relation could be shown regarding egg quality and size of the female. Not clearly dependent upon the length of the female was the size of the larvae, the mortality during the embryonic and larval period, and the growth rate of juveniles up to a length of about 4 cm.

WILLIAMS, J. E.

1952   Northern pike management. Michigan Conservation 21(2):5–7.

Brief history of pike fishing regulations in Michigan from 1875, outlining the changes in attitude from an extermination policy to one of conservation.

1955   Determination of age from the scales of northern pike (*Esox lucius* L.). Ph.D. thesis, University of Michigan. 185 pp.

1959a   Techniques for management of warm-water fish. Sampling of lake fish populations with seines and toxicants. Michigan Department of Conservation, Dingell-Johnson Report F-15-R-1/Job 3.

1959b   Techniques for management of warm-water fish. Evaluation of mortality of northern pike from hooking and natural mortality. Michigan Department of Conservation, Dingell-Johnson Report F-15-R-1/Job 7.

1959c   Techniques for management of warm-water fish. Evaluation of reproduction of northern pike in controlled marshes. Michigan Department of Conservation, Dingell-Johnson Report F-15-R-1/Job 8.

1960a   Techniques for management of warm-water fish. Evaluation of mortality of northern pike from hooking and natural causes. Michigan Department of Conservation, Dingell-Johnson Report F-15-R-2/Job 6.

1960b   Techniques for management of warm-water fish. Evaluation of reproduction of northern pike in controlled marshes. Michigan Department of Conservation, Dingell-Johnson Report F-15-R-2/Job 7.

1960c   Techniques for management of warm-water fish. Preparation of a monograph on northern pike and muskellunge. Michigan Department of Conservation, Dingell-Johnson Project F-15-R-2, Job 14:11–16.

1961a   Techniques for management of warm-water fish. Sampling of lake fish populations with seines and toxicants. Michigan Department of Conservation, Dingell-Johnson Report F-15-R-3/Job 2:1–5.

1961b   Techniques for management of warm-water fish. Creel census of population control lakes. Michigan Department of Conservation. Dingell-Johngon Report F-15-R-3/Job 5.

1961c   Techniques for management of warm-water fish. Evaluation of mortality of northern pike from hooking and natural causes. Michigan Department of Conservation, Dingell-Johnson Report F-15-R-3/Job 6.

1961d   Techniques for management of warm-water fish. Evaluation of reproduction of northern pike in controlled marshes. Michigan Department of Conservation, Dingell-Johnson Report F-15-R-3/Job 7.

1962a   Techniques for management of warm-water fish. Evaluation of reproduction of northern pike in controlled marshes. Michigan Department of Conservation, Dingell-Johnson Report F-15-R-4/Job 7.

1962b   Techniques for management of warm-water fish. Sampling of lake fish populations with seines and toxicants. Michigan Department of Conservation, Dingell-Johnson Report F-15-R-4/Job 2:1–6.

1962c   Techniques for management of warm-water fish. Analysis of predatory fish food and feeding habits as observed in the laboratory. Michigan Department of Conservation, Dingell-Johnson Report F-15-R-4/Job 9.

1963a   Research and management of sport fisheries of Michigan. Development and evaluation of techniques for management of warm-water fishes. Evaluation of reproduction of northern pike in controlled marshes. Michigan Department of Conservation, Dingell-Johnson Report F-27-R-1/Wk.Pl. 3/Job 7.

1963b   Research and management of sport fisheries of Michigan. Development and evaluation of techniques for management of warm-water fishes. Evaluation of reproduction of northern pike in controlled marshes. Michigan Department of Conservation, Dingell-Johnson Report F-27-R-1/Wk.Pl. 3/Job 9.

1963c   Research and management of sport fisheries of Michigan. Development and evaluation of techniques for management of warm-water fishes. Preparation of a monograph on northern pike and muskellunge. Michigan Department of Conservation, Dingell-Johnson Report F-27-R-1/Wk.Pl. 3/Job 13.

1965a   Research and management of sport fisheries of Michigan. Evaluation of fish management procedures. Test of the effects of protective regulations for northern pike. Michigan Department of Conservation, Dingell-Johnson Report F-27-R-2/Wk.Pl. 2/Job 1.

1965b   Research and management of sport fisheries of Michigan. Development and evaluation of techniques for management of warm-water fishes. Analysis of predatory fish food habits in lakes. Michigan Department of Conservation, Dingell-Johnson Report F-27-R-2/Wk.Pl. 3/Job 6.

1965c   Research and management of sport fisheries of Michigan. Development and evaluation of techniques for management of warm-water fishes. Management of impoundments containing populations of slow-growing northern pike. Michigan Department of Conservation, Dingell-Johnson Report F-27-R-2/Wk.Pl. 3/Job 13.

1966a   Research and management of sport fisheries of Michigan. Development and evaluation of techniques for management of warm-water fishes. Determination of the growth of northern pike on various diets in ponds and lakes. Michigan Department of Conservation, Dingell-Johnson Report F-27-R-4/Wk.Pl. 3/Job 8:1–3.

1966b   Research and management of sport fisheries of Michigan. Development and evaluation of techniques for management of warm-water fishes. Analysis of predatory fish food habits in lakes. Michigan Department of Conservation, Dingell-Johnson Report F-27-R-3/Wk.Pl. 3/Job 6:1.

1966c   Research and management of sport fisheries of Michigan. Development and evaluation of techniques for management of warm-water fishes. Management of impoundments containing populations of slow-growing northern pike. Michigan Department of Conservation, Dingell-Johnson Report F-27-R-3/Wk.Pl. 3/Job 13:1–4.

1967   Research and management of sport fisheries of Michigan. Development and evaluation of techniques for management of impoundments containing populations of slow-growing northern pike. Michigan Department of Conservation, Dingell-Johnson Report F-27-R-4/Wk.Pl. 3/Job 13:1–5.

1968   Warmwater fish biology and population ecology. Management of an impoundment containing a population of slow-growing northern pike. Michigan Department of Conservation, Dingell-Johnson Report F-29-R-1/Job 6:1–5.

WILLIAMS, J. E. and B. L. JACOB
1971   Management of spawning marshes for northern pike. Michigan Department of Natural Resources, Research and Development, Report 242:1–22.
         Management involved maintaining high water levels, controlling stocking rate, eliminating fish predators and competitors, and getting better growth and survival through fertilization. Discusses problems of variable fingerling production and high loss of spawners.

WILLIAMS, M. Y.
1922   Biological notes along 1400 miles of the MacKenzie River system. Canadian Field-Naturalist 36:61.

WILLIAMSON, L. O.
1940   Length-weight relationship of fish. Wisconsin Conservation Bulletin 5(9): 37–39.

1942   Spawning habits of muskellunge, northern pike. Wisconsin Conservation Bulletin 7(5):10–11.
         Observations pertain to season, grounds, behaviour, age at sexual maturity, fecundity, and natural hybridization.

WILLIS, D. W., J. E. SMELTZER and S. A. FLICKINGER
1984   Characteristics of a crappie population in an unfished small impoundment containing northern pike. North American Journal of Fisheries Management 4:385–389.

WILLOCK, T. A.
1969   Distributional list of fishes in the Missouri drainage of Canada. Journal of the Fisheries Research Board of Canada 26:1439–1449.

WILSON, C. B.

1916   Copepod parasites of freshwater fishes and their economic relations to mussel *Glochidia*. U.S. Bureau of Fisheries Bulletin 34:333–374.

1920   Food and parasites of the fishes of Lake Maxinkuckee. Lake Maxinkuckee: a physical and biological survey. Indiana Department of Conservation, pp. 291–305.

WILSON, J.

1977   A specimen fishing year. London, A. & C. Black.

WILSON, M. V. H.

1980   Oldest known *Esox* (Pisces: Esocidae), part of a new Paleocene teleost fauna from western Canada. Canadian Journal of Earth Sciences 17:307–312.

1981   Eocene freshwater fishes from the Coalmont Formation, Colorado. Journal of Paleontology 55:671–674.
       Early Eocene freshwater fish bones and scales from the upper member of the Coalmont Formation, northern Colorado, include remains of Esocidae. Includes the first Eocene record of the pikes. The relatively narrow dimensions of the scales resemble those of the modern *E. lucius* more than *E. masquinongy*.

WILSON, M. V. H. and P. VEILLEUX

1982   Comparative osteology and relationships of the Umbridae (Pisces: Salmoniformes). Zoological Journal of the Linnean Society 76:321–352.

WINBERG, G. G.

1956   Rate of metabolism and food requirements of fishes. Nauchnye Trudy Belorusskovo Gosudarstvennovo Universiteta imeni. V. I. Lenina, Minsk. (Trans. from Russian by Fisheries Research Board of Canada Translation Series 194:1–253.)

WINKELMAN, B.

1977   Hammerhandles or lunkers. Which will it be? Fins and Feathers, June 1977.

1978a Strategy for cold water pike. Fishing Facts, October 1978, pp. 42–45.
       Hints on angling for pike in cold waters, including different movement patterns of pike in lakes with different prey.

1978b Where to find northern pike throughout the year. Fins and Feathers Fishing Annual, 1978, pp. 4–8, 10–11.
       Locations of pike depends upon: 1) lake type, 2) time of year, 3) predator-prey relationships, and 4) forage fish base (predators adapt feeding habits to environment). Information to aid anglers.

WINNICKI, A. and J. DOMURAT

1964   Wytrzymalosc oslonek jajowych niektorych ryb rozwijajacych sie w roznych srodowiskach. [Resistance of egg membranes of some fishes reproducing in various environments.] Zeszyty Naukowe Wyzszej Szkoly Rolniczej w Olsztynie 18(3):315–324.
       Studies on the durability of egg shells of rainbow trout, brook trout, vendace and pike during the whole embryonal period.

WINQUIST, G., O. LJUNGBERG and B. HELLSTROM

1968   Skin tumors of northern pike (*Esox lucius* L.). II. Viral particles in epidermal proliferations. Bulletin de l'Office International des Epizooties 69/7–8: 1023–1031.
       Describes the light and electron microscopy of sarcoma-like skin tumours and epidermal swellings found in pike from a brackish archipelago of the Baltic.

WINQUIST, G., O. LJUNGBERG and B. IVARSSON

1973   Electron microscopy of sarcoma of the northern pike *Esox lucius*. *In* Dutcher, R. M., and L. Chieco-Blanchi, eds., Unifying concepts of leukemia. Basel, Karger.

WINTEMBERG, W. J.

1936   Roebuck prehistoric village site Grenville, Co., Ontario. National Museum of Canada, Bulletin 83, Anthropological Series, 19:1–178.

1946   The Sidey-Mackay village site. American Antiquities 11:154–184.

WIRTH, T. L.

1960   Exploitation of fish populations by anglers in Wisconsin lakes. Wisconsin Conservation, December 1960, 4 pp.

WISTROM, C. A., B. APELGREN and C. W. THREINEN

1957   Northern pike *Esox lucius*. Data for Handbook of Biological Data. 7 pp.

WITA, I.

1971   *Naupliicola ergasili* new species parasite of *Ergasilus sieboldi* larvae from Poland. Bulletin de l'Academie Polonaise des Sciences, Serie des Sciences Biologiques 19:351–353.

1972   *Parastasiella ergasili* new species parasite of *Ergasilus sieboldi* eggs in Poland. Bulletin de l'Academie Polonaise des Sciences, Serie des Sciences Biologiques 20:133–137.

1974   Three new speciesof *Paradistigma* new genus *euglenoidina parasitica* parasitizing *Ergasilus sieboldi* copepoda from *Esox lucius* of Mazurian lakes in Poland. Acta Parasitologica Polonica 22(35–44):365–391.

WITCOMB, D.

1966   The importance of aquatic weeds in the general economy of freshwater habitats. *In* Jones, J. W., and P. H. Tombleson, eds., Proceedings of the 2nd British Coarse Fish Conference, Liverpool, 1965, pp. 49–56.

WITHLER, I. L.

1956   A limnological survey of Atlin and southern Tagish lakes. British Columbia Game Commission, Management Publication 5:1–36.

WIZIGMANN, G., C. BAATH and R. HOFFMAN

1980   Isolation of viral hemorrhagic septicemia virus from fry of rainbow trout, pike and grayling. Zentralblatt fuer Veterinaermedizin 27:79–81.
         During a natural outbreak of disease, viral hemorrhagic septicemia virus was isolated from fry of pike.

WOHLSCHLAG, D. E.

1953   Some characteristics of the fish populations in an Arctic Alaskan lake. Current Biological Research in the Alaskan Arctic 11:19–29.

1954   Growth peculiarities of the cisco, *Coregonus sardinella* (Valenciennes), in the vicinity of Point Barrow, Alaska. Stanford Ichthyological Bulletin 4(3):189–209.

WOJDA, S.

1972   Szczupak. [The pike.] Wiadomosci Wedkarskie 279:12–13.
         Fishing gear and methods of pike catches.

WOLF, K.

1972   Advances in fish virology: a review 1966–1971. *In* Mawdesley Thomas, L. E., ed., Diseases of fish, Symposia of the Zoological Society of London (30). London, Academic Press, pp. 305–327.

1974   Rhabdovirus disease of northern pike fry. U.S. Fish and Wildlife Service
        FDL-37:1–4.
WOLFERT, D. F. and T. J. MILLER
1978   Age, growth and food of northern pike in eastern Lake Ontario. Transactions
        of the American Fisheries Society 107:696–702.
        Results of pike sampled by gill nets and trap nets in 1972–73. Electivity
        indices for three most common species in diet.
WONDARK, P.
1974   Morphologische Untersuchungen am Hoden des Hechtes (*Esox lucius* L.).
        Ph.D. thesis, Gartenbau Technological University. 23 pp.
WONDRA, K.
1981   Die Hechterbruetung. [Pike breeding.] Fischerei Teichwirt 32(4):98–101.
        Pike stocks are endangered by angling and by changes in the environment.
        Through embankment spawning grounds are lost. Eutrophication and pollu-
        tion disturb development of eggs and larvae so that stocking operations are
        necessary. Artificial reproduction, breeding and rearing are described.
WONG, B. and T. WHILLANS
1973   Limnological and biological survey of Hottah Lake, Northwest Territories
        Environment Canada Technical Report Series CENT-73–6:1–69
        Assessment of length, weight, age, and stomach contents of pike caught by
        gill nets during summer of 1972. General notes on angling.
WOODBURY, L. A.
1942   A sudden mortality of fishes accompanying a supersaturation of oxygen in
        Lake Waubesa, Wisconsin. Transactions of the American Fisheries Society
        71:112–117.
        A heavy algal bloom and surface oxygen values of 30–32 ppm were associ-
        ated with mortality of pike. Death of fish was attributed to blocking of circu-
        lation through gills by gas bubbles with consequent respiratory failure.
WOODING, F. H.
1959   The angler's book of Canadian fishes. Don Mills, Collins. 303 pp.
WOODLING, J.
1984   Game fish of Colorado; an identification guide for sport fish commonly
        caught in Colorado. Denver, Colorado Division of Wildlife.
WOODS, C. E.
1971   Helminth parasites of fishes from the Forest River, North Dakota. American
        Midland Naturalist 86:212–215.
WOOLMAN, A. J.
1896   Report upon ichthyological investigations in western Minnesota and eastern
        North Dakota. Report of the U.S. Commission of Fish and Fisheries for 1893,
        app. 3, pp. 343–373.
WORLEY, D. E. and R. V. BANGHAM
1952   Some parasites of fishes of the upper Gatineau River Valley. Ohio Journal of
        Science 25:210–212.
WORTHINGTON, E. B.
1949   An experiment with populations of fish in Windermere 1939–48. Proceed-
        ings of the Zoological Society of London 120:113–149.
WOYNAROVICH, E.
1955   Biological observation in relation to artificial propagation of fish. Acta Biolo-
        gica Academiae Scientiarum Hungaricae 6(1/2):149–169.

1960   Oxygen consumption of the larvae of pike (*Esox lucius* L.) and sheat-fish (*Silurus glanis* L.) at temperatures of 0.5 to 28 C. Ann. Biol. Tihany 27:183–191.

1962   Erfolgreiche kunstliche Befruchtung vom Hechtrogen. Allgemeine Fischerei-Zeitung 87:346–348.

1963   Artificial fertilization of pike eggs. Halaszat 9(2):58. [in Hungarian]

WRIGHT, A. H. and A. A. ALLEN

1913   The fauna of Ithaca, N.Y. Fishes. *In* Field note-book of fishes, amphibians, reptiles and mammals. Ithaca, pp. 4–6.

WRIGHT, E. P.

1878   Die Entwicklung des Knochenhechts und der Schollen. Kosmos 4:312–315.

WRIGHT, K. J.

1971   Mississippi River special tailwater sport fishing creel census in pool 7, March 1, 1969 - April 30, 1969. Wisconsin Department of Natural Resources, Management Report 45.

WRIGHT, R.

1892   Preliminary report on the fish and fisheries of Ontario. Ontario Game and Fish Commission Report for 1892, pp. 419–476.

WRZESZCZ, J.

1960   Ryby drapiezne potoku Trzebiocha i charakter ich presji na mlodziez troci (*Salmo trutta morpha lacustris* L.) z jeziora Wdzydze. [Predatory fishes of Trzebiocha Stream and their impact on juvenile trout (*Salmo trutta morpha lacustris* L.) in Lake Wdzydze.] M.S. thesis. 44 pp.
          Characteristics of the food of pike and the impact of predatory fishes on juvenile lake trout.

WUNDER, W.

1927a   Wie findet der Hecht seine Beute. Fischerei-Zeitung

1927b   Sinnesphysiologische Untersuchungen uber die Nahrungsaufnahme verschiedener Knochenfischarten. Zeitschrift fur vergleichende Physiologie 6:67–98.

1936   Physiology of the fresh-water fishes of central Europe. Handbuch der Binnenfischerei Mitteleuropas, vol. 2B. Stuttgart, E. Schweizerbart. (Trans. from German by Stanford University, WPA Project 50–11861, 1941.}

1949   Ein Fall von Wirbelsaulenverkurzung beim Hecht (*Esox lucius*). Archiv fur Hydrobiologie 42:470–473.

1960   Missbildungen bei kleinen Hechten. Fischwirt 10(2):35–40.

1961   Massenhaftes Auftreten von Missbildungen bei kleinen Hechten (*Esox lucius* L.). Zoologischer Anzeiger 166:42–55.

1972   Sinnesphysiologische Untersuchungen uber die Nahrungsaufnahme verschiedener Knochenfischarten. Zeitschrift fur vergleichende Physiologie 6:67–98

1976   Curvature of the spine and shortening of the fins in the zander *Lucioperca sandra* caused by waste water from the households in the Eder Valley Dam Reservoir. Zoologischer Anzeiger 197:356–376.

1978   Ein Hecht (*Esox lucius*L.) mit vollkommenem Bruch der Wirbelsaeule und Querschnittslaehmung des Rueckenmarks. [A pike (*Esox lucius* L.) with a total fracture of the spine and a severing of the spinal cord with resulting paralysis.] Archiv fuer Hydrobiologie 84:247–255. [in German, English summary]

Description of a pike with a broken spine. Photos of the behaviour of the fish and of the vertebrae. Discussion of the literature.

1982   Wundheilung, Regeneration und Missbildungen bei Fischen. Versuche bei kleine Hechten uber die Regeneration des Schwanzes. Fischer u. Teichwirt 35(5):135–136.

WUNDSCH, H. H.

1929   Untersuchungen uber die Kiemenfaule bei Fischen (XII). (Eine besondere Art der "Kiemenfaule" bei Hechten und Schleien (II)). [Investigations on gill rot in fish (XII). A special kind of "gill rot" in northern pike and tench (II).] Zeitschrift fuer Fischerei und deren Hilfswissenschaften 27:287–293.

1930   XV. Untersuchungen uber die diemenfaule bei fischen. III. Weitere beobachtungen an *Branchiomyces demigrans* als erreger der kiemenfaule beim Hecht. Zeitschrift fuer Fischerei und deren Hilfswissenschaften 28:391–402.

WUNSCHE, J. and W. STEFFENS

1968   Der Gehalt an eesentiellen Aminosauren im Protein von Karpfen (*Cyprinus carpio*), Regenbogenforelle (*Salmo gairdneri*), Kleiner Marane (*Coregonus albula*), Hecht (*Esox lucius*) und Aal (*Anguilla anguilla*). Zeitschrift fuer Fischerei und deren Hilfswissenschaften 16(3/4):301–304.

WURTZ, A.

1945   Developpement, biologie et nutrition des jeunes alevins de brochet (*Esox lucius* L.). Bulletin Francais de Pisciculture 135:57–69.

WURTZ-ARLET, J.

1952   Le black-bass en France: Esquisse Monographique. Annales de la Station Centrale d'Hydrobiologie Aphiquee 4:203–286.

WYDALLIS, E. A.

1960   Observations on the scale development patterns of the eastern chain pickerel, northern pike, Great Lakes muskellunge, Ohio muskellunge, and yellow walleye with respect to age and length. Ohio State University, Fisheries Research Report 1959–60:1–142.

WYDOSKI, R. S.

1977   Relation of hooking mortality and sublethal hooking stress to quality fishery management. *In* Barhart, R. A., and T. D. Roelofs, eds., National symposium on catch and release fishing. Humboldt State University, pp. 43–87.

WYDOSKI, R. S. and D. H. BENNETT

1981   Forage species in lakes and reservoirs of the western United States. Transactions of the American Fisheries Society 110:764–771.
        Brief discussion of how pike introductions affected forage species populations.

WYGANOWSKI, J.

1957   Wedkarstwo. [Angling.] Warsaw, PWRiL. 487 pp.

1974   Poradnik wedkarski. [Angler's manual.] Warsaw, PWRiL. 161 pp.

WYNNE-EDWARDS, V. C.

1947   Northwest Canadian fisheries survey. Chapter 3, The Mackenzie River. Fisheries Research Board of Canada Bulletin 72:21–30.

1952   Freshwater vertebrates of the arctic and subarctic. Fisheries Research Board of Canada Bulletin 94:1–28.

YAMAMOTO, T., R. K. KELLY and O. NIELSEN
  1984   Epidermal hyperplasias of northern pike (*Esox lucius*) associated with herpes
          virus and C-type particles. Archives of Virology 79:255–272.
YEFIMOVA, A. I.
  1949   The pike of the Ob'-Irtysh basin. 1. Izvestiya Gosudarstvennogo Nauchno-
          UIssledovatel'skogo Instituta Ozernogo i Rechnogo Rybnogo Khozvaistva
          28:114–117.
YUSUPOV, O. Y. and A. N. URAZBAEV
  1980   Parasitic ciliates *Peritricha* Urceolariidae of fishes from the Aral Sea. Parazi-
          tologiya 14:504–510.

ZABA, B. N. and E. J. HARRIS

    1978   Accumulation and effects of trace metal ions in fish liver mitochondria. Comparative Biochemistry and Physiology 61C:89–94.

ZADUL'SKAYA, E. A.

    1960   Feeding and food relationships of predatory fishes in the northern part of Rybinsk reservoir. Translated from Russian by U.S. Department of Commerce, Technical Service.

ZAITZEV, A. V.

    1955a   The annual cycle of testes in pike. Comptes Rendus de l'Academie des Sciences 101:185–187.

    1955b   A histological investigation of the annual changes of the thyroid gland of the pike and the neuro-secretory activity of the hypothalamic nuclei in the seasonal change of the thyreotropic function of the hypophysis. Doklady Akademii Nauk SSSR 104:315–318.

ZALACHOWSKI, W.

    1965a   Wzrost szczupalka z Jezior Leginskich. [The growth of pike (*Esox lucius* L.) in Leginskie Lakes.] Zeszyty Naukowe Wyzszej Szkoly Rolniczej w Olsztynie 20:181–193.
            Rate of pike growth as compared to data from lakes in other regions.

    1965b   Odzywianie sie szczupaka z Jezior Leginskich. [The feeding of pike from Leginskie Lakes.] Zeszyty Naukowe Wyzszej Szkoly Rolniczej w Olsztynie 20(2):195–212.
            Feeding behaviour of pike and its effect upon prey fishes.

    1970   Biologie rozwoju larw szczupaka w grupie jezior Leginskich. [Biology of pike larval development.] Roczniki Nauk Rolniczyck 92H(3):93–119.
            Changes in pike biology connected with its morphological development; the effect of different ecological conditions upon the course of these changes.

    1973   Szczupak. [The pike.] Warszawa, PWRiL. 251 pp.

ZAMOJSKA, B.

    1967   Struktury wielkosci ofiar szczupaka i okonia w kilku rozniacych sie limnologicznie i rybacko jeziorach. [Size structure of pike and perch prey in some lakes differing as regards limnology and fishery type.] Ph.D. thesis, 61 pp.
            Species composition of the food of predatory fishes. Size structure of roach and perch; i.e., of species most frequently consumed by adult pike and perch.

ZARNECKI, S.

    1928   Szczupak. [The pike.] Przeglad Rybacki 1(9):349–351.
            Some comments on general morphology of pike body and on its biology.

    1964   Z biologii szczupaka (*Esox lucius* L.). [On pike biology (*Esox lucius* L.).] Wszechswiat 3:64–66.
            Description of some unknown facts on the behaviour of pike.

ZAROV, A. I.

    1964   Zametki o pitanii scuki i ariskogo zerecha v Farchadskom vodochranilisce. Izvestiya Akacemii Nauk Tadzhikskoi SSR Otdelenie Biologicheskikh Nauk 3(17):89–90.

ZARYANOVA, Y. B.

    1962   The reproduction of the pike in the first years of the establishment of Volgograd Reservoir. Trudy Saratovskogo Otdeleniya Vsesoyuznogo Nauchno-Issledovatel-skogo Instituta Ozernogo i Rechnogo Rybnogo Khozyaistva 7:243–259.

ZAWADOWSKA, B. and W. KILARSKI

1984a   Histochemical adaptation of an eye muscle system to the type of behaviour of the two teleost species *Cyprinus carpio* and *Esox lucius*. Journal of Muscle Research and Cell Motility 5:212. [Summary]

The fundamental organization of the extrinsic eye muscles of the teleosts is alike. Histochemical analysis showed the obvious diversity of the muscle fibre population among both investigated species. It is thought this is an adaptation to the different mode of life of these two species.

1984b   Histochemical characterization of the muscle fiber types of the teleost (*Esox lucius* L.). Acta Histochemica 75:91–100.

Four types of muscle fibres are described in pike body musculature on the base of the actomyosin ATP-ase activity and succinate dehydrogenase (SDH) activity.

ZAWISZA, J.

1953   Wzrost ryb w jeziorze Tajty. [The growth of fish in Lake Tajty.] Roczniki Nauk Rolniczych, Ser. D, 67:221–255.

Analysis of the rate of growth of economically important fish species made in order to serve as a basis for proper planning of lake management.

1961   The growth of fishes in lakes of Wegorzewo district. Roczniki Nauk Rolniczyck 77B:731–748. [in Polish, English summary]

ZBIKOWSKA, L.

1980a   Cechy merystyczne szczupaka (*Esox lucius* L.) z jeziora Sniardwy. [Meristic features of the pike (*Esox lucius* L.) from Lake Sniardwy.] Zeszyty Naukowe Akademii Rolniczo-Technicznej w Olsztynie, Ser. Ochrona Wod i Rybactwo Srodladowe 10:105–116.

Meristic features and their statistical analysis. Calculations are given of the arithmetic mean, standard deviation of coefficients of variability.

1980b   Cechy biometryczne szczupaka (*Esox lucius* L.) z jeziora Sniardwy. [Biometric features of the pike (*Esox lucius* L.) from Lake Sniardwy.] Zeszyty Naukowe Akademii Rolniczkj Technicznej w Olsztynie 11:89–99. [in Polish, English summary]

ZDANKO, A.

1969   Szczupak. [The pike.] Wiadomosci Wedkarskie 238:4.

Pike biology. Methods of angling in various seasons of the year.

ZENKIN, G. M. and I. N. P. PIGAREV

1970   Specific elements in retina and level of ganglionic cells of pike. Biologiya Vnutrennykh Vod Informatsionii Byulleten 5:45–48.

ZHITENEVA, L. D.

1969   Fishes of the settlement of Mayaki (end of 3000 years B.C.). Zoologicheskii Zhurnal 48:93–98. [in Russian, English summary]

ZHUKOV, P. I.

1968   The routes of penetration of Ponto-Caspian ichthyofauna into the rivers of the Baltic Sea basin. Zoologicheskii Zhurnal 47:1417–1419. [in Russian, English summary]

ZIEBA, J.

1956   Die Blutgefasse des Dottersackes des Hechtes (*Esox lucius* L.). Odbitka zego numeru Biuletynu, Zakladu Biologii Stawow Poiskiej Akademii Nauk, pp. 17–18.

ZIEBARTH, G.
　　1983　Ein Versuch zum Vorstrecken von Hechtbrut in Kleinsilos. Zeitschrift fuer
　　　　　Binnenfischerei 30(5):168–169.
ZIELINSKA, K.
　　1975　The Golgi apparatus in cells of the olfactory epithelium in the pike. Folia
　　　　　Morphologica 34:485–492.
　　　　　This study of the Golgi apparatus used classical impregnation methods, the
　　　　　refractometric method, and histochemical test for TPPase.
　　1976　Mitochondria and respiratory and hydrolytic enzymes in the cells of the olfac-
　　　　　tory epithelium in the pike. Folia Morphologica 35:21–29.
　　　　　Mitochondria in the cells of the olfactory epithelium of the pike were studied
　　　　　by the use of the classical staining method, by the refractometric method, and
　　　　　by histochemical tests for the respiratory enzymes, cytochrome oxidase, and
　　　　　succinate dehydrogenase.
ZIMAKOV, I. E.
　　1978　A radiochemical method of analysis for study of trace quantities of mercury
　　　　　in food products. Voprosy Pitaniya 3:64–69.
ZINOV'YEVA, S. N. and V. P. KOTOV
　　1969　The pike of Votkinsk Reservoir. Uchenya Zapisko Permskii Gosudarstvennyi
　　　　　Universitet Imeni A. M. Gor'kogo 217:77–88.
ZITNAN, R.
　　1971　Rafidaskaroza - zavazna parazitarna choroba nasich pstruhov. [Raphidas-
　　　　　carosis - a severe parasitary disease of trouts in Czechoslovakia.] Polov. a
　　　　　Ryb. 22(6):4.
　　　　　Describes the life cycle of *Raphidascaris ocus* which parasitizes pike. The
　　　　　parasite was fairly widespread in the locality of the Dobsina Dam.
ZOTOV, A. F.
　　1958　Antibakterial'nye svoistva organov i tkanei presnovodnykh. [Antibacterial
　　　　　properties of the organs and tissues of freshwater fish.] Voprosy Ikhtiologii
　　　　　10:157–161.
　　　　　Antibacterial properties were found in pike. Organs and tissues showed anti-
　　　　　bacterial influence of gram-positive and gram-negative bacteria. Antibac-
　　　　　terial principles were not found in gills, muscles, or intestines. No seasonal
　　　　　pattern could be established.
ZUBENKO
　　1975　The role of the perch in the food of the pike and the pike-perch of Kremen-
　　　　　chug Reservoir. Rybnoe Khozyaistvo Respublikankii Mezhvedomstvennyi
　　　　　Tematicheskii Nauchnyk Sbornik 20:101–105.
ZUROMSKA, H. and W. KORZYNEK
　　1958　Zroznicowanie miejsca i czasu tarla szczupaka. [Differentiation of place and
　　　　　timing of pike spawning.] Gospodarka Rybna 10(5):20–21.
　　　　　Analysis of fyke-net catches in Masurian lakes. Conclusions for managers.
ZWIRZ, B.
　　1975　Proven methods for walleye, pike and muskie. Fishing Guide, pp. 56–61,
　　　　　121.
ZYLINSKI, R.
　　1958　O ochronie szczupaka slow kilka. [Some comments on the protection of
　　　　　pike.] Wiadomosci Wedkarskie 19:11–12.
　　　　　Changes of angling rules. Shortening of protective period by two weeks.

Subject Index

LEONARD, V. J. 1963
LIND, E. A. and E. KAUKORANTA 1975a, Finland
LIND, E. A. and E. KAUKORANTA 1975b, Finland
LIPSIT, J. H. 1977, Great Lakes
LUGOVAYA, T. V. 1967, USSR
LUGOVAYA, T. V. 1973, USSR
MACAN, T. T. , England
MACINS, V. 1972, Ontario
MAFTEI, D. V. 1963
MAKSUNOV, V. A. 1956, USSR
MAKSUNOV, V. A. 1972, USSR
MANN, R. H. K. 1971b, England
MANN, R. H. K. 1975b, England
MANN, R. H. K. 1976, England
MARSHALL, W. S. and N. C. GILBERT 1905, Wisconsin
MCCARRAHER, B. 1960, Nebraska H
MCCARRAHER, D. B. 1957a, Nebraska
MCCORMACK, J. 1965, England
MENDIS, A. S. 1956, Saskatchewan
MILLER, J. and K. BUSS n.d., Pennsylvania
MILLER, R. B. and W. A. KENNEDY 1948
MONTPETIT, A. N. 1897, Canada
MORRIS, J., L. MORRIS and L. WITT 1972, Nebraska
MORROW, J. E. 1964, Alaska
MOSINDY, T. 1980, Ontario
MUENCH, B. 1964, Illinois
MUNRO, W. R. 1957, Scotland
NAWRATIL, O. 1954, Austria
NELSON, M. N. and A. D. HASLER 1942, Wisconsin
NEW YORK DEPARTMENT OF CONSERVATION 1969, New York
NIKITINA, A. G. 1958, USSR
NITSKANSKII, S. G. 1961, USSR
NOLAND, W. E. 1951, Wisconsin
NYBELIN, O. 1943, Sweden
OATIS, P. H. and J. G. LINDENBERG 1979, Massachusetts
OSBURN, R. C. 1901, Ohio
PARAGAMIAN, V. L. 1976, Wisconsin
PATERSON, R. J. 1968, Alberta
PEARSE, A. S. 1922, Wisconsin
PIHU, E. 1961
POPOVA, O. A. 1960, USSR
POPOVA, O. A. 1962, USSR
POPOVA, O. A. 1965, USSR
POWELL, T. G. 1972b, Colorado
RAWSON, D. S. 1932, Saskatchewan
RAWSON, D. S. 1951, Northwest Territories

RAWSON, D. S. 1957, Saskatchewan
RAWSON, D. S. 1959, Saskatchewan
RIDENHOUR, R. L. 1955, Iowa
RIDENHOUR, R. L. 1957, Iowa
RIDENHOUR, R. L. 1960, Iowa
SCHMITZ, W. R. 1953, Wisconsin
SEDLAR, J. 1971
SHAFI, M. 1974, England
SHAFI, M. and P. S. MAITLAND 1971, Scotland
SHILENKOVA, A. K. 1956., USSR
SNOW, H. E. 1969a, Wisconsin
SOLMAN, V. E. F. 1940, Manitoba
SVETOVIDOVA, A. A. 1960, China
TARNAVSKII, N. P. 1967, USSR
VALKEAJARVI, P. 1983, Finland
VAN ENGEL, W. A. 1940, Wisconsin
VAN OOSTEN, J. 1937, Great Lakes
VASHCHENKO, D. M. 1958a, USSR
VORONIN, F. N. and V. V. KRYLOV 1971, USSR
VOSTRADOVSKA, M. 1978, Czechoslovakia
VOSTRADOVSKY, J. 1983, Czechoslovakia
WAINIO, A. 1966b, Great Lakes
WESLOH, M. L. and D. E. OLSON 1962, Minnesota
WONG, B. and T. WHILLANS 1973, Northwest Territories
YEFIMOVA, A. I. 1949, USSR
ZALACHOWSKI, W. 1965a, Poland
ZAWISZA, J. 1961, Poland
ZINOV'YEVA, S. N. and V. P. KOTOV 1969, USSR

AGE AND GROWTH DETERMINATION
ANWAND, K. 1969
ASTANIN, L. P. 1947
BACKIEL, T. 1968, Poland
CARLANDER, K. D. and L. L. SMITH, Jr. 1945, Minnesota
CASSELMAN, J. M. 1967, Ontario
CASSELMAN, J. M. 1974b, Ontario
CASSELMAN, J. M. 1978a, Ontario
CASSELMAN, J. M. 1979, Ontario
CASSELMAN, J. M. 1983a, Ontario
CASSELMAN, J. M. 1983b, Ontario
CRAGG-HINE, D. 1966, England
CROSSMAN, E. J. 1979b, Ontario
DEBONT, A. F. 1967
DRAIGHIN, P. A. 1958, USSR

FROST, W. E. and C. KIPLING 1959, England

FROST, W. E. and C. KIPLING 1961, England

HARRISON, E. J. and W. F. HADLEY 1979, New York

INLAND FISHERIES TRUST , Ireland

MASSE, G. 1979, Quebec

PHILLIPS, R. 1974

POUPE, J. 1973, Czechoslovakia

SHENTYAKOVA, L. F. 1966, USSR

SHENTYAKOVA, L. F. 1969, USSR

SUNDBACK, K. 1971, Finland

SYCH, R. 1971

TERSKOV, I. A., E. A. VAGANOV and V. V. SPIROV 1976, USSR

VOSTRADOVSKY, J. 1970a, Czechoslovakia

VOSTRADOVSKY, J. 1977, Czechoslovakia

WAINIO, A. 1966a, Great Lakes

WILLIAMS, J. E. 1955, Michigan

AGE AND GROWTH STUDIES

AKOS, H. 1981, Hungary

ALM, G. 1959, Sweden

ANONYMOUS 1933, Poland

ANWAND, K. 1971, East Germany

ARKHIPTSEVA, N. T. 1974, USSR

AUSTIN, P. 1954a, Ireland

AUSTIN, P. 1954b, Ireland

AUSTIN, P. 1958, Ireland

AUTKO, B. F. 1964, USSR

BASHMAKOVA, A. Y. 1930, USSR

BEYERLE, G. B. 1973a, Michigan

BRACKEN, J. J. 1973, Ireland

BRACKEN, J. J. and W. S. T. CHAMP 1968, Ireland

BRACKEN, J. J. and W. S. T. CHAMP 1971, Ireland

BRETT, J. R. 1979

BUSS, K. and J. MILLER 1961, Pennsylvania

BUSS, K. and J. MILLER 1962, Pennsylvania

CALDERONI, P. 1965, Italy

CARBINE, W. F. and V. C. APPLEGATE 1948, Michigan

CASSELMAN, J. M. 1967, Ontario

CASSELMAN, J. M. 1972, Ontario

CASSELMAN, J. M. 1974b, Ontario

CASSELMAN, J. M. 1978a, Ontario

CASSELMAN, J. M. 1983a, Ontario

CASSELMAN, J. M. 1983b, Ontario

CASSELMAN, J. M. and E. J. CROSSMAN 1986, Ontario H

CASSELMAN, J. M. and H. H. HARVEY 1975, Ontario

CHRISTIANSEN, D. G. 1976, Northwest Territories

CIEPIELEWSKI, W. 1970, Poland

CLARK, C. F. 1957, Ohio

CLARK, C. F. and F. STEINBACH 1959, Ohio

CUERRIER, J. L. and A. COURTEMANCHE 1954, Quebec

DIANA, J. S. 1979a, Alberta

DIANA, J. S. 1981, Michigan

DIANA, J. S. 1983b, Michigan

DOMANEVSKY, L. N. 1963, USSR

ECOLE, R. A. 1979, France

EDDY, S. and K. CARLANDER 1939, Minnesota

EDDY, S. and K. CARLANDER 1942, Minnesota

EDDY, S. and K. D. CARLANDER 1940, Minnesota

FILIPSSON, O. 1972, Sweden

FROST, W. E. 1963, England

FROST, W. E. and C. KIPLING 1965, England

FROST, W. E. and C. KIPLING 1967, England

FROST, W. E. and C. KIPLING 1968a, England

FUHRMANN, O. 1934a

GABEL, J. A. 1974, South Dakota

GEE, A. S. 1978, England

GOTTBERG, G. 1917a, Finland

HALNON, L. 1960, Vermont

HART, P. J. B. and T. J. PITCHER 1969b, England

HARTMANN, J. 1978, West Germany

HASSLER, T. J. 1969, South Dakota

HELSTROM, N. 1978, Finland

HICKLEY, P. and A. SUTTON 1984, England

HILE, R. 1931, Indiana

INSKIP, P. D. 1980, Wisconsin

IOWA CONSERVATION COMMISSION 1961, Iowa

JOHAL, M. S. 1978, Czechoslovakia

JOHNSON, L. D. 1961b, Wisconsin

JUDAY, C. and C. L. SCHLOEMER 1936, Wisconsin

JUDAY, C. and C. L. SCHLOEMER 1938, Wisconsin

KAJAVA, R. n.d., Finland
KAPCZYNSKA, A. and T. PENCZAK 1969, Poland
KARZINKIN, G. S. 1939, USSR
KENNEDY, M. and P. FITZMAURICE 1969, Ireland
KIPLING, C. 1983a, England
KIPLING, C. and W. E. FROST 1970, England
KORWIN-KOSSAKOWSKI, M. 1976, Poland
KREUZER, R. O. and J. G. SIVAK 1984, Ontario
KULEMIN, A. A., I. I. MAKKOVEYEVE and M. I. SOLOPOVA 1971, USSR
KUPCHINSKAYA, E. S. 1985, USSR
LAARMAN, P. W. 1964a, Michigan
LUX, F. E. 1960, Minnesota
MACDONALD, P. D. M. and PITCHER, T. J. 1979, Ontario
MACKENTHUN, K. M. 1948, Wisconsin
MAFTEI, D. V. 1963
MAGNIN, E., E. MURAWSKA and V. LEGENDRE 1973, Quebec
MAKOWECKI, R. 1973a, Alberta
MAKOWECKI, R. 1973b, Alberta
MAKSUNOV, V. A. 1972, USSR
MANN, R. H. K. 1971a, England
MANN, R. H. K. 1971b, England
MANN, R. H. K. 1976, England
MASSE, G. 1979, Quebec
MCCAULEY, R. W. and J. M. CASSELMAN 1981, Ontario
MEIEN, V. A. 1926, USSR
MILLER, J. and K. BUSS n.d., Pennsylvania
MONGEAU, J.-R. 1960, Quebec
NELSON, W. R. 1974, South Dakota
NIKITINA, A. G. 1958, USSR
OCVIRK, J. 1984, Czechoslovakia
OLIVA, O. 1956, Czechoslovakia
OLIVA, O. and A. S. NAIKSATAM 1979, Czechoslovakia
OLSSON, M. 1976, Sweden
ONTARIO DEPARTMENT OF LANDS AND FORESTS 1953, Ontario
ORLOVA, E. L. and G. K. AZHIGALIYEVA 1984, USSR
PERMITIN, I. E. 1959, USSR
PETERS, J. C., ed. 1964, Montana
PUPYRNIKOVA, A. V. 1953, USSR
QADRI, S. U. and P. J. RUBEC 1977, Ontario

RIDENHOUR, R. L. 1960, Iowa
ROSEBOROUGH, D. 1957, Great Lakes
SCHULTZ, F. H. 1955, Saskatchewan
SEABURG, K. G. and J. B. MOYLE 1964, Minnesota
SEDLAR, J. 1971
SNOW, H. E. 1969a, Wisconsin
SNOW, H. E. and T. D. BEARD 1972, Wisconsin
SOLONINOVA, L. N. 1976, USSR
SVETOVIDOV, A. N. 1929, USSR
SVETOVIDOVA, A. A. 1960, China
TANDON, K. K. and O. OLIVA 1978, Czechoslovakia
THOMPSON, D. 1979
VAN ENGEL, W. A. 1940, Wisconsin
VAN OOSTEN, J. 1937, Great Lakes
VOSTRADOVSKY, J. 1977, Czechoslovakia
VOSTRADOVSKY, J. 1980, Czechoslovakia
WAINIO, A. 1966b, Great Lakes
WILLEMSEN, J. 1967b, Netherlands
WILLEMSEN, J. 1978, Netherlands
WOLFERT, D. F. and T. J. MILLER 1978, Great Lakes
ZALACHOWSKI, W. 1965a, Poland
ZAWISZA, J. 1961, Poland

ANATOMY, MORPHOLOGY, AND HISTOLOGY

ABASHIDZE, V. S. 1969
ADELMAN, I. 1969, Minnesota
ALEEV, Y. G. 1969
ALLIS, E. P., JR. 1905
AMBROSINUS, B. 1642
ANDREW, W. 1959
ARENDT, E. 1822
BACHOP, W. E. 1958, Ohio
BAKHTIN, Y. K. 1976, USSR
BARAUSKAS, R. 1978, USSR
BAUMGARTEN, H. G., B. FALCK and H. WARTENBERG 1970
BAUMGARTEN, H. G. and H. WARTENBERG 1970
BERG, L. S. 1899, USSR
BERG, L. S. 1936, USSR
BERNATOWICZ, S. 1948, Poland
BESRUKOW, E. A. 1928, USSR
BEZRUKOVA, E. A. 1928, USSR
BIELEK, E. 1974, Austria
BIELEK, E. 1976, Austria

BLASIUS, G. 1692
BLOT, J. 1968
BOGOSLOVSKAIA, E. I. 1960, USSR
BOLDYREFF, E. B. 1935
BOYTSOV, M. P. 1974, USSR
BRAEKEVELT, C. R. 1973, Manitoba
BRAEKEVELT, C. R. 1974, Manitoba
BRAEKEVELT, C. R. 1975, Manitoba
BRIDGES, C. D. B. 1969
BRINLEY, F. J. 1940
BUCKE, D. 1971
BYCZKOWAKA-SMYK, W. 1959
BYZOV, A. L., Y. A. TRIFONOV, L. M.
    CHAILAHIAN and K. W. GOLUBTZOV
    1977
BYZOV, A. L., Y. A. TRIFONOV and L. M.
    CHAILAKHYAN 1973, USSR
CAMERON, J. N. 1974, Alaska
CAMERON, J. N. 1975, Alaska
CASSELMAN, J. M. 1974a, Ontario
CASSELMAN, J. M. 1979, Ontario
CASSELMAN, J. M. 1980, Ontario
CASSELMAN, J. M., E. J. CROSSMAN,
    P. E. IHSSEN, J. D. REIST and H. E.
    BOOKE 1986, Ontario H
CASSERIUS, J. 1552
CIHAR, J. 1955, Czechoslovakia
COCKERELL, T. D. A. 1913, Ohio
CROSSMAN, E. J. and J. M. CASSELMAN
    1969, Ontario
CSENGO, N. 1914
DABROWSKI, J. 1961, Poland
DE BEER, G. R. 1937, England
DEMCHENKO, I. F. 1963, USSR
DEVILLERS, C. and J. CORSIN 1968,
    France
DEVITSINA, G. V. and T. A. BELOUSOVA
    1978, USSR
DEVITSINA, G. V. and G. A. MALYUKINA
    1977, USSR
DEVITSYNA, G. V. 1973, USSR
DEVITSYNA, G. V. 1977, USSR
DISLER, N. N. 1967, USSR
DISSELHORST, R. 1904, Germany
DORNESCU, G. T. and D. MISCALENCU
    1968a
DORNESCU, G. T. and D. MISCALENCU
    1968b
DOVING, K. B., M. DUBOIS-DAUPHIN, A.
    HOLLEY and F. JOURDAN 1977
DZHUMALIYEV, M. K. 1977
FALCON, J. 1979a
FALCON, J. 1979b

FALCON, J., M. T. JUILLARD and J. P.
    COLLIN 1980a
FALCON, J., M. T. JUILLARD and J. P.
    COLLIN 1980b
FALCON, J. and H. MEISSL 1980
FALCON, J. and H. MEISSL 1981
FALCON, J. and J. P. MOCQUARD 1979
FRANCOIS, Y. 1966
FROST, G. A. 1926
GEORGES, D. 1964, France
GILTAY, C. M. 1832
GILTAY, C. M. 1833
GOROVAIA, S. L. 1969
GRASSE, P. P. 1958
GREGORY, W. K. 1933
GRODZINSKI, Z. 1971, Poland
GROSS, G. W. and G. W. KREUTZBERG
    1978, West Germany
HARRIS, J. E. 1938
HEROLD, R. C. 1971a
HEROLD, R. C. 1971b
HEROLD, R. C. and L. LANDINO 1970
HEROLD, R. C. B. 1974, Pennsylvania
HEROLD, R. C. B. 1975, Pennsylvania
HILGENDORF, F. M. 1872
HILGENDORF, F. M. 1880
HOFER, B. 1901
HOFFMANN, R., P. WONDRAK and W.
    GROTH 1980, Germany
HUBBS, CARL L. 1920
HUBBS, CARL L. 1921
HUBBS, CARL L. 1922, Michigan
IVANOV, M. E. 1956, USSR
IVANOV, N. M. 1978, USSR
IVANOVA, M. N.
JAKUBOWSKI, M. 1965
JAKUBOWSKI, M., W. BYCZKOWSKA-
    SMYK and Y. MIKHALEV 1969
JANEC-SUSLOWSKA, W. 1957,
    Poland
JASINSKI, A. 1965, Poland
JASINSKI, A. 1977a, Poland
JASINSKI, A. 1977b, Poland
JOLLIE, M. 1975, Illinois
JUSZCZYK, D. 1975
KALGANOV, V. M. 1949
KALLIO, D. M., P. R. GARANT and C.
    MINKIN 1971
KARAMIAN, A. I. 1949, USSR
KEAST, A. and D. WEBB 1966, Ontario
KILARSKI, W. 1966, Poland
KLEERKOPER, H. 1969
KOLGANOV, D. I. 1968, USSR

KOROVINA, V. M., A. I. LYUBITSKAYA and E. A. DOROFEEVA 1965, USSR

KOROVINA, V. M. and N. E. VASIL'EVA 1976, USSR

KOSHELEV, B. W. 1961, USSR

KOURIL, J. and J. HAMACKOVA 1977, Czechoslovakia

KRAUSE, R. 1923, Germany

KREUTZBERG, G. W. and G. W. GROSS 1977, West Germany

KRUTZBERG, G. W. and G. W. GROSS 1977

KUPERMAN, B. I. and V. V. KUZ'MINA 1984

LAWLER, G. H. 1960b, Manitoba

LAWLER, G. H. 1961b, Manitoba

LAWLER, G. H. 1961c, Manitoba

LAWLER, G. H. 1964b, Manitoba

LAWLER, G. H. 1966a, Manitoba

LAWLER, G. H. 1966b, Manitoba

LEHTONEN, H., P. BOHLING and M. HILDEN 1983

LEKANDER, B. 1949

LEVINE, J. S. and E. F. MACNICHOL 1982

LINSS, W. 1969a

LINSS, W. 1969b

LINSS, W. 1969c

LINSS, W. 1969d

LINSS, W. and G. GEYER 1968

MAFTEI, D. V. 1963

MAKSIMOVA, E. M. 1969

MAKSIMOVA, E. M. and V. V. MAKSIMOV 1972

MAKSUNOV, V. A. 1956, USSR

MALCOLM, J. 1975

MARKIEWICZ, F. 1960

MARS-VALLETT, A. E. 1968

MAVRINSKAYA, L. F. 1956

M'DONNELL, R. 1864, Ireland

MECKLENBURG, C. VON 1974, Sweden

MERRILEES, M. J. 1972, Ontario

MERRILEES, M. J. and E. J. CROSSMAN 1973, Ontario

MERRILEES, M. J. and E. J. CROSSMAN 1974, Ontario

MIDTTUN, B. 1980, Norway

MIDTTUN, B. 1981, Norway

MIDTTUN, B. 1983, Norway

MINOR, J. D. 1976, Canada

MISRA, P. M. 1966

MONOD, T. 1968

NECRASOV, O. 1968

NELSON, G. J. 1969

NELSON, G. J. 1972

NYSTROM, M. 1979, Finland

OBERSZTYN, A. 1953

OLIVA, O. 1965, Czechoslovakia

ORSKA, J.

OWMAN, C. and C. RUDEBERG 1970

PEACH, U. A. and V. A. REMOROV, eds. 1977

PEHRSON, T. 1944

RAMANUJAM, S. G. M. 1966

REIFEL, C. W. and A. A. TRAVILL 1978a, Ontario

REIFEL, C. W. and A. A. TRAVILL 1978b, Ontario

REIST, J. C. 1978, Alberta

REIST, J. D. 1985, Ontario

RIEHL, R. and E. SCHULTE 1977, West Germany

RUDEBERG, C. 1969

RUDEBERG, C. 1971

SAVAGE, A. G. 1983, Ireland

SBIKIN, Y. N. 1974, USSR

SCHAUINSLAND 1906, Germany

SCHMIDT, B. 1913

SCHNAKENBECK, W. 1936

SCHOOTS, A. F. M., J. J. M. STIKKEL-BROECK, J. F. BEKHUIS and J. MANUEL DENUCE 1982, Netherlands

SCHWARZ, S. S., V. G. ISTSCHENKO, L. A. DOBRINSKAYA, A. Z. AMSTISLAVSKII, I. N. BURSYNINA, I. A. PARAKETZOV and A. S. YAKOLEVA 1968

SHAMARDINA, I. P. 1957, USSR

SHCHERBUKHA, A. Y. 1974, USSR

SHKOL'NIK-YARROWS, E. G. 1975, USSR

SKURDAL, J. 1981

SOKOLOV, B. M. 1961, USSR

SOKOLOV, L. I. 1971, USSR

SOROKIN, V. N. and A. A. SOROKINA 1979, USSR

SROCZYNSKI, S. 1972, Poland

SROCZYNSKI, S. 1976, Poland

STAMMER, A. 1969, Hungary

STAMMER, A., I. HORVATH, M. CSOKNYA and K. HALASY 1978a, Hungary

STAMMER, A., I. HORVATH, M. CSOKNYA and K. HALASY 1978b, Hungary

STARKS, E. C. 1916, California

STARKS, E. C. 1930, California

STERNFELD, A. 1882

STUDNICKA, F. K. 1944

SUNDARARAJ 1958

SUSLOWSKA, W. 1971, Czechoslovakia
SZLAMINSKA, M. 1980, Poland
SZUBA, Z. 1971, Poland
TEN KATE, J. H. 1973, Ontario
TEN KATE, J. H. and J. W. KUIPER 1970
TEODORESCU, A.-C. 1970
TERESHENKOV, I. I. 1972, USSR
TOWARNICKI, R. 1962, Poland
TOWARNICKI, R. 1963, Poland
TRAUTMAN, M. B. and C. L. HUBBS 1936,
    Michigan
TRAUTMAN, M. B. and C. L. HUBBS 1948,
    Michigan
TYSZKIEWICZ, K. 1969, Czechoslovakia
VINNIKOV, Y. A., V. I. GOVARDOVSKII
    and I. V. OSIPOVA 1965
WAINIO, A. 1978, Ontario
WALLS, G. L. 1942, Michigan
WEISS, J. 1979, East Germany
WILSON, M. V. H. and P. VEILLEUX 1982
WONDARK, P. 1974, Germany
ZARNECKI, S. 1928, Poland
ZBIKOWSKA, L. 1980a, Poland
ZBIKOWSKA, L. 1980b, Poland
ZENKIN, G. M. and I. N. P. PIGAREV 1970,
    USSR
ZIELINSKA, K. 1975, Poland
ZIELINSKA, K. 1976, Poland

ANGLING AND RECORD CATCHES

ANDRZEJCZYK, T. 1972, Poland
ANON, W. T. 1884, Ontario
ANONYMOUS 1888, England, Ireland
ANONYMOUS 1906, Poland
ANONYMOUS 1908, Poland
ANONYMOUS 1937, Poland
ANONYMOUS 1938, Poland
ANONYMOUS 1957, Poland
ANONYMOUS 1960a, North Dakota
ANONYMOUS 1973a, Saskatchewan
ANONYMOUS 1976b
ANONYMOUS 1976e
ANONYMOUS 1977
BAILEY, J. and M. PAGE 1985, England
BAJKOV, A. 1932, Manitoba
BARTA, A. 1877, Poland
BARTLES, B. 1973, England
BERGH, K. 1977
BEUKEMA, J. J. 1970
BLACK, R. D. C. 1981, Ireland
BROWN, J. J. 1876, USA
BULLER, F. 1979, England

BULLER, F. 1981, England H
CAINE, L. S. 1949a
CAINE, L. S. 1949b
CAMP, R. R. 1951
CARLANDER, K. D. 1956, Iowa
CARLSON, R. M. and R. CAPLE 1980,
    Great Lakes
CARPENTER, R. G. and H. R. SIEGLER
    1947, New Hampshire
CASSELMAN, J. M. and E. J. CROSSMAN
    1986, Ontario H
CECILIA, A. 1973, Spain
CHABAN, R. 1973, Morocco
CHOYNOWSKI, J. 1936, Poland
CHURCHILL, W. and H. SNOW 1964,
    Wisconsin
COOPER, G. P. and W. C. LATTA 1954,
    Michigan
CROSSMAN, E. J. 1979a, Ontario
CSANDA, D. 1981, Great Lakes
CSANDA, D. and T. PORTINCASO 1981,
    Canada
CZAPLICKI, J. 1964, Poland
DAVIS, J. 1983, Ontario
DEAN, T. 1982, South Dakota
DICONSTANZO, C. J. and R. L.
    RIDENHOUR 1957, Iowa
EGGERS, J. 1983, Netherlands
ELSER, H. J. 1961, Maryland
ERICKSON, G. 1978
ERIKSON, G. 1978
FALK, M. R. and D. V. GILLMAN 1980,
    Northwest Territories
FALKUS, H. and F. BULLER 1975, England
FELLEGY, J. 1975, Minnesota
FERNANDEZ ROMAN, E. 1982
FICKLING, N. 1982a, England
FITZMAURICE, P. 1978, Ireland
GABELHOUSE, D. W., Jr. 1981
GASBARINO, P. 1985, Ontario
GAY, M. 1975, England
HAMER, C. 1975, Minnesota
HAMPTON, J. F. 1948, Europe
HANSEN, J. P. 1983
HENEGAR, D. 1960a, North Dakota
HUGGLER, T. 1975
HURUM, H. J., England
HUTCHINSON, H. G. 1904
JAMSON, G. C. 1973, Michigan
JANISZEWSKI, M. 1934, Poland
JANISZEWSKI, M. 1938a, Poland
JANISZEWSKI, M. 1938b, Poland
JENKINS, R. M. and D. I. MORAIS 1971

JONES, R. H. 1982, Ontario
KACZYNSKI, C. 1976, Poland
KELEHER, J. J. 1961, Northwest Territories
KENDALL, W. C. 1918, Maine
KNOWELDEN, M. 1984
KOBES, R. 1982, USA
KORULCZYK, T. and L. KOZLOWSKA 1970, Poland
KORZYNEK, W. 1960, Poland
KORZYNEK, W. 1962, Poland
LEHTONEN, H. and K. SALOJARVI 1981, Finland
LEONARD, N. A. 1952, Ontario
LINDNER, A. 1976
LINDNER, B. 1978
LINDNER, R. and J. ZERNOV 1975
LUCAS, J. 1953
LUCAS, J. 1960
MADIGAN, P. 1978, Ontario
MAKOWSKI, M. L. 1966, Poland
MANN, K. 1982
MARION, R. 1976
MARLBOROUGH, D. 1969, England
MARSHALL, S. 1950, Poland
MATHER, F. 1898
MCCARRAHER, D. B. 1955, North America
MCCLANE, A. J. 1954, USA
MCCLANE, A. J. 1976
MEAD, C. W. 1915, New York
MIGDALSKI, E. C. 1962, North America
MOYLE, J. B. 1955, Minnesota
MYERS, B. J. 1979, Ontario
NEW YORK DEPARTMENT OF CONSERVATION 1969, New York
NICHOLS, J. T. and V. HEILNER 1920, North America
NORRIS, T. 1864, USA
NORTH, E. 1980
OCVIRK, J. 1982, Czechoslovakia
O'NEILL, R. H. 1932, Canada
ORGAN, W. 1960, Manitoba
PAGEAU, G., Y. GRAVEL and V. LEGENDRE 1979, Quebec
PEARCE, W. A. 1961, New York
PENNEL, H. C. 1863, England
PROROK, P. 1983
QUIGLEY, D. T. 1982, Ireland
RAHN, M. 1975
RICKARDS, B. 1976, England
RICKARDS, B. 1978, Scotland
RICKARDS, B. 1980, Ireland
RICKARDS, B. and R. WEBB 1971, England

RICKARDS, B. and K. WHITEHEAD 1976, England
RICKARDS, B. and K. WHITEHEAD 1977, England
RIEMENS, R. G. 1977, Netherlands
RIEMENS, R. G. 1978, Netherlands
RIPLEY, O. 1932
ROACH, L. S. 1948
ROBINSON, G. 1941
RULEWICZ, M. 1974, Poland
SCHMIDTT, H. 1980, Germany
SCHUPP, D. H. 1974, Minnesota
SCHWARTZ, F. J. and H. J. ELSER 1962, Maryland
SMITH, O. W. 1922
SPENCE, E. F. 1928, England
SPOTSWOOD, L. 1985, Ontario
STANGE, D. 1986a, Manitoba
STANGE, D. 1986b
STIGER, H. , Germany
STOCKWELL, G. A. 1875, Great Lakes
STONE, P. 1977, England
SZTRAMKO, L. and PAINE, J. R. 1982, Great Lakes.
TAVERNER, E. and MOORE, J. 1935, England
TAYLOR, F. 1962, England
THOMPSON, W. 1883, Great Lakes
TOWNSEND, D. C.
TURRELL, W. J. 1910, England
WALKER, R. 1953, England
WALTON, I. and C. COTTEN 1835
WEBB, R. and B. RICKARDS 1976, England
WEITHMAN, A. S. and R. O. ANDERSON 1976, Missouri
WESTMAN, J. 1961
WHITEHOUSE, F. C. 1948, Canada
WILSON, J. 1977, England
WINKELMAN, B. 1977
WINKELMAN, B. 1978a
WINKELMAN, B. 1978b
WIRTH, T. L. 1960, Wisconsin
WOJDA, S. 1972, Poland
WOODING, F. H. 1959, Canada
WYDOSKI, R. S. 1977, California
WYGANOWSKI, J. 1957, Poland
WYGANOWSKI, J. 1974, Poland
ZDANKO, A. 1969, Poland
ZWIRZ, B. 1975

BEHAVIOUR
ABROSIMOVA, A. M. 1975

BAERENDS, G. P. 1957
BALAYCO, L. A. 1981
BEUKEMA, J. J. 1970
BRAUM, E. 1963, West Germany
CHRISTIANSEN, D. G. 1976, Northwest
  Territories
CHUMAKOV, K. A. 1963, USSR
CLARK, J. (2) 1972a, Colorado
DOMBECK, M. P. 1979, Wisconsin
FARABEE, G. B. 1970, Missouri
GRAFF, D. R. 1972, Pennsylvania
HELFMAN, G. S. 1979
HOOGLAND, R., D. MORRIS and N. TIN-
  BERGEN 1957
HOWARD, H. C. and R. E. THOMAS 1970,
  Nebraska
HUCHSON, D. R. and J. M. SHEPPARD
  1963, Ontario
IVANOVA, M. N. 1969, USSR
IVANOVA, M. N. and A. N. LOPATKO
  1983, USSR
JOHNSON, L. 1960, England
JOHNSON, L. D. 1962a, Wisconsin
JONES, F. R. H. 1963, England
KASHIN, G. M., L. K. MALININ and G. N.
  ORLOVSKY 1976, USSR
KASHIN, S. M., L. K. MALININ, G. N.
  ORLOVSKY and A. G. PODDUBNY
  1977, USSR
KONOBEEVA, V. K., A. G. KONOBEEV
  and A. G. PODDUBNYI 1980, USSR
LAWLER, G. H. 1953, Manitoba
LAWLER, G. H. 1969b, Manitoba
LEWINGTON, J. 1973a, Northwest Terri-
  tories
MAGNUSON, J. J. and D. J. KARLEN 1970,
  Wisconsin
MAGNUSON, J. J. and B. PETROSKY 1973,
  Wisconsin
MALININ, L. K. 1969, USSR
MALININ, L. K. 1970, USSR
MALININ, L. K. 1971a, USSR
MALININ, L. K. 1971b, USSR
MALYUKINA, G. A., N. G. DMITRIEVA,
  E. A. MARUSOV and G. V. YURKEVICH
  1977
MANTEIFEL, B. P., I. I. GIRSA, T. S.
  LESHCHEVA and D. S. PAVLOV 1965,
  USSR
MARS-VALLETT, A. E. 1968
MCNAMARA, F. 1937, Michigan
MOODY, R. C., J. M. HELLAND and R. A.
  STEIN 1983, Ohio

NEILL, S. R. ST. J. and J. M. CULLEN 1974
NELSON, L. R. 1983, Alberta
NURSALL, J. R. 1973, Alberta
OHLMER, W. and I. SCHWARTZKOPFF
  1959
PETROSKY, B. R. and J. J. MAGNUSON
  1973, Wisconsin
PODDUBNYI, A. G., L. K. MALININ and V.
  V. GAIDUK 1970
RUDAKOVSKIY, L. G., L. N. SOLODI-
  LOV, V. R. PROTAXOV and V. M. KRU-
  MIN 1970, USSR
VERHEIJEN, F. J. 1969
WEBB, P. W. 1984a, Michigan H
ZARNECKI, S. 1964, Poland

COMMERCIAL FISHING
ALM, G. 1957, Sweden
ANDERSON, A. W. and C. E. PETERSON ,
  USA
ANISHCHENKO, V. 1965
ANONYMOUS 1983, Netherlands
ANWAND, K. 1971, East Germany
ANWAND, K. 1972
BAJKOV, A. 1930, Canada
BALDWIN, N. S., R. W. SAALFELD, M. A.
  ROSS and H. J. BUETTNER 1979, Great
  Lakes
BERKA, R. 1980, Czechoslovakia
CARLANDER, K. D. 1942, Minnesota
CARLANDER, K. D. 1947, Minnesota
CARLSON, R. M. and R. CAPLE 1980,
  Great Lakes
CLEMENS, W. A., J. R. DYMOND and N.
  K. BIGELOW 1924, Ontario
DERKSEN, A. J. 1978, Manitoba
DOMANEVSKII, L. N. 1958, USSR
DYMOND, J. R. 1922, Great Lakes
DYMOND, J. R. 1939, Ontario
DYMOND, J. R. and J. L. HART 1927,
  Ontario
DYMOND, J. R., J. L. HART and A. L.
  PRITCHARD 1929, Great Lakes
EL-BASTAVIZI, A. M. and G. A. SMIR-
  NOVA 1972
EVERMANN, B. W. 1905
FOOD AND AGRICULTURE ORGANIZA-
  TION OF THE UNITED NATIONS 1977
GENGERKE, T. 1977, Iowa
HALME, E. and S. HURME 1952, Finland
HARKNESS, W. J. K. 1936a, Ontario
HARKNESS, W. J. K. 1936b, Ontario

HARKNESS, W. J. K. 1936c, Ontario
HELMS, D. 1976, Iowa
HELMS, D. R. 1975, Iowa
KACZYNSKI, C. 1976, Poland
KARDASHEV, A. V. and A. R. SHAMUN 1984, USSR
KARPOVICH, I. Y. 1968
KENNEDY, W. A. 1954, Northwest Territories
KIPLING, C. 1972, England
KOZMIN, A. K. 1952, USSR
KUZNETSOV, V. A. 1980, USSR
LANTZ, A. W. and D. G. IREDALE 1966, Ontario
LANTZ, A. W. and D. G. IREDALE 1971, Manitoba
LAPITSKII, I. I. 1958, USSR
LEBEDEV, V. D. 1961, USSR
LEHNHERR, H. R. 1981, Switzerland
LEHTONEN, H. and M. HILDEN 1980, Finland
LEHTONEN, H. and K. SALOJARVI 1981, Finland
LJUNGBERG, O. 1963, Sweden
MALLEY, M. W. and S. M. BROWN 1983, Ireland
MILLER, R. B. and M. J. PAETZ 1959, Alberta
NIKANOROV, Y. I. 1962, USSR
PAGEAU, G., Y. GRAVEL and V. LEGENDRE 1979, Quebec
PERVOZVANSKIJ, V. Y. 1984, USSR
PETERKA, J. J. and L. L. SMITH, JR. 1970, Minnesota
REICHENBACH-KLINKE, H. H. 1970, Austria
ROZANSKI, M. 1913a, Poland
RUDNICKI, A., J. WALUGA and T. WALUS 1971, Poland
SMITH, H. M. and M.-M. SNELL 1891, Great Lakes
TSEPKIN, E. A. 1976, USSR
TSEPKIN, E. A. 1977, USSR
TSEPKIN, E. A. 1978, USSR
TSEPKIN, E. A. 1980, USSR
U.S. BUREAU OF COMMERCIAL FISHERIES 1965

CREEL CENSUS AND ANGLING STATISTICS

ANDERSON, A. W. and C. E. PETERSON , USA
ANONYMOUS 1966, Wisconsin
BABALUK, J. A., B. M. BELCHER and J. S. CAMPBELL 1984, Manitoba
BRUEDERLIN, B. and B. H. WRIGHT 1981, Manitoba
BRUEDERLIN, B. B. 1982, Manitoba
BRYNILDSON, C., D. B. IVES and H. S. DRUCKENMILLER 1970, Wisconsin
CUERRIER, J. P. and J. C. WARD 1952
CUERRIER, J. P. and J. C. WARD 1953
CUERRIER, J. P. and J. C. WARD 1954
DUNNING, D. J., J. T. EVANS and M. J. TARBY , New York
ESCHMEYER, R. W. 1935, Michigan
ESCHMEYER, R. W. 1936, Michigan
ESCHMEYER, R. W. 1938, Michigan
FALK, M. R. and L. W. DAHLKE 1974, Northwest Territories
FALK, M. R., D. V. GILLMAN and L. W. DAHLKE 1974, Northwest Territories
GIANOTTI, F. S. and G. GIOVINAZZO 1975, Italy
GIANOTTI, F. S., G. GIOVINAZZO and L. GORI 1975, Italy
GREENBANK, J. 1957
GROEBNER, J. F. 1960, Minnesota
HAZZARD, A. S. and R. W. ESCHMEYER 1936, Michigan
HORLER, A., M. E. JARVIS and R. A. C. JOHNSTON 1985, Yukon
HUBER, E. H. and H. R. KITTEL 1961, Minnesota
JOHNSON, M. W., W. J. SCIDMORE, J. H. KUEHN and C. R. BURROWS 1957, Minnesota
KOSHINSKY, G. D. 1969, Saskatchewan
LANDHURST, R. S. 1978, Wisconsin
LOEFFLER, H. 1977, West Germany
LUX, F. E. and L. L. SMITH, Jr. 1960, Minnesota
MILLER, J. G. 1954, New York
MITZNER, L. 1971, Iowa
MOYLE, J. B. and D. R. FRANKLIN 1955, Minnesota
MUIR, B. S. 1957, Great Lakes
PEARCE, W. A. 1961, New York
REID, D. J. 1977, Ontario
SNOW, H. E. 1978a, Wisconsin
SNOW, H. E. 1978b, Wisconsin
SNOW, H. E. 1982, Wisconsin
THUEMLER, T. G. 1982, Wisconsin
TODD, A. 1968, Ontario
WILLIAMS, J. E. 1961b, Michigan

WRIGHT, K. J. 1971, Wisconsin

CULTURE AND ARTIFICIAL PROPAGATION

AGAPOV, J. D. and V. N. ABROSOV 1967, USSR

ALESSIO, G. 1983, Italy

ANONYMOUS 1892, Poland

ANONYMOUS 1908, Poland

ANONYMOUS 1965b, Poland

ANONYMOUS 1969, Poland

ANONYMOUS n.d.b

ANWAND, K. 1963

ANWAND, K. 1965a

ANWAND, K. 1966a

ANWAND, K. 1967b

ARRIGNON, J. 1972, France

BALVAY, G. 1983

BELINA, T. 1956, Poland

BENECKE, B. 1885

BENNETT, L. H. 1947, Minnesota

BENNETT, L. H. 1948, Minnesota

BENOIT, D. S. R. and J. G. HALE 1969, Minnesota

BERKA, R. 1980, Czechoslovakia

BILLARD, R. 1983, France

BILLARD, R., M. DEBRUILLE, J. P. GERARD and G. DE MONTALEMBERT 1976, France

BILLARD, R. and J. MARCEL 1980, France

BILLARD, R., J. MARCEL and G. DE MONTALEMBERT 1983, France

BILLARD, R., ed. 1980b, France

BILLARD, R., ed. 1983a, France

BLACK, J. D. and L. O. WILLIAMSON 1947, H

BOOTSMA, R. 1971, Netherlands

BOOTSMA, R. 1973, Netherlands

BOOTSMA, R. and C. J. A. H. V. VAN VORSTENBOSCH 1973, Netherlands

BOOTSMA, R., P. DE KINKELIN and M. LEBERRE 1975, Netherlands

BORDES, G. 1979

BRY, C., R. BILLARD and G. DE MONTALEMBERT, 1978, France

BRY, C. and C. GILLET 1980a, France

BRY, C. and C. GILLET 1980b, France

BRY, C., Y. SOUCHON and G. NEVEU 1984, France

BUSS, K. 1968

CARBINE, W. F. 1942b, Michigan

CATAUDALLE, S. and P. MELOTTI n.d., Italy

CHABAN, R. 1973, Morocco

CHAUVEHEID, A. and R. BILLARD 1983, France

CHIKOVA, V. M. 1966, USSR

CHIMITS, P. 1947, France

CHIMITS, P. 1951, France

CHIMITS, P. 1956, France

CHODOROWSKI, A. 1973a

CHODOROWSKI, A. 1973b

CHODOROWSKI, A. 1975

CLARK, C. F. and E. D. NOW 1954, Ohio

CLARK, C. F. and E. D. NOW 1955, Ohio

CLARK, J. (2) 1972b, Colorado

CLARK, J. H. 1974, Colorado

CLARK, J. H. 1975, Colorado

CLARK, T. L. 1975, Pennsylvania H

CONSEIL SUPERIEUR DE LA PECHE 1976, France

CZAPIK, A. 1961, Poland

DAUPHIN, R. 1983, France

DAVIS, H. S. 1953, California

DAWSON, L. 1959, Nebraska

DEL CAMPILLO, C. and P. A. PELLITERO 1973, Spain

DEMCHENKO, I. 1959, USSR

DEXTER, R. W. and D. B. MCCARRAHER 1967, Nebraska

DOMURAT, J. 1958, Poland

DRIMMELEN, D. E. VAN 1969, Netherlands

DUBRAVIUS, J. 1547

EISLER, R. 1957, Washington

FAGO, D. 1971a, Wisconsin

FAGO, D. 1971b, Wisconsin

FAGO, D. M. 1977, Wisconsin

FORNEY, J. L. 1968, New York

GALINA, N. V., E. F. MARTINSON and V. I. REDIKSON 1958, USSR

GAMMON, J. R. 1965, Indiana

GENINA, N. V., E. F. MARTINSEN and V. Y. REDIKSON 1958, USSR

GENSCH, R. 1979, West Germany

GOTTWALD, S. 1956, Poland

GOTTWALD, S. 1958a, Poland

GOTTWALD, S. 1958b, Poland

GOTTWALD, S. 1960, Poland

GOTTWALD, S. 1966a, Poland

GOTTWALD, S. 1966b, Poland

GOTTWALD, S. 1970, Poland

GOTTWALD, S., Z. KLEBUKOWSKA and A. WINNICKI 1965, Poland

GOTTWALD, S. and Z. PLACZKOWSKI 1958, Poland

GOUBIER, J. and Y. SOUCHON 1982, France

GRAFF, D. R. 1968, Pennsylvania

GRAFF, D. R. 1978, Pennsylvania H

GRAFF, D. R. and L. SORENSON 1969, Pennsylvania H

GRAFF, D. R. and L. SORENSON 1970, Pennsylvania H

GROCHOWALSKI, J. 1954, Poland

GUERIN, F. 1984, France

GUEST, W. C. 1977, Texas

GULIDOV, M. V. 1969a, USSR

GUTIERREZ-CALDERON, E. 1955, Spain

HAIME, J. 1874, Europe

HAMACKOVA, J., J. KOURIL and S. CHA-BERA 1977, Czechoslovakia

HASSLER, T. J. 1982, South Dakota

HAWDY, P. W. , Arizona

HENEGAR, D. 1969, North Dakota

HINER, L. E. 1961, North Dakota

HORVATH, L. 1983, Hungary

HOWARD, H. C. and R. E. THOMAS 1970, Nebraska

HUET, M. 1948, France

HUET, M. 1960, France

HUET, M. 1970, France

HUET, M. 1972a, France

HUET, M. 1972b, France

HUET, M. 1976, France

HUET, M. and J. A. TIMMERMANS 1958, France

HUET, M. and J. A. TIMMERMANS 1959, France

HUISMAN, E. A. 1975

JACOB, B. 1969, Michigan

JAEGAR, T., H. DAUSTER and A. KIWUS 1980

JARVENPA, O. M. and W. KIRSCH 1969, Minnesota

JOHNSON, L. D. 1958, Wisconsin

JORDAN, M. and Z. SREBRO 1956, Poland

KENDALL, W. C. 1918, Maine

KISTELSKI, B. 1933, Poland

KLEINERT, S. J. and D. F. MRAZ 1965b, Wisconsin

KLEINERT, S. J. and D. F. MRAZ 1965d, Wisconsin

KONOVALOV, P. M. and T. V. LUGA-VAYA 1968, USSR

KOURIL, J. and J. HAMACKOVA 1978, Czechoslovakia

LANGLOIS, T. H. 1927

LANOISELEE, B. 1984, France

LASSLEBEN 1960

LAYCOCK, G. 1966

LEACH, G. C. 1927

LIEPOLT, R. and E. PESCHECK 1958

LILLELUND, K. 1958, Germany

LUCCHETTA, J. C. 1983, France

LUKOWICZ, M. VON 1983, West Germany

MANN, R. H. K. 1971a, England

MARCEL, J., G. DE MONTALEMBERT and R. BILLARD 1983

MATVEEVA, R. P. 1955, USSR

MCCARRAHER, B. 1958b, Nebraska

MCCARRAHER, D. B. 1957c, Nebraska

MCCARRAHER, D. B. 1963, Nebraska

MEADE, J. W., W. F. KRISE and T. ORT 1983, Pennsylvania H

MICHAELIS, A. 1911

MOEN, T. and M. LINDQUIST 1954, Iowa

MOEN, T. E. 1953, Iowa

MOEN, T. E. 1955, Iowa

MORRIS, J. W. 1974, Nebraska

MRAZ, D. F. 1961, Wisconsin

MRAZ, D. F. 1962a, Wisconsin

MULLER, H. 1954, Germany

NEVEU, G. and C. BRY 1983, France

OEHMCKE, A. and K. WALKER 1969, Wisconsin

OEHMCKE, A. A. 1949, Wisconsin

ORME, L. E. 1978, South Dakota H

PECHA, O. 1983, Czechoslovakia

PECKHAM, R. 1968, Nebraska

PECOR, C. H. 1978, Michigan H

PECOR, C. H. 1979, Michigan H

PETLINA, A. P. 1980, USSR

PIENING, H. 1970, Wisconsin

PRATT, K. 1975, Michigan.

PREISSER, E. 1976

PRIVOLNEV, T. I. 1951, USSR

PROTAL, J. 1947

RADCLIFFE, W. 1921

RAHN, J. 1978, Germany

REZNICHENKO, P. N., N. V. KOT-LYAREVSKAYA and M. V. GULIDOV 1966, USSR

REZNICHENKO, P. N., N. V. KOT-LYAREVSKAYA and M. V. GULIDOV 1967, USSR

ROGALSKI, J. 1937, Poland

ROTH, H. 1960

ROYER, L. M. 1971, Saskatchewan

ROZANSKI, M. 1913b, Poland
ROZNIAKOWSKI, J. 1957, Poland
SAKOWICZ, L. and W. URBANOWSKI 1933, Poland
SANDERSON, C. H. and Z. BEAN 1974, H
SCHINDLER 1946
SCHOETTGER, R. A. and E. W. STEUCKE, Jr. 1970a, Wisconsin
SCHOETTGER, R. A. and E. W. STEUCKE, Jr. 1970b, Wisconsin
SCHULTZ, F. H. 1956, Saskatchewan
SCHUMANN, G. O. 1963
SHARP, R. W., L. H. BENNETT and E. C. SAEUGLING 1952, Minnesota, Iowa
SIMONTACCHI, C., C. BOITI, N. BONALDO, P. COLOMBO BELEVEDERE and L. COLOMBO 1983, Italy
SKIBINSKI, L. 1910, Poland
SMISEK, J. 1967a, Czechoslovakia
SMISEK, J. 1967b, Czechoslovakia
SMISEK, J. 1968a, Czechoslovakia
SMISEK, J. 1968b, Czechoslovakia
SORENSON, L., K. BUSS and A. D. BRADFORD 1966, Pennsylvania
STRZELECKI, J. 1929, Poland
SURBER, E. E. 1929
SZCZERBOWSKI, J. A. 1965, Poland
TIMMERMANS, G. A. 1979
URBANOWSKI, W. 1937, Poland
U.S. FISH AND WILDLIFE SERVICE 1974, USA
VOUGA, M. 1939
WALKER, K. W. 1968
WEBSTER, J., A. TRANDAHL and J. LEONARD 1978, USA
WESTERS, H. 1979, Michigan H
WIKTOR, J. and C. ZUKOWSKI 1962, Poland
WILLEMSEN, J. 1958, Netherlands
WONDRA, K. 1981, Germany
WOYNAROVICH, E. 1955, Hungary
WOYNAROVICH, E. 1963, Hungary

DISTRIBUTION AND RANGE

ACKERMAN, B. 1955, USA
AGASSIZ, J. L. R. 1854, Alabama
AGASSIZ, L. 1850, Great Lakes
ALLISON, D. and H. HOTHEM 1975, Ohio
ALT, K. T. 1977, Alaska
ALT, K. T. 1980, Alaska
ANDERSON, R. M. 1913, Yukon
ANONYMOUS 1961a, Quebec
BACKUS, R. H. 1957, Labrador
BAJKOV, A. 1927, Alberta
BEAN, T. H. 1892, Pennsylvania
BEAN, T. H. 1903b, New York
BICH, J. P. and C. G. SCALET 1977, South Dakota
BLANC, M., P. BANARESCU, J.-L. GAUDET and L.-C. HUREAU 1971, Europe
BODALY, R. A. and C. C. LINDSEY 1977, Yukon
BUSS, K., and J. MILLER, n.d., Pennsylvania
CARL, C. G. and W. A. CLEMENS 1948, British Columbia
CARL, C. G., W. A. CLEMENS and C. C. LINDSEY 1959, British Columbia
CARLANDER, K. D. 1948, Minnesota
CARUFEL, L. H. 1958, North Dakota
CHAMBERS, K. J. 1963, Ontario
CHAMPEAU, A., A. GREGOIRE and G. BRUN 1978, France
CLARK, G. 1955, Canada
CLARKE, C. H. D. 1940
CLEARY, R. E. 1956, Iowa
CLEMENS, W. A., R. V. BOUGHTON and J. A. RATTENBURY 1945, British Columbia
CONNECTICUT BOARD OF FISHERIES AND GAME 1959, Connecticut
COOPER, G. P. 1941, Maine
COPE, E. D. 1864, Michigan
COPE, E. D. 1865, Michigan
COPE, E. D. 1870, North Carolina
COPE, E. D. 1877, North Carolina
CORKUM, L. D. and P. J. MCCART 1981, Northwest Territories, Yukon
COWARD, T. A. 1914, England
COX, P. 1899, Quebec
CROSSMAN, E. J. 1978, Ontario
CUERRIER, J. P. 1962, Quebec
CUERRIER, J. P., F. E. J. FRY and G. PREFONTAINE 1946, Quebec
DALL, W. H. 1870, Alaska
DAY, F. 1884, England, Ireland
DEMEL, K. 1933, Poland
DICK, M. M. 1964
DICKINSON, W. E. 1960, Wisconsin
DUKRAVETS, G. M. and Y. A. BIRYUKOV 1976, USSR
DULMA, A. 1973, USSR
DUNBAR, M. J. and H. H. HILDEBRAND 1952, Canada
D'URBAN, W. S. M. 1859, Quebec
DYMOND, J. R. 1922, Great Lakes

DYMOND, J. R. 1923, Ontario
DYMOND, J. R. 1926, Ontario
DYMOND, J. R. 1936, British Columbia
DYMOND, J. R. 1937, Ontario
DYMOND, J. R. 1939, Ontario
DYMOND, J. R. 1947, Canada
DYMOND, J. R. 1964, Canada H
DYMOND, J. R. and J. L. HART 1927,
    Ontario
DYMOND, J. R., J. L. HART and A. L.
    PRITCHARD 1929, Great Lakes
DYMOND, J. R. and W. B. SCOTT 1941,
    Ontario
EDDY, S. and T. SURBER 1947, Minnesota
EDDY, S. and T. SURBER 1960, Minnesota
EDDY, S., R. C. TASKER and J. C.
    UNDERHILL 1972, Minnesota
EDDY, S. and J. C. UNDERHILL 1978, Min-
    nesota
EGERMAN, F. F. 1936, USSR
EIGENMANN, C. H. 1894, Canada,
    USA
EVERMANN, B. W. 1916, Kentucky,
    Tennessee
EVERMANN, B. W. and E. L. GOLDSBOR-
    OUGH 1901, New York
EVERMANN, B. W. and E. L. GOLDSBOR-
    OUGH 1902, New York
EVERMANN, B. W. and E. L. GOLDSBOR-
    OUGH 1907a, Alaska
EVERMANN, B. W. and E. L. GOLDSBOR-
    OUGH 1907b, Canada
EVERMANN, B. W. and W. C. KENDALL
    1896, Vermont
EVERMANN, B. W. and W. C. KENDALL
    1902a, Great Lakes
EVERMANN, B. W. and W. C. KENDALL
    1902b, New York
EVERMANN, B. W. and W. C. KENDALL
    1902c, New York
FAGO, D. 1983, Wisconsin
FAGO, D. 1985, Wisconsin
FORBES, S. A. and R. E. RICHARDSON
    1908, Illinois
FORTIN, P. 1864
FOWLER, H. W. 1915, Canada
FOWLER, H. W. 1918a, USA
FOWLER, H. W. 1919, Pennsylvania
FOWLER, H. W. 1948, Northwest Territories
FRY, F. E. J. and V. B. CHAPMAN 1948,
    Ontario
FRY, F. E. J. and J. P. CUERRIER 1941,
    Quebec

GARRARD, J. 1886, Wisconsin
GEE, A. S. 1978, England
GEORGE, C. J. 1980, New York
GERKING, S. D. 1945, Indiana
GERKING, S. D. 1959
GILL, T., ed. 1898, New York
GRAY, T. E. 1850, Yukon
GREELEY, J. R. 1934, New York
GREELEY, J. R. 1938, New York
GREELEY, J. R. 1939a, New York
GREELEY, J. R. 1939b, New York
GREELEY, J. R. 1940, New York
GREELEY, J. R. and S. C. BISHOP 1932,
    New York
GREENBANK, J. 1954
GREENBANK, J. 1957
GREENE, C. W. 1935, Wisconsin
HAAS, R. L. 1943, Illinois
HALKETT, A. 1898, Arctic
HALKETT, A. 1913, Canada
HANKINSON, T. L. 1908, Michigan
HANKINSON, T. L. 1916, Michigan
HANKINSON, T. L. 1920, Michigan
HANKINSON, T. L. 1929, North Dakota
HARKNESS, W. J. K. and J. L. HART 1927,
    Ontario
HARPER, F. 1948, Northwest Territories
HARPER, F. 1961, Quebec
HARRISON, J. S. 1963
HEARD, W. R., R. L. WALLACE and W. L.
    HARTMAN 1969, Alaska
HENDERSON, N. E. and R. E. PETER 1969,
    Alberta
HOKE, R. A., M. J. NORROCKY and B. L.
    PRATER 1975, Ohio
HOLT, P. C., ed. 1972
HUBBS, CARL L. 1926, Great Lakes
HUBBS, CARL L. 1979, California
HUBBS, CARL L. and D. E. S. BROWN
    1929, Ontario
HUBBS, CARL L. and C. W. GREENE 1928,
    Great Lakes
HUBBS, CARL L. and K. F. LAGLER 1941,
    Great Lakes
HUBBS, CARL L. and K. F. LAGLER 1949,
    Great Lakes
HUBBS, CARL L. and K. F. LAGLER 1957,
    Great Lakes
HUBBS, CARL L. and K. F. LAGLER 1958,
    Great Lakes
HUBBS, CARL L. and A. M. WHITE 1923,
    Minnesota
HUBBS, CLARK 1972, Texas

HUET, M., A. LELEK, J. LIBOSVARSKY and M. PENAZ 1969, Czechoslovakia
HUVER, C. W. 1960, Connecticut
JASKOWSKI, J. 1962, Poland
JENKINS, R. E., E. A. LACHNER and F. J. SCHWARTZ 1972
JONES, A. N. 1972, Wales
JORDAN, D. S. 1888
JORDAN, D. S. 1890, USA
JORDAN, D. S. 1905b
JORDAN, D. S. and B. W. EVERMANN 1902, North America
JORDAN, D. S., B. W. EVERMANN and H. W. CLARK 1930, North America
KENDALL, W. C. 1895, Maine
KENDALL, W. C. 1909, Labrador
KENDALL, W. C. 1920, Saskatchewan
KOSSWIG, C. 1969, Asia
KOSTER, W. J. 1957, New Mexico
KOZHOV, M. 1963, USSR
KRULL, J. N. 1968, New York
LAWLER, G. H. and N. H. F. WATSON 1958, Manitoba
LEFEBRE, P. 1977, Quebec
LEGENDRE, V. 1954, Quebec
LINDBERG, G. U. 1936, USSR
LINDEBORG, R. G. 1941, Ontario
LIVINGSTONE, D. A. 1951, Nova Scotia
LOW, A. P. 1895a, Labrador
LOW, A. P. 1895b, Labrador
MACOUN, J. 1888, Northwest Territories
MAGNIN, E. 1964, Quebec
MARLBOROUGH, D. 1969, England
MAY, S. P. 1858, Ontario
MCALLISTER, D. E. 1962b, Arctic
MCALLISTER, D. E. and B. W. COAD 1974, Ontario
MCCARRAHER, D. B. 1961b, North America
MCCORMICK, L. M. 1892, Ohio
MEEK, A. 1916
MEEK, S. E. 1899, Ontario
MEEK, S. E. and H. W. CLARK 1902, Ontario
MILLER, R. B. 1946, Northwest Territories
MILLER, R. B. 1949, Alberta
MONGEAU, J., A. COURTEMANCHE, G. MASSE and B. VINCENT 1974, Quebec
MONGEAU, J.-R., J. LECLERC and J. BRISEBOIS 1980, Quebec
NEEDHAM, J. G. 1922, New York
NELSON, E. W. 1887, Alaska
NELSON, M. N. and A. D. HASLER 1943, Wisconsin
NEWDICK, J. 1979, England
ODELL, T. T. 1931, New York
OMAND, D. N. 1950, Ontario
ORTENBURGER, A. I. and C. L. HUBBS 1926, Oklahoma
PAGEAU, G., Y. GRAVEL and V. LEGENDRE 1979, Quebec
PARSONS, R. F. n.d., Labrador
PEARSON, W. D. and L. A. KRUMHOLZ 1984, Tennessee
PECZALSKA, A. 1953, Poland
PECZALSKA, A. 1954, Poland
PENCZAK, T. 1969a, Poland
PENCZAK, T. 1969b, Poland
PFLIEGER, W. L. 1971, Missouri
POTVIN, C. 1973, Quebec
PREBLE, E. A. 1908, Northwest Territories
PREFONTAINE, G. 1941, Quebec
QUEBEC MINISTERE DES PECHERIES ET DE LA CHASSE 1961, Quebec
QUEBEC MINISTERE DU TOURISME, DE LA CHASSE, ET DE LA PECHE 1966, Quebec
RADFORTH, I. 1944, Ontario
RANEY, E. C. and W. H. MASSMAN 1953, Virginia
RAWSON, D. S. 1947a, Northwest Territories
RAWSON, D. S. 1947b, Northwest Territories
RAWSON, D. S. 1949, Saskatchewan
RAWSON, D. S. 1960b, Saskatchewan
REICHENBACH-KLINKE, H. H. 1970, Austria
REMBISZEWSKI, J. M. and H. ROLIK 1975, Poland
RICHARDSON, L. R. 1935, Quebec
RICHARDSON, L. R. 1944, Quebec
RUDNICKI, A. 1965, Poland
RYDER, R. A., W. B. SCOTT and E. J. CROSSMAN 1964, Ontario
SCOTT, W. B. 1958, Canada, Alaska
SCOTT, W. B. and E. J. CROSSMAN 1969, Canada
SMALL, H. B. 1883, Ontario
SMITH, H. M. 1893, North Carolina
SMITH, H. M. 1907, North Carolina
SMITH, H. M. and T. A. BEAN 1899, D.C.
SMITH-VANIZ, W. F. 1968, Alabama.
SOLJAN, T. 1946, Italy
SOOT-RYEN, T. 1926, Finland

STORER, D. H. 1848, Vermont
SYMINGTON, D. F. 1959, Saskatchewan
SZCZERBOWSKI, J. A. 1972, Poland
TACK, E. 1972
THOMPSON, E. S. 1898, Manitoba
THOMPSON, Z. 1853, Vermont
THORPE, L. M. and D. A. WEBSTER , Connecticut
TONER, G. C. 1943, Ontario
TRAUTMAN, M. B. 1957, Ohio H
TUBB, R. A., F. A. COPES and C. JOHNSTON 1965, North Dakota
TURNER, L. M. 1886, Alaska
UNDERHILL, J. C. and J. B. MOYLE 1968, Great Lakes
VASILIU, G. D. and C. SOCA 1968, USSR
VLADYKOV, V. D. 1958, Quebec
VLADYKOV, V. D. and D. E. MCALLISTER 1961, Quebec
WALECKI, A. 1889, Poland
WALKER, C. E., R. F. BROWN and D. A. KATO 1974
WALKER, S. J. 1931, Manitoba
WALTERS, V. 1953, Arctic
WALTERS, V. 1955, Arctic
WEBSTER, D. A. 1942, Connecticut
WEED, A. C. 1922
WENT, A. E. J. 1957, Ireland
WHEELER, A. 1977, British Isles
WHITWORTH, W. R., P. L. BERRIEN and W. T. KELLER 1968, Connecticut.
WILIMOVSKY, N. J. 1954, Alaska
WILKENS, H. and A. KOEHLER 1977, West Germany
WILLIAMS, M. Y. 1922, Northwest Territories
WILLOCK, T. A. 1969, Canada
WITHLER, I. L. 1956, British Columbia
WOOLMAN, A. J. 1896, Minnesota, North Dakota
WRIGHT, A. H. and A. A. ALLEN 1913, New York
WYNNE-EDWARDS, V. C. 1947, Northwest Territories
WYNNE-EDWARDS, V. C. 1952, Arctic
ZHUKOV, P. I. 1968, USSR

EARLY DEVELOPMENT
BALON, E. K. 1974, Ontario
BALON, E. K. 1984, Ontario
BALVAY, G. 1983
BILLARD, R. 1980, France

BLAXTER, J. H. S. 1986
BRYAN, J. E. 1967, Minnesota
BUYNAK, G. L. and H. W. MOHN, JR. 1979, Pennsylvania
CHICEWICZ, M. and I. MANKOWSKA 1970, Poland
CIHAR, J. 1956, Czechoslovakia
DAMURAT, J. n.d., Poland
DANIL`CHENKO, O. P. 1982, USSR
DANIL`CHENKO, O. P. and N. S. STROGANOV 1975, USSR
DEVILLERS, C. 1947, France
DOMURAT, J. 1966, Poland
DORIER, A. 1938
DORIER, A. 1939
DURAND, J.-P. and J.-M. GAS 1976, France
FRANKLIN, D. R. 1960, Minnesota
FRANKLIN, D. R. and L. L. SMITH, Jr. 1960b, Minnesota
FRANKLIN, D. R. and L. L. SMITH, Jr. 1960c, Minnesota
FUIMAN, L. 1982, Great Lakes
GALAT, D. L. 1973
GIHR, M. 1957
GRODZINSKI, Z. 1971, Poland
GULIDOV, M. V. 1969a, USSR
GULIDOV, M. V. 1969b, USSR
HAKKILA, K. and A. NIEMI 1973, Finland
HASSLER, T. J. 1970, South Dakota
HASSLER, T. J. 1982, South Dakota
HOKANSON, K. E. F., J. H. MCCORMICK and B. R. JONES 1973, Minnesota
HUBBS, CARL L. 1922, Michigan
IGNAT`EVA, G. M. 1974b
IGNAT`EVA, G. M. and N. N. ROTT 1970
IGNATIEVA, G. M. 1976a
IGNATIEVA, G. M. 1976b
IVLEV, V. S. 1939a, USSR
KENNEDY, M. 1969, Ireland
KERNEHAM, R. J. 1976
KOSTOMAROVA, A. A. 1959, USSR
KOSTOMAROVA, A. A. 1961, USSR
KOTLYAREVSKAYA, N. V. 1969, USSR
KUZNETSOV, V. A. 1972, USSR
LEBEDEVA, O. A. and M. M. MESHKOV 1968, USSR
LECYK, M. 1965, Poland
LEREBOULLET, A. 1853, France
LEREBOULLET, A. 1854, France
LEREBOULLET, A. 1861, France
LEREBOULLET, D. A. 1854, France
LEREBOULLET, D. A. 1862a, France
LEREBOULLET, D. A. 1862b, France

LEYCK, M. 1965

LYUBITSKAYA, A. I. 1961

MANSUETI, R. 1954, Maryland

MATVEEVA, R. P. 1955, USSR

MONTEN, E. 1948

OLIPHAN, L. V. 1940, USSR

PITKYANEN, G. B. and Y. A. ZAITSEV 1974

PIWERNETZ, D. 1968a

PIWERNETZ, D. 1968b

PRICE, J. W. 1957, Ohio

REZNICHENKO, P. N. 1958, USSR

SCHAPERCLAUS, W. 1940, Germany

SCHOOTS, A. F. M., P. A. C. M. EVERTSE and J. M. DENUCE 1983

SIEFERT, R. E., W. A. SPOOR and R. F. SYRETT 1973, Minnesota

SMITH, L. L., Jr. and D. M. OSEID 1974, Minnesota

STROGANOV, N. S. and O. P. DANIL'CHENKO 1973, USSR

STUDNICKA, F. K. 1944

SZLAMINSKA, M. 1980, Poland

VOLODIN, V. M. 1960, USSR

WINNICKI, A. and J. DOMURAT 1964, Poland

WURTZ, A. 1945

WYDALLIS, E. A. 1960, Ohio

ZALACHOWSKI, W. 1970, Poland

FOOD AND FEEDING HABITS

AGAPOV, J. D. and V. N. ABROSOV 1967, USSR

ALLEN, K. R. 1939, England

ANONYMOUS 1934, Poland

ANTONESCU, C. S. 1933

ANTOSIAK, B. 1961, Poland

ANWAND, K. 1966a

ARKHIPTSEVA, N. T. 1974, USSR

BAGENAL, T. B. 1971, England

BALVAY, G. 1983

BEYERLE, G. B. 1971c, Michigan

BEYERLE, G. B. 1973a, Michigan

BIALOKOZ, W. and T. KRZYWOSZ 1976b, Poland

BIALOKOZ, W. and T. KRZYWOSZ 1979, Poland

BILLARD, R. 1980, France

BLAXTER, J. H. S. 1986

BODNIEK, V. M. 1976, USSR

BRAUM, E. 1963, West Germany

BRAUM, E. 1967, Germany

BRUYENKO, V. P. 1976, USSR

BUBINAS, A. D. 1976, USSR

BUBINAS, A. P. 1976, USSR

BUCKE, D. 1971

CHRISTIANSEN, D. G. 1976, Northwest Territories

CIHAR, J. 1955, Czechoslovakia

CLEMENS, W. A., J. R. DYMOND and N. K. BIGELOW 1924, Ontario

COPLAND, W. O. 1956, Scotland

CORBIN, G. B. 1873, England

CUERRIER, J. L. and A. COURTEMANCHE 1954, Quebec

DABROWSKI, K. R. 1982

DENCE, W. A. 1938, New York

DIANA, J. S. 1979a, Alberta

DIANA, J. S. 1979c, Alberta

DZIEKONSKA, J. 1954

FORBES, S. A. 1878, Illinois

FORBES, S. A. 1888, United States

FORBES, S. A. 1890, Illinois

FROST, W. E. 1954, England

FROST, W. E. and C. KIPLING 1970, England

FUHRMANN, O. 1934a

GRIMAS, U. and N.-A. NILSSON 1965, Sweden

GUTIERREZ-CALDERON, E. 1957, Spain

HARTLEY, P. H. T. 1940, England

HARTLEY, P. H. T. 1948, England

HELSTROM, N. 1978, Finland

HUNT, B. P. and W. F. CARBINE 1951, Michigan

HUNT, R. L. 1965, Wisconsin

HYSLOP, E. J. 1980

IVANOVA, M. N. 1959, USSR

IVANOVA, M. N. 1963, USSR

IVANOVA, M. N. 1966, USSR

IVANOVA, M. N. 1970, USSR

IVANOVA, M. N. and A. N. LOPATKO 1983, USSR

IVANOVA, M. N. and A. N. LOPATKO 1983, USSR

IVLEV, V. S. 1961, USSR

JOHNSON, L. 1966c, England

JOHNSON, L. D. 1959, Wisconsin

JOHNSON, L. D. 1961a, Wisconsin

JOHNSON, L. D. 1962b, Wisconsin

JOHNSON, L. D. 1969, Wisconsin

JOHNSON, L. D. n.d., Wisconsin

KARZINKIN, G. S. 1939, USSR

KEAST, A. and D. WEBB 1966, Ontario

KEDLEC, J. 1952, Michigan

KOKES, J. 1977
KUPCHINSKAYA, E. S. 1985, USSR
LARSEN, K. 1951a, Denmark
LARSEN, K. 1966, Denmark
LAWLER, G. H. 1965, Manitoba
LEONARD, V. J. 1963
LIPSIT, J. H. 1976a, Great Lakes
LUGOVAYA, T. V. 1971b, USSR
LUX, F. E. and L. L. SMITH, Jr. 1960, Minnesota
MA MANZUDU, B. 1984, Belgium
MANN, R. H. K. 1976, England
MANN, R. H. K. 1982, England
MARSHALL, W. S. and N. C. GILBERT 1905, Wisconsin
MARTYNIAK, A., J. TERLECKI and J. A. SZCZERBOWSKI 1976, Poland
MATHERS, R. A. and P. H. JOHANSEN 1985, Ontario
MATVEEVA, R. P. 1955, USSR
MCCARRAHER, D. B. 1959c, Nebraska
MCNAMARA, F. 1937, Michigan
MELLEN, I. 1927
MISRA, P. M. 1966
NURNBERGER, P. K. 1930, Minnesota
OBER, R. D. 1976, North Dakota
OMAROV, O. P. and O. A. POPOVA 1985, USSR
ORLOVA, E. L. and G. K. AZHIGALIYEVA 1984, USSR
PENN, G. H. 1950, USA
PIKHU, E. K. and E. R. PIKHU 1969, USSR
PUPYRNIKOVA, A. V. 1953, USSR
QUEIRAZZA, G., E. SMEDILE and E. TIBALDI 1969
RIDENHOUR, R. L. 1960, Iowa
SALMI, J. 1982, Finland
SEABURG, K. G. 1957
SEABURG, K. G. and J. B. MOYLE 1964, Minnesota
SIBLEY, C. K. 1922, New York
SIBLEY, C. K. and V. RIMSKY-KORSAKOFF 1931, New York
SJOBERG, G. 1983, Sweden
SOKOLOV, L. I. 1962, USSR
SOROKINA, A. A. 1977, USSR
SPANOVSKAYA, V. D. 1963, USSR
SPRULES, W. M. 1946, Manitoba
TEPLOVA, V. N. and V. P. TEPLOV 1953, USSR
TURNER, L. J. 1984, Alberta
VOLKOVA, L. A. 1973, USSR
VOSTRADOVSKY, J. 1971, Czechoslovakia
VOSTRADOVSKY, J. 1980, Czechoslovakia
WAINIO, A. 1966b, Great Lakes
WILLEMSEN, J. 1965, Netherlands
WILLEMSEN, J. 1967a, Netherlands
WILLEMSEN, J. 1967b, Netherlands
WILLEMSEN, J. 1978, Netherlands
WILLIAMS, J. E. 1962c, Michigan
WILSON, C. B. 1920, Indiana
WOLFERT, D. F. and T. J. MILLER 1978, Great Lakes

FOSSILS AND ARCHAEOLOGY

AGASSIZ, L. 1842
BALON, E. K. 1968a, Czechoslovakia
BERG, L. S. 1947, USSR
BLAND, J. K. and D. BARDACK 1973, Great Lakes
BOISAUBERT, J.-L. and J. DESSE 1975, Switzerland
BRINKHUIZEN, D. C. 1979, Netherlands
CAVENDER, T. M., J. G. LUNDBERG and R. L. WILSON 1970
CROSSMAN, E. J. and C. R. HARINGTON 1970, Yukon, Ontario
DRIESCH, A. VON DEN 1982, West Germany
FREY, D. G. 1964
HEINRICH, D. 1981, West Germany
LEBEDEV, V. D. 1961, USSR
MCALLISTER, D. E. 1959, Ontario
MCALLISTER, D. E. 1962a, Ontario
MCALLISTER, D. E. 1963, Yukon
MCALLISTER, D. E. 1968, Ontario
MCALLISTER, D. E. 1975, Quebec
MCALLISTER, D. E. and D. ST-ONGE 1981, Northwest Territories
MOHL-HANSEN, U. 1954
MORALES, A. 1980, Spain
MURCHISON, C., ed. 1868, England
NIKOLSKY, G. 1946, USSR
OSBORNE, P. J. and F. W. SHOTTON 1968, England
PAUL, A. 1980, Germany
ROSENLUND, K. 1976, Denmark
SLOKA, J. 1977, USSR
SMITH, C. L. 1962, Kansas, Oklahoma, Nebraska
SOKOLOV, L. I. and E. A. TSEPKIN 1969, USSR
SPENCER, P. J. 1979, England
SYTCHEVSKAYA, E. C. 1974, USSR
SYTCHEVSKAYA, E. C. 1976, USSR

TELLER, S. and D. BARDACK 1974, Great
  Lakes
TSEPKIN, E. A. 1972, USSR
TSEPKIN, E. A. 1981, USSR
VORONONKOVA, L. D. 1964, USSR
WHEELER, A. 1978, England
WILSON, M. V. H. 1980, Canada
WILSON, M. V. H. 1981, Colorado
WINTEMBERG, W. J. 1936, Ontario
WINTEMBERG, W. J. 1946
ZHITENEVA, L. D. 1969, USSR

GENERAL ACCOUNTS
ALDINGER, H. 1965
ALTMAN, P. L. and D. S. DITTMER, eds.
  1972
ANONYMOUS 1964, Poland
ANONYMOUS 1973b, Poland
BAJKOV, A. 1930, Canada
BLAIR, F. W. 1957, USA
BULLER, F. 1971, England
BULLER, F. 1981, England H
BURNAND, T. 1963, Italy
CARLANDER, K. D. 1950, Iowa
CARLANDER, K. D. 1953, Iowa
CARLANDER, K. D. 1969, Canada, USA H
CHOLMONDLEY-PENNEL, H. 1865, Eng-
  land
CLARK, C. F. 1958, Canada, USA
CROSS, F. B. 1967, Kansas
CVANCARA, V. and C. PONTO 1981
CVANCARA, V. A. 1977
CVANCARA, V. A. 1978
CVANCARA, V. A. 1979
CVANCARA, V. A. 1980
CVANCARA, V. A. and L. P. PAULUS 1976
DE BOISSET, L. 1948, France
EDDY, S. and T. SURBER 1943, Minnesota
EDDY, S. and J. C. UNDERHILL 1974, Min-
  nesota
FOOD AND AGRICULTURE ORGANIZA-
  TION OF THE UNITED NATIONS 1959
FORBES, S. A. and R. E. RICHARDSON
  1920, Illinois
FOURNIER, H. 1980, Quebec
FREEMAN, R. B. 1980, England
FROST, W. and C. KIPLING 1967, England
HAKOKONGAS, M. 1971, Finland
HARLAN, J. R. and E. B. SPEAKER 1956,
  Iowa
HARTLEY, P. H. T. 1947a, England
HARTLEY, P. H. T. 1947b, England

HEARTWELL, C. and L. HESS 1977, West
  Virginia H
HEGEMANN, M. 1964, Germany
HENSHALL, J. A. 1919
HERBERT, H. W. 1851, North America
HOLCIK, J. and J. MIHALIK 1968
HUNTER, J. G. 1968, Quebec
INSKIP, P. D. 1982a
JARDINE, A. 1898
JENNINGS, J. T. 1954, British Isles
JORDAN, D. S. 1877a, North America
JORDAN, D. S. 1907
KARVELIS, E. G. 1964, North America
KENDALL, R. L., ed. 1978
KENDALL, W. C. 1919, USA
KOSHINSKY, G. D. 1979, Saskatchewan
LAGLER, K. F., J. E. BARDACH and R. R.
  MILLER 1962
LANGLOIS, T. H. 1954, Great Lakes
LAWLER, G. H. 1964a, Manitoba
LEACH, G. C. 1927
LELEK, A. 1980, Europe
LINCOLN, R. P. 1953
LINDBERG, G. U. 1974
LINDROTH, A. 1946, Sweden
LIPSIT, J. H. 1976b, Great Lakes
LUNDSTROM, D. L. n.d.
MACKAY, H. H. 1963, Ontario
MCALLISTER, D. E. and E. J. CROSSMAN
  1973, Canada
MCCARRAHER, D. B. 1957b, Nebraska
MCPHAIL, J. D. and C. C. LINDSEY 1970,
  Canada
MELANCON, C. 1958, Quebec
NATIONAL GEOGRAPHIC SOCIETY 1965
NIKOL'SKII, G. V. 1961, USSR
NIKOLSKY, G. V. 1963, USSR
OPUSZYNSKI, K. 1979, Poland
PAETZ, M. J. and J. S. NELSON 1970,
  Alberta
PENA, J. C. 1985, Europe
PINCHER, C. 1948, USA
PLISZKA, F. 1964, Poland
PORTER, L. R. 1977, Minnesota
PRATT, H. S. 1935, USA
PRAWOCHENSKI, R. 1976, Poland
RAAT, A. J. P. 1987
REECE, M. 1963
REGAN, C. T. 1911, British Isles
ROZWADOWSKI, J. 1904, Poland
RUDNICKI, A. 1951, Poland
SCOTT, W. B. 1954, Canada
SCOTT, W. B. 1967, Canada

SCOTT, W. B. and E. J. CROSSMAN, 1973, Canada
SEKUTOWICZ, S. 1938, Poland
SPEIRS, J. M. 1952, Great Lakes
STANGENBERG, M. 1966, Poland
STARMACH, K. 1951a, Poland
STEFFENS, W. 1961
STERBA, G. 1963
TOMLIN, W. D. 1892
TONER, E. D. 1966
TONER, E. D. and G. H. LAWLER 1969
UMINSKI, W. 1917, Poland
VAN OOSTEN, J. 1946, USA
VAN OOSTEN, J. 1960, USA
VARLEY, M. E. 1967, England
VESEY-FITZGERALD, B. and F. LAMONT eds., n.d.
ZALACHOWSKI, W. 1973, Poland

GENETICS
BARTHOLOMEW, M. A., J. DIVALL and J. E. MORROW 1962, Alaska
BEAMISH, R. J., M. J. MERRILEES and E. J. CROSSMAN 1971, Ontario
BHUSHANA RAO, K. S. P. and C. GERDAY 1973a
BHUSHANA RAO, K. S. P. and C. GERDAY 1973b
CAINE, L. S. 1949a
COHEN-SOLAL, L., M. LE LOUS, J. C. ALLAIN and F. MEUNIER 1981
DAVISSON, M. T. 1972, Pennsylvania H
DRILHON, A., J. M. FINE and E. MAGNIN 1961
DUFOUR, D. and D. BARRETTE 1967, Quebec
ECKROAT, L. R. 1969, Pennsylvania
ECKROAT, L. R. 1974, Pennsylvania
FERGUSON, A. and F. M. MASON 1981, Ireland
FICKLING, N. 1982b, England
FOCANT, B. and F. HURIAUX 1976
FOCANT, B., F. HURIAUX and I. A. JOHNSTON 1976
FRANKENNE, F., L. JOASSIN, J. CLOSSET and C. GERDAY 1971, Belgium
FRANKENNE, F., L. JOASSIN and C. GERDAY 1973, Belgium
GIBB, B., I. BECKER and M. KRAEMER 1974
GOLD, J. R., W. J. KAREL and M. R. STRAND 1980

GOSSELIN-REY, C., G. HAMOIR and R. K. SCOPES 1968
HAEN, P. J. and F. J. O'ROURKE 1969a, Ireland
HAEN, P. J. and F. J. O'ROURKE 1969b, Ireland
HEALY, J. A. and M. F. MULCAHY 1979, Sweden
HEALY, J. A. and M. F. MULCAHY 1980
HUNN, J. B., R. A. SCHOETTGER and E. W. WHEALDON 1968
KIRSIPUU, A. 1975
KREUZER, R. O. and J. G. SIVAK 1984, Ontario
KUZNETSOV, V. A. 1975, USSR
LOCASCIO, N. J. 1969, Pennsylvania
LYSLOVA, E. M., T. P. SEREBRENIKOVA and N. A. VERZHBINSKAYA 1975
MASSARO, E. J. and C. L. MARKERT 1968
MULCAHY, M. F. 1969, Ireland
MULCAHY, M. F. 1970a, Ireland
NOGUSASHY, S. 1960
NYGREN, A., P. EDLUND, U. HIRSCH and L. AHSGREN 1968, Sweden
PERRIER, H., J. P. DELCROIX, C. PERRIER and J. GRAS 1974
PRAKKEN, R., J. BEKENDAM and G. A. PIETERS 1955
ROSSI, A., P. DAMIANI and E. DONATI 1973, Italy
SCHOOTS, A. F. M. and J. M. DENUCE 1981, Netherlands
SCHOOTS, A. F. M., B. J. A. JANSSEN and J. M. DENUCE 1981, Netherlands
SVARDSON, G. and T. WICKBOM 1939, Sweden
UTHE, J. F., E. ROBERTS, L. W. CLARKE and H. TSUYUKI 1966, British Columbia
VASIL'YEV, V. P. 1980, USSR
WEISS, D. G., V. KRYGIER-BREVART, G. W. GROSS and G. W. KREUTZBERG 1978, West Germany

HABITAT AND ENVIRONMENTAL FACTORS
ADELMAN, I. 1969, Minnesota
ADELMAN, I. R. and L. L. SMITH, Jr. 1970b
AHOKAS, J. T., N. T. KARKI, A. OIKARI and A. SOIVIC 1976, Finland
ANNETT, C. S. and F. M. D'ITRI 1978, Michigan

ANTONESCU, C. S. 1933

ARMSTRONG, F. A. J. and D. P. SCOTT 1979, Ontario

ARRIGNON, J. 1966, France

ASH, G. R., N. R. CHYMKO and D. N. GALLUP 1974, Alberta

ATTON, F. M., R. P. JOHNSON and N. W. SMITH 1974, Saskatchewan

BALDWIN, R. E., D. H. STRONG and J. H. TORRIE 1961, Wisconsin

BALL, R. C. 1950, Michigan

BALON, E. K. 1974, Ontario

BARTEHLMES, D. and H. WALDOW 1978, Germany

BEARD, T. D. 1971, Wisconsin

BENSON, N. G. 1980, Montana

BERNATOWICZ, S. 1955, Poland

BEVELHIMER, M. S., R. A. STEIN and R. F. CARLINE 1981, Ohio H

BILLARD, R. 1983, France

BODALY, R. A. and L. F. W. LESACK, 1984, Manitoba

BONIN, J. D. and J. R. SPOTILA 1978, New York H

BOUCHER, R. and E. MAGNIN 1979, Quebec

BOYTSOV, M. P. 1974, USSR

BRETT, J. R. 1979

BRINKHURST, R. O. 1969, Great Lakes

BRYAN, J. E. 1967, Minnesota

CARLANDER, K. D., J. S. CAMPBELL and R. J. MUNCY 1978a, North America

CARLANDER, K. D., J. S. CAMPBELL and R. J. MUNCY 1978b, North America

CARLSON, R. M. and R. CAPLE 1980, Great Lakes

CASSELMAN, J. M. 1972, Ontario

CASSELMAN, J. M. 1978a, Ontario

CASSELMAN, J. M. 1978b, Ontario

CASSELMAN, J. M. and H. H. HARVEY 1975, Ontario

CHAPMAN, C. A. and W. C. MACKAY 1984a, Alberta

CHAPMAN, C. A. and W. C. MACKAY 1984b, Alberta

CHUMAKOV, K. A. 1963, USSR

CIEPIELEWSKI, W. 1970, Poland

CLARK, E. R. and J. A. L. FRASER 1983

COOPER, G. P. and G. N. WASHBURN 1949, Michigan

CRAIG, J. F. and C. KIPLING 1983, England

CROOKS, S. 1972, Ontario

CVANCARA, V. A., S. F. STIEBER and B. A. CVANCARA 1977

DABROWSKI, K. R. 1982

DEALTRY, J. T. 1970, England

DOAN, K. H. 1964, Manitoba

DOUDOROFF, P. and D. L. SHUMWAY 1970

DRYDEN, R. L. and C. S. JESSOP 1974, Northwest Territories

DUNNING, D. J., J. T. EVANS and M. J. TARBY , New York

EDDY, S. 1938, Minnesota

EDDY, S. and K. D. CARLANDER 1940, Minnesota

EUROPEAN INLAND FISHERIES ADVISORY COMMITTEE 1968

FORTIN, R., P. DUMONT and H. FOURNIER 1983, Quebec

FROST, S., R. I. COLLINSON and M. P. THOMAS 1978

FROST, W. E. and C. KIPLING 1968b, England

FRY, F. E. J. 1947, Ontario

FRY, F. E. J. 1960, Ontario

GABOURY, M. N. and J. W. POTALAS 1982, Manitoba

GARDNER, J. A. 1926, England

GEE, J. H., R. F. TALLMAN and H. J. SMART 1978, Manitoba

GOETHBERG, A. 1976

GREGORY, R. W., A. A. ELSER and T. LENHART 1984

GROEN, C. L. and T. A. SCHROEDER 1978, Kansas

GULIDOV, M. V. 1969a, USSR

GUTIERREZ-CALDERON, E. 1955, Spain

HAKANSON, L. 1980

HALL, D. J. and E. E. WERNER 1977, Michigan

HALLOCK, C. 1886, Australia, Java

HANNON, M. R., Y. A. GREICHUS, R. L. APPLEGATE and A. C. FOX 1970, South Dakota

HARRISON, E. J. and W. F. HADLEY 1978, New York

HARTMANN, J. 1978, West Germany

HARVEY, H. H. 1980, North America

HARVEY, H. H. and J. F. COOMBS 1971, Ontario

HASSELROT, T. B. 1968, Sweden

HENLEY, D. T. and R. L. APPLEGATE 1982, South Dakota H

HICKS, D. E., K. COOK and P. MAUCK 1970, Oklahoma

HILDEN, W., R. HUDD and H. LEHTONEN 1982, Finland

HILL, K. 1974, Iowa

HOKANSON, K. E. F. 1977, Minnesota

HOKANSON, K. E. F., J. H. MCCORMICK and B. R. JONES 1973, Minnesota

HOLCIK, J. and I. BASTL 1973, Czechoslovakia

HOLCIK, J. and I. BASTL 1976, Czechoslovakia

HOLLAND, L. E. and M. L. HUSTON 1984, Wisconsin

HOOPER, F. F. 1951, Minnesota

HURLEY, D. A. and W. J. CHRISTIE 1977, Great Lakes

INSKIP, P. D. 1982b

JENKINS, R. M. 1968

JENKINS, R. M. 1969

JENKINS, R. M. and D. I. MORAIS 1971

JOHNSON, L. D. 1962c, Wisconsin

JOHNSON, M. G., J. H. LEACH, C. K. MINNS and C. H. OLVER 1977, Ontario

JUNE, F. C. 1976, South Dakota

KAMPS, L. R., R. CARR and H. MILLER 1972, D.C.

KENNEDY, W. A. 1947, Northwest Territories

KLYSZEJKO, B. 1973, Poland

KOSHELEV, B. W. 1961, USSR

KULIKOV, N. V. and V. G. KULIKOVA 1977, USSR

LAPITSKII, I. I. 1958, USSR

LAPKIN, V. V., A. G. PODDUBNYY and A. M. SVIRSKIY 1983, USSR

LECYK, M. 1965, Poland

LEHTONEN, H. and M. HILDEN 1980, Finland

LEINERTE, M. P., D. R. VADZIS, Z. K. KALNINYA and Y. Y. SLOKA 1974, USSR

LEVIN, A. A. 1970, Ohio

LEWINGTON, J. 1973a, Northwest Territories

LEWINGTON, J. 1973b, Northwest Territories

LEYCK, M. 1965

LILLELUND, K. 1967, West Germany

LINDSEY, C. C., K. PATALAS, R. A. BODALY and C. P. ARCHIBALD 1981, Yukon

LUX, F. E. and L. L. SMITH, Jr. 1960, Minnesota

LYUBITSKAYA, A. I. 1961

MACAN, T. T. 1970, England

MACHNIAK, K. 1975

MACHON, A., M. J. NORTH, N. C. PRICE and D. E. WELLS 1984

MACKENTHUN, K. M. and E. F. HERMAN 1948, Wisconsin

MAGNUSON, J. J. and D. J. KARLEN 1970, Wisconsin

MAGNUSON, J. J. and B. PETROSKY 1973, Wisconsin

MAKOWECKI, R. 1973a, Alberta

MAKOWECKI, R. 1973b, Alberta

MALININ, L. K. 1971a, USSR

MALININ, L. K. 1971b, USSR

MALLEY, M. W. and S. M. BROWN 1983, Ireland

MAREAN, J. B. 1976, Great Lakes

MARKOV, V. I. 1962, USSR

MATHER, F. 1881

MCCARRAHER, D. B. 1962, Nebraska

MCCARRAHER, D. B. 1971, Nebraska

MCCAULEY, R. W. and J. M. CASSELMAN 1981, Ontario

MCGOVERN, S. P. 1983b, Manitoba

MILLER, R. B. and M. J. PAETZ 1959, Alberta

MOORE, W. G. 1942a

MOORE, W. G. 1942b

MORAWSKA, B. 1968, Poland

MOREAU, G. and L. LEGENDRE 1979

MOSKALENKO, B. K. 1956, USSR

MOSSIER, J. N. 1971, North Dakota

MOYLE, J. B. and W. D. CLOTHIER 1959, Minnesota

MULLER, H. 1966, Germany

NELLEN, W. 1965, Germany

NETH, P. C. 1978, New York

NETSCH, N. F. 1975, Alaska

NORTH, E. 1980

NUORTEVA, P., M. LODENIUS and S.-L. NUORTEVA 1979, Finland

ODELL, T. T. 1932, New York

OIKARI, A. 1975a, Finland

OIKARI, A. 1975b, Finland

OLSSON, M. and S. JENSEN 1975, Sweden

OSBORN, T. C., D. B. ERNST and D. H. SCHUPP 1981, Minnesota

PAGEAU, G., Y. GRAVEL and L. LEVESQUE 1971, Quebec

PARSONS, R. F. n.d., Labrador
PATRIARCHE, M. H. 1963, Michigan
PATRIARCHE, M. H. 1966, Michigan
PATRIARCHE, M. H. and H. GOWING
   1961, Michigan
PATRIARCHE, M. H. and H. GOWING
   1962b, Michigan
PATRIARCHE, M. H. and J. W. MERNA
   1970, Michigan
PERSSON, P. E. 1980
PETERKA, J. J. 1972, North Dakota
PETERKA, J. J. and J. S. KENT 1976, North
   Dakota
PETIT, G. D. 1973, Ohio
PETROSKY, B. R. and J. J. MAGNUSON
   1973, Wisconsin
PETTERSEN, S. 1980, Norway
PHILLIPS, G. R. and R. W. GREGORY
   1979, Montana
PHILLIPS, G. R., T. E. LENHART and R. W.
   GREGORY 1980, Montana
PIETERS, H., J. SPEUR and P. G.
   WASSENAAR-SCHOLTZ 1983, Nether-
   lands
PRIVOLNEV, T. I. 1963, USSR
PRIVOLNEV, T. I. 1964a, USSR
PRIVOLNEV, T. I. and N. V. KOROLEVA
   1953, USSR
RAWSON, D. S. 1948, Manitoba
RAWSON, D. S. and J. E. MOORE 1944,
   Saskatchewan
ROSS, M. J. and D. B. SINIFF 1980
ROSS, M. J. and J. D. WINTER 1981, Min-
   nesota
RUNDBERG, H. 1977, Sweden
SACKMAUEROVA, M., O. PAL'USOVA
   and A. SZOKOLAY 1977, Czechoslovakia
SCHLESINGER, D. A. and H. A. REGIER
   1983
SCHULTZ, F. H. 1955, Saskatchewan
SCIDMORE, W. J. 1970
SCOTT, D. P. 1964, Ontario H
SEDLAR, J. 1969, Czechoslovakia
SELBIG, W. 1970
SHCHERBUKHA, A. Y. 1971, USSR
SIEFERT, R. E., W. A. SPOOR and R. F.
   SYRETT 1973, Minnesota
SPRULES, W. M. 1947, Manitoba
STELLA, E., L. FERRERO and F. G. MAR-
   GARITORA 1978, Italy
STREL'TSOVA, S. V. 1970, USSR
STROGANOV, N. S. and V. G. KHO-
   BOTJIEV 1968, USSR

SUOMINEN, H. 1980, Finland
SVARDSON, G. and G. MOLIN 1981,
   Sweden
SWIFT, D. R. 1965, England
SYCHEVA, V. N. 1965, USSR
SZMANIA, D. 1973, Wisconsin
THREINEN, C. W., Wisconsin
THREINEN, C. W. 1969, Wisconsin
TRESSLER, W. L., L. H. TIFFANY and W.
   P. SPENCER 1940, Ohio
TRIPLETT, J. R., D. A. CULVER and G. B.
   WATERFIELD 1981, Ohio
TROCHERIE, F. and B. MIGEON 1984,
   France
TSVETKOV, V. I. 1969, USSR
TURNER, L. J. 1984, Alberta
U.S. FISH AND WILDLIFE SERVICE 1976,
   New York
U.S. FISH AND WILDLIFE SERVICE 1981
VOINO-YASENETSKII, A. V. 1958, USSR
VOLKOVA, L. A. 1973, USSR
VOLODIN, V. M. 1960, USSR
VUORINEN, P. and M. B. AXELL 1980,
   Finland
WAJDOWICZ, Z. 1958, Poland
WHEELER, A. 1969, England
WITCOMB, D. 1966
WOODBURY, L. A. 1942, Wisconsin
ZIMAKOV, I. E. 1978, USSR

HISTORICAL ACCOUNTS

ANON, W. T. 1884, Ontario
ANONYMOUS 1550, England
BAGENAL, T. B. 1970a, England
BALDWIN, N. S., R. W. SAALFELD, M. A.
   ROSS and H. J. BUETTNER 1979, Great
   Lakes
BAUMANN, P. C., J. F. KITCHELL, J. J.
   MAGNUSON and T. B. KAYES 1974,
   Wisconsin
BENSON, N. G. 1968, Montana
BIGGAR, H. P., ed. 1922
BIGGAR, H. P., ed. 1925
BIGGAR, H. P., ed. 1929
BIGGAR, H. P., ed. 1932
BILLINGS, E. 1857, Canada
BULLER, F. 1981, England H
CLINTON, D. 1815, New York
CROSSMAN, E. J. 1971, Ontario
DUBRAVIUS, J. 1547
ENDRES, A. 1969, France
GESNER 1558, Germany

HEDERSTROM, H. 1959, Sweden
HEINRICH, D. 1980, East Germany
MARSTON, R. B. 1889, Ireland
MATHER, F. 1881
MEYER, P., ed. 1901, France
NECKHAM, A. 1863, England, Scotland, Ireland
NORMAN, J. R. 1930
NORRIS, T. 1864, USA
PERGAMINUS, N. 1480
RADCLIFFE, W. 1921
RULEWICZ, M. 1974, Poland
SHANDON 1889, Ireland
SMITH, H. M. and M.-M. SNELL 1891, Great Lakes
SMITT, F. A. 1892, Sweden
SOLMAN, V. E. F. 1950, Vermont
TURRELL, W. J. 1910, England
VINCENT OF BEAUVAIS 1624
WEBSTER, J., A. TRANDAHL and J. LEONARD 1978, USA
WENT, A. E. J. 1957, Ireland

HYBRIDS

ANDERSON, R. O. 1973, Missouri H
ANONYMOUS 1952, H
ARMBRUSTER, D. 1966
BEVELHIMER, M. S. 1983, Ohio H
BEVELHIMER, M. S., R. A. STEIN and R. F. CARLINE 1981, Ohio H
BEVELHIMER, M. S., R. A. STEIN and R. F. CARLINE 1985, Ohio H
BEVELHIMER, M. S., R. A. STEIN and R. F. CARLINE n.d.,   H
BEYERLE, G. B. 1973b, Michigan H
BEYERLE, G. B. 1981, Michigan H
BEYERLE, G. B. 1984, Michigan H
BLACK, J. D. and L. O. WILLIAMSON 1947, H
BONIN, J. D. and J. R. SPOTILA 1978, New York H
BULLER, F. 1981, England H
BUSS, K. 1960, Pennsylvania H
BUSS, K. 1963, Pennsylvania H
BUSS, K. 1966a, Pennsylvania H
BUSS, K., J. MEADE, III and D. R. GRAFF 1978, Pennsylvania H
BUSS, K. and J. MILLER 1967, Pennsylvania H
CAMERON, G. S. 1948, Ontario H
CARLANDER, K. D. 1969, Canada, USA H

CASSELMAN, J. M. and E. J. CROSSMAN 1986, Ontario H
CASSELMAN, J. M., E. J. CROSSMAN, P. E. IHSSEN, J. D. REIST and H. E. BOOKE 1986, Ontario H
CLARK, T. L. 1975, Pennsylvania H
COPELAND, J. 1975, H
CROSSMAN, E. J. 1965, Ontario H
CROSSMAN, E. J. and K. BUSS 1965, North America H
CROSSMAN, E. J. and J. W. MEADE 1977, North America H
DAVISSON, M. T. 1972, Pennsylvania H
DYMOND, J. R. 1964, Canada H
EDDY, S. 1941a, Minnesota H
EDDY, S. 1941b, Minnesota H
EDDY, S. 1944, Minnesota H
EMBODY, G. C. 1918, H
GIBSON, M. B. and J. W. MACPHERSON 1954, Ontario H
GILLEN, A. L., R. A. STEIN and R. F. CARLINE 1981, Ohio
GODDARD, J. A. and L. C. REDMOND 1978, Missouri H
GODFREY, J., Jr. 1945, H
GRAFF, D. R. 1968, Pennsylvania
GRAFF, D. R. 1978, Pennsylvania H
GRAFF, D. R. and L. SORENSON 1969, Pennsylvania H
GRAFF, D. R. and L. SORENSON 1970, Pennsylvania H
HEARTWELL, C. and L. HESS 1977, West Virginia H
HENLEY, D. T. and R. L. APPLEGATE 1982, South Dakota H
HESS, L. 1980a, West Virginia H
HESS, L. and C. HEARTWELL 1977, West Virginia H
HESS, L. and C. HEARTWELL 1979, Pennsylvania H
HESSER, R. B. 1978, Pennsylvania H
HOTTELL, H. E. 1976, Georgia H
HUBBS, CARL L. 1955, H
HUBERT, W. A. 1980, Iowa H
JENNINGS, T. L. and F. FRANK 1965 H
JOHNSON, L. D. 1978, Wisconsin H
JOHNSON, R. E. 1945, Minnesota H
MCCABE, B. C. 1958, Massachusetts H
MCCARRAHER, B. 1960, Nebraska H
MCCARRAHER, D. B. 1960, Nebraska H
MEADE, J. and D. R. GRAFF 1978, Pennsylvania H

MEADE, J. W., W. F. KRISE and T. ORT 1983, Pennsylvania H

NANSEN, C. 1973, H

NIKOLYUKIN, N. I. 1935, H

NIKOLYUKIN, N. I. 1963, USSR H

OEHMCKE, A. A. 1951, Wisconsin H

OEHMCKE, A. A., L. JOHNSON, J. KLING-BIEL and C. WISTROM 1965, Wisconsin H

ORME, L. E. 1978, South Dakota H

PECOR, C. H. 1978, Michigan H

PECOR, C. H. 1979, Michigan H

RANEY, E. C. 1955, Massachusetts H

SANDERSON, C. H. and Z. BEAN 1974, H

SCHWARTZ, F. J. 1962, Maryland H

SCHWARTZ, F. J. 1972, Maryland H

SCOTT, D. P. 1964, Ontario H

SERNS, S. L. and T. C. MCKNIGHT 1977, Wisconsin H

SLASTENENKO, E. P. 1956, H

SLASTENENKO, E. P. 1957, H

STEIN, R. A. 1979, Ohio H

STEIN, R. A., R. F. CARLINE and R. S. HAYWARD 1981, H

STEIN, R. A., R. F. CARLINE and R. S. HAYWARD 1982, Ohio H

TOMCKO, C. M. 1982, Ohio H

TOMCKO, C. M., R. A. STEIN and R. F. CARLINE 1984, Ohio H

TRAUTMAN, M. B. 1957, Ohio H

UNDERHILL, A. H. 1939, New York H

VAN OOSTEN, J. 1957, H

WAHL, D. H. and R. A. STEIN 1985, Ohio H

WEBB, P. W. 1978a, Michigan H

WEBB, P. W. 1978b, Michigan H

WEBB, P. W. 1980, Michigan H

WEBB, P. W. 1982, Michigan H

WEBB, P. W. 1984a, Michigan H

WEBB, P. W. 1984b, Michigan H

WEBB, P. W. and J. M. SKADSEN 1980, Michigan H

WEBSTER J., A. TRANDAHL and J. LEONARD 1978, USA

WEITHMAN, A. S. 1975, Missouri H

WEITHMAN, A. S. and R. O. ANDERSON 1976, Missouri H

WEITHMAN, A. S. and R. O. ANDERSON 1977, Missouri H

WESTERS, H. 1978, H

WESTERS, H. 1979, Michigan H

WICH, K. and J. W. MULLAN 1958, Massachusetts H

IDENTIFICATION

ARMBRUSTER, D. 1966

CASSELMAN, J. M. 1980, Ontario

CASSELMAN, J. M., E. J. CROSSMAN, P. E. IHSSEN, J. D. REIST and H. E. BOOKE 1986, Ontario H

DECKER, D. J., R. A. HOWARD, JR. and W. H. EVERHART 1978, New York

FICKLING, N. 1982b, England

FUIMAN, L. 1982, Great Lakes

HUBBS, CARL L. and K. F. LAGLER 1939, Great Lakes

KELSEY, P. M. 1968, New York

LAWLER, G. H. 1960b, Manitoba

LAWLER, G. H. 1961b, Manitoba

LAWLER, G. H. 1961c, Manitoba

LESLIE, J. K., and GORRIE, J. F. 1985, Ontario

LOPINOT, A. , Illinois

LOPINOT, A. C. n.d., Illinois

MACKAY, H. H. 1931, Ontario

MCALLISTER, D. E. and E. J. CROSSMAN 1973, Canada

MILLER, J. and K. BUSS 1962, Pennsylvania

SEAMAN, W. 1968

WAINIO, A. 1978, Ontario

WHITWORTH, W. R., P. L. BERRIEN and W. T. KELLER 1968, Connecticut.

WOODLING, J. 1984, Colorado

INTRODUCTIONS AND STOCKING

ANDERSON, R. O. 1973, Missouri H

ANONYMOUS 1965a, Morocco

ANONYMOUS 1966, Wisconsin

ANONYMOUS 1975a, Oklahoma

ANWAND, K. 1965b

ANWAND, K. 1967a

BAXTER, G. T. and J. R. SIMON 1970, Wyoming

BERNATOWICZ, S. 1938, Poland

BEVELHIMER, M. S., R. A. STEIN and R. F. CARLINE 1985, Ohio H

BEYERLE, G. B. 1970a, Michigan

BEYERLE, G. B. 1973b, Michigan H

BEYERLE, G. B. 1978, Michigan

BEYERLE, G. B. 1980, Michigan

BEYERLE, G. B. 1984, Michigan H

BEYERLE, G. B. and J. E. WILLIAMS 1972, Michigan

BEYERLE, G. B. and J. E. WILLIAMS 1973, Michigan

BORTKIEWICZ, K. 1967, Poland
BRY, C. 1980, France
BRY, C., V. SOUCHON, G. NEVEU and L. TREBAOL 1983b, France
BRY, C. and Y. SOUCHON 1982, France
BRY, C., Y. SOUCHON, G. NEVEU and L. TREBAOL 1983a, France
BUSS, K. 1968
CARLANDER, K. D. 1957, Iowa
CARLANDER, K. D. and J. G. ERICKSON 1953, Iowa
CARLANDER, K. D. and R. RIDENHOUR 1955, Iowa
CARLINE, R. F. 1979, Ohio
CHABAN, R. 1973, Morocco
CHAUDERON, L. 1969
CHENEY, A. N. 1885, New York
CLARK, C. F. 1960, Ohio
CLARK, J. (1) 1908, England
COOK, K. D. 1978, Oklahoma
DES CLERS, S. and J. ALLARDI 1983, France
FLICKINGER, S. A. and J. H. CLARK 1978, Colorado
GIERALTOWSKI, M. 1938, Poland
GREGORY, R. W. and T. G. POWELL 1969, Colorado
GRIMM, M. P. 1982a, Netherlands
GRIMM, M. P. 1982b, Netherlands
GRIMM, M. P. 1983b
GUTIERREZ-CALDERON, E. 1952, Spain
GUTIERREZ-CALDERON, E. 1969, Spain
GUTIERREZ-CALDERON, E. and E. SCAPARDINI-ANDREU 1950, Spain
HARRISON, H. M., C. O'FARRELL and T. E. MOEN 1961, Iowa
HEADRICK, M. R., M. S. BEVELHIMER, R. F. CARLINE and R. A. STEIN 1981, Ohio
HEADRICK, M. R. and R. F. CARLINE 1980, Ohio
HESSEN, D. O. 1985, Norway
HICKS, D. 1972a, Oklahoma
HICKS, D. 1972b, Oklahoma
HOTTELL, H. E. 1976, Georgia H
HUBBS, CLARK 1972, Texas
HUNER, J. V. and O. V. LINDQUIST 1983, Finland
JOHNSON, L. D. 1971, Wisconsin
JOHNSON, L. D. 1978, Wisconsin H
KEMPINGER, J. J. 1966a, Wisconsin
KEMPINGER, J. J. 1967a, Wisconsin
KLEBERT, E. 1904, Poland

KLEINERT, S. J. 1967b, Wisconsin
KLEINERT, S. J. and D. F. MRAZ 1965a, Wisconsin
KLUPP, R. 1978, West Germany
KROHN, D. C. 1968a, Wisconsin
KROHN, D. C. 1969, Wisconsin
KUHNE, E. R. 1939, Tennessee
LEHTONEN, H. 1981, Finland
LEHTONEN, H. and M. PETTERSSON 1973, Finland
LE LOUARN, H. 1983, France
LEWIS, S. A. 1975, Oklahoma
LYNCH, T. M. 1957, Colorado
MALONEY, J. and D. SCHUPP 1977, Minnesota
MARSHALL, T. L. and R. P. JOHNSON 1971, Saskatchewan
MCCABE, B. C. 1943, Massachusetts
MCCARRAHER, D. B. 1959a, Nebraska
MCCARRAHER, D. B. 1961b, North America
MORRIS, J. W. 1972, Nebraska
MORRIS, J. W. 1973, Nebraska
MORRIS, J. W. 1974, Nebraska
MOULTON, J. 1975, Connecticut
MOULTON, J. C. 1978, Connecticut
MRAZ, D. F. 1961, Wisconsin
MRAZ, D. F. 1962a, Wisconsin
MRAZ, D. F. 1963, Wisconsin
MULLER, H. 1959, Germany
NASH, C. W. 1913, Ontario
PATTERSON, R. R. 1971, New Mexico
PEARSON, W. D. and L. A. KRUMHOLZ 1984, Tennessee
PENA, J. C. n.d., Spain
POWELL, T. G. 1972a, Colorado
POWELL, T. G. 1972c, Colorado
POWELL, T. G. 1973, Colorado
PRIEGEL, G. R. 1965, Wisconsin
PRIEGEL, G. R. 1967, Wisconsin
RAJAD, M. n.d., Morocco
RUNNSTROM, S. 1950, Sweden
SAKOWICZ, L. 1939, Poland
SCHWARTZ, F. J. 1960b, Maryland
SMITH, H. M. 1896, California
SNOW, H. E. , Wisconsin
SNOW, H. E. 1967a, Wisconsin
SNOW, H. E. 1967b, Wisconsin
SNOW, H. E. 1974, Wisconsin
SOUCHON, Y. 1980, France
STEIN, R. A. 1979, Ohio H
STEIN, R. A., R. F. CARLINE and R. S. HAYWARD 1981, H

STEIN, R. A., R. F. CARLINE and R. S. HAYWARD 1982, Ohio H
STEUCKE, W. 1975, North Dakota
SUMARI, O. and K. WESTMAN 1969b, Finland
THREINEN, C. W. and A. OEHMCKE 1950, Wisconsin
TYMOWSKI, J. 1951, Poland
VASEY, F. W. 1968, Missouri
VASEY, F. W. 1974, Missouri
VOOREN, C. M. 1972, Netherlands
WAHL, D. H. and R. A. STEIN 1985, Ohio H
WELCOMME, R. L. 1979
WESLOH, M. L. and D. E. OLSON 1962, Minnesota
WILLEMSEN, J. 1955, Netherlands
WYDOSKI, R. S. and D. H. BENNETT 1981, USA

LENGTH-WEIGHT RELATIONSHIPS

ALESSIO, G. 1975b, Italy
ANTOSIAK, B. 1961, Poland
BALON, E. K. 1964, Czechoslovakia
BALON, E. K. 1965, Czechoslovakia
BECKMAN, W. C. 1948, Michigan
BROWN, E. H., Jr. and C. F. CLARK 1965, Ohio
BUSS, K. and J. MILLER 1961, Pennsylvania
CARBINE, W. F. 1945, Michigan
CARLANDER, K. D. 1943, Minnesota
CARLANDER, K. D. 1944, Minnesota
CASSELMAN, J. M. 1982, Ontario
CIHAR, J. 1955, Czechoslovakia
FROST, W. E. and C. KIPLING 1967, England
GREENBANK, J. 1950
GREENBANK, J. 1957
KUEHN, J. H. 1949, Minnesota
KULEMIN, A. A., I. I. MAKKOVEYEVE and M. I. SOLOPOVA 1971, USSR
KUPCHINSKAYA, E. S. 1985, USSR
LAARMAN, P. W. 1964b, Michigan
LIND, E. A. 1974, Finland
MACHNIAK, K. 1975
MACKENTHUN, K. M. 1948, Wisconsin
MUENCH, B. 1963, Illinois
NECRASOV, O. 1968
OLIVA, O. 1956, Czechoslovakia
SCHNUTE, J. and D. FOURNIER 1980

SHCHERBUKHA, A. Y. 1971, USSR
STRAUB, M. 1984, Switzerland
VOSTRADOVSKY, J. 1970b, Czechoslovakia
WILLIAMS, J. E. 1960c
WILLIAMS, J. E. 1963c, Michigan
WILLIAMSON, L. O. 1940, Wisconsin

LIFE HISTORY AND HABITS

ANONYMOUS 1903, Poland
BAGENAL, T. B. 1971, England
BALFOUR-BROWNE, F. 1906, England
BREGAZZI, P. R. 1978, England
BUSS, K. 1961a, Pennsylvania
CARBINE, W. F. 1942a, Michigan
CARBINE, W. F. and V. C. APPLEGATE 1948, Michigan
CHENEY, W. L. 1971, Alaska
CHENEY, W. L. 1972, Alaska
EMBODY, G. C. 1910, New York
FINNELL, L. 1984, Colorado
FINNELL, L. 1985, Colorado
FISH, M. P. 1932, Great Lakes
FRANKLIN, D. R. 1959, Minnesota
FRANKLIN, D. R. and L. L. SMITH, Jr. 1963, Minnesota
FROST, W. E. and C. KIPLING 1967, England
HARRISON, E. J. 1978, New York
HARRISON, E. J. and W. F. HADLEY 1983, New York
HAWDY, P. W. , Arizona
HOLCIK, J. 1968, Czechoslovakia
IVANOVA, M. N. 1970, USSR
KENDALL, A. W., Jr. and J. B. MARLIAVE, eds. 1985
KENDALL, W. C. 1918, Maine
LEPAN, S. R. 1985, New York
OEHMCKE, A. A., L. JOHNSON, J. KLINGBIEL and C. WISTROM 1965, Wisconsin H
RANEY, E. C. 1959, New York
RUTLEDGE, W. P. and J. A. PRENTICE 1973, Texas
SAMOKHVALOVA, L. K. 1974, USSR
SCHINDLER 1946
THREINEN, C. W., C. A. WISTROM, B. APELGREN and H. E. SNOW 1966, Wisconsin
VASEY, F. W. 1974, Missouri
VELAZ DE MEDRANO, L. 1949, Spain

MANAGEMENT

ANDERSON, R. O. 1973, Missouri H
ANDERSON, R. O. and A. S. WEITHMAN 1978
ANONYMOUS 1958, Poland
ANONYMOUS n.d.b
ANONYMOUS n.d.c
ANTOSIAK, B. 1958, Poland
BAGENAL, T. B. 1982, England
BALDWIN, N. S. 1946, Ontario
BARTA, A. 1877, Poland
BASTL, I., J. HOLCIK and A. KIRKA 1975, Czechoslovakia
BENNETT, G. W. 1962a
BENNETT, G. W. 1962b
BENSON, N. G. 1976, Montana
BENSON, N. G., J. R. GREELEY, M. I. HUISH and J. H. KUEHN 1961, Canada, USA
BEUKEMA, J. J. 1970
BEVELHIMER, M. S. 1983, Ohio H
BEYERLE, G. B. 1970b, Michigan
BEYERLE, G. B. 1971d, Michigan
BEYERLE, G. B. 1980, Michigan
BEYERLE, G. B. and J. E. WILLIAMS 1965, Michigan
BEYERLE, G. B. and J. E. WILLIAMS 1968, Mighican
BEYERLE, G. B. and J. E. WILLIAMS 1972, Michigan
BEYERLE, G. B. and J. E. WILLIAMS 1973, Michigan
BILLARD, R., ed. 1983a, France
BOUCHER, R. and E. MAGNIN 1979, Quebec
BOUQUET, H. G. J. 1979
BREGAZZI, P. R. 1978, England
BROUGHTON, N. M. and K. A. M. FISHER 1981, England
BRY, C. 1980, France
BRY, C., V. SOUCHON, G. NEVEU and L. TREBAOL 1983b, France
BRY, C. and Y. SOUCHON 1982, France
BRY, C., Y. SOUCHON, G. NEVEU and L. TREBAOL 1983a, France
BRY, C., Y. SOUCHON and G. NEVEU 1984, France
BRYNILDSON, C. 1958, Wisconsin
BRYNILDSON, C. 1970, Wisconsin
BUSS, K. 1961a, Pennsylvania
CARLANDER, K. D. 1957, Iowa
CARLANDER, K. D. and L. E. HINER 1943b, Minnesota
CARLANDER, K. D. and J. W. PARSONS 1949, Iowa
CARTER, E. R. 1955, Kentucky
CASSELMAN, J. M. 1969, Ontario
CASSELMAN, J. M. 1974a, Ontario
CASSELMAN, J. M. 1975, Ontario
CASSELMAN, J. M. 1978b, Ontario
CASSELMAN, J. M. and H. H. HARVEY 1975, Ontario
CHAPLEAU, D. and G. THELLEN 1979, Quebec
CHRISTENSEN, K. E. 1959, Michigan
CHRISTENSEN, K. E. 1960a, Michigan
CHRISTENSEN, K. E. 1960b
CHRISTENSEN, K. E. 1961a, Michigan
CHRISTENSEN, K. E. 1961b, Michigan
CHRISTENSEN, K. E. 1961c, Michigan
CHRISTENSEN, K. E. 1962a, Michigan
CHRISTENSEN, K. E. 1962b, Michigan
CHRISTENSEN, K. E. 1962c, Michigan
CHURCHILL, W. and H. SNOW 1964, Wisconsin
CLARK, J. H. 1975, Colorado
COLORADO DIVISION OF WILDLIFE 1974, Colorado
COSTEA, E. and V. CURE 1971, Romania
DIANGELO, S. 1961, Michigan
DIUZHIKOV, A. 1959, USSR
DRAGANIK, B. and J. A. SZCZERBOWSKI 1963, Poland
DUBE, J. and Y. GRAVEL, ed. 1979, North America
DUNNING, D. J., Q. ROSS and J. GLADDEN 1982, New York
ENDRES, A. 1969, France
FAUBERT, N., M. DUBREUIL, L.-R. SEGUIN and D. ROY 1979, Quebec
FITZMAURICE, P. 1983, Ireland
FORNEY, J. L. 1967, New York
FRANKLIN, D. R. and L. L. SMITH, Jr. 1960a, Minnesota
GABELHOUSE, D. W., Jr. 1981
GEIGER, W., H. J. MENG and C. RUHLE 1975
GIBSON, R. J. and C. E. HUGHES 1969, Manitoba
GODDARD, J. A. and L. C. REDMOND 1978, Missouri H
GRAVEL, Y. and J. DUBE 1979, Quebec
GREEN, D. M., Jr. 1978, New York
GREGORY, R. W., A. A. ELSER and T. LENHART 1984

GRIMM, M. P. 1983b

GROEN, C. L. and T. A. SCHROEDER 1978, Kansas

HALNON, L. C. 1959, Vermont

HANSON, H. 1958, Minnesota

HARRISON, H. M., C. O'FARRELL and T. E. MOEN 1961, Iowa

HART, P. J. B. and B. CONNELLAN 1979, England

HASSLER, T. J. 1982, South Dakota

HAZZARD, A. S. 1945

HAZZARD, A. S. and R. W. ESCHMEYER 1936, Michigan

HESS, L. and C. HEARTWELL 1979, Pennsylvania H

HESSER, R. B. 1978, Pennsylvania H

INLAND FISHERIES TRUST 1972, Ireland

INLAND FISHERIES TRUST 1977, Ireland

JANISCH, J. L. 1976, Indiana

JARVENPA, O. 1962, Minnesota

JARVENPA, O. M. 1962, Minnesota

JARVENPA, O. M. 1963, Minnesota

JARVENPA, O. M. and W. KIRSCH 1969, Minnesota

JENKINS, R. M. 1970

JENKINS, R. M. 1973

JOHNSON, F. H. and J. B. MOYLE 1969, Minnesota

JOHNSON, M. K. 1960, Iowa

JOHNSON, M. W., W. J. SCIDMORE, J. H. KUEHN and C. R. BURROWS 1957, Minnesota

KAJ, J. 1958, Poland

KAJ, J. and B. WLOSZCZYNSKI 1957, Poland

KEMPINGER, J. J. 1966b, Wisconsin

KEMPINGER, J. J. 1967b, Wisconsin

KEMPINGER, J. J. 1972, Wisconsin

KEMPINGER, J. J. and R. F. CARLINE 1978a, Wisconsin

KEMPINGER, J. J. and R. F. CARLINE 1978b, Wisconsin

KIPLING, C. and W. E. FROST 1972, England

KLEINERT, S. J. 1970, Wisconsin

KLUPP, R. 1978, West Germany

KUZNETSOV, V. A. 1980, USSR

LAGLER, K. F. 1939, Ohio

LAGLER, K. F. 1956, Michigan

LANGFORD, T. E. 1966, England

LATTA, W. C. 1971, Michigan

LATTA, W. C. 1972, Michigan

LAWLER, G. H. 1978, Manitoba

LEALOS, J. M. and G. G. BEVER 1982, Wisconsin

LE LOUARN, H. 1983, France

LENKIEWICZ, D. 1939, Poland

LIPSIT, J. H. 1977, Great Lakes

LUKOWICZ, M. VON 1983, West Germany

MAKOWECKI, R. 1973a, Alberta

MAKOWECKI, R. 1973b, Alberta

MANN, R. H. K. 1985, England

MCCARRAHER, D. B. 1959b, Nebraska

MCCLENDON, E. W. 1976

MCGOVERN, S. P. 1983a, Manitoba

MILLER, R. B. 1950a, Alberta

MILLER, R. B. 1950b, Alberta

MILLER, R. B. and R. C. THOMAS 1956, Alberta

MORRIS, J. W. 1973, Nebraska

MORRIS, J. W. 1974, Nebraska

MOYLE, J. B. 1949a, Minnesota

MOYLE, J. B. and W. D. CLOTHIER 1959, Minnesota

NELSON, W. R. 1978, South Dakota

NEWBURG, H. 1973, Minnesota

NIKANOROV, Y. I. 1962, USSR

NIKOLSKII, G. V. 1969, USSR

ORLOVA, E. L. and O. A. POPOVA 1976, USSR

PAGEAU, G., Y. GRAVEL and V. LEGENDRE 1979, Quebec

PATRIARCHE, M. H. 1963, Michigan

PATRIARCHE, M. H. 1966, Michigan

PATRIARCHE, M. H. 1968, Michigan

PATRIARCHE, M. H. 1971, Michigan

PATRIARCHE, M. H. and H. GOWING 1962a, Michigan

PEARSON, J. 1980, Indiana

PECKHAM, R. 1970, Nebraska

PECKHAM, R. D. 1973, Alaska

PHENICIE, C. K. and J. R. LYONS 1973

PIROZHNIKOV, P. L., A. F. KARPEVICH, A. I. ISAYEV and V. I. KARPOVA 1969, USSR

POLLOCK, K. H. and R. H. K. MANN 1983, England

PRIEGEL, G. R. 1969, Wisconsin

RAGAN, J. E. 1970, North Dakota

RAWSON, D. S. and F. M. ATTON 1953, Saskatchewan

ROZANSKI, M. 1914, Poland

SALOJARVI, K., H. AUVINEN and E. IKONEN 1981, Finland

SALOJARVI, K., H. AUVINEN and E. IKONEN 1982, Finland

SCHOENECKER, W. 1970, Nebraska
SCHOETTGER, R. A. and E. W. STEUCKE,
    Jr. 1970a, Wisconsin
SCHOETTGER, R. A. and E. W. STEUCKE,
    Jr. 1970b, Wisconsin
SCHULTZ, F. H. 1955, Saskatchewan
SCHWALME, K., W. C. MACKAY and D.
    LINDNER 1985, Alberta
SCIDMORE, W. J. 1964, Minnesota
SCIDMORE, W. J. 1970
SELBIG, W. 1970
SHENTIAKOV, V. A. 1963, USSR
SMITH, M. W. 1950, Canada
SNOW, H. E. 1961, Wisconsin
SNOW, H. E. 1974, Wisconsin
SNOW, H. E. 1982, Wisconsin
SNOW, H. E. and T. D. BEARD 1972,
    Wisconsin
SNOW, H. E. n.d., Wisconsin
SOLMAN, V. E. F. 1945, Manitoba
SOLMAN, V. E. F. 1950, Vermont
SPRULES, W. M. 1947, Manitoba
STRICKER, J. D. 1969
STRZELECKI, J. 1929, Poland
SULLIVAN, M. G. 1985, Alberta
SUMARI, O. and K. WESTMAN 1969b, Fin-
    land
SWIDERSKI, E. 1908, Poland
SZCZERBOWSKI, J. A., A. MARTYNIAK
    and J. TERLECKI 1976, Poland
THOMPSON, G. J. and H. C. GILSON 1952,
    England
THREINEN, C. W., C. A. WISTROM, B.
    APELGREN and H. E. SNOW 1966,
    Wisconsin
VAN OOSTEN, J. 1957, H
VASEY, F. W. 1968, Missouri
VASHCHENKO, D. M. 1958b, USSR
VIBERT, R. (ed.) 1967
VOSTRADOVSKY, J. 1983,
    Czechoslovakia
VOSTRADOVSKY, J. and M. VOSTRA-
    DOVSKA 1973, Czechoslovakia
WEBSTER, J., A. TRANDAHL and J. LEO-
    NARD 1978, USA
WERNER, R. G. and N. H. RINGLER 1980,
    New York
WILLIAMS, J. E. 1952, Michigan
WILLIAMS, J. E. 1965a, Michigan
WILLIAMS, J. E. 1965c, Michigan
WILLIAMS, J. E. 1966c, Michigan
WILLIAMS, J. E. 1967, Michigan
WILLIAMS, J. E. 1968, Michigan

WILLIAMS, J. E. and B. L. JACOB 1971,
    Michigan
WRIGHT, R. 1892, Ontario
WYDOSKI, R. S. 1977, California
ZAWISZA, J. 1953, Poland
ZYLINSKI, R. 1958, Poland

MARKING AND TAGGING

ALLAN, J. W. 1957, Great Lakes
BAGENAL, T. B. 1967b, England
BEYERLE, G. B. and J. E. WILLIAMS 1972,
    Michigan
BEYERLE, G. B. and J. E. WILLIAMS 1973,
    Michigan
CARBINE, W. F. and V. C. APPLEGATE
    1948, Michigan
CARLANDER, K. D. and J. G. ERICKSON
    1953, Iowa
CARLANDER, K. D. and R. RIDENHOUR
    1955, Iowa
CHAPMAN, C. A. and W. C. MACKAY
    1984a, Alberta
COOK, M. 1985a, Colorado
COOK, M. F. and E. P. BERGERSEN n.d.,
    Colorado
COOPER, G. P. 1951, Michigan
COULLOUDON, J. 1960, Quebec
CUNNINGHAM, C. R., J. F. CRAIG and W.
    C. MACKAY 1983
DES CLERS, S. and J. ALLARDI 1983,
    France
DIANA, J. S. 1979b
DIANA, J. S. 1980, Alberta
DIANA, J. S., W. C. MACKAY and M. EHR-
    MAN 1977, Alberta
DUERRE, D. C. 1966a, North Dakota
DUERRE, D. C. 1966b, North Dakota
FAGO, D. 1971a, Wisconsin
FAGO, D. 1971b, Wisconsin
FICKLING, N. 1982b, England
GOTHBERG, A. 1977
GRIMM, M. P. 1981a, Netherlands
GRIMM, M. P. 1982b, Netherlands
GROEBNER, J. F. 1964, Minnesota
HALME, E. 1957, Finland
HALME, E. 1958, Finland
HARRISON, E. J. 1978, New York
HART, P. J. B. and T. J. PITCHER 1969a,
    England
HELMS, D. 1976, Iowa
HELMS, D. R. 1975, Iowa

HENLEY, D. T. and R. L. APPLEGATE 1982, South Dakota H

HILL, W. J. 1969, North Dakota

JARVI, T. H. 1931, Finland

KAUKORANTA, E. and E. A. LIND 1975, Finland

KENDLE, E. R. and L. A. MORRIS 1972, Nebraska

KIPLING, C. and W. E. FROST 1970, England

KIPLING, C. and E. D. LE CREN 1975, England

KIPLING, C. and E. D. LE CREN 1984, England

KOSHINSKY, G. D. 1972, Saskatchewan

KOVAL, N. V. 1969

LEHTONEN, H. 1972, Finland

LIND, E. A. and E. KAUKORANTA 1975b, Finland

MALININ, L. K. 1970, USSR

MANN, R. H. K. 1980, England

MANN, R. H. K. 1985, England

MCDONALD, D. B. 1969, Alberta

MOEN, T. and D. HENEGAR 1971, South Dakota, North Dakota

MRAZ, D. F. 1962b, Wisconsin

NISSINEN, T. 1965b, Finland

NISSINEN, T. 1971, Finland

OLIVA, O. 1960, Czechoslovakia

PATRICK, B. and R. HAAS 1971

POLLOCK, K. H. and R. H. K. MANN 1983, England

PRIEGEL, G. R. 1968a, Wisconsin

PRIEGEL, G. R. 1969, Wisconsin

RHUDE, L. 1980, Alberta

RIDENHOUR, R. L. 1957, Iowa

ROSS, M. J. and C. F. KLEINER 1982, Minnesota

ROSS, M. J. and J. D. WINTER 1981, Minnesota

RUNNSTROM, S. 1950, Sweden

SCHOENECKER, W. 1961, Nebraska

TROCHERIE, F. and C. BERCY 1984, France

VALKEAJARVI, P. 1983, Finland

VOSTRADOVSKY, J. 1969a, Czechoslovakia

VOSTRADOVSKY, J. 1969c, Czechoslovakia

VOSTRADOVSKY, J. 1975, Czechoslovakia

WHITE, W. J. and R. J. BEAMISH 1972

MOVEMENT AND ACTIVITY

ABROSIMOVA, A. M. 1975

ABROSIMOVA, A. M., S. G. VASINA and S. B. GUMENYUK 1971

BLAXTER, J. H. S. 1969

BREDER, C. M. 1926

CARBINE, W. F. and D. S. SHETTER 1944, Michigan

CARLANDER, K. D. and E. CLEARY 1949, Iowa

CARLANDER, K. D. and R. RIDENHOUR 1955, Iowa

CARTER, E. R. 1955, Kentucky

CASSELMAN, J. M. 1972, Ontario

COOK, M. F. and E. P. BERGERSEN n.d., Colorado

DIANA, J. S. 1979b

DIANA, J. S. 1980, Alberta

DIANA, J. S., W. C. MACKAY and M. EHRMAN 1977, Alberta

DOMBECK, M. P. 1979, Wisconsin

GOTTBERG, G. 1922, Finland

HADLEY, W. F. 1970, Minnesota

HALME, E. and E. KORHONEN 1960, Finland

HARAM, O. J. 1966

HART, J. L. 1931, Ontario

HEADRICK, M. R. and R. F. CARLINE 1980, Ohio

JOHNSON, T. and K. MUELLER 1978, Sweden

JONES, D. R., J. W. KICENIUK and O. S. BAMFORD 1974, Northwest Territories

KELEHER, J. J. 1963, Northwest Territories

LEHTONEN, H. 1973, Finland

LIND, E. A. 1960, Finland

LIND, E. A. 1974, Finland

MACKAY, W. C. and J. F. CRAIG 1983

MACKENZIE, R. A. 1930

MAGNUSON, J. J. and B. PETROSKY 1973, Wisconsin

MALININ, L. K. 1969, USSR

MALININ, L. K. 1971a, USSR

MALININ, L. K. 1971b, USSR

MCKENZIE, R. A. 1930, Ontario

MILLER, R. B. 1948

MOEN, T. and D. HENEGAR 1971, South Dakota, North Dakota

NISSINEN, T. 1971, Finland

PAVLOV, D. S., A. D. MACHEK and S. N. KAPUSPIN 1981

PRIEGEL, G. R. 1968a, Wisconsin

RAGAN, J. E. 1975, North Dakota

ROSS, M. J. and J. D. WINTER 1981, Minnesota
SUMARI, O. 1965, Finland
VOSTRADOVSKY, J. 1969a, Czechoslovakia
VOSTRADOVSKY, J. 1975, Czechoslovakia
WEBB, P. W. 1978a, Michigan H
WEBB, P. W. 1983, Michigan

NUTRITION

BACKIEL, T. 1971, Poland
BALAGUROVA, M. V. 1967, USSR
BEVELHIMER, M. S., R. A. STEIN and R. F. CARLINE 1981, Ohio H
BIALOKOZ, W. and T. KRZYWOSZ 1976b, Poland
BIALOKOZ, W. and T. KRZYWOSZ 1978, Poland
BIALOKOZ, W. and T. KRZYWOSZ 1979, Poland
CERNOHOUS, L. 1974, North Dakota
CHODOROWSKA, W. 1973
CHODOROWSKA, W. and A. CHODOROWSKI 1969
CHODOROWSKA, W. and A. CHODOROWSKI 1975
CHODOROWSKI, A. 1976
COPELAND, J. 1975, H
DIANA, J. S. 1979a, Alberta
DIANA, J. S. 1979c, Alberta
DIANA, J. S. 1982, Alberta
DIANA, J. S. 1983a, Alberta
FORTUNATOVA, K. R. and O. A. POPOVA 1973, USSR
HASHIMOTO, Y. 1975
HEALEY, M. C. 1972, Scotland
IVANOVA, M. N. 1968, USSR
IVANOVA, M. N. and A. N. LOPATKO 1979, USSR
IVANOVA, M. N., A. N. LOPATKO and L. V. MALTSEVA 1982, USSR
JOHNSON, L. 1960, England
JOHNSON, L. 1966b, England
KARZINKIN, G. S. 1935, USSR
KETOLA, H. G. 1978, New York
KOSTOMAROVA, A. A. 1959, USSR
KOSTOMAROVA, A. A. 1961, USSR
LUGOVAYA, T. V. 1967, USSR
LUGOVAYA, T. V. 1971b, USSR
LUQUET, P. and J. F. LUQUET 1983, France
LYAKHNOVICH, V. P., T. I. NEKHAYEVA and T. M. SHEVTSOVA 1973, USSR

MEDFORD, B. A. 1976, Alberta
MONGEAU, J.-R. 1954, Quebec
MONGEAU, J.-R. 1955a, Quebec
MONGEAU, J.-R. 1955b, Quebec
SAMOKHVALOVA, L. K. 1976, USSR
SHERSTYUK, V. V. 1965, USSR
SPATARU, P. 1969, Hungary
TYMOWSKI, J. 1939, Poland
WILLEMSEN, J. 1965, Netherlands
WILLIAMS, J. E. 1966a, Michigan
WINBERG, G. G. 1956, USSR

PARASITES, PATHOLOGY, AND DISEASES

AHNE, W. 1978
AHNE, W. 1980, Germany
AISA, A. 1976, Italy
AISA, A. and P. GATTAPONI 1974, Italy
AKHERMOV, A. K. and E. A. BOGDANOVA 1961, USSR
ALLISON, L. N. 1953, Michigan
AMIN, O. M. 1979, Wisconsin
AMIN, O. M. 1981, Wisconsin
ANDREASSEN, J. and H. MADSEN 1970, Denmark
ANDRIC-ESPERANTO, M. J. 1985, Yugoslovia
ANONYMOUS 1928, Poland
ANONYMOUS 1961b
ARAI, H. P. and S.-M. CHIEN 1973, Alberta
ARTAMOSHIN, A. S. 1978, USSR
ARTAMOSHIN, A. S. and V. I. KHODAKOVA 1976, USSR
ARTAMOSHIN, A. S. and L. I. PROKOPENKO 1980, USSR
ARTHUR, J. R., L. MARGOLIS and H. P. ARAI 1976, Yukon
AVDOS'EV, V. S., I. R. DEMCHENKO, I. M. KARPENKO and O. P. KULAKOVSKAYA 1962, USSR
BANFIELD, W. G., C. J. DAWE, C. E. LEE and R. SONSTEGARD 1976
BANGHAM, R. 1946, Wisconsin
BANGHAM, R. V. and J. R. ADAMS 1954, British Columbia
BANGHAM, R. V. and G. HUNTER 1939, Great Lakes
BANINA, N. N. 1969
BARYSHEVA, A. F. and O. N. BAUER 1961, USSR
BAYLIS, H. A. 1928, England
BAYLIS, H. A. 1939, England

BEKESI, L., G. MAJOROS and E. SZABO 1984, Hungary

BLIZNYUK, I. D. 1969

BOOTSMA, R. 1971, Netherlands

BOOTSMA, R. 1973, Netherlands

BOOTSMA, R. and C. J. A. H. V. VAN VORSTENBOSCH 1973, Netherlands

BOOTSMA, R., P. DE KINKELIN and M. LEBERRE 1975, Netherlands

BORGSTROM, R. 1970, Norway

BORRONI, I. and E. GRIMALDI 1974, Italy

BOWER, S. M. and P. T. K. WOO 1977a, Ontario

BOWER, S. M. and P. T. K. WOO 1977b, Ontario

BROWN, E. R., W. C. DOLOWY, T. SIN-CLAIR, L. KEITH, S. GREENBERG, J. J. HAZDRA, P. BEAMER, and O. CAL-LAGHAN 1976, Illinois

BROWN, E. R., L. KEITH, J. J. HAZDRA and T. ARNDT 1975

BROWN, E. R., L. KEITH, J. B. G. KWAPINSKI, J. HAZDRA and P. BEA-MER 1973

BUCK, O. D. and J. L. CRITES 1975, Great Lakes

BUCKE, D., J. FINLAY, D. MCGREGOR and C. SEAGREAVE 1979, England, Wales

BURROWS 1974, Minnesota

BUTLER, E. P. 1919, Michigan

CALENIUS, G. 1980, Finland

CALENIUS, G. and G. BYLUND 1980, Finland

CARBINE, W. F. 1942c, Michigan

CASEY, N., M. MULCAHY and W. O'CONNELL 1975, Ireland

CHAPPELL, L. H. 1967, England

CHAPPELL, L. H. and R. W. OWEN 1969, England, Ireland

CHERNYSHEVA, N. B. 1976, USSR

CHINNIAH, V. C. and W. THRELFALL 1978, Labrador

CHIZHOVA, T. P. 1956, USSR

CHUBB, J. C. 1963a

CHUBB, J. C. 1963b, England

CHUBB, J. C. 1963c, England

CHUBB, J. C. 1968, England

COPLAND, W. O. 1956, Scotland

CROSSMAN, E. J. 1962a, Ontario

CROSSMAN, E. J. 1984, Ontario

DAVIES, E. 1966, England

DAVIES, E. H. 1967, England

DAVIES, E. H. 1968, England

DAVIS, H. S. 1953, California

DAWE, C. J., W. G. BANFIELD, R. SONSTEGARD, C. W. LEE and H. J. MICHELITCH 1977, Canada

DAWE, C. J., D. G. SCARPELLI and S. R. WELLINGS, eds. 1976

DECHTIAR, A. O. 1972a, Great Lakes

DECHTIAR, A. O. 1972b, Ontario

DE KINKELIN, P., B. GALIMARD and R. BOOTSMA 1973, France

DEL CAMPILLO, C. and P. A. PELLITERO 1973, Spain

DEUFEL, J. 1964, Ireland

DOAN, K. H. n.d., Canada

DOBIE, J. 1966, Minnesota

DOGIEL, V. A., G. K. DETRUSHEVSKI and I. I. POLYANSKI, eds. 1961

DOLLFUS, R. F. 1968, France

DORSON, M., P. DE KINKELIN and C. MICHEL 1983

DYKOVA, I. and J. LOM 1978, Czechoslovakia

ECONOMON, P. 1960, Minnesota

EKBAUM, E. 1937, Ontario, Manitoba

ENGASHEV, V. G. 1965, USSR

ENGELBRECHT, H. 1958, Germany

ERGENS, R. 1966, Czechoslovakia

ERGENS, R. 1971, Czechoslovakia

ESLAMI, A. H., M. ANWAR and S. KHA-TIBY 1972, Iran

FISCHTHAL, J. H. 1947, Wisconsin

FISCHTHAL, J. H. 1950, Wisconsin

FISCHTHAL, J. H. 1952, Wisconsin

FROLOVA, E. N. and T. V. SHCHERBINA 1975, USSR

FROST, W. E. 1977, England

GORDON, D., N. A. CROLL and M. E. RAU 1978, Quebec

GRABDA, J. 1971, Poland

GRABDA-KAZUBSKA, B. and L. EJSYMONT 1969

GRIFFIN, P. J. 1953, West Virginia

GRIMALDI, E. 1974, Italy

GRUPCHEVA, G. I. 1966, Bulgaria

GUILFORD, H. G. 1965, Great Lakes

HALVORSEN, O. 1968, Norway

HALVORSEN, O. and K. ANDERSEN 1973, Norway

HARRISON, E. J. and W. F. HADLEY 1982, New York

HEGEMANN, M. 1958b, Germany

HINTON, D. E., E. R. WALKER, C. A.
PINKSTAFF and E. M. ZUCHEL-
KOWSKI 1984, West Virginia
HIRAKI, S., M. F. MULCAHY and L. DMO-
CHOWSKI 1978
HOFFMAN, G. L. 1967, North America
HUGGHINS, E. J. 1959, South Dakota
HUNTER, G. W., III and J. S. RANKIN
1941, Connecticut
IZYUMOV, N. A. 1959, USSR
JARA, Z. 1968, Poland
KEARN, G. C. 1966
KOGTEVA, E. P. 1961, USSR
KOSHEVA, A. F. 1957, USSR
KOVAL, V. P. 1969, USSR
KOZICKA, J. 1953, Poland
KOZICKA, J. 1971, Poland
KRITSCHER, E. 1975, Austria, Hungary
KULAKOVSKAYA, O. P. 1976
KULMATYCKI, W. 1929, Poland
KUPERMAN, B. I. and R. E. SHUL'MAN
1972, USSR
LAIRD, M. 1961, Northwest Territories, Que-
bec
LAMBERT, A. 1978, France
LARUE, G. R. 1926
LAWLER, G. H. 1959, Canada
LAWLER, G. H. 1969a, Manitoba
LAWLER, G. H. 1969c, Sweden
LAWLER, G. H. 1970
LAWLER, G. H. and W. B. SCOTT 1954,
North America
LEONG, T. S. and J. C. HOLMES 1981,
Alberta
LETENDRE, G. C., C. P. SCHNEIDER and
N. F. EHLINGER 1972
LJUNGBERG, O. 1963, Sweden
LJUNGBERG, O. 1976, Sweden
LJUNGBERG, O. 1977, Sweden
LJUNGBERG, O. and J. LANGE 1968,
Sweden
LOM, J. 1970
LOM, J. 1973
MALMBERG, G. 1970, Finland, Norway,
Sweden
MARGOLIS, L. 1951, Quebec
MARGOLIS, L. 1952, Quebec
MARITA, N. M. 1959, USSR
MARKIEWICZ, F. 1967, Poland
MARSHALL, W. S. and N. C. GILBERT
1905, Wisconsin
MATSKASI, I. 1969
MEIER, W. 1981

MEIER, W. and P. E. V. JORGENSEN
1979a, Switzerland
MEIER, W. and P. E. V. JORGENSEN
1979b, Switzerland
MELLORS, P. J. and R. W. OWEN 1980,
England
MESZAROS, F. 1969, Hungary
MEYER, F. P. and J. A. ROBINSON 1973,
North America
MEYER, M. C. 1954, Maine
MICHAJLOW, W. 1933
MICHAJLOW, W. and I. WITA 1976
MILLER, R. B. 1943, Alberta
MILLER, R. B. 1944, Alberta
MILLER, R. B. 1950a, Alberta
MILLER, R. B. 1952, Canada
MILLER, R. B. and H. B. WATKINS 1946,
Alberta
MISHRA, T. N. and J. C. CHUBB 1969, Eng-
land
MITENEV, V. K. 1975, USSR
MOLNAR, K. 1976, Hungary
MOLNAR, K. 1980, Hungary
MORAVEC, F. 1977, Czechoslovakia
MORAVEC, F. 1978a, Czechoslovakia
MORAVEC, F. 1978b, Czechoslovakia
MORAVEC, F. 1979, Czechoslovakia
MORAVEC, F. and I. DYKOVA 1978,
Czechoslovakia
MULCAHY, M. 1970, Ireland
MULCAHY, M. F. 1963, Ireland
MULCAHY, M. F. 1969, Ireland
MULCAHY, M. F. 1970b, Ireland
MULCAHY, M. F. 1975, Ireland
MULCAHY, M. F. 1976, Ireland
MULCAHY, M. F. and A. O'LEARY 1970,
Ireland
MULCAHY, M. F. and F. J. O'ROURKE
1964a, Ireland
MULCAHY, M. F. and F. J. O'ROURKE
1964b, Ireland
MULCAHY, M. F., A. SAVAGE and N.
CASEY 1983, Ireland
MULCAHY, M. F., G. WINQUIST and C. J.
DAWE 1970, Ireland
MUNRO, A. L. S., J. LIVERSIDGE and K.
G. R. ELSON 1976, Scotland
NAGIBINA, L. F. 1961, USSR
NICHOLSON, D. 1932
NIGRELLI, R. F. 1947
NIGRELLI, R. F. 1953, North America
NUHI, A. and Y. KHORASANI 1981, Iran
NURNBERGER, P. K. 1930, Minnesota

NYSTROM, M. 1979, Finland
NYSTROM, M. 1982, Finland
ODENING, K. 1974
ODENING, K. 1976, East Germany
ODENING, K. and I. BOCKHARDT 1976,
 East Germany
PALMIERI, J. R. 1975
PAPAS, T. S., J. DAHLBERG and R. A.
 SONSTEGARD 1976, Ontario
PAPAS, T. S., M. SHAFFER, T. PRY and R.
 A. SONSTEGARD 1977, Ontario
PENNELL, D. A. 1969, Washington
PERLOWSKA, R. 1969, Poland
PETERS, L., D. CAVIS and J. ROBERTSON
 1978, Michigan
PETRUSHEVSKII, G. K., ed. 1961, USSR
POJMANSKA, T., B. GRABDA-
 KAZUBSKA, S. L. KAZUBSKI,
 JADWIGA and K. NIEWIADOMSKA
 1980, Poland
PRIBYSLAVSKY, J. and Z. LUCKY 1967
PRICE, C. E. 1969, Denmark
PROKOPENKO, L. I., A. S. ARTAMOSHIN
 and A. A. FROLOVA 1978, USSR
PRONINA, S. V. 1977a, USSR
PRONINA, S. V. 1977b, USSR
PRONINA, S. V., E. D. LOGACHEV and N.
 M. PRONIN 1981, USSR
PRONINA, S. V. and N. M. PRONIN 1982,
 USSR
PUCILOWSKA, A. 1969, USSR
REED, G. B. and G. C. TONER 1941,
 Ontario
REED, G. B. and G. C. TONER 1942,
 Ontario
REICHENBACH-KLINKE, H. H. 1971
REICHENBACH-KLINKE, H. H. 1974
RIBELIN, W. E. and G. MIGAKI, eds. 1975
RICHARDSON, L. R. 1941, Quebec
RIZVI, S. S. H. 1969, England
ROUSSOW, G. 1960
SCHAFERNA, K. 1944
SCHWARTZ, J. J. 1974
SELL, J. 1974, Poland
SELL, R. J. 1952, Ohio
SHETTER, D. S. 1949, Michigan
SHLYAPNIKOVA, R. L. 1961, USSR
SISOVA-KASATOCKINA, O. A. and A. J.
 DUBOVSKAJA 1975
SKRYABINA, E. S. 1978, USSR
SNIESZKO, S. F. 1952
SNIESZKO, S. F. and G. L. BULLOCK
 1968

SONSTEGARD, R., K. NIELSEN and L. A.
 MCDERMOTT 1970, Ontario
SONSTEGARD, R. A. 1975, Ontario
SONSTEGARD, R. A. 1976, Ontario
SONSTEGARD, R. A. and J. G. HNATH
 1978, Ontario
SONSTEGARD, R. A. and J. F. LEATHER-
 LAND , Great Lakes
SONSTEGARD, R. A. and T. S. PAPAS
 1977, Ontario
STAFFORD, J. 1904, Canada
STUCKY, N. P. 1973, Nebraska
SUPRYAGA, V. G. and A. A. MOZGOVOI
 1974, USSR
SWEETING, R. A. 1976
THOMPSON, J. S. 1982, Finland
THOMPSON, P.-A. and W. THRELFALL
 1978, Quebec
THRELFALL, W. and G. HANEK 1970,
 Labrador
TROFIMENKO, V. Y. 1969, USSR
UNGUREANU, E. M., A. C. DRANGA and
 R. P. MARINOV 1970
VAUGHAN, G. E. and D. W. COBLE 1975,
 Wisconsin
VOLCHUK, H. L. 1976, New York
VOTH, D. R. and O. R. LARSON 1968,
 North Dakota
WASHBURN, F. L. 1886, Minnesota
WATSON, R. A. and T. A. DICK 1980, Man-
 itoba
WHANG-PENG, J., R. A. SONSTEGARD
 and C. J. DAWE 1976, USA
WILLEMSE, J. J. 1968, Netherlands
WILLEMSE, J. J. 1969, Netherlands
WILSON, C. B. 1916
WILSON, C. B. 1920, Indiana
WINQUIST, G., O. LJUNGBERG and B.
 HELLSTROM 1968, Sweden
WINQUIST, G., O. LJUNGBERG and B.
 IVARSSON 1973
WITA, I. 1971, Poland
WITA, I. 1972, Poland
WITA, I. 1974, Poland
WIZIGMANN, G., C. BAATH and R. HOFF-
 MAN 1980, Germany
WOLF, K. 1972
WOLF, K. 1974
WOODS, C. E. 1971, North Dakota
WORLEY, D. E. and R. V. BANGHAM 1952
WUNDER, W. 1936, Europe
YAMAMOTO, T., R. K. KELLY and O.
 NIELSEN 1984, Alberta

YUSUPOV, O. Y. and A. N. URAZBAEV
1980, USSR
ZITNAN, R. 1971, Czechoslovakia

PHYSIOLOGY AND BIOCHEMISTRY
ACOLAT, L. 1955, France
ADELMAN, I. R. and L. L. SMITH, Jr.
1970a
AHOKAS, J. T., N. T. KARKI, A. OIKARI
and A. SOIVIC 1976, Finland
ALLEN, J. L., C. W. LUHNING and P. D.
HARMAN 1972, Georgia
ANANICHEV, A. V. 1961
ANANICHEV, A. V. 1963, USSR
ANONYMOUS n.d.a
ANWAND, K. 1963
ANWAND, K. 1966b
ASTER, P. L. 1975
ASTER, P. L. 1976, Alberta
ATWATER, W. O. 1892, USA
BALK, L., J. W. DEPIERRE, A. SUND-
VALL and U. RANNUG 1982
BALK, L., S. MAANER, A. BERGSTRAND
and J. W. DEPIERRE 1985, Sweden
BALK, L., J. MEIJER, A. ASTROM, R.
MORGENSTERN, J. SEIDEGAARD and
J. W. DEPIERRE 1980
BALK, L., J. MEIJER, A. BERGSTRAND,
A. AASTROEM, J. SEIDEGAARD and J.
W. DEPIERRE 1982, Sweden
BALK, L., J. MEIJER, J. W. DEPIERRE and
L.-E. APPELGREN 1984, Sweden
BALK. L., A. KNALL and J. W. DEPIERRE
1982
BEVELHIMER, M. S. 1983, Ohio H
BEVELHIMER, M. S., R. A. STEIN and R.
F. CARLINE 1985, Ohio H
BEVELHIMER, M. S., R. A. STEIN and R.
F. CARLINE n.d.,   H
BHUSHANA RAO, K. S. P. 1970, Belgium
BIELEK, E. 1980, Austria
BILLARD, R. 1982, France
BILLARD, R. and B. BRETON 1976, France
BILLARD, R. and J. E. FLECHON 1969,
France
BILLARD, R., W. C. MACKAY, and J.
MARCEL 1983, Alberta
BILLARD, R., J. MARCEL and G. DE
MONTALEMBERT 1983, France
BODROVA, N. V. and B. V. KRAIUKHIN
1959, USSR

BODROVA, N. V. and B. V. KRAIUKHIN
1960a, USSR
BODROVA, N. V. and B. V. KRAIUKHIN
1960b, USSR
BODROVA, N. V. and B. V. KRAIUKHIN
1961a, USSR
BODROVA, N. V. and B. V. KRAIUKHIN
1961b, USSR
BODROVA, N. V. and B. V. KRAIUKHIN
1963, USSR
BOGDANOV, G. N. and S. V.
STRELTSOVA, 1953, USSR
BONIN, J. D. and J. R. SPOTILA 1978, New
York H
BORG, H., A. EDIN, K. HOLM and E.
SKOLD 1981
BURLAKOV, A. B. and N. E. LEBEDEVA
1976, USSR
BYZOV, A. L., Y. A. TRIFONOV and L. M.
CHAILAKHYAN 1973, USSR
CAMERON, J. N. 1973, Alaska
CARDOT, J. and J. RIPPLINGER 1967
CARLSSON, S. 1978, Sweden
CARLSSON, S. and K. LIDEN 1977, Sweden
CARLSTROM, D. and J. E. GLAS 1959
CASSELMAN, J. M. 1972, Ontario
CASSELMAN, J. M. 1974b, Ontario
CASSELMAN, J. M. 1978a, Ontario
CERVINKA, S. and O. PECHA 1975,
Czechoslovakia
CHAIKOVSKAYA, A. V., E. T. USKOVA
and S. I. DAVIDENKO 1981
CHERNIKOVA, V. V. 1966, USSR
CLEERE, W. F., S. BREE and M. P.
COUGHLAN 1976, Ireland
CLERX, J. P. M. 1978, Netherlands
CLERX, J. P. M., A. CASTEL, J. F. BOL and
G. J. GERWIG 1980
CORDIER, G. 1959
CRAIK, J. C. A. 1982
CRUEA, D. D. 1969, Wyoming
CVANCARA, V. A. 1969
CVANCARA, V. A. and W. HUANG 1978
CZELZUGA, B. 1977, Poland
CZELZUGA, B. 1978, Poland
DAWE, C. J. 1970
DAWSON, V. K. and P. A. GILDERHUS
1979
DE JAGER, S., M. E. SMIT-ONEL, J. J.
VIDELER, B. J. M. VAN GILS and E. M.
UFFINK 1976, Netherlands
DE LIGNY, W. and B. L. VERBOOM 1968,
Netherlands

DIANA, J. S. 1979a, Alberta

DIANA, J. S. 1982, Alberta

DIANA, J. S. and W. C. MACKAY 1979, Alberta

DIPLOCK, A. T. and G. A. D. HASLE-WOOD 1967

DI PRISCO, G. L., G. MATERAZZI and G. CHIEFFI 1970

DOCKRAY, G. J. 1974a

DOCKRAY, G. J. 1974b

DOCKRAY, G. J. 1975

DOLININ, V. A. 1973, USSR

DOLININ, V. A. 1974, USSR

DOLININ, V. A. 1975a, USSR

DOLININ, V. A. 1975b, USSR

DOLININ, V. A. 1976, USSR

DRAKENBERG, T., M. SWAERD, A. CAVE and J. PARELLO 1985, Sweden

DUSHAUSKENE-DUZH, N. F., G. G. POLI-KARPOV and B. I. STYRO 1969

DYER, W. J. 1952, Nova Scotia

EALES, J. G. 1969, Manitoba

ERIKSSON, L.-O. and S. ULVELAND 1977, Sweden

FABRI, Z. J. 1984

FELDT, W. and M. MELTZER 1978

FERREIRA, J. T., H. J. SCHOOBEE and G. L. SMIT 1984

FILOSOFOVA-LYZLOVA, E. M. 1972

FITZPATRICK, D. A. and K. F. MCGEE-NEY 1975

FLEROVA, G. I., V. I. MARTEM'YANOV and R. A. ZAPRUDNOVA 1980, USSR

FLOURENS, P. 1957

FOX, D. L. 1957

GAGE, S. H. 1942

GARDNER, J. A. 1926, England

GARDNER, J. A. and G. KING 1923, England

GEE, J. H., K. MACHNIAK and S. M. CHALANCHUK 1974, Manitoba

GEE, J. H., R. F. TALLMAN and H. J. SMART 1978, Manitoba

GELINEO, S. 1969

GEOFFROY, C. J. 1735

GEORGESCAULD, D and H. DUCLOHIER 1969

GERDAY, C. 1976

GILDERHUS, P. A., B. L. BERGER, J. B. SILLS and P. D. HARMAN 1973

GIRSA, I. I. 1969

GLASS, R. L., T. P. KRICK and A. E. ECK-HARDT 1974

GLASS, R. L., T. P. KRICK, D. L. OLSON and P. L. THORSON 1977

GLAZUNOVA, G. A. 1974

GRIER, H. J. and J. R. LINTON 1977

GROSS, G. W. and G. W. KREUTZBERG 1978, West Germany

GULIDOV, M. V. 1969a, USSR

HABEKOVIC, D. 1979

HAKANSON, L. 1980

HAMACKOVA, J., Z. SVOBODOVA and J. KOURIL 1975, Czechoslovakia

HANSON, A. 1966

HOFFMANN, R., C. PFEIL-PUTZIEN and M. VOGT 1978, Germany

HOLAK, H., B. JARZAB, A. BALDYS and B. WITALA 1979, Poland

HUGGINS, A. K., G. SKUTSCH and E. BALDWIN 1969

HUNN, J. B. 1972a

HUNN, J. B. 1972b, Wisconsin

IL'YENKO, A. I. 1970, USSR

IL'YENKO, A. I. 1972, USSR

INCE, B. W. 1979, England

INCE, B. W. and A. THORPE 1975, England

INCE, B. W. and A. THORPE 1976a, England

INCE, B. W. and A. THORPE 1976b, England

INCE, B. W. and A. THORPE 1978, England

IVLEV, V. S. 1939b, USSR

IVLEV, V. S. 1954, USSR

JALABERT, B. 1976, France

JALABERT, B. and B. BRETON 1974, France

JOASSIN, L., F. FRANKENNE and C. GER-DAY 1971

JURKOWSKI, M. K. 1976, Poland

KANGUR, A. 1968

KAUSHIK, S. J., K. DABROWSKI and P. LUQUET 1985, France

KERR, T. 1942

KETZ, H. A., G. ASSMANN and H. WITT 1960

KIERMEIR, A. 1939

KIME, D. E. 1978, England

KIME, D. E. and E. A. HEWS 1978, England

KIRSIPUU, A. 1964a, USSR

KIRSIPUU, A. 1964b

KLUYTMANS, J. H. F. M. and D. I. ZAN-DEE 1973a, Netherlands

KLUYTMANS, J. H. F. M. and D. I. ZAN-DEE 1973b, Netherlands

KLUYTMANS, J. H. F. M. and D. I. ZAN-
DEE 1974, Netherlands
KLYSZEJKO, B. 1973, Poland
KORZHUEV, P. A. and T. N. GLAZOVA
1968, USSR
KOTLYAREVSKAYA, N. V. 1966,
USSR
KRISTOFFERSSON, R. and S. BROBERG
1972, Finland
KRISTOFFERSSON, R., S. BROBERG and
A. OIKARI 1972, Finland
KRISTOFFERSSON, R., S. BROBERG and
A. OIKARI 1973, Finland
KRISTOFFERSSON, R., S. BROBERG, A.
OIKARI and M. PEKKARINEN 1974, Fin-
land
KRUGLOVA, E. E. 1971a
KRUGLOVA, E. E. 1971b
KULIKOV, N. V. 1970, USSR
KURSIPUU, A. 1971
KUZ'MINA, V. V. 1977, USSR
KUZ'MINA, V. V. 1981, USSR
KUZ'MINA, V. V. 1984, USSR
KUZ'MINA, V. V. and I. L. GOLO-
VANOVA 1980, USSR
KUZ'MINA, V. V. and E. N. MOROZOVA
1977, USSR
KUZ'MINA, V. V. and L. P. ZHILINA 1974,
USSR
LAPKIN, V. V., A. G. PODDUBNYY and A.
M. SVIRSKIY 1983, USSR
LAVROVA, Y. A. and Y. V. NATOCHIN
1974, USSR
LINDROTH, A. 1947, Sweden
LINDSTEDT, P. 1914
LINHART, O. 1984a, Czechoslovakia
LINZEL, W., H. PFEIFFER and I. ZIPPEL
1939
LOCASCIO, N. J. T. and J. E. WRIGHT, Jr.
1973
LOEFFLER, C. A. 1971, Sweden
LOFTS, B. and A. J. MARSHALL 1957
LUBITSKAYA, A. I. and E. A. DORO-
FEEVA 1961, USSR
LUPO DI PRISCO, C., G. MATERAZZI and
G. CHIEFFI 1970
LUSTIG, V. and J. A. KELLEN 1971
MACKAY, W. C. 1967, Alberta
MACKAY, W. C. and D. D. BEATTY 1968,
Alberta
MALYUKINA, G. A., G. V. DEVITSYNA
and E. A. MARUSOV 1974
MANOHAR, S. V. 1970, Manitoba

MANOHAR, S. V. and H. BOESE 1971,
Manitoba
MARTEM'YANOV, V. I. and R. A.
ZAPRUDNOVA 1982, USSR
MAVRINSKAYA, L. F. 1956
MCCAY, C. M. 1931
MEDFORD, B. A. 1976, Alberta
MEDFORD, B. A. and W. C. MACKAY
1978, Alberta
MEDVEDKIN, V. N., Y. V. MITIN and E. A.
PERMYAKOV 1984, USSR
MEZQUITA, J., R. BARTRONS, G. PONS
and J. CARRERAS 1981
MINAKOWSKI, W. 1962, Poland
MINAKOWSKI, W. and Z. NOWICKA 1962
MOLNAR, G. and E. TAMASSY 1970, Hun-
gary
MOLNAR, G., E. TAMASSY and I. TOLG
1967, Hungary
MOLNAR, G. and I. TOLG 1963, Hungary
MORRE, J. and J. BARRET 1963
MULCAHY, M. F. 1970a, Ireland
MUSACCHIA, X. J., B. J. SULLIVAN and
C. G. WILBER 1957, Arctic
NEUMAN, W. F. and B. J. MULRYAN 1968
NEUMAYER, L. 1895
NIENSTEDT, W., I. NIENSTEDT and J.
MANNISTO 1981, Finland
NOMURA, S., T. IBARAKI, H. HIROSE and
S. SHIRAHATA 1972, Japan
NONNOTTE, G. 1981, France
OBERSZTYN, A. 1953
OIKARI, A. 1975a, Finland
OIKARI, A. 1975b, Finland
OIKARI, A. 1978, Finland
OIKARI, A. and A. SOIVIO 1975, Finland
OIKARI, A. and A. SOIVIO 1977, Finland
OLIPHAN, L. V. 1940, USSR
PARISI, G. 1968
PENNOCK, J. F., R. A. MORTON, D. E. M.
LAWSON and D. L. LAIDMAN 1962
PERMYAKOV, E. A., L. P. KALINI-
CHENKO, V. N. MEDVEDKIN, E. A.
BURSTEIN and C. GERDAY 1983, Bel-
gium
PHILLIPS, G. R. and R. W. GREGORY
1979, Montana
PICOS, C. A., G. NASTASESCU and G.
IGNAT 1969, Romania
PIEZ, K. A.
PIEZ, K. A. and J. GROSS 1960
PLACK, P. A. 1964
PLACK, P. A. and S. K. KON 1961

PLISZKA, F. 1956, Poland
POLYAK, S. 1957
PRAVDINA, N. I. and M. A. CHEBO-
  TAREVA 1971
PRAVDINA, N. I., M. A. CHEBOTAREVA
  and E. E. KRUGLOVA 1974
PRIVOLNEV, T. I. 1954, USSR
PRIVOLNEV, T. I. 1964b, USSR
RAFFIN, J. P. and C. LERAY 1980
REAY, G. A. 1939
REMOROV, V. A. 1966, USSR
SCHOOTS, A. F. M., R. J. G. OPSTELTEN
  and J. M. DENUCE 1982, Netherlands
SCHWALME, K. 1984, Alberta
SCHWALME, K. and W. C. MACKAY
  1985a
SCHWALME, K. and W. C. MACKAY
  1985b, Alberta
SEREBRINIKOVA, T. P. and E. M.
  LYZLOVA 1977, USSR
SHAMARADINA, I. P. 1954, USSR
SHENTIAKOV, V. A. 1963, USSR
SHKORBATOV, G. L. 1965a, USSR
SHKORBATOV, G. L. 1965b, USSR
SHLYUMPBERGER, V. 1966, USSR
SILLS, J. B., J. L. ALLEN, P. D. HARMAN
  and C. W. LUHNING 1973, Wisconsin,
  Georgia
SIMONTACCHI, C., C. BOITI, N.
  BONALDO, P. COLOMBO
  BELEVEDERE and L. COLOMBO 1983,
  Italy
SIMONTACCHI, C., D. CASCIOTTI and C.
  BOITI 1982, Italy
SMIRNOV, A. A. and E. V. CHIR-
  KOVSKAYA 1969, USSR
SOIVOI, A. and A. OIKARI 1976, Finland
SPECKERT, W., B. KENNEDY, S. L. DAIS-
  LEY and P. DAVIES 1981
STARMACH, K. 1951b, Poland
STEIN, H. 1981
STEIN, H. and H. BAYRLE 1978
STEIN, H. and H. ENZLER 1983, Germany
STRATILS, A., V. TOMASEK, J. CLAMP
  and J. WILLIAMS 1985, Czechoslovakia
STROGANOV, N. S. and I. A. LASH-
  MANOVA 1968, USSR
TAN, E. L. and T. WOOD 1969
THORPE, A. 1976, England
THORPE, A. and B. W. INCE 1974a, Eng-
  land
THORPE, A. and B. W. INCE 1974b, Eng-
  land

THORPE, A. and B. W. INCE 1976
TIMOSHINA, L. A. 1970
VAN NOORDEN, S. and G. J. PATENT
  1978
VENDRELY, R. and C. VENDRELY 1950
VERZHBINSKAYA, N. A., L. I. PERSHINA
  and V. G. LEONT'EV 1977, USSR
VOINO-YASENETSKII, A. V. 1958, USSR
WEISS, D. G. 1980, West Germany
WEISS, D. G., G. W. GROSS and G. W.
  KREUTZBERG 1978b, West Germany
WELCH, H. E. 1968
WESSLER, E. and I. WERNER 1957
WESTERS, H. 1978, H
WIEBE, A. H. 1931
WILBER, C. G. 1955, Missouri
WILDING, J. L. 1939
WINBERG, G. G. 1956, USSR
WOYNAROVICH, E. 1960, Hungary
WUNSCHE, J. and W. STEFFENS 1968
ZAITZEV, A. V. 1955b, USSR
ZAWADOWSKA, B. and W. KILARSKI
  1984a, Poland
ZAWADOWSKA, B. and W. KILARSKI
  1984b, Poland
ZOTOV, A. F. 1958, USSR

POPULAR ACCOUNTS
ANONYMOUS 1877
ANONYMOUS 1902a
ANONYMOUS 1902b
ANONYMOUS 1960b, North Dakota
ANONYMOUS 1975b
ANONYMOUS 1976a
ANONYMOUS 1976b
ANONYMOUS 1976c
ANONYMOUS 1976d
ANONYMOUS 1985
ANONYMOUS n.d.d, Saskatchewan
ANONYMOUS n.d.f, USA
BAUER, P. 1971
BRERETON, G. E. and J. M. FERRIER, eds.
  1981
BROWN, L., England
BRUHL, L. 1925, Germany
BRUHL, L. 1927a, Germany
BRUHL, L. 1927b, Germany
BRUNNER, G. and H. REICHENBACK-
  KLINKE 1961, Germany
BUSS, K. 1966b, Pennsylvania
BUSS, K. and A. LARSEN 1961, Great Lakes
CACUTT, L. 1979, England

CAINE, L. S. 1949b
CARBINE, W. F. 1938, Michigan
CARLANDER, K. D. 1952, Iowa
CECILIA, A. 1973, Spain
CHENEY, A. N. 1893, New York
CHENEY, A. N. 1897
CHENEY, A. N. 1898, New York
CIRCLE, H. n.d., USA
COOK, M. 1985a, Colorado
COOK, M. 1985b, Colorado
CORBIN, G. B. 1873, England
CROSSMAN, E. J. 1984, Ontario
CULL, J. L. 1934
DIANGELO, S. and J. E. WILLIAMS 1962, Michigan
DONAIRE, J. A. 1976, Spain
DUNHAM, D. K. 1956
EGGERS, J. 1984
FERNANDEZ ROMAN, E. 1982
FLEGEL, E. 1965
GABRIELSON, I. N. and F. LAMONTE 1950, USA
GIBBS, J. 1976
GORSLINE, T. 1981, Ontario
HAEGEMAN, J. 1979, Ontario
HAFFNER, C. 1912
HALLOCK, C. 1877, North America
HALME, E. 1957, Finland
HALME, E. 1958, Finland
HENEGAR, D. 1960b, North Dakota
HUGHES, T. , England
HUNER, J. V. 1983
KING, F. A. 1959
LOPINOT, A. 1958, Illinois
LUCAS, J. 1963, North America
MACFIE, J. A. n.d., Ontario
MARZAL, M. 1958, Spain
MARZAL, M. 1967, Spain
MCCARRAHER, B. 1956, Nebraska
MCCLANE, A. J. 1961
RAY, J. n.d., Kansas
SCHWARTZ, F. J. 1960a, Maryland
SEAMAN, W. 1968
SMITH, L. L., Jr. 1941, Minnesota
SMITH, L. L., Jr. and N. L. MOE, (Compilers) 1944, Minnesota
SNOW, H. 1958, Wisconsin
SNOW, H. E. 1973, Wisconsin
THOMPSON, D. 1979
TONER, G. C. n.d., Canada
WILLIAMS, J. E. 1952, Michigan

POPULATION DYNAMICS

ADELMAN, I. 1969, Minnesota
ALESSIO, G. 1984, Italy
ALM, G. 1959, Sweden
ANDERSON, R. O. and S. J. GUTREUTER 1981
ANDERSON, R. O. and A. S. WEITHMAN 1978
ANWAND, K. 1971, East Germany
ANWAND, K. 1972
AUTKO, B. F. 1960, USSR
AUTKO, B. F. 1964, USSR
BACKIEL, T. 1971, Poland
BAGENAL, T. B. 1977, England
BALON, E. K. 1968b, Czechoslovakia
BANKS, J. W. 1970, England
BECKMAN, L. G. and J. H. ELROD 1971, South Dakota
BEYERLE, G. B. 1970b, Michigan
BEYERLE, G. B. 1971a, Michigan
BEYERLE, G. B. 1971c, Michigan
BEYERLE, G. B. 1973a, Michigan
BEYERLE, G. B. 1973b, Michigan H
BEYERLE, G. B. 1978, Michigan
BEYERLE, G. B. 1980, Michigan
BILLARD. R. 1980, France
BIMBER, D. L. and S. A. NICHOLSON 1981, New York
BODALY, R. A. and L. F. W. LESACK, 1984, Manitoba
BOLOTOVA, T. G., and A. N. BURLAKOVA, 1975, USSR
BRAUM, E. 1967, Germany
CAPLAN, D. L. 1982, Wisconsin
CARLANDER, K. D. 1955, Iowa
CARLANDER, K. D. and J. G. ERICKSON 1953, Iowa
CARLANDER, K. D. and L. E. HINER 1943b, Minnesota
CARLANDER, K. D. and J. W. PARSONS 1949, Iowa
CARLINE, R. F. 1979, Ohio
CASSELMAN, J. M. and H. H. HARVEY 1975, Ontario
CHAPMAN, D. W. 1967
CHATELAIN, R. and G. MASSE 1980, Quebec
CHRISTENSEN, K. E. and J. E. WILLIAMS 1969, Michigan
CHRISTENSON, L. M. 1957, Minnesota
CHRISTENSON, L. M. and L. L. SMITH 1965, Minnesota
CHURCHILL, W. S. 1961, Wisconsin

CHURCHILL, W. S. 1962, Wisconsin

CIEPIELEWSKI, W. 1973, Poland

CIEPIELEWSKI, W. 1981, Poland

COOPER, G. P. 1951, Michigan

COOPER, G. P. and W. C. LATTA 1954, Michigan

COOPER, G. P. and R. N. SCHAFER 1954, Michigan

DOBIE, J. and J. B. MOYLE 1962, Minnesota

DOLZHENKO, M. P. and V. P. VLASOV 1961, USSR

DOMANEVSKII, L. N. 1959, USSR

DOMANEVSKII, L. N. 1963, USSR

DOMANEVSKY, L. N. 1964, USSR

DONETZ, J. E. 1982, Ontario

DUBE, J. and Y. GRAVEL, eds. 1979, North America

DUNST, R. 1966, Wisconsin

DUNST, R. C. 1969, Wisconsin

ECOLE, R. A. 1979, France

ELKINS, W. A. 1937, Wisconsin

ELROD, J. H. and T. J. HASSLER 1969, South Dakota

FALK, M. R. and D. V. GILLMAN 1975a, Northwest Territories

FEDIN, S. P. 1958, USSR

FETTERROLF, C. M., Jr. 1952, Michigan

FINNELL, L. 1984, Colorado

FINNELL, L. 1985, Colorado

FITZMAURICE, P. 1978, Ireland

FLICK, W. A. 1977, Quebec

FORNEY, J. L. 1977, New York

FORTIN, R., P. DUMONT, H. FOURNIER, C. CADIEUX and D. VILLENEUVE 1982, Quebec

FRANKLIN, D. R. 1959, Minnesota

FRANKLIN, D. R. and L. L. SMITH, Jr. 1963, Minnesota

FROST, W. E. 1946, England

FROST, W. E. and C. KIPLING 1968a, England

FROST, W. E. and C. KIPLING 1970, England

FRY, F. E. J. 1955, Ontario

GABOURY, M. N. 1982, Manitoba

GENGERKE, T. 1977, Iowa

GOEDDE, L. E. and D. W. COBLE 1981, Wisconsin

GOLDSPINK, C. R. and J. W. BANKS 1975

GREEN, D. M., Jr. 1978, New York

GRIMALDI, E. 1972, Italy

GRIMM, M. P. 1980, Netherlands

GRIMM, M. P. 1981a, Netherlands

GRIMM, M. P. 1981b, Netherlands

GRIMM, M. P. 1983a, Netherlands

GROEBNER, J. F. 1960, Minnesota

GROEBNER, J. F. 1964, Minnesota

GROEN, C. L. and T. A. SCHROEDER 1978, Kansas

GULIN, V. V. and G. P. RUDENKO 1974, USSR

GYURKO, S. and Z. I. NAGY 1971

HAGENSON, I. and J. F. O'CONNOR 1979, Manitoba

HAIDER, G. and U. PAGGA 1983, West Germany

HAKKARI, L. and P. BAGGE 1983, Finland

HART, P. J. B. and T. J. PITCHER 1969b, England

HASSLER, T. J. 1970, South Dakota

HAZZARD, A. S. 1935, Utah

HEARD, W. R., R. L. WALLACE and W. L. HARTMAN 1969, Alaska

HEESE, L. W. and B. A. NEWCOMB 1982, Nebraska

HELLAWELL, J. 1966, England

HELMS, D. 1976, Iowa

HELMS, D. R. 1966, Iowa

HELMS, D. R. 1975, Iowa

HESS, L. 1980a, West Virginia H

HESS, L. 1980b, West Virginia

HESS, L. and C. HEARTWELL 1977, West Virginia H

HICKS, D. E., K. COOK and P. MAUCK 1970, Oklahoma

HILL, K. 1974, Iowa

HILL, W. J. and A. H. WIPPERMAN 1978, Montana

HOLCIK, J. 1970, Czechoslovakia

HOLCIK, J. 1977, Czechoslovakia

HOLCIK, J. and I. BASTL 1973, Czechoslovakia

HOLCIK, J. and K. PIVNICKA 1972, Czechoslovakia

HURLEY, D. A. and W. J. CHRISTIE 1977, Great Lakes

INSKIP, P. D. and J. J. MAGNUSON 1983, Wisconsin

JENKINS, R. M. 1968

JENKINS, R. M. 1982

JESSOP, C. S., T. R. PORTER, M. BLOUW and R. SOPUCK 1973, Northwest Territories

JOHNSON, F. H. and A. R. PETERSON 1955, Minnesota

JOHNSON, L. 1966c, England
JOHNSON, L. 1973, Northwest Territories
JOHNSON, L. 1981
JOHNSON, L. D. 1981, Wisconsin
JOHNSON, R. E. 1949
JUNE, F. C. 1976, South Dakota
KEAST, A. 1970, Ontario
KEAST, A. 1978, Ontario
KEMPINGER, J. J. and R. F. CARLINE 1977, Wisconsin
KEMPINGER, J. J. and R. F. CARLINE 1978a, Wisconsin
KEMPINGER, J. J. and R. F. CARLINE 1978b, Wisconsin
KEMPINGER, J. J. and W. S. CHURCHILL 1970, Wisconsin
KEPLER, P. 1973, Alaska
KIPLING, C. 1976, England
KIPLING, C. 1983b, England
KIPLING, C. and W. E. FROST 1969, England
KIPLING, C. and W. E. FROST 1970, England
KIPLING, C. and E. D. LE CREN 1975, England
KULEMIN, A. A., I. I. MAKKOVEYEVE and M. I. SOLOPOVA 1971, USSR
LARSEN, K. 1961, Denmark
LATTA, W. C. 1971, Michigan
LATTA, W. C. 1972, Michigan
LAWLER, G. H. n.d., Manitoba
LE CREN, E. D., C. KIPLING and J. C. MCCORMACK 1971, England
LE CREN, E. D., C. KIPLING and J. C. MCCORMACK 1972, England
LE CREN, E. D., C. KIPLING and J. C. MCCORMACK 1977, England
LEOPOLD, M. and B. DABROWSKI 1975, Poland
LEOPOLD, M., T. KORULCZYK, W. NOWAK and L. SWIERZOWSKA 1975a, Poland
LEOPOLD, M., T. KORULCZYK, W. NOWAK and L. SWIERZOWSKA 1975b, Poland
LEOPOLD, M., T. KORULCZYK, L. SWIERZOWSKA and W. NOWAK 1975a, Poland
LEOPOLD, M., T. KORULCZYK, L. SWIERZOWSKA and W. NOWAK 1975b, Poland
LEROUX, D. 1984, Manitoba

LIND, E. A. and E. KAUKORANTA 1975b, Finland
LUSK, S. 1981, Czechoslovakia
MACDONALD, P. D. M. and PITCHER, T. J. 1979, Ontario
MALLEY, M. W. and S. M. BROWN 1983, Ireland
MANN, R. H. K. 1971b, England
MANN, R. H. K. 1975a, England
MANN, R. H. K. 1975b, England
MANN, R. H. K. 1980, England
MANN, R. H. K. and T. PENCZAK 1984, Poland
MCCARRAHER, B. 1960, Nebraska H
MCCORMACK, J. C. 1970, England
MISIK, V. 1964, Czechoslovakia
MONGEAU, J.-R. 1976, Quebec
MONTEN, E. 1949
MORGAN, N. C. 1972
MORIN, R., J. DODSON and G. POWER 1980, Quebec
MORRISON, B. 1976
MOULTON, J. C. 1978, Connecticut
MOYLE, J. B. 1949a, Minnesota
MOYLE, J. B., J. H. KUEHN and C. R. BURROWS 1948, Minnesota
NIKOLSKII, G. V. 1969, USSR
NOWAK, W. 1971, Poland
O'GRADY, M. F. 1983, Ireland
OLIVA, O. 1960, Czechoslovakia
OTTO, C. 1979, Sweden
PAGEAU, G., Y. GRAVEL and L. LEVESQUE 1971, Quebec
PALOHEIMO, J. E. 1958
PARAGAMIAN, V. L. 1976, Wisconsin
PENCZAK, T. 1981, Poland
PENCZAK, T., M. ZALEWSKI and M. MOLINSKI 1976, Poland
PETERSON, J., M. TAYLOR and A. HANSON 1980, Nebraska
PLISZKA, F. R. 1954, Poland
PODDUBNY, A. G. 1976
QADRI, S. U. and P. J. RUBEC 1977, Ontario
RAGAN, J. E. 1975, North Dakota
RAWSON, D. S. 1947c, Northwest Territories
RAWSON, D. S. 1960a, Saskatchewan
REED, E. B. 1962, Saskatchewan
REGIER, H. A., Great Lakes
RICKER, W. E. 1975
RICKER, W. E., ed. 1968
RIDENHOUR, R. L. 1960, Iowa

RUDENKO, G. P. 1971, USSR
RUDENKO, G. P. and Y. P. VOLKOV 1974,
   USSR
RUNDBERG, H. 1977, Sweden
RUTLEDGE, W. P. and S. G. CLARKE
   1971, Texas
RYDER, R. A. and S. R. KERR 1978, Ontario
RYDER, R. A., S. R. KERR, K. H. LOFTUS
   and H. A. REGIER 1974,
   Ontario
SCHMIDTT, H. 1980, Germany
SCHNEiDER, J. C. 1971, Michigan
SCHUPP, D. H. 1974, Minnesota
SCIDMORE, W. J. 1955, Minnesota
SEDLAR, J. 1969, Czechoslovakia
SHAFI, M. 1969, Scotland
SHAFI, M. 1974, England
SHARONOV, I. V. 1961, USSR
SJOBERG, G. 1983, Sweden
SMITH, L. L., D. R. FRANKLIN and R. H.
   KRAMER 1958, Minnesota
SNOW, H. E. 1961, Wisconsin
SNOW, H. E. 1967c, Wisconsin
SNOW, H. E. 1978a, Wisconsin
SNOW, H. E. 1978b, Wisconsin
SNOW, H. E. and T. D. BEARD 1972,
   Wisconsin
SNOW, H. E. n.d., Wisconsin
SOUCHON, Y. 1980, France
STENSON, J. A. E. 1982
SULLIVAN, M. G. 1985, Alberta
SVARDSON, G. 1976, Sweden
SZCZERBOWSKI, J. A. 1969, Poland
SZMANIA, D. 1973, Wisconsin
TEODORESCU-LEONTE, R. 1969,
   USSR
THREINEN, C. W. 1969, Wisconsin
TONN, W. M. and J. J. MAGNUSON 1982,
   Wisconsin
TOWNSEND, A. H. and P. P. KEPLER 1974,
   Alaska
TURNER, L. J. and W. C. MACKAY 1985
VASHCHENKO, D. M. 1958a, USSR
VILHANEN, M., H. KOKKO and V.-M.
   KAIJOMAA 1982, Finland
VOSTRADOVSKY, J. 1969b, Czechoslo-
   vakia
VOSTRADOVSKY, J. 1983, Czechoslovakia
VOSTRADOVSKY, J. and M. VOSTRA-
   DOVSKA 1973, Czechoslovakia
WEITHMAN, A. S. 1975, Missouri H
WEITHMAN, A. S. and R. O. ANDERSON
   1977, Missouri H

WERNER, R. G. and N. H. RINGLER 1980,
   New York
WILLIAMS, J. E. 1959b, Michigan
WILLIAMS, J. E. 1960a, Michigan
WILLIAMS, J. E. 1961c, Michigan
WILLIS, D. W., J. E. SMELTZER and S. A.
   FLICKINGER 1984, Kansas
WOHLSCHLAG, D. E. 1953, Alaska
WORTHINGTON, E. B. 1949, England

PREDATOR-PREY RELATIONSHIPS

ANDERSON, R. O. and A. S. WEITHMAN
   1978
ANDORFER, B. 1980
ANDREEV, V. L. 1968
ANTOSIAK, B. 1958, Poland
ANTOSIAK, B. 1963, Poland
ARRIGNON, J. 1966, France
BAGENAL, T. B. 1977, England
BAJKOV, A. D. and A. H. SHORTT 1939,
   Manitoba
BAKSHTANSKII, E. L. and V. D.
   NESTEROV 1976
BEARD, T. D. 1971, Wisconsin
BERNARD, H. 1934, Quebec
BEYERLE, G. B. 1970a, Michigan
BEYERLE, G. B. 1971a, Michigan
BEYERLE, G. B. 1971b, Michigan
BEYERLE, G. B. and J. E. WILLIAMS 1965,
   Michigan
BEYERLE, G. B. and J. E. WILLIAMS 1968,
   Mighican
BIALOKOZ, W. and T. KRZYWOSZ 1976a,
   Poland
BIALOKOZ, W. and T. KRZYWOSZ 1979,
   Poland
BLAXTER, J. H. S. 1986
BRY, C. and C. GILLET 1980a, France
BRY, C. and C. GILLET 1980b, France
BRYNILDSON, C., D. B. IVES and H. S.
   DRUCKENMILLER 1970, Wisconsin
CARLANDER, K. D. 1957, Iowa
CHAPMAN, C. A. and W. C. MACKAY
   1984a, Alberta
CHAPMAN, C. A. and W. C. MACKAY
   1984b, Alberta
CHRISTIANSEN, D. G. 1976, Northwest
   Territories
COBLE, D. 1973, Wisconsin
CROSSMAN, E. J. 1962b, Ontario
DOBBEN, W. H. VAN 1952, Netherlands

DOBIE, J. n.d., Minnesota
DOBLER, E. 1977, Germany
DOMANEVSKII, L. N. 1962, USSR
DOORNBOS, G. 1979, Netherlands
DOXTATER, G. 1967, Indiana
DUNSTAN, T. C. and J. F. HARPER 1975, Minnesota
ERLINGE, S. 1968, Sweden
ERLINGE, S. 1969, Sweden
FORTUNATOVA, K. R. 1955, USSR
FORTUNATOVA, K. R. and O. A. POPOVA 1973, USSR
FOWLER, H. W. 1913
FROST, W. E. 1954, England
FROST, W. E. 1963, England
GILES, N. 1984
GILLEN, A. L., R. A. STEIN and R. F. CARLINE 1981, Ohio H
GREEN, R. 1976, Scotland
GRIMM, M. P. 1981a, Netherlands
GRIMM, M. P. 1981b, Netherlands
GRIMM, M. P. 1983a, Netherlands
GULISH, W. J. 1970, Indiana
HAKKINEN, I. 1978, Finland
HALLET, C. 1977, Belgium
HARRINGTON, R. W., Jr. 1947, New Hampshire
HARRIS, A. J. 1980, England
HART, P. J. B. and B. CONNELLAN 1979, England
HART, P. J. B. and B. CONNELLAN 1984, England
HOOGLAND, R., D. MORRIS and N. TINBERGEN 1957
HOROSZEWICZ, L. 1964, Poland
HUBLEY, R. C., Jr. 1961, Wisconsin
HUNTER, M. 1907, Quebec
HUNTINGFORD, F. A. 1976
HUNTINGFORD, F. A. 1982
HURLEY, D. A. and W. J. CHRISTIE 1977, Great Lakes
IVANOVA, M. N. 1959, USSR
IVANOVA, M. N. 1963, USSR
IVANOVA, M. N. 1968, USSR
IVANOVA, M. N. 1969, USSR
IVANOVA, M. N. 1970, USSR
IVANOVA, M. N. and A. N. LOPATKO 1979, USSR
JACOBSSON, S. and T. JARVI 1976
KASHIN, S. M., L. K. MALININ, G. N. ORLOVSKY and A. G. PODDUBNY 1977, USSR
KEAST, A. 1979, Ontario

KENNEDY, W. A. and W. M. SPRULES 1967
KIPLING, C. and W. E. FROST 1972, England
KOIVUSAARI, J. 1976, Finland
KOLI, L. and M. SOIKKELI 1974, Finland
KUSHNARENKO, A. I. 1978, USSR
LAGLER, K. F. 1956, Michigan
LAWLER, G. H. 1965, Manitoba
LEBEDEVA, N. E. and Y. L. CHERNYAKOV 1978, USSR
LEEUWEN, J. L. VAN and M. MULLER 1983, Netherlands
LEMMETYINEN, R. and J. MANKKI 1975, Finland
MACLEAN, J. and J. J. MAGNUSON 1977
MAITLAND, P. S. 1969, Scotland
MANN, R. H. K. 1982, England
MANN, R. H. K. 1985, England
MANN, R. H. K. and W. R. C. BEAUMONT 1980, England
MANTEIFEL, B. P., I. I. GIRSA, T. S. LESHCHEVA and D. S. PAVLOV 1965, USSR
MANTEIFEL, B. P., ed. 1965
MAUCK, W. L. 1970, Missouri
MAUCK, W. L. and D. W. COBLE 1971, Missouri
MCKNIGHT, T. C. and S. L. SERNS 1974, Wisconsin
NEILL, S. R. ST J. and J. M. CULLEN 1974
NURSALL, J. R. 1973, Alberta
NURSALL, J. R. and M. E. PINSENT 1969, Alberta
OMAROV, O. P. and O. A. POPOVA 1985, USSR
ORLOVA, E. L. 1976, USSR
ORLOVA, E. L. and O. A. POPOVA 1976, USSR
PECK, J. W. 1974, Great Lakes
PENA, J. C., F. J. PURROY and J. DOMINGUEZ n.d., Spain
PENCZAK, T. 1966, Poland
PENCZAK, T. 1970, Poland
PHILLIPS, G. R. and R. W. GREGORY 1979, Montana
PITMAN, C. R. S. 1961, Canada
PLATONOVA, O. P. 1966, USSR
POPOVA, O. A. 1961, USSR
POPOVA, O. A. 1967, USSR
POWELL, T. G. 1973, Colorado
PRITCHARD, D. L., O. D. MAY and L. RIDER 1976

RAWSON, D. S. 1948, Manitoba
REIST, J. C. 1978, Alberta
REIST, J. D. 1980, Alberta
REIST, J. D. 1983b, Alberta, Saskatchewan
RIZVANOV, R. A. 1971, USSR
SALYER, J. C., II and K. F. LAGLER 1949,
    Michigan
SAMOKHVALOVA, L. K. 1976, USSR
SCHUMANN, G. O. 1963
SNOW, H. E. 1974, Wisconsin
SOLMAN, V. E. F. 1945, Manitoba
STEIN, R. A., R. F. CARLINE and R. S.
    HAYWARD 1981, H
STIRLING, A. B. 1863
SUMARI, O. 1971, Finland
SWEETING, R. A. 1977, England
SZCZERBOWSKI, J. A. 1963, Poland
TOMCKO, C. M. 1982, Ohio H
TOMCKO, C. M., R. A. STEIN and R. F.
    CARLINE 1984, Ohio H
TONER, E. D. 1959a, Ireland
TONER, E. D. 1959b, Ireland
TURNER, L. J. 1984, Alberta
VASHCHENKO, D. M. 1958b, USSR
VASHCHENKO, D. M. 1958c, USSR
VASHCHENKO, D. M. 1962a, USSR
VASHCHENKO, D. M. 1962b, USSR
VERHEIJEN, F. J. 1963
VERHEIJEN, F. J. and H. J. REUTER 1969
WAGNER, W. C. 1972, Great Lakes
WEBB, P. W. 1978b, Michigan H
WEBB, P. W. 1980, Michigan H
WEBB, P. W. 1982, Michigan H
WEBB, P. W. 1984a, Michigan H
WEBB, P. W. 1984b, Michigan H
WEBB, P. W. and J. M. SKADSEN 1980,
    Michigan H
WEITHMAN, A. S. and R. O. ANDERSON
    1977, Missouri H
WILLIAMS, J. E. 1965b, Michigan
WILLIAMS, J. E. 1966b, Michigan
WRZESZCZ, J. 1960, Poland
WYDOSKI, R. S. and D. H. BENNETT 1981,
    USA
ZADUL'SKAYA, E. A. 1960, USSR
ZALACHOWSKI, W. 1965b, Poland
ZAMOJSKA, B. 1967, Poland
ZUBENKO 1975, USSR

PROJECT REPORTS
ALT, K. T. 1968, Alaska
ALT, K. T. 1969, Alaska

ANONYMOUS 1966, Wisconsin
ANONYMOUS 1975a, Oklahoma
ANONYMOUS n.d.a
ANONYMOUS n.d.e, Ohio
BEARD, T. D. 1971, Wisconsin
BEARD, T. D. and H. E. SNOW 1970,
    Wisconsin
BEYERLE, G. B. 1970b, Michigan
BEYERLE, G. B. 1971b, Michigan
BEYERLE, G. B. 1971c, Michigan
BEYERLE, G. B. 1971d, Michigan
BEYERLE, G. B. 1973a, Michigan
BEYERLE, G. B. 1973b, Michigan H
BEYERLE, G. B. 1975, Michigan
BOUSSU, M. F. 1954, South Dakota
BOUSSU, M. F. 1959a, South Dakota
BOUSSU, M. F. 1959b, South Dakota
BOUSSU, M. F. 1959c, South Dakota
BOUSSU, M. F. 1961, South Dakota
BUCK, O. D. and J. L. CRITES 1975, Great
    Lakes
CARLINE, R. F. 1979, Ohio
CHRISTENSEN, K. E. 1959, Michigan
CHRISTENSEN, K. E. 1960a, Michigan
CHRISTENSEN, K. E. 1960b
CHRISTENSEN, K. E. 1961a, Michigan
CHRISTENSEN, K. E. 1961b, Michigan
CHRISTENSEN, K. E. 1961c, Michigan
CHRISTENSEN, K. E. 1962a, Michigan
CHRISTENSEN, K. E. 1962b, Michigan
CHRISTENSEN, K. E. 1962c, Michigan
CHURCHILL, W. S. 1961, Wisconsin
CHURCHILL, W. S. 1962, Wisconsin
CLARK, J. (2) 1972a, Colorado
CLARK, J. (2) 1972b, Colorado
COLE, W. D. 1967, Kansas
COLORADO DIVISION OF WILDLIFE
    1974, Colorado
COOK, K. D. 1978, Oklahoma
CRABTREE, J. E. 1969, Texas
DEAN, B. C. 1957, Michigan
DIANGELO, S. 1960, Michigan
DIANGELO, S. 1962, Michigan
DUERRE, D. C. 1966a, North Dakota
DUERRE, D. C. 1966b, North Dakota
DUNST, R. 1966, Wisconsin
FAGO, D. 1971a, Wisconsin
FAGO, D. 1971b, Wisconsin
FINNELL, L. 1984, Colorado
FINNELL, L. 1985, Colorado
FINNELL, L. M. 1983, Colorado
FOGLE, N. E. 1961, South Dakota
FOGLE, N. E. 1963a, South Dakota

FOGLE, N. E. 1963b, South Dakota
FOGLE, N. E. 1965, South Dakota
GREEN, D. M., Jr. 1978, New York
GREGORY, R. W. and T. G. POWELL 1969, Colorado
HALNON, L. 1960, Vermont
HALNON, L. C. 1959, Vermont
HEADRICK, M. R., M. S. BEVELHIMER, R. F. CARLINE and R. A. STEIN 1981, Ohio
HEADRICK, M. R. and R. F. CARLINE 1980, Ohio
HEARTWELL, C. and L. HESS 1977, West Virginia H
HENEGAR, D. 1969, North Dakota
HESS, L. 1980a, West Virginia H
HESS, L. 1980b, West Virginia
HESS, L. 1980c, West Virginia
HICKS, D. 1972a, Oklahoma
HICKS, D. 1972b, Oklahoma
HICKS, D. 1972c, Oklahoma
HICKS, D. E., K. COOK and P. MAUCK 1970, Oklahoma
HILL, W. J. 1969, North Dakota
JOHNSON, L. D. 1961a, Wisconsin
JOHNSON, L. D. 1961b, Wisconsin
JOHNSON, L. D. 1962a, Wisconsin
JOHNSON, L. D. 1962b, Wisconsin
JOHNSON, L. D. 1962c, Wisconsin
JOHNSON, L. D. 1965, Wisconsin
JOHNSON, L. D. 1971, Wisconsin
JOHNSON, L. D. n.d., Wisconsin
KEMPINGER, J. J. 1966a, Wisconsin
KEMPINGER, J. J. 1966b, Wisconsin
KEMPINGER, J. J. 1967a, Wisconsin
KEMPINGER, J. J. 1967b, Wisconsin
KEMPINGER, J. J. 1972, Wisconsin
KEMPINGER, J. J. and W. S. CHURCHILL 1970, Wisconsin
KEMPINGER, J. J., W. S. CHURCHILL, G. R. PRIEGEL and L. M. CHRISTENSON 1975, Wisconsin
KLEINERT, S. J. 1967a, Wisconsin
KLEINERT, S. J. 1967b, Wisconsin
KLEINERT, S. J. and D. F. MRAZ 1965a, Wisconsin
KLEINERT, S. J. and D. F. MRAZ 1965b, Wisconsin
KLEINERT, S. J. and D. F. MRAZ 1965c, Wisconsin
KLEINERT, S. J. and D. F. MRAZ 1965d, Wisconsin

KLEINERT, S. J. and D. F. MRAZ 1965e, Wisconsin
KROHN, D. C. 1968a, Wisconsin
KROHN, D. C. 1968b, Wisconsin
LAARMAN, P. W. 1964a, Michigan
LEWIS, S. A. 1975, Oklahoma
MITZNER, L. 1971, Iowa
MOULTON, J. C. 1978, Connecticut
MRAZ, D. F. 1961, Wisconsin
MRAZ, D. F. 1962a, Wisconsin
MRAZ, D. F. 1962b, Wisconsin
MRAZ, D. F. 1963, Wisconsin
NEWBURG, H. 1973, Minnesota
PATRIARCHE, M. H. 1963, Michigan
PATRIARCHE, M. H. 1966, Michigan
PATRIARCHE, M. H. 1968, Michigan
PATRIARCHE, M. H. 1971, Michigan
PATRIARCHE, M. H. and H. GOWING 1961, Michigan
PATRIARCHE, M. H. and H. GOWING 1962a, Michigan
PATRIARCHE, M. H. and H. GOWING 1962b, Michigan
PATTERSON, R. R. 1971, New Mexico
PETERS, J. C., ed. 1964, Montana
PHILLIPS, C. L. 1971, Rhode Island
PHILLIPS, C. L. 1972, Rhode Island
PHILLIPS, C. L. 1980, Connecticut
PRIEGEL, G. R. 1965, Wisconsin
PRIEGEL, G. R. 1967, Wisconsin
PRIEGEL, G. R. 1969, Wisconsin
PRIEGEL, G. R. and D. C. KROHN 1971, Wisconsin
RAGAN, J. E. 1970, North Dakota
RAGAN, J. E. 1975, North Dakota
RUTLEDGE, W. P. and S. G. CLARKE 1971, Texas
RUTLEDGE, W. P. and J. A. PRENTICE 1973, Texas
SCHRYER, F. and W. D. COLE 1966, Kansas
SCHRYER, F. and V. EBERT 1968, Kansas
SCHRYER, F., V. W. EBERT and L. DOWLIN 1971, Kansas
SHIELDS, J. T. 1956, South Dakota
SHIELDS, J. T. 1957, South Dakota
SMITH, L. L., D. R. FRANKLIN and R. H. KRAMER 1958, Minnesota
SNOW, H. E. 1967a, Wisconsin
SNOW, H. E. 1967b, Wisconsin
SNOW, H. E. 1967c, Wisconsin
SNOW, H. E. 1969b, Wisconsin
SPRAGUE, J. W. 1961, South Dakota

STEIN, H. and H. ENZLER 1983, Germany
VASEY, F. W. 1968, Missouri
VASEY, F. W. 1974, Missouri
WHITNEY, A. N. 1953, Montana
WICKLUND, R. B. and S. DIANGELO
    1959, Michigan
WILLIAMS, J. E. 1959a, Michigan
WILLIAMS, J. E. 1959b, Michigan
WILLIAMS, J. E. 1959c, Michigan
WILLIAMS, J. E. 1960a, Michigan
WILLIAMS, J. E. 1960b, Michigan
WILLIAMS, J. E. 1960c, Michigan
WILLIAMS, J. E. 1961a, Michigan
WILLIAMS, J. E. 1961b, Michigan
WILLIAMS, J. E. 1961c, Michigan
WILLIAMS, J. E. 1961d, Michigan
WILLIAMS, J. E. 1962a, Michigan
WILLIAMS, J. E. 1962b, Michigan
WILLIAMS, J. E. 1962c, Michigan
WILLIAMS, J. E. 1963a, Michigan
WILLIAMS, J. E. 1963b, Michigan
WILLIAMS, J. E. 1963c, Michigan
WILLIAMS, J. E. 1965a, Michigan
WILLIAMS, J. E. 1965b, Michigan
WILLIAMS, J. E. 1965c, Michigan
WILLIAMS, J. E. 1966a, Michigan
WILLIAMS, J. E. 1966b, Michigan
WILLIAMS, J. E. 1966c, Michigan
WILLIAMS, J. E. 1967, Michigan
WILLIAMS, J. E. 1968, Michigan

REPRODUCTION
ADOLFSON, I. 1949, Sweden
ARGILLANDER, A. 1753
AUTKO, B. F. 1964, USSR
BAGENAL, T. B. 1967a, England
BAGENAL, T. B. 1971, England
BANENENE, Y. K. 1978, USSR
BANIONIENE, J. 1979, USSR
BEAULIEU, G. 1961, Quebec
BIALOKOZ, W. 1974, Poland
BILLARD, R. 1978, France
BILLARD, R. 1982, France
BILLARD, R. and B. BRETON 1976, France
BILLARD, R., W. C. MACKAY, and J.
    MARCEL 1983, Alberta
BILLARD, R., J. MARCEL and G. DE
    MONTALEMBERT 1983, France
BILLARD, R., ed. 1983a, France
BLACKMAN, B. G. n.d., Great Lakes
BOGOSLOVSKAIA, E. I. 1960, USSR

BRY, C., R. BILLARD and G. DE MON-
    TALEMBERT, 1978, France
BULGAKOVA, E. I. 1965, USSR
BUTLER, G. E. 1949, Manitoba
CARBINE, W. F. 1944, Michigan
CASSELMAN, J. M. 1969, Ontario
CASSELMAN, J. M. 1973, Ontario
CASSELMAN, J. M. 1974a, Ontario
CASSELMAN, J. M. 1975, Ontario
CHABAN, R. 1973, Morocco
COURTEMANCHE, A. 1954, Quebec
CRAIG, J. F. and C. KIPLING 1983, England
DABROWSKI, T. and M. SALACKI 1964,
    Poland
DABROWSKI, T. and M. SALACKI 1965,
    Poland
DAHL, J. 1961
DANILENKO, T. P. 1983, USSR
DE MONTALEMBERT, G., C. BRY and R.
    BILLARD 1978
DE MONTALEMBERT, G., B. JALABERT
    and C. BRY 1978
DE MONTALEMBERT, G., J. MARCEL and
    R. BILLARD 1980
DIANA, J. S. 1983b, Michigan
DONALDSON, E. M. 1977
DUMONT, P., R. FORTIN and H. FOUR-
    NIER 1979, Quebec
DUPLINSKY, P. D. 1982, Rhode Island
DURAND, J.-P. and J.-M. GAS 1976,
    France
EKSTROM, V. C. 1835
EPLER, P. and K. BIENIARZ 1978
GAJDUSEK, J. and V. RUBCOV 1983
GOEDMAKERS, A. and B. L. VERBOOM
    1974
GOTTWALD, S. and A. WINNICKI 1966,
    Poland
HICKS, D. 1972c, Oklahoma
HOCHMAN, L. 1964
IGNAT'EVA, G. M. 1974a
JALABERT, B. 1976, France
JALABERT, B. and B. BRETON 1974,
    France
JUNE, F. C. 1970, South Dakota
JUNE, F. C. 1971, South Dakota
JUNE, F. C. 1977, South Dakota
KIPLING, C. and W. E. FROST 1969, Eng-
    land
KLEINERT, S. J. 1967a, Wisconsin
KMIOTECK, S. and J. M. HELM 1961,
    Wisconsin
KONONOV, V. A. 1957, USSR

KORWIN-KOSSAKOWSKI, M. 1976,
  Poland
KOTLYAREVSKAYA, N. V. 1966, USSR
KOURIL, J. 1975, Czechoslovakia
KOURIL, J. and J. HAMACKOVA 1975,
  Czechoslovakia
KOURIL, J. and J. HAMACKOVA 1977,
  Czechoslovakia
KOURIL, J., J. HAMACKOVA and Z. SVO-
  BODOVA 1976, Czechoslovakia
KROHN, D. C. 1968b, Wisconsin
KULIKOV, N. V., V. G. KULIKOVA and S.
  A. LYUBIMOVA 1971, USSR
LAFRANCE, J.-M. 1974, Quebec
LETICHEVSKY, M. A. 1946, USSR
LILLELUND, K. 1967, West Germany
LINHART, O. 1984a, Czechoslovakia
LINHART, O. 1984b, Czechoslovakia
LOFTS, B. and A. J. MARSHALL 1957
MACHNIAK, K. 1975
MANN, R. H. K. 1976, England
MARCEL, J., G. DE MONTALEMBERT and
  R. BILLARD 1980, France
MOCZARSKI, K. M. and I. KOSCIUSZKI
  1983, Poland
MUNTYAN, S. P. 1978, USSR
PONEDELKO, B. I. 1957, USSR
POTOPOVA, O. I. 1966, USSR
POUVREAU, M. 1980, France
POUVREAU, M., G. MAISSE, B. JALA-
  BERT and B. BRETON 1983, France
QUILLIER, R. and R. LABAT 1977,
  France
RIEHL, R. and E. SCHULTE 1977, West
  Germany
SAZONOVA, Y. A. 1979, USSR
SCHOOTS, A. F. M., R. J. G. OPSTELTEN
  and J. M. DENUCE 1982, Netherlands
SCHOOTS, A. F. M., J. J. M. STIKKEL-
  BROECK, J. F. BEKHUIS and J.
  MANUEL DENUCE 1982, Netherlands
SENTEIN, P. and P. REBOULIN 1969
SHIKHSHABEKOV, M. M. 1978, USSR
SHILIN, Y. A. 1972, USSR
SIMONTACCHI, C., C. BOITI, N.
  BONALDO, P. COLOMBO
  BELEVEDERE and L. COLOMBO 1983,
  Italy
SIMONTACCHI, C., D. CASCIOTTI and C.
  BOITI 1982, Italy
SIMONTACCHI, C., D. CASCIOTTI, M.
  SILVESTRELLI and C. BOITI 1981, Italy
SOLONINOVA, L. N. 1975, USSR

SOUCHON, Y. 1979, France
SOUCHON, Y. 1983, France
SPANOVSKAYA, V. D. and L. M. SOLONI-
  NOVA 1983a, USSR
SPANOVSKAYA, V. D. and L. N. SOLONI-
  NOVA 1983b, USSR
STEIN, H. and H. BAYRLE 1978
SUKHANOVA, G. I. 1979, USSR
SVARDSON, G. 1945, Sweden
SVARDSON, G. 1949b, Sweden
SWIFT, D. R. 1965, England
TERLECKI, J. 1973, Poland
TROCHERIE, F. and B. MIGEON 1984,
  France
TRUMAN, E. B. 1869
VESSEL, M. F. and S. EDDY 1941, Min-
  nesota
ZAITZEV, A. V. 1955a, USSR
ZARYANOVA, Y. B. 1962, USSR

SAMPLING TECHNIQUES
BAGENAL, T. B. 1972, England
BAGENAL, T. B. 1979
BEAMISH, R. J. 1973, Ontario
BEUKEMA, J. J. 1970
BODROVA, N. V. and B. V. KRAIUKHIN
  1959, USSR
BODROVA, N. V. and B. V. KRAIUKHIN
  1960a, USSR
BODROVA, N. V. and B. V. KRAIUKHIN
  1960b, USSR
BODROVA, N. V. and B. V. KRAIUKHIN
  1961a, USSR
BODROVA, N. V. and B. V. KRAIUKHIN
  1961b, USSR
BODROVA, N. V. and B. V. KRAIUKHIN
  1963, USSR
BROUGHTON, N. M. and K. A. M. FISHER
  1981, England
CARBINE, W. F. and D. S. SHETTER 1944,
  Michigan
CASSELMAN, J. M. 1978b, Ontario
CASSELMAN, J. M. and H. H. HARVEY
  1973, Ontario
DERKSEN, A. J. 1978, Manitoba
ELLIS, J. E. and E. N. PICKERING 1973,
  Great Lakes
JESTER, D. B. 1977, New Mexico
KIPLING, C. 1975, England
LARSEN, K. 1961, Denmark
LAWLER, G. H. 1950, Manitoba
LAWLER, G. H. 1963, Manitoba

LE CREN, E. D., T. B. BAGENAL and C. KIPLING 1975, England

LEOPOLD, M., T. KORULCZYK, W. NOWAK and L. SWIERZOWSKA 1975a, Poland

LEOPOLD, M., T. KORULCZYK, W. NOWAK and L. SWIERZOWSKA 1975b, Poland

LEOPOLD, M., T. KORULCZYK, L. SWIERZOWSKA and W. NOWAK 1975a, Poland

LEOPOLD, M., T. KORULCZYK, L. SWIERZOWSKA and W. NOWAK 1975b, Poland

MANN, R. H. K. and T. PENCZAK 1984, Poland

MOYLE, J. B. 1949b, Minnesota

MOYLE, J. B., J. H. KUEHN and C. R. BURROWS 1948, Minnesota

MOYLE, J. B. and R. LOUND 1960, Minnesota

NEWBURG, H. 1973, Minnesota

OIKARI, A. and A. SOIVIO 1975, Finland

WHITNEY, A. N. 1953, Montana

WILLIAMS, J. E. 1959a, Michigan

WILLIAMS, J. E. 1961a, Michigan

WILLIAMS, J. E. 1962b, Michigan

SPAWNING

ALLDRIDGE, N. A. and A. M. WHITE 1980, New York

ALLEN, A. A. 1913, New York

AUTKO, B. F. 1964, USSR

BENSON, N. G. 1980, Montana

BERNATOWICZ, S. 1955, Poland

BERNATOWICZ, S. 1962, Poland

BOLOTOVA, T. G., and A. N. BURLAKOVA, 1975, USSR

BOUSSU, M. F. 1959a, South Dakota

BOUSSU, M. F. 1959b, South Dakota

BOUSSU, M. F. 1959c, South Dakota

BOUSSU, M. F. 1961, South Dakota

BREDER, C. M., Jr. and D. E. ROSEN 1966

BROOK, G. 1887, Scotland

BRUENKO, V. P. 1976, USSR

BRUYENKO, V. P. 1976, USSR

BYKOV, N. E. 1974, USSR

CAHN, A. R. 1927, Wisconsin

CASSELMAN, J. M. 1969, Ontario

CASSELMAN, J. M. 1973, Ontario

CLARK, C. F. 1950, Ohio

COLE, W. D. 1967, Kansas

CORNELL, J. H. 1968

DES CLERS, S. and J. ALLARDI 1983, France

ENDRES, A. 1969, France

FABRICIUS, E. 1950, Sweden

FABRICIUS, E. and K.-J. GUSTAFSON 1958, Sweden

FAGO, D. 1973, Wisconsin

FORTIN, R., P. DUMONT and H. FOURNIER 1983, Quebec

FORTIN, R., P. DUMONT, H. FOURNIER, C. CADIEUX and D. VILLENEUVE 1982, Quebec

GRAVEL, Y. and J. DUBE 1979, Quebec

GRAVEL, Y. and J. DUBE 1980, Quebec

HAMES, R. 1970, Connecticut

JARVENPA, O. 1962, Minnesota

JARVENPA, O. M. 1963, Minnesota

JOHNSON, F. H. 1957, Minnesota

JUNE, F. C. 1977, South Dakota

KENNEDY, M. 1965, Ireland

KENNEDY, M. 1969, Ireland

KLEINERT, S. J. and D. F. MRAZ 1965e, Wisconsin

KORZYNEK, W. 1956, Poland

LAFRANCE, J.-M. 1975, Quebec

LAFRANCE, J.-M. 1976, Quebec

LEPAN, S. R. 1985, New York

MAKHOTIN, Y. M. 1977, USSR

MAREAN, J. B. 1976, Great Lakes

MCCARRAHER, D. B. and R. E. THOMAS 1972, Nebraska

MCNAMARA, F. 1937, Michigan

MISSISSIPPI RIVER WORK UNIT 1978, Wisconsin

MONTEN, E. 1949

NEBOL'SINA, T. K. 1956, USSR

NELSON, W. R. 1978, South Dakota

NETH, P. C. 1978, New York

OSBORN, T. C., D. B. ERNST and D. H. SCHUPP 1981, Minnesota

PLISZKA, F. R. 1954, Poland

POTOPOVA, O. I. 1966, USSR

PRIEGEL, G. R. and D. C. KROHN 1971, Wisconsin

PRIEGEL, G. R. and D. C. KROHN 1973, Wisconsin

ROBERTSON, M. R. 1969, Alberta

SCHRYER, F. and W. D. COLE 1966, Kansas

SCHRYER, F. and V. EBERT 1968, Kansas

SCHRYER, F., V. W. EBERT and L. DOWLIN 1971, Kansas

SCHULTZ, F. H. 1955, Saskatchewan
STRZYZEWSKA, K. 1957, Poland
SUKHANOVA, G. I. 1979, USSR
SVARDSON, G. 1949a, Sweden
THREINEN, C. W. , Wisconsin
WILKONSKA, H. and H. ZUROMSKA
  1967, Poland
WILLEMSEN, J. 1979, Netherlands
WILLIAMSON, L. O. 1942, Wisconsin
ZUROMSKA, H. and W. KORZYNEK 1958,
  Poland

TAXONOMY, NOMENCLATURE, AND SYSTEMATICS

AGASSIZ, L. 1842
ANONYMOUS 1946, Ontario
AYRES, W. O. 1849
BAILEY, R. M., J. E. FITCH, E. S.
  HERALD, E. A. LACHNER, C. C.
  LINDSEY, C. R. ROBINS, and W. B.
  SCOTT 1970, Canada, USA
BAJKOV, A. 1927, Alberta
BERG, L. S. 1947, USSR
BERKES, F. and M. MACKENZIE 1978,
  Quebec
BILLINGS, E. 1857, Canada
BRACKEN, J. J. and M. P. KENNEDY 1967,
  Ireland
CASSELMAN, J. M., E. J. CROSSMAN,
  P. E. IHSSEN, J. D. REIST and H. E.
  BOOKE 1986, Ontario H
CAVENDER, T. 1969, Oregon
CHICIAK, M. 1947, Poland
COPE, E. D. 1869, Michigan
CROSSMAN, E. J. 1960, Ontario
CROSSMAN, E. J. 1971, Ontario
CROSSMAN, E. J. 1978, Ontario
DE KAY, J. E. 1842., New York
EDDY, S. 1957
EDDY, S. and T. SURBER 1947, Minnesota
EDDY, S. and T. SURBER 1960, Minnesota
EVERMANN, B. W. 1898
EVERMANN, B. W. 1902
FARRAN, G. P. 1946, Ireland
FORELLE, F. 1857, Canada
FOWLER, H. W. 1918b, Michigan
FOWLER, H. W. 1948, Northwest Territories
GERKING, S. D. 1955, Indiana
GILL, T. N. 1896
GIRARD, C. F. 1854
GORDON, W. J. , England
GOSLINE, W. A. 1960, England

GRASSE, P. P. 1958
GUNTHER, A. 1866, England
HUBBS, CARL L. 1924, Michigan
HUBBS, CARL L. 1926, Great Lakes
JORDAN, D. S. 1877b
JORDAN, D. S. 1880, North America
JORDAN, D. S. 1882, Ohio
JORDAN, D. S. 1885
JORDAN, D. S. 1918, California
JORDAN, D. S. 1925
JORDAN, D. S. and B. W. EVERMANN
  1917
JORDAN, D. S. and C. H. GILBERT 1882,
  North America
KALABINSKI, E. 1909, Poland
KIRTLAND, J. P. 1844, Great Lakes
KIRTLAND, J. P. 1854, Great Lakes
KNAUTHE, K. 1902, Germany
LEGENDRE, V. 1954, Quebec
LESLIE, J. K., and J. F. GORRIE 1985,
  Ontario
LESUEUR, C. A. 1821
LESUEUR, C. A. 1818, North America
MACLEOD, R. D. 1956, England
MCALLISTER, D. E. 1968, Ontario
MEEK, S. E. and R. G. NEWLAND 1886
MEZHNIN, F. I. 1980
MILNER, J. W. 1876
MITCHILL, S. L. 1815, New York
MYERS, G. S. 1958a
MYERS, G. S. 1958b
NEEDHAM, W. 1720
NELSON, G. J. 1969
NELSON, G. J. 1972
NOGUSASHY, S. 1960
REIST, J. D. 1983a, Ontario
ROSEN, D. E. 1974
ROYAL ONTARIO MUSEUM 1946, Ontario
SCOTT, W. B. and E. J. CROSSMAN 1969,
  Canada
SHERWOOD, F. 1978, Ontario
SMALL, H. B. 1883, Ontario
SOIN, S. G. 1980
STARKS, E. C. 1904, Massachusetts
THOMPSON, Z. 1850
WALECKI, A. 1864, Poland
WALTERS, V. 1955, Arctic
WILSON, M. V. H. and P. VEILLEUX 1982

TOXICOLOGY AND CONTAMINANTS

ADELMAN, I. R. and L. L. SMITH, Jr.
  1970b

ANDERSSON, O. and G. BLOMKVIST 1981, Sweden

ANNETT, C. S. and F. M. D'ITRI 1978, Michigan

ARMSTRONG, F. A. J. and D. P. SCOTT 1979, Ontario

BADSHA, K. S. and C. R. GOLDSPINK 1982, England

BAUDO, R., G. GALANTI, B. LOCHT, H. MUNTAU and P. G. VARINI 1981, Italy

BERGER, B. L., R. E. LENNON and J. W. HOGAN, 1969

BJOERKLUND, I. and L. NORLING 1980, Sweden

BODALY, R. A. and R. E. HECKY 1979, Manitoba

BODALY, R. A., R. E. HECKY and R. J. P. FUDGE 1984, Manitoba.

BROWN, E. R., W. C. DOLOWY,. T. SIN-CLAIR, L. KEITH, S. GREENBERG, J. J. HAZDRA, P. BEAMER and O. CAL-LAGHAN 1976, Illinois

BROWN, E. R., L. KEITH, J. J. HAZDRA and T. ARNDT 1975

BROWN, E. R., L. KEITH, J. B. G. KWAPINSKI, J. HAZDRA and P. BEA-MER 1973

BROWN, J. R. and L. Y. CHOW 1977, Ontario

BULL, K. R., A. F. DEARSLEY and M. H. INSKIP 1981, England

CHARBONNEAU, S. M., I. C. MUNRO, E. A. NERA, R. F. WILLES and T. et al. KUIPER-GOODMAN 1974

CHODYNIECKI, A., M. KURPIOS, M. PROTASOWICKI and J. JURAN 1974, Poland

DANIL'CHENKO, O. P. and N. S. STRO-GANOV 1975, USSR

DE FREITAS, A. S. W., M. A. J. GIDNEY, A. E. MCKINNON and R. J. NORSTROM 1977

DE FREITAS, A. S. W., S. U. QADRI and B. E. CASE 1974

DUPLINSKY, P. D. 1982, Rhode Island

EATON, J. G., J. M. MCKIM and G. W. HOLCOMBE 1978, Minnesota

FAGERSTROM, T., B. ASELL and A. JER-NELOV 1974, Sweden

FAGERSTROM, T., R. KURTEN and B. ASELL 1975, Sweden

FIMREITE, N. and L. M. REYNOLDS 1973, Ontario

FRANCO, J. M. 1973, Spain

GENGERKE, T. 1977, Iowa

GILDERHUS, P. A., B. L. BERGER and R. E. LENNON 1969

GOTHBERG, A. 1977

GOULD, W. R., III and W. H. IRWIN 1965

HAKKILA, K. and A. NIEMI 1973, Finland

HANNERZ, L. 1968

HANNON, M. R., Y. A. GREICHUS, R. L. APPLEGATE and A. C. FOX 1970, South Dakota

HASANEN, E. and J. K. MIETTINEN 1963, Finland

HASANEN, E. and V. SJOBLOM 1968, Fin-land

HASSELROT, T. B. 1968, Sweden

HASSELROT, T. B. and A. GOTHBERG 1974, Sweden

HASSINGER, R. and D. WOODS 1974, Min-nesota

HATTULA, M. L., J. JANATUINEN, J. SARKKA and J. PAASIVIRTA 1978, Fin-land

HELDER, T. 1980, Netherlands

HOLCIK, J. 1966, Czechoslovakia

HOLDEN, A. V. 1973

HUISMAN, E. A., J. H. KOEMAN and P. V. I. M. WOLFF 1971

JARVENPAA, T., M. TILLANDER and J. K. MIETTINEN 1970

JOHANSSON, N. and J. E. KIHLSTROM 1975, Sweden

JOHNELS, A. G., M. OLSSON and T. WES-TERMARK 1968, Sweden

JOHNELS, A. G. and T. WESTERMARK 1969, Sweden

JOHNELS, A. G., T. WESTERMARK, W. BERG, P.I. PERSSON and B. SJOS-TRAND 1967, Sweden

KARLSSON, S. and K. LIDEN 1977, Sweden

KELSO, J. R., H. R. MACCRIMMON and D. J. ECOBICHON 1970, Ontario

KEMPF, C. and B. SITTLER 1977, France

KLAVERKAMP, J. F., D. A. HODGINS and A. LUTZ 1983, Manitoba

KLEINERT, S. J., P. E. DEBURSE and T. L. WIRTH 1968, Wisconsin

KOIVUSAARI, J. 1976, Finland

KRISTOFFERSSON, R., S. BROBERG and A. OIKARI 1973, Finland

385

LANDNER, L., K. LONDSTROEM, M. KARLSSON, J. NORDIN and L. SOERENSEN 1977

LINKO, R. R., J. KAITARANTA, P. RANTAMAKI and L. ERONEN 1974, Finland

LINKO, R. R. and K. TERHO 1977, Finland

LJUNGBERG, O. 1976, Sweden

LOCKHART, W. L., J. F. UTHE, A. R. KENNEY and P. M. MEHRLE 1972, Ontario

LOCKHART, W. L., J. F. UTHE, A. R. KENNEY and P. M. MEHRLE 1973, Ontario, Manitoba

MACK, G. L., S. M. CORCORAN, S. D. GIBBS, W. H. GUTENMANN, J. A. RECKAHN and D. J. LISK 1964, New York

MARKING, L. L. 1967

MARKING, L. L. 1969a

MARKING, L. L. 1969b

MARKING, L. L. 1970, Wisconsin

MARTIN, N. V. and D. C. SCOTT 1959

MATHERS, R. A. and P. H. JOHANSEN 1985, Ontario

MATHERS, R. A. S. 1984, Ontario

MAWDESLEY-THOMAS, L. E. and J. S. LEAHY 1967, England

MCFARLANE, G. A. and W. G. FRANZIN 1980, Manitoba

MCKIM, J. M., J. W. ARTHUR and T. W. THORSLUND 1975, Minnesota

MCKIM, J. M., J. G. EATON and G. W. HOLCOMBE 1978, Minnesota

MIETTINEN, V., E. BLANKENSTEIN, K. RISSANEN, M. TILLANDER and J. K. MIETTINEN 1970

MIETTINEN, V., Y. OHMOMO, M. VALTONEN, E. BLANKENSTEIN, K. RISSANEN and J. K. MIETTINEN 1969

MILLER, C. T., Z. ZAWIDZKA, E. NAGY and S. M. CHARBONNEAU 1979, Ontario

MOILANEN, R., H. PYYSALO, K. WICKSTROM and R. LINKO 1982, Finland

MOORE, J. W. and D. J. SUTHERLAND 1980

MORRIS, R. L. and L. G. JOHNSON 1971, Iowa

MORSTROM, R. J., A. E. MCKINNON, A. S. W. DE FREITAS and D. R. MILLER 1975

MUNTYAN, S. P. 1978, USSR

OHMONO, Y., V. MIETTINEN, E. BLANKENSTEIN, M. TILLANDER and K. RISSANEN 1969

OIKARI, A. and A. SOIVIO 1977, Finland

OLSSON, M. 1976, Sweden

OLSSON, M. and S. JENSEN 1975, Sweden

PAASIVIRTA, J., J. SAERKKA, K. SURMA-AHO, T. HUMPPI, T. KUOKKANEN and M. MARTTINEN 1983, Finland

PAASIVIRTA, J., J. SAERKKAE, M. AHO, K. SURMA-AHO, J. TARHANEN and A. ROOS 1981, Finland

PANCHENKO, S. E. 1972

PECHKURENKOV, V. L. and G. L. POKROVSKAYA 1978, USSR

PECHKURENKOV, V. L., I. A. SHEKHANOVA and I. G. TELYSHEVA 1972, USSR

PERSSON, P.-E., H. PENTTINEN and P. NUORTEVA 1978, Finland

PRAVDA, O. 1973, Czechoslovakia

PROTASOWICKI, M. and A. OCIEPA 1978, Poland

SAUTER, S., K. S. BUXTON, K. J. MACEK and S. R. PETROCELLI 1976

SCOTT, D. P. 1974, Ontario

SCOTT, D. P. and F. A. J. ARMSTRONG 1972, Manitoba, Ontario

SLOTERDIJK, H. 1979, Quebec

SMITH, E. C., F. BERKES and J. A. SPENCE 1975, Quebec

SMITH, L. L., Jr. and D. M. OSEID 1970, Minnesota

SMITH, L. L., Jr. and D. M. OSEID 1974, Minnesota

SMITH, L. L. and D. M. OSEID 1972, Minnesota

SPEYER, M. R. 1980, Quebec

STAINTON, M. P. 1971

SVOBODOVA, Z. and M. HEJTMANEK 1976, Czechoslovakia

TONG, S. C., W. H. GUTENMANN, D. J. LISK, G. E. BURDICK and E. J. HARRIS 1972, New York

TURNER, M. A. and A. L. SWICK 1983, Ontario

VAN LOON, J. C. and R. J. BEAMISH 1977, Manitoba

WACHS, B. 1982, West Germany

WALTER, C. M., F. C. JUNE and H. G. BROWN 1973, South Dakota

ZABA, B. N. and E. J. HARRIS 1978, Wales